NAPLES AND NAPO

Naples and Napoleon

Southern Italy and the European Revolutions (1780–1860)

JOHN A. DAVIS

OXFORD
UNIVERSITY PRESS

OXFORD
UNIVERSITY PRESS

Great Clarendon Street, Oxford OX2 6DP

Oxford University Press is a department of the University of Oxford.
It furthers the University's objective of excellence in research, scholarship,
and education by publishing worldwide in

Oxford New York

Auckland Cape Town Dar es Salaam Hong Kong Karachi
Kuala Lumpur Madrid Melbourne Mexico City Nairobi
New Delhi Shanghai Taipei Toronto

With offices in

Argentina Austria Brazil Chile Czech Republic France Greece
Guatemala Hungary Italy Japan Poland Portugal Singapore
South Korea Switzerland Thailand Turkey Ukraine Vietnam

Oxford is a registered trade mark of Oxford University Press
in the UK and in certain other countries

Published in the United States
by Oxford University Press Inc., New York

First published 2006
First published in paperback 2008

British Library Cataloguing in Publication Data
Data available

Library of Congress Cataloging in Publication Data
Data available

Typeset by SPI Publisher Services, Pondicherry, India
Printed in Great Britain
on acid-free paper by
the MPG Books Group

ISBN 978–0–19–820755–7(Hbk.) 978–0–19–955230–6(Pbk.)

1 3 5 7 9 10 8 6 4 2

Acknowledgements

I thank the European University Institute, the British Academy, and the John Simon Guggenheim Foundation for fellowships that have enabled me to research this book in Italy and France, and would like to acknowledge the support provided by the Emiliana Pasca Noether Chair in Modern Italian History at the University of Connecticut. Sabbatical leave gave me the opportunity to start writing the book, and a generous invitation from Professor Lester Little to spend time at the American Academy in Rome as a Resident provided an unforgettably congenial and stimulating environment in which to do so.

It is a pleasure to record my thanks to the countless archivists and librarians who have offered guidance and assistance; in particular, the directors and staff of the *Archivio di Stato* in Naples, the *Archivio di Stato* in Foggia, the *Archives Nationales* in Paris, the *Archives de Guerre* at Vincennes, and the *Public Record Office* in London. My thanks also to Prince Murat and his family for permission to consult and quote from the papers of Joachim and Caroline Murat. In Naples, as well as the librarians and staff at the *Biblioteca Nazionale Vittorio Emmanuele II*, I am especially grateful to the staff of the city's wonderful *Biblioteca di Storia Patria* and to its present and former directors, Professor Renata de Lorenzo and Professor Giuseppe Galasso. My thanks also to the staff of the *Istituto per la Storia del Risorgimento* in Rome, and its director, Professor Giuseppe Talamo; to Christina Huemer, the Librarian at the AAR; to the staff and directors of the *Biblioteca Nazionale* and the *Biblioteca di Storia Moderna e Contemporanea* in Rome, of the *Biblioteca Civica* in Cosenza, and of the British Library; and to Peter Allison and his colleagues at the University of Connecticut's Homer Babbidge Library.

Naples has been an extraordinarily welcoming and rewarding city in which to work. The *Istituto Italiano per gli Studi Filosofici*, its director, Avvocato Gerardo Marotta, and its administrator, Professor Antonio Gargano, have for many years provided me with opportunities to teach and discuss my work with Italian students and scholars, for which I am very grateful. I also thank Angela Catello, Gabriella Corona, Ermelinda De Rosa and her family, Cesare and Tullia de Seta, Gennaro and Cristina Incarnato, Paolo Macry, Giovanni and Linda Muto, Walter Palmieri, Anna Maria Rao, Maria Gabriella Rienzo, and Giulia Rispoli and her family for their friendship and generous hospitality over many years. It is a great sadness that I did not finish the book in time to share it with Luigi de Rosa and Filippo Mazzonis, two generous scholars and close friends whose presence I greatly miss.

On this side of the Atlantic, my thanks to the East Coast *italianisti*—Ruth Ben Ghiat, Mary Gibson, Stephen Hughes, Alice Kelikian, David Kertzer, Silvana Patriarca, Marta Petrusewicz, Jane and Peter Schneider, and Nadia Urbinati—and to the members of the Columbia Italian History seminar whose comments on different parts of this study have been very helpful. I also acknowledge the support of my colleagues in the History Department at the University of Connecticut, and I especially thank Fakhreddin Azimi, Joel Blatt, Richard D. Brown, Frank Costigliola, Michael Dintenfass, Ken Gouwens, Bob Gross, Kathryn Myers, and Sylvia Schafer for their friendship and intellectual fellowship.

Louis Bergeron, Giuseppe Galasso, Adrian Lyttelton, Alfonso Scirocco, Pasquale Villani, and Stuart Woolf at different stages and in different ways have all helped me shape this project, and I am especially indebted to my friends Alex Grab, John Robertson, and Desmond Ryan who generously agreed to review and comment on an earlier draft of the book. When it came to pulling together its different strands and arguments, their insights proved invaluable, although it goes without saying, of course, that I alone am responsible for everything that follows, errors and inaccuracies included.

Elissa Papirno helped proof the final draft and at Oxford University Press Rupert Cousens, Eva Nyika, Charles Lauder, Mary Payne, and Zoe Washford have taken the book through the final stages. Mr Nicholas Hall at Christie's, New York, kindly helped obtain permission to reproduce the cover portrait of Caroline Murat. Without Martha McCormick's efficient management of my office I don't think I would ever have found the time to write it in the first place. But the biggest thanks of all I owe to my wife Elaine, to whom this book is lovingly dedicated.

Coventry, Connecticut

May Day 2006

Contents

List of Maps

Introduction

Naples, Napoleon, and the Origins of the Two Italies

For nearly ten years, from 1806 to 1815, Naples and southern Italy formed part of Napoleon's continental enterprise. Although Napoleon never once set foot in Naples, during this brief decade southern Italy was a peripheral but also an integral part of the imperial system. Like the other territories ruled directly and indirectly by France, the Kingdom's function was to supply men, equipment, and money for the emperor's wars, raw materials for French manufactures, and markets for French products. However, because the French never succeeded in dislodging the former Bourbon rulers and their British allies from Sicily, the long coastlines of the southern Italian mainland formed the empire's most southerly frontier and for almost ten years only the narrow Straits of Messina separated the emperor's troops from those of France's principal adversary.[1]

Napoleon's Mediterranean Kingdom also had an important part to play in the dynastic politics of empire. Its first ruler was the emperor's brother Joseph, until he was moved to Madrid in 1808 to fill the recently vacated Spanish throne and succeeded by Napoleon's brother-in-law, Joachim Murat. The tensions with Paris that developed after Murat's arrival in Naples would vividly expose the deep contradictions on which the imperial project was founded, and in 1811 Murat came very close to sharing the fate of Louis Bonaparte, who had been deposed as king of Holland a year earlier. Unlike Louis, Murat survived but the tensions remained, and in the hope of retaining his kingdom in 1814 Murat joined forces with the emperor's enemies. A year later Murat rallied once again to the imperial cause after Napoleon's flight from Elba, but his defeat shortly afterwards by the Austrians at the battle of Tolentino in May 1815 brought the 'Napoleonic episode' in Italy to a final close, although Murat's personal denouement was still to come.[2]

The history of Napoleon's Mediterranean Kingdom illustrates many of the broader contradictions on which the short-lived imperial enterprise was

[1] 'The southern end of the Italian peninsula was, in one sense, the strategic centre or turning point of the great war between France and England': Johnson (1904) i., p. viii. However, that is more true for the period before rather than after 1806; see Mackesy (1957).

[2] For the 'Napoleonic episode' see Bergeron (1972). The principal modern biographers of Murat are Valente (1941/65) and Tulard (1983), but the most comprehensive modern historian of the period is Pasquale Villani (see Villani, 'Il decennio francese', in Galasso and Romeo (eds.) (1986), now reprinted in Rao and Villani (1995), 179–282).

founded.[3] But what has attracted attention above all to the brief interlude of French rule in southern Italy are the reforms that were undertaken. Within months of taking control, the new French rulers set about remodelling the Kingdom in accordance with the templates established by the revolution in France and its aftermath. Feudalism was abolished and the monarchy was reorganized around the system of central and local administration established by the Constitution of Year VIII in France. The tax system was similarly brought into line with France, and direct taxes were reorganized around a single land tax. The debts of the previous monarchy were redeemed through the sale of the lands of over 1,300 religious houses, the *Code Napoléon* was introduced and the administration of justice reorganized. In 1810 Joachim Murat established a feudal commission that visited every community in the Kingdom to resolve outstanding litigation over former feudal rights, and at the same time divided the former feudal and common lands amongst the inhabitants of the rural communities.

Writing shortly after the event, Pietro Colletta claimed that 'Never has society undergone political convulsions comparable to those experienced in the Kingdom of Naples at the start of the nineteenth century.'[4] Allowing for a degree of exaggeration, it was nonetheless true that there was nothing comparable in the other territories ruled directly or indirectly by France to the reforms that took place in southern Italy. Yet for over a century, historians of modern Italy have argued that the failure of those reforms to take root in the South marked the decisive moment when the destinies of the two Italies—the North and the South—became finally and irrevocably set on different and divergent paths. While the rest of Italy embraced modernity and moved closer to the political and cultural models set by the most advanced western European nations, the South turned its back and limped into the nineteenth century still shackled to the *ancien régime.*

These arguments were not made at the time, however, but much later in the closing decade of a century that had seen Italy achieve independence and nationhood. Yet, while the first generation of Italian historians was hard at work celebrating Italy's heroic struggles for independence and forging the founding myths of the new nation, the country faced a prolonged economic and political crisis that came close to overthrowing the fragile constitutional monarchy established barely three decades earlier. In addition to serious and widespread internal unrest that resulted in the military occupation of Sicily in 1893 and of the city of Milan in 1898, Italy also suffered a devastating and humiliating colonial defeat at the battle of Adowa in 1896 that came as a heavy psychological blow to the most ardent supporters of the new nation.[5]

[3] '[T]he very notion of Napoleon's empire as a conceivable, potentially durable form of European international politics, or as a leading one, is a contradiction in terms': Schroeder (1994), 394.

[4] Colletta (Cortese, 1957), ii. 214.

[5] On Italian insecurities, see Chabod (1962); the most thorough English account of the crisis of the 1890s is Duggan (2002), 640–7.

It was in this context of apprehension and introspection that the 'Southern Problem' forced itself on the attention of the new nation. There had been serious unrest in the South in the years immediately after Unification, the scale of which the authorities attempted to minimize by dismissing the disturbances as mere acts of brigandage. However, more troops were needed to suppress the so-called brigandage, and more lives were lost than in all the Italian wars of independence.[6] By the 1890s, although the epicentre of popular unrest had shifted to the North, the discontents of the South had exposed the desperate conditions of poverty and distress that persisted there thirty years after Unification. The evident disparities between the two Italies were an open contradiction to claims that the Risorgimento had unified Italians, while the mass emigration that followed, as at first thousands and then millions of southerners abandoned their homes in search of work and better lives across the Atlantic, raised even greater fears. Many of the new nation's staunchest supporters saw in the mass exodus a haemorrhage of the nation's life-blood that posed a mortal threat to its survival.[7]

Against these forebodings, ways had to be found to defend the Risorgimento, reassert national unity, and absolve the new Italy of responsibility for the conditions of the South. Not for the first time history came to be written backwards, and the creative force of the Risorgimento was salvaged by insisting that the Southern Problem was primarily a legacy of the past. The principal architect of this interpretation was one of the most formidable intellectual champions of the Risorgimento, the Neapolitan philosopher and historian Benedetto Croce.

A southerner himself, and deeply proud of his southern origins, Croce was among the first to argue that centuries of foreign misrule and exploitation had turned the South into 'a paradise inhabited by devils'.[8] It was Croce who first adopted and adapted the term 'passive revolution' to describe the South's failure to respond to the innovative forces of the modern era. The phrase had originally been coined by Vincenzo Cuoco, a member of the Neapolitan Republic in 1799 who shortly afterwards became its first historian, but it was only when Croce borrowed it a century later that the 'passive revolution' came to encapsulate everything that had made the pre-Unification South different. For Croce, the deep moral decay of southern society was the reason the emancipating forces unleashed by the Enlightenment and the European revolutions had resulted in nothing more than a 'passive revolution' in the South. The forces of change had evoked strongly positive responses, but only from a progressive and isolated minority, which was why the reform movement that had flourished in Naples in the second half of the eighteenth century failed to achieve significant or lasting changes. However, for Croce nothing demonstrated more dramatically or tragically the backwardness

[6] Davis (1988), 168–86; Riall (1997).

[7] On perceptions of the South before and after Unification see Dickie (1999) and Moe (2002).

[8] Davis (1999), 350–7. On the origins of the 'paradise inhabited by devils' see Croce's often misrepresented essay in *Uomini e cose della vecchia Italia* (1956), i. 69–87.

and corruption of southern society than the fate of the short-lived Neapolitan Republic of 1799.

The Republic had been established following the defeat of the royal army in the winter of 1798, and after the king of Naples had unwisely yielded to pressure from his British allies to attack the small French garrison that had occupied Rome and set up a Republic there earlier in the year. The defeat of the Bourbon army and the flight of the king and his courtiers to Sicily on Nelson's men-o'-war, led to a French invasion and the declaration of a Republic in Naples in January 1799. The Neapolitan Republic had a very short life and like its sister republics elsewhere in Italy was left defenceless once the French Directory decided to withdraw its troops from the Italian peninsula in April. But when the Republic fell in June, the immediate agents of its destruction were Admiral Lord Nelson's warships and the counter-revolutionary masses that rallied enthusiastically to the banners of the Holy Faith—the *Santafede*—raised by Cardinal Fabrizio Ruffo.

Writing a century after the event, Croce transformed the rise and fall of the Neapolitan Republic of 1799 into one of the founding myths of the new Italian state. The young visionaries who had supported the Republic were portrayed as the first martyrs of the new Italy, although Croce also argued that their lives had been sacrificed in a noble but hopeless cause. Although they had allowed themselves to be influenced too heavily by foreign political models, the cultural backwardness of the South meant that their lofty ideals could never have been realized. In any case the true voices of the South in 1799 were not theirs, but those of the ignorant and brutish masses who flocked to the banners of the *Santafede*, urged on by a fanatical clergy and a corrupt ruling class.

For Croce, the triumph of the counter-revolution in 1799 revealed why in the South the innovative and creative forces of the revolutionary era were destined to lead only to forms of 'passive revolution'. When another French army invaded the South in 1806 to place Joseph Bonaparte on the throne of Naples, the outcome would inevitably be the same. As a good Italian nationalist, Croce again refused to accept that reforms introduced by a foreign force of occupation could have any constructive force. In any case it was already too late; everything creative in the South had already been destroyed in the tragedy of the Republic. The reforms introduced by the French were bound to fail. They were based on alien models imposed from above and took little account of Neapolitan customs and culture. Above all they evoked no creative responses in a society that was irretrievably corrupted and incapable of achieving its own redemption.[9]

By demonstrating that the regeneration of the pre-Unification South could not come from within, but only through the emancipating force of the liberal values and institutions of which the new Italy was the bearer, Croce brilliantly reconciled the backwardness of the South with the creative spirit of the Risorgimento. Once stamped with the authoritative *imprimatur* of the leading champion of

[9] Croce (1897), pp. vi–x; idem (1924/1967), 197–212.

Italy's liberal Risorgimento, the 'passive revolution' and the backwardness the South thereafter acquired a central place in the master narratives of the new Italy.[10]

The South soon found a similar place in the annals of Napoleonic Europe. The numerous studies published shortly after the turn of the new century to mark the centenary celebrations of France's first empire included a closely documented study of Joseph Bonaparte's reforms in Naples by the distinguished French archivist Jacques Rambaud. In keeping with the spirit of the time, Rambaud portrayed Napoleon as a stern but wise schoolmaster who had brought the lessons of modernity to a continent still locked in the black night of the *ancien régime*. In this perspective, the Neapolitans inevitably figured as inattentive pupils who had been unwilling to learn from the models set by the *Grande Nation*, and Rambaud sadly concluded that there was no clearer warning of the fate that awaited those who failed to heed the empire's civilizing mission than the sad state of southern Italy a century after the French had departed.[11]

In the meantime, as the rapid industrialization of many parts of northern Italy further accentuated the relative backwardness of the South, Croce's optimistic claim that the new Italy would solve the problems of the South was coming under increasingly critical scrutiny. For socialists, in particular, the backwardness of the South revealed not only the limits of national unity but was also the principal obstacle to the progress of democracy in Italy.[12] Once the crisis that followed the First World War had swept away Italy's fragile constitutional monarchy and led to the establishment of the Fascist dictatorship, those arguments were taken up and developed by one of Mussolini's most eminent victims, the communist leader Antonio Gramsci.

Gramsci devoted his long and painful confinement in Fascist jails to reworking Croce's liberal master narrative of the Risorgimento in Marxist terms, and in what would later be known as the *Prison Notebooks* the struggles for Italian Unification were portrayed instead as the victory of a narrow and deeply conservative ruling class that never fully acquired the qualities of a modern capitalist bourgeoisie. Following the lead given by earlier socialist observers like Gaetano Salvemini, Gramsci argued that the backwardness of the South was the rock on which the democratic aspirations of the Risorgimento had foundered.

At this point Gramsci also invoked Vincenzo Cuoco's 'passive revolution', although unlike Croce he acknowledged that the abolition of feudalism at the beginning of the nineteenth century had brought important changes in the South, most notably the wholesale expropriation of the southern peasantry who lost the

10 See Davis (1999), 350–7.

11 'Educateurs sévères et peu modérés sur le prix de leurs lecons, les Français n'ont pas trouvé l'affection de leurs élèves: c'est le sort des "professeurs d'energie". Cependant les Français étaient la nation la plus capable de sympathies pour Naples . . . On peut déplorer pour le pays lui-meme qu'il n'ait pas consenti à se plier avantage à la forte et nécessaire discipline, qui peuvent peut-être faire de l'Etat de la péninsule le plus vaste et le plus peuplé, le promoteur de la fédération, sinon de l'unité italienne': Rambaud (1911), 555–6.

12 Villari (1961/70), Part II, 181–490.

customary rights they formerly exercised on the feudal estates and the common lands of the rural communities. However, Gramsci insisted that the French reforms had failed to create a new capitalist landowning class, leading instead to a 'passive revolution' that both anticipated and determined Italy's later 'missing bourgeois revolution'. Just as the backward and reactionary South had blocked the democratic forces of the Risorgimento, once Unification had been achieved the backward South and its reactionary landowners remained the principal obstacles to the political development of the new Italian state.[13]

When Gramsci's prison writings were published posthumously after the fall of Mussolini's regime they ensured that the South would hold a central place in the debates on the historical roots of Fascism that followed. But the South was already at the centre of Italy's new political agendas. The southern regions had borne the brunt of the interwar Depression and the Fascist regime's economic and colonial policies, and following the invasion of Sicily in 1943 had for two years been subject to military operations and Allied occupation. The damage to the economy and the sufferings of the civilian population were as terrible as anywhere in Europe, and lay behind the social unrest and political protests that continued well after the end of the Second World War.

Among the political parties that founded Italy's new democratic Republic in 1947 there was broad agreement that the need to find a solution to the 'Southern Problem' was one of the most pressing challenges for Italy's reborn democracy.[14] However, those concerns were also shared outside Italy, and as fears grew that the discontents of the southern population might give rise to communist infiltration the South ceased to be simply an Italian problem, and the Italian Mezzogiorno was to be the theatre for the biggest internationally funded rural development programme in post-Second World War Europe. Economists, anthropologists, and sociologists came from all over the world, but mainly from the United States, to test the latest development theories and turn the South into the foremost site of pre-modernity in contemporary Europe.[15]

Meanwhile, the South was acquiring notoriety through other channels, first literature and then cinema. The South was the leading protagonist in both of Italy's post-war international best-selling novels—Carlo Levi's *Christ Stopped at Eboli* and Tomasi di Lampedusa's *The Leopard*. In both the South was portrayed as a world that had somehow remained outside history and resisted the encroaching forces of modernity. Through cinema and television those images reached even wider international audiences and turned the South into a universally recognizable metaphor of pre-modernity.[16]

[13] See especially 'Alcuni temi della quistione meridionale' (ed. De Felice and Parlato, 1966), 121–60, but also Fubini (ed.) (1959) and Hoare and Nowell Smith (1971).

[14] Allum (1973), Tarrow (1973).

[15] D'Antone (ed.) (1996).

[16] While there are now a number of studies on earlier stereotyping of the South (e.g. Dickie, 1999; Moe, 2003), much less has been written about contemporary perceptions of the South. For the South in contemporary Italian literature, however, see Dombroski in Schneider (ed.) (1998) 261–76.

As those metaphors have become more universal they have inevitably also moved further and further from both present and past realities, while more recent research has begun to question many of the fundamental assumptions on which they are premised. Quite apart from the sheer improbability that a chunk of pre-modern Europe might miraculously survive unchanged down to the present, the images of backwardness and immobility are of little help in explaining why the South is still in many respects a problem today. The rural world that constituted the 'Southern Problem' after the Second World War has long since vanished. Living standards in the South today are around the national norms, while levels of consumption are comparable to those in the wealthiest parts of Europe. Yet levels of productivity in southern Italy also remain among the lowest in Europe, economic and social infrastructures are poor, and organized crime, mafia, and political corruption persist.[17] The problems present in the South today seem, however, to be more directly the consequence of the ways in which the southern regions have been incorporated into the modern Italian state than that of some vague and in any case immeasurable notion of 'backwardness'.[18]

Rethinking what makes the South different today raises questions about the past, and above all about the ideological models that have reduced Italian history to a simple Manichean struggle between modernity and backwardness embodied by the North and the South. That dichotomy is based on nineteenth-century notions about state building and progress that can only appear outdated at a time when historians are more ready to acknowledge both the inherently contradictory forces of modernity and the persistence of the Old Order in even the most advanced of the nineteenth-century states.[19] But these dichotomies also derive from abstract and often deeply ahistorical generalizations that fit the North no better than the South, and take little if any account of the deep economic, political, cultural, and historical diversities that feature no less prominently in the North than in the South. Even in geographical terms the boundaries that separate the North from the South remain elusive.[20]

Although outdated these dichotomies continue to colour the ways in which Italy's political and social histories in the age of the Risorgimento and since are portrayed.[21] It is the central contention of this book, however, that the neat

17 See Bevilacqua (1994), Lumley and Morris (eds.) (1997), and the special issue of the *JMIS* (2006, vol. 11/2) on political development since 1945. See also Allum (1973), Tarrow (1967), and Ginsborg (2003).

18 e.g. De Rosa (2004), 129–36.

19 See for example Mayer (1981), but see also Breuilly, in Rowe (ed.) (2003), 121–53.

20 On the false North–South distinctions see Bevilacqua (1994), *Questione Settentrionale* (Meridiana 16, 1993) and Meriggi (1996). For a critical review of these debates in English see Davis (1998), 205–24; Riall (1998), 32–57; Lumley and Morris (1997); Schneider (ed.) (1998).

21 For a recent unreconstructed Crocean view see the editor's Introduction to Imbruglia (ed.) (2000), 1: 'An eighteenth century state, the Kingdom of the Two Sicilies was constituted, developed and died between 1734 and 1799. It was born as a monarchy in 1734, and ended as a revolutionary Republic in June 1799. Conquered again by the Bourbons, after a phase of anarchy, it became a sort of Mediterranean despotism, a Catholic variant of Asian or Moslem despotic states. Its destiny—monarchy, republic, anarchy, despotism—could well be taken from the pages of the *Esprit des Lois*.

contrasts between a modernizing North and a backward South are anachronisms that have subsequently come to distort the history of the North before Unification no less seriously than that of the South. A reconsideration of what made the South different before Unification therefore calls for a more general reconsideration of the dynamics of political change in Italy as a whole in the century before Unification.

This book began as a study of the brief period of Napoleonic rule at the start of the nineteenth century that was supposedly the site of the original 'passive revolution'. In the light of modern scholarship on the Napoleonic enterprise, however, both the notion of the 'passive revolution' and that of the exceptionality of the South in the century before Unification become questionable. Seen in the broader context of Napoleonic Europe, southern Italy was not the norm but an anomaly. No comparable reforms were attempted in any of the other peripheral imperial territories. In Poland, for example, even the political privileges of the nobility survived, and despite the abolition of feudalism the seigneurial order was not touched in the German territories. The reasons for this seemed obvious enough to Count Beugnot, one of the empire's most seasoned administrators, who reported that feudalism was so deeply embedded in the fabric of the countries that made up the Kingdom of Westphalia that to eradicate it would take decades, perhaps even centuries: 'one would have to go back four or five centuries to find similar examples in France'.[22] But even in those states that were closer to France in terms of political and institutional organization, recent studies show that the reforming zeal of the French administrators has often been exaggerated. Despite the emperor's obsessive insistence, attempts to implement key reforms—for example, the introduction of the *Code Napoléon*—were generally minimalist, and very often it was the local elites who took the initiative to rewrite imperial prescriptions to suit their own political agendas.[23]

Why, then, the attempt to make Naples a model of the empire's modernizing mission? Once that question is posed, the weakness of the claim that everything was imposed from above becomes evident. There was nothing in the career profiles of either Joseph Bonaparte or Joachim Murat to indicate an active commitment to reform. To be sure, the men Napoleon sent to advise his brother were 'experts in the business of annexation'.[24] All were seasoned administrators who were also deeply skilled in the more sinister political arts, but all but one left with Joseph in 1808. Thereafter, Murat relied more heavily on Neapolitan administrators, but although their roles were important, their presence and collaboration alone are not sufficient to explain either the momentum of change or the very varied responses to change.

But it was dramatic history'. An even more extreme version of the Manichaean view of the historical origins of the North–South divide can be found in Putnam (1994).

[22] Woolf (1991), 52.

[23] Fahrmeir, in Rowe (ed.) (2003), 107–20.

[24] Woolf (1991), 50.

To a far greater extent than historians have been prepared to acknowledge, the changes that took place in southern Italy after 1806 were driven and shaped from below. In part, the scale of the French reforms reflected the gravity of the crisis of the *ancien régime* monarchy in the South, which confronted the French invaders with challenges that could not safely be deferred. Public finances were on the point of collapse and the creditors of the *ancien régime* monarchy were threatened with ruin. There was no cash in the government treasuries and taxes were not being raised. Public administration and the administration of justice were in chaos and needed to be completely reconstructed.

From the moment that the French rulers set about these tasks, however, their initiatives were shaped by the interventions of different social groups and interests. To explain why, it is necessary to turn back to the earlier period of Bourbon reformism, which is where this book begins. The pursuit of dynastic autonomy led the Kingdom's new Bourbon rulers to copy initiatives being taken by other Italian and European rulers in the same period. It was not the initiatives taken to strengthen the monarchy and its resources that made the South different, but the context in which these were attempted. As these questions carry us backwards in time into the eighteenth century, the images of an immobile and unchanging South begin to disintegrate and instead reveal a society, an economy, and a political system inseparably caught up in the changes that were everywhere beginning to undermine the fabric of the European *ancien régime*.

The changes taking place in the South in the half century that preceded the revolution in France were often experienced in particularly intense and disruptive forms, but they differed in degree, not in kind, from those concurrently taking place elsewhere in Italy and Europe. The same was true of the political crisis that overwhelmed the Bourbon monarchy in the final decade of the eighteenth century. In every Italian state, attempts by the rulers to establish more effective forms of centralized bureaucratic government created deep political divisions, gaining support in some quarters but provoking powerful resistance in others. While in some important respects distinctive, in substance the crisis in the South was rooted in the same contradictions and tensions that caused the Habsburg rulers of Tuscany and Lombardy to abandon reform and reverse measures already implemented.[25]

In the South, those reactions were particularly polarized, but were not essentially different, nor did the crisis of the *ancient régime* monarchy in the South follow lines essentially different from those of other Italian states. In reality the South in 1799 never quite lived up to its later notoriety as the home of the Italian counter-revolution. The savagery of the Neapolitan Sanfedists was not invented and quickly acquired a notoriety that haunted successive generations

[25] For the economic forces that were transforming the European *ancien régime*, see Aymard (1978). For the political repercussions in the Habsburg territories see Capra (2005), for Tuscany, see Turi (1969/1999).

of southern liberals. But the carefully contrived retrospective reconstructions of the fate of the Neapolitan Republic deliberately failed to acknowledge that in 1799 Italy as a whole was the theatre for a second Vendée, or that the Neapolitan Republic was in all essential respects remarkably similar to its sister republics in the rest of Italy.

The exceptionality of the South has been heavily overstated, but what is missing most crucially from the imagery of the 'passive revolution' are the quite exceptional forms of political mobilization taking place in many different parts of the South by the end of the eighteenth century. These found expression in the political battles that followed the founding of the Republic, but they can also be traced to the earlier campaigns against feudalism. There were many reasons for this, not least being the monarchy's efforts to recruit the local communities to its campaign against feudal privilege. The actions of the royal courts, together with the presence of the masonic lodges that with government support spread to the most remote provincial centres in the closing decade, all contributed to generate forms of political mobilization that had no parallels elsewhere in Italy.

As a result, local conflicts in the South were drawn into broader political and juridical struggles whose vocabularies they assimilated. This would be evident in the struggles that followed the founding of the Republic in 1799, and again during the short period of French rule. As in the rest of Italy, French rule in the South met with fierce opposition as well as active support and collaboration. Like the other Italian states, the South paid heavy sacrifices to the imperial cause in terms not only of lives and tributes, but also of persistent danger and disorder. The Kingdom was permanently at risk of attack and invasion, while the escalation of brigandage was a direct consequence not only of conscription and economic hardship but also of the massive volume of contraband goods that flooded into southern Italy as a direct result of the emperor's Continental blockade.

Murat's own insecurity in the imperial enterprise and the Kingdom's vulnerable position on the frontier of empire created important political opportunities that the southern elites did not let pass, and in particular gave rise to demands for constitutional government that found wide support in southern Italy during the final years of French rule. The breadth of support for the constitutional project is not easily reconciled with the later imagery of the 'passive revolution', and suggests that the South had embarked on a path of political development that was not so much different but in some respects precocious in comparison with the other Italian states.

Those differences were also evident in 1815 when the restored Bourbon rulers retained the administrative and institutional changes made by their French predecessors more fully than any other Italian rulers. Indeed, in 1816 these were extended to Sicily as well, which as a result lost its centuries-old autonomy as a separate crown. The consolidation of a post-feudal bureaucratic autocracy gave new impetus to the demands for constitutional government, which found expression in the revolutions of 1820–1 on the mainland and in Sicily.

The nine months of constitutional government and freedom of speech that followed demonstrate how profoundly the retrospective lens of the 'passive revolution' has distorted the histories of both the North and the South before Unification. The revolutions of 1820–1 in the South were the epilogue to the decade of French reforms, and the debates that took place in the local and regional assemblies and in the petitions submitted to the National Parliament focused above all on the threats that the centralist and autocratic reorganization of the state posed to regional and local autonomies.

Although those debates took place only in the South in 1820–1, similar developments were taking place in every other Italian state. Everywhere the post-feudal order was founded on the expansion and extension of centralized power at the expense of local autonomies, and especially the powers formerly exercised at local levels by sections of the elites. Everywhere in Italy these tendencies were the principal cause of political tension in the Restoration states, and everywhere opposition to the new forms of centralized autocracy came as much from the old patrician families who were the principal victims of the new forms of autocratic power as from the elites of more recent origin.[26] The difference was that in the South these changes had come earlier and more abruptly. This was partly because of the scale of the crisis of the *ancien régime* monarchy and partly because of the ways in which forms of agrarian paternalism and deference that in other parts of Italy would survive until much later in the century were eroded at a much earlier stage.

In March 1821 the precocious political dialogue in the South was abruptly cut off by the Austrian invasion, which was also a reminder that political developments in pre-Unification Italy were determined as much by realities of imperial subordination as by the force of revolution. The South was not unique in this respect either: all the Italian rulers, even the House of Savoy, were dependent on direct or indirect foreign support. But again the consequences were especially acute in the South, where the Bourbon dreams of dynastic autonomy had been amongst the first victims of the revolutionary wars. In 1815 the South passed from formal imperial subjection to France and informal colonial subordination to Great Britain to become a satellite of the Habsburg monarchy. In 1821 Habsburg bayonets enabled the Bourbon rulers to regain their throne, but the realities of colonial subordination caused the monarchy to make a bid for autonomy by promoting the Kingdom's economy and protecting its nascent industrial centres. That bid ended in conflict with Great Britain and failure, but even though the Bourbon bid for economic autonomy was motivated exclusively by dynastic objectives it anticipated the policies that would be adopted by the rulers of the Kingdom of Piedmont–Savoy two decades later.

Retrospectively, Italians wrote the history of Unification around the idea of the nation and nationalism, so it is easy to forget the other forces that made the

[26] On the importance of patrician discontent as a factor in opposition to Habsburg rule in Lombardy see Meriggi (1983, 1987), and on Tuscany see the important recent study by Thomas Kröll (2005).

survival of independent dynastic states on the Italian peninsula increasingly difficult. Even the most powerful, the Kingdom of Piedmont–Sardinia, survived the crisis by ceasing to be a regional dynastic state. The forces that brought about the collapse of the Bourbon monarchy in the South were essentially the same as those that undid the other Italian rulers.

The retrospective contrasts between a modernizing North and a backward South have not only imposed differences that did not exist, but also obscured those that did. The Napoleonic decade was a critical moment in the history of the Italian South, as it was in the histories of the Italian peninsula and of Europe. However, it was not the decisive turning point that subsequently came to dominate the master narratives of Italian history. The political and social changes taking place in the South in the half century before Italian Unification mirrored, and in many cases even anticipated, those occurring in other parts of Italy. Everywhere in Italy those changes brought new insecurities, even though in the South the impact of these changes would prove to be especially disruptive.

Two final points: throughout this Introduction and in the pages that follow the South refers to the Kingdom of the Two Sicilies, in other words the southern mainland and Sicily. But although Sicily has a critical role in different parts of the narrative that this book seeks to unfold, it is not treated in as much detail as the mainland or as it deserves. The reasons for this are essentially practical. Sicily and the mainland were different countries, with different institutions, laws, and customs. To have written as fully about Sicily as the mainland provinces would have required extensive additional archival research that would have made a long book even longer, but this inevitably results in imbalances of which I am very much aware.

Secondly, anyone writing about this period must be enormously indebted to the remarkable expansion in historical research and debate on the pre-Unification South in recent decades. Some of the breadth of that research will be evident from the bibliographies that follow, without which this study could not have been attempted. Since overwhelmingly this is the work of Italian historians, which is not easily accessible to those who do not read Italian, it is important to remind anglophone readers that far from travelling some distant or exotic *terre incognitae* the chapters that follow move across some of the most deeply researched and closely debated territories in modern Italian history.

PART I

ABSOLUTIST NAPLES

Italy in 1748, from G. Holmes (ed.), *The Oxford Illustrated History of Italy* (Oxford: Oxford University Press, 1997).

1

The *Ancien Régime* in the South

INTRODUCTION: HOW THE EUROPEAN REVOLUTION CAME SOUTH

Sir William Hamilton, who from 1763 served for thirty-six years as Britain's special envoy to the rulers of the Kingdom of the Two Sicilies, liked to describe his posting as a 'remote and indolent corner of the world'. In the closing years of the century, however, this remote corner of the world found itself at the centre of the political storms that swept through Europe in the wake of the revolution in France.[1] In part this was because the central and eastern Mediterranean had in the intervening decades come to acquire new importance in European politics. Trade between the Mediterranean countries and northern Europe had increased notably in these years, but the region's new strategic importance derived above all from the colonial struggles between Britain and France that after the American War of Independence had shifted to the Indian subcontinent. In the meantime, the expansionist projects of Tsarist Russia had led to a sequence of conflicts with the Ottoman Turks that culminated in the Russian annexation of the Crimea in 1783 and a major war begun in 1787 and fought by the Russians and the Austrians against the Turks. These conflicts were a new cause of political uncertainty for the whole of south-eastern Europe and for the states that bordered on the Adriatic and the eastern Mediterranean.

Those broader connections would become apparent when Napoleon Bonaparte's invasion of Egypt in 1798 threw southern Italy into crisis. The expedition's aim was to cut England's lines of communications with India, a project that was wrecked by Nelson's victory at the battle of the Nile on 1 August 1798. The wider significance of Nelson's victory was evident not only from the baronetcy and the acclaim won by the British admiral, but also from the handsome cash bounty he received from the grateful governors of the East India Company.[2]

Naples and its rulers were less fortunate. After his victory, the hero of the Nile headed for Naples to repair his ships, recover from his wounds, and become

[1] Sir William served as the British envoy in Naples until 1799; see Constantine (2001) and Fothergill (1969).

[2] Vincent (2003), 272.

infatuated with Sir William Hamilton's young wife, Emma. The crisis of the Neapolitan monarchy quickly followed. The king of Naples, Ferdinand IV, had already been pressed into the coalition against France in 1793, and now he came under renewed pressure from Nelson, the Hamiltons, and the queen to launch an offensive against the French forces that had occupied Rome earlier in the year.

The campaign was a disaster. The Neapolitan army was defeated and disintegrated; the king fled and was carried on Nelson's ships with his courtiers to the safety of Sicily. The mainland, in the meantime, was invaded by a French army and in January 1799 a republican government was proclaimed in Naples. In June the monarchy was restored, thanks to Nelson's ships and a popular royalist insurrection, aided and directed by Russian and Turkish troops.

The presence of the Russian, Albanian, and Turkish troops that joined the assault on the Republic and its French ally in 1799 was a clear sign of the broader dimensions of the conflict that momentarily converged on the central Mediterranean and the Italian peninsula. But only the particular constellation of powers and forces was new. Like the other Italian states southern Italy was used to living on the peripheries of empire and its destinies had always been shaped by the shifting alignments and counter-alignments of Europe's power politics.[3]

The immediate cause of the crisis of the Neapolitan monarchy in 1799 was the renewal of war in Europe, but it was also driven by internal tensions and conflicts directly linked to the attempts by the Bourbon rulers to transform their kingdom into a viable dynastic state. Before it became an independent dynastic state in 1734, the Kingdom of the Two Sicilies had for two centuries been the eastern frontier of the Spanish empire and its first line of defence against the Ottoman Turks.[4] After a brief interlude of Austrian government the Kingdom acquired its autonomy with the accession of a cadet branch of the Spanish Bourbons. The Kingdom's new rulers were now faced with the same challenges that confronted their counterparts throughout Europe. To secure their kingdom and their dynastic ambitions, the new rulers needed to improve its defences and strengthen its military forces. However, that required revenues and resources that the monarchy did not have and could only acquire by increasing its power and authority. That in turn meant diminishing the autonomous jurisdictions, the privileges, and monopolies exercised by the feudal nobility, by the Church, and by the self-governing corporations with which the *ancien régime* princes shared power.[5]

It was not the dynastic ambitions of the Neapolitan Bourbons that were unusual, but the scale of the obstacles to achieving them. The Kingdom was poor and weak. It had no effective army or navy, while the royal administration was limited. The Kingdom consisted of the separate crowns of Naples and Sicily that were joined only in the person of the ruler: both Kingdoms had their own laws, customs, institutions, and constitutions, and in both Naples and Sicily the privileged orders exercised independent jurisdictions, and enjoyed wide fiscal

[3] See Galasso (1994). [4] Ibid. [5] Scott (ed.) (1990); Bonney (ed.) (1999).

exemptions and many important exclusive rights. The monarchy's jurisdictions were limited, and to make matters worse most of its revenues had been permanently disposed of by the Spanish rulers in the previous century. During the early years of Spanish rule the Kingdom's financial and administrative institutions had been extensively reorganized, but these constructive developments had been overthrown in the financial crisis that overwhelmed the Spanish monarchy in the seventeenth century when the Kingdom's principal assets and revenues were plundered to finance Spain's European wars and pay its creditors. The beneficiaries were the privileged orders and corporations who exploited the needs and weaknesses of the Spanish monarchy to increase their privileges, powers, and exemptions, as well as hordes of small investors who purchased venal offices and shares in the tax farms put up for sale.[6]

By the start of the eighteenth century, therefore, both the degree to which power was decentralized in the South and the institutional weakness of the southern monarchy were indeed exceptional in comparison with the other major Italian principalities. Much of the Kingdom was ruled not by the royal courts, but by the feudal courts that answered to lay and ecclesiastical feudatories or to the tribunals that represented powerful corporate bodies like the city of Naples.

The new rulers nonetheless tried to follow the lead set by other European princes to acquire the revenues without which neither the trappings nor the substance of dynastic autonomy could be attained. As the king's chief minister, Bernardo Tanucci, put it: 'Principini, ville e casini: Principoni armate e cannoni.'[7] The Bourbon rulers of Naples wanted big palaces, big guns, big armies, and big ships, too. Yet none of these could be achieved without reducing the fiscal exemptions, autonomous jurisdiction, and power sharing on which the whole political edifice of the *ancien régime* in the South was founded. That meant conflict with the most powerful interests in the Kingdom: the privileged orders, the Church, and the great self-governing corporations.

Similar dramas were being played out in absolutist states throughout Europe, and although from state to state the balances between the different forces varied, everywhere the Old Order resisted. As in the rest of Europe, the dynastic projects of the Bourbon rulers were also played out against a backdrop of changes that were undermining the economic as well as the political foundations of the European *ancien régime*. Even though the origins of these changes were often distant, they nonetheless had far-reaching consequences throughout the European peripheries, including the Italian peninsula. One of the most tangible signs of the changes that were the source of new wealth and a new capacity for consumption could be seen in the growing numbers of curious foreign travellers who tramped the itineraries

6 The tax farms were known as *arrendamenti*, from the Spanish word *arrendar* ('to yield'). See De Rosa (1958/2005) and Calabria (1991).

7 'Little princes need little palaces and little villas: big princes need big armies and big guns.' Simioni (1925), 40.

of the Grand Tour. Many began to find their way to Naples, where they might well have been entertained by Sir William Hamilton, who even wrote to London to express his concern over the amounts of money they spent.[8]

These wealthy travellers were living testimony of the consumer revolutions taking place by the mid-century elsewhere in Europe.[9] They did not bring these revolutions to Italy, but the growing numbers of foreign merchant ships beginning to visit the Mediterranean ports revealed how economic expansion in other parts of Europe was already giving rise to new demand for goods that the Mediterranean economies produced in plenty, in particular grain, olive oil, silk, wool, and citrus fruits. Especially during the years of the long European peace that preceded the revolutionary wars, British and French merchants and shipping were only the most prominent among those visiting the ports of the Mediterranean and the Levant. Exports grew at quite a modest pace, but enough to cause commodity prices to rise and generate powerful new incentives for increasing agricultural output.[10]

The consequences were deeply contradictory. Except in the fertile Po valley and the irrigated lower Milanese plain that won the admiration of the English agronomist Arthur Young at the end of the century, in most parts of Italy farming was geared mainly to subsistence needs and access to more distant markets was limited.[11] In most cases, agricultural production could be increased only by bringing more land under cultivation. But everywhere land was a scarce and inelastic resource. In part, geography and climate were the reasons for this since much of the Italian peninsula is dominated by the chain of the Apennine Mountains that runs from the Alps to Sicily. Outside the Po valley, good irrigated farmland was hard to find, and many of the principal cereal-growing regions—such as the Apulian plateau known as the Tavoliere or the hinterlands of central Sicily—suffered from lack of irrigation and severely inadequate rainfall, which resulted in thin and infertile topsoils that required extended periods of fallow and grazing between crops.

There were also pockets of more fertile land, of course, which in the South were often found close to the main cities—the Neapolitan *Campagna Felix*, the Terra di Bari, and the area around Reggio Calabria: in Sicily, Palermo's fabled Conca d'Oro and the areas surrounding Messina, Catania, Siracusa, and Noto. However, over the centuries soil erosion had also turned vast areas of previously fertile farm land into malaria-infested and uninhabitable swamps, a problem aggravated by the clearance of woodland from the lower upland slopes that caused thin topsoils to be washed from the hillsides by spring rains. As demand for wheat and other cash-crops grew, woodland clearances were already assuming a scale in many parts of southern Italy that seriously alarmed contemporaries.[12]

[8] Acton (1965), 169. [9] De Seta (1996).

[10] Caracciolo (1973); Chorley (1965); Romano (1951).

[11] See Cafagna (1962). For Arthur Young see Okey (ed.) (1915).

[12] Sereni (1961/89); Bevilacqua (1988), 337–62; Corona and Bevilacqua (1998), pp. xi–xvii, 27–62, 191–201.

The scarcity of land was also a consequence of feudalism. In eighteenth-century Europe feudalism took many different forms. While serfdom survived only in the East, in many parts of western Europe feudatories no longer exercised independent jurisdictions, although they did enjoy important fiscal and political privileges. In Italy, the meaning of feudal titles and the scale of feudal property varied not only from state to state, but also within states. In the Tuscan Grand Duchy it was unknown, but remained extensive in Piedmont and Lombardy, although in both cases the fiscal and political privileges of the feudatories had in most cases been heavily curtailed.[13]

In the South by no means was all land held in feudal tenure, but feudal property was nonetheless more extensive than in any other part of Italy or indeed western Europe. In most parts of the Kingdom, feudal courts were responsible for the day-to-day administration of justice and the maintenance of order. Feudal landowners were entitled to raise levies over the local communities subject to their feudal jurisdiction. These rights and levies were countered, without being balanced, by the numerous collective use-rights that the local communities exercised on feudal land as well as on the extensive common lands that constituted one of the principal resources of the rural poor. These included the right to pasture animals at certain times of year, to fell timber for fuel and building, to glean after the harvest, to gather chestnuts, to hunt for game in the woodlands, or to fish in the ponds and swamps. Unlike private property, the ownership of feudal land was therefore strictly conditional and the land remained subject to multiple uses and rights.[14]

As unprecedented rates of demographic expansion caused demand for land to increase during the course of the eighteenth century, the constraints imposed by feudal obligations and collective use-rights became more visible and vexatious, and the title by which both were exercised began to be challenged. As these rights became more contentious, so did all forms of property rights, giving rise not only to growing confusion but also to conflict. In response to rising commodity prices and land rents, the feudal landowners were often the first to violate feudal regulations by creating illegal enclosures, denying the local communities their collective use-rights, or occupying sections of the common lands. Given the inelastic supply of land, these actions threatened the livelihood of the rural communities, whose survival depended on their customary and seasonal use-rights on feudal land and access to common land. The assault on these collective rights triggered reactions similar to those that brought market forces and the moral economies of the rural communities into conflict in eighteenth-century England.[15]

In many parts of southern Italy these developments gave rise to conflicts not only between rural communities and neighbouring lay and ecclesiastical feudatories, but also between neighbouring villages. The situation was further

[13] Villari (1961). [14] Villani (1974); Villari (1961).

[15] On the ways in which rising prices and population growth caused the relative value of feudal revenues to decline, see Aymard (1978), 1155–69, Thompson (1994).

complicated by the prevalence of transhumant grazing along most of the Apennine chain in central and southern Italy. Every spring and autumn, millions of sheep made their way back and forth between upland summer pastures and winter grazing on the coastal plains. For these seasonal migrations to take place, the flocks enjoyed rights of passage across private and public land that had been protected by law since the fifteenth century. However, as enclosures spread, as more land came under the plough and as woodland was cleared, the transit routes were threatened, which created other potentially dangerous conflicts. Powerful interests were at stake, and it was no accident that brigandage and the transhumant economy were closely linked since many of the larger flocks were owned by powerful landowners who did not hesitate to employ armed retainers to defend their property and their rights.[16]

Changes being felt throughout all the agrarian economies of the Italian peninsula, therefore, were often experienced in particularly dramatic and disruptive form in the South. Not all parts of southern Italy and Sicily were affected in equal ways, or indeed even at the same time. However, the fragility of the southern economies, the delicate balances between scant resources and the needs and interests of different sections of the population, made change not only difficult, but also ensured that it could rarely be achieved gradually. As a result, the forces of change often gave rise to conflicts that challenged the foundations of the agrarian order and undermined the forms of agrarian paternalism and deference that in other parts of Italy would survive until much later.

Unwittingly, the monarchy's campaign against feudalism in the South served to exacerbate these conflicts. Throughout Europe, more or less enlightened attempts by the rulers to reduce feudal privileges and give more freedom to market forces gave rise to varied forms of popular resistance, which in many cases caused these initiatives to be abandoned. This was the case both in Austria and in Lombardy, where in the final decade of the eighteenth century many of Joseph II's earlier reforms were abandoned or even reversed. The same happened even in the proverbially tranquil Grand Duchy of Tuscany, where at the end of the century popular resistance also caused many of the liberal reforms introduced by Grand Duke Peter Leopold to be abandoned.[17]

In southern Italy, however, the impact of the monarchy's campaign against feudalism was different. Because the monarchy had no bureaucracy of its own, it relied primarily on the royal courts and tribunals to challenge and check feudal privileges. For that reason, the crown's agents actively encouraged local communities to bring legal suits against powerful feudal neighbours. Ironically, these attempts to use feudal law—as opposed to more arbitrary and absolutist measures—to combat feudal abuses brought the campaign against feudalism to

[16] See esp. Villari (1961), 14–58; Marino (1988), 255–9; Russo (2002).

[17] On the Habsburg territories see Capra (2005) 218–33; on Tuscany, Cochrane (1973), Lichfield (1986), and Turi (1969/99).

the most distant towns and villages of the Kingdom and played an important part in escalating local conflicts that neither the crown nor the courts had the means to resolve.[18]

The monarchy's campaign against feudalism in the South therefore also played a critical part in undermining local systems of power and authority. The projects and ideas of the reformers played a part in this, too, of course, and especially as their projects began to be debated in the provinces, thanks mainly to the rapid increase in masonic lodges, whose numbers multiplied in the last decades of the century, often with the open support of the government.[19]

Well before the revolution of 1789 and the crisis of the Neapolitan monarchy, there were clear signs that the European revolutions had found their way to the South by many different paths. By the closing years of the century these gentlemanly debates were taking place against a noisier background of conflicts in which the voices of the rural poor could also be clearly heard. The South was not a world locked into some timeless past, where every attempt at change met with resistance and failure. In every aspect of political, social, economic, and social life, the prevailing idiom had become change, often radical and deeply disruptive change. Indeed, it was the deeply disruptive impact of change on the fragile foundations of southern society that explains why the crisis of the *ancien régime* monarchy at the end of the century opened the way to a broader crisis of social as well as political institutions. The crisis that affected the Italian *ancien régimes* as a whole came in the South to take forms that were also distinctive.

SEEKING SECURITY

Before they could change their Kingdom, its new rulers first had to secure it. From 1504 to 1707 the crowns of Naples and Sicily had been possessions of the Spanish monarchy, ruled by Spanish viceroys whose courts were respectively in Naples and Palermo. The independent dynastic state that came into being in 1734 was a direct consequence of the decline of Spanish power, and specifically of the War for the Spanish Succession that followed the death of the last Spanish Habsburg emperor, Charles II, in 1700.[20]

The conflicts lasted nearly half a century and focused on Spain's possessions in Italy, which as well as Naples and Sicily included Milan and Sardinia. First the Spanish were driven out of southern Italy by the Austrians, who in 1707 placed

[18] See especially Rao (2002), 63–113, and Rao (2005), 142–67. Sicily was different: see Chapter 3.

[19] Giarrizzo (1995), 406–20. See also Ferrone (1982/1995, 1989/2000); Chiosi (1986, 1992).

[20] The result was not one but three wars, which started when Louis XIV of France declared his grandson, the Duke of Anjou, successor to the Spanish crown (the War of the Spanish Succession (1702–14)), followed by the War of the Polish Succession (1733–8), and finally the War of the Austrian Succession (1740–8).

a Habsburg Archduke on the throne of Naples.[21] The Austrians occupied Sicily in 1720 and held the South until the War of the Polish Succession, when Bourbons once again regained the upper hand. In 1733 it was agreed that the son of King Philip V of Spain, the Spanish Infante Don Carlos who had inherited from his mother the title of Duke of Parma, should become the ruler of what would be an independent kingdom of Naples and Sicily.[22] In 1734 a Spanish army retook Sicily and Naples; Philip V renounced his own claims in favour of Don Carlos, who became king. The Habsburg emperor Charles VI grudgingly agreed and in return the Bourbons acknowledged Habsburg claims to Milan, the Duchies of Parma and Piacenza, and the Grand Duchy of Tuscany. They also pledged that the thrones of Sicily and Naples should never revert to the Spanish monarchy.[23]

The first priority for Charles of Bourbon[24] was to secure the safety of his Kingdom. Spain was too weak to offer effective protection, and for two centuries the Kingdom had relied on Spanish armies and navies for its defence. As a result the Kingdom had only a small army and no navy, even though its extensive coastline was exposed to attack by other European powers and by Barbary corsairs that marauded on the Kingdom's merchant shipping and fishing vessels. The crumbling watch towers that remain to this day had been built to warn inhabitants of the coastal settlements of impending raids, whose principal aim was to capture prisoners to be sold as slaves in North Africa.[25]

The new Kingdom had more powerful enemies, however. Austria remained hostile, as did Great Britain. When Spain and France went to war over the Austrian Succession in 1740, the new Austrian empress Maria Theresa worked hard to foment opposition to the new dynasty amongst the Neapolitan and Sicilian nobles, many of whom remained strongly pro-Austrian. But when Naples remained stubbornly neutral, Commodore Martin led a British naval squadron into the Bay of Naples on 18 August 1742 and threatened to bombard the city unless the Bourbon rulers joined the coalition against France.[26] The pro-Austrian revolt by the nobles never materialized, however, and two years later at the battle of Velletri the king of Naples got the better of an Austrian army that had been sent to depose him.[27]

[21] In 1713 Spain lost Sicily, which under the terms of the Treaty of Utrecht passed to the Duke Victor Amadeus II of Savoy, whose family finally acquired an ardently coveted royal title. When the Austrians occupied Sicily in 1720 the Piedmontese rulers had to make do with the less desirable island of Sardinia, which nonetheless still carried a royal title that the rulers of the House of Savoy kept until they became kings of Italy in 1861.

[22] To win the support of Philip V of Spain, the French monarchy offered to drop its claims to the Medici and Farnese inheritance in Italy: this was the inheritance of Philip's wife, Elizabeth Farnese, the last surviving descendant of the two great families that had dominated central Italy since the sixteenth century; see Lynch (1989), 137–41.

[23] At the Peace of Vienna 1735, which was reconfirmed in 1738.

[24] Don Carlos took the titles Charles VII in Naples and Charles III in Sicily; however, he is always referred to by the title he assumed upon becoming king of Spain in 1759: Charles III.

[25] See Colley (2002).

[26] This was the first of four threats by the British navy to bombard Naples in the century that followed: the threats were repeated in 1799, 1815, and 1840.

[27] Treaty of Fontainebleau, 25 October 1743: see Barra (no date), 4–6.

Commodore Martin's visitation exposed the Kingdom's extreme military and naval vulnerability, and it was only when the Treaty of Aix-la-Chapelle in 1748 brought the War of the Austrian Succession to an end that the Bourbon monarchy in the South could finally enjoy some degree of security. This enabled Charles to turn his attention to reorganizing his Kingdom and building palaces, but his days in Naples were numbered. Following the death of his hopelessly insane half-brother, he inherited the throne of Spain and took his leave for Madrid in 1759.[28] Since his own eldest son was also mad, his second son took the title of Infante of Spain, while the crowns of Naples and Sicily went to his eight-year-old third son, whose own mind was far from stable. The boy-king took the titles of Ferdinand IV of Naples and Ferdinand III of Sicily,[29] and until he came of age in 1767 the kingdom was governed by a Regency Council headed by Bernardo Tanucci, the Tuscan lawyer who served as principal minister throughout Charles's time in Naples.[30]

Charles's departure to Spain occurred in the middle of the Seven Years War (1756–63), the bloodiest and most costly of Europe's eighteenth-century conflicts that nonetheless finally caused France and Austria to become allies. That alliance brought western Europe the relatively long period of peace that lasted until 1792 that was the background for the numerous experiments in absolutist reform and the intellectual debates of the Enlightenment.[31] It also saw Naples leave the diplomatic protection of Madrid to enter the orbit of Habsburg Vienna, a diplomatic shift that was consummated in 1768 when Ferdinand of Naples married the sixteen-year-old daughter of the Austrian empress Maria Theresa, the Archduchess Maria Carolina.[32]

The Neapolitan marriage marked an important extension of Habsburg influence in Italy. Maria Carolina's bother, the emperor Joseph II, escorted her on her nuptial journey to Naples. Another brother, Peter Leopold, was Grand Duke of Tuscany, while her sister Maria Amalia was married to the Duke of Parma, Don Felipe of Bourbon, who was the first cousin of the king of Naples.[33] After giving birth to her first male child in 1776, the young queen exercised her right to become a member of the Council of State and within a year had engineered Tanucci's downfall.

Tanucci's fall after forty-four years in government marked the defeat of the 'pro-Spanish' party in Naples, and the queen quickly set about constructing her own party while the king spent most of his time hunting.[34] The young queen's aim was

[28] Philip V died in 1746 and was succeeded by Charles's half-brother, who ruled as Ferdinand VI until his death in 1759 at the age of forty-six without heirs.

[29] He is generally known by the Neapolitan title, until the Act of Union in 1816 when he became Ferdinand I.

[30] Bernardo Tanucci (1698–1793).

[31] Schroeder (1994), 3–52.

[32] Maria Carolina (1752–1814) bore Ferdinand 17 children.

[33] Another sister, Maria Cristina, was governor of the Low Countries, while in 1770 yet another sister, Marie Antoinette, would of course marry the future Louis XVI and in 1774 become the queen of France: Dumas (1864), i. 190.

[34] In 1787 Goethe commented, 'Naples itself appears to be happy, free and lively, vast numbers of people running about in mingled confusion, the king is out hunting, the queen is expecting

to imitate the reforms being introduced in Vienna by her brother, the emperor Joseph II, and she needed a minister willing to assert the power of the monarchy over the feudal nobility and the Church and build a dynastic army and navy. She found her man in 1778 when her brother Peter Leopold sent an energetic administrator named John Acton to Naples to advise on building a navy.

Born in France but descended from an English Jacobite family, Acton had served in the French navy before going to Tuscany to advise the Grand Duke on naval matters. He now followed Tanucci's footsteps from Florence to Naples, where his task initially was to advise on naval matters. However, the queen soon gave him the job of reorganizing the army and expanding the Kingdom's economy and trade. Within two years of his arrival, Acton was the queen's favourite and by repute also her lover. In 1779 he was appointed Secretary for the Navy and in 1780 acquired the posts of Secretary for War and Finances, making him the most powerful minister at the Neapolitan Court.[35]

Acton's project for building an independent navy and reorganizing the army gave the government's reform programme a new sense of urgency. Anxious to acquire British approval Acton sought the good offices of the British envoy, Sir William Hamilton. The new relations between Naples and Vienna had made the British less hostile to the Neapolitan government, and as commercial competition between Britain and France increased, and as the size of France's Mediterranean fleet grew, Britain's interest in developing new markets in the Two Sicilies and in gaining access to the Sicilian ports had also grown. Although Britain's principal trade entrepôt in the western Mediterranean was Livorno in the Grand Duchy of Tuscany, apart from Gibraltar and the Balearic Islands Britain had no secure naval stations in the Mediterranean and few allies capable of providing port facilities in times of war.[36]

The Neapolitan government was also interested in finding ways to promote its foreign trade. New commercial treaties were negotiated with the Habsburg Empire, the Ottoman Porte, the Bey of Tripoli, Denmark, the Dutch Republic, Morocco, Sardinia, and Russia. Negotiations with Britain collapsed, however, when the British refused to give up the major commercial privileges they enjoyed under the terms of a very one-sided treaty signed with Spain in 1667.[37]

Despite this failure, the volume of British imports—especially salt cod, and colonial and manufactured goods—grew rapidly in the second half of the century and faster than France's trade with Naples, which was also expanding.[38] This was a source of great alarm for the reformers who feared that the Kingdom risked

a child, and so things could not be better' (Naples, 25 February, 1787): cited in Saine and Sammons (1989), 152.

[35] See entry by Nuzzo, in *DBI*, i. 206–10; Barra (no date), 108.

[36] De Divitiis and Giura (1997).

[37] The privileges included a flat rate reduction on all landing duties and the right not to be inspected by Neapolitan customs officers. See Nuzzo (1971), 280–1.

[38] Nuzzo (1990), 457.

becoming a colonial supplier of raw materials to Britain.[39] These fears also fuelled rumours that the queen and Acton were agents of British commercial interests, and these were eagerly seized on by the remnants of the pro-Spanish faction that had never hidden its hostility to the Austrian queen.[40] But those attacks were also directed at the increasingly absolutist and arbitrary style of government adopted by the queen and her favourite minister.

THE CHURCH

Perhaps the most dangerous enemy of the new dynasty was the Pope. For centuries the papacy had claimed that the rulers of the Kingdom were its feudal vassals, which meant that the Pope claimed the exclusive right to sanction any change of dynasty. In symbolic recognition of their status as vassals the rulers of Naples every year made the gift to the Pope of a white palfrey (known as the *chinea*) laden with gold and precious jewels.[41] However, the Pope's power in the Kingdom was far from symbolic, and as well as important jurisdictional rights and the revenues attached to them Rome was the source of extensive and very lucrative ecclesiastical patronage. For that reason it also exercised great political influence, and had many committed supporters amongst the feudal aristocracy as well as the clergy.

In the early eighteenth century Rome's power and patronage in the Kingdom came under attack. The case against Rome was set out most cogently in Pietro Giannone's *Civil History of the Kingdom of Naples*, a treatise first published in 1723 which subsequently became an obligatory point of reference for the later Neapolitan reform movement. In his tract, Giannone depicted the history of the South as a prolonged struggle for freedom from the papacy, which had always been the ally of the Kingdom's foreign invaders. He concluded that the Kingdom would never be free of papal oppression until it was ruled by an independent secular prince.[42]

Giannone's treatise drew on a much older tradition of hostility to the papacy, and earlier Neapolitan writers had frequently depicted Spain as the papacy's accomplice in suppressing Neapolitan liberties. In the seventeenth century, papal hostility to all forms of new learning, to science and the new rationalist philosophies, had encouraged the popularity of 'libertine', rationalist, and secularist philosophies in southern Italy. Since the university was closely controlled by the

[39] Galanti, *Breve Descrizione* (1792), ii. 334–5. The surplus with France probably offset the deficit in the Kingdom's accounts through bills discounted in England and Holland, but either way this was clear evidence that the volume of the Kingdom's foreign trade was increasing in the second half of the century: see Salvemini in Imbuglia (2000), 44–69; also Chorley (1965), 13–38; Romano (1951), 92–5.

[40] Nuzzo (1990), 437–535.

[41] This ceremony was one of the most colourful of the annual pageants of papal Rome: Tanucci threatened to end it in 1767 but this did not happen until 1788 at the height of the anti-curial campaign: see Rambaud (1908), 294.

[42] Chiosi (1987), 371–467.

Spanish vice-regal authorities and supporters of papal supremacy, a strong tradition of private schools had also taken root in Naples.[43]

In the new political circumstances following the founding of an independent dynastic state, opposition to Rome would play an important role in creating the intellectual background from which the Neapolitan reform movement would emerge. However, hostility to Rome also went hand in hand with asserting the autonomy of the new dynastic rulers, and helps explain the enthusiastic reception for Freemasonry in southern Italy. It was the first patron of Freemasonry in Naples, the Prince of Sansevero, who in 1744 appealed to Charles III to follow the example of the Elector of Prussia and declare himself a mason, create a new aristocracy of the virtuous, and establish a national army.[44]

The king did not respond to that appeal, but in 1741 the government had negotiated a new Concordat in which Rome made important concessions, including waiving certain tax exemptions for religious houses. The Concordat also enabled the government to begin reducing the number of convents and religious houses in the Kingdom considered to be excessive.[45] However, the standing of the new ruler with the opponents of papal power was greatly enhanced in 1744 when the Archbishop of Naples, Cardinal Spinelli, was accused of secretly plotting with Rome to introduce the Inquisition into Naples. The charges against Spinelli mobilized all the opponents of Rome, and the king's decision to order an inquiry that confirmed the accusations was warmly greeted by the anti-papal faction. It also revealed the highly divisive nature of ecclesiastical politics, however. In Rome the royal intervention was furiously attacked and opposition to the papal curia in Naples was attributed to the spread of 'a Republican and British spirit' encouraged by the unchecked circulation of works by Giannone, Locke, and Montesquieu.[46] In Naples, however, the Pope's protests also found many supporters, including the Jesuits, most of the regular clergy, and S. Alfonso Maria di Liguori, the city's most popular and influential preacher who in his widely attended sermons regularly denounced all those who challenged the authority of Rome as libertines and Freemasons.[47]

THE CAPITAL

The Kingdom that Charles of Bourbon inherited in 1734 was not only the oldest monarchy on the peninsula, but also the largest.[48] At the time of Charles's accession the population of the mainland was estimated at four million, with nearly

43 Chiosi (1987), 371–467. 44 Ibid.; Ferrone (1989/2000); Giarrizzo (1995).

45 Moricola (1994) 27–8: 22% of the 75,000 priests and clerics in the Kingdom resided in Naples.

46 Chiosi (2000), 452–4. 47 Ibid.

48 Before the House of Savoy—the oldest ruling dynasty in Italy, indeed in Europe according to their apologists—acquired their royal title in 1713, the only other Italian ruler with the title of king was the Pope; the *papa-re*.

another million in Sicily. The Kingdom also contained Italy's two largest cities. Naples, whose population was estimated at between 350,000 and 400,000 at the end of the eighteenth century, was still the third largest city in Europe after London and Paris. Palermo, with around 120,000 inhabitants was much smaller, but at the end of the century still slightly larger than Rome. The other southern cities were both smaller and less numerous than their northern counterparts.[49]

For the French traveller Charles de Brosse, Naples was the only Italian city in the eighteenth century that had the feel of a capital, and the new Bourbon rulers set out to make it a monument to their dynastic ambitions.[50] Naples was in many respects the perfect theatre for such an enterprise. Set in surroundings of extraordinary natural beauty and drama, the city was also a treasure-trove for eighteenth-century tastes. Here the traveller could admire the spectacle of Mount Vesuvius in eruption, visit the sites of the ancient cities of Herculaneum and Pompeii where excavations had recently begun to yield remarkable artefacts of antiquity, or tour the fabled Phlegrean Fields, which offered an unrivalled choice of classical sites, mythological references, and natural wonders.

As well as some of the finest Baroque architecture in Italy, the city's streets and public squares were a constant pageant of folklore and festival that was outshone only by papal Rome. Scarcely a day passed without processions to celebrate a neighbourhood saint or patron, in which monks and friars from the many religious houses, members of the lay confraternities, the penitents, the sick, the halt, the maimed, the lame, and the blind formed the permanent supporting cast. Nor could the visitor miss the famous *lazzaroni*, most often depicted as exotic beggars idly reclining in picaresque semi-nudity on the harbour walls.[51]

Even more exotic was the fabled *cuccagna*, an elaborately choreographed spectacle that was part public charity and part display of royal munificence. For days food, flour, wine, meats, and live animals—cows, calves, goats, kids, sheep, lamb, geese, capons, and other fowl—were piled high on towers constructed in one of the main *piazze* of the city. On the appointed day and hour a signal was given, the guards stood back and the populace invaded the *piazza* to take whatever could be carried. The pell-mell that ensued took place under the benevolent gaze of the prince and his courtiers, who watched from the lofty safety of a balcony.

More often cited than seen, the *cuccagna* embodied the exotic and the barbaric that caught the travellers' fascination. But if the city's pageantry had deep roots in

49 The next largest on the mainland was Foggia with 20,000 inhabitants, followed by a number of towns whose populations varied between 10,000 and 20,000. In Sicily, Catania and Messina were the largest cities after Palermo, with a number of other towns of around 8,000 inhabitants: see Galasso (1997), 42–4.

50 Many other reactions were far less complimentary; discerning discourses in travellers' tales are a flourishing industry: see Calaresu (1999), Moe (2002), Naddeo (2005), but the fullest critical anthologies remain Mozzillo (1992) and Venturi (1972). See also Galasso, 'Lo stereotipo del napoletano', in idem (1994), 171–225.

51 Johann Wolfgang von Goethe noted perceptively that they were not beggars, but stevedores whose brief work shifts were combined with long periods of enforced idleness: Naples May 28, 1787, in Saine and Sammons (1989), 262–7; cf. also Boyle (1992), 458–66, 478–81.

the culture of its popular neighbourhoods, much had also been invented in the course of the eighteenth century as the city became the principal site for parading the glory and grandeur of the new dynasty. Once the Kingdom had been secured from foreign enemies, Charles III set about making his capital reflect to the glory of the new dynasty. The result was an unprecedented building spree designed to rank Naples with the leading capital cities in Europe, embellished with a dazzling array of sumptuous royal palaces, villas, hunting lodges, theatres, and monuments in and around the capital that aimed to surpass the grandest princes in Europe.[52]

The greatest of these projects was the vast palace built on the principal landward approaches to the city at Caserta. Designed by Luigi Vanvitelli, work begun in 1754 and was completed within only twenty-two years.[53] But Caserta was only one of the many grandiose new monuments that transformed the appearance of Naples and its surrounding area. Work also began to enlarge the royal palace in the centre of the Naples, while new royal residences were built at Capodimonte, at Portici, and near the recently opened excavations at Herculaneum, all of which were accompanied by sumptuous and elegant new villas built for wealthy courtiers and nobles.[54] Elegant hunting lodges and follies paid tribute in addition to the king's passion for hunting, which was inherited as an obsession by his third son who in 1767 would succeed him as Ferdinand IV.

These great building projects brought artists and craftsmen from all over Europe to the city, among them the Bohemian painter Antol Raffael Mengs, who had accompanied Charles III's child-bride, Maria Amalia[55] from her father's Court in Dresden, Angelika Kauffmann,[56] Philip Hackert,[57] and Wilhelm Tischbein,[58] who first came to Naples with Goethe and was later appointed director of the *Accademia delle Belle Arti* in 1789.[59]

Among the numerous portraits commissioned to celebrate the new dynasty, the most prominent background themes were the buried Roman cities of Pompeii and Herculaneum, and Mount Vesuvius.[60] Excavation of the archaeological sites

[52] See especially De Seta (1981, 1992, 1999).

[53] Luigi Vanvitelli's (1700–73) reputation had been made in Rome where he had been the chief architect and supervisor of buildings at St Peter's in the 1720s. As well as a new harbour for the papal port of Ancona and the monumental cemetery at the shrine of the Madonna of Loreto, he also designed the Jesuit chapel in Lisbon and the residence of the Habsburg Archduke of Milan.

[54] On the 'ville vesuviane' see De Seta (1981), 152–83.

[55] The daughter of the Elector of Saxony (and King of Poland) who became Charles's child-bride in 1737 at the age of 13.

[56] Angelika Kauffmann (1741–1807): born in Switzerland she worked in London from 1766 to 1781, then moved to Italy with her husband Antonio Zucchi.

[57] Philip Hackert (1737–1807): a Prussian landscape painter who moved from Rome to Naples where he was appointed court painter by Ferdinand IV.

[58] Wilhelm Tischbein (1751–1829) was director of the Academy from 1789 to 1799, then returned to Germany and became the court painter to the Duke of Oldenburg at Eutin. See Boyle (1992), 392–3.

[59] See F. Haskell (1981), 15; Sloan, in Jenkins and Sloan (1996), 25–7; Spinosa (1981), 55–155; Marandel (1981), 156–82.

[60] Sloan (1996), 27.

at Herculaneum had begun in the 1730s, and the fame of the Roman paintings and designs and of the remarkable collections of papyri found in the villas of Herculaneum and Pompeii, and other sites at Castellamare, spread across Europe thanks to the lavishly illustrated volumes published by the royal printing house in Naples in the 1750s. These were followed by colour reproductions of paintings on the Greek and Roman vases found at the same sites in volumes edited by mysterious Baron d'Hancarville and Sir William Hamilton.[61] The city as a result came to be closely identified with the new enthusiasm for neo-classical art, and it also provided the English pottery-master Josiah Wedgwood with the design for the highly successful line of Etruria ware that was directly inspired by Hamilton's reproductions of the classical paintings found at Pompeii and Herculaneum.[62]

Vesuvius was hardly less important in linking the city to contemporary fascination with the natural sciences, although few observers could resist the unscientific temptation of linking the volcano to the character of the Neapolitans. Sir William Hamilton was not only the volcano's indefatigable record keeper but also its principal publicist. He made the difficult and frequently dangerous ascent to the crater almost seventy times, generally in the company of a retinue of foreign visitors and often immediately after major eruptions.[63]

The city had much else to reflect the glory of the new dynasty and long before the arrival of the Bourbons was famed as the 'European capital of music'.[64] With four conservatories the city continued to attract the leading musical talents of the age, among them Paisiello and Cimarosa.[65] In addition to its rich tradition of street theatres and puppet stalls, where *Pulcinella* and his entourage drew on an older Neapolitan tradition of the *commedia dell'arte*, the city also boasted five permanent theatres.[66]

One of Charles III's first initiatives was to rebuild and enlarge the San Carlo theatre to keep an eye, so it was said, on what his nobles were doing at night. But the broader significance of the monarchy's role as leader and arbiter of cultural taste was unmistakable.[67] The new theatre was connected to the royal palace, making it an extension of the Court. 'Groundlings' were admitted on occasion, but only the nobility and wealthiest non-noble families were eligible for subscriptions to the boxes, which were allocated personally by the king. The season ran from the Christmas holidays to Lent and was where the nobility met, entertained,

[61] And came to play an important role in establishing the neo-classical style: see Jenkins in Jenkins and Sloan (1996), 40–60.

[62] Ibid.

[63] See Constantine (2001), 195; on Baron d'Hancarville see Rousseau, in Rousseau and Porter (1987).

[64] The first performance of Pietro Mestasio's *Didone Abbandonata* in 1724 made Naples the birthplace of European melodrama. Handel's opera *Partenope* was first performed in 1730, while Giovanni Pergolesi's *Serva Padrona* launched the new fashion for *opera buffa* that would quickly be taken up in all the courts and capitals of Europe: De Benedetto in Imbruglia (2000), 135–50.

[65] Ibid.

[66] The *San Carlo*, the *Fiorentino*, the *Teatro Nuovo*, the *San Carlino*, and the *Teatro del Fondo*.

[67] Croce, *I Teatri* (1947).

played cards, ate, drank, and conversed while following the action on stage by means of mirrors set at the rear of the boxes.[68]

The king was not the only source of artistic patronage, however, as there were also many private patrons in the city. In the past, the great religious houses and churches had been the principal patrons of artists and architects, but in the eighteenth century wealthy lay patrons became more prominent. The glory of the great palaces built by the new rulers was reflected in those of leading nobles like the Duke della Torre and the Prince of Francavilla, which also housed outstanding collections of paintings and fine art. The splendid baroque family chapel of the Prince of Sansevero with its famous masonic devices was built during the reign of Charles III, while the 'Vesuvian villas' built for leading courtiers and noblemen at Herculaneum were the finest expression of the Indian summer of the Kingdom's eighteenth-century cultural renaissance. Numerous private patrons played their part in this, including Tanucci's friend, the wealthy Tuscan banker Bartolomeo, who funded the new chair in political economy at the University of Naples—the first not only in Italy but in Europe—created in 1754 for Antonio Genovesi. But wealthy patrons were active in many other branches of the arts, especially music and the theatre.[69]

By contrast, the monarchy's promotion of the arts and sciences was always politically motivated and selective. Tanucci was no friend of the new ideas of the Enlightenment, but he understood that the arts, sciences, and learning were essential trappings of the modern prince.[70] He was responsible for founding the *Accademia del Disegno* in 1752, which later became the *Accademia delle Belle Arti* and three years later the *Accademia Reale Ercolanese*, which was responsible for cataloguing the papyri and other treasures discovered during the excavations at Herculaneum.

The complaint most frequently heard in the 1780s, however, was that royal patronage of the arts and sciences was penny-pinching and uncertain. Whatever funds were available were directed to prestigious regalian monuments, and even the plans to transfer the collection of artworks that Charles inherited from his mother Elizabeth Farnese to Naples ran into major problems. Nor was the monarchy willing to support wider academic and scientific projects, and despite repeated appeals from the world of letters and learning the *Royal Academy for Sciences*

[68] Rosselli (1984), 82–3; Sorba (2001), 93–153.

[69] Francesco Saverio de Rogati, a jurist and a music lover, was the protégé of Vito Giuseppe Millico, who was the most acclaimed Neapolitan castrato of the time. De Rogati was director of the Royal College of Music (later the Conservatory of San Pietro a Majella). The Prince of Campofranco and the Lucchesi Palli family were also leading patrons of musicians and the theatre: see Di Benedetto in Imbruglia (2000), 148–9.

[70] He banned possession of Voltaire's *Dictionary* and Fénélon's *Reflections on the Conscience of a King* as an offence punishable by two years imprisonment on the grounds that 'We do not hold it advisable to place in the hands and mouths of the common people ideas that criticise our rulers.' See Rotondo (1984), 492; on censorship and publishing in Naples see Rao (1998) and Luise (2001).

founded by the Austrian government in 1732 was not re-established until 1778 and even then suffered from severe lack of resources.[71]

Nonetheless, by the end of the century Naples had become an established station on the European Grand Tour. That was good for business, but not good enough to make a significant contribution to the city's economy. In economic terms, the greatest impact of the monarchy's initiatives came from the work and demand created by its building projects, and when it came to promoting trade and manufacturing enterprises royal interventions followed conventional mercantilist logic. Charles III's government established a variety of royal manufactures whose main purpose was to provide luxury goods and apparel for use at court and to reduce the need for imports.[72] There were also a number of more utopian initiatives, and after the expulsion of the Jesuits in 1767 the convents of San Giuseppe di Chiaia and of the Carminello were converted into pauper schools under royal patronage.[73]

The most unusual of these utopian schemes came toward the end of the century when in 1789 the *Royal Silk Works* was founded at San Leucio near the royal palace at Caserta. The aim was to improve the quality of silk fabrics by using the most modern techniques, but what made the project remarkable were the utopian regulations for the community of silk workers introduced three years later and supposedly drafted by the king himself. They and their families were provided with housing, schools, and medical services, while strict equality between the sexes was to be observed and dowries were banned.[74]

The San Leucio colony was established after the revolution in France and just before the monarchy cut all its ties with the reform movement and was most probably inspired by the utopian colonies founded by the Jesuits in Paraguay. Similar South American models also inspired the greatest monument to the monarchy's paternalism, the *Royal Hospice for the Poor* (*Reale Albergo dei Poveri*) in Naples.

This too had been started by Charles III, to match the monumental poorhouse built earlier in the century by the Austrians in Palermo. The Neapolitan project was designed on a massive scale by the architect Ferdinando Fuga, and consisted of a complex of workhouses, hospitals, orphanages, and asylums for the mentally ill. Its façade measured nearly 500 metres, making it one of the largest poorhouses in Europe.[75]

Naples already possessed an immensely rich and varied assortment of charitable foundations, hospices, and hospitals run by religious and lay groups. The decision

[71] Chiosi (2001), 122–3.

[72] These included a royal craft school modelled on the Gobelins factory in Paris, an *Academy for the Design and Working of Precious Stones* at S. Carlo la Mortella, a coral factory, a factory for making crystal glass, a lace factory, and a silk works. His first and showiest project, however, was the *Royal Porcelain Works*, which was built in 1742 next to the splendid new palace at Capodimonte and modelled directly on the famous Meissen factory of Charles's father-in-law, the Elector of Saxony.

[73] The Carminello housed 200 orphan girls, who were taught to spin and weave hemp, and to make lace and silk *merletti*. Ferdinand IV later added a dyeing shop, spinning works, and weaving shed and turned the Carminiello into the first royal silk factory in the kingdom.

[74] Tescione (1961), 178–89.

[75] See Guerra (1996), 153–215.

to build the new poorhouse reflected the growing scale of poverty in the city, which was exacerbated by rising prices, by the closure of many monasteries, and by the difficulties facing many of the city's confraternities and mutual aid associations.[76] But the decision to build the new poorhouse was taken at a moment when economists in Italy, as in the rest of Europe, were arguing that the indiscriminate provision of charity by such institutions was the cause not the cure of poverty and unemployment. The project for the Royal Poorhouse in Naples was untouched by such considerations, however, and was inspired instead by the great missionary churches that had been built in Mexico and other parts of Spanish America to draw the heathen Indians to the true faith. In Fuga's plan, the central core of the hospice was a vast church that would perform a similar missionary function in this teeming European metropolis.[77]

Although never completed, Fuga's vast project nonetheless effectively conveyed the monarchy's paternalist concern for its subject. Less intentionally, its very scale signalled the inability to devise effective responses to problems that many were beginning to argue epitomized deeper inadequacies of the *ancien régime*: the alarming increases in pauperism and the excessive size of a city that lacked any means to support itself beyond revenues drawn from the provinces. In a metaphor that gained currency in the second half of the century, Naples was a swollen head that lived parasitically off the shrunken corpse of the provinces.

BEYOND THE CAPITAL

In some respects that image was exaggerated. As the Kingdom's principal commercial as well as political and cultural centre, the capital generated consumer needs that supported commercial networks that extended from the farms of the fabled *Campania Felix* to the towns along the Bay of Naples—Portici, Torre del Greco, Torre Annunziata, and Castellamare di Stabia—to more distant centres like Campobasso, Nola, Salerno, and Avellino.[78] Naples was also the hub for the pivotal commercial axis that linked the capital with Apulia and the Adriatic coast where the city's grain was grown, since this could be carried by ship more easily and at less cost than overland transport from provinces closer to the city.

Bari and the Adriatic ports were also at the centre of other commercial networks that connected with the Papal States, the Republic of Venice, Trieste, the Dalmatian and Croatian ports, and the eastern Mediterranean. But it was an increasing source of resentment in the provinces that the lion's share of foreign trade was monopolized by Naples. Olive oil, grain, silk, and other products from the mainland provinces and from Sicily could only enter the export trade after

[76] At the end of the century there were 146 convents and monasteries, 44 conservatories for women, 4 hospitals and hospices, and 8 colleges and seminaries in the capital. See Moricolo (1994), 26, 73–9.

[77] Id.; Valenzi (1995); Migliorini (1992).

[78] Marin, in Clark and Lepetit (1997), 143–216, and Ringrose in ibid. 217–40.

being shipped through Naples, from where the Kingdom's products were exported to Livorno, Genoa, and Marseilles.[79] The capital was also the principal point of entry for imports from France, Spain, Britain, Holland, and the German states.[80]

Despite these constraints, many provincial centres were showing unmistakable signs of steady commercial expansion in the second half of the eighteenth century. This was the case of towns like Bari, Molfetta, and Trani on the Adriatic coast, which were the principal outlets for the wheat grown in Capitanata.[81] Further south, Gallipoli was the principal commercial outlet for the olive oil produced in Apulia and northern and eastern Calabria, nearly all of which was exported directly to Naples. Despite the decline of the silk industry, Reggio was another prosperous commercial centre with trading networks that extended throughout southern Calabria and with strong commercial links with both Naples and the Sicilian towns.

In western Sicily, Palermo replicated the role of Naples, while in the east Catania and Siracusa were both important commercial centres where revenues from the wealthy lay and ecclesiastical properties in the rural hinterland were consumed. These towns were also centres for smaller independent commercial networks that stretched into the rural interior. Messina, by contrast, had not recovered from the earthquake of 1743, and like the rest of north-eastern Sicily would be badly damaged again by the devastating earthquake of 1783, whose epicentre was on the mainland. The rise of Trapani, which became the second largest port in western Sicily after Palermo, was a further sign of the impact of rising demand.[82] So too was the arrival of foreign merchants like the Liverpool merchants John Woodhouse and another Englishman Benjamin Ingham, who in the closing years of the century set up an export–import business in Marsala wine and other Sicilian export goods. Their enterprise did not prosper until after the turn of the century, but like the French merchants who came to buy raw silk in large quantities in the Calabrian market towns their presence indicated how the Kingdom was already being drawn into Europe's rapidly expanding commercial networks.[83]

The new rulers invested principally in Naples, but did not ignore Palermo, which was the seat of a Royal Viceroy. Numerous public and private palaces were built and rebuilt, new *piazze* and thoroughfares were created, and during the

79 In the 1770s, the English traveller Henry Swinburne listed the Kingdom's principal exports as 'wheat, barley, legumes, Indian corn, hemp, linen, cumin, fennel, honey, wax, fruit, manna, saffron, potash, brimstone (sulphur), nitre, pitch, sumac, skins, cattle, oranges, lemons, brandy, vinegar'. The single most important export commodity was olive oil (especially from Bari, Otranto, Gallipoli, and the provinces of the Abruzzi) and the soap industry of Marseilles was its principal foreign buyer. Merchants from Lyons were also among the leading purchasers of the Kingdom's raw silk. The principal imports were colonial goods, especially 'sugar, coffee, and spices, as well as fine fabrics, textiles, household goods, gun barrels, German, Austrian and Brescian ironworks and quality clothing'. Swinburne (1783), 79–81.

80 Chorley (1965); Romano (1951).

81 Chorley (1965), 38.

82 Benigno (1982).

83 Trevelyan (1973); d'Angelo (1988), 47–52.

Viceroyalty of the Marchese Caracciolo in the 1780s the city's famed Botanical Gardens were laid out. Catania was Sicily's second city and one of its most prosperous, drawing on a fertile agricultural hinterland whose bounty financed the splendid baroque towns that had been built in south-eastern Sicily following the devastating earthquake of 1684.[84]

On the mainland, towns like Salerno, Nola, Campobasso, Teramo, Foggia, Bari, Lecce, Gallipoli, Potenza, Cosenza, and Reggio Calabria were also important centres of civil and ecclesiastical administration, and here too there were signs of cultural as well as commercial change. Amongst these was the growing number of petitions for licences to open theatres, which greatly alarmed Tanucci, who feared that the provincial theatres would encourage licentiousness and give rise to disorder.[85] Private salons where the local elites met to exchange ideas and discuss public affairs were also becoming more active and visible in many of these provincial centres. So too were the masonic lodges that in the closing decades of the century played an even greater role in bringing the debates taking place in the capital to the most remote parts of the kingdom.[86]

The emergence of these provincial voices was inseparable from economic and commercial changes that, however uncertain, were beginning to focus attention on the Kingdom's political and administrative institutions. As these debates broadened, the damaging impact of the capital's privileges and in general of the mass of monopolies, restrictions, controls, and levies that burdened producers in the provinces came under increasing scrutiny. When in 1763 the Kingdom was struck by one of the most terrible famines of the century, Naples came to embody all the ills of the *ancien régime* and everything that stood in the way of the economic and civil regeneration of what was already being described not as the Kingdom but as the nation.

[84] De Seta and Di Mauro (1980), 120. [85] Croce (1947), 275.
[86] Giarizzo (1995); Ferrone (1989); Chiosi (2001).

2

Projecting Reform

THE GREAT FAMINE 1763–4

In 1763 and 1764 the worst famine of the century struck Italy. Mortality rates were extremely high in all the major cities, but even worse in rural areas. Like the earlier Lisbon earthquake of 1755, the famines played an important part in shaping the reform movements that developed in the Italian states in the following decades. Although the causes were natural, many were convinced that their consequences had been needlessly exacerbated by bad institutions and harmful regulations.[1]

The effects were especially dramatic in Naples, where it had been clear from the spring of 1763 that the coming harvest was likely to fail almost completely. But no measures were taken, and by the summer there was serious unrest in the capital and throughout the Kingdom. In August, the carriage carrying the young king to hear mass in the church of San Maria del Carmine was stopped by a crowd of women protesting against high food prices and shortages. The government feared a major revolt in the city and to prevent this a military expedition was sent to Apulia to seize whatever grain could be found to secure the supplies needed for the capital.

Grain was forcibly requisitioned in the provinces to feed Naples, causing thousands of starving people to head to the capital in search of food. As news spread in the following spring that the coming harvest was expected to fail as well, as many as forty thousand starving immigrants were estimated to have flooded into the city from the provinces. Daily processions of religious relics were staged in an attempt to lower tensions, but there was no relief and in April plague began to spread and carried off an estimated two to three hundred thousand souls.[2]

The crisis grew worse but the government was unable to intervene because the city's provisioning regulations were the exclusive monopoly of the municipal government and its tribunals in the city and in the provinces, and of the small aristocratic elite who controlled them. When the noble junta proved unable to agree on how to act, Bernardo Tanucci, who was head of the Regency government, authorized the city merchants to purchase grain abroad. He even contemplated

[1] Venturi (1973a), 394–472. [2] Ibid. 436.

transferring part of the city's bloated population to new settlements in the provinces, but once the danger passed he admitted that the government was powerless against the noble oligarchy that governed the city, which he described as 'a Hydra, a beast with many heads'.[3]

The famine had dramatically exposed the problems posed not only by the privileges enjoyed by the capital and the small aristocratic elite that governed the city, but also by the whole system of regulations and monopolies that seemed to obstruct every form of production and commercial exchange in the Kingdom. As a result, Naples would come to epitomize the evils of the archaic and irrational institutions on which the *ancien régime* was founded and in the debates that followed a new group of writers, thinkers, and teachers began to make institutional and political reform the premise for the Kingdom's economic recovery and the civil regeneration.

THE OBSTACLES TO REFORM

By the time that Charles III left for Spain in 1759, the monarchy's attempts to increase its authority and revenues had done little more than reveal the scale of the obstacles that confronted it. In an attempt to overcome the jurisdictions that limited the monarchy's ability to govern in 1739 Bernardo Tanucci had created an ad hoc tribunal, the *Supreme Magistracy of Commerce*, with the very broad task of promoting the Kingdom's internal and external trade and improving the state of 'agriculture, manufacture and commerce'. To enable it to override the jurisdictions of all other tribunals, the Magistracy was given a number of extraordinary powers. But when the existing tribunals refused to recognize these, the new tribunal was powerless. Similar reactions followed when Tanucci attempted to reorganize the administration of justice, revise the legal codes, and redeem venal offices, but with the same results.[4]

Nor was progress made towards increasing the crown's revenues. As a result of the earlier crisis of the Spanish monarchy, excise duties on the production and sale of silk, oil, tobacco, manna, soap, playing cards, and countless other goods had been permanently lost. The revenues were raised by tax farms known as *arrendamenti*, which the Spanish viceroys had sold to private investors. The taxes continued to be raised, but the greater part went to support hordes of holders of venal office, many of which were hereditary, and to pay the annual interest owed to those who owned or had inherited shares in the *arrendamenti*.

By mortgaging the kingdom's future fiscal revenues to its creditors, the Spanish viceroys had turned the *arrendamenti* into a form of consolidated national debt in

[3] Venturi (1973a), 444.

[4] These tribunals were the *Camera della Sommaria*, the *Magistrato del Commercio*, the *Sopraintendenza della Reale Azienda*, and the *Tribunale della Dogana di Foggia*. Chiosi (1987), 371–467.

which all sections of Neapolitan society and all public foundations held shares.[5] The *arrendamenti* had as a result become one of the most important financial institutions of the *ancien régime* monarchy, but could not safely be touched unless some way was found to redeem the existing creditors. The Kingdom's French rulers would later do this by means of mass sales of church lands, but that was not a conceivable option for the *ancien régime* rulers, who were forced to see a large portion of the monarchy's fiscal revenues go to pay the interest owed to the holders of *arrendamenti* and to support a huge class of hereditary venal office holders.[6]

The situation was made worse by the scale of feudal exemptions and ecclesiastical mortmain in the Kingdom. As a partial remedy a new hearth tax was introduced in 1737 to increase direct revenues, which were assessed through a new tax survey (*catasto*) of every town and village on the mainland. But since the monarchy did not have the administrative means to attempt the more accurate geometric tax surveys being adopted in the Habsburg lands, the new tax was based on simple estimates. Because all feudal and ecclesiastical properties remained exempt, the new levy fell almost entirely on the poor.[7]

For all forms of extraordinary expenditure the monarchy relied on the customary grants voted by the feudatories. When Charles III needed to raise funds for the war against Austria in 1744, for example, the lay and ecclesiastical feudatories granted him a feudal *donativo*, but in return he was required, as was customary, to confirm all their privileges and exemptions. By the end of the century little had changed, and the monarchy remained dependent on the *donativi* and other levies that could only be raised with the consent of the feudatories.

The crown's fiscal and financial difficulties were reflected in its administrative weaknesses. Not only did it rule Naples and Sicily on different terms, but most of the Kingdom was governed not by the crown but by the feudatories, the Church, and great self-governing corporations like the cities of Naples and Palermo. As one contemporary put it, the Kingdom was divided up into 'as many little different monarchies as there are Feudatories'.[8]

In this respect at least, southern Italy was more similar to countries like Poland or Hungary on Europe's eastern peripheries. In the other Italian states, feudal jurisdictions remained powerful only in the Papal States, in Friuli, and in Savoy and Sardinia. In the Grand Duchy of Tuscany feudalism in its classical form had never taken root, while in Austrian Lombardy and in the lands of the House of Savoy—except in the hereditary Duchy of Savoy—the privileges of the lay and ecclesiastical nobility and of the Church had been severely curtailed since the previous century. By the early eighteenth century the House of Savoy in Piedmont and the Habsburg rulers in Lombardy had both established effective centralized administrations. In both cases the nobles continued to exercise

[5] De Rosa (1958/2005), pp. x–xii, 3–17.
[6] On France see Doyle (1996).
[7] Villani (1974), 192–5.
[8] Rao (1984), 41.

important government functions, but they did so as agents of the crown and not as independent sources of power and authority.[9]

In the South, however, the crown's authority was much more limited. Even where the royal writ did run on the mainland, royal administration was conducted on the king's behalf by three ancient tribunals in the capital. These tribunals combined juridical and administrative roles in ways that were typical of the European *ancien régime*, and their task was to oversee the administration of the royal towns and cities (*università*), resolve litigation between the crown and the feudatories, and settle controversies between local communities and their neighbouring lay or ecclesiastical feudatories.[10]

The tribunals were controlled by a small but immensely powerful oligarchy of senior magistrates known as the *togati* (literally 'men of the robe'). Despite the title, they were not the equivalent of the French *noblesse de la robe* since there were no institutions on the mainland comparable to the French *Parlements* or Estates General.[11] Their power derived from the centuries of Spanish rule, when the royal tribunals had become instruments for defending the independence and privileges of the Neapolitan 'nation' against the pretensions of the Spanish monarchy, the feudatories, and the Church. This illustrated another important distinction between Naples and Sicily: the establishing of the Holy Office of the Inquisition in Sicily, but not in Naples. This was partly because the Spanish rulers considered Naples to be 'an indomitable and uncontrollable city', but above all because of the fierce opposition of the *togati*.[12]

The *togati* numbered no more than seventy senior magistrates, but they made themselves indispensable intermediaries between the Spanish monarchy and the most powerful interest groups in the Kingdom. A self-recruiting oligarchy, they firmly controlled public administration and their power was reinforced by the monopoly they exercised over the technical procedures of the law, the *arcanum juris*.[13] The *togati* were as a result one of the most powerful and independent corporations of the *ancien régime*, without whose cooperation the monarchy could take few political or administrative initiatives.

The monarchy's control over its own administration was severely limited in other respects. The Kingdom's army was small, but the feudal nobility exercised the exclusive right of preferment to all commissions. That had major implications for civil administration too, since following Spanish practice this was conducted in each province by military tribunals, *Udienze*, presided over by governors known as *Presidi*. Since these were military offices, the nobility again exercised the exclusive right of preferment.

[9] On Piedmont see Ricuperati, in Merlin et al. (1994), 448–57, 648–64; on Lombardy Capra (2005), 218–33.

[10] The *Camera di Santa Chiara*, the *Sacro Reale Consiglio*, and the *Camera della Sommaria*. See Villani (1974), 69–75.

[11] Except in Sicily, but the Sicilian Parliament was dominated by the great lay and ecclesiastical feudatories not by the *togati*.

[12] Rovito (1982), 5.

[13] Ajello (1976).

As the terrible famine of 1763–4 had shown, however, the most extreme example of the nobility's corporate power was the city of Naples. The city's government was controlled by a small and exclusive oligarchy of feudal noblemen, to which only those whose families formed the *nobilità di Piazza*, the inner elite of the Neapolitan aristocracy, were admitted. This oligarchy controlled the Tribunal of San Lorenzo, which was responsible for 'policing and maintaining public order and public morality in the capital'. The municipal officials were all noblemen, including the *Eletto del Popolo*, who represented the city guilds and corporations; the *Regio Portolano*, who was responsible for the use of public land and spaces; and the *Regio Giustiziere*, who regulated the city's markets and commodity prices.[14]

The leader of the municipal junta was appointed by the king and held the title of *Presidente dell'Annona*, indicating that the most important of the Tribunal's responsibilities was management of the regulations that governed the provisioning of this vast metropolis. For this reason the Tribunal exercised a massive array of powers and jurisdictions throughout the Kingdom, and through tribunals in the provinces the prices at which staple necessities—primarily grain and olive oil but also silk, wool, and other raw materials needed for the city's many small manufactures and craftsmen—were purchased by the city's provisioning authorities (the *Annona*). The authority of the city government therefore stretched to every corner of the Kingdom, and imposed regulations and restrictions now being identified as the principal cause of the poverty of the provinces.

REFORM AS CIVIL MISSION

In the decades after the famines the condition of the Kingdom and its institutions, economy, trade, commerce, agriculture, and populations for the first time began to come under close critical scrutiny. The terms of these debates were set out most fully in the writing and teaching of Antonio Genovesi. The son of a shoemaker, Genovesi entered the priesthood to make a living and then turned to philosophy. He was widely sought after as a teacher and thanks to the patronage of a wealthy Tuscan banker, Bartolomeo Intieri, was appointed in 1754 to the first chair in political economy, not only at the University of Naples but in all of Europe.[15]

[14] Also known as the *Corpo degli Eletti*, but nearly always referred to as the *Corpo della Città*, this consisted of an executive (the *Sedili*) nominated by 5 electoral chapels (the *piazze*) whose members came from a list of only 119 noble families that formed the *Nobili di Piazza*, an additional piazza of 'heads of distinguished families' made up of many lesser noble families, as well as some non-nobles who were nominated from each of the city's 29 administrative districts known as *ottine* (subdivisions of the city's 9 *quartieri*). From those nominated, the king appointed 29 *capitani di ottina* and 58 *procuratori di ottina* who collectively constituted the *Piazza del Popolo* from which the king again nominated a single *eletto* and 10 *consultori* who formed the '*governo della Piazza*'. The '*eletto del Popolo*', along with one '*eletto*' nominated from each of the noble *piazze*, constituted the Tribunal of San Lorenzo. See Battaglini (1992), 114.

[15] Antonio Genovesi (1713–69): the patrons who organized the appointment were the Chaplain Royal, Celestino Galiani, and the wealthy Tuscan administrator and intellectual Bartolomeo Intieri. See Pii (1984); Villari (1959); Venturi (1962), 3–32.

Genovesi's *Lectures on Commerce* published after the famine in 1765 made him the pivotal figure in the reform movement in Naples. Contrasting the economic conditions of the Kingdom with those of Britain, France, and Spain, Genovesi argued that economic development could not be achieved without rational institutions and laws that reflected just and progressive social values. Genovesi's ideas drew heavily on those of earlier Neapolitan writers, especially Giannone and Giambattista Vico, and his ideas travelled freely between economics and moral philosophy. He rejected Rousseau's idealization of the primitive and insisted that trade and commerce were the attributes of civilization (*incivilmento*) and could flourish only in societies whose institutions encouraged individual liberty. Freedom, honest industry, and civil responsibility were the mainsprings of commercial expansion and public prosperity; reform was essentially a civil and a civilizing mission, an ethical mission whose aim was the regeneration of the nation.

Genovesi was a pragmatist, however, who believed that reform could be achieved by practical and empirical means and in the words of one of his most famous students: '. . . Genovesi turned philosophy away from theological and metaphysical abstractions to face reality.'[16] He also identified those who were to accomplish that mission:

> In every civilised country to be found in Europe today the tone of society is set neither by the populace nor by the great, but rather by the middling order, by which I mean priests, friars, teachers of letters, magistrates and private gentlemen. A proper education such as will form good minds and robust bodies must have its beginnings with such persons. Yet there are still countries in Europe where these same people are still amongst the worst educated, and this renders those states arrogant, ignorant and impossible to reason with.[17]

The reformers' first task, therefore, was to educate the middle class and their second task was to educate those who governed.

For Genovesi, feudal and mercantilist institutions were the principal obstacles to the regeneration of Neapolitan society. Feudalism was wicked because it had created irrational and evil institutions and because the feudal mentalities of privilege, exemption, and idleness had corrupted the nation and prevented Neapolitans from asserting their independence. Genovesi also frequently contrasted the present state of the Kingdom with the prosperity it had enjoyed in the distant past before it was subject to foreign invasion and occupation, a long history of exploitation that had begun when the Romans conquered the South. The rediscovery of the peoples who had inhabited the South before the Roman conquest—the Daunites, the Lucanians, the Irpinians, and others—gave the writings of the Neapolitan reformers a strongly nationalist cast. Following Giannone's claim that only an independent secular prince could restore to the South its long lost independence, the reformers also looked to the new rulers to realize their great project of national regeneration.

[16] Vincenzo Cuoco, cited in Sofia (1988), 145.

[17] Venturi (1962), 28.

Feudalism was the great symbol of past oppression and the principal cause of the present decay. It was feudalism that made the nation 'inferior' to other leading European and Italian states and its abolition was the great task awaiting the new prince who after centuries of foreign oppression would restore the Kingdom's lost independence. These were even more central themes in the writings of Gaetano Filangieri, whose magisterial *Scienza della Legislazione* was written in the decade of the American Revolution and published in the one that followed.

Filangieri insisted on the interlocking and interdependent nature of feudal institutions, which, he argued, could only be destroyed by abolishing their juridical premises:

> In the present condition of the nations of Europe everything belongs to the few. What is needed is that everything should belong to the many.

Yet this could not be achieved merely by abolishing internal customs duties and *gabelles*, nor even by abolishing particular feudal rights and feudal entails (known as *maggioraschi* and *fidecomessi*) that gave the feudatories a monopoly over land for which the interests of younger sons were sacrificed. What was needed above all was reform of the law and the magistracy, and the creation of primary schools, technical schools, and colleges to raise the skills of the population and its moral awareness. Progress, education, and moral values were inseparable, because without the support of an informed civil society no reform could succeed.[18]

Filangieri was Genovesi's intellectual heir, but the *Scienza della Legislazione* set out a much broader project that would necessitate uprooting the fundamental institutions of the *ancien régime*. Only then could the forces needed to give new vitality to the nation be emancipated. But Filangieri was no less committed than Genovesi to the need for practical action and intervention: 'The glory of the man of letters is to prepare information that will be of use to those who govern.'[19] In a nation where education for the masses did not exist, reform could be achieved only through the intervention of an enlightened prince. It was the philosopher's duty to enlighten the princes, and for that reason, albeit with great reluctance, Filangieri was prepared to accept appointments from the monarchy.

Filangieri's prodigious correspondence brought him into contact with leading reform writers and thinkers in both Europe and North America, and his voluminous correspondence reveals how much the intellectual and political world had changed in the brief period since Genovesi's first publications. He corresponded prolifically with Benjamin Franklin on the new constitution of the United States, and as elsewhere in Europe the American War of Independence and the founding of the new American republic gave new strength in Naples to the belief that progress and reason were unstoppable.[20]

[18] Ibid. 618–19. [19] Chiosi (1987), 66.

[20] In 1784 Franklin invited the Neapolitan philosopher to Virginia to observe the new political order at firsthand: Lo Sardo (1999), 7–8, 108–24.

DISCOVERING THE NATION

By the time Filangieri died in 1788, a generation of writers inspired by Genovesi's call for useful knowledge were already documenting the state of the realm and its economy. In 1770 the marquis Domenico Grimaldi, a wealthy and widely travelled Calabrian landowner, drew attention to the disastrous consequences of the regulations imposed by the *arrendamenti* on the production of oil and silk in Calabria.[21] The marquis Giuseppe Palmieri, a wealthy landowner from the Terra di Otranto, published a detailed study of the obstacles to the production and export of olive oil (*Degli Ulivi*, 1794), and the abbé Francesco Longano wrote the first detailed account of economic conditions in the provinces of Molise and Capitanata, the principal sources of the capital's wheat. From Teramo in the mountainous Abruzzi province, Melchiorre Delfico denounced the damage to agriculture caused by taxes, collective customary rights, and transhumant grazing and argued the benefits of new crops like rice.[22]

The most comprehensive survey of the Kingdom was the work of Giuseppe Maria Galanti, who between 1782 and 1785 travelled tirelessly through the mainland provinces. The result was the *Nuova Descrizione Storica e Geografica delle Sicilie*, a work of extraordinary breadth and detail acclaimed throughout Europe as a pioneering and incomparable exercise in the new science of statistics.[23]

Galanti's purpose was to document Genovesi's premise that the disastrous condition of the Kingdom was the work of man, not nature:

> Men have always toiled to turn into horrible calamities the precious gifts which nature has bestowed on them. Today we have come to understand that the noble and useful application of power derives from imposing the rule of law to make men more virtuous, more tranquil and more enlightened.

Better governance and better laws were the secret to moral and economic progress, and Galanti's confidence in the restorative power of rational laws and rational institutions was reinforced by his conviction that the natural resources of the South were abundant and plentiful: 'Nowhere outside this Kingdom is there greater variety and abundance of nature and land: but everything here tends to render the property of the industrious man uncertain and precarious and hence oppress agriculture.'[24] Reform was, therefore, essentially a matter of liberating the Kingdom's natural and human resources.

21 *Saggio sopra l'economia campestre della Calabria.*

22 Venturi (1962), 1096–171. See also Chorley (1965), 141–203; Marcy (1974), 399–413; Marino (1988), 35–8, 245–59.

23 An enthusiastic Christian Joseph Jagemann declared from Weimar, 'there is surely no comparable treatise on the constitution of any other European nation today', and Jean-Marie Alquier would later describe Galanti as 'the author of one of the finest compilations of statistics that have been achieved in Europe'. Venturi (1958), 973; Sofia (1988), 123. On Galanti see Villani (1989), 247–60.

24 G. M. Galanti, *Nuova Descrizione Storica e Geografica delle Sicilie* (henceforth, NDG) (1786), ii. 7.

THE CAPITAL DENOUNCED

Although Galanti's main concern was the depressed condition of the provinces, his starting point was the capital whose privileges he like many others now believed were the principal cause of the poverty of the provinces.

By the closing decade of the century that swollen head was inhabited by some 550,000 souls, of whom 380,000 lived in the parishes of Naples, with a further 130,000 in the outlying *casali* and about 40,000 were soldiers and temporary residents.[25] By Galanti's estimate some 25,000 noble families lived in the capital,[26] whose exclusive core was the *nobiltà di piazza*, the hundred or so families that constituted the four noble *Sedili*. Galanti had little to say about their economic condition, but Henry Swinburne, an English Catholic educated in France who visited Naples in 1776, was struck by the extravagant behaviour of the 'grandees' and by the huge numbers of their retainers and hangers-on, which was why they were heavily indebted and rarely entertained foreigners. By English standards he considered the marriage portions modest, and he noted that the nobles no longer wore swords, although the dress of the middle classes had become increasingly luxurious.[27]

Then came the lawyers, a class Galanti scathingly dismissed as people 'maintained by the litigious character of this nation': he estimated that there were about 6,000 employed in the law courts in the capital and 26,000 in the Kingdom as a whole. Then there were the 10,000 physicians, doctors, apothecaries, and leeches practising in the capital and in the nearby city of Salerno, which was the seat of the Kingdom's ancient medical school. Galanti had little to say about the numerous secular and regular clergy, although he did praise the parish clergy for their role in maintaining public order and the continuous 'brilliant festivals' organized by the parish churches and lay confraternities that kept the lower classes entertained and out of mischief.[28]

Henry Swinburne was struck by the orderliness of the city, and commented that despite its size there was no drunkenness, little theft, and few murders, which led him to claim that its populace compared very favourably with 'the mobs of London and Edinburgh'. Galanti reported that there were fewer than 40 murders a year in the city, but expressed great alarm at the growth in the number of beggars and vagrants. The supposed cause was that many artisans were unable to save to provide for their old age, but Galanti echoed

25 NDG, i. 190, 311–18.

26 Of these, 1,500 were *nobili di piazza*, *fuori piazza*, feudatories, *nobili viventi*, and soldiers. Another 4,500 noble families lived in the provinces.

27 Swinburne also noted that 'it does not cost a nobleman more to marry a daughter than to make her a nun'. Entering a nunnery, he was informed, cost about 1,000 pounds sterling, but did require in addition an annual pension and a portion of the inheritance. On the other hand, 'servants and artificers of the city give from 50 to 100 ducats with their daughters: peasants and countrymen go as far as 300 ducats' ((1783), i. 65–9).

28 NDG, i. 378.

the reformers' conviction that the indiscriminate charity provided by the excessive numbers of religious foundations was the main cause of indigence in the capital.[29]

From Galanti's description, Naples emerges as a city full of shops, taverns, ice-cream parlours, and above all coffee shops, crammed with clients at all times of day and the principal meeting place for all classes: 'even for the humblest workmen who now regularly drink coffee in the morning since they believe it to be beneficial for the digestion'. However, the working classes also attracted the reformers' disdain: 'The lower classes of the capital are a little doltish (*goffo*), they do everything to live and sell their services cheaply.'[30]

Amongst the city's working people, domestic servants, porters, carriage drivers, retainers, and flunkeys were the largest occupational groups. At the bottom of the social scale were the '*mascalzoni*, also known disparagingly as *lazzari* because of their nudity.... Nearly all are foundlings who live in the street and congregate especially around the Mercato district where the poorest, most undisciplined and most rebellious sections of the populace of Naples reside'. However, Galanti dismissed as gross exaggeration travellers' stories that the *lazzaroni* formed a corporate body that elected their own leader and dealt directly with the authorities.[31] By contrast Henry Swinburne considered the large and relatively prosperous community of fishermen and their families in the nearby Santa Lucia district to be 'the handsomest men in Naples: they have true Grecian features and are the most substantial and best lodged portion of the Neapolitan populace'.[32]

The large number of artisans and merchants reflected the city's role as the principal centre of consumption on the mainland. They included silversmiths, silk-makers, carriage builders and repairers, ceramic makers, and cordswainers, as well as a growing number of foreign merchants. For Galanti, however, the expansion of consumption was a source of great misgiving: 'in general our workshops and manufactures are inferior to those of foreigners, and especially of the English, since our national spirit is not directed at these affairs. The king has attempted to set good examples, but these have been little followed.' Luxury consumption was doubly dangerous: it encouraged the consumption of foreign goods that the Kingdom could ill afford and promoted a culture of idleness and indulgence instead of stimulating interest in new forms of production. The mania for foreign consumer goods also reinforced the prejudice against manual labour that led persons of talent and ability to seek more socially acceptable forms of employment, with the result that rather than engage in trade or industry, 'our people prefer to make money through litigation'.

If the Kingdom was not to become a commercial colony of the English or the French, Galanti concluded, it must learn to satisfy its own needs from its own

[29] Galanti, *Breve Descrizione di Napoli e del Suo Contorno* (henceforth, BDN) (1792), i. 273.

[30] BDN, i. 270, 383.

[31] NDG, i. 169, 268: see Goethe's comments above p. 27.

[32] Swinburne (1783), i. 65

resources. Naples in particular should not be content to consume foreign commodities but must learn to develop its own industries.[33]

THE PROVINCES REVEALED

However, that would never happen until the city learned to live off its resources, rather than those it drained from the provinces:

> The city of Naples enjoys the right to devour the provinces because it has the right to take for itself their livestock and the fruits of their agriculture, just as Constantinople does from the provinces of the Ottoman Empire.

The sad result was that Naples 'has unhappily swallowed the entire kingdom, making it poor, oppressed and deserted'.[34]

The reformers' great mission was, therefore, to reveal the causes of the impoverished state of the provinces because 'in Naples more is known about the condition of the island of Tahiti than of our own provinces'.[35] Such ignorance was not easily overcome, since the disastrous state of communications made all forms of overland travel difficult, slow, and in many seasons of the year impossible. 'Our kingdom is a peninsula with swamps along its coasts that lie covered in stagnant water that the unhealthy air has made uninhabitable.' Ancient neglect had been aggravated by the uncontrolled clearance of woodland in more recent times, which accelerated the processes of soil erosion and landslides that clogged the streams and rivers of the valley bottoms, creating vast and unhealthy swamps. Even in the fertile province of Campania, huge areas of fertile agricultural land had been overtaken by swamps. On the mouth of the Volturno River, the ancient port of Literno had been swallowed up by marshes that had formed around Vico di Partano. Swamps had also invaded the land between Salerno and Agropoli, and the Sarno River, navigable in classical times, was no longer passable. The Marchesato Plain on the Ionian coast between Squillace and the river Neti was flooded, leaving Crotone as the only city to have survived.[36]

In other parts of the Kingdom, lack of rainfall and irrigation were the main reasons for the population's decline and the agricultural decay. The Terra d'Otranto had more than two hundred miles of coast, but contained only four thinly populated towns. Apulia was 'a real desert' where the land could only be worked thanks to seasonal migrants from the Abruzzi Mountains. In the Calabrian provinces the population was low: the Marchesato Plain was almost uninhabited, while the province of Cosenza was empty in winter and spring when its inhabitants left to work on the harvest on the eastern coast.[37]

33 BDN, i. 263. 34 Ibid. 264; iii. 309.

35 Cited in Venturi (1962), 973: for debates on luxury in Italy see Wahnbaeck (2004).

36 NDG, iii. 122. 37 Ibid. iii. 124–5, 195–6.

These migrations were an essential part of the agrarian economies of the Mezzogiorno. The timing of the harvest in each province varied slightly and from the late spring onwards huge armies of migrant labourers were on the move seeking work as reapers, gleaners, olive pickers, or whatever was available. As a result, much of the lowland population and even higher percentages of the upland and mountain communities led nomadic lives for part of the year.

The reformers believed lack of population to be the principal cause of the decline of agriculture in many parts of the South, but they also noted that in the Campania, Molise, the upland regions stretching from Benevento to Avellino, and the river Ofanto there were signs that rapid population expansion was causing acute problems of land shortage.[38]

These comments, together with the numerous references to the ecological problems caused by woodland clearances, were indications of important changes taking place as the reformers were writing. These were also evident in the account that Henry Swinburne gave of his travels through the mainland provinces in 1777. Before setting out on his journey Swinburne spent some months in Naples where he became acquainted with Galanti and his circle, and as a result obtained invitations to visit many prominent reforming landowners and provincial intellectuals.

In contrast to the patronizing tones and exotic fantasies that dominated the tales of most foreign travellers, Swinburne's observations were remarkably sober. He took care to explain Neapolitan leases, farming techniques, and customs in terms his anglophone readers would recognize. His itinerary took him from Naples along the principal overland route to the Adriatic provinces by way of Avellino to Foggia and then to Manfredonia and Barletta on the coast. At Trani the local governor supplied him with letters requiring all convents to provide him with hospitality: 'except for letters to private families, there is no better method to be pursued in a tour through a country so ill-provided with Inns.' He noted that much wheat was exported from the Adriatic coastal towns, but added, 'I am afraid that industry has taken a long farewell of most of the cities of the coast.'[39]

He still found much to admire, including many prosperous monasteries and especially the huge Dominican house he visited in Giovinazzo. After a short pause at Bari, the Kingdom's principal and busiest Adriatic port, he made his way to Francavilla where he was the guest of the Prince of Oria. He was filled with admiration for the model agricultural estate:

> At present very little remains unlet; the rents are paid as the crops are got in and sold, not at stated days of payment. All tithes belong to the Lord of the Manor, who is the lay impropriator; for the Church has only its glebe. Many gentlemen of secondary rank hold their land of the prince as under-tenants by payment of a fixed fine of investiture nearly in the same manner as our copy-holders make surrenders and hold estates by copy of court-roll. There are besides many owners of land, not of noble degree, who pay the tenth of their crops to the Prince.[40]

[38] BDG, iii. 260: on the *demani* see pp. 58–9.
[39] Swinburne (1783), i. 181.
[40] Ibid. i. 219.

Swinburne also visited the nearby Imperiali estates belonging to the Prince of Francavilla, where cotton had been introduced in rotation with wheat, barley, and oats before the land was turned over to sheep-grazing for a year. The Imperiali estates were worked in partnership—'the proprietor tills it the first time; the tenant gives it four subsequent ploughings and furnishes seed; the expense of the harvest is born equally by both and the profits halved between them.'

Taranto was less to his liking: 'it is without doubt the most disgusting habitation of human beings in Europe, except perhaps the Jewish ghetto in Rome', but here he met with another leading figure of the Neapolitan reform movement, Monsignore Capecelatro, the Archbishop of Taranto, whom the English traveller acknowledged to be one of his most widely informed sources. Swinburne then resumed his journey southwards along the difficult roads leading to Calabria, following the Bradano River to Metapontum and then onwards by way of Policoro, where he admired another huge estate that had formerly belonged to the Jesuits.[41]

As he moved further south and through Calabria, however, Swinburne's comments on the landowners became less admiring:

> The Barons are in general very far from considering themselves as the protectors, the political fathers of their vassals, but encroach so much on the commons and the cultivated grounds for the sake of extending their chase that the peasants have neither room nor opportunity to raise sufficient food for their support: they therefore fly to the mendicant and other religious orders of friars and take religious habit to procure their subsistence. The father of a family when pressed for the payments of taxes and sinking beneath the load of hunger and distress *va alla montagna*, that is he retires to the woods where he meets with fellow sufferers, turns smuggler and becomes by degrees an outlaw, a robber and an assassin.[42]

It was not only in Calabria that the rural poor seemed overwhelmed by taxation and exclusion from the land. 'Throughout the realm the situation of the husbandmen is truly deplorable: everything is excised and the mode of collecting is cruel and pernicious.'[43] Crossing the plain of Sibari, Swinburne noted how the collapse of the complex irrigation systems of antiquity had turned one of the greatest cities of *Magna Graecia* into a malarial swamp.

After taking shelter at Capo Rizzuto to avoid a raiding party of Barbary pirates, Swinburne reached Catanzaro, the principal administrative town of lower Calabria whose 12,000 inhabitants 'live by the law and the sale of corn, silk and oil'. Leaving Catanzaro for Reggio by way of Gerace, Swinburne was fascinated by the Albanian settlement he visited at Bora, one of the many Greek Orthodox communities in Calabria and the Abruzzi that dated back to the fifteenth century.

[41] Before their expulsion it had supported over 5,000 sheep, 300 cattle, 400 buffalo, 400 goats, and 200 horses and provided work for more than 200 families, but when Swinburne saw it the farms had fallen into decay. Ibid. 236, 278.

[42] Ibid. i. 282.

[43] Ibid. i. 285.

In Reggio, Swinburne was impressed by the fertility of the land around the city and its thriving silkworm industry, although he noted that the workers were 'less expert than the Tuscans, who although more northerly manage to produce two or three hatchings per year. The silk work houses are owned by wealthy families in Reggio who furnish rooms, leaves, eggs and every necessary implement; take two thirds of the profit and leave the rest for the attendant.' However, the industry had a strongly subordinate structure. The eggs were not raised locally but imported from Livorno, while the raw silk was exported without being worked, one reason, Swinburne argued, being the unjust character of the tax system that took a fixed percentage in weight of the crop: 'In general the profits of the silk trade in this country centre on the Barons and the Revenue Offices.' But although the high levels of taxation gave rise to widespread smuggling, Swinburne reckoned that Reggio still earned around half a million ducats a year from olive oil exports alone.[44]

Swinburne's own interest in the Kingdom's resources and products was designed to satisfy the curiosity of readers in England, and was therefore another illustration of the reasons Sir William Hamilton's 'remote corner' was becoming less distant. But Swinburne's account provides further evidence that incentives derived from increasing demand were causing existing constraints to be more apparent and less easily accepted.

FEUDALISM: 'THE CRUELLEST ENEMY OF CIVIL LIBERTY'

Among the reform writers a consensus was gaining ground that the Kingdom was rich in natural resources but impoverished by evil institutions: there were too many taxes, too many monopolies, too many idle monks and friars, too few roads, too many consumers, too few producers, too much luxury, too much poverty, too little knowledge or learning. But the root cause of all these evils was feudalism. Galanti wrote:

> It is feudalism that has burdened agriculture and society with the monopolies, exactions and regulations that have impoverished the many to the advantage of the few.... Feudal government is the cruellest enemy of civil liberty... and it has survived more extensively in the Kingdom of the Sicilies than in any other part of Italy.[45]

Feudalism had sapped the spirit of enterprise and industry itself so that 'in the course of time all land in the kingdom will finish in the hands of idle persons who live only from their revenues and who have destroyed all spirit of industry'.[46]

[44] Swinburne (1783), i. 357–8. [45] NDG, i. 273–4. [46] Ibid. iii. 261–9.

How had this come about? Popes, barons, Viceroys, bad laws, tax-farms, the courts? All these have contributed to the fact that the very nature of the soil and the people has been changed, causing the nation's ancient population to fall by two-thirds... Our laws, because governed by the maxims of feudal government, have made the condition of our agriculture wretched and have benefited only a class of idle men... All those amongst us who have talent and some little fortune turn to the courts or to medicine as a career, or else become notaries or priests, in such ways we seek to provide for our needs... From this derives the life of idleness and inactivity that renders sad and consumes the inhabitants of our small provincial towns. The rest of the nation is mainly employed in selling goods made in foreign countries, in a variety of small artisan enterprises or else as servants to the rich.[47]

Galanti estimated that only one million of the more than four million souls living on the mainland were free of feudal obligations and taxes.[48] The heaviest burdens fell on those who lived in towns and villages subject to feudal jurisdictions, who in addition to the tithes paid to the feudatory and the Church also paid taxes to the crown and to the provincial administration for poor relief, the militia, and other services. In most parts of the Kingdom, waterways, mills, and public bread ovens were monopolies of the feudal landowners, abbeys, or convents. The peasant farmer was taxed 'to grind his own corn and bake the bread for his own family' and in the Terra d'Otranto even sea salt and pebbles were feudal monopolies.

The consequences were clear to see: the inhabitants of feudal towns lived in 'pitiful hovels roofed with wood and straw where a single bed shares space with the swine and beast of burden'.[49] Although the feudatories no longer had the right to impose capital punishment, their courts were responsible for maintaining order and administering justice at a local level. Their orders were carried out by feudal officers with various titles—*mastrodatti*, *portolani*—and enforced by armed retainers known as *armigeri* or *sbirri*.

Feudal landowners were exempt from most of the taxes paid by the rest of the population. Galanti calculated that of the two and a half million ducats paid annually in direct taxes, less than one quarter of a million ducats was paid by the barons. Nor was feudal land subject to the hearth tax introduced in 1737.[50] The feudatories were supposed to pay tax to both the crown and to the local communities for land they held by private as opposed to feudal title,[51] but they generally avoided doing so.

As feudatories, the barons paid a direct tax called the *adoa*, which had originated in the sixteenth century as a commutation of feudal services. Originally set at 26 per cent of revenues, inflation had by the eighteenth century made the returns derisory. They were also subject to a heavy inheritance tax at death, the rate being half an estate's estimated revenues.[52] But the estimates were always contested so that payment was deferred often for generations. The heaviest taxes

[47] Venturi (1962), 974. [48] BDN, iii. 37. [49] NDG, i. 279.
[50] The *catasto onciario*: see Villani (1968), 56–63. [51] Termed *burgensatici*.
[52] The *rilievo*.

paid by the feudatories were the *donativi* that the crown was entitled to raise on the occasion of major royal events or war. But in return, the crown was obliged to confirm the feudatories' rights and privileges.[53]

The reformers noted that despite the feudatories' insistence on their exemptions and privileges, feudal estates were still freely bought and sold and were attractive to purchasers because of the various forms of patronage, ecclesiastical benefices, and social status attached to them. This blurred distinctions between feudal and non-feudal property and was another item on the growing list of objections to feudalism. An important contribution to that debate came from the cadet sons of noble families who were disinherited by the system of entails that had been introduced to protect the integrity of family patrimonies from creditors.[54] Cadets excluded from direct inheritance instead received a simple allowance (known as a *secondagenitura)* to enable them to 'live nobly or enter military service'. In the absence of male heirs, women might inherit an estate, but to avoid this, right of succession had been extended to the 'fourth degree when there is descendence in the direct male line from the original holder of the title'.[55]

Some of the most outspoken opposition to feudalism came from the cadets of noble families, of whom Gaetano Filangieri was the most famous. But this was only one aspect of a broader crisis of identity within the feudal nobility that became increasingly evident in the final decades of the eighteenth century. As the debates on feudalism developed the nobles and the clergy became divided. Some rallied to defend feudal practice and privilege, while others denounced the narrow oligarchy of noble families that governed the capital and monopolized senior commissions in the army. As in the rest of Europe, the debates on the virtues and functions of a genuine aristocracy reflected a deeper crisis of identity within the nobility. Very similar divisions were apparent within the ranks of the clergy, and explain why in 1799 many aristocrats and senior churchmen would see the Republic as an opportunity to restore both the nobility and religion to their rightful place in society.

THE AFRICAN DESERT AND BARBAROUS TARTARY: THE PASTORAL ECONOMY

Feudalism was the principal but not the only enemy. Echoing ideas that had first been voiced by the French economists known as the Physiocrats, many Neapolitan writers were especially outraged by the survival of what they considered to be one of

[53] Charles III raised 5,255,000 ducats in *donativi* from the feudatories between 1734 and 1759, including a *donativo* of 1 million ducats in 1736 to mark his accession to the throne; another million in 1738 on the occasion of his marriage to Maria Amalia of Saxony; 500,000 ducats in 1741 on the birth of his daughter; 700,000 ducats in 1748 on the birth of Prince Filippo. The remainder took the form of war subsidies raised in 1742, 1744, 1746, and 1747. NDG, ii. 44, 123–4.

[54] Known as *maggioraschi* and *fidecomessi:* see Villani (1968), 81–97, and Cooper, in Goody (ed.) (1976), 192–326.

[55] NDG, i. 280.

the surest signs of the primitive state of agriculture: the extensive transhumant pastoral economy that subjected vast stretches of land to collective use.[56] For the reformers the regulations that protected rights of passage and permitted promiscuous grazing along the routes the sheep followed on the biennial migrations were archaic and intolerable obstacles to the introduction of more rational and intensive forms of rotation.

The reality was, of course, more complex. As in other parts of the Mediterranean world, these seasonal migrations played a critical role in integrating the different economies of southern Italy. Sheep rearing and its allied industries (textiles, leather, and cheese production) brought together the economies of the mountain communities and those of the plains. The migrant sheep left behind the only natural enrichment available on these barren and rain-starved soils, making their presence during the winter essential to the success of the spring grain harvests on the coastal plains.

The transhumant system was closely integrated into prevailing natural conditions and resources, and over time had been regulated in ways designed to reconcile the potentially conflicting interests of pasture and agriculture. Those regulations had been institutionalized in the fifteenth century during the reign of Alfonso of Aragon, when the transhumant economy was placed under the protection of the crown. The system of regulations guaranteed seasonal rights of transit and established three separate transit routes (known as *tratturi*) for the biennial migrations. The destination for the flocks that in summer grazed on the Apennine uplands was the northern Apulian plateau, where a vast tract of land known as the *Tavoliere* was reserved for winter grazing.[57]

The seasonal migrations and the leasing of the pasture were administered by the royal customs office known as the *Dogana delle Pecore della Puglia* in Foggia. When Henry Swinburne visited Foggia in 1777 he described the *Dogana* as 'one of the richest mines of wealth belonging to the Crown of Naples' and estimated that between revenue from leases and taxes on sales in Foggia it yielded around 400,000 ducats and provided winter grazing for over a million sheep.[58]

[56] The most prominent members of the 'school' were Quesnay, Mirabeau père, P. Mercier de la Rivière, G. F. L. Trosen, P. S. Dupont de Nemours, and N. Baudeau. The ideas of the Physiocrats were known in Naples primarily through the writings of the abbe' Ferdinando Galiani, who from 1759 to 1769 was secretary to the Neapolitan ambassador in Paris. A close friend of Denis Diderot and Madame d'Epinay, he set out his copious commentaries on the writings of the French economists in his *Dialogues sur le commerce des blés*, published anonymously in Naples in 1770. Galiani recognized the broader virtues of laissez-faire principles, but he also argued that the prevailing economic condition of the Kingdom made the need for government intervention overwhelming. See L. De Rosa (1995), 125. On Galiani see also Steegmuller (1991). Robertson (1997), 667–97, sets the Neapolitan writers in the context of Enlightenment debates on political economy.

[57] Marino (1988).

[58] The *Dogana*'s revenue derived in part from leases paid by the shepherds and owners of the flocks and in part from taxes imposed at the Foggia market. Swinburne was told that the shepherds paid 13.20 ducats to graze five score sheep for the season starting in November, and were in addition obliged to sell all their produce (milk, cheese, wool, skins) only on the market at Foggia. Swinburne also described the vast underground deposits where the summer grain was stored, and he noted that during the summer when all were working in the fields the town was virtually empty, while during the winter grazing season it had more than 20,000 inhabitants: Swinburne (1783), i. 145.

The Neapolitan reformers did not share Swinburne's enthusiasm for either Foggia or the *Dogana*. For Ferdinando Galiani the *Tavoliere* had 'No parallels in civilised Europe, but only in the African desert and in Barbarous Tartary'.[59] Melchiorre Delfico decried what he called the 'barbarism of the pastoral economy' and claimed that the subjection of the Apulian plain to promiscuous grazing had destroyed its agriculture, leaving the Kingdom's oldest and most fertile granary barren. To remove the threat of famine and to improve the Kingdom's foreign trade he pleaded for the immediate abolition of the *Dogana* and for the sale of the pastures owned by the crown. Sold as copy-hold lease these would yield greater revenues for the crown and at the same time encourage the development of more productive forms of agriculture.[60]

Nicola de Dominicis was one of the few who argued that grazing made an essential contribution to the southern economy, and that what mattered was how the competing interests might be reconciled and mediated.[61] But his was a lone voice. Galanti favoured the suppression of the *Dogana* and the sale of the crown pastures. He acknowledged that the *Dogana* had been created to mediate between the conflicting interests of agriculture and pasture, and between the owners of large flocks and poorer grazers. But over time the sheep runs had fallen into the hands of a small group of graziers who now monopolized all the pasture on the *Tavoliere*, threatening to deprive the poorer sheep-owners of access to pasture. The continuing high demand for pasture kept the price of leases high and removed any incentive to release the land for agriculture.[62]

THE CONTRADICTIONS OF CHANGE

The projects that the reformers had begun to formulate ran far beyond the absolutist objective of the monarchy's own initiatives, however, even though for a brief period the two seemed to many to be moving in harmony. That was an illusion, since the rulers wanted to modify feudalism while the reformers wanted to do away with it. But the reformers' descriptions also gave a clear picture of how agrarian realities in southern Italy were changing, and with them feudalism. They described feudalism in the South as a 'ghost', not because it was dead, but because its original purposes had been destroyed. Instead of mediating between potentially conflicting interests, feudalism had been stripped of its original elements of reciprocity. It was increasingly seen simply as an instrument of tyranny in the hands of feudatories who wanted to transform their feudal estates into what would later be referred to as *latifundia*—large monopolistic but private properties. The reciprocal obligations that had once been inherent in feudal landownership were destroyed, and the collective rights on which the livelihood of most rural communities depended were increasingly at risk.

[59] F. Galiani, *De Moneta*, 1780—cited in Marino (1988), 245.
[60] Venturi (1962), 1171.
[61] Marino (1988), 38.
[62] NDG, ii. 295–303; Marino (1988), 257.

Yet the reformers' critique took little account of the different interests at stake. Against the evils of feudalism, they insisted on the creative force of the market and like the advocates of economic liberalism elsewhere in Europe the Neapolitan reformers showed little sympathy for the moral economies of the rural communities.[63] For all their emphasis on pragmatism, the reformers' confidence in the abstract theories and the moral certitudes of the political economists was unshakeable.

[63] Villari (1961), 45.

3

Undermining the Old Order

INTRODUCTION

Change came to the South in many different forms. The most conspicuous resulted from the actions and interventions of the monarchy and its agents, while the most audible were the speculations and projects of the reformers. But the market was also at work in its own sometimes visible, sometimes invisible, ways, shaped and directed nonetheless by the reactions of a crowd of different agents, each with their own interests—landowners, feudatories, clerics, priests, and also the rural communities. For that reason, the changes taking place in southern Italy never conformed to a neat antithesis between the narrow aims of an absolutist monarchy and the broader projects of the reformers. The intentions of both were complicated by more autonomous developments profoundly changing the foundations of the social as well as the political order in the South.

For similar reasons, the appearances of unity given by the campaign against feudalism proved deceptive. At first the campaign seemed to offer opportunities to harmonize the interests of the princes and the philosophers in an alliance that Gaetano Filangieri hailed with high expectations in 1783. But those hopes were founded on profound misunderstandings. The monarchy and the reformers had quite different objectives, while the campaign gave rise to complex and often contradictory alignments. On one hand, the feudatories fought to protect their rights while at the same time disregarding the constraints imposed by feudal title to enclose their land and deny access for those who enjoyed customary use rights. On the other, the local communities rallied to the monarchy's campaign against feudal abuses, in the belief that the royal courts would remove abuses and force the feudatories to honour their collective use-rights. As the monarchy's war on feudal exemptions and privileges led its agents to mobilize the rural communities to enforce feudal law custom, its interventions proved an additional source of conflict in a world of growing discord.

THE PRINCES AND PHILOSOPHERS

The great famine of 1763–4 had played an important part in shaping the aims of the reform movement, but when the government's interest in reform revived in the 1770s it was inspired by the more narrowly defined absolutist ambitions of Maria Carolina and her minister John Acton. The broader model came from reforms being introduced in the Habsburg territories by Emperor Joseph II that moved to a broader attack on the Church's remaining jurisdiction in civil affairs and on feudal privilege.[1] In Naples even before the fall of Tanucci and in line with the other Catholic princes the government's anti-papal stance had hardened. In 1767, the Jesuits were expelled and the Order's extensive properties in the Kingdom were placed under royal administration.[2] After the fall of Tanucci, other religious orders were suppressed and the government adopted a more aggressive policy when it began to nominate leading figures in the anti-curial movement to vacant bishoprics. Papal authority in the Kingdom was made subject to royal authorization and the crown claimed the right of preferment to all abbeys and benefices, as well as a share of their revenues.[3] The government's initiatives were a much weaker version of the measures adopted in Vienna, and reflected the decline in the international authority of the papacy in the last quarter of the century. While they won enthusiastic support from the predominantly anti-curial senior secular clergy in Naples, they also provoked equally strong opposition from those who supported the papacy's jurisdictional claims in the Kingdom.[4]

Once Acton was established as the queen's principal minister, many of Tanucci's earlier initiatives were revived and in 1782 a *Supreme Council of Finance* was created. This was similar in many respects to the earlier *Magistracy of Commerce*, and its task was to recommend ways to revive the Kingdom's economy. The difference was that the government invited leading members of the reform movement to serve on the council, which as a result briefly came to embody the alliance between the prince and the philosophers. A year after the creation of the Supreme Council Filangieri dedicated the third volume of his *Scienza della Legislazione* to the queen, with the hope that reform would unite the 'peaceful philosophers' and an enlightened prince in a common enterprise.

For the government, the philosophers were welcome allies. The ascendancy of the queen and the Kingdom's new Austrian connection had been fiercely opposed by the pro-Spanish party at court, whose attacks took the form of a viciously defamatory campaign directed above all against the queen. Like Marie Antoinette and Catherine the Great, Maria Carolina was portrayed as a depraved harlot with

[1] In 1783 civil marriage was separated from church marriage, and in 1791 criminals' right to seek sanctuary in holy places was abolished. The monarchy's civil and criminal law codes were revised, new measures to limit feudalism were introduced, and in May 1789 an imperial edict made it lawful for peasants to redeem certain feudal obligations and authorized the sale of feudal lands. See Beales (2005), 156–81, 207–55.

[2] On instruction from the former king and with strong encouragement from the French minister Choiseul: Chadwick (1981), 345–68.

[3] Tanucci threatened to abolish the *chinea* in 1767 but that was not done until 1788. Rambaud (1908), 294.

[4] One of the most contentious nominations was that of Andrea Serrao, a leading opponent of papal supremacy, as Bishop of Potenza: see Chiosi (1981), 267–86. On the decline of papal authority see Chadwick (1981), 345.

insatiable sexual appetites, and these attacks came to a head in 1784 when the Spanish minister Floridablanca called for the queen's removal from politics on the grounds of moral turpitude. But Madrid's patently partisan intervention was deflected by the queen's Austrian protectors, and also served to strengthen the alliance with the reformers.[5]

Until it was disbanded in 1792, the Supreme Council of Finance was the principal forum for public debate on the means to improve the state of the realm. Gaetano Filangieri, Giuseppe Palmieri, Domenico di Gennaro, the Duke of Cantalupo, and Ferdinando Galiani were amongst the leading figures in the reform movement who accepted the government's invitation to serve. To carry out its brief the Council commissioned Domenico Grimaldi, Giuseppe Palmieri, and Giuseppe Maria Galanti to prepare reports on the state of the Kingdom's olive oil and silk trades.[6] In the meantime Acton was busy with projects designed to increase trade and commerce. In 1785 he went to study the commercial reforms introduced by Grand Duke Peter Leopold in Tuscany. His greatest achievement, however, was a round of commercial treaties that concluded with a trade agreement signed with Russia in 1787.[7]

The practical results were disappointing, however. In 1779 the *arrendamento* on tobacco had been abolished, but an attempt to reform the more powerful *arrendamanto della Seta* foundered in 1780. In 1786 the monopolies exercised by the custom houses of Naples, Salerno, and Cava were abolished, but the growing burden of Acton's expenditure on the army and navy meant that the government could ill afford to forgo even small revenues.[8] By the early 1790s the reformers were frustrated and the government had lost interest. Its priority had always been to reorganize the army and build a navy, aims that overrode all other concerns and came to rely on increasingly absolutist measures.

THE ARMY AND THE NOBLES

The project for reforming the army proved to be especially divisive. It met with strong support from the reformers, who believed that the creation of a national army was an essential step towards national regeneration. It also found support amongst many sections of the nobility, but absolute resistance by others. The reform project began in 1782 when Acton created new militias, and was extended in 1784 with the creation of an *Intendenza Generale* with a budget of 2.4 million ducats whose task was to oversee the reorganization of the army and to create a navy. Foreign generals were brought to Naples to reorganize and train the infantry along French lines, and the nobility was deprived of its monopoly over senior

[5] Ajello (1991), 716–33. [6] Chorley (1965), 16, 132; Macry (1974), 457–84.

[7] Nuzzo (1971), 457.

[8] The Council abolished a number of the smaller *arrendamenti* (on manna in 1785 and on *acquavite* in 1786), but the means for any broader reform of the tax-farms did not exist.

military positions. Between 1768 and 1777, expenditure on the navy had run at around 650,000 ducats per annum: in 1788 this jumped to 1,023,000 ducats, and then between 1791 and 1794 rose again to over 1.5 million.[9]

These measures provoked fierce opposition from the noble families that enjoyed exclusive rights over commissions in the army, but were welcomed by those that did not. The same would happen when the Nunziatella military academy government was reorganized with the aim of creating a modern officer corps trained in the latest branches of military science and technology and with a strong sense of dynastic loyalty. This again divided the nobles, and found considerable support among young noblemen who came from families that did not enjoy privileged preferments and commissions. Many of the young cadets who were trained at the Nunziatella in the late 1780s and early 1790s would rally to the Republic at the end of the decade.[10] But the defenders of feudal privilege also mobilized to denounce the government's resort to absolutist measures and to the outrage of the queen the young Principino of Canosa claimed that feudal privilege was the only defence against royal tyranny.[11]

DEVOLUTION

From much earlier in the century the government had been exploring ways to change feudalism from within by means of the crown's right to take possession of feudal properties when the owner died without heirs. Historically the crown had not exercised this right of devolution, but when the last Duke of Atri, Rudolfo Acquaviva, died without an heir, the *Regia Camera della Sommaria* invoked and placed the vast Atri estates (known as the 'State of Atri') under crown administration.

The 'State of Atri' in the Abruzzi caught the interest of reformers who urged the crown to take the opportunity to strip these estates of their feudal title and sell them as private property. In nearby Teramo, both the bishop and Melchiorre Delfico debated how these properties could be disposed of to create a new class of independent, small peasant farms that would regenerate the local economy.[12]

What followed revealed the obstacles to what might at first sight appear a simple solution. First, the crown's claim to the estate was contested, causing years of delay. Then the reformers proved to be hopelessly divided in their recommendations, and when Delfico and Galanti finally agreed that the estate should be sold as private property, the crown's own lawyers rejected this. They argued that since the estates had reverted to the crown under feudal law they could not be alienated

[9] Simioni (1920–1), 61; Rao (1987), 623–77; idem (2000), 95–117.

[10] Chiosi (2000), 118–34; Rao (ed.) (1995), 15–20; see also Barberis (1988) and Ferrone (1993) for similar developments in Piedmont and other Italian states.

[11] On Canosa, see Villani (1974), 177–88.

[12] Rao (1984), 54; Incarnato (1993), 43–5.

or sold, but they could be leased as private property, a solution that Tanucci also supported on the grounds that it would purge the estates 'of the tyrannical oppressions that resulted from the fact that the feudatories had controlled the exercise of justice'. In other words, remove abusive practices without abolishing feudal tenure or feudal dues. Since the crown administration was also the beneficiary of these dues, however, it had little incentive to abolish them.[13]

No clear plan had been agreed for the 'State of Atri' when in 1792 the death without heirs of the Prince of Riccia caused another large feudal estate to devolve to the crown. The outcome again proved to be higher on expectations than results. The legality of the sequestration was challenged and subsequent litigation revealed centuries of unresolved disputes to rights and titles in all the neighbouring communities. The most important part of the estate was a *difesa*, a term that described any part of a feudal estate that had been enclosed and freed from promiscuous or customary rights. But since only feudal property was subject to 'devolution', could the *difesa* also be legally sequestered?

No one knew, and the crown's agents were never able to resolve whether the estate was feudal property. Their investigations did reveal, however, that the previous owners had treated parts of the estate as feudal or allodial (that is to say, as private property), depending on which category was most fiscally advantageous, a practice similar to manipulating modern tax codes but without risk of audit.

The same investigations unearthed litigation that stretched back centuries over contested claims to the various feudal or non-feudal titles under which different parts of the estates were held, the dues and levies exacted, and the rights of usage to which different parts of the estates were subject. What emerged from these investigations was the extreme uncertainty that surrounded all titles, property, and levies. As the crown courts tried to challenge or verify these titles, the uncertainty and confusion increased. It also became clear that it was much easier for the crown administrators to simply pocket the revenues of the estates under their care than to identify the origins and legitimacy of those revenues.[14]

THE *DEMANI*

Similar situations were revealed in what was the largest reform initiative attempted by the monarchy and the final achievement of the alliance between the throne and the reformers. This was the edict of 1792 that ordered the division of all common lands on the mainland, which were to be allocated to those with title to exercise use-rights on them.

As in much of the rest of Europe, the common lands (*demani*) in southern Italy took a variety of forms: some belonged to the crown, others formed part of feudal estates subject to seasonal public access, while others had been granted to

[13] Rao (1984), 42. [14] Ibid. 35.

local communities as the original source of revenue and to make land available for grazing or cultivation. Over time, however, the demarcations of the *demani* had frequently been lost or became contested. As pressure on land grew in the eighteenth century, these issues became increasingly contentious and rival claims to ownership or use of the *demani* were a frequent cause of conflict within and between communities throughout southern Italy.[15]

The reformers saw the opportunity for a fundamental reform. Since the royal domains were not subject to feudal titles and jurisdictions, the crown could dispose of them as it wished. The best place to start, they argued, would be the crown's extensive property on the Apulian *Tavoliere* that was reserved for sheep-grazing. Sold as private property, or leased as quit-rents, this land could be converted into thousands of small farms that would turn Capitanata into one of the most productive provinces in the Kingdom. The same solution could be applied in other regions where the crown owned extensive domain lands, such as the Sila Forest in Calabria.[16]

From the crown estates it was a small step to envisage the privatization of the common lands of the local communities, which offered the opportunity for an even more general reform. In this case, however, the government first had to restore the village commons to their original state, using the courts to get rid of those who had abusively occupied them. The commons could then be restored to local communities and divided amongst the inhabitants as small-holdings, or divided amongst those holding rival claims in proportion to their rights.[17]

The principles on which this massive operation were to be based were simple and rational. By settling the disputed ownership of the common lands a dangerous source of conflict would be removed, at the same time creating a new financial base around which local administration could be reorganized. The project promised one of those virtuous cycles close to the hearts of reformers, but the symmetry of their logic underestimated the enormous technical problems posed by such a reform. The government did not have the means to resolve the huge number of disputes over illegal occupations of common land, while many argued that the divisions in any case would be disastrous for the pastoral economy and would deprive the rural communities of their main source of livelihood.

The edict of 1792 proclaiming the division of the common lands throughout the mainland was, nonetheless, the government's single most important reform initiative. Once again, however, it revealed that the government did not have the means to implement such a measure, which was delegated to courts already swamped by existing litigation. Far from resolving these disputes, the edict of 1792 was another example of how government intervention raised expectations that it had no means of satisfying, further heightening local tensions, and making property rights even more uncertain.[18]

[15] Corona (1995), 23–62. [16] Ibid. 79–127. [17] Ibid. 79–94.
[18] Ibid. 179–212.

ABSOLUTIST ALTERNATIVES

Sicily

The alternative to changing feudalism from within was absolutism, which was first experimented with in Sicily when in 1781 the government gave its Viceroy emergency powers to challenge the autonomy of the Sicilian feudatories. Not only was Sicily an independent crown, but the monarchy's jurisdictions in Sicily were even more limited than on the mainland, while the privileges of the Sicilian feudatories were sanctioned by the island's Parliament. The powers of the royal Viceroy in Palermo were severely limited and government at all levels was largely in the hands of the lay and ecclesiastical feudatories. When the crown had attempted to challenge those privileges in 1773, the Sicilian nobility had responded by staging a revolt in Palermo.

It was a sign of the monarchy's new assertiveness, therefore, when in 1781 the marchese Domenico Caracciolo was sent to Palermo with special powers to reduce the influence of the Sicilian barons and the Parliament.[19] Domenico Caracciolo was a man of the Enlightenment who at the time of his appointment was serving in the Neapolitan diplomatic mission in Paris. He had previously represented the Neapolitan government in London, enjoyed close contacts with the Neapolitan reformers and with the intellectual salons of Paris, and was an outspoken champion of the anti-curial movement. When he finally reached Palermo, Caracciolo began by abolishing the Inquisition and then introduced measures to reduce the power of the clergy and the jurisdictions exercised by the barons. He instructed the Sicilian courts to demand valid title from all feudal property and revenues. He intervened to challenge baronial interference in the exercise of justice and in local administration, and attempted to organize a land survey that would serve as a basis for the introduction of a new tax. Following what had been proposed in Naples after the famine of 1764, the Viceroy also reduced Palermo's right to impose provisioning regulations in the rest of Sicily, and introduced measures to encourage free trade. He even tried to promote the formation of small peasant properties by establishing rural credit banks (*monte di pietà*).[20]

As had occurred on the mainland, these measures were strongly supported by the progressive sections of the Sicilian nobility and clergy. But when in 1782 the Sicilian Parliament rejected Caracciolo's proposals as an infringement of Sicilian liberties, the monarchy's support for its Viceroy crumbled. Even though the government issued Pragmatic Sanctions in 1788 that flatly rejected the claim that Sicilian feudal possessions were free of all obligations to the crown, Caracciolo received no support. When a year later the Viceroy tried to broaden the reform programme by encouraging the sale and lease of the common lands, he was recalled to Naples. Although he blamed the failure of his mission in part

[19] Marquis Domenico Caracciolo (1715–89).

[20] Giarizzo (1985), 193–212.

on the hostility of the Sicilian barons, Caracciolo held the government in Naples primarily responsible.[21]

Calabria and the Cassa Sacra

The second experiment in absolutist government took place on the mainland following the terrible earthquake of 1783 that devastated southern Calabria and much of eastern Sicily. Casualties were impossible to assess and the damage to property incalculable. The government declared a state of emergency and despatched an expedition headed by Francesco Pignatelli of Strongoli, with the title of Royal Vicar General, emergency powers to override all existing jurisdictions, and 100,000 silver ducats. To recover the expedition's costs, the government decreed the suppression of all the religious houses in the devastated regions and incorporated their assets to create a fund known as the *Cassa Sacra*.[22]

Many Calabrian landowners sympathetic to the principles of the reform movement saw the catastrophe and funds amassed by the *Cassa Sacra* as an opportunity to put into practice the projects that reformers had been proposing for more than a decade. To give an example, Domenico Grimaldi at once set to work to repair the massive damage that had been done to his experimental farms at Seminara. Another prominent landowner whose property suffered extensive damage was Andrea Serrao, the Bishop of Potenza, who was the feudal owner of the town of Castelmonardo, which was completely destroyed. Like Grimaldi, the bishop took charge of rebuilding the town, which he renamed Filadelfia, a clear sign of the principles that inspired the project.[23]

The reformers confidently predicted that the sale of the lands of the religious houses would bring into being a class of sturdy peasant farmers, whose energies and labour, they claimed, would revitalize the economy of the devastated provinces. In reality, few if any small properties were created and the land sales instead proved to be a bonanza for wealthy landowners, among them Bishop Serrao, who made extensive purchases of land in Maida, Acconia, and Francavilla from the *Cassa*. But few of these buyers shared the progressive ideas of the Bishop of Potenza, while the peasants suffered a double loss. Few had the means to take part in the land sales, while most who had been tenants of the monasteries lost their leases when the land passed to new owners. Numerous peasant families were driven off the land, and even the government was soon forced to admit that for the rural poor the operations of the *Cassa Sacra* had been an even greater affliction than the earthquake. It was also rumoured that the Vicar General had made huge personal profits and had returned to Naples laden with plate plundered from Calabrian convents.[24] To raise cash quickly the lands of the Calabrian religious houses had been sold off at low prices to wealthy landowners, and little of the

[21] In Naples he succeeded the Duke of Sambuca as the chief minister, but died a year later.

[22] Placanica (1970, 1985); Cingari (1978), 25–38.

[23] Chiosi (1981), 296–300.

[24] Cortese (1965), 79–115.

proceeds were reinvested in Calabria. What was not pillaged by General Pignatelli went to shore up the monarchy's rising expenses on the army and navy.

The experience of the *Cassa Sacra* in Calabria also indicated the difficulty of applying the reformers' neat principles to the harsh realities of the rural South. The rural poor were unable to compete with powerful landowners without more direct assistance and protection. They had no means to purchase even small plots of land, and without capital or credit had no means to work it. The *Cassa Sacra* would, however, prove to be only the first of many schemes designed to benefit the rural poor that instead deprived them of the lands they had worked as tenants.

'An Inexplicable Mystery': The Sila Forest

The government's involvement in Calabria after the earthquake had drawn attention to the state of lawlessness and unrest that had for some time existed in the neighbouring region of the Sila Forest, which resulted in an official investigation in 1790. This was as much a pretext as a reason for the investigation, however, since the government's interest in the Sila Forest related primarily to the heavy increase in demand for timber resulting from Acton's shipbuilding programme. The Sila Forest was the principal source of timber on the mainland, but it was also part of the crown's domain that over time had been the subject of widespread illegal occupations. Its need for timber as prices rose therefore gave the government new reasons for recovering property that had been illegally occupied and in reasserting its jurisdictions.

A senior royal magistrate named Giuseppe Zurlo, who was a prominent member of the anti-feudal movement in Naples, was sent to investigate. He quickly discovered that the whole Sila region had been subject to systematic illegal occupations at the expense not only of the crown but also of the common lands of the local communities and other landowners, and his report in 1790 revealed what one later commentator referred to ironically as the 'inexplicable mystery of the Sila'.[25]

Zurlo's report explained that the royal domain properties in the Sila Mountains were particularly extensive and had formerly provided the crown with important revenues. They also served to guarantee adequate common pasture for the local communities, and to prevent illegal clearances of woodland. But over time these common lands had been abusively taken over by a small number of wealthy landowners who included the owners of the largest herds of sheep and livestock. These illegal occupations, Zurlo concluded, were the principal causes of the lawlessness that prevailed throughout the Sila region, and those principally responsible were the powerful landowners who employed armed bands to protect their animals and their pasture.

[25] Bianchini (1839), 418–19—ironical since it was no mystery. See also Villani (1974), 222. Luigi de' Medici was also sent by the government to investigate the impact of the *Cassa Sacra* in Calabria in 1790; see Cortese (1965), 100–8.

Zurlo's account was yet another illustration of how the erosion of public access to land lay at the heart of the rural conflicts spreading to many different parts of the South. In the case of the Sila, the usurpations of the common lands had impoverished the rural communities. But they could not escape the struggles between powerful landowners and graziers, leaving many villagers with no alternative but to join the bands of brigands. Zurlo also noted that those responsible for the usurpations had established powerful connections in public administration to ensure that they would be protected and their unlawful actions go unpunished. The Sila was 'an inexplicable mystery' only because an explanation obvious to all was one that in the absence of effective royal government was too dangerous to be told.[26]

Zurlo's report offered important insights into the conflicts bringing lawlessness and violence to many parts of the Mezzogiorno at the close of the century, but also revealed that even when it was aware of what was going on the government lacked the means to intervene.

FEUDALISM UNDER REVIEW

The government's urgent need for resources and revenues lay behind its increasingly interventionist although rarely effective actions. But similar difficulties faced many landowners too, with consequences that served to accelerate changes taking place from below. Clear evidence of this is provided by the estate records of two major feudal landowners who were both, although for different reasons, looking for ways to increase their estate revenues in the final decade of the century. In both cases this resulted in a thorough survey of the principles on which their estates were managed and the introduction of a series of innovations.[27]

In 1789 Antonio Maresca, the Duke of Serradicapriola, decided to make a thorough review of the management of his estates because he had been appointed to serve as the Neapolitan ambassador at the Court of the Russian Tsar. But no less important than his imminent departure for St Petersburg, where he would remain for forty years, were the heavy losses he had suffered from his investments in various *arrendamenti* whose yields had plummeted in the 1780s due to the government's financial difficulties. To restore the lost income the duke needed to increase the revenues from his estates.

The review carried out gives a clear picture of the scale of property of a leading, but by no means very wealthy, feudal family. The core of the family's extensive feudal holdings was in the fertile north-eastern corner of Capitanata, with other properties on the Piano di Sorrento and in Naples where the family owned

[26] Ibid. The situation in the Sila region suggests interesting parallels with the conflicts in the royal forests of 18th-century England described by E. P. Thompson in *Whigs and Hunters* (1975).

[27] My thanks to M. L. Storchi for assistance in selecting these examples from the numerous records available in the section of *Archivi Privati* in the ASN.

a *casa nobile* in the fashionable Chiaja district. Their total value was estimated at 308,203 ducats. The single largest asset, however, was the family's holdings in various *arrendamenti*, valued, in 1782, at 140,183 ducats, that provided an annual income of 5,465 ducats.[28]

Returns from the family's feudal possessions were much higher, however. The estates in Serracapriola alone averaged 3,972 ducats per year, those at Chieuti 4,255 ducats, although non-feudal revenues (*burgensatici*) in both towns were much lower. Expenses, including taxes owed to the towns (for *buonatenenza*) and to the crown (*catasto*), amounted to 1,159 ducats, leaving a net annual income of just over 8,000 ducats (not including 'the costs of cultivation and improvement').[29] The family also owned eight farms (*massarie*) between Chieuti, Serracapriola, and the Marina di Serracapriola, whose capital value was estimated at 31,140 ducats.[30]

The stereotypes of the feudal landowner are not easily reconciled with the meticulous bookkeeping maintained by the administrators of the Serradicapriola estates, whose accounts were submitted regularly to Naples for further scrutiny by the owners' accountants and attorneys before being forwarded to St Petersburg. The revenues of each estate were recorded separately, and income from feudal rights was listed separately from leases and income from livestock and crops.

When Antonio Maresca decided to disinvest his shares in the *arrendamenti*[31] in 1789, he instructed his accountants to carry out a complete survey of the revenues from his estates and to identify alternative and more rewarding investment opportunities. This search would thereafter remain the principal theme of the duke's correspondence with his administrator in Naples, Francesco Roddi, whose brother was the manager of the estates in Chieuti.

Before leaving for Russia, the duke leased the estates to his brother, the marchese Don Benedetto Maresca, and when in 1803 the lease came up for renewal, he urged Roddi to demand a 30 per cent increase on the grounds that over the previous twenty years 'all manner of goods with no exception have at least doubled in value, as can easily be seen from the great rise in living costs here in the Capital'. He complained that most of the additional profits from his farms had been taken by the merchants who purchased grain in Capitanata, and he instructed Roddi to

[28] Land, property, and mortgage loans in the Piano di Sorrento amounted to 62,031 ducats, and loans in Naples to 26,779 ducats. The family's *casa nobile* in Naples was valued at 57,500 ducats and the *difesa* of Crepacuore in Capitanata at 20,479 ducats.

[29] ASN, Archivi Privati: Archivio Maresca di Serra di Capriola: B 167, Stato dei beni di Duca Antonio Maresca, 1782.

[30] Ibid. The first specialized in raising cattle, the second pigs, the third brood mares, the fourth sheep and goats, the fifth buffalo. They owned two other mixed farms where livestock rearing was combined with the cultivation of wheat and forage crops. The most profitable was the pig farm, because the investment was low and the return from the lease relatively high. The least rewarding were the brood mares, while all the other operations had an annual yield of over 15%.

[31] The *arrendamenti* in the Dogana di Napoli, Farina Vecchia, Olio e Sapone, worth 68,918 ducats because they were yielding between only 2.8 and 3.2%.

organize with other landowners to sell their grain independently and cut out the middle men. He also suggested that longer leases would give leaseholders greater security and incentives to improve the land, which he believed would enable them to pay higher leases.[32] Roddi replied that the 30% increase was impractical and patiently suggested that a better alternative would be to speculate on rising olive oil prices. The speculation would be relatively safe, the risks low, and the potential profits high.[33]

Although a single example, the Duke of Serradicapriola's review of the management and revenues of his estate was closely connected to broader structural developments: on one hand, the decline in income from the *arrendamenti* and, on the other, the rapid increase in commodity prices. But debt was another powerful incentive for maximizing revenues, as illustrated by the second example. When in 1788 Don Nicola Toccò Cantelmo Stuard, the Duke of Apice and Sicignano, became the Duke of Montemiletto, he also inherited his father's debts. To meet these, he appointed a lawyer named Gaetano Celani as his 'Vicar' to reorganize the administration of his feudal properties in Ajello. Two additional agents were subsequently employed to review the management and leases of his estates at Apice in Principato Ultra and for smaller feudal estates in the Abruzzo. In the 1790s the review was extended to the estates at Montemiletto in Principato Ultra and to the duke's more scattered properties in Calabria.

This was a major operation, and it was not until 1797 that Don Michele Bianco was appointed as 'General Agent and Procurator' to coordinate the different reports, in which he was assisted by the duke's treasurer, Gaetano Colella. Together they wrote a report that gave a clear picture of the organization and administration of this major feudal property. It began with a detailed description of the town of Montemiletto and 'the Palace that is by no means undistinguished and with all the facilities to be expected in the residence of a great Lord' that housed the duke's staff. These estates consisted of seven separate *feudi*, overseen by three Governors of Justice (*Governadori di Giustizia).*

Bianco's first recommendation was that the duke should take advantage of the rising cost of timber resulting from the government's shipbuilding programme. He also recommended that fewer loans should be made to the peasant farmers, because this encouraged 'idleness'. To encourage the peasants to improve the land, he recommended that leases be extended to eight years and argued that the three-year leases customarily used in the region were ruinous for agriculture. He concluded by recommending that the duke invest in planting trees and repairing the mills, calculating that an initial investment of 23,130 ducats would result in an increased annual income of 3,550 ducats that could be expected to grow by a further 2,544 ducats over a ten-year period.[34]

[32] Ibid. B 126 Copia lettere, 1803–4. [33] Ibid.

[34] ASN, Archivi Privati: Archivio Toccò di Montemiletto: B 123 fascio 532, Descrizione del feudo di Montemiletto.nell'anno, 1799.

Earlier in 1798 the duke sent his 'secretary and chaplain' Don Fileno de Pompeis to reorganize his estates in Calabria. Don Fileno spent a year on the estates, replaced dishonest administrators, organized the new leases, and recovered various properties belonging to the landowner. But the timing was not good. At the beginning of the year the king had fled to Sicily and in January the Republic was declared in Naples. When de Pompeis arrived to conduct his visitation of a feudal property near Amantea in March 1799, he was caught in the middle of a royalist uprising. Since it was known that the duke was a supporter of the Republic in Naples (for which his lands would shortly be sequestrated by the crown) his agent de Pompeis 'was seized by the inhabitants of that Town and shamefully arrested'.[35]

The upheavals of 1799 meant that the planned reorganization of the Montemiletto estates in Calabria was not carried out. In the meantime, however, with the assistance of the commercial firm of Becchi in Florence the duke became active in international trade. His first ventures resulted in heavy losses, but undeterred he invested in trading oil and wheat from Apulia and sulphur from Sicily. A year later his business improved, and he was working with other noblemen who were trading on their own account, among them the Prince of Trabia in Palermo, who exported sulphur from his own estates, and the Prince Belmonte di Pignatelli, who acted as his agent in Rome. Montemiletto was soon corresponding with a wide range of commercial houses in London, Hamburg, Amsterdam, Milan, Livorno, and Venice who supplied him with information about commodities in demand and market prices.[36]

These examples indicate that the world of these great feudal landowners was far from static. Both reveal the different pressures—debts, the crisis of public finances, rising commodity prices, and even speculative opportunities—that were encouraging landowners to increase their incomes and to develop new investment strategies. Both suggest that the outcomes could be very contradictory, leading to new forms of investment but also more effective exaction of existing revenues, and feudal revenues in particular.[37] The fate that nearly overtook Don Fileno de Pompeis in Calabria in March 1799 also indicates the reactions such initiatives might provoke.

PROVINCIAL VOICES

The efforts of these two feudal landowners illustrate the many different ways in which forces of change were being transmitted to the rural South. Another clear sign of the wider impact of these changes lay in the emergence of new provincial voices. They were predominantly those of the priests, administrators, prelates, and

[35] ASN, Archivi Privati: Archivio Toccò di Montemiletto: B 123 fascio 532, Descrizione del feudo di Montemiletto.nell'anno, 1799.

[36] Ibid. f. 191–4.

[37] For similar developments in Sicily see Aymard (1971–2), 67–85.

gentlemen that Genovesi had hailed as the makers of the new age, and they were especially audible in the regions most directly exposed to new economic and commercial forces where an important refrain was protest at the constraints and restrictions to which provincial producers were subject.

After the famine of 1764, merchants and producers in the Apulian provinces had challenged the legality of the regulations imposed by the provisioning authorities in Naples and by the *arrendamenti*. In Calabria, too, the damage done by these regulations to the producers of olive oil and raw silk was a dominant theme in the salons of the reform-minded gentry. But the ideas of the reformers were also taken up in Molise where the expansion of wheat production in the second half of the century had brought obstacles to economic growth into sharp focus. The most obvious of these was the lack of communications, which meant that although Campobasso was less than a hundred kilometres from Naples it was more economical to bring grain by sea from the more distant Apulian provinces.[38]

Campobasso was the chief administrative town in the province after Foggia[39] and an important administrative centre where the reform ideas found a wide audience. The group who began to meet regularly in the town included Giuseppe Maria Galanti, the brothers Giuseppe and Biase Zurlo, Paolo Nicola Giampaolo, Domenico di Gennaro, Vincenzo Cuoco, Alessandro Petitti, and Francesco De Attalis. All came from the province and nearly all went on to serve as administrators in the Bourbon government in the 1780s and early 1790s. Many would reappear in the administrations of Joseph Bonaparte and Joachim Murat after 1806.

They all, too, had similar career profiles. Giuseppe Maria Galanti came from a 'distinguished and wealthy family' in Santa Croce di Morconei, where he had first acquired his hatred of feudalism from the priests who ran the local school, whom he described as strongly committed to the anti-curial movement and outspoken critics of the feudal order. At the age of nine Galanti moved to Naples to continue his studies under the guidance of an uncle in clerical orders, where his ideas were shaped by the teachings of Genovesi and Filangieri.

The brothers Giuseppe and Biase Zurlo also attended schools in Molise before going to Naples to train as lawyers. Once qualified, they returned to Campobasso and started their careers by pleading the cases of Molisan villages against neighbouring feudatories. Vincenzo Cuoco, the future historian of the Republic of 1799 and later member of Joachim Murat's administration, was another member of the group whose career followed a similar path.[40]

In Teramo, one of the principal towns in the northern Abruzzi, another group was headed by Melchiorre Delfico and his brother Berardino and included the *abate* Berardino Quartapelle, Giovanni Bernadino Thaulero, Alessi Tulli, and

38 See Marin, in Clark and Lepetit (1997), 143–216, and Macry (1974), 402–22.

39 Strictly speaking Molise did not exist in the eighteenth century: administratively it was part of Capitanata and only became a separate administrative entity when the French rulers created the kingdom's 15 provinces in 1806.

40 R. Lalli, Introduction to G. Zurlo, 8–15, and De Francesco (1997), 4–9.

Baron Sterlich, one of the wealthiest landowners in the province.[41] In Lecce, the marchese Giuseppe Palmieri, the Bishop of Lecce, Filippo Briganti of Gallipoli, and the physician Giovanni Presto were founders of an agricultural society whose purpose was to improve local agriculture, especially the production of olive oil, and debate 'matters of public interest'.[42] In Calabria, a similar group of reform-minded gentry and churchmen met regularly in Cosenza, and before the earthquake many visitors travelled to admire Domenico Grimaldi's experimental estates at Seminara near Reggio where new oil presses from Genoa and Piedmontese organzine looms for reeling silk had been imported.[43]

Nor were these innovations taking place only on the mainland. During the winter in Florence after the revolution in France Arthur Young was surprised and delighted to meet the renowned Sicilian agronomist Paolo Balsamo, who was returning from a visit to study agriculture in England.

> A professor of agriculture, in Sicily, being sent by his sovereign, and wisely sent, to England for instruction in agriculture appears to me to be an epoch in the history of the human mind. From that island, the most celebrated in Antiquity for fruitfulness and cultivation... whose practice the greatest nations considered as the most worthy of imitations: at a period too when we were in the woods, condemned to Barbarity and hardly considered worth the trouble of conquering. What has effected so enormous a change? Two words explain it: we are become free and Sicily enslaved.[44]

In 1792 Galanti appealed for agricultural associations to be set up in every province of the realm. Citing Domenico Grimaldi's experimental farms in Calabria as a model, Galanti claimed that the need to improve agriculture was the most pressing challenge facing the nation. Agricultural associations would enable landowners, estate administrators, and farmers to learn how to apply the most modern agricultural procedures of the day, and because of their importance for the progress of the nation Galanti proposed that they be called Patriotic Societies.[45]

In addition to the salons of the provincial nobility and prelates, masonic lodges were also multiplying in the main provincial cities and towns in the 1780s, with the government's full support. Following the example of her brother Joseph II, the queen made herself the patroness of freemasons throughout the Kingdom and leading courtiers were appointed to preside over the rapidly expanding lodges, which included a lodge for noblewomen founded by the Princess Ottaiano.[46]

41 Incarnato (1991), 42–9; Clemente (1981), 344–467.

42 Venturi (1962), 1096–7.

43 Ibid. 409–28; Chorley (1965), 160–75.

44 Arthur Young (1915), ed. T. Okey, 277.

45 Just as well that Galanti was unaware of Arthur Young's scathing comments after visiting the Patriotic Society in Milan: 'I looked about me to see a practical farmer enter the room, but I looked in vain. A goodly company of i Marchesi, i Conti, i Cavalieri, i Abati but not one close-cropped wig or a dirty pair of breeches to give authority to their proceedings.' Ibid. 235. See also Villani (1989), 247–60, and De Lorenzo (1998), 1–88.

46 H. Acton (1956), 151: the Princess Ottaiano was one of the queen's favourites, and also the sister of Luigi de' Medici, who was suspected as a Jacobin in the 1790s but served the monarchy after the restoration of 1799, and became the leading minister after the restoration of 1815 and again after the revolutions of 1820–1.

As they spread to the provinces and to Sicily in the 1780s, the lodges provided the provincial gentry with cultural and political networks much broader than the salons of the aristocracy, and quite different from the lay confraternities.[47] But Galanti's appeal for the formation of Patriotic Societies came too late. By 1794 the government had abandoned all interest in reform, whose supporters were now treated with suspicion and viewed as potential Jacobins. The masonic lodges and many of those whose voices had formerly been heard most clearly from the provinces now found themselves under arrest.

CASACALENDA

The voices of the local communities could also now be heard, although in most cases only through the mediation of those who took up their cause against abuses of feudal power. One especially well-documented case was the town of Casacalenda in Molise, whose struggles were recorded in particular detail because the town was represented by the brothers Giuseppe and Biase Zurlo.[48]

Beyond the particular issues at stake, Casacalenda revealed conflicts being repeated in similar forms throughout southern Italy. The petition the brothers Zurlo made on the town's behalf set out the origins of the litigation that the community had brought against the 'past and present Possessors of the town of Casacalenda in the local courts, the royal courts, and the superior courts of Lucera and Foggia and which had over time had created a chaos of undecided litigation'.[49] The town claimed that the feudal owners of Casacalenda had 'always been intent on depriving the community of its property and its rights, and had for centuries buried it under a mass of costly law suits':

> Royal Governors, Royal *Uditori*, *Caporota*, and Provincial Fiscal officials, Fiscal Officials and magistrates from the *Regia Camera*, *Tavolarj*, Engineers, Agrarian Surveyors, *Attitanti*, scribes and all the people that are necessary in these legal procedures have been frequent visitors to the town.

When the costs of litigation bankrupted the town, the feudatory demanded immediate settlement of everything he claimed. Unable to afford recourse to the courts, the community appealed directly to the king. The petition showed that the town was engaged in over 200 separate law suits with this single feudatory, many of which dated back more than a century. If the feudatory's claims were upheld, the community stood to lose 'thousands of acres of land, houses and buildings, as well as its rights on the Feudal and Demanial lands'. The jurisdictions that the feudatory abusively claimed would deprive the community of its 'civic rights, the customary rates at which *fide* and *terraggi* were paid' and leave it subject to

[47] Giarizzo (1995), 406–20. [48] For other examples see e.g. Corona (1995), 195–202.
[49] ASN: Min Fin f. 1627 (23 June 1802).

'exactions in kind without proven title, deforestation of feudal land and the loss of its common lands'.[50]

This tale of long-standing abuses and exploitation reached a climax in the second half of the century in ways that vividly reveal the convergence of forces undermining the fabric of agrarian order in the South. Behind the abuses denounced in the petition can be detected the new pressures to enclose and privatize, which threatened the lands of all the rural towns and villages. The interventions of the royal tribunals and of lawyers like the Zurlo brothers did not bring solutions, but they did legitimize the claims of the rural communities.

There were prices to be paid, however. In Casacalenda the struggle against the feudatory was led by the mayor, Domenico di Gennaro, who was also closely involved in the reform movement in Naples. When in 1794 the government moved against a suspected pro-Jacobin conspiracy in the capital, di Gennaro was arrested and imprisoned for two years. He had been denounced by none other than the Duke of Sangro, the feudatory of Casacalenda who in 1799 when the Republic was declared in Naples would take his revenge. Arming 10,000 Albanians from a neighbouring settlement, Casacalenda was sacked and Domenico de Gennaro brutally put to death.[51]

CONCLUSION

Although the Bourbon experiments in absolutism did not attain their declared goals, they succeeded only too well in exacerbating local conflicts and undermining the legitimacy of the *ancien régime* in the South. By bringing the war against feudalism to the remotest corners of the mainland provinces, the crown, its agents, and the reformers unwittingly inflamed conflicts that could not easily be contained.

The critical role played by the monarchy in exacerbating these disputes is best illustrated by the contrast with Sicily, where the underlying tendencies were similar to those on the mainland. In Sicily important changes were taking place, and here too the feudal order was also changing from within. The lay and ecclesiastical feudatories were also increasingly dividing into reactionary and progressive factions. Although widely resisted, Caracciolo's moves to partition the common lands and challenge feudal titles in the 1780s marked the beginning of something similar. But resistance by the feudatories was more effective, and it was not until the following century that feudalism became a focus for political conflicts similar to those already present on the mainland in the final decades of the eighteenth century. These conflicts were not the reason the Bourbon monarchy collapsed in 1798, but they helped shape the civil war that followed.

[50] ASN: Min Fin f. 1627 (23 June 1802); *fide* and *terragi* were dues paid, respectively, for pasture and sowing of the feudal *demani*.

[51] Martelli, in Rao (2002), 717–43.

4

1799: The Rise and Fall of the Republic

Italy in 1797, from G. Holmes (ed.), *The Oxford Illustrated History of Italy* (Oxford: Oxford University Press, 1997).

NAPLES AND THE REVOLUTION IN FRANCE

The revolution in France had at first caused little concern in Naples. Melchiorre Delfico and Giuseppe Maria Galanti both believed that the events in France would serve to revive the monarchy's reform initiatives, and the government, for its part, looked to profit from the difficulties facing the French rulers. In 1790 Maria Carolina and Ferdinand IV travelled to Vienna[1] and when they returned new restrictions were imposed on French merchant shipping, while Acton renewed efforts to establish closer ties with Great Britain.

The situation changed following the imprisonment of Louis XVI and Marie Antoinette in 1792. In September, Naples refused to recognize the representative of the French Republic, Citizen Armand Mackau. Relations worsened when the French government discovered that Naples had urged the Sublime Porte not to recognize the representative of the French Republic. In retaliation Rear-Admiral Latouche-Tréville was ordered to station a squadron of French warships off the Bay of Naples in December 1792 on the pretext of a courtesy visit.[2]

The Neapolitan government was careful not to give offence, but when in January 1793 the French vice-consul replaced the Bourbon family emblems with the new republican insignia unknown persons smeared them with filth.[3] The executions of Louis XVI in January and of Marie Antoinette in October 1793 pushed Naples decisively closer to France's enemies, and in July the Kingdom secretly entered an offensive treaty with Britain and Austria.[4] A week after reporting that Naples would stay out of the war in August 1793, the French consul informed Paris that he had been wrong and was leaving Naples immediately.[5]

The treaty gave the British navy access to the Neapolitan and Sicilian ports, and in return Naples agreed to participate in the expedition that Britain and Spain were preparing against Toulon.[6] But the expedition turned into a military and diplomatic disaster that convinced the king that he had been exploited and reinforced the reformers' belief that England's aim was to make the Kingdom a colonial market for their goods and manufactures. The toll in lost lives and equipment was heavy, but even worse Naples lost its neutral status and was thrown into deeper commercial recession.

The most serious consequence of the Toulon expedition for the allies was the defection of Spain, which in September 1795 became France's ally. By freeing France from the threat of attack on its southern land borders, the Spanish alliance enabled the Directory to embark on a major war in Europe. The principal target was the Rhineland, but two diversionary operations were planned. General

[1] For the coronation of the former Tuscan Grand Duke Peter Leopold after the death of his brother Joseph.

[2] Nicolini (1939), 7–53; Barra (1997), i. 133–41.

[3] AAEP: Corr Politique (Naples), 38 (1793–1805), 11, 29 Jan 1793.

[4] Ibid.

[5] Ibid., 24 August/ 31 August 1793: Lallement to Paris.

[6] Niccolini (1939), 45–53; Nuzzo (972), 22–6.

Hoche was to raise an insurrection in Ireland, while another French army would invade northern Italy in the classic move designed to force the Austrians to split their forces on two fronts.[7]

The Directory's plans were thrown out of kilter when the rapid and unexpected victories of the *Armée d'Italie*, commanded by a 26-year-old general from Corsica, Napoleon Bonaparte, forced the Austrians to abandon most of northern Italy. The Piedmontese army was defeated in April, then the Austrians at Lodi (10 May), and five days later Bonaparte entered Milan. The remaining Austrian forces regrouped in the stronghold of Mantua, but Verona, the papal legation cities of Bologna and Ferrara, and the Duchy of Modena all fell to the French. As the French advanced, the Neapolitan government urgently sued for an armistice, to which Bonaparte agreed on 5 June. In return, Naples was obliged to pay a large cash indemnity, to observe strict neutrality, and to close its ports to British shipping.

During the winter and spring of 1796–7 Bonaparte was busy organizing the northern Italian republics, and during the summer held court in the magnificent Mombello palace on Lake Como.[8] His political influence grew further when in early September he intervened against a threatened monarchist revolt in Paris.[9] Much more controversial, however, were the terms of the peace of Campoformio signed with Austria in October with little consultation with the government in Paris. But Bonaparte's most ardent Italian supporters were outraged when the former Venetian Republic passed to Austria in return for the cession of the southern Netherlands and Lombardy to France.[10]

After Campoformio, Bonaparte returned to Paris with plans to invade England. But these were postponed in favour of a project that he had outlined to Talleyrand, the French foreign minister, after occupying the Adriatic port of Ancona in October 1796: 'Let us now concentrate all our activities on the navy and destroy England. That done, Europe is at our feet.'[11] That was the object of the large French expeditionary force that sailed from Toulon in the spring of 1798, whose undeclared destination was Egypt. The conquest of the Middle East would place France in control of the Mediterranean and at the same time cut Britain's communications with its new colonial empire in India.

As it passed to the west of Sicily en route for Malta, Napoleon's fleet caused great concern in Naples. After Austria's defeat and Britain's decision to withdraw its navy from the Mediterranean, the Kingdom was without allies and in a high state of alarm following the French occupation of Rome in February 1798, the arrest of the Pope, and the declaration of a Republic.[12]

7 Woolf (1991), 162–67; Grab (2003), 154–9.

8 The Cisalpine Republic was proclaimed in Milan on 29 June 1797, and the creation of the Ligurian Republic brought the port of Genoa under French control. On 14 May Bonaparte ordered that Venice be occupied and plundered, bringing to an end the ancient Republic of St Mark.

9 The coup of 18 Fructidor Year V: 4 September 1797.

10 Treaty of Campoformio, 17 October 1797.

11 Hardmann (1908), p. x.

12 See Caffiero (2005); Tulard (1983), 48–9; Zaghi (1986), 32–88: The pretext for the French invasion was the death of the French General Duphot, who was accidentally killed by the Pope's

Paris continued to insist that it had no hostile intent, provided that the Neapolitan government continued to observe the armistice. But Napoleon's Egyptian expedition meanwhile played into the hands of the allies and ensured that France's control of the Mediterranean would be short-lived. The French occupation of Malta had outraged the Russian Tsar, Paul I, and the Knights of the Order of St John of Jerusalem who ruled the island and were under his protection, appealed for his assistance. Meanwhile Bonaparte's invasion of Egypt had also brought the Ottoman sultan into the coalition against France.

Bonparte's plan was wrecked when on 1 August Rear Admiral Horatio Nelson destroyed the French fleet in an especially bloody engagement off Aboukir Bay. For the allies this was an ideal moment to counter-attack in Italy. A large French force was still stranded in Palestine and the British navy once again controlled the Mediterranean. St Petersburg and the Sublime Porte were ready, but the problem was to get the Austrians back into combat. For this, the king of Naples was to be the bait and in the months that followed Naples came under intense pressure to launch an offensive against the French forces occupying Rome.

The Neapolitans were already heavily compromised since in direct violation of the armistice with France Nelson had been permitted to provision his ships at Messina and Syracuse en route to Egypt. The violation was even more flagrant when Nelson returned to Naples after the battle of the Nile to repair his badly damaged ships and to recuperate from the serious wound he received during the engagement. He was feted as a hero by the Neapolitan government, while Sir William and Emma Hamilton took charge of his convalescence. So began his affair with Lady Hamilton and the no less public cuckolding of Sir William. But Emma Hamilton was already a close—it was rumoured even an intimate—confidante of the queen, and Nelson and the Hamiltons now worked in concert with Maria Carolina and Acton to persuade the king to attack the French in Rome.

On 24 November King Ferdinand set off at the head of an army of more than 50,000 men against the small and scattered French forces in the Papal States. The attack on Rome was to be coordinated with a naval operation in which Nelson's ships would land 10,000 Neapolitan troops in Livorno to cut the lines of the retreating French armies. Russia and the Ottoman Porte would engage the French in the Adriatic. To complete the trap, it was hoped that the Austrian emperor would resume hostilities in northern Italy and retake Mantua.

None of this happened. Unlike Caesar who 'came, saw and conquered', King Ferdinand 'came, saw and fled'.[13] The Neapolitan army entered Rome on 29 November but disintegrated when General MacDonald's[14] much smaller

police while trying to control a pro-republican demonstration in December 1797. The Directory ordered Marshal Berthier to occupy Rome and set up a republican government. Pope Pius VI fled to Tuscany, where he was arrested and taken to France and died a year later in captivity at Valence.

[13] Simioni (1921), 185.

[14] General Jacques-Etienne Joseph-Alexandre MacDonald (1765–1840).

forces regrouped and counter-attacked. As well as its equipment, the Neapolitan army lost nearly 2,000 dead and wounded and another 10,000 prisoners.[15]

The headlong flight was led by the king, who paused in Naples only long enough to collect his family, closest courtiers, the crown jewels, and the cash deposits of the public banks. On 22 December the royal family and its entourage embarked on Nelson's *Vanguard* and after weathering a terrible gale reached the safety of Palermo. In the meantime, General Championnet,[16] who had been despatched from the Po valley with 12,000 men to reinforce MacDonald in Rome, invaded the Kingdom. After a month of negotiation and confusion, on 21 January 1799 a Republic was declared in Naples and on the following day Championnet's forces entered the city where they encountered fierce popular resistance.

THE CRISIS OF THE MONARCHY

Defeat in 1798 was in large part a result of the financial and political strains caused by the preparations for war that had begun in 1793, but it had deeper financial and political roots. Acton's earlier attempts to reorganize the army and build a navy had placed massive strains on the monarchy's finances, while the government's increasingly absolutist measures had alienated virtually all its supporters.

Signs of the impending financial crisis came with the suspension of payments on various *arrendamenti*. In 1790 the crown raised a feudal *donativo* from the barons, and then in 1792 called for a feudal *relievo* two years before it was due.[17] The Toulon expedition in 1794 made the situation even more desperate and new taxes were levied on ecclesiastical revenues and the exemptions agreed in the Concordat of 1741 were withdrawn. More religious houses were suppressed and their assets sold. A forced loan was imposed on the city of Naples, another on the barons, while all churches were ordered to surrender their plate to the crown.[18] The banks were authorized to issue uncovered promissory notes, causing their value to fall by over 80 per cent, at which point the government seized their deposits and created a new *Banca Nazionale* directly under its control.[19]

These measures struck indiscriminately at the privileged orders and pushed through the absolutist measures that had been attempted but not implemented in the previous decade. To make matters worse, the threat of famine returned in 1793, evoking memories of the disaster of 1764. This time there was no question

[15] The Neapolitan operations were directed by the Austrian general Karl von Leiberich Mack (1752–1823), who was later court-martialled after surrendering the the imperial army without resistance at Ulm in 1805. Nelson later commented, 'Let not General Mack be employed; for I knew him at Naples to be a rascal, a scoundrel, and a coward.'

[16] Jean-Antoine-Etienne Championnet (1761–1800).

[17] Massafra (1969), 637.

[18] 103,000 and 120,000 ducats, respectively; Colletta (Cortese, 1957), i. 305–8. See also Ermice (2005), 31–4.

[19] Estimated by Colletta to be worth 13 million ducats; Frigione (1941), 48.

of forcible requisitioning from the provinces because the war had already brought foreign trade to a standstill and economic conditions in Apulia and Calabria were disastrous.[20] Instead the government authorized the city to incur debts to purchase grain abroad. New loans were raised and for the first time the controls on food prices in the capital were lifted, with the result that bread prices rose to market levels. The *arrendamenti* on grain and other staple foodstuffs were suspended to prevent prices rising too fast, but new excise duties on wine, building materials, and luxury goods were introduced in an attempt to maintain the payments owed to the holders of these *arrendamenti*.[21]

The government proved unable to prevent food prices from rising in the capital, the payments to holders of the *arrendamenti* had been reduced or suspended, and it had violated one of the most prized privileges of the nobility. Then in the spring of 1794 a major Jacobin conspiracy was discovered. More than four hundred arrests were made in Naples alone, and all those who had associated with Latouche-Tréville and his officers or who were suspected of supporting the revolution came under suspicion. The supposed leaders were executed, and others were exiled or chose to leave the Kingdom.[22] The works of Gaetano Filangieri were banned and the government's fitful support for Galanti's statistical inquiries was abruptly suspended: in 1795 he, too, was subject to investigation on suspicion of treason. In February 1796 Mario Pagano, who had succeeded Filangieri as the leading proponent of reform, was arrested and held in prison until he was exiled two years later.[23]

The police operations in 1794 revealed the existence of at least two Jacobin clubs in Naples: the *Club Romo* (*Republic Or Death*) and the *Club Lomo* (*Liberty or Death*).[24] Among the organizers were the *abate* Jerocades, an influential teacher, and his student, Carlo Lauberg, a priest who taught chemistry at the Nunziatella Academy. This was especially alarming because Lauberg had acquired an enthusiastic following amongst the young cadets at the military academy. In exile in Paris he would soon become the pivotal figure in the diaspora of the Neapolitan 'patriots'.[25]

Whatever Maria Carolina's sympathies with the reform project might once have been, the execution of her sister Marie Antoinette had transformed the queen into an even more committed counter-revolutionary. The government's suspicions now extended beyond the intellectuals and reformers to the propertied classes as a whole, and in April 1795 in a letter to the marquis di Gallo the queen told of her outrage at what she believed to be the treachery of the nobility:

> the nobility is the most corrupted and evil of all classes because it wants to have a king who has no authority, no force, no power and no rights: a mere puppet so that they may be

[20] Chorley (1965), 38. [21] De Rosa (1958), 6.

[22] Rao (1992), 63–6; Battaglini (1992), 18.

[23] Colletta (Cortese, 1957), i. 313–17. On Pagano see Venturi (1962), 785–832; Galasso (1984), 69–105. [24] Rao, *JMIS* (1999, 4/3), 360.

[25] Battaglini (1992), 18; Rao (1979), 91; De Lorenzo (2001), 17–37.

grand . . . they are true vipers. The worst of all classes, the pits. Their young men who study or become soldiers are equally corrupt. The people can be trusted, but those who work for the nobles are under their influence.[26]

The government had already moved against the freemasons and in 1791 Luigi de' Medici[27] had reported that the 'events in France are not unknown' to the members of the masonic gatherings in Cosenza and smaller Calabrian towns. Orders were given for the closure of the masonic lodges, and in 1797 the marchese Domenico Grimaldi was arrested and imprisoned, along with other members of the Reggio lodge.[28] Mario Pagano, the Prince of Colonna, and the Dukes of Cassano, Canzano, and Cantalupo as well as Luigi de' Medici were among those interrogated by a special Police Junta set up by Acton and the queen to investigate all those suspected of having contacts with freemasons and Jacobins.[29]

In 1791 the monarchy abruptly dropped its anti-curial policies and began to repair its relations with the Church. The Cardinal Archbishop of Naples was asked to assist in setting up popular devotional societies to counter the freemasons and their 'libertine' ideas. The first of the popular royalist clubs took the name *Arcadia Reale* and was founded days before the discovery of the Jacobin conspiracy in 1794. Enthusiasm for what another Catholic royalist, Francesco Gusto, was already calling 'a counter-revolutionary crusade' grew and similar societies were established elsewhere in the Kingdom, especially in Salerno and the Cilento.[30]

After 1794 the government had severed its ties with the reformers and was already mobilizing the most reactionary forces in the Kingdom. But despite the armistice signed by Bonaparte in June 1796 the army remained fully mobilized, while an additional armed militia of 10,000 men was also raised in the same year.[31] To pay for this, an extraordinary war *decima*[32] on all feudal and allodial property was demanded in May 1796, which provoked angry protest from the privileged orders. Churches, religious houses, and private families were all required to surrender their plate and silver, the bank deposits were again looted, and coin virtually disappeared in the capital. Total bank deposits had fallen from an estimated 12,000,000 in 1788 to only 3,500,000 by 1796, and nearly all of this had been appropriated by the crown.[33]

The government's increasingly despotic actions left it with few supporters, while the financial and military situation continued to deteriorate. It proved impossible to raise militias in the provinces for lack of funds, and in 1796 as many as 18,000 soldiers died of fevers in their summer encampments. The Venetian ambassador reported that there was little enthusiasm for the war because 'the country is already exhausted and oppressed by so many previous burdens'.[34]

26 Weil (1902), cited in Battaglini (1992), 22.

27 Luigi de' Medici, Prince of Ottaiano (1760–1830); in 1791 de' Medici was a government minister.

28 Battaglini (1992), 15; Venturi (1962), 429.

29 Colletta (Cortese, 1957), i. 348–53.

30 Chiosi (1992), 249.

31 Simioni (1921), 172.

32 Equivalent of the ecclesiastical tithe: 10% *ad valorem*.

33 Frigione (1941), 52–3.

34 Simioni (1921), 176.

By 1799 the military mobilization had become almost impossible to sustain, and the decision to launch an offensive against the French forces in Rome was in part an attempt to break out of the trap. But it was both unwise and unnecessary. The Directory's Ambassador at Naples, General Brune, had repeatedly given reassurance that the French occupation of Rome was purely punitive and that France had no designs on the Kingdom.[35] Bonaparte had opposed the occupation of Rome, which he believed had dangerously extended the French lines of communications, and the French representative in Naples informed Paris that there would be no military advantages from invading Naples. But in July 1798 the newly arrived French vice-consul, Joseph Sièyes,[36] reported that the French were completely shunned in Naples, trade with France was at a standstill, and British ships were freely entering the port of Messina contrary to the terms of the Franco–Neapolitan treaty.[37]

The king's hesitations were finally overcome by Nelson's victory on the Nile in August 1798, and he allowed himself to be persuaded that an offensive against the French forces in Rome could not fail. Yet there were signs that the expedition had failed before it began. In September a further levy was raised to bring the theoretical strength of the army to 60,000 men. Only 25 ducats were needed to purchase exemptions, so that the burden fell entirely on the poorest and was fiercely resisted even in the frontier provinces and in the towns of Portici, Barra, and Resina near the capital provoked open rebellion.[38]

There were also ominous signs of insubordination in the officer corps and hostility between the old nobles and younger officers trained at the Nunziatella. Incapable of imposing discipline and to cover his own incompetence, General Mack blamed the defeat on his officers: 'one sixth traitors, four sixths cowards, and only what remain men of honour'. Francesco Pignatelli of Strongoli, the Bourbon field marshal, claimed that the offensive had been sabotaged by commanders who secretly sympathized with the French.[39]

THE REPUBLIC

Before abandoning Naples to its fate on 21 December, the king nominated the deeply unpopular Marshall Pignatelli Strongoli as his Vicar General with full powers. On 12 January 1799 Pignatelli signed an armistice with the French commander Championnet, whose forces had reached Sparanise. The nearby fortress of Capua and the city of Naples were surrendered and it was agreed that an indemnity of 2,500,000 ducats would be paid to the French.[40]

[35] AAEP, CC, Naples 38: buste 104, Nivose Year VI (22 January 1798).

[36] Joseph Sièyes (1763–99).

[37] AAEP, CC, Naples 38: buste 116, 7 Messidore Year VI (25 June 1798).

[38] Ibid.; Simioni (1921), 200.

[39] Gabriele Manthoné and Oronzio Massa were specifically accused of deliberately failing to pass on orders; Simioni (1921), 200–1.

[40] Rao (1987/1995), 475. General Francesco Pignatelli had served as Vicar General in Calabria in 1783. He was the brother of Prince Pignatelli of Strongoli and two of his nephews (Ferdinando Prince

Carlo De Nicola, a Neapolitan lawyer whose meticulously maintained diary has survived, recorded the changing reactions in the city. After the flight of the king the situation was relatively quiet, even though there was no coin to be found and paper bills had become almost valueless. But 'the people, Thank God, are quiet. The urban militia has now been formed.'[41] The situation changed completely, however, when the armistice and the imminent French occupation became known.

After the flight of the king, the nobles formed a *Deputazione del Buongoverno* to organize the defences of the city, raise a civic militia, maintain law and order, and take charge of provisioning and the day-to-day government of the city. But the powers of the king's Vicar General had not been clearly defined, and were now challenged by the nobles, who claimed that in time of war or emergency they alone had the constitutional right to govern in the absence of the king.[42] The *Deputazione* therefore appointed two nobles[43] to act as 'leaders of the People', whose task was to arm the city's fortresses (the Castel Nuovo, Castel dell'Ovo, S. Elmo, and the Carmine) and win the support of the people through distributions of 'bread, wine, cheese, *acquavite* and money'.[44]

Carlo Lauberg and Vincenzio Russo[45] were among the Neapolitan exiles who accompanied Championnet on his march to Naples, and they warned him that the aim of the nobles in the city was to establish 'an Aristocratic Republic like that of Venice or Genoa'. Inside the city there was also opposition to the aristocratic *Eletti* from those who wanted Championnet to enter the city immediately and declare a republic. These 'patriots' now looked for leadership to the Prince of Moliterno, who as 'Commander General of the People' had built up a strong popular following.[46]

De Nicola described how tensions in the city rose as the noble *Eletti* and their opponents began to compete for popular support. On 13 January he noted, 'There has been some violence because two parties have been formed, one for the City the other for Pignatelli and both are believed to be armed.' Serious rioting began two days later and mobs began attacking those suspected of sympathizing with the French, the 'patriots'. De Nicola noted with alarm, 'The popular revolt continues and has become more dangerous than I can say. The trouble started when flyers were distributed before the armistice was signed and was then aggravated by the order that no offence be given the French when they enter the city.'

Against a background of rising popular unrest, the Vicar General fled the city on 16 January. Moliterno renewed the efforts to maintain order by distributing money and at the same time setting up gallows in the main *piazze* to deter looters. On 18 January De Nicola reported that the city was quieter 'and everywhere full of processions of penitents organized by the religious orders. The Gerolomini

of Strongoli and his brother Mario) were condemned to death for supporting the Republic in 1799, while two others—Francesco and Vincenzo—became generals in Murat's army. See Colletta (Cortese, 1957), i. 390 and n. 274.

[41] On De Nicola's diary see especially De Lorenzo (2001). [42] Battaglini (1992), 114–15.

[43] Girolamo Pignatelli, Prince of Moliterno (1774–1848), and Lucio Carraciolo, Duke of Roccoromana (1771–1836). [44] Battaglini (1992), 132.

[45] Vincenzio Russo (1770–99). [46] Battaglini (1992), 124.

fathers walked the streets with bare feet, the Dominicans and Conventuals were all out in force.'[47]

Moliterno was already negotiating secretly with the 'patriots'. He then released the political prisoners from the jails and formed a republican committee, and during the night of 19 January the patriots took control of the S. Elmo fortress that dominated the upper part of the city. When it became known that Moliterno was negotiating the entry of the French troops, the mobs took to the streets. Amongst their prime targets were noblemen suspected of being pro-French. Ascanio Filomarino, Duke della Torre, and Clemente Filomarino were dragged from their houses and butchered; the palaces of the Duke of Melissano and the Duke of Solimena and the monastery of S. Gaudioso were burned down; the house of the marquis di Rosa was attacked.

In an attempt to restore order on 20 January the sacred relics of San Gennaro were processed and accompanied by huge crowds, but to no effect. On the following day De Nicola simply stated, 'Today has been a day of the worst horrors that I cannot begin to describe.'[48]

His despair was echoed by another diarist, the *abbate* Pietrabondo Drusco:

> the anarchy had reached a state of fury and was directed entirely against the Jacobins and to plunder. The plebs are by nature insane and when they found themselves in power it is easy to imagine what licence followed. The lives and property of every citizen were in danger, and in search of safety many voluntarily took refuge in the St Elmo Castle.[49]

From there on 21 January the Republic was declared and on the following day Championnet's troops entered Naples through the Porta Capuana.[50] The violence now reached its peak, as De Nicola recorded with alarm:

> The events that have taken place in the lower part of the city will not be believed and cannot be described. Enough to say that we have seen the heart of our city become the theatre for a violent war.

The people continued to pursue suspected Jacobins 'as the supporters of the French are now known' and they fought fierce battles with the French troops around the Porta Capuana and the Largo delle Pigne.[51]

Even royalists were taken by surprise at the popular resistance to the French and loyalty to the monarchy. Relaying information from the Court in Palermo, Sir William Hamilton reported to Lord Grenville in London on 17 January that 'the Neapolitan Nobility has shown no loyalty to the Bourbons, but the People appear to be violently anti-French and loyal to their Sovereign'.[52] The following day he reported on Pignatelli's 'shameful armistice' and stated that the '*Lazzaroni* and populace of the city are in ferment and the Nobility are trying to calm them'.

[47] Carlo De Nicola, *Diario Napoletano*: 6, 13, 16, 17, 18, 25, 27, 30, 31 January 1799.

[48] De Nicola, 21 January, 39.

[49] Drusco (1884), 23 (19 January).

[50] Ibid. 157; Rao (1987/1995), 475.

[51] De Nicola, 22 January, 42.

[52] PRO London FO 70, vol. 12, Hamilton to Lord Grenville, 17 January 1799.

But he also expressed privately the view that the monarchy had little support and that there is 'universal complaint of a total want of Justice and good governance throughout the Kingdom of Naples and that the provinces are in the most extreme want and misery, so that few, should it come to trial, would think such a government worth fighting for'.[53] When news reached Palermo of the popular revolt against Pignatelli, Hamilton warned that 'it will in all probability end in the Nobility calling the French army into Naples to quell the populace and save their persons'.[54] But by 29 January, when news had still not reached Palermo of the entry of the French army into Naples a week earlier, Hamilton had changed his tune: 'The Neapolitan people have no love for the French, but if by their means the price of bread and oil could be lowered, they would become their friends immediately for a true Patriotic Spirit does not, I believe, exist in Italy.'[55]

THE PROVISIONAL GOVERNMENT

Within twenty-four hours of entering the city, Championnet restored order with the help of the patriots and San Gennaro whose blood, with some encouragement from French artillery, obligingly performed a miraculous but unscheduled liquefaction. On 23 January Championnet formally established a provisional republican government pending approval from Paris that never arrived. Carlo Laubert, the most prominent of the exiles, was nominated to preside over a government composed of fifteen members who formed six separate Committees.[56]

The provisional government was dominated by the exiles, who were referred to simply as Jacobins.[57] In Paris their contacts with Filippo Buonarroti had made Lauberg and Giuseppe Abbonamonti suspect as 'anarchists' after the coup of Thermidor, which was why they like many other Italian exiles left Paris to join the French armies in Italy in 1796. In Italy, some of the exiles were involved in a Jacobin-organized revolt at Oneglia in Piedmont in 1796. Giuseppe Abbonamonti, Matteo Galdi, Saverio Massa, and Francesco Saverio Salfi took part in the Cisapline Republic, but were expelled from Milan by the French authorities. Mario Pagano and Vincenzio Russo both took part in setting up the Roman Republic in February 1798.[58]

The difficulties that faced the provisional government were immense. The capital had to be pacified and measures to procure food supplies, restore the currency, and revive the economy were needed. The provisional government had also to

[53] Ibid. [54] Ibid. [55] Ibid., 29 January.

[56] Executive, Legislative, Internal Affairs, War, Finance, Police and Justice.

[57] 'Jacobin' was initially the term used by the royalists to denounce all the supporters of the Republic, but as divisions among the republicans grew, the moderates were referred to as 'patriots' and the radicals as 'Jacobins'.

[58] Filippo Michele Buonarroti (1761–1837) was heavily implicated in the pro-Jacobin plot in Paris in May 1796 known as the 'Conspiracy of the Equals'. See Rao (1992), 477.

assert its authority in the provinces, which had been thrown into confusion by the collapse of the monarchy. Throughout the frontier regions, the retreat of the royal army, the French invasion, and the king's appeal for a mass rising against the invaders had created a situation of utter disorder that threatened to escalate into civil war as towns and villages declared for and against the new government. To make matters worse the provisional government also had to raise 2,500,000 ducats from the capital to pay the indemnity to the Directory and a further 15,000,000 from the provinces.[59]

Championnet was inflexible in insisting that the indemnity be paid within two months, but his close adviser and fellow Jacobin Marc-Antoine Jullien[60] warned that the French demands would make it impossible to establish stable government. The only way to prevent the currency collapsing, he argued, would be to sell the lands of the crown and the Church.[61]

Another French official warned of the seriousness of the situation:

> In Naples we arrived as Liberators. We freed the wealthy classes who are also the patriots. We have powerful support from the ex-Nobles, the wealthy and the enlightened classes. They have welcomed us with great enthusiasm, but it is easy to discourage them. We have demanded from them 60 million francs. This is an exorbitant sum. Everyone knows that Ferdinand has bankrupted Naples and robbed them even of their plate. He took huge sums of money with him to Sicily and there is hardly any silver coin to be found. There is no way that this town can pay 60 millions, and even to raise part of this we shall lose very many of our supporters.... The populace of Naples is ignorant, highly superstitious, fanatically loyal to Ferdinand and hostile to the French. Had they the opportunity and the means they would not let one escape. They are terrifying because there are so many of them. If the English come and bombard the city and make allies of the *lazzaroni* we will be in the greatest of danger.... The French seem to have forgotten that we are in the land of the Sicilian Vespers.[62]

Carlo De Nicola also noted fearfully that 'the French troops are not sufficiently numerous to hold Naples in check and put down the insurrections in the kingdom'. On 3 February he reported that a militia of 1,100 men was to be established: 'all the good patriots are at its head with various ranks, and the rest have been enrolled from the former nobles and gentry'.[63] But the militia consisted of only six hundred men. All were armed and mounted, but property qualifications were set deliberately high to keep out the urban poor.[64]

The militia patrolled the city in the company of French troops, searching for arms and for those who had led the popular rising. These patrols were also responsible for setting up Trees of Liberty, the symbol of the new order, in the principal

59 Colletta (Cortese, 1957), ii. 20–1.

60 Marc-Antoine Jullien (1775–1848).

61 Battaglini (1997), 240.

62 AAEP, CP, Naples, 126: M. David, 'Notes sur la révolution de Naples', 10 February 1799 (22 Piovoso an VII).

63 De Nicola, 3 February 1799, i. 61.

64 Pietro Colletta later commented, 'few citizens were entered on the lists of the armed militia, but many were entered on the tax registers'. Colletta (Cortese, 1957), ii. 22.

piazze. The clergy was mobilized to celebrate the Republic with *Te Deums* and processions through the city.

De Nicola continued to emphasize the hostility felt by every class of citizen to the new government, however, which he attributed in part to the 'impertinence' of the French officers and the tensions caused by the billeting of French troops. But a wider cause of grievances came from continuing 'taxes, the shortages of food and the almost complete absence of coin':

> The price of food is getting higher every day, while everyone who owns any property is tormented by new taxes which hurt the rest of the population, and in any case fewer and fewer have anything to spend. Those who have no jobs or who formerly worked for the Court no longer have clients, so that the artisans are also without work: this causes the discontent to grow and those who formerly supported the change in government have begun to change their tune.[65]

This did not deter the government from attempting to reorganize the Kingdom along republican lines. On 25 January the former *Corpo della Città* was abolished and replaced by a municipality consisting of twenty-five members, most of whom were selected from the old nobility. The provinces were reorganized and renamed by a French official on Championnet's staff, Jean Bassal. Measures were taken to restore the currency and prevent the collapse of public finances: on 29 January the National Debt was guaranteed, but all payments from the banks, whose last deposits had been looted by the fleeing monarchy, were suspended and they were placed under armed guard.[66]

THE DIRECTORY AND THE REPUBLIC

The political affairs of the Neapolitan Republic were from the start closely controlled by the government of the Directory in Paris, which on 27 February ordered that Championnet be arrested and recalled to France for disobeying orders. He was succeeded by his rival General MacDonald, who remained in command until ordered to abandon the city early in May. In February Guillaume Charles Faypoult was appointed political commissar, but a month later was replaced by André Joseph Abrial.

It is unclear whether the Directory's decision to arrest Championnet was motivated by his undisguised Jacobin sympathies or by the well-documented reports that his generals were out of control and looting at will. The complaints that led to his arrest came, however, from the Civil Commissar, Guillaume Faypoult.[67] The two had been at loggerheads long before they reached Naples,

[65] De Nicola, 1 March 1799, 87. [66] Frigione (1941), 54.

[67] Guillaume Faypoult (1752–1817): Neapolitan historians generally see Faypoult as the villain, but see Godechot (1937), ii. 242–62.

and Faypoult had specifically denounced Championnet for failing to consult him before signing the armistice and negotiating with the patriots:

> He has taken control of every branch of government. He will not even speak to me. This strange behaviour will almost certainly result in anarchy.[68]

In protest at Championnet's arrest, the provisional government sent a delegation headed by the Prince of Moliterno to Paris to convey its dismay both at Championnet's dismissal and at the 'more austere and severe' bearing of his successor. But this was also a pretext to protest against the obstacles that the policies of the French government and its agents placed in the path of the new Republic.

Despite its best efforts, they argued, the provisional government's attempts to raise the money demanded by France had 'yielded only small sums, and even these are soaked in bitter and justified tears'. There was little more that could be done given the rapidly deteriorating situation in the provinces. The Neapolitan patriots 'deserve the most special consideration from *la Grande Nation*' and in the present circumstances 'the Government is paralysed in all its operations by the lack of financial means', which made it impossible to supply men or money to *la Grande Nation*. The government's great mission was 'to set the people on the right path', but to do this the people had first to be 'caressed and raised up from their abject state rather than oppressed' and the delegation implored the Directory to waive or defer its demands for payment of the indemnity.[69]

Moliterno's delegation was not even received in Paris since the Directory refused to acknowledge its legitimacy on the grounds that Championnet had had no authority to establish the provisional government in Naples. On 25 Ventoso (12 March) the provisional government tried another tack and instructed the delegation's secretary, Francesco Antonio Ciaja, to point out that the survival of the Republic was the only way to stop the British and Russians from attacking the south of France.[70] That appeal did not get a hearing either.

MACDONALD AND FAYPOULT

Two weeks after his arrival, Faypoult reported that only 1,000,000 ducats had been paid towards the maintenance of the French army since January. He therefore demanded the immediate surrender of all the royal palaces, the estates of the Medici and Farnese families, the lands and goods of the Order of Malta and the Neapolitan chivalric orders, and the lands of all emigrés, which France now claimed by right of conquest. He agreed, however, that cash indemnity could be paid in the form of jewels and plate.[71]

[68] AAEP, CP, Naples, 126, 9 Piovoso an VII (28 January 1799); BSPN Documenti Originali, ms xxxvi a 8, p. 61.
[69] BSPN Documenti Originali, ms xxxvi, pp. 8–33.
[70] Ibid. 41.
[71] BSPN Documenti Originali, ms xxvi a 8, p. 43; Helfert (1885), 144.

In a separate report, MacDonald complained about the ineffectiveness of the provisional government: 'the most difficult thing here is to make the government effective. It is flawed in every respect, makes every manner of promises and deliberates endlessly but never does anything. There is never any agreement . . . it has no power, no credibility and no energy.'[72]

The Legislative Committee set up by Championnet included Mario Pagano, Domenico Forges Davanzati, Giuseppe Albanesi, and Giuseppe Luogoteta, and was responsible for drawing up a constitution and drafting laws to abolish feudalism and reform the judicial system. But it had little freedom of choice, since the only constitution acceptable to Paris was the French constitution of Year III.[73]

On the question of the common lands (the *demani*) the situation was clearer because in 1792 the Bourbon government had already decreed they should be divided amongst those with use-rights. But like the Bourbon government, the provisional government lacked the means to implement such a project. Feudalism, not unexpectedly, proved even more controversial and the Legislative Committee immediately split into radical and moderate tendencies when Mario Pagano proposed that the abolition of entails should be made retroactive.[74]

As news reached Naples of opposition to the Republic in the provinces, demands that the provisional government move quickly to abolish feudalism became more insistent. On 16 February the *Monitore Napolitano* appealed for 'the law that will be most useful for the provinces—the abolition of feudalism'.[75] This, it argued, was the surest way to end the revolts against the Republic. Two days later the provisional government debated two proposals, one drafted by Giuseppe Albanese and Domenico Forges Davanzati, the other a more moderate alternative drawn up by Mario Pagano. The sticking point was the issue of compensation and when discussion resumed on 25 February the split between radicals and moderates widened. On 7 March two more proposals were again discussed,[76] and a compromise draft was finally submitted to MacDonald on 26 March. Two days later the provisional government urged MacDonald to enact the law quickly:

> The delay of your reply regarding approval of the law relating to the abolition of feudal fiefs, which will dissipate the insurrections as the sun melts the clouds and bring the people to actively support the revolution, has caused us the greatest concern.[77]

MacDonald's approval was postponed, however, until the arrival of the new Commissar, André Joseph Abrial.

[72] A de G (Vincennes), B3*** 321, MacDonald to Directory, 6 Ventoso (24 February 1799) and 1 Germile (21 March 1799).

[73] Rao (1995), 32–47; Galasso (1984), 69–105.

[74] Ibid.

[75] *Monitore Napoletano* (5), 28 Piovoso Year VII/I (16 February 1799).

[76] One by Giuseppe Cestari and supported by Carlo Laubert and Cesare Paribelli, the other by Pagano: see Galasso (1984), 69–105.

[77] Battaglini and Placanica (2000–1), ii. 154: Doc 672. 28 March 1799.

COMMISSAR ABRIAL

Abrial reached Naples on 28 March (8 Germinal) and at once reported that there was total confusion. He blamed Championnet, who had ignored the ruling that in all 'occupied territories' a Political Commissar should be in charge of public administration. But since it was too late to undo Championnet's errors without alienating France's strongest supporters, Abrial decided to create a new five-member Executive Commission and reorganize the larger twenty-five-member Legislative Commission. The new Executive Commission would have no powers to issue orders without the approval of the Political Commissar, making it 'a mere façade', but a useful one since 'the People see only Neapolitans and in the division of powers they see the image of a true Republic'.[78]

Abrial admitted that he knew no one in Naples, so he turned to the patriots and the 'popular clubs': 'I asked them to recommend individuals of real capability. Endless lists of names poured into my office.' After careful scrutiny, the Commissar had created 'a really excellent government', two-thirds of whom had originally been appointed by Championnet.[79]

The Commissar now urged the provisional government to get rid of Championnet's unworkable administration, create an effective National Guard, and rescue the currency. He also took up the proposals for the abolition of feudalism that were still awaiting MacDonald's approval.

On 9 April Eleonora Fonseca di Pimentel published in the *Monitore Napletano* a long commentary on the debates.[80] All were agreed, she claimed, that all forms of personal service should be abolished and the disagreements were over the compensation that should be paid for the abolition of '*diritti reali*'—land and levies owned in feudal title. The radicals claimed that since feudalism was the result of theft perpetrated against the nation by the different invaders of the past—'The Barbarians from the North'—now that the people ('the Nation') was free, it had the right to reclaim what was its own.

For the moderates, Mario Pagano argued for a more pragmatic solution and proposed excluding 'dues such as tithes and the *terratico* that arise from contracts made between noble landowners and peasant farmers'. He also argued that the feudatories should be compensated for the loss of feudal *demani*: 'To abolish everything, or to leave everything to the barons would be equally unjust.'[81]

[78] Battaglini (1992), 252.

[79] The new Legislative Commission included Mario Pagano, Domenico Cirillo, and Giuseppe Maria Galanti, while Giuseppe Abamonti, Ercole d'Agnese, Giuseppe Albanesi, Ignazio Ciaja, and Melchiorre Delfico (who never reached Naples) formed the Executive. Abrial also established four ministries: the Interior (De Filippis), Justice and Police (Pigliceli), War (Manthoné), and Finance (Macedonio). Helfert (1882), 146; Rao (1995), 51–2.

[80] *Monitore Napoletano*, Decadì 20 Germile Year VII/I1 (Tuesday 9 April)—this issue reported the debate held earlier on 7 March. In the meantime Lauberg and Cestari—the main supporters of the radical proposal—had left Naples. See Battaglini and Placanica (2000–1), ii. 133.

[81] Ibid.; Venturi (1962), 829; Galasso (1964), 69–105; Rao (1995), 37–47.

Fonseca Pimentel clearly sympathized with the radicals, but Giuseppe Maria Galanti was among those to urge caution:

> It has not escaped my notice that with the abolition of feudalism and feudal tithes there are those who wish an agrarian law like that of the republics of ancient times. But history constantly warns us . . . of the grave discord to which this would give rise.

Such a law, Galanti warned, would found the new Republic ' on civil discord, on injustice and bad faith'.[82]

Carlo De Nicola had also noted in his diary at the end of March that the Legislative Committee was divided into three factions. The radicals were led by Carlo Lauberg and included Domenico Bisceglia, Prosdocimo Rotondo, and Cesare Paribelli. They were opposed by the 'good republicans', amongst whom De Nicola included Mario Pagano, Ignazio Ciaja, and Domenico Forges Davanzati. Only the latter had the support of the Civil Guard, he claimed, and alone understood that it was essential to find ways of collaborating with the Directory. Finally there was a third group made up of aristocrats, and included Luigi de' Medici, the ex-Prince of Colobritano, and the ex-Prince Santangelo. De Nicola believed that their aim was to take advantage of the divisions between the radicals and the patriots in the 'hope of gaining control of affairs and forming an aristocratic government; but they are being closely watched'.[83]

Commissar Abrial was sympathetic to the radicals, but also believed that the provisional government had become dangerously unpopular and in early April he expelled Lauberg. Unlike MacDonald, however, Abrial preferred the more radical law on feudalism; the draft finally approved on 26 April still contained many compromises.[84] Nevertheless, the Commissar insisted that it conformed fully to 'the principles of French law'. The law was finally published on 27 April and abolished all feudal dues, 'leaving the ex-Barons with only those lands that were not subject to the right of devolution to the crown'.[85]

Carlo De Nicola was sceptical: 'We still await the other law that will abolish the tax on wheat and wine and reduce the tithe by one third. The Government's idea is to make the concessions in order to let the provinces understand the advantages of the Revolution and so bring the revolts to an end. But they should have done this sooner.' [86]

THE PROVINCES

By April, however, the end had already begun. The Russian–Austrian offensive in the north forced the Directory to withdraw its armies from Italy, while in the

[82] Battaglini and Placanica (2000–1), ii. 138–46 (Doc 669).
[83] Battaglini (1992), 238; De Nicola, 14 April 1799, 135.
[84] Battaglini and Placanica (2000–1), ii. 132–3. [85] Ibid.
[86] De Nicola, 27 April 1799, 150.

South the royalists had already taken control of the provinces and on 2 April Nelson's warships had begun to blockade the Bay of Naples.

In the provinces the first republics had been declared well before the Republic was established in Naples. The French armies that invaded the Kingdom in December 1798 had first occupied the frontier fortress of Civitella del Tronto, and on 11 December the Abruzzi town of Teramo was the first to set up a republican administration. Its lead was followed by L'Aquila, which on 16 December became the administrative centre of the new republican provincial administration.[87]

Other towns in Abruzzi declared for the monarchy, however, making communication with the capital difficult, problems exacerbated by the bands of royalist irregulars that were harassing the French invaders in the frontier regions of the Abruzzi and the Terra di Lavoro. Although the French held the major strongholds of Gaeta, Capua, and Caserta, their communications were still exposed to attacks by bands of royalist irregulars. One of the largest bands was based near the town of Itri and was led by Michele Pezza, better known as Fra Diavolo. Another royalist force led by Mammone was based nearby at Sora, from where his men could raid the French positions and their troops as they moved along the highway that was the principal line of communication between Naples and Rome. In Molise, republican administrations were set up in Isernia, Venafro, Sulmona, and Campobasso, but here too many smaller towns joined the royalists.[88]

In the provinces not directly exposed to the French invasions, most of the principal towns opted initially for the Republic. In Apulia, the Terra di Bari was a republican stronghold by the end of January. The neighbouring towns of Trani, Bari, Altamura, Ruvo, Corato, Grumo, Gravina, Canosa, and Spinazzola all initially declared for the Republic, as did Ascoli Satriano and Foggia in Capitanata. Potenza, the provincial capital of Basilicata (Principato Ultra), had also declared for the Republic, but many smaller towns remained loyal to the king.[89]

The first spate of anti-republican insurrections began in late January and February. An important catalyst was the arrival of agents from the provisional government in Naples known as 'democratisers' who were sent to reorganize provincial administration and to raise taxes. The immediate response in many towns that had originally declared for the Republic was to raise the royal insignia and revolt.

The revolt spread and early in February Championnet dispatched General Duhesme with 6,000 men to impose the republican order in Capitanata and Apulia. Making Foggia his base, Duhesme joined forces with Ettore Carafa, Count of Ruvo,[90] who had raised an army from his feudal estates in Apulia, and had laid siege to the royalist town of Andria. When it fell an estimated 4,000 inhabitants were massacred. Next Ruvo and Duhesme took and sacked the town of Sansevero.[91]

[87] Republican administrations were set up in the neighbouring towns of Pescara (24 December), Chieti (25 December), and Lanciano (1 January 1799).

[88] Battaglini (1992), 172–4.

[89] Rao (1995), 97–100.

[90] Ettore Caraffa, Count of Ruvo (1763–99): a leading feudal landowner, he was involved in the Jacobin conspiracy in Naples in 1794 and had fled to France. See Nicolini (1939), 100–20.

[91] 23 February: Helfert (1885), 139, 155; Rao (1995), 99.

The Calabrian provinces were the furthest removed from the French invasions, but also the closest to the Court and its British allies in Sicily. Even here, however, support for the Republic was initially solid. Following the *Cassa Sacra*, hostility to the former Bourbon government was strong, and in 1798 unrest and lawlessness had forced the government to abandon attempts to introduce conscription.

In January Cosenza had been the first major city in Upper Calabria to declare for the Republic, and its lead was copied by the other principal towns: Castrovillari, Paolo, S. Lucido, Amantea, and Rossano. In Lower Calabria, the royal governor, Antonio Winspeare, fled to join the Court in Sicily, and Reggio also joined the Republic. But here too many smaller towns remained loyal to the king.[92]

The supporters of the Republic suffered a severe blow, however, when a joint Russian and Turkish force captured Corfu on 1 March, which left all the republican towns along the Adriatic coast dangerously exposed to attack. Then in April a small royalist force led by Cavalier Antoine Micheroux[93] landed near Brindisi. That was the signal for defections, which spread rapidly and culminated in the fall of Foggia, the principal republican stronghold in the east, on 23 May.

By then royalist insurrections were sweeping through other provinces that had initially declared for the Republic. In Basilicata, Matera defected in February and the republican administration in Potenza was also overthrown. In the Cilento, a royalist rising at Montesano on 17 February gave the cue for revolts that spread through the Diano, Policastro, and Lucania valleys.[94]

When Cardinal Ruffo landed in Calabria on 8 February, the initial response to his appeal for a 'Holy Crusade' against the foreign invaders and their Neapolitan sympathizers had been cool. But at the end of February Monteleone surrendered to Ruffo's forces, and from there he moved to take Catanzaro and then Cotrone. With Lower Calabria in the hands of the royalists, the revolts spread to Upper Calabria. On 15 March Cosenza fell and was sacked. Still moving cautiously, Ruffo advanced northwards, taking and sacking the republican stronghold of Altamura at the end of April. There he waited for reinforcements before advancing by way of Gravina to Spinazzola, Venosa, and then Melfi.

On 2 June Ruffo reached Bovino, where he waited to join forces with Micheroux. From Bovino, he made contact with the royalist forces led by Giuseppe Pronio in the Abruzzi, while Micheroux was in communication with the bands led by Fra Diavolo and Gaetano Mammone that controlled much of the Terra di Lavoro. On 6 June Micheroux reported that the whole of the Terra di Bari, Capitanata, Molise, and the Terra di Lavoro had been recaptured for the king with the assistance of 'four Russian frigates, 320 soldiers, 120 sailors and 20 pieces of Russian artillery'.[95] On June 8 Ruffo entered Avellino and five days later was at the gates of Naples.

[92] Cingari (1957), 117, 139–40.

[93] Antoine Micheroux (1776–1805) was a Belgian Walloon officer serving in the Bourbon army who also performed diplomatic functions.

[94] Cassese (1970), 97.

[95] Maresca (1894), 287–92; on Ruffo see Cingari (1957), 191–210, 242; Helfert (1885), 182.

THE END OF THE REPUBLIC

On 30 March MacDonald announced that the royalist insurrections in the Adriatic provinces had been crushed and that communications had finally been reopened with Apulia. A week later he received news that General Giuseppe Schipani, who had been sent to put down insurrections in the Cilento and Calabria, had been defeated by royalist irregulars led by Sciarpa.[96]

Naples itself was now under direct threat of attack. On 2 April, coinciding with the Austro-Russian offensive in northern Italy a squadron of British warships commanded by Commander Troubridge[97] had occupied the islands of Procida, Ventotenne, Ponza, and Capri and placed the capital under blockade. On 11 April MacDonald reported to Paris that the French position in Naples was no longer tenable. His communications were overextended and his force of 16,000 men was every day reduced by disease and attacks by brigands. He could no longer hold the lines from Naples and Salerno to Rome and Ancona, as well as those from Naples to Apulia and the Terra di Bari.

> Every day there are fresh attacks and acts of brigandage, the patriots are weak, we lack local resources, there are no supplies or forage, no silver, no corn so that we can only obtain what we need by force of arms. Since the English squadron has taken up position off the coast the revolts have increased, the people become more insolent and many patriots are already leaving in fear because of the feebleness of our forces . . . and because of the number of placards and incendiary proclamations that seem to presage a general rising.[98]

The general ordered that grain from Apulia be sent to Rome to supply his retreating army, even at the risk of letting Naples starve. On 22 April the French army moved from Naples to the safety of Caserta, leaving behind a small but well-supplied garrison in the S. Elmo fortress. MacDonald told the provisional government that the National Guard should be mobilized. Three days later four of his battalions were recalled to join the *Armée de l'Italie* in the North and MacDonald ordered his officers to abandon Apulia and the Abruzzi. On 1 May he informed Paris that he was leaving Naples 'to its own resources' on the following day, although his withdrawal was delayed until the 7th.[99] Abrial stayed until 28 May, and before leaving he told the provisional government that it was now completely free to act as it wished.[100]

Despite the desperate military situation, on 11 May Eleonora Fonseca di Pimentel hailed the French withdrawal as the moment when the Republic was finally free.

> Patriots, citizens of the Neapolitan Nation, You are now finally in control of your own destiny and have the opportunity that other reborn Nations have vainly desired: this is the moment to show your wisdom, to unite your minds, your strength and will so that you

[96] Cassese (1970), 110. [97] Thomas Troubidge (1750–1810).
[98] A de G (Vincennes), B***321, 22 Germinal (11 April 1799).
[99] A de G (Vincennes), B3*** 321, 2–18 Flóreal Year VII (21 April 1799).
[100] AAEP: Corr Politique (Naples), 126.

may soon proclaim your Constitution. From this moment you have the opportunity to show the august French Nation and the whole of Europe whether or not you deserve to be a free People.[101]

There was a renewed spate of legislative activity and renewed efforts to win over the *popolaccio*. But the government's politics took a more repressive turn after the discovery on 5 April of a royalist conspiracy. Two brothers named Baccher were discovered to be in communication with the Court in Palermo, but many aristocrats were also involved in the conspiracy, among them Andrea Sanfelice, the Duke of Calabritto, the Duke of Salandra and Sanfelice's wife, Luisa de Molino. It was the latter who revealed the conspiracy, making her one of the principal targets of the later Royal Terror.

On 12 April a Committee of Public Safety (the Court of Censorship) was set up to impose more severe police measures. A Patriotic Society modelled on the Jacobin Club in Paris was also established with power to scrutinize and interrogate all public officials. Carlo De Nicola reported that this was 'composed of many zealous citizens who meet regularly to examine objectively all those who are deemed unreliable and seek to have them arrested'.[102] Subsequently other Patriotic Societies were set up and similarly demanded the right to select magistrates and public officials. De Nicola was outraged when the *Sala Patriotica* of Santa Lucia was addressed by 'a commoner from the Mercato district'. But he added, 'I think that these people must all have been bribed, because the people are all Royalists and I know that they are just waiting for the King's army to arrive and meanwhile are making cartridges.'[103]

Tensions between the Jacobins and the patriots were increasing and on 26 May De Nicola reported that Mario Pagano and Domenico Cirillo had accused the leaders of the government of imitating Robespierre's Terror.[104] In an attempt to restore confidence and alleviate popular discontent on 9 May the government abolished consumption taxes on wheat and seized the property of the monarchy to guarantee the bank deposits.[105] On 14 May (25 Fiorile) a radical reform of the judiciary and legal system was announced and on 29 May the lands and goods of those who had accompanied the Court to Palermo were sequestered.[106]

THE FINAL ACT

By now the enemies of the Republic were nearly at the gates and as they drew closer to the capital in the first week of June the outlying hamlets declared for the king. A sliver of hope came, however, with the news that the French fleet had slipped the

101 *Monitore Napoletano*, Duodì 22 Fiorile Year VII (Saturday 11 May 1799).
102 De Nicola, 18 April 1799; Colletta (Cortese, 1957), ii. 28; Rao (1995), 53.
103 De Nicola, 29 May, 193; see also Cuoco (ed. Villani, 1974), 115–18 and Rao (1999), 364.
104 De Nicola, 26 May 1799; see also Cuoco (ed. Villani, 1974), 153.
105 De Nicola, 9 May 1799, 167–8; Colletta (Cortese, 1957), ii. 69–71.
106 Rao (1999), 491.

British blockade off Brest and that Admiral Bruix was headed for the Mediterranean with the aim of joining forces with the Spanish fleet and engaging the British fleet.

The same news forced Nelson to change course. On 13 June he had set sail from Palermo to command the action in the Bay of Naples, but Lord Keith now ordered him to take up station off the west of Sicily to await the expected Franco-Spanish attack. Nelson ordered Captain Troubridge to join him with the ships blockading Naples, leaving only some smaller gunboats under the command of Captain Edward James Foote to keep up the bombardment of the republican strongholds along the coast.

The respite was only temporary, however, and even before the return of the main British battle squadron Foote's small flotilla had sufficient fire-power to enable the royalists to take Castellamare. On 13 June, the feast day of St Anthony of Padua, Ruffo's forces finally reached the city gates.[107] A fierce fight for control of the Ponte della Maddelena lasted all day, but in the early evening Ruffo's Calabrian irregulars and a detachment of Micheroux's Turks forced an entry through the Porta Capuana. The republican defenders of the Carmine fort were overcome and put to the sword, and by midnight the royalists were in control of the lower part of the city.[108]

The patriots, however, still held the principal forts: the Castel Nuovo, the Castel dell'Ovo, and the S. Elmo castle. The latter not only commanded the higher ground but was garrisoned by the small and well-equipped French force commanded by Colonel Joseph Méjean. For as long as they held these positions the patriots were impregnable and had most of the city under their cannon.

Ruffo and Micheroux could see no way to dislodge the patriots from the forts, and were increasingly concerned by the anarchy that had overwhelmed the lower parts of the city where the *Sanfedisti* and the people were indiscriminately slaughtering suspected supporters of the Republic. With the full agreement of the commanders of the Russian and Turkish contingents and of Captain Foote, Ruffo and Micheroux therefore began negotiating an armistice with the patriots. The terms permitted the republicans and the French garrison to leave the forts under guarantee of safe conduct and made available transports to take them and their families and possessions safely to France.

The armistice was agreed, and for the English signed by Captain Foote on behalf of Troubridge who was still with Nelson. The next act in the tragedy of the Neapolitan Republic began on 24 June when Nelson's flagship, the *Foudroyant*, weighed anchor in the Bay of Naples. Nelson immediately declared the armistice null and void: for two days Ruffo and Micheroux protested and resisted, but Nelson held firm. Then on the 26 June he appeared to change his mind: that afternoon the republicans came voluntarily out of the forts and were shown full military honours by the Russian and Turkish commanders, whose troops escorted

[107] The royalists had little faith in the traditional protector of Naples, St Gennaro, the miraculous liquefaction of whose blood had taken place despite the presence of the French invaders in the city.

[108] Helfert (1885), 143–4.

them through the mob to embark on the *polacche* that were to carry them and their families to France.

On 27 June Ruffo celebrated Nelson's agreement to the terms of the capitulation with a Te Deum sung in the cathedral, but on the following day—and for reasons that remain disputed to this day—Nelson ordered his ships to change position and bring the transports under their guns.[109] British marines made their way through the transports, arresting those suspected of being leading republicans who were then made prisoners once more in the forts they had voluntarily abandoned on the previous day.

On 29 June, Nelson authorized the court martial of Francesco Caracciolo,[110] a former Neapolitan naval officer who had taken command of the Republic's small navy and had been captured while trying to escape. The court martial was conducted by a panel of Neapolitan officers but on board the *Foudroyant*. Carracciolo was convicted of treason against his sovereign and without awaiting superior orders Nelson insisted that the sentence be carried out immediately. On the same afternoon Carracciolo was hanged from the yard-arm of the Neapolitan warship the *Minerva*.

The final and longest act of the tragedy followed when King Ferdinand left Palermo for Naples in July. When the royal flotilla reached the Bay of Naples the king did not disembark, but while the city remained menaced by the guns of the British and Neapolitan warships the Royal Terror began. A special Junta was constituted with the power to arrest, interrogate, and judge those guilty of unlawful rebellion against their sovereign ruler. The hangings and beheadings that began in July would keep the public executioners and the scaffold in the Piazza del Carmine fully employed until September of the following year.[111]

109 Whether Nelson deliberately tricked the republicans into leaving the forts, which were impregnable, or whether he acted after receiving explicit orders from the Court in Palermo has been debated ever since. See Guttridge (1903), pp. lix–cviii and the attached documents, and Giglioli (1903), 306–21. The debates are reviewed in Davis, in Rao (ed.) (2002), 393–400.

110 Francesco Caracciolo (1752–99) was a rear admiral in the Bourbon navy who on 8 April took command of the republican navy: Cortese (1965), 157–74.

111 See Battaglini and Placanica (2000–1), ii. 579–614: 3,818 individuals were tried, of whom 216 were executed, 492 exiled, and the remainder given lesser sentences; 107 royalists were convicted and executed during the Republic.

5

Jacobins and Patriots

HOW THE REPUBLIC BECAME A LEGEND

In the closing years of the nineteenth century, the events of 1799 were brilliantly transformed into one of the great founding myths of the new Italian nation. The year 1799 came to represent a watershed, the turning point that separated Italy's two destinies. In the North it was during the republican experiments between 1796 and 1799 that the first explicit proposals were made for the creation of an independent and unified Italian state, which many hailed as the beginning of the process that would lead to Italy's political unification half a century later. The South, however, was already different. Here it was not the republicans but the counter-revolutionary Sanfedists that triumphed. The North had taken the path of progress and modernity, the South the path of backwardness.

The distinctions were not made by contemporaries, and indeed they ran directly counter to one of the most striking features of this period when in exile Italians from all over the peninsula were for the first time discovering a sense of common destiny, if not identity.[1] Nor is this surprising, since in most essential respects the history and the fate of the Republic in Naples were very similar to those of the other Italian republics. Nor was the South ever the only site of popular counter-revolutions that were no less intense or widespread in the North after the French invasions in 1796.

Like its sister republics in northern and central Italy, the Neapolitan Republic was founded under the intrusive guardianship of French armies. Its actions were subordinated to the politics of the Directory, whose principal object was extortion, plunder, and pillage. Like the other Italian republics, the Neapolitan Republic depended on the support of a small minority drawn from a cross section of the propertied and educated classes, and like them it failed to win the support of the masses. It fell because the Directory was forced to withdraw its troops from Italy in April 1799, leaving all the Italian republics defenceless against the allied counter-offensive. In its objectives, in its support, and in the reasons for its collapse the Neapolitan Republic was essentially similar to the other Italian republics.

[1] The literature on the political significance of the republic triennium is vast. In English see Woolf (1979), 157–74, and Lyttelton (1993), 63–105; for excellent overviews of the Italian literature see Rao (2002), 63–116 and Caffiero (2005), 19–58.

What did differ in the South was, however, the scale of the crisis of the monarchy that these events revealed.

It was only later that the emphasis shifted to what had made the Neapolitan Republic different, and certainly nothing contributed more decisively to transforming the Neapolitan Republic of 1799 into myth than its tragic end.[2] Even at the time this quickly assumed symbolic significance, not least because the Neapolitan Republic marked both the furthest geographical reach of the republican experiment that had started seven years earlier in France and the beginning of its end.[3]

The fanaticism of the counter-revolution, and above all the cold-blooded savagery of the Royal Terror in Naples whose victims included many from the most noble families in the Kingdom, inspired genuine revulsion. In the fierce political debates in Paris that preceded the coup of 18th Brumaire (November 1799) later in the same year, Championnet cited the fate of the Neapolitan Jacobins to denounce the Directory for betraying the Italian republics and to warn what could be expected in France should the *ci-devant* monarchy and its supporters ever triumph.[4] Hearing the tales of the Neapolitan exiles who had made their way to Paris, Maria Helen Williams was also persuaded that the royalist vengeance in Naples matched only Robespierre's Terror in scale and inhumanity.[5]

The comparison was questionable, but the revulsion was real. Even in Britain, the behaviour of the king of Naples and Nelson's apparent complicity were the subject of an outraged denunciation when in the House of Commons in February 1800 Charles James Fox accused the hero of the Battle of the Nile of knowingly participating in an atrocity. A decade later in his *Life of Nelson* Robert Southey described what had happened in the Bay of Naples in 1799 as:

> A deplorable transaction, a stain on the memory of Nelson and upon the honour of England. To palliate it would be vain: to justify it would be wicked. There is no alternative for one who will not make himself a participant in guilt but to record the shameful story with sorrow and shame.[6]

What subsequently fixed the image of the Republic of 1799 most lastingly, however, was the *Historical Essay Concerning the Late Revolution in Naples* by Vincenzo Cuoco, published in Milan in 1801. Cuoco had been a member of the provisional republican government in Naples in 1799 and had been arrested in May but escaped and made his way to France, where like many other Italian exiles he found himself far from welcome in the sombre political climate after Brumaire.[7] After Bonaparte's victory over the Austrians at Marengo in June 1800, Cuoco like many of his fellow countrymen moved to Milan where he wrote his account of the Neapolitan Republic.

Cuoco acknowledged that the Republic's fate had been sealed by the withdrawal of MacDonald's armies in May, but he also insisted that the republican

[2] Rao (1999, 2002). [3] Vovelle (1999), 43–59. [4] Rao (1992), 165–82.
[5] Rao, in Di Lorenzo (ed.) (2003), 708–39. [6] Southey (1813), i. 170.
[7] Di Francesco (1997), 29–38; Rao (1992), 393–515.

government had failed to develop coherent policies or strategies. He was especially strident in his criticism of the leaders of the Republic, most of whom he claimed were self-serving aristocrats. They had been eager to pass laws from which they alone would benefit, such as abolishing the entails that in aristocratic families cut off cadet sons from the line of inheritance. But when it came to the broader question of abolishing feudalism, these aristocratic republicans had proved reluctant. Cuoco's other target was the exiles, whom he accused of blindly supporting the French authorities and of imposing reforms based uncritically on French models ill-suited to the political and cultural realities of Naples.

As a result, the provisional government had failed to win over the provinces, raise a republican army, abolish feudalism until too late, or create democratic institutions that might have found roots in Neapolitan society. For that reason, Cuoco argued, the republican experiment in Naples had been a 'passive revolution', inspired by foreign models and guided by leaders who lacked understanding of local conditions and failed to establish any following among the masses who remained loyal to the monarchy and their own popular religious practice.[8]

Cuoco's account was subsequently taken as persuasive evidence that the paths of the two Italies had critically diverged during the years of the Jacobin Republics. Writing a century after the event, Benedetto Croce saw in Cuoco's 'passive revolution' confirmation of his own conviction that there had been no possibility of achieving progress in the pre-Unification South. Centuries of foreign oppression, exploitation, and misrule had corrupted and destroyed southern society. This made the ignorant masses facile tools in the hands of a reactionary ruling class, abetted by a corrupt and superstitious clergy. Against the forces of reaction the small group of idealists who had tried to lead the Republic was helpless. For Croce, what Vincenzo Cuoco had described as the 'passive revolution' was the inevitable consequence of the moral and material backwardness that in 1799 made the fanatical Sanfedist counter-revolution the true voice of the South.[9]

In Croce's master-narrative of the Risorgimento, the heroic sacrifice of the Neapolitan republicans—the martyrs of 1799—became one of the most potent founding myths of the new state. Not surprisingly, therefore, in his Marxist counter-narrative Antonio Gramsci placed even greater but equally retrospective importance on Cuoco's 'passive revolution'.[10] Today, Cuoco's essay is known primarily through these two influential, but equally retrospective and ideological commentaries. In both cases Cuoco's arguments were drilled to serve the needs of two very different ideological constructs, both of which identified 1799 as the moment when modern Italy's two souls parted ways. But more recent studies suggest that in the process Cuoco's arguments have been twisted almost beyond recognition.

Cuoco's *Essay* was written and published at a moment of great political uncertainty when the Italian exiles and survivors of the earlier republics like Cuoco had

[8] Cuoco (ed. Villani, 1980), 90. [9] Croce (1924/1967), 204–12.
[10] See Introduction, pp. 4–6.

returned to Milan but were more likely to be treated as suspect 'anarchists' than as friends by the French. Nonetheless, many of the exiles continued to hope that Napoleon would support the earlier republican project, among them Francesco Lomonaco, whose *Report to Citizen Carnot* was published in August 1800.

Lomonaco's brief tract was written in the form of an open letter to the French foreign minister, and it appealed to France to support the creation of an independent Italian republic. Its author had also participated in the Republic in Naples in 1799, and it coupled a proud defence of the Neapolitan Jacobins with a searing attack on the Directory and the French commander in Naples, Joseph Méjean, whose decision to surrender the impregnable S. Elmo fortress had sent the patriots to certain death.[11] Lomonaco gave a detailed description of the horrors of the Royal Terror and the counter-revolution in Naples, but clearly with the intent of persuading France's new government that the only way to guarantee the security and political stability of the Italian peninsula was to create an independent and unified Italian Republic.[12]

When Vincenzo Cuoco's *Essay* appeared a year later, the political climate in Milan had become even more threatening. A conspiracy involving a number of Neapolitans had been discovered in the summer of 1801, many exiles had been arrested, the masonic lodges suspected of providing refuge for 'anarchists' and 'terrorists' had been closed down, and the fate of the former Cisalpine Republic was still uncertain.[13]

In these circumstances, Cuoco needed to use great caution. He, too, was a prominent Jacobin and like Lomonaco believed that Italy's political development could not take place without France's support. But he also believed that France must be made to understand that the Italian Republic could be built only by Italians and, like Lomonaco, Cuoco held that the policies of the Directory had been the main reason the republican experiment in Italy had failed. But in the present circumstances any direct accusations against France would have been both dangerous and counter-productive, which may explain why Cuoco chose to blame the leaders of the Neapolitan Republic for errors that had clearly been the responsibility of Championnet, MacDonald, Faypoult, Abrial, and Paris.[14]

It was France that had forced the Republic to accept the conservative French constitution of Year III, France that had made financial stability impossible, France that had imposed an unworkable reorganization of provincial administration, and France that had refused to allow the Republic to raise its own army. The greatest political error of all, Cuoco claimed, had been the failure to devise an effective policy toward the provinces. 'Their first error was to fear the capital

[11] Francesco Lomonaco, *Rapporto al Cittadino Carnot* (ed. De Francesco, 1999), 224–76. Lomonaco (1772–1810) was a young democrat from Basilicata who had taken part in the Republic in Naples where he published a translation of Mably's *Rights and Duties of the Citizen.*

[12] De Francesco (1999), 254; Rao (1992), 429–40.

[13] De Francesco (1999), 60–1.

[14] De Francesco (1997), 1–21; for an alternative view see Tessitore (1985), 329–69, and Villani, Introduction to Cuoco, *Saggio Storico sulla rivoluzione napoletana del 1799* (1980), pp. xvii–xlix.

too much and the second was not to fear the provinces enough.'[15] Yet the new administrative system in Naples had been imposed, as Cuoco well knew, by Championnet's assistant, Jean Bassal, two days after the founding of the Republic. In April, Abrial had not hesitated to describe Bassal's project, which had thrown all the existing administrative hierarchies into confusion, as an unworkable disaster. By then, of course, it was too late.

The Directory's insistence that Naples pay a huge indemnity had wrecked the chances of rescuing the government from its desperate financial state. Marc-Antoine Jullien had argued in January that the immediate sale of *beni nazionali* was the only way to avert catastrophe. But after Jullien's arrest, Faypoult had claimed all the crown and public lands as France's legitimate war booty. The Directory's fiscal demands had also been the reason for the fatal decision to send 'democratizers' to the provinces, the disastrous consequences were compounded by the imposition of republican rituals that 'wounded everything that the people held most sacred, their gods, their customs and even the very names of their towns'.[16]

Like Lomonaco, Cuoco had two aims. First to persuade his fellow Italians of the need to unite, and second to persuade the French of the advantages that a unified Italian Republic would bring them. The great lesson of 1799 was that the Italian republics could not stand alone, but nor could they unite without the support of the *Grande Nation*. The overriding need, however, was for unity between the Italian republics, and hence for unity amongst Italians. It was this that led Cuoco in his *Essay* to focus on the abyss that had been revealed between the elites and the masses in the South.

As Giovanni Gentile noted long ago, this reveals above all Cuoco's debt to the ideas of another great Neapolitan thinker, Giambattista Vico. Like Vico, Cuoco was convinced that no political revolution could succeed unless it was linked to a broader process of social but above all cultural regeneration. As a public official in the South later during the Napoleonic period, like many other former Jacobins, Cuoco would have the opportunity to put those ideas into practice in urging the case for educational reforms. But his emphasis on the abyss that separated the elites from the masses in the South in 1799 was designed to illustrate a problem that existed not only throughout Italy but indeed most of Europe.[17]

Vincenzo Cuoco's *Essay* is a remarkable analysis of the complex interactions between politics and culture in a moment of revolutionary upheaval. But for this the South was essentially an example, albeit one that Cuoco could describe from direct personal experience. His purpose was to expose the obstacles facing republicans throughout Europe and Italy, which in the South had taken forms specific but not unique. How, why, and whether the South was different were questions his *Essay* did not seek to address.

[15] Cuoco (ed. Villani, 1980), 141–5. [16] Ibid. 143.
[17] See Gentile (1909), 3–83. See also Dainotto (2001).

THE REPUBLICAN MOMENT IN NAPLES

Writing about the popular movement in the French Revolution, Richard Cobb once commented that the reasons for its failure were obvious, but overlooked the much more interesting question of why France had a popular movement in the first place. In Italy, there was no popular movement comparable to that of Paris but Cobb's comment can equally well be applied to the significant minority who under conditions of great risk and danger supported the Italian republican projects.[18]

Everywhere in Italy the supporters of the republics were small minorities who never succeed in developing a popular following. Circumstances rarely allowed their projects to be translated into reality, but nonetheless the republics did offer the first brief moment of freedom of speech in modern Italy and one that would not be repeated until the revolutions of the nineteenth century.[19] It was during this brief period that it became possible to see how deeply the cultural and political developments of the previous decade both within and outside Italy had taken root. This also explains why not only the projects but also the political strategies employed by the Italian republicans were similar from one end of the peninsula to the other.

An example of this was the ways in which the republican elites understood and tried to overcome an isolation that was as much cultural as political.[20] In Naples, the provisional government and its numerous committees were the principal forum for political debates, but these were also conducted in a variety of public places and in the numerous newspapers, journals, and broadsheets launched after the founding of the Republic.[21] These publications were also indicative of the strength of a new print culture that had taken root in the last decades of the century. Like many other Italian states, Naples had developed an important publishing industry and book trade in the eighteenth century, and despite censorship books circulated with ease and in great numbers among the elites.[22]

Of the many journals and broadsheets that came into being after the declaration of the Republic, the one closest to the government was the *Monitore Napolitano*, which first appeared on 2 February 1799—'Saturday 14 Piovoso Year VII of Liberty, Year I of the Neapolitan Republic One & Indivisible'—with the stirring declaration:

> Finally we are free, and for us too the day has come when we too can finally pronounce the sacred words Liberty and Equality and announce ourselves to the Mother Republic as worthy sons, and to the free Peoples of Italy and Europe as their worthy brothers. . . .[23]

[18] Cobb (1970), p. xiv.

[19] Censorship in Napoleonic Italy was pervasive and more effective than under the *ancien régime*: see Davis in Goldstein (ed.) (2000), 85–7.

[20] For Rome see Caffiero (2004), 3–140.

[21] The most important source is a remarkable collection of documents published and edited by Mario Battaglini and Augusto Placanica: Battaglini and Placanica (2000–1).

[22] See Rao (ed.) (1998), and Luise (2001).

[23] *Monitore Napolitano* (1), 2 February 1799.

A government announcement stated that the *Monitore* would 'give account of all the operations of the Government'. It was edited by Eleonora Fonseca di Pimentel[24] and supported by the government although also privately funded. It ran to thirty-five issues, the last appearing on 8 June, five days before the fall of the Republic.[25] Other journals included the *Veditore Repubblicano, Il Vero Repubblicano, Il Giornale Estemporaneo, Il Corriere di Napoli e di Sicilia,*[26] which all offered a variety of commentaries on the government and its deliberations. But the fullest accounts of the provisional government and in particular the debates on the abolition of feudalism were published in the *Monitore.*

The press offered unique opportunities for exchanging ideas and debating political projects, but the supporters of the Republic well knew that print was not a medium that enabled them to reach the masses. From the early days of the Republic numerous attempts were made to reach the people and in February the first Halls of Public Education were opened, where patriotic lectures were given.[27]

Popular republican 'catechisms' were also seen as an important means of educating the people, and the Interior Minister, Gianfrancesco Conforti, insisted on the great influence of the theatre: 'the theatres constitute a form of public education of the greatest importance not only for the young but also for adults who have been the subject of stultifying effects of long lasting despotism.... Here instruction can be presented to the citizen in the guise of entertainment.' But he also held that censorship was necessary: 'since the theatre can as easily portray vice as virtue... it should be the subject of rigorous scrutiny by the public authorities who must ensure that the people are not moved by sentiments other than patriotism, virtue and sound morality.'[28] The government also expressed concern that freedom of speech should not be a licence for sedition and warned against the dangers of seditious meetings and forbade the formation of private societies and associations.[29]

Republican ritual was seen as an even more important means of communication that was deliberately grafted onto existing civil, religious, and royal rituals. The key symbol of the new regime was the Liberty Trees set up in the major squares and public sites in both the capital and the provincial towns. The clergy and civil authorities participated in these rituals, just as they had in those of the *ancien régimes*, singing *Te Deums* to consecrate the new regime and to celebrate major public events.

The provisional government was well aware of the hardship facing the majority of citizens at a time when commerce was at a standstill and the political crisis had thrown thousands of public employees out of work. Much energy was devoted

[24] Eleonora Fonseca di Pimentel (1752–99) had moved from Rome to Naples. In 1794 she had been arrested as a suspected Jacobin and again in November 1798. She was among the political prisoners released in January 1799 and edited the *Monitore Napolitano*; she was hanged on 20 August 1799.

[25] Quarterly subscription cost 6 carlini. See Battaglini and Placanica (2000–1), ii. 83.

[26] Battaglini (1988).

[27] Rao (1999), 358–64.

[28] Croce (1947), 275.

[29] Rao (1999), 367.

to public charity and welfare, and the physician Domenico Cirillo proposed establishing a system 'of Republican charity to help the great number of people who because of the change in government have been thrown into destitution'.[30]

The government had scant means, however, to redress the growing hardships that faced the population of the capital. When the French army departed in April, Eleonora Fonseca di Pimentel and the Calabrian ex-monk Francesco Saverio Salfi appealed for more energetic action to win over the people, especially the use of dialect, street theatre, puppet shows, and ballads to take the message of Liberty and Equality to the masses.[31] But by then the city was without food or currency, was under blockade by Nelson's warships, and was threatened by Cardinal Ruffo's rapidly advancing Sanfedist army.

Popular religious sensibilities played an important part in the fall of the Republic, but its supporters had been aware of this danger from the very start, Championnet having been warned by Marc-Antoine Jullien as they marched towards Naples in December 1798 that it was essential to avoid giving offence.[32] That was one reason, of course, for the repeated homage paid to the cult of San Gennaro. Championnet attended an unscheduled performance of the miracle of the liquefaction of the saint's blood the day he entered the city, and MacDonald attended the scheduled miracle in May. The report that appeared the following day in the *Monitore* reflected the unease of the Republic's secular supporters, but also an acknowledgement of the ritual's political importance:

> Even San Gennaro has become a Jacobin! So let the first Voice of the People be heard! Can any Neapolitan not be what San Gennaro is? Long Live the REPUBLIC.[33]

As in the other Italian republics, these gestures to popular folklore were supported by more measures indicating that strong religious convictions were as much a component of Italian republicanism as anti-clericalism.[34] In Naples, efforts were made from the outset to win the support of the clergy and in February Championnet appointed Gianfrancesco Conforti to direct the Ministry of the Interior. Formerly a leading figure in the Bourbon government's earlier anti-curial campaign, Conforti was widely respected among the anti-curial clergy and he now worked closely with the pro-republican Cardinal Archbishop of Naples, Giuseppe Maria Capece Zurlo.[35] They made a number of innovations designed specifically to make the Republic more popular, including abolition of the deeply resented fees charged by the clergy for granting marriage dispensations and measures to shorten the time needed to train and consecrate new priests in order to recruit clerics sympathetic to the Republic.[36]

[30] De Nicola, 10 April, 133. [31] Salfi (1821).
[32] Imbruglia, in Rao (ed.) (2002), 295–324.
[33] *Monitore Napoletano*. Decadì 20 Fiorile Year VII/1 (Thursday 9 May 1799).
[34] On the Roman Republic see Caffiero (2005), 99–140.
[35] Stella, *DBI*, xviii. 462–4; Parente, in Scaramella (ed.) (2000), 45–106.
[36] See Imbruglia, in Rao (ed.) (2002), 295–324; Lomonaco, in ibid. 168–96.

In the end, it was not that the republicans did not try to appeal to popular religious sensibilities, but rather that those sensibilities were manipulated more skilfully by their enemies. Prominent amongst these were those groups that had previously been most vehement in their opposition to the monarchy's anti-curial and anti-papal policies: not only had they been been reconciled with the monarchy after 1794 but they had been charged with mobilizing against the threat of atheist republicanism.[37]

1799: THE REPUBLICANS

Who were the republicans in 1799? Contemporaries emphasized how many were nobles. The diarist Carlo De Nicola divided the members of the provisional government into three groups: the patriots ('the good republicans'), the Jacobins ('aspirant despots'), and the 'aristocrats'.[38] This closely reflected Vincenzo Cuoco, who singled out the aristocrats for an especially scathing attack:

> The first Republicans were all from the most distinguished families in the capital and in the provinces: many were noblemen, all members of the wealthy gentry and full of learning, and indeed it was an excess of learning, which far outran their years and experience, that led them to think that it was easy to do things that in fact proved to be quite impossible because of the conditions in which the *popolaccio* lived.[39]

Looking for a more general profile of the supporters of the Republic, Benedetto Croce cited the chant of the Neapolitans who went to the barricades to prevent Championnet's army from entering the city: 'Chi tenga vino ha da esse Giacobin' ('Those who live well are the Jacobins').[40]

The Republic's supporters came from the propertied and educated classes, but they were not a homogeneous group. Taking the exiles as a statistical base, Anna Maria Rao has shown that 'the majority of the Neapolitan republicans came from the families of the professional, land-owning or mercantile middle class, who had grown up and been educated during the reform decades.' Slightly more than half the exiles were younger than thirty, and nearly 70% were under thirty-five.[41]

Attempts to press the sociological distinctions further and to associate the supporters of the Republic with a rising professional and landed bourgeoisie are not convincing, however. In part this was because the republicans represented a 'middle class that had grown up in the shadow of the feudal nobility' so that the boundaries between the two remained uncertain and confused.[42] But most of the leading royalists came from similar backgrounds, while a great many families followed a well-established and universal strategy and split both ways.

[37] Chiosi (1992), 261–3. [38] De Nicola, 22 March, 107.
[39] Cuoco (ed. Villani, 1980), 5–6 (Cuoco's Preface to the 1806 edn. of the *Saggio*).
[40] Croce (1897), 47. [41] Rao (ed.) (2002), 516.
[42] Ibid., but see also Petraccone (1989), 329–35.

The boundaries between the capital and the provinces were also confused, and the generation that adopted the republican programme most readily was as often provincial as metropolitan in origin. Vincenzo Cuoco is a good example since his career was similar to that of many other young professionals from the provinces who had become involved in the struggles against feudalism and the feudal landowners before becoming supporters of the Republic.

Born in Civitacamporomano in Molise in 1772, Cuoco had moved to Naples to study law in 1787. He had powerful connections in the capital, especially through his uncle Nicola Vivenzio, who was Procurator Fiscal to the Camera della Sommaria and in 1792 drafted the edict that restored the *demani* to the local communities.[43] Like many other lawyers newly arrived from the provinces, Cuoco represented his town in litigation against its powerful feudal neighbour, the Duke of Sant-Andrea. He also served as an assistant to Giuseppe Maria Galanti, but then found himself in a politically more radical circle of Domenico Cirillo, Francesco Conforti, Melchiorre Delfico, Mario Pagano, and Vicenzio Russo.[44]

Cuoco was not involved in the Jacobin clubs discovered in Naples in 1794, but many other young men from the provinces were, including Domenico Tatà from the Molisan town of Casalcalendo. His friend Domenico di Gennaro was the mayor who headed the campaign against the local feudal landowner, the Duke of Sangro, and Tatà's arrest in Naples in 1794 led the authorities to trace a network of connections to the salon run by the wealthy landowner Francesco Carbone and his wife in the nearby town of Castalbottaccio. That gave the Duke of Sangro the opportunity to denounce di Gennaro as a Jacobin, and he was duly arrested in 1795. In 1799, as we have seen, di Gennaro paid with his life.[45]

Not everyone marched to the same step. The Zurlo brothers had been deeply committed to the anti-feudal movement before 1799, but remained carefully invisible during the revolution. Giuseppe Maria Galanti was also firmly opposed to the Republic and feared that the law abolishing feudalism would provoke a civil war. Yet others who had been prominent in the earlier reform movement now participated actively in the Republic. In Teramo, Melchiorre Delfico had been arrested in December 1798, but was then elected president first of the new republican municipality and then of the Regional Administration of the Lower Abruzzi. In nearby Chieti, Baron Nolli, a leading landowner who had founded the town's Patriotic Society, was also elected president.[46]

The Republic found particularly strong support among the secular clergy, including more than thirty bishops.[47] In many cases this was simply a matter of rendering unto Caesar what was Caesar's and in his Easter pastoral letter in 1799 the Cardinal Archbishop of Naples, Capece Zurlo,[48] exhorted the faithful to

[43] De Francesco (1997), 4–5; Corona (1995), 104–20.
[44] De Francesco (1997), 7.
[45] Martelli, in Rao (ed.) (2002), 724–43. See also Chapter 3.
[46] De Lorenzo, in Rao (ed.) (2002), 654–7 and 667–72.
[47] Miele, in Scaramella (ed.) (2000), 3–41.
[48] Chiosi, 'Capece Zurlo', *DBI*, xviii. 462–4; Parente, in Scaramella (ed.) (2000), 45–106.

'give obedience to the government, not out fear but as a duty of conscience with all their hearts and sincerity as is owed to the temporal power'.[49]

Clerical support for the Republic also reflected the deeper convictions of those who had formerly been active in the monarchy's campaign against Rome. Gianfrancesco Conforti, for example, was strongly committed to the Jansenist-inspired project for a spiritual reorganization of the Italian churches whose principal spokesman in Italy had been Scippione de' Ricci, the Bishop of Pisa and architect of the religious policies of Grand Duke Peter Leopold in Tuscany.[50] But when the Bourbon government mended its quarrels with Rome in 1791, Conforti was first dismissed, then arrested in 1796 before being released and exiled in 1798.[51]

The absolutist reaction after 1794 persuaded Conforti that the republican project offered a means to reform and reconstitute the Church along Jansenist lines. The views of Andrea Serra, Bishop of Potenza, were similar. He too had played a leading role in the monarchy's campaign against Rome and in 1799 was prominent in organizing support for the Republic.[52] Domenico Forges Davanzati, Bishop of Canosa, was a member of the provisional government, and Giuseppe Capecelatro, the Cardinal Archbishop of Taranto, was another prominent supporter. A writer, collector of antiquities, and a friend of Sir William Hamilton, Capecelatro was also an energetic reformer who believed firmly that the clergy should share useful and practical knowledge and had reorganized the curriculum of the seminaries in his diocese.[53]

The Republic also found ardent champions among the lesser clergy, especially the numerous class of abbés.[54] The abbé Vincenzo Troysi composed a 'Republican Mass', the abbé Michelangelo Cicerone translated the Gospel of St John the Evangelist into dialect, whereas the abbé Giuseppe Bellini 'preached the religion of Liberty and Equality in the piazza Nazionale'.[55] There were even some regulars amongst its supporters, including Uombuono dell Boccacche, the former Franciscan friar who recorded events in the Abruzzo town of Lanciano.

Municipal allegiances were more complex and expediency was often the decisive factor. For the towns and villages in the frontier provinces that were in the line of the invading French armies, the only way to avoid destruction was to raise the Liberty Tree and sport the republican red cockade, although even that did not spare them having to pay heavy cash indemnities to the French commanders who then set up republican municipalities.

The military strength of the French was overwhelming and the royalist leader, Antoine Micheroux, later claimed that the expected arrival of a large French army was the reason why the leading administrative and commercial cities in Apulia had opted for the Republic in January and February.[56] But this does not explain

[49] Helfert (1885), 143–4.
[50] See Cochrane (1973). On popular resistance to Jansenist policies see also Turi (1969/1999).
[51] Lomonaco, in Rao (ed.) (2002) 189–96. [52] Chiosi (1981), 319–41.
[53] See entry on Giuseppe Capecelatro (1744–1836) by Chiosi, in *DBI*, xviii. 448–51.
[54] In Italian *abate*: the title of those who had taken religious instruction without being ordained.
[55] Helfert (1885), 143–4. [56] Maresca (1894), 515.

support for the Republic in Calabria, Molise, Basilicata, and the Salernitano, provinces that were distant from the invading French armies. These provinces were all untouched by the invasions, but were nonetheless caught up in the collapse of the royal government after the flight of the king in December.

Local considerations always predominated, but for those with power and influence at a local level once the Republic had been declared in Naples in January with the approval of the king's Vicar General it became the legitimate government. As a result, many former royal officials and provincial landowners initially rallied to the Republic, normally with scrupulous attention to proper legal forms, and the establishment of the new republican municipal authorities was nearly always preceded by the convocation of the town or village *parlamenti*, and duly solemnized by the religious and civil authorities.

In sociological terms the alignments were very untidy. In Apulia, the Republic was supported by many powerful feudal families, including Ettore Caraffa, Conte di Ruvo.[57] In Calabria, the leading feudal families—the Serra Cassano, the Gerace, the Pignatelli, the Montemiletto, the Canzano, the Auletta, the Marsico, and the Roccaromana—were also prominently represented amongst supporters of the Republic in Naples, although almost exclusively by cadets with no expectation of inheritance.[58]

There were very few clear patterns. In some Calabrian towns the new administrations were composed of families hostile to the local feudatories, while in others, like Cosenza, most of the republicans were nobles.The feudal owner of the Calabrian town of Cirò, Princess Spinelli, supported the Republic in Naples and ordered her agents in Cirò to support the Republic against the local *galantuomini*, who had joined the royalists. Prince Diego Pignatelli, marquis of Vaglio and Monteleone, supported the Republic in Naples and instructed his agents in Calabria to follow his lead. The agent of the Prince of Montemiletto was nearly lynched as a Jacobin near Monteleone in March 1799, as we have seen, when it became known locally that his master was a supporter of the Republic in Naples. In Catanzaro, however, the republican government was headed by a former royal official and was supported by both feudal and non-feudal landowners. The same was true at Tropea, formerly a royal town where the Republic was supported by noble and non-noble landowners alike.[59]

Local issues determined local alignments and in his account of the Republic Vincenzo Cuoco insisted on the importance of local disputes, factional struggles, and municipal rivalries in shaping alignments for and against the Republic. Another astute observer, Luigi Blanch, made the same point:

> what determined how local factions would take a stand for or against the new order depended on whether they were friends or enemies of the baron who owned the most land

[57] Lucarelli (1934), 44.

[58] These were the families listed by Maria Carolina when she instructed Ruffo to confiscate their lands: Helfert (1885), 120.

[59] Cingari (1957), 119, 137, 162, 165.

in the locality. If the barons supported the Republic in Naples, this gave their enemies in the provinces the opportunity to declare for the king. Most of the provincial landowners were enemies of the barons as a result of municipal litigation, but the barons' staff and servants and their families were the ones who really exercised power at a local level and made their living from doing so. They were deeply attached to the order that provided them with all these benefits and hence fiercely hostile to anything that threatened it.[60]

Blanch's analysis captured the complexity of the interests at stake and the reasons the republican experiment easily collapsed into civil war. The monarchy's earlier campaign against feudal privileges had seriously undermined the feudal order, which now faced an even greater danger. At the same time, the enthusiasm for the Republic in the provinces was also driven by expectations of greater local autonomy. However, the reorganization of provincial administration threatened the municipal hierarchies that played a critical role in the *ancien régime* organization of provincial life, while the Republic's attempts to assert its own authority also ran directly counter to provincial aspirations to greater freedom. For that reason, the Republic became the catalyst for conflicts rooted in the crisis and collapse of the monarchy.

[60] Blanch (Croce, ed., 1945), i. 44; on Luigi Blanch (1784–1872), see the entry by Cortese in *DBI*, x. 771–6.

6

The Counter-revolution

THE MYTHS OF THE *SANTAFEDE*

The second great myth of 1799 is the *Santafede*, the fanatical popular counter-revolution that retrospectively became inseparable from the image of the Neapolitan Republic. In modern Italian, the term *Sanfedist* still refers to any form of reactionary populism, an association that reflects how the memory of the *Santafede* echoed Genovesi's fear of the 'Hottentots that stand at our gates' and haunted generations of liberals for years to come.

The Sanfedists had their champions, of course, the first being the apologists of the Bourbon monarchy. They were followed by nationalist historians in the early twentieth century who reinvented the Sanfedists as precocious patriots, and since then all manner of militant causes have claimed them as their own.[1] But although the legend remained strong, the *Santafede* never recurred. In 1806 the monarchy tried every means to resuscitate popular royalism, but without success. During the revolutions of 1820–1 there was no Sanfedist reaction, and although there were many peasant revolts in 1848 none adopted the throne and altar as its banner. Similarly, after the collapse of the Kingdom in 1860 popular discontent and protest in the South stubbornly refused to make royalism its cause and the feared Sanfedist reaction never materialized.[2]

The reason the *Santafede* never became a southern Italian variant of Spanish Carlism was quite simply that the counter-revolution of 1799 was never quite what the later myths described.[3] During the months that preceded the fall of the Republic, Ruffo and the royalist leaders were struggling to discipline and give direction to highly localized insurrections. It was only in the eyes of the republicans awaiting the onslaught in Naples and from the perspective of posterity that these coalesced into a single counter-revolution, driven by a fanatical and single-minded desire to restore the monarchy and the Holy Faith.

A second legend would also have it that the South was the principal theatre of popular counter-revolution in Italy. After the first French invasions in 1796, however, popular insurrections took place throughout Italy: in Liguria (1797),

[1] See, e.g., Lumbroso (1932); Rodolico (1926); Dante (1980).
[2] Davis, in Davis and Ginsborg (1991), 1–25.
[3] On Spanish Carlism see Blinkhorn (1975).

in the Valtellina (1798), and throughout central Italy after the occupation of Rome in February 1798. Following the Russo-Austrian offensive in the spring of 1799, Italy could rightly claim to be the new *Vendée*, and popular insurrections in support of the legitimist rulers and the true faith occurred in Piedmont, Lombardy, the Veneto, the central duchies and Tuscany, Umbria, the Marche, and Lazio.

Many of these risings had strong devotional and even messianic overtones. In Lombardy, a peasant named Viora Branda dreamed that he had been summoned by Christ to punish the infidel invaders. He and his followers called themselves the *Massa Cristiana* and joined the Austrians to drive the French and their sympathizers out of Piedmont. Peasants in Tuscany rallied to the banners of the Virgin Mary. To the cry of *Viva Maria!* they threw themselves on the retreating French armies, hunted down and killed suspected 'Jacobins' who fell into their hands, and laid waste to the Jewish ghettos in Livorno and Siena.[4]

What took place in the South bore similarities to these movements, but there were also striking differences, not least the lack of religious motivation that Cardinal Ruffo repeatedly lamented. The extent to which the counter-revolution was 'popular' also merits closer attention and the Sanfedists were by no means recruited only from the poorest. Most important of all, the term *Santafede* did not describe a spontaneous phenomenon, but was a name chosen deliberately by Ruffo in an attempt to impose some appearance of unity and purpose on insurrections that took many different forms: some were counter-revolutions, others were more institutionalized, while others looked more like civil war.

ORGANIZED RESISTANCE: THE FRONTIER PROVINCES

Calabria did not become involved until later, however. The first royalist insurrections were in the northern frontier provinces of the Terra di Lavoro, the Abruzzi, and Molise that Rodolico later called the Italian *Vendée*. These were the provinces that bore the full weight of the invading French armies, and here popular resistance was essentially institutionalized.

In all the frontier towns there were standing militias, known as *masse*. In times of peace they were responsible for maintaining order, but in times of war they acted as reserves to assist the regular army to defend the Kingdom's frontiers. The landowners in each town were required to provide mounts and muskets for the *miliziotti*, who were recruited from the wealthier peasants, although in times of emergency, such as the autumn of 1798, the net was thrown wider. The *miliziotti* were paid 3 *carlini* a day and the money was raised through taxes on local communities. The *masse* were commanded by local landowners, who delegated the task to professional soldiers or others who acted as *capo-massa*.[5]

[4] See Capra (1978), 364–70; on Piedmont and Lombardy, Ruggiero (1979), 69–70; for Umbria, Tsoukas (1988); on Tuscany, Tognarini (ed.) (1985) and Turi (1969/1999).

[5] Simoni (1921), 175.

After the defeat of the royal army in November 1798, the *masse* in the frontier provinces formed the Kingdom's first line of defence. They were mobilized when the king ordered a *levée en masse* before leaving for Sicily. As news reached the Abruzzi town of Lanciano, the pro-republican former Franciscan monk, Uombuono delle Boccache, recorded that 'the enthusiasm of the people to take up arms was incredible, inspired by the appeal of their king, by the appeals of the royal and baronial officers, by the regular and secular clergy, and many of the latter by exaggerating the threatened dangers awakened in the hearts of the more courageous the desire to become leaders of the *masse* and the people or even generals of a province, to the point that they showed no shame in calling themselves a sovereign people and the People of God.'[6]

In the neighbouring town of Teramo the royalist priest Angelo de Jacobis told a different tale, however. When the city *parlamento* had been summoned in September, the news of a general levy was greeted with dismay: 'this threatened every family with ruin, and especially those of the peasants, working men and those who were heads of households'.[7] A second appeal was made in January but when few responded the *Preside* of Chieti tried to make up numbers by recruiting prisoners from the jails who immediately rebelled and fled.[8]

Even before the royal offensive began in November 1798 the French occupation of Rome earlier in the year had provoked insurrections to the north of the Kingdom's frontiers. When the king issued the appeal for a *levée en masse* in the frontier provinces the situation quickly became very confused. The Court in Palermo tried to maintain contact with the *capi-masse*, and in December, for example, the leader of one of the largest bands of royalist irregulars in the Abruzzi, Giuseppe Pronio, was given 200 muskets by the Bourbon General de Gambs, who before fleeing to join the king in Sicily put him under the orders of the royalist Baron Luigi de Riseis.[9] As the French forces advanced, communications with the *capi-masse* became increasingly difficult and by January the *masse* were operating autonomously and supplied themselves by raiding towns and villages that had surrendered to the French and joined the Republic.

The *capi-masse* had no common career profile. Some had previous military experience, others had served as guards for the administration of local feudatories. Most came from families of wealthy peasants, artisans, or craftsmen, a few from the poorest sections of rural society. But the most successful already had powerful networks of kinsmen and clients. Pronio, for example, had been a priest before becoming an armed retainer in the service of the Duke of Vasto and had many followers in his native town of Introdacqua.[10] Gaetano Mammone, one of two brothers from Sora who became feared *capi-masse*, was by contrast a miller whose signature was to drink the blood from the decapitated heads of his victims.

[6] Uombuono delle Boccache, 'Saggio storico-critico della città di Lanciano', in Coppa-Zuccari (ed.) (1927), i. 30.

[7] Angelo de Jacobis, 'Cronaca degli Avveniment in Teramo 1796–1823', in ibid. iii.

[8] Della Boccache, in ibid. i. 47. [9] Maresca (1893–4), 283. [10] Helfert (1885), 137.

Among the most notorious of the *capi-masse* was Michele Pezza of Itri in the Terra di Lavoro, better known by his *nom de guerre*, Fra Diavolo. The son of an olive oil dealer and a small landowner in Itri, Pezza had been sentenced to death for two murders in 1796. The sentence was commuted to service in the Royal Fusiliers, but Pezza took to the hills rather than perform military service. When French troops occupied Itri in 1798, they killed Pezza's father, and Michele joined forces with bands from neighbouring towns to take up the royalist cause. In February 1799 he was leading some 600 men who harried the French lines of communication to the north of Naples.[11] He maintained close contacts with the Court in Palermo, attended a war council to plan the final attack on Naples held in April on board HMS *Culloden* off the coast near Gaeta, and was given a royal commission.[12]

MUNICIPAL RIVALRIES

As French forces penetrated more deeply into these provinces, what had begun as institutionalized resistance became more disorganized. Communications broke down and the actions of the bands and the troops pursuing them took the form of reprisals and counter-reprisals from which the rural communities had no means of escape.

The cycles of violence intensified as conflicts within communities and between neighbouring communities grew. The contrasting accounts chronicled by Angelo de Jacobis in Teramo and Uombuomo delle Boccache in Lanciano reveal how internal conflicts were inseparable from rivalries between neighbouring towns and over municipal hierarchies.

As a French army advanced on Teramo in December 1798, a section of the wealthier classes decided to allow the troops to enter the town unopposed, and in return the French commander appointed the same men to form a republican administration. Angelo de Jacobis was scandalized by the way the new republican administration tried to win the support of the *bassa gente* of the town with three days of feasting:

> And so we came to see the common folk stuff themselves until they were bursting with macaroni, stew, and bread, quaffing wine at the tables, pausing only to jump to their feet to declaim 'Long Live Freedom'. The king was denounced, images of the royal couple were defaced, it was announced that taxes would be reduced and there would be equal justice for all.[13]

Although a royalist sympathizer himself, when the same *bassa gente* staged a royalist rising shortly afterward de Jacobis had deep reservations about their motives:

> What a terrible sight to see the people go berserk and tear down, break and splinter fences, doors, balconies, iron railings, burn linen, mattresses, blankets, utensils, books, documents

[11] Cingari (1976), 38–59. [12] Ibid. 59.
[13] De Jacobis, in Coppa-Zuccari (ed.) (1927), 86 (24 January 1798).

and everything they can lay their hands on, breaking open barrels of wine and spilling oil and corn. How many precious legal documents were destroyed, how many pieces of fine antique furniture burned, because these are the houses of lawyers and gentlemen! What an uncontrolled mob that under the pretext of fighting for the Crown seeks only to take from the rich and for that reason calls them Jacobins![14]

The royalist revolt in Teramo was short-lived and on 22 December a detachment of French troops returned to the town, which, to the horror of de Jacobis, was sacked: 'Ill-fated families, ill-fated store-rooms: everything has been carried off!' The French took everything they found in the houses of the merchants and of the 'lesser gentlemen', they sacked the bishop's palace, and they destroyed the church bells. They 'shot a number of peasants', arrested the leading royalists, and before leaving restored the republican administration.[15]

When neighbouring Lanciano became the target of a royalist insurrection in early February, the reactions of the pro-republican friar Uombuono delle Boccacche were similar and he too claimed that the instigators of the revolt were motivated by 'the desire to oppress the rich under the false pretext of defending God, the king, the state and the country'.[16]

Both accounts reveal the class hatreds that permeated these rural communities, but they also show that far from being spontaneous the popular revolts were in most cases directed by factions within the elites. As in Teramo, when the first French forces reached Lanciano in early January, the leading families had agreed to surrender and had donned the 'tricolour cockade'. General Duhesme ordered that a new town council be elected by public vote. The nobleman 'Citizen Felice dei baroni Gigliani' and a wealthy merchant, Francesco Paolo de Bucachi, were put in charge of the new council, which immediately lowered taxes and abolished the 'levy imposed on every head and pair of arms that was formerly paid by the artisans and labourers of the city'.[17]

The revolt that followed was plotted by Vincenzo Giordano and his son Fioravante, who were described as 'strong supporters of the Crown and wealthy public merchants'. But although wealthy, Giordano and his son did not have a strong popular following in Lanciano, so they had to look outside. That led them to make contact with the royalist *capo-massa*, Pronio, which broadened the conflict since Pronio also needed more men. To get them, he went to villages known to have grudges against Lanciano.

By the last day of Carnival everything was ready. Pronio and his men lay in wait until Giordano's followers staged a tumult, the pre-arranged signal to enter the town. Many republicans were killed in the fighting and their houses burned down, those that remained alive were arrested, and a general *parlamento* was held in piazza S. Maria la Nuova where Giordano was elected head of a new administration that declared its loyalty to the king.

[14] Ibid. 77. [15] Ibid. 67–8 (22 December–6 January).
[16] Della Boccache, in Coppa-Zuccari (ed.) (1927), i. 148. [17] Ibid. 62.

Within days a detachment of French cavalry reoccupied Lanciano. The royalists were imprisoned, and Giordano escaped execution only because one of the republican families pleaded for mercy. The republicans were rewarded, Lanciano was raised to the rank of provincial administrative centre and the republican landowner Felice Gigliani became president of the provincial government.[18]

The conflicts in Lanciano followed fault lines marked out by factional rivalries, and similar patterns were evident in other regions. In the Val di Diano the first revolt against the Republic took place in Montesano and was the continuation of much older struggles among three prominent families—the Cestari, Gerbasio, and Abbatemarco—to win control of the town's administration and its assets.

At the time of the fall of the monarchy, Don Nicola Cestari was a man of great wealth and influence in the town. He enjoyed extensive contacts in Naples, but was unpopular in Montesano because of the control that he and his family exercised over public administration and town lands. He became even more unpopular in 1796 when he took responsibility for enforcing the government conscription quotas. His rivals leveraged this discontent to have the village *parlamento* elect two popular leaders in his place. But Cestari used his political influence in Naples to have the election overturned by the *Corte della Sommaria*.

In January 1799 Cestari declared his support for the new republican government in Naples, and began to organize and arm a civic guard. But when he convened the town *parlamento* to approve new taxes to pay for the civic guard on 17 February, his rivals organized a popular revolt in the name of the king and Cestari was murdered. His long-standing rival, Don Emerico Gerbasio, was declared president of the municipality, and immediately ordered the seizure of the goods and property of the Cestari family and also of his former ally, the Abbetemarco.[19]

In Potenza, in Basilicata, the royalist riot that led to the murder of Bishop Andrea Serrao in January reflected similar factional struggles and Pietro Colletta later noted that 'none of his assassins were plebeian'. Serrao's attempts to settle contested rights on *demani* near Potenza and to reorganize the diocese made him the declared enemy of a number of powerful feudal families and of the local clergy.[20]

Similar tales unfolded elsewhere. There was initially strong support for the Republic in the Apulian provinces, but here too municipal rivalries were the catalyst of royalist revolts. As Vincenzo Cuoco later acknowledged, 'there is nothing more delicate in the course of a revolution than the way you change local government'.[21] When Trani, the seat of the former Royal *Udienza*, opted for the Republic in January, the employees of the royal tribunals, supported by out-of-work sailors led by a watchmaker, overthrew the new city junta and declared for the king.[22] Matera abandoned the republican cause as soon as the French raised its rival, Altamura, to the status of the principal administrative town of Basilicata.

[18] Della Boccache, in Coppa-Zuccari (ed.) (1927), 195.

[19] Cassese (ed. Cestaro and Laveglio 1970), 97.

[20] Chiosi (1981), 337–41.

[21] Cuoco (ed. Villani), 153.

[22] Lucarelli (1934), 53–77.

Similarly in the Abruzzi, opposition to the republican order swept through the smaller towns and villages when Chieti was designated the provincial capital and given responsibility for raising taxes.

Taxation was a critical issue, of course, and explains why the arrival of the democratizers often marked the beginning of a more general revolt against the Republic. In Lanciano Uombuono dell Boccacche simply recorded:

> This tax has caused great dismay, since immediate payment in coin is demanded, and great lamentations are to be heard especially in the smaller villages and hamlets since many believed that when the French arrived they would not impose additional taxes, but would instead have removed those taxes that oppress our people.[23]

At Ostuni, in the Terra d'Otranto, the arrival of the democratizers sparked a popular revolt and the massacre of the republican *galantuomini*. The same occurred at Trani and at Molfetta, while at Cirò in Calabria the people simply declared 'We don't want the Republic if we must pay the same taxes as before.'[24]

Local autonomies were the central issues and the driving force of the revolt of the provincial republics when the provisional government in Naples tried to assert its authority. As Pietro Colletta later noted, the collapse of the monarchy had inevitably brought much older municipal rivalries into play: 'being governed as a republic or a monarchy had little to do with political convictions, but was everywhere a pretext for the display of much older hatreds.'[25]

The crisis of the monarchy gave the poorer towns and villages the opportunity to challenge their subordination to the main provincial centres, and the first bids for freedom came from the outlying hamlets and villages of the major towns. Since the latter had initially opted for the Republic, it followed that the lesser towns were soon enthusiastic converts to the royalist cause. Therefore when Bari declared for the Republic, its outlying *casali* immediately became royalist. This was repeated in Calabria and when Monteleone, Cosenza, and Catanzaro declared for the Republic, their *casali* rebelled in the name of the king. In Molise, the Albanian settlements, which were amongst the most impoverished and disenfranchised in the Kingdom, were the first to rise in the name of the king. In Calabria, however, the Albanian communities were equally rebellious but also staunchly republican.[26]

Administrative hierarchies did not exhaust the sources of municipal rivalries, nor were these conflicts shapeless. The southern peasants, it was said, wore thick boots but had sharp minds,[27] and these apparently random conflicts had roots in disputes that were inseparable from the rapid erosion of the older feudal agrarian

[23] Della Boccache, in Coppa-Zuccari (ed.) (1927), i. 71.

[24] Colletta (Cortese, 1957), ii. 26; Helfert (1885), 137; Cingari (1957), 300.

[25] Colletta (Cortese, 1957), ii. 38. [26] Cingari (1957), 123–7.

[27] Lucarelli (1934), 59–62; on the anti-republican insurrections see also Colapietra (1981), 6; Cassese, in Cestaro and Laveglia (ed.) (1970), 63–5; Ciasca (1926), 631–51; Caldora (1965), 11–60; Genoino (1931); Fortunato (1899), 223–45. For the most comprehensive review of the literature on the counter-revolutions see the Introduction to Rao (ed.) (1999), 9–36.

regime. The breakdown of order caused by the French invasion was often no more than the opportunity to settle by force older grievances that the royal courts failed to resolve, as occurred when the inhabitants of the village of Orsogna in the Abruzzi settled long-standing disputes by wiping out the neighbouring village of Guardagrele.[28]

COLLECTIVE VIOLENCE

Contemporaries were nonetheless horrified by the acts of violence involving whole communities that seemed inseparable from these conflicts, and even if many of the accounts were exaggerated there can be no doubt that collective violence was used widely and even systematically. Many of the stories of cannibalism and other atrocities are probably best understood as part of an older collective folk memory, but there were other cases where acts of collective violence seem to have been a deliberate manifestation of the involvement of the whole community. In Potenza, for example, the heads of Bishop Serrao and his followers were paraded through the city on pikes. At Trani, when the republicans were massacred in the prisons on Easter Monday their mutilated corpses were dragged through the streets and according to some accounts their livers were hacked out and sold for meat. At Montesano, Nicola Cestari's head was paraded through the streets accompanied by crucifixes before his decapitated body was mutilated and his house pillaged and burned.[29] In Lanciano, when the Giordano family regained power after the fall of the Republic in Naples they took their final revenge on the Carabba, who only two months earlier had intervened to spare their lives:[30] Carabba and his wife were hacked to death, and their naked and mutilated bodies were then paraded through the streets on pikes to shouts of 'Viva la Regina di Francia'.[31]

Less publicized amongst all this brutality were the attempts made to reconcile opposing factions and to prevent the conflicts from spreading. Aside from the intervention of the Carabba family in Lanciano to save the Giordano family, another occurred during the royalist rising in Teramo. When the insurgents seized members of the leading families—Tulii, Thaulero, Michitelli, Nardo, and the priest Bernardo Quartapelle—the bishop and the *preside* Giamberardino Delfico intervened to secure their release.[32] In Chieti, the *preside* even persuaded the *masse* to leave the province in January to enable the French occupation to take place with minimal upheaval.[33] The leader of the first royalist rising in Chieti, Dott. Pasquale Tamburri, was also spared: 'so terrified was he of the prospect of punishment' that

[28] Colapietra (1981), 6. See also Spagnoletti, in Rao (ed.) (2002), 635–52.
[29] Lucarelli (1934), 72; Cassese, in Cestaro and Lavegglia (ed.) (1970), 96.
[30] Della Boccache, in Coppa-Zuccari (ed.) (1927), i. 173–4. [31] Ibid. 178.
[32] On the Delfico family see Clemente (1988), 365–85; idem, *DBI*, xxxvi. 527–39; Incarnato (1995), 3–62; and Petraccone (1989), 203–7.
[33] Della Boccache, in Coppa-Zuccari (ed.) (1927), i. 47.

he returned to the town and after explaining his behaviour was restored to good standing by the supporters of thc Republic.[34]

In these uncertain times, mercy was not only a valuable currency of patronage but one that might also provide useful future insurance in a time of rapidly changing political fortunes. The willingness to spare the leaders of opposing factions was rarely extended to the *bassa gente* and the *cafoni*, however. When the French suppressed the royalist rising in Teramo large numbers of '*plebe e nobili*' were arrested; the *nobili* were released on payment of three to four hundred ducats, but the French insisted on shooting some seventeen 'leaders of the yokels and so-called brigands'.[35] None of the commentators showed any concern for the 'peasants, yokels and bandits' who were the most frequent victims of the disorders, and both Uombuono delle Boccacche and Angelo de Jacobis illustrated the fear and loathing in which they were held by the educated classes. When it was known in Teramo, for example, that the royalist *capo-massa* Sciabolone was headed for nearby Ascoli, de Jacobis noted, 'It is rumoured that the men of the mountains, in other words these brigands and yokels, plan to plunder our city.'[36]

The cycles of disorder were also fuelled by the cruel and brutal measures employed by the French armies. Any town or village that showed signs of resistance, or that did not immediately opt for the Republic and agree to pay taxes, was liable to 'military execution': it was first surrounded by troops then torched, and the inhabitants shot down as they tried to escape.

As the royalist revolts spread, MacDonald in early March ordered his commanders to adopt even more severe measures. Every insurgent town or village should be destroyed, all 'Cardinals, Archbishops, Bishops, Abbots and Curés and other ministers of Religion shall be held collectively responsible for any armed garnering or revolt. As soon as these occur, no matter where or when, the ministers of Religion of the jurisdiction where these events occur must go at once to persuade the rebels to disperse. Any failure to do this will incur the same punishment for the minister of Religion as for the rebels.' The military commanders were authorized to shoot all rebels caught with arms, all ring leaders, and any priest found amongst the insurgents. Any village or town in which an insurrection occurred was to be held collectively responsible. Towns loyal to the republic, on the other hand, were to be exempted from military billeting and requisitioning provided they had paid all taxes owed. It was forbidden to ring church bells as a sign of alarm without permission, and the bells of all rebel towns were to be destroyed.[37]

The peasants who joined the royalist insurrections responded in kind, and during the retreat from Naples MacDonald vividly described the terror this inspired amongst his troops. In May one of his detachments had been attacked near the papal frontier at Antrodoco 'by a prodigious number of peasants'. After fighting

[34] Ibid. 77.
[35] De Jacobis, in Coppa-Zuccari (ed.) (1927), iii. 67–8 (22 December–6 January).
[36] Ibid. 90 (26 January).
[37] A de G (Vincennes), B3*** 321. Decree 14 Ventoso (4 March 1799).

for ten hours, the French column finally escaped, but only after losing over three hundred men and all its equipment. MacDonald concluded, 'It would be very difficult, I can assure you, to take these troops back into that country since they have the greatest distaste for the cruel and barbarous war in which they have been engaged with the peasants.'[38]

CARDINAL FABRIZIO RUFFO AND THE *SANTAFEDE*

Cardinal Fabrizio Ruffo's correspondence is an invaluable and curiously neglected source for understanding the dynamics of the counter-revolutions in the South in 1799. Ruffo was far from the fanatical *condottiere* of popular legend, but a man of considerable political and administrative experience who had begun his career as a protégé of Giovanni Braschi, who as Pope Pius VI had made him Treasurer General. This earned him a cardinal's hat in 1791, but Ruffo fell victim to plots in the Roman *curia* and returned to Naples where he was made responsible for the royal silkworks at S. Leucio.[39]

Acton was jealous of him and the queen disliked him, but he was appointed Vicar General with full powers to reconquer the Kingdom on 25 January 1799 mainly because the Court feared that Messina would declare for the Republic at the first opportunity. While Ruffo also had powerful family connections in Calabria, he received little support beyond promises of assistance from the English fleet in the Tyrrhenian, and from the Russian and Turkish troops that were to be sent to the Adriatic coast.[40]

Accompanied by Antonio Winspeare, the former *Preside* of the province, Ruffo landed in Calabria on the estates of his brother, the Duke of Baronello, near Scilla, but was not greeted with enthusiasm. On 9 February he reported to Acton, 'I do not have the men to resist the torrent that has engulfed these provinces.' Even on his brother's estate he succeeded in raising only eighty volunteers, whom he described as 'former guards from the feudal estates and criminals—people of no good intent or reliability'.[41]

The responses from the local clergy and religious houses proved more positive, however, and with support from the Bishop of Mileto and with funds raised by the Carthusian monastery of S. Stefano in Bosco and by the monastery of S. Domenico di Soriano, the number of his followers began to grow rapidly by the end of the month.[42]

On 28 February the situation turned in Ruffo's favour when the republican town of Monteleone surrendered without resistance. Royalist insurrections then quickly spread through Lower Calabria, and by the beginning of March Ruffo's

[38] A de G (Vincennes), B3* 322 MacDonald to Minister of War, 23 Floréal Year VII (12 May 1799).
[39] Piscitelli (1951), 71–148. [40] Helfert (1885), 87–8.
[41] Croce (1943), 14–15; Cingari (1978), 180–5. [42] Helfert (1885), 103.

following had increased to about 1,500 men, most of whom were soldiers from disbanded units of the royal army or members of the militias of the royal courts and administration.[43]

Ruffo was still deeply suspicious of his followers. According to a later royalist apologist, 'they included priests of all ranks, many wealthy landowners as well as workmen and peasants, some were honest and were motivated by attachment to the King and public order but others were simply assassins and robbers driven by the hope of plunder, vendetta and murder'.[44]

In March Ruffo refused to move against the republican stronghold of Crotone, giving the indiscipline of his followers as his reason:

> Were I at the head of a regular force I would not hesitate: but with these people I cannot take the risk because they do not understand me, they will not follow me and I run the risk of losing everything that has so far been gained.[45]

The localized nature of the conflicts meant that his 'army' could disappear as quickly as it had been formed. It was for that reason that Ruffo decided to impose on his followers the emblems and insignia of a royalist crusade, delaying at Mileto to organize them into three companies under the command of regular officers. For the same purpose and in order to better identify his followers, Ruffo devised the insignia of the *Santafede*: the white Bourbon cockade set in a crucifix. The insignia was meant to impose some semblance of religious purpose and legitimacy on men whom he continued to mistrust and believed to be 'of no good intent and without any permanency'. But the Cardinal was neither a fanatical *condottiere* of the monarchy nor of the church militant, and he told Acton that his sole purpose in adopting the religious insignia was 'so that the people may know that our purpose is to defend religion'.[46]

Ruffo was also a pragmatist who believed that guns, supplies, and money were more important for the success of the undertaking than religious enthusiasm: 'religious fervour and devotion to the person of the King may yield excellent results. But if we want to maintain the vassals of His Royal Highness in a state of calm and loyalty to our good cause, a well-filled war chest is indispensable.'[47] At Monteleone he had begun to raise taxes and levies. The revenues of pro-republican absentee landowners were sequestered to pay the royalist *masse*, and he appointed a wealthy landowner from Bagnara, Don Pasquale Versace, to act as Treasurer for the expedition.[48]

A month later, the fall of Cosenza and Catanzaro gave the royalists control of the Calabrias. But Ruffo was still reluctant to move north, and his misgivings about his followers, now some 4,000, had grown:

> I still consider this to be a miracle of Providence, since those who follow me are not the same from one place to the next, but come from the neighbourhood of the towns we wish

[43] Ibid. 107. [44] Sacchinelli (1836), 95.
[45] Croce (1943), 29—26 February, Mileto. [46] Croce (1943), 55.
[47] Ibid. 2—Ruffo to Acton 25 January, Palermo. [48] Helfert (1885), 106.

to besiege: they are perfectly free to join us or not as they choose, but thank God that so far we have never been short of them.[49]

There was still no single *Armata Cristianissima*, but rather a mass of localized followings that reconstituted themselves at each new town and village that was to be taken. Ruffo continued to deny that religious enthusiasm or devotion to the monarchy were drawing the people to the counter-revolution, but insisted that the root cause of what he termed the 'anarchy' was the neglect of religion for which he blamed the monarchy for joining in the persecution of the Church.

In a revealing *Pro-Memoria* written at Maida after the fall of Catanzaro, Ruffo argued that the disaster in Calabria was a consequence of the weakness of the Church, which he blamed on the monarchy and specifically on the operations of the *Cassa Sacra* after the earthquake of 1783. Most of the monasteries in the region had been closed: at Maida, for example, where there had once been five, there was now not one. As a result 'the labourers in the Lord's vineyard are so few in number that these people have been deprived of proper teaching in their Christian duties.' But the secular clergy had suffered equally: 'Because the church no longer has sufficient land to finance the priesthood, most parish priests do not have any form of stipend and are so poor they must beg for their bread. In short, the sacred cult is in a state of total abandonment.'[50]

Critical of the monarchy's anti-curial policies, as befitted the holder of a cardinal's hat, Ruffo was also hostile to the Jansenist sympathies of the predominantly anti-curial Calabrian prelacy. He had been a strong supporter of the devotional mysticism promoted by the followers of S. Alfonso di Liguori, and had been one of the founders of the anti-republican and anti-masonic societies that had been established in Naples after 1794.[51] For Ruffo, therefore, the counter-revolution was an opportunity to reverse the gains that had been made in the previous century by the anti-curialists and the Jansenists, and to correct the errors of the monarchy's anti-curial campaign.[52] Such views, however, did not not endear him to his royal masters in Palermo.

By the end of March, Ruffo's more immediate concern was to bring an end to the violence spreading within the regions that had been retaken by the royalists. But this again brought him into conflict with Acton and the queen. The first clash occurred when Maria Carolina instructed him to pre-empt the French by abolishing feudalism: 'and especially introduce in advance all those measures that when they arrive the French will introduce, so that we may in this way win for ourselves the support of the people'.[53]

Ruffo refused, arguing this would alienate the landowners whose allegiance he was trying to regain. When the queen demanded that he seize the estates of the

[49] Croce (1943), 67—Ruffo to Acton, 14 March.

[50] Ibid. 55—Ruffo to Acton, 8 March.

[51] See Chiosi (1984). On the Calabrian clergy see Cingari (1978), 93–8.

[52] Making him the perfect counterpart of Gianfranco Conforti, who saw the Republic as the means to achieve the Jansenist reform project.

[53] Helfert (1885), 16—Maria Carolina to Ruffo, 26 February.

Principe di Gerace, of the Cassano Serra, and of the Vaglio Monteleone who had accepted office in the 'so-called Republic' the cardinal again prevaricated, arguing that it would be wiser to raise indemnities from republican towns and to invite donations from royalist landowners: 'I am making the barons pay only what they can, taking their corn, silk, oil and horses when I can find them.' He had reduced the taxes paid by the poorest and had halved the 'hearth tax and the tax on labour paid by the poor in the royalist towns, to incite jealousy between the people and the middling classes and to lessen the burdens on the people who are truly oppressed by taxes, yet without abolishing them altogether'.[54] A week later Ruffo again informed Acton that his aim was 'to moderate the taxes owed to the barons without destroying them, to reduce the taxes paid by the poor and to try to get trade and commerce moving again if possible'.[55]

The more general reform desired by the queen, Ruffo feared, would alienate the landowners and allow the popular movement to get completely out of control. By contrast, his tactic was to win over the sections of the propertied and privileged classes who had rallied to the Republic. His aim, he told Acton, was not to terrorize but to encourage the republicans to defect:

> It is like the old medieval wars between the barons, and I find that by dividing them with flattery and rewards, privileges and gifts one half will soon get the rest under control and will do the task with enthusiasm. But what is the point in punishing them, indeed how is it possible to punish them when they are so many without resorting to methods of excessive cruelty?[56]

Ruffo saw himself in the midst of two wars. One was being fought between the barons and *ceto medio*, whom the Republic had divided into opposing factions, or whose pre-existing factional alliances had regrouped along the division between royalists and republicans. The other was the war being fought by the people, and Ruffo agreed that they suffered intolerable burdens (*soverchi aggravi*). But these burdens could not be lessened without alienating the landowners and provoking a social war that could not be controlled.

The best way to defeat the republicans, Ruffo insisted, was to make it as easy as possible for them to recant: 'The Calabrians in general are loyal to the king and many joined the rebellion through fear rather than enthusiasm.'[57] When the republicans in Ascoli Satriano were threatened by a royalist revolt and sued for terms, he sent a detachment of mounted troops to protect them from the insurgents. He was furious when he learned that Captain Troubridge's men had massacred all the Jacobins they captured on the island of Procida, arguing that this would only make the republicans in Naples more intransigent.[58]

Ruffo's concern about restoring order was shared by other royalist leaders. In the Cilento, Bishop Ludovisi of Policastro had voiced his alarm at the lawlessness

[54] Croce (1943), 45—Ruffo to Acton, 3 March.
[55] Ibid. 67—14 March.
[56] Ibid. 154—Ruffo to Acton, 30 April (Policoro).
[57] Ibid. 39, 45.
[58] Lucarelli (1934), 113.

that accompanied the spread of anti-republican revolts. He instructed the parish priests to organize armed *masse* to keep the royalist insurgents in check. When this failed to stop the violence, he appealed to both Troubridge and Ruffo for assistance. Ruffo sent a thousand men headed by the *capo-massa* Nicola Gualtieri, known as *Panedigrano*, to restore order in the Val di Diano and in the townships around Potenza, which had been in the hands of royalists since the end of March.[59]

In Apulia, Antoine Micheroux also stated that it was more difficult to restore order than to defeat the republicans. As the royalist revolts spread, he told Acton that 'a Robesperrian Terror rules everywhere, and the People have brought down their legitimate governors and magistrates'.[60] Like Ruffo, he too emphasized the importance of mending the divisions within the ruling classes, which he considered to be the cause of the popular anarchy. In contrast to the massacres and reprisals inflicted by the French and by Ettore Caraffa's followers, whenever possible Micheroux offered the republicans terms and protection. When General Duhesme had taken Sansevero in March, he had executed six popular royalist *caporioni* and confiscated the property of the feudatories and landowners who had supported the monarchy. By contrast, Micheroux deliberately adopted a more conciliatory line when he captured the republican stronghold of Foggia on 23 May. The royalist prisoners in the city were released and funerals were held for the royalists who had been killed following the declaration of the Republic, but he refused to take action against the republican leaders or to seize their lands.[61]

Neither Ruffo nor Micheroux could restrain the violence of *capi-masse* like the Mammone brothers and Fra Diavolo, whose actions were condoned by the Court. But Ruffo feared that this would wreck his own efforts to win over the republicans by negotiation.[62] His outcry following the massacres on the Ponte della Maddelena after the *Sanfedisti* had forced their way into Naples in June expressed his sense of impotence:

> The responsibility of governing, although it would be more accurate to say trying to control, a people raised in total anarchy and of giving orders to twenty illiterate and insubordinate leaders of irregular troops, all of whom have no interest other than plunder, massacre, rape and violence, is something so horrible that it quite exceeds my strength! They have now brought to me some 1,300 Jacobins and I have nowhere safe to keep them so they remain here with us on the bridge: some 50 have already been slaughtered and shot before my eyes without me being able to do anything, while at least 200 more have been dragged here wounded and naked.[63]

Well before Ruffo agreed to the armistice that Nelson and the government later declared null and void, the royalist leaders had been at loggerheads with the Court. Disgraced and threatened with arrest, Ruffo left Naples in July for Rome to attend

[59] Cassese, in Cestaro and Laveglia (eds.) (1970), 108–9.

[60] Lucarelli (1934) 45; Maresca (1894), 106–22.

[61] Maresca (1894), 258–60.

[62] Ibid. 289; Cingari (1978), 54–5.

[63] Maresca (1894), 277, Ruffo to Acton, 21 June.

the convocation that had been summoned to elect a successor to his former patron, Pius VI. Far from rallying the masses and the landowners around the monarchy, the counter-revolution had exacerbated older conflicts, although it was not until after the fall of the Republic that the full scale of the collapse became evident.

THE RESTORATION

The Capital

For the diarist Carlo De Nicola, the end of the Republic was simply the start of 'the third anarchy'. In Naples, this took the form first of the popular revolt against the 'giacobini' and then the Royal Terror. Two days after entering the city, Ruffo set up a *Giunta di Stato* to try those accused of treason, hoping that this would calm the popular fury directed at the patriots. But Ruffo's judges were soon replaced by the king's appointees, whose arrival in Naples marked the start of a more systematic persecution of suspected republicans.

Some 8,000 individuals were charged with treason and in Naples alone more than a hundred executions were carried out between July 1799 and September 1800. Those who died included two women who had played different roles in the Republic. Eleonora Fonseca di Pimentel, who had edited the *Monitore Napoletano,* was among the first of those to die when she went to the scaffold on 20 August 1799. Luisa Sanfelice, who had inadvertently betrayed the royalist Baccher conspiracy, was among the last when she was hanged on 11 September 1800.

The monarchy also settled its scores with the nobility. A royal decree dated 25 April 1800 set out the bill of attainder against those who were supposed to be the crown's most solid pillar, its strongest ally and most glorious embellishment. Instead, during the revolt, 'The *Sedili,* known also as the *Piazze* of the City of Naples, remained quite indifferent to the fate of the State and allowed their authority to be exercised by a group of corrupted youths who lacked all sense of duty to God and to their King and, as is now known, permitted them to attack Our Supreme Authority.'

Hence the monarchy decreed that it must give 'new form to the Nobility of Naples' and to that effect:

> we do abolish in perpetuity the *Piazze* or *Sedili* of the City of Naples and we prohibit any meeting of that body which from henceforth will be considered a felony. We do hereby also abolish entirely the *Corpo degli Eletti,* otherwise known as the Tribunal of San Lorenzo, and all the other Deputations of the City.[64]

In their place a new *Supremo Tribunale Conservatore della Nobiltà* was created, to which only nobles of 'proven loyalty' could be admitted. The capital would now

[64] ASN: Min. Finance 1532: Decree 25 April 1800.

be governed by a *Regio Senato*, and its seat was moved to the former monastery of Monte Oliveto. The other city deputations were also abolished and replaced by new administrations. The members of all of these new administrations were to be appointed by the king.[65]

As Luigi Blanch later noted, the abolition of the *Corpo della Cittá* was the culmination of the monarchy's earlier attempts to reduce the political powers of the nobility. The one remaining political constraint on the monarchy had been removed and the nobles became simply a privileged administrative class.[66]

The Provinces

Under the reign of terror instituted in July 1799 order was quickly restored in the capital, but in the provinces the state of lawlessness grew worse. In April, Ruffo had warned Acton that brigandage and vendettas were bringing chaos to the Calabrian towns occupied by the royalists. In Apulia, Micheroux had expressed similar concerns. Many of the *capi-masse* in the northern provinces refused to disband after the fall of the Republic, and were operating as bandits, making raids deep into the Papal States on the pretext of pursuing fleeing republicans. The notorious Fra Diavolo refused to obey orders to disband and was arrested in Rome, but escaped to Palermo to plead his case to the Court, which offered him a pension of 2,500 ducats (that was never paid). Scarpia, a former corporal in the guard of the Royal *Udienza* in Salerno who became the principal royalist *capo-massa* in the Cilento, had better luck and received an estate near Polla worth 3,500 ducats a year.[67]

To restore order and to punish those who had supported the Republic, the government sent out teams of Royal Visitors to the provinces early in 1800. Their task initially was to bring those charged with treason to Naples for trial, to investigate local grievances, and to report on the state of each province. In the provinces it was widely believed that the Royal Visitors 'have been charged to take account of all those subjects who during the recent emergency in the Kingdom have shown themselves to be meritorious and to have made financial sacrifices, so that they may be compensated from the lands of those guilty of treason'.[68] But these expectations were quickly disappointed. Ruffo had already warned the government that the leading republicans from Calabria were all cadets of the major feudal families and so had few personal possessions.[69]

The monarchy's freedom to pursue its vendetta against the former republicans ended abruptly when in the spring of 1800 Napoleon Bonaparte led a French army back to northern Italy and defeated the Austrians at Marengo. Fearful for its safety, the Neapolitan government sued for terms that proved onerous.

[65] ASN: Min. Finance 1532: Decree 25 April 1800.
[66] Blanch (ed. Croce, 1945), i. 35–6.
[67] Cassese, in Cestaro and Laveglia (eds.) (1970), 114.
[68] ASN: Min. Finance 1532.
[69] Cingari (1976), 38–59.

The Kingdom was also obliged to pay heavy cash indemnities to compensate France for the Neapolitan offensive in 1798 and the subsequent French invasion of the Kingdom. In addition it was now to pay the upkeep of a French *Army of Observation* to be stationed in the Abruzzi and at Otranto to enforce the terms of the treaty, to return all lands seized from the republicans and the *rei di stato* (traitors), to end the executions, to offer amnesty to the surviving supporters of the republic, and to allow the exiles to return.[70]

These terms were deliberately designed to humiliate the Neapolitan government, which was no longer free to conduct its own domestic policy. But they were also ruinous and came as the final blow to the already catastrophic state of the monarchy's finance. In a desperate bid to repair the damage the government called on Giuseppe Zurlo, the lawyer from Baranello in Molise to make a final experiment in absolutist reform.

Zurlo had risen to the ranks of the *togati* in 1789 and had conducted the investigation into the royal domains in the Sila in 1790. In 1798, on the eve of the Republic, he had been appointed Director of Finances (*Segreteria d'Azienda*), the most senior position in the government. He had played no part in the Republic and now in its chaotic aftermath he was given the task of conducting a complete reform of the Kingdom's administration.

In the circumstances the task was impossible, but Zurlo nonetheless showed remarkable energy and commitment. The whole set of earlier reform schemes, from proposals to abolish the *Dogana di Foggia* and the *Tavoliere* to projects to drain the swamps on the Volturno basin and the legislation of 1792 on the division of the common lands, was dusted off, and time was even found to reconsider treatises pressing the advantages of the cultivation of maize in place of wheat. Now that the nobility had been defeated Zurlo also set about reorganizing local administration, creating the new post of the Royal Intendent to represent the government in each province. He even planned to make government departments prepare budgets, to reform the banks, and to establish a national debt.[71] But the government had neither the material nor the political means nor indeed the time to realize any of these projects.

The Provincial Visitations

Zurlo stripped the Royal Visitations of their original punitive functions and saw the opportunity to use the special powers conferred on the royal agents as the means to enact a wholesale reform of public administration in the provinces. The Royal Visitors now became Economic Visitors, whose task was to report on what was needed to revive the provinces. But their reports revealed above all the extent to which government in the provinces had collapsed.

[70] The armistice of Foligno (18 February 1801) was followed by the Treaty of Florence (28 March 1801), which was negotiated by Joachim Murat the future king of Naples.

[71] Villani (1955), 19–78 (now in Villani 1974); Rao (1986), 1–27; De Lorenzo (1998), 35–40.

A year after the fall of the Republic, most of the South was still in a state of anarchy. In November 1800 the Royal Visitor in Molise reported that troops were urgently needed to 'put an end to the lawlessness of the dissolute soldiery that have been left behind by an army that has disintegrated and has been despoiled of all its equipment and which even now has not been restored to its former state'.

There was no money or coin to be had because of the 'seizures made by the French, the collapse of the banks and family trusts (*monti*) and the gathering of many persons in *masse* who, under the pretext of defending the Kingdom, have in reality pursued their own particular vendettas and robbed any village they might'. In the absence of regular troops, it was impossible to enforce the king's or a court's authority. Instead 'the mass of people who were released from jail during the recent disturbances now roam openly through the countryside.... They have created a situation of perfect anarchy, greater even than that unleashed by the ferocity of those miscreants commonly known as the *Sanfedists* and may well lead to civil war.'

Taxes needed to be levied on every town to raise an armed troop of *Cacciatori di Montagna*, but the revenues of the charitable foundations (*Pii Laicali*) in most villages had 'scandalously been expropriated by the despot *Gualantuomini*'. The guards of the former royal tribunals had been disbanded 'so that the poor shepherds and farmers on the Tavoliere are every day robbed and murdered'.[72]

In Basilicata, the town of Melfi that had rallied to Ruffo in 1799 was still in a state of 'perfect anarchy and controlled by a band of criminals led by the Cabelli and Franchi families'.[73] In the Val di Diano the winning factions and communities had occupied the lands and property of their rivals, making enclosures and clearing huge tracts of woodland and forest. In the neighbouring Cilento the relatives and supporters of Don Antonio Gariglia were 'murdering and terrorising anyone who attempted to give evidence against them', and the official begged the king to warn Gariglia and his followers 'not to gather in armed and mounted bands, not to sing provocative songs, nor to beat or threaten any person ... and not to fire their muskets inside the towns or put up notices of proscription during the night'.[74]

In the Abruzzi 'in most towns public administration is in the hands of persons of no ability or honesty' and every form of public and municipal revenue was controlled by private individuals:

> What is the total amount of all the taxes paid in this province? What is the yield of each different tax? What is the state of each revenue? What proportion should be spent within the Province to meet ordinary and extraordinary expenses? What part should be sent to the General Treasury in Naples? I will not be speaking insolently if I hazard to say that Your Excellency does not know the answer to these questions, because neither does the *Camera*

72 ASN: Min. Finance 1643: 16 November 1800.

73 ASN: Min. Finance 1533: 26 August 1801.

74 Ibid. 1643 n.d. 1800: see Cassese, in Cestaro and Laveglia (eds.) (1970), 115.

della Sommaria, nor do the Provincial Delegates nor even do I myself despite the fact that I have made every possible inquiry here at source.[75]

The resulting 'uncertainty and chaos makes the Royal Court and its Ministers appear ignominious.... The weak, the evil minded, the jealous and all those who are enemies of public order and prosperity, in other words all those whom your Excellency has succeeded in expelling from the Administration because unworthy to be part of it, lose no opportunity to spread the word that the Provinces are being exhausted and that all their money is being taken away to Naples.'[76]

These findings were confirmed by Angelo Masci, a close confidant of Zurlo:

> the extreme poverty of this province [L'Aquila]... is principally due to the fact that the town taxes fall entirely on the Poor, which renders them incapable no matter how much they may work to support the means of subsistence and at the same time pay also what they must to the crown and find money to cultivate their land, take care of their livestock, provide pasture and conduct their trades.... In every town I have found a group of intriguers who have long since usurped control over all elections and over the administrators.... The elections are always 'fixed' and as soon as they are over the fraud and the manoeuvres by which they succeed in dilapidating public funds begin again.[77]

THE COLLAPSE OF THE MONARCHY

The Visitors' reports revealed problems whose origins long predated the events of 1799 but which the monarchy was no longer in any condition to address. In 1801 the Peace of Amiens had offered the Kingdom a momentary respite, but when the war in Europe started again another French *Army of Observation* returned to Apulia in 1803. The cost was 4,000,000 ducats, nearly one-third of the government's normal annual revenues. The Russian and Turkish governments also submitted their accounts for military services rendered in 1799. The harvest failed in 1802, there was virtually no currency in circulation, and by 1803 the bank notes that Zurlo had issued under guarantee two years earlier had fallen to 30 per cent of their original value.[78]

Zurlo became the scapegoat and was replaced by Luigi de' Medici, Prince of Ottaiano. The cadet of a noble family, the dukes of Sarno, de' Medici had been arrested first as a suspected Jacobin in 1794 and then in 1799 by the French as a suspected royalist, so his political credentials were in good order after the Restoration. He would later prove to be an able financier, but in 1803 there was no room for manoeuvre. The budget deficits could not be reduced, payments to public employees were in arrears, the banks' promissory notes remained almost

75 ASN: Min. Finance 1630. 76 Ibid.
77 ASN: Min. Finance 1634: Relazione di Angelo Masci a Giuseppe Zurlo, 25 December (L'Aquila).
78 Villani (1984), 279–304.

valueless, and the payment of interest on most of the *arrendamenti* had been suspended. Divisions within the government were also deepening. Acton's star had fallen and Cardinal Ruffo was recalled in 1802.[79]

The government faced imminent collapse. The only hope was that the French would be defeated, and so when it became known that England was trying to reactivate the coalition against France the Neapolitan envoy in London was instructed in 1805 to renew the alliance. As a result, the Kingdom once again went to war with France and was once again invaded by a French army. The Bourbon rulers again sought safety in Palermo under the protection of the British navy, but this time the French would retain control of the mainland for nearly ten years.

CONCLUSION

The Neapolitan Bourbons were not the only Italian rulers whose government was thrown into crisis by the events that followed the revolution in France. The British minister in Turin had been warning since the early 1790s that war with France threatened to bring about the financial collapse of the Piedmontese monarch, while even the Habsburg rulers faced similar difficulties.[80]

The invasions exposed strong social tensions in most of the Italian states, even in the proverbially peaceful Grand Duchy of Tuscany, where the popular *Viva Maria!* insurrections gave vent to the resentments of the urban and rural poor against the liberal reforms of Peter Leopold. Throughout Italy, sections of the clergy were actively mobilizing popular opposition to the atheist republican invaders and their Italian sympathizers, and in the papal territories public order had collapsed well before the French occupation of Rome. Nor was it easily restored. In August 1799 a Neapolitan army occupied Rome and oversaw the restoration of papal administration, but central Italy remained in chaos.

The upheavals in the South were part of a broader pattern of political crisis and social protest whose immediate causes were the French invasion and the allies' counter-offensives. Nonetheless, in the South the crisis was also a consequence of the collapse of the monarchy, and exposed the conflicts and insecurities that had been accumulating over the previous decades. By the eve of the next French occupation, the feudal order was visibly disintegrating as were the fragile structures of government and authority.

[79] Blanch (ed. Croce, 1945), i. 27–9, and Villani (1984), 275–325.

[80] For example, a decade earlier Britain's envoy in Turin, Sir John Trevor, had warned that mobilization for war might bring about the financial collapse of the Piedmontese monarchy (Trevor to Lord Camarthen, 27 October 1784, PRO FO 67/6).

PART II

NAPOLEONIC NAPLES

7

Naples in the Imperial Enterprise

Southern Italy in 1806, from R. M. Johnston, *The Napoleonic Empire in Southern Italy*, vol. i (London: Macmillan, 1904).

NAPOLEONIC ITALY 1800–1806

On 27 December 1805, following Napoleon's victory at Austerlitz, a peremptory imperial edict from the Schönbrunn Place in Vienna proclaimed that 'the Bourbon dynasty of Naples had ceased to reign'. The invasion of southern Italy that followed two months later was ostensibly to punish the Neapolitan Bourbons for treacherously allying with the emperor's enemies while signatories to a peace treaty with France. That treachery made the survival of the Bourbon rulers incompatible with the honour of the emperor's crown, and Marshal Masséna with an army corps of 40,000 men was sent to install the emperor's brother, Prince Joseph, on the throne of Naples.[1]

The treachery of the Bourbon rulers was no more than a pretext for an invasion that Napoleon had contemplated much earlier and which had a clearly defined part to play in the broader plan of empire. Well before Austerlitz, France was securely in control of much of northern and central Italy. In January 1802 the former Cisalpine Republic was reconstituted as the Italian Republic, which after the proclamation of the empire was renamed the Kingdom of Italy in March 1805 under the titular vice-regal government of the emperor's step-son Eugène Beauharnais. The former papal territories of Emilia were already part of the Kingdom, which after Austerlitz in addition acquired Austria's former Venetian provinces and Istria. Geographically the Kingdom was divided in two by the Duchies of Parma, Piacenza and Guastalla, which were occupied by France and nominally ruled by the emperor's sister Pauline.[2] Piedmont had been annexed to France, and Liguria occupied while Elisa Bonaparte and her husband Felice Bacciocchi ruled the small duchies of Piombino and Lucca.[3] Out of deference to the alliance with Spain that continued to assure France a free hand in the rest of Europe, the former Grand Duchy of Tuscany had been turned into the ostensibly independent Kingdom of Etruria for the former Duke of Parma, Louis of Bourbon, and his wife, the Spanish *Infanta* Maria Luisa. But this was little more than a mask for French occupation and became redundant as soon as the Spanish alliance collapsed: in 1807 Tuscany was occupied and a year later annexed to France.[4]

Political considerations similarly deferred full French occupation of the Papal State, since Napoleon initially hoped to win the Pope's support to heal the dangerous legacy of conflicts over religion that France had inherited from the revolution. The new pope Pius VII at first seemed compliant and a concordat was agreed on 16 July 1801, but Napoleon's repeated refusal to comply with its terms and his occupation of Bologna and the northern papal territories caused relations with the

[1] Schroeder (1994), 264, 257–76.

[2] Pauline Bonaparte (1780–1825). In 1797 Pauline married General Victor Emmanuel Leclerc, and after his death the Roman Prince Camillo Borghese became her second husband in 1803.

[3] Liguria was annexed in 1805, the duchies in 1808; Zaghi (1986), 367–8; Woolf (1991), 191–3.

[4] Louis of Bourbon, formerly the Duke of Parma, became king of Etruria but died in 1803.

papacy to deteriorate rapidly.[5] In October 1805 French troops occupied the papal port of Ancona and then Civitavecchia in May 1806. Two years later Rome was occupied on the pretext that the Pope was trading with France's enemies, and like his predecessor Pius VII became the emperor's prisoner.[6]

The occupation of Rome in 1808 consolidated France's control of the mainland Italian peninsula, which had been significantly extended by the invasion of southern Italy two years earlier. The intention had been to conquer Sicily as well, but despite an easy victory over the Bourbon army on the mainland in March 1806, Napoleon's armies never managed to cross the narrow Straits of Messina that separated Sicily from the mainland. In 1810 a major expedition was prepared but then abandoned, so that the long coastlines of the southern mainland remained the most southerly frontier of Napoleon's continental empire.

Naples was ruled first by the emperor's brother Joseph and then by his brother-in-law, Joachim Murat. Napoleon often referred dismissively to his Mediterranean Kingdom and in 1808 while trying to persuade his brother to accept the Spanish throne he described Naples as 'the end of the world'.[7] But the emperor had his own way with words, and in the same week he told Joachim Murat that Naples was one of the most beautiful kingdoms in Europe. More revealing than these casual comments, however, was that the invasion of Rome in 1808 was justified not once but on three separate occasions by the overriding need to protect the security of the Kingdom of Naples.[8]

There were many reasons why Naples mattered. Apart from its role as a frontier it had a critical role to play in the attempt to exclude British trade from the European continent. Geographically it was also the key to establishing French domination of the Adriatic and challenging British naval supremacy in the Mediterranean. Its ports offered opportunities to rebuild the Mediterranean fleet that Nelson destroyed at the Battle of the Nile, a need made even more pressing by the more recent losses at Trafalgar. Nor had Napoleon abandoned the idea of re-launching the Egyptian enterprise that had been interrupted by Nelson's victory in 1798. Once the European foundations of the imperial project had been secured, southern Italy offered the jumping-off point for the conquest of the Middle East and North Africa.

None of these more ambitious projects would be realized, but that still left the Kingdom with a critical role to play in enforcing the blockade against British goods and providing billets for imperial armies during the brief intermissions between campaigning. Like France's other colonies, Naples would provide constant flows of men, money, materials, and provisions needed to sustain the empire's wars and France's economy. It was believed to be a land rich in fabulous

[5] Barnaba Chiaramonti (1740–1823) was elected Pope Pius VII on 14 March 1800 at the conclave held under Austrian protection in Venice. Bologna and Ferrara were annexed to the Italian Republic in 1802. The Pope attended the emperor's coronation in Paris in December 1804, but Napoleon still refused to make concessions.

[6] Menozzi (1985), 169–82.

[7] Tulard (1983), 124.

[8] Rambaud (1908), 294.

and hitherto untapped natural resources that would offer an abundance of raw materials for French manufactures, as well as captive markets for French exports. It also offered a valuable source of fat pensions for the emperor's most trusted officers and an endless supply of jobs for the hordes of place-seekers, adventurers, artists, soldiers, sailors, and out-of-work administrators that all empires spawn.

Napoleon's Mediterranean Kingdom was not remarkable in any of these respects, but the deep contradictions on which the imperial enterprise was founded would be very vividly exposed in the exceptionally stormy relations between Naples and Paris, especially after the arrival of Joachim Murat in 1808. Down to the final days of the empire, the relations between Naples and Paris exposed both the remarkably dysfunctional nature of the Bonaparte family enterprise and the extreme forms of colonial subordination on which this short-lived imperial project was founded. That makes Naples an excellent vantage point for understanding the broader mechanisms of the imperial enterprise, but also raises questions about why the French rulers attempted to reorganize the southern state at a moment of severe colonial exploitation, prolonged commercial and financial crisis, and constant political upheaval.

TAKING NAPLES

The opportunity for invading southern Italy came as a direct result of Britain's efforts to revive the coalition against France after the collapse of the Peace of Amiens. But in the end it was Napoleon not the British who pushed the allies into action when he crowned himself King of Italy in Milan in March 1805 and annexed Genoa.[9] Austria mobilized, Russia rejoined the coalition, and as before, the allies chose Naples as their jumping-off point for an offensive in Italy. A British force of 6,000 men sailed for the Mediterranean, where they were to be joined by 10,000 Russian and 7,000 Neapolitan troops.[10]

What for the Neapolitan government in 1798 had been a gamble was now an even more desperate bid to rid the Kingdom of a financially ruinous French army of occupation. Despite the fact that his government had already secretly entered an agreement with the allies, in September the Neapolitan ambassador in Paris renewed the treaty of neutrality with France. As a result, the commander of the French Army of Observation in Apulia withdrew his army to join the campaign against Austria in the North. Shortly after, the Russian and British troops disembarked in Naples.

The allies' expectations were raised when news of Nelson's final victory at Trafalgar reached Naples in October, and then dashed in December by news of

[9] As Paul Schroeder puts it, 'the coalition had been planned by Britain and Russia but it was Napoleon who brought it into being.' Schroeder (1994), 264, 257–76.

[10] Johnson (1904), i. 75. See also Flayhart (1992), 54–169.

Napoleon's decisive victory at Austerlitz. King Ferdinand wanted to issue an appeal for a *levée en masse*, but was advised by his allies that resistance was impossible. Two days later the commander of the British troops in Naples, General Sir James Craig, was instructed to withdraw to Sicily 'with or without the permission of His Sicilian Majesty'. The Russians did likewise.[11] Convinced they had been betrayed by their allies, as in 1798 Ferdinand and Maria Carolina took refuge in Palermo, leaving the hereditary Prince to organize the military defence of the Kingdom in Calabria.

From his military headquarters at Fiorentino, Prince Joseph-Napoleon Bonaparte, Grand Elector of the Empire, Lieutenant of the Emperor, and Commander-in-Chief of the Army of Naples, issued a proclamation to the people of the Kingdom of Naples that mimicked the timeless rhetoric of invading armies:

> The French Emperor and King of Italy being desirous to spare you the Calamities of war signed a treaty of Neutrality with your Court.... But despite confirming this treaty, the King of Naples has joined the Coalition. The Army that I command is marching to punish this perfidy. But you, the People, have nothing to fear. Our arms are not directed against you. Your altars and your Ministers of Religion are the same as ours. Your laws and your property will be respected. Your Magistrates will remain in their posts. The French soldiers will be your brothers.[12]

A week later Masséna's *Armée de Naples* crossed the frontier of the Terra di Lavoro on 9 February 1806.[13] The commanders of the Bourbon army, General Roger Damas and the Hereditary Princes Leopold and Francis, planned to fall back and give battle in Calabria, where the queen's agents were busy preparing a second *Sanfedist* rising. But in January Uombuono delle Boccache noted that the queen's hopes for another 'Great Neapolitan Vespers' in the frontier provinces had failed. Attempts to raise a *leva di massa* were abandoned when the government learned that the *galantuomini* were opposed, while the Minister of Police, the Duke of Ascoli, prevented the movement of spies sent by the queen 'who were plotting to massacre the so-called friends of the French and the families of all those who were unwilling to rise against them'.[14]

Angelo de Jacobis recorded that when the people of Teramo were informed that the king had appealed for a *leva in massa* 'those charged with this duty met with no response, because during the first war against the French the People had been

[11] Johnson (1904), i. 75.

[12] BNN (Bancone 8 B 21): Napoleon used similar terms at Cairo and two decades later the French invasion of Algeria was justified in identical language: see Burke (2002), 41–8.

[13] General André Masséna, Duke of Rivoli, Prince of Essling and Maréchal of France (1758–1817) served in the *Armée d'Italie* 1792–8, and led the occupation of Rome in 1798 but was accused of wide-scale looting and was recalled by the Directory. In November 1799 he replaced Championnet as commander of the *Armée d'Italie*. In 1805 he was again appointed commander of the *Armée d'Italie* (in place of General Joubert), and in December 1805 commander of the *Armée de Naples* and commanded the siege of Gaeta February to June 1806, then took over command in Calabria. In 1807 he rejoined the *Grande Armée*.

[14] Delle Boccache, in Coppa-Zuccari (ed.) (1927), 565 (January 1806).

forced to make too many sacrifices . . . only a few charitable foundations gave some money, but not much'.[15] In February another appeal for a draft was made but 'this really distressed the people'. The *Preside* withdrew and the *parlamento* was reconvened and immediately voted to establish 'a civic guard to maintain order'.[16] When the first French troops arrived in nearby Lanciano on 23 March, de Jacobis simply noted that all those who had brought denunciations against the Jacobins in Teramo in 1799 were immediately arrested.[17]

The fortresses of Capua and Caserta surrendered to Masséna's army, but a well-supplied garrison under the command of Prince Hesse Philippsthal continued to hold the fortress of Gaeta.[18] Taking charge of the siege, Masséna sent General Partouneaux[19] with a small force to occupy Naples, which he did on 14 February but in circumstances very different from Championnet's entry seven years earlier. The Regency government surrendered the city's forts, and organized a mounted civic guard composed of the 'wealthiest gentlemen together with certain magistrates and men of letters'.[20] Carlo De Nicola noted with relief in his diary that the propertied classes had enrolled enthusiastically in the civic guard: 'The people remain calm since in any case these measures have placed them in greater subjection.' When Prince Joseph Bonaparte entered the city he was welcomed by the civic authorities and the clergy, while San Gennaro obliged again with another unscheduled miracle.[21]

The Ministries of Police and the Interior were among the first to be set up. On 3 March the French authorities appointed Police Commissars in each district, supported by Inspectors of police and a force of Gendarmes. The Commissars were given powers to arrest suspected enemies of the state, to impose censorship, control and inspect the mails, to issue licenses for carrying firearms, to regulate all public meetings, markets, and fairs, and in particular to detain all 'vagabonds, beggars and unknown persons'.[22] On 12 March the Duke of Lauranzana, who had been amongst those charged with treason in 1799, was appointed head of the Commissariat and given the task of purging it of former royalist magistrates and office holders.

THE CALABRIAN REVOLT

Meanwhile Masséna had sent General Reynier[23] with 11,000 men to pursue the retreating Bourbon army, which he caught up with on 6 March near Lagonegro

[15] De Jacobis, in Coppa-Zuccari (ed.) (1927), 215–27 (January 1806).

[16] Ibid., 215–16 (8 February 1806).

[17] Ibid., 233 (30 March 1806).

[18] William II (1777–1847), Elector of Hesse.

[19] Louis Comte Partouneaux (1770–1835) (G. Six, (1934), ii. 289).

[20] The members of the Regency were General Naselli, the Prince of Canosa, and a senior magistrate, Michelangelo Cianciulli.

[21] De Nicola, 11 February 1806, 202.

[22] Ibid. 3 March 1806, 200.

[23] General Jean-Louis Ebenezer Reynier (1771–1814), Swiss officer who killed General Destaing in a duel in 1802 and was sent to the *Armée d'Italie* in exile. Commanded the right wing of Masséna's army in 1806 and then the conquest of Calabria. Awarded the *Legion d'Honneur* in May and in July

and four days later in fog and snow attacked the Bourbon positions on the heights of Campotenese. Abandoning their equipment, the remnants of the Bourbon army fled south towards Castrovillari and Reggio seeking to escape to Sicily. Reynier reached Cosenza on 21 March and the new government's official newspaper, the *Monitore Napoletano*, announced the collapse of the 'comic defence of the Calabrias'.[24] By early in April the conquest seemed secure, and Reynier raised no objection when Prince Joseph became the first ruling Neapolitan monarch to journey in person through the Calabrian provinces when he visited Cosenza and Crotone at the beginning of April, before returning to Naples by way of Taranto, Matera, and Gravina.

On 30 March Napoleon conferred the title of King of Naples and Sicily on his brother, who on 16 April paraded through the streets of Naples accompanied by his victorious generals.[25] But the triumph proved premature. In March military commissions had been set up and *colonne mobili* were despatched to put down minor revolts, but in April the *Monitore Napoletano* reported more serious insurrections in the northern provinces.[26]

The surrender of Gaeta in July made it more difficult for the British and the Sicilians to get supplies to the royalist *capi-masse* operating in the North. But in the meantime, Reynier's advance into Calabria had dangerously strung out the French forces, and to take advantage of this a small British force commanded by Sir John Stuart landed in the Bay of S. Eufemia on 28 June. The aim was to draw French troops away from Gaeta, at the same time cut Reynier's communications with Masséna in the North and with the rest of the French troops in Cosenza.[27] Caught in a trap, Reynier decided to attack the British company of more than 5,000 men drawn up in defensive positions near the village of Maida on 2 July, but was repulsed with heavy casualties.[28]

The victory at Maida resonated loudly because it was the allies' first success against troops of the reputedly invincible *Grande Armée*. But Stuart was unable to exploit the victory. Summer fevers had broken out amongst his troops and the expedition was shipped back to Sicily.[29] Nonetheless, the British victory was the signal for a general revolt in the Calabrian provinces. Catanzaro declared for the Bourbons and soon the entire Sila region was again in revolt. By the time that Joseph Bonaparte left for Spain in 1808 order had only precariously been restored and would remain uncertain throughout the period of French rule.

was defeated by Sir John Stuart at Maida. Resumed command in Calabria from Masséna 12 January 1807, retook Amantea (6 February), Crotone (10 June), and Scilla (February 1808). Replaced as military commander in Calabria by General Maurice Mathieu 28 February 1808 and appointed Minister of War and provisional Commander-in-Chief, *Armée de Naples*; rejoined the *Grande Armée* in July 1808 and fought in Spain (1810) and Russia (1812).

[24] *Monitore Napoletano*, no. 7, 21 March 1806.

[25] Ibid., no. 17, 25 April; no. 19, 2 May; no. 21, 9 May; no. 22, 13 May; no. 23, 16 May.

[26] Ibid., no. 4, 11 March. [27] Bunbury (1854), 233.

[28] Ibid., Reynier to Joseph Bonaparte (Marina di Catanzaro, 13 July 1806).

[29] Bunbury (1854), 230–50; Johnson (1904), i. 113–26; Mackesey (1957), 140–6.

JOSEPH BONAPARTE

It was a sign of the importance Napoleon attached to his Mediterranean Kingdom that he should have placed his eldest brother on the throne. Born in Corsica in 1767, Joseph-Napoleon Bonaparte[30] had studied law at the University of Pisa, where he became a close friend of his fellow Corsican, Antoine Christophe Saliceti,[31] whose commitment to the Corsican nationalist cause he shared. In 1788 Joseph returned to Ajaccio and with his younger brother Napoleon became prominent in the pro-French faction led by Saliceti. The opposing faction that favoured independence was led by the legendary Pasquale Paoli, who in 1793 opposed union with France and placed Corsica under the protection of the British navy.[32]

Paoli's move forced the Bonaparte brothers to flee to France, where thanks to Saliceti's patronage Joseph found lucrative employment as a commissar to the army. In 1794 he married Julie Clary, the daughter of a wealthy Marseilles merchant, and moved to Genoa where he took up trade. The defeat of the royalist insurrections in Paris on 12 Vendémiaire (5 October 1795) marked the start of his brother's ascendancy and also brought Joseph to prominence. In October 1796 he commanded the expedition that brought Corsica back under French control, and was responsible for setting up a new administration dominated by the Bonaparte clan and its allies.

Elected to the Council of Five Hundred in Paris as a Corsican deputy in April 1797, Joseph subsequently served as the French minister at the Court of the Duke of Parma and then as Minister Plenipotentiary to the Holy See.[33] In Rome, Joseph was probably responsible for the pro-French demonstrations that led to the death of General Duphot in December, after which he returned to Paris where government service had brought him rich rewards. In October 1798 he purchased the sumptuous chateau of Mortefontaine, fifty kilometres from Paris, which became an important meeting place in the months leading up to the Coup of 18–19 Brumaire (November) 1799.

After Brumaire, Joseph was appointed to the Council of State and played a leading role in negotiating an agreement with the United States and the Treaty of Lunéville with Austria.[34] The concordat with the papacy was signed on 21 June 1801 in his latest and even more regal residence, the Hotel Marbeuf in the rue du

[30] Napoleon was born in 1769, Lucien in 1775, Elisa (Maria-Anna Eliza) in 1777, Louis in 1778, Paoletta in 1780, Maria Annunziata (Caroline) in 1782, Jerome in 1784.

[31] See below pp. 166–9.

[32] Pasquale Paoli (1725–1807) led the Corsican revolt against Genoa in 1755 and opposed Genoa's cession of the island to France in 1768. Defeated by the French he went into exile in England but after the revolution in France was elected Governor of Corsica. In 1793 he was accused of counter-revolution but with the support of Admiral Hood drove out the French and their supporters (including the Bonaparte family). When the French regained control of the island in 1795 Paoli again went into exile in London where he died in 1807.

[33] March–May 1797.

[34] 3 October 1800; 9 February 1801.

Faubourg Saint-Honoré. He also led the negotiations with Lord Cornwallis that resulted in the Peace of Amiens.[35]

Relations between Joseph and his brother became strained, however, when Napoleon took the title of Consul for Life.[36] Because Napoleon's marriage with Josephine de Beauharnais[37] remained childless, Joseph demanded that as head of the family Napoleon should name him as heir, but his brother refused. Then when in May 1803 war with England resumed, Joseph was put in charge of preparing the invasion forces and was at Boulogne in May 1804 when the constitution of Year XII making Napoleon hereditary emperor was approved in the Senate. In November this was confirmed by plebiscite and Joseph acquired the rank of Grand Elector of the Empire and the title of his Serene Imperial Highness, Prince Joseph-Napoleon.

A RELUCTANT KING

After his coronation in Paris on 2 December 1804, Napoleon offered Joseph the throne of the Kingdom of Italy but he refused because this would have meant renouncing his claims as Napoleon's heir in France. When the crown of Naples and Sicily became vacant a year later, Napoleon was not prepared to accept another refusal. In a private interview in Paris on 30 January 1806, he instructed André Miot,[38] whom he had appointed to serve as Joseph's Minister of War in Naples, to give his brother the following message:

> Tell him that I am making him King of Naples and a Grand Elector of the Empire, and that I will make no change to his situation in France: but tell him also that the slightest hesitation, the slightest indecision and he will lose everything.... If he accepts, I shall call him Napoleon and he will become my son.... It was his refusal to accept the throne of Italy that forced me to nominate Eugène as my son. But I am determined to nominate someone else if Joseph refuses. All feelings of affection must now give way to *raison d'Etat*. I only recognise as relatives those who serve me. It is no longer the name of Bonaparte, but only that of Napoleon that binds my family together now. It is not with the thing in my breeches that I make sons, but with my fingers. I cannot now love anyone whom I do not esteem. Joseph must forget all the bonds of childhood and make himself worthy of my esteem.

The emperor would make available 40,000 men led by Marshal Masséna for the invasion, but warned Joseph to ensure that 'Masséna be prevented from stealing' in view of the 'shocking plundering' for which he had been responsible in Venice: 'I do not fear my generals and I will not indulge them.' The emperor also decided to send his fellow Corsican Antoine Christophe Saliceti to Naples, but

[35] 27 March 1802. [36] 2 August 1802.

[37] Josephine Tascher de la Pagerie (1763–1814), widow of the Vicomte de Beauharnais, had married Napoleon on 9 March 1796.

[38] See below pp. 165–6.

warned that Joseph should watch him closely and not allow him to steal: 'He is a man of character who will prove useful, but he has only agreed to go because he thinks he can steal another few millions even though he has already made himself rich enough.'

Napoleon's understanding of empire was very clearly set out when he explained what he expected of Naples and its rulers: 'I desire that he will make the people of Naples pay for everything needed by my troops and my State and that he should not squander money fattening *frippons*.' Miot was to impress on Joseph that 'I intend to create a family of kings, or rather of Viceroys, since the king of Italy, the king of Naples and others whom I have yet to name will form part of a federal system (système fédératif).'[39]

Talleyrand, Napoleon's Foreign Minister, offered similar but also contradictory advice: 'He recommended that the King follow a course of blind devotion and count on no demonstration of tenderness. . . . Once on the throne of Naples, he should not make any constitution, leave the nobility and all institutions as they are and only give office to Frenchmen. If he gives any to Neapolitans, he will have to rely on local factions.'[40]

When he reached Naples on 15 February, Joseph informed the emperor that he had at once attended a mass celebrated by the Cardinal Archbishop 'and I made San Gennaro a very nice present'.[41] He believed that public opinion was the key to consolidating the occupation, and that this could be won over by wooing the propertied classes. As well, Joseph was mindful of the need to satisfy 'the five hundred thousand souls who make up the population of the capital', so he lowered the price of oil and bread and adopted more effective measures against the Barbary pirates whose raids threatened the livelihood of the Neapolitan fishermen and sailors.[42]

The emperor wanted more strenuous measures: 'Arm your forts! Disarm, DISARM, the Neapolitans! Believe me, you will never hold on to the country just by winning over public opinion, because sooner or later you will have an insurrection.'[43] He told Joseph that he must raise taxes as soon as possible and was convinced that at least 30,000,000 francs could be had at once from Naples. 'Naples is richer than Vienna or Milan.' To raise the money Joseph should do what Napoleon claimed he had done himself in Cairo during the Egyptian expedition: 'deport fifteen thousand *lazzaroni*, surround the city with mortar batteries and seize all lands belonging to the royal domain'.[44]

The imperial decree of 30 March 1806 that made Joseph king also laid down the terms on which he held the throne of Naples. The decree, to which the imperial administration in Paris always subsequently referred simply as the 'constitution of 30 March 1806', reserved to the emperor command of the French army in

[39] ANP: AFiv 1714d: Notes prises chez M. le Conte Miot de Melito pendant son séjour à Naples 1806–8.
[40] Ibid., Talleyrand to Miot.
[41] ANP: AFiv 1714c: 16 February 1806.
[42] Ibid. 22 February 1806.
[43] ANP: AFiv 1714d: 17 March 1806.
[44] Ibid., Miot Journal, 17 March 1806.

Naples as well as the courts and required Naples to provide the imperial treasury with an annual revenue of 1,000,000 francs, to be paid directly to the emperor 'in compensation for military expenses and for his personal distribution'.[45]

Like Eugène Beauharnais in Milan, the king of Naples was required to consult the emperor before introducing any new law or making any appointment. During Joseph's brief reign the legislation needed to refashion the Neapolitan monarchy along the lines of the centralized bureaucratic autocracy that had emerged from the revolution in France was introduced. But there were exceptions and Joseph successfully resisted the emperor's demands that he introduce conscription and the *Code Civil*. When Joseph left Naples for Spain in May 1808 most of the new legislation was still to be implemented and order had barely been restored in the Calabrian provinces.

Joseph's transfer from Naples to Madrid in the spring of 1808 was determined by the broader reorganization of the empire after the defeat of Prussia in October 1806 and the peace with Russia concluded at Tilsit in July 1807. This left England alone against France and meant that Napoleon was now free to pursue the project of the Continental blockade in the attempt to destroy Britain's trade. The peremptory demand in August 1807 that the Tagus be closed to British shipping was simply the pretext for the French invasion of Portugal and Spain.

In Italy, the end of the alliance with Spain opened the way for France to occupy Livorno and annex Tuscany and the Papal States while in Spain, the overthrow of the king started the chain of events that would take Joseph Bonaparte from Naples to Madrid. The emperor had first informed Joseph of the project in Venice in December 1807, but the decision was not confirmed until the following May.[46] Joseph Bonaparte entered Madrid on 20 July 1808, but eleven days later he was forced to abandon the city for safer quarters and did not return until the following January.[47] Joachim Murat meanwhile was making his way to Naples.

JOACHIM MURAT

Joachim Murat was born in 1767 at La Bastide-Fortunière (now La Bastide-Murat) near Cahors. The son of a provincial merchant and innkeeper, his mother wanted him to be a priest and Murat studied briefly at a seminary in Toulouse before joining the army.[48] A forthright anti-royalist, Murat's career began to progress after the flight of Louis XVI. He fought in Belgium and Holland and rose through the ranks, but his strong Jacobin sympathies put him at risk after the fall of Robespierre. It was the attempted coup of 12–13 Vedémiaire Year III

[45] ASN, Min Esteri f. 5490 fascic 193 Champagny to di Gallo (29 March 1809); see also Rambaud (1911), 214.

[46] ANP: AFiv 1714d: 16 December 1807, Miot.

[47] Grab (2003), 130: Joseph—known henceforth in Spain as *Pepe Botella*—returned to Madrid in January 1809 and remained there until 1813.

[48] 21st Light Cavalry regiment, the *Chasseurs d'Auvergne*; see Tulard (1983), 7.

(5 October 1795) when the Convention in Paris was threatened by a royalist insurrection that caused the careers of Joachim Murat and Napoleon Bonaparte to cross. General Paul Barras turned for help to Bonaparte, but it was Murat's action in seizing the forty guns in the artillery depot at Sablons that provided Napoleon with the 'whiff of grapeshot' needed to disperse the insurrection.[49]

Murat was quickly rewarded. In February 1796 he commanded the cavalry in the campaign in northern Italy and became part of the inner group of Bonaparte loyalists. In April 1798 he joined the expedition to Egypt, where he distinguished himself and survived a pistol shot that passed from one cheek to the other.[50]

The Coup of 18–19 Brumaire was the next step. On 9 November 1799 Bonaparte addressed the Council of Five Hundred that had been convened in the chateau of Saint-Cloud and proposed a change of government. But he utterly failed to win over the deputies who began to heckle. On orders from Napoleon's younger brother Lucien, Murat escorted the shaken general to safety before returning with a detachment of grenadiers to empty the chamber and announce: 'Citizens, you are dissolved.'[51]

Murat's promotions and rewards increased. He was appointed Commander-in-Chief of the Consular Guard and on 18 January 1800 he married Bonaparte's youngest sister, Caroline.[52] The Murats took up residence in the Tuilleries and were given a large country mansion by the First Consul. Still on active service, during the winter of 1799–1800 Murat was busy preparing for the coming campaign at Dijon and Chalons. On 20 April 1800 he was appointed lieutenant general in chief of the *Armée d'Italie* and commander of the cavalry. He took part in the crossing of the Alps and after pursuing the retreating Austrians entered Milan on 2 June. He fought at Marengo (14 June), but was then ordered back to Paris to take command of the division of grenadiers.

Murat's next appointment was to the Army of Observation in Italy.[53] He occupied Bologna and then Florence in January 1801, where he dictated the armistice with the Kingdom of Naples and the more punitive terms that Napoleon imposed in the Treaty of Florence.[54] Murat was also given the difficult mission of reassuring the Pope of the emperor's friendly intentions. Back in Florence he oversaw the creation of the Kingdom of Etruria, before moving to Milan where he quickly fell out with Melzi d'Eril, the Lombard patrician whom Bonaparte had nominated President of the Italian Republic when it was founded in January 1802.

In August 1803 Murat returned to Paris, where Caroline had amassed an impressive collection of properties, furnishings, and art works, and had taken up residence in the opulent Hotel Thelusson in the rue de la Victoire. New honours

[49] Tulard (1983), 7–24. [50] Ibid. 43. [51] Ibid. 48.

[52] Maria Annunziata Bonaparte (1782–1839): the religious marriage was only celebrated two years later, on 4 January 1802, when Louis Bonaparte married Hortense de Beauharnais.

[53] 20 November 1800.

[54] Tulard (1983), 61. The armistice of Foligno, 18 February 1801; Treaty of Florence, 29 May 1801.

followed and in January 1804 Murat was appointed to the lucrative post of military governor of Paris, which was how he came to be directly involved in the kidnapping and execution of the Duke of Enghien in March 1804.[55] As commandant of the chateau of Vincennes, Murat was responsible for selecting the court martial that would sentence the Bourbon prince. He first prevaricated but then complied with Napoleon's demands, making himself both an accomplice and a target for later royalist vengeance.[56]

The royalist conspiracy provided Napoleon with the pretext for establishing the empire, as a result of which Murat was nominated Marshal of the Empire and Imperial Grand Admiral. In March 1805 he purchased the Elysée Palace where he, Caroline, and their three children took up residence.[57] When the war against Austria resumed in September 1805, Murat and his cavalry participated in the French victories at Ulm and Austerlitz. But he was deeply slighted when the emperor's step-son, Eugène Beauharnais, was made Viceroy of Italy, nor was he satisfied when Napoleon made him Grand Duke of Berg.[58]

The Grand Duchy secured Napoleon's control of the Rhine, but despite Berg's economic and industrial importance Murat was disappointed, his ambitious and jealous wife even more so. He made his triumphal entry into Düsseldorf on 24 March, but he spent little time in the Duchy, which was administered directly from Paris by the French Minister of Finance, Gandin, because Napoleon claimed that when Murat acted alone 'he only makes a mess of things'.[59] However, Murat did manage to secure a personal fortune reputedly worth 3,000,000 francs by 1808, and his successor, Count Jacques Claude Beugnot, claimed that he had 'squeezed the Grand Duchy like an orange until the pips cracked'.[60]

Caroline Bonaparte never visited Berg, but remained in Paris where she was reputedly the lover first of General Jounot and then of the dashing young Austrian ambassador, Count Clemenz von Metternich. But both she and Murat were now deeply involved in the rivalries that had emerged within the imperial family. They were hostile to Josephine and the Beauharnais, and were also jealous of Louis Bonaparte, the king of Holland, who had married Josephine's daughter Hortense and whose son, Napoleon Charles, the heirless Napoleon seemed inclined to adopt.[61]

By September 1806 Murat was back in arms, and his cavalry fought at Jena (14 October) and Prenzlow (29 October 1806). En route to Russia, Napoleon's armies were greeted as liberating heroes in Poland, and Jean Tulard claims that the

[55] The discovery in March 1804 of a royalist plot against the First Consul in which generals Pichegru and Moreau were both implicated led Napoleon to order the kidnapping and execution of the Bourbon Duke of Enghien.

[56] Tulard (1983), 70. According to Talleyrand the execution was 'worse than a crime, it was a mistake'.

[57] Ibid. 73: the children were Achille, Letitia, and Lucien—Louise was born in 1805.

[58] 15 March 1806: a newly created principality that included the Duchies of Berg and Cleves, which were ceded to France by Prussia under the terms of the Treaty of Pressburg.

[59] Tulard (1983), 65. [60] Ibid. 63. [61] Ibid. 94.

tumultuous welcome that Murat received in Warsaw converted him to the cause of Polish unification and independence.[62] But whatever hope he had of becoming king of Poland vanished when the war with Russia ended.[63] Murat returned to Paris, where Caroline was now a major figure in both the imperial court and the city's social and cultural life. Without leaving Paris Murat showed new interest in the affairs of his Grand Duchy, where he was represented by an able administrator and fellow Cahorsin, Jean-Antoine-Michel Agar.[64]

Duty next took Murat to Spain where he acted as the emperor's lieutenant at Bayonne in February 1808. On 2 May Murat's Polish cavalry, Egyptian Mamelukes, and dragoons savagely crushed the popular rising in Madrid,[65] and on the same day the emperor offered him a choice: the throne of Naples or Portugal. Napoleon urged his brother-in-law to take the former: Naples, he said, was 'much better than Spain' and would soon be reunited with Sicily. Nor need Murat fear that his military career would suffer, since his wife Caroline 'is quite capable, should need arise, to be regent'.

Unknown to Murat, Napoleon had previously offered the throne of Naples to his brother Lucien on condition that he divorce his wife, but Lucien had refused.[66] There was no universal rejoicing in the Bonaparte camp when it was known that Murat was be king, however, and many felt that Caroline should have been named regent. The youngest of Napoleon's sisters, she was also the closest to him. Talleyrand claimed that she had 'the head of Cromwell on the shoulders of a beautiful woman', while Napoleon himself later claimed that 'She had a lot of drive, heaps of personality and boundless ambition'.[67]

Caroline also had excellent contacts at the highest level of the imperial administration. She was a close confidante of Napoleon's much feared chief of police, Joseph Fouché, and of the long-standing Bonaparte family patron, Antoine Christophe Saliceti, who was already in Naples. Murat, by contrast, had few political skills and would have to seek his own advisers since Napoleon provided none. Although he tried to keep Caroline's political role to a minimum, she was from the start the more powerful of the two and in Naples would become the dominant partner.

After returning to Paris, Murat and Caroline left for Italy at the end of August. They made their way to Naples through Turin, Reggio Emilia, Ancona, and Rome, where the Pope did not offer to receive them. From Rome they continued to Gaeta, then by way of Capua and Aversa to Naples, where they made their triumphal entry on 6 September 1808.[68]

[62] Tulard (1983), 104. [63] Ibid. 108–9. [64] See below.
[65] Tulard (1983), 123. [66] Ibid. 124. [67] Ibid. 159. [68] Ibid. 137.

8

The Costs of Empire

THE TREATY OF BAYONNE

The Kingdom's colonial status had already been made clear in the obligations placed on Joseph Bonaparte. Like the empire's other colonies, its function was to satisfy the insatiable demands of the imperial treasuries and armies, enforce the Continental blockade against British goods, supply French manufactures with raw materials, and French producers with markets. With the accession of Joachim Murat in 1808, however, these terms became even more onerous and were formalized in the treaty that Murat signed at Bayonne on 30 March 1808.

The treaty granted Murat the throne of Naples in perpetuity with succession through the male line only, although Caroline Bonaparte was to succeed as queen in the event of his death. The treaty was offensive and defensive, and obliged the king of Naples in time of war to contribute 18,000 infantry, 3,000 cavalry, and a train of twenty-five pieces of artillery to France, the costs to be met entirely by the Neapolitan treasury wherever they served. The Neapolitan government was in addition required to meet the full cost of the upkeep of the French troops stationed in the Kingdom, and to build and supply six ships of the line, the first two to be delivered to France by the end of 1809. Finally, the king of Naples had to undertake to enforce in every way 'the blockade against England to ensure the destruction of its trade'.[1]

The secret clauses attached to the treaty placed all of the Murats' now extensive property in France in the emperor's hands as a surety for their good conduct. The inventory of their assets illustrates the rewards acquired by those who rose to high rank in the emperor's service and included 'their palace in Paris, their house at Neuilly, the Stables at Artois, the estate at La Motte' and 'in general all the goods that they possess in France without exception and including all moveables, furniture and furnishings in their palaces and houses, all paintings, statues and any other artistic or decorative object whatever its nature'.[2]

The emperor made some concessions. He promised Murat the Farnese properties in Rome that belonged to the Neapolitan Bourbons and agreed to an annual subsidy of half a million francs, which effectively halved the annual charge of land

[1] BSPN: ms XXI B5. [2] Ibid.

rents that Naples had to pay personally to the emperor. However, all the properties and annual rents owed to the emperor were to be paid in full to the imperial treasury by January 1809. In addition, Murat was required to furnish rents to fund 'six Great Fiefs of the Empire' in the Kingdom[3] and to contribute to funding the *Legion d'Honneur*.[4]

OPENING QUARRELS

The first disputes with Paris focused on the chaotic state in which Joseph had left the Kingdom's finances. Before leaving for Spain at the end of July Joseph's finance minister, Pierre-Louis Roederer, handed over direction of finances to Prince Pignatelli. Although he admitted to the emperor that the bank had suffered because of the withdrawals needed to meet the cost of Joseph's transfer to Spain, Roederer nonetheless insisted that the financial situation of the Kingdom was flourishing.[5]

Pignatelli soon discovered that Roederer had left no accounts, and that before leaving for Madrid Joseph had made generous settlements in favour of his ministers, favourites, and mistresses.[6] The French *chargé d'affaires*, D'Aubusson de la Feuillette,[7] later reported to Paris in scandalized terms that Joseph's lover, Maria Giulia Colonna, Duchess of Atri—who bore him two children—had been given a gift of 5,000 ducats, while another woman 'who was not even a mistress' received 2,000 ducats. D'Aubusson estimated that in total Joseph's largesse amounted to as much as 11,000,000 francs.[8]

Roederer did not record what he himself had received, although he did inform Joseph that he needed to raise a loan from the Swiss banker Falconnet because he had no desire to arrive at the Court of the King of Spain 'like an indebted old courtesan'.[9]

Early in September Murat complained to Napoleon of the 'terrible state of my finances'. But these complaints carried little weight since Murat had left a similar

[3] The creation of 'imperial feofs' in the satellite kingdoms was standard practice and similar obligations were placed on the Kingdom of Italy after Austerlitz where twelve imperial duchies were established. See Zaghi (1986), 367.

[4] ASN, Min Esteri f. 5490 fascic.193: di Gallo to Champagny, 25 January 1809; memo sur les dettes.

[5] *ANP*: AFiv 1714a: 27 July 1808, Roederer to Napoleon.

[6] ANP: Fonds Joseph Bonaparte 381 AP3: 14 June 1808, Roederer to Joseph Bonaparte, and ibid., 2 July 1808. Amongst the recipients were the Generals Matthieu, Saligny, Jourdan, and Reynier, the Foreign Minister Di Gallo, and the banker Falconnet, 'who of all the merchants in Naples has been the most zealous in the service of Your Majesty'. Additional gifts of 3,000 ducats in annual rents had been given to the Duke of Noia, 4,000 ducats in rents to General Dumas, another cash gift of 18,975 ducats to di Gallo, and a fictitious sale of domain land valued at 50,440 ducats (but really worth 80,000 ducats) to the Minister of Justice, Francesco Ricciardi.

[7] D'Aubusson de la Feuillette served as *chargé d'affaires* from January 1808 until he was replaced by Hue de Grosbois in 1810.

[8] AAEP: CP, Naples 133: D'Aubusson to Champagny, 2 January 1809.

[9] ANP: Fonds Joseph Bonaparte 381: 7 July, Roederer acknowledged that the emperor had given him 55,000 *livres* of rent and estates worth 40,000 *livres*.

situation of financial chaos in Berg.[10] Pignatelli warned Murat, however, that a month previously the emperor had suspended payment of the half-million ducats that he had promised towards the cost of maintaining French troops in the Kingdom, making the Kingdom's financial situation untenable. The principal of a loan that Joseph's government had raised in Holland in 1806 had been exhausted, and Joseph's considerable removal costs had left the treasury and the banks without cash. Declaring the situation to be beyond him, Pignatelli asked to resign.[11]

D'Aubusson confirmed Murat's description of the situation: 'It is my duty to say, and with the greatest regret, that a change was overdue here.' The financial situation was desperate, there was no proper accounting, everything was haphazard and confused, and pay for the army and public works was all in arrears. Joseph's administration was filled with 'favourites and cliques', the Council of State 'was for the greater part composed of men with no vision or ability, who were opposed to any form of innovation or liberal ideas, and especially to the establishment of the Napoleonic Code without changes being made to it'. Murat's description had 'contained nothing that is not accurate.... Since Joseph had never reviewed his troops, no-one knew who was being paid and who was not', but the army's pay was at least nine months in arrears when he left for Spain.[12]

An even sharper confrontation followed when Murat announced on 15 November that he had lowered the interest paid on the Public Debt from 5 to 3%. The French ambassador in Naples, D'Aubusson, again defended Murat, but Napoleon was incensed. Murat, he insisted, had acted without his permission and he denounced the reduction in interest rates as a violation of Treaty of Bayonne that tarnished the honour of the empire.[13]

The wrangling over the Kingdom's obligations and failure to meet them became interminable. In the first of many stern warnings, the Imperial Minister for External Affairs, Count Jean-Baptiste de Champagny, informed the Marchese di Gallo, the Neapolitan ambassador in Paris, that Murat's failure to settle the outstanding arrears was considered by the emperor to be a second violation of the Treaty of Bayonne. Champagny warned Murat that the emperor 'wishes it to be understood that whatever the King of Naples might consider to be the advantage of building roads or establishments of education, he must first and foremost ensure that my troops are paid and that there are no arrears'. He instructed Murat to implement the terms of the Treaty of Bayonne at once and in full and to introduce the Napoleonic Civil Code without further delay or modification.[14]

In December 1808 Murat requested permission to appoint Agar, his former minister of finance in Berg. When the imperial administration in Paris approved, Caroline's secretary noted that 'Agar's nomination was indispensable here, even

10 See Schmidt (1905), 68.

11 AAEP CP, Naples 133: D'Aubusson to Champagny 24 February 1809. He described Prince Pignatelli of Cerchiara as 'absolument incapable et *frippon*'.

12 Ibid.—1 January.

13 Le Brethon, vi. 410: Murat to Napoleon, 15 November 1808; D'Aubusson to Champagny.

14 Ibid.

though we have had to wait long time. There is no-one capable of taking on this ministry, which is a real Augean stable. Even Agar, despite his intelligence and energy, will have to work day and night for at least two years before he gets things in order. It is not an enviable task and I defy those who are against him from stirring up envy.'[15]

Murat again pointed out that his government ministries required 1,000,000 ducats a month and there were currently only 193,000 ducats available.[16] His protest was ignored, and when the first payments to France under the terms of the Treaty of Bayonne fell due (1st January 1809), Champagny formally protested that the Neapolitan government had defaulted on its obligations. Paris now demanded the immediate transfer of the estates required to fund the six Imperial fiefs and the settlement of the arrears owed for the maintenance of French troops.

Di Gallo replied that 'everything which his Imperial and Royal Majesty orders will be done'. But he also argued that the demands were unreasonable. The heavy expenses incurred during the first six months of the reign, the payments made to cover the arrears on pay for the army and civil administration, the cost of the military operation to regain Capri, and preparations for an expedition to invade Sicily had prevented Murat from meeting other obligations. He closed by warning Champagny that malicious gossip was being spread in Paris by sympathizers of the *ci-devant* monarchy who were looking to discredit the new ruler.[17]

In February 1809 D'Aubusson wrote to defend Murat's achievements in Naples. Amongst these he listed the raising of two corps of an elite praetorian guard (the *Veliti*[18]) and the reorganization of the Provincial Militia, which had taken over public order duties from the French regiments being withdrawn for the campaign against Austria in northern Italy.

Reassurance came from Paris too, first from Saliceti, who reported early in March that he had spoken to the emperor and that all was well: 'The Emperor is the centre of all the dynasties that he has founded and he wishes to direct the operations of each to ensure that they work together to create the great system that will set the destiny of the world.'[19]

Marshal Berthier also wrote to reassure Murat of the emperor's favourable disposition: 'This, Sire, is what you must do: Be a King amongst your subjects, but with the Emperor be a Vice-Roy. Be a Frenchman and never a Neapolitan. Consult his Imperial Majesty in everything: those things which may seem at this moment harmful to your subjects are in reality to their advantage, because everything that the Emperor desires forms part of the vast plan of his projects and his ideas, while the well-being of the nations that are governed by his dynasty depends on the success of his lofty vision: it is for us simply to follow and obey his orders and plans without trying to understand their depth.'[20]

15 Le Brethon, vi. 458: 24 February 1809.
16 Le Brethon, vi. 478: Murat to Napoleon, 6 January 1809.
17 ASN: Min Esteri f. 5490, fascic 193: 5 February 1809.
18 See p. 253.
19 Le Brethon, viii. 3835, 53; Saliceti to Murat from Paris, 5 March 1809.
20 Ibid., 3838, 59; Berthier to Murat, 5 March 1809.

The controversy dragged on throughout Murat's reign without resolution. At the end of 1809 the imperial administrators calculated that the total Neapolitan debt had risen from 5.7 to 6.5 million francs. In 1810 relations became even more strained and in January Champagny threatened military action and warned the new Neapolitan ambassador in Paris, the Duke of Monteleone, that the emperor 'considers all commitments made to him to be inviolable and he is accustomed to make even the most powerful Princes honour their obligations. Should the government of the Two Sicilies continue to refuse to meet its obligations, he will be forced to order his generals to take the appropriate measures to ensure the payment of these sums.' On 22 January the French ambassador D'Aubusson and the *chargé d'affaires* Gosbois were recalled to Paris.[21]

In April 1810 Murat made a final appeal that the contribution of 1,200,000 francs to the *Legion d'Honneur* be waived, since his government was maintaining 10,000 French troops, as well as paying for 50,000 Neapolitan soldiers, the navy, the cost of preparations for the invasion of Sicily, and the cost for the ships being built for France at Castellamare under the terms of the Treaty of Bayonne. To reduce current costs, Murat again asked permission to put his army on a peace footing and to dismiss the French employees who duplicated his own staff and cost 1,800,000 francs a year.[22] Paris refused to acknowledge any of these pleas, and on 23 June Naples was forced to acknowledge debts of more than 9,000,000 francs.[23]

TRADING DISPUTES

Paris and Naples were also in dispute over commercial matters and the enforcement of the blockade. At least initially, Napoleon had been convinced that the Kingdom of Naples was a land of untold natural wealth waiting only to be exploited. That illusion was still alive in 1809 when a report prepared by the *Council for Trade and Industry* in Paris described Naples as: 'the promised land . . . unlike Peru where you have to dig for gold in the bowels of the earth in Naples it lies glittering on the surface'.[24]

Those expectations were soon disappointed, but nonetheless French commercial interests focused on the Kingdom's raw materials: olive oil for the Marseilles

[21] ASN, Min Esteri f.5490 fascic. 193: Champagny to Monteleone, 10 January 1810.

[22] ANP: AFiv 1714a, 8 April 1810.

[23] ANP, 31 AP 575: Extraits de la convention signée à Paris 23 juin 1810. These included an outstanding debt of 2,519,444 francs to be settled in 'domain lands situated near Naples', an annual debt of 1,280,000 francs to the *Legion d'Honneur*, 1,275,035 francs for the upkeep of French troops, 3 million francs for the repayment of loans from France, to be consolidated on the Public Debt; and a further debt of 1,289,562 francs to the Kingdom of Italy for the cost of maintaining Neapolitan troops during the campaign of 1809.

[24] ANP: F12 549–50.210, Mémoire sur un project de traité de commerce avec le Royaume de Naples.

soap industry, silk yarn for the Lyons weaving industries, and wool ('very white, fine and strong') for the cloth industries of Aix-la-Chapelle, Rouen, Liège, and Beauvais, as well as liquorice and cotton. But it was also believed that Naples could offer markets for 'the fine and middle range woollens' from Abbeville, Elbeuf, Languedoc, Liège, and Aix-la-Chapelle, as well as for other 'small cloths' and for 'tanned leather goods'.[25]

The emperor's irritation increased, therefore, when Murat refused to acknowledge French commercial privileges and failed to enforce the Continental blockade. As early as December 1808 Murat was denying that he had permitted British goods to enter his Kingdom: 'Sire, I can only answer your accusations by saying that I am neither a rebel, nor an ingrate, nor am I mad, and that I would indeed deserve to be sent to the *Petites Maisons* (the madhouse) and every ignominy had I been capable of such actions.'[26]

Champagny asked D'Aubusson directly whether Murat was allowing British and colonial goods to be freely imported, but the French *chargé d'affaires* flatly denied that this was true. When Champagny renewed the accusation a few days later, D'Aubusson again denied it.[27] M. Blanc, the French consul in Naples, agreed that he had not seen any 'English colonial goods' in Naples, but added, 'I have had cause, however, to inform His Excellency M. D'Aubusson la Feuillade of my concerns regarding the interlope trade carried out by the English with the ports of Trieste, Fiume and other ports in the Morea.' He claimed that it was common knowledge that there were huge stocks of English goods in both Sicily and Malta, many of which were being smuggled into the Kingdom. But they were almost impossible to trace since he did not have agents in every Neapolitan port, and in any case the goods were landed on empty beaches.[28]

The priorities of the imperial administration were clearly set out in the instructions given to Blanc's successor, M. Doriol. He was to ensure that 'the Imperial laws against trade with England are being fully observed', to check personally the certificates of origin for all goods entering the city, and to report to Paris 'anything that might be of interest'. While 'the close ties between the emperor and king Murat meant that the Neapolitan government could have no interest contrary to that of the French government, laxities might still occur through the negligence or corruption of the secondary authorities', which should be reported.[29] Doriol needed little encouragement and sent off a string of complaints about the failure of the 'intermediary authorities to observe the Imperial decrees', claiming that large quantities of English contraband goods were coming into Apulia from Albania and the Morea.[30]

The consul's complaints raised another dispute. In 1806 Joseph's government had abolished all existing commercial treaties, and stated that trade relations

[25] ANP: F12 549–50.210, Mémoire sur un project de traité de commerce avec le Royaume de Naples.
[26] Le Brethon, vi, n.3651, 442: Murat to Napoleon, 9 December 1808.
[27] AAEP: CP Naples, 132: 7 December 1808, 11 December 1808.
[28] AAEP: CC Naples, 39, 1806–11, 102: 6 December 1808.
[29] Ibid. 120: March 1809.
[30] Ibid. 135: 12 May 1809, Doriol to Champagny.

between Naples and France would be regulated by a new agreement. In 1808 Paris had imposed a highly disadvantageous commercial treaty on the Kingdom of Italy, and was eager to extend the same terms to Naples but Murat resisted.[31]

In July 1809, D'Aubusson cut across these exchanges with a report on the damage that renewal of war with Austria had caused to Neapolitan trade:

The situation is getting worse by the day. The King tells me that he is hoping that His Majesty will permit him to allow American ships to enter the ports so that he may trade with them to raise some money to meet the cost of the administration, and especially to pay the army. The Tour d'Auvergne battalion is virtually without clothing or boots.[32]

In September, Murat requested the emperor's permission to trade with American vessels:

Sire, the commerce of my Kingdom is absolutely nil: the granaries, depots and warehouses are filled with goods but the land is no longer cultivated and there are even some fears for the harvest. As a result it is impossible to raise taxes. In a word . . . I no longer know how to pay my troops and at the same time keep the government going.

He requested that he at least be allowed to sell olive oil to the Americans.[33]

Napoleon refused Murat permission to trade with the Americans and instead demanded that the import duties on French cloth and other manufactures in Naples be halved. Murat was astounded: 'If your Majesty's intentions are put into effect, he will with a single order have pronounced the total ruin of my Kingdom.' Attached to Murat's letter was a memo drafted by Agar, which argued that 'on the day when French manufactured goods are admitted free of duty, we shall have to abandon all forms of manufacture in this kingdom'.[34] Privately Agar told Murat that the French demands would be a 'mortal blow' that would leave 60,000 without employment in the province of Naples alone and damage even the production of coarse cloth used by the 'inferior classes'.[35]

Nonetheless, on 12 November the French *chargé d'affaires* 'delivered a demand that French cloth be allowed to enter Naples free of duty' on the grounds that this duty contravened traditional French privileges. He also raised new complaints against infringements of French consular privileges, navigation rights, and the denial of warehousing facilities to French ships.[36]

The situation deteriorated further when in April 1810 the emperor doubled the duties on Neapolitan cotton imported to France. Murat objected that this measure 'can have no object other than that of destroying this new industry which I have tried to establish in the kingdom'.[37] In October, the emperor escalated the commercial offensive, decreeing that France enjoyed the exclusive privilege of

31 Zaghi (1986), 132.
32 AAEP: CP Naples, 133: D'Aubusson to Champagny, 1 July 1809.
33 ANP: AFiv 1714a, 16 September 1809. 34 ANP: AFiv 1714a, 28 October 1809.
35 ANP: 31AP43, Mosbourg to Murat 27 October 1809.
36 AAEP: CP Naples, 133, 12 November 1809. 37 ANP: AFiv 1714a, 8 April 1810.

exporting cotton and silk cloth to Naples without duties, a measure that Murat claimed 'will deprive my treasury of a revenue which is not borne by French trade but by my subjects who are the consumers of these goods'.[38]

Murat again begged the emperor to relieve him of the cost of maintaining French troops in the Kingdom, which since 1808 had risen from 17,404 to 40,154 men: 'this makes it quite impossible to balance the budget of my state'.[39] During the autumn the situation in the Kingdom had become even more grave and a poor harvest now threatened a serious subsistence crisis in the capital. Murat renewed his pleas for permission to trade with the Americans and pointed out that imperial decrees requiring the destruction of all goods seized from English vessels had caused numerous bankruptcies in Naples. He complained bitterly about the behaviour of French agents in Naples, his principal target, although unnamed, being Consul Doriol: 'In the name of God, Sire, bring to an end the painful situation in which I find myself, I no longer have the strength to struggle against perfidy and bad faith!'[40]

November brought a further disappointment. Export licences arrived from Paris, but only for trade with Africa, the Ottoman Porte, and the Kingdom of Italy. However, permits were not required since Naples was at peace with all these states. By contrast, there were no permits for trade with Britain, even though licences issued in Bordeaux now permitted trade with Britain by way of American ships.[41]

The subsistence crisis facing Naples and the Kingdom was still serious in the early months of 1811, and Murat's government adopted a more hostile posture. The new *chargé d'affaires* Hue de Grosbois reported in January that the Neapolitan government was deliberately flouting the imperial decree that gave privileged status to French textiles.[42] In March, Doriol reported that the government was openly supporting the anti-French attitude of its officers.[43] In April exports of cotton seed had been banned, a measure Doriol believed was designed to destroy attempts to cultivate cotton in France and in the Papal States and was therefore contrary to the emperor's plan 'to encourage the production of colonial products in order to break the British monopoly'.[44]

In September, Doriol reported that the government had increased duties on colonial goods brought into Naples as prizes by French corsairs. Grain exports in ships of more than 60 tons had also been banned, which Doriol claimed was an attempt to exclude France from the carrying trade although Murat said it was to prevent large cargoes falling into the hands of British privateers. Doriol concluded that this measure would mean that the 8 to 10 million francs that France was losing each year on its trade with Naples would increase, while France 'must in

[38] ANP: AFiv 1714a, Murat to Napoleon, 20 October 1810. [39] Ibid., 31 October 1810.
[40] Ibid., Murat to Napoleon, 9 November 1810. [41] Ibid., 16 November 1810.
[42] AAEP: CP Naples, Gosbois to Duke of Cadore (formerly Champagny), 2 January 1811.
[43] AAEP: CC Naples, 39, 312: 21 March 1811. [44] AAEP: CP Naples, 136, 4 April 1811.

addition now pay for charters while her own ships rot in the harbour'. The quarantine regulations were also being used to deter French shipping.[45]

THE SICILIAN EXPEDITION, 1810

In 1810 another dangerous quarrel developed that did even greater damage to Murat's relations with the emperor. The cause was the expedition that Murat prepared for the invasion of Sicily in the summer of 1810. As one of the emperor's most renowned commanders, it was not surprising that Murat should have been eager to demonstrate his military prowess in his own kingdom. In October 1808 he had achieved an easy but important propaganda success by recapturing Capri from the small British garrison that Joseph had been unable to dislodge. However, the emperor's new war against Austria in the spring of 1809 had revealed the difficulty of reconciling the Kingdom's military needs with those of the empire. The recall of the French forces had left the Kingdom dangerously exposed to counter-attack by the British and the Sicilians, who had immediately seized the opportunity to assemble a major expeditionary force.[46] The threatened Anglo-Sicilian invasion never materialized, but nonetheless it convinced Murat of the need to dislodge the British from Sicily.

By 1810, however, Murat had other compelling reasons for wanting to get the British and the Bourbons out of Sicily. For both Murat and Caroline Bonaparte, Napoleon's decision to resolve the problems posed by the absence of an heir by divorcing Josephine and marrying an Austrian princess was a double blow. Not only was the new marriage likely to produce the long-awaited Bonaparte heir, but even worse, the emperor's proposed bride, the Archduchess Marie Louise, was a favourite granddaughter of Queen Maria Carolina of Naples. Murat and Caroline were not alone in drawing the conclusion that this could be the prelude to an accommodation with the Neapolitan Bourbons that might easily cost them their throne. The danger was the greater because it was well known that Maria Carolina was at loggerheads with her English protectors and was widely suspected to be secretly negotiating with the emperor. For Murat, the conquest of Sicily was as much a dynastic as a military necessity.

When Napoleon announced his plan to divorce Josephine Beauharnais at the family conference held in Paris in December 1809, only Murat and Cambacérès openly opposed it. But when Murat travelled to Paris for the imperial wedding in March 1810, first on the list of his requests to the emperor was permission to go ahead with the invasion of Sicily. After lengthy waits and many calculated rebuffs, he finally got what he wanted and immediately returned to Naples to start preparations for the expedition.

45 AAEP: CC Naples, 39, 401, 22 October 1811; 413, 23 December 1811.

46 BNP; Fonds Italiens 1125 (vol. 2): Rapports au Roi 1809; Cavaignac to Murat, 6 July 1809.

The emperor's agreement was only provisional, however, and in April Colonel Leclerc was sent to Naples on a secret mission to report on the feasibility of the project. Leclerc's report reached Paris in May and convinced Napoleon that the expedition could not succeed. But he decided that it would be useful to let it proceed simply to force the English to divert troops from the Iberian peninsula to defend Sicily.[47]

When Murat returned to Naples he ordered his War Minister, Hector Daure, to prepare an invasion force of 22,000 men and to requisition transports for crossing the Straits of Messina. On 16 May Murat left Naples with the advance guard of his army, declaring that he would be in Palermo within two months. Early in June he established his headquarters at Scilla, above the Straits of Messina. In June the Imperial Minister of War, Baron Clarke, informed him that 15,000 French and 2,000 Corsican troops would be available for the expedition, command of which would be entrusted to a French general nominated by the emperor.[48]

This was a terrible blow to Murat, who was still unaware that the emperor was using the threatened invasion simply as a diversion. In that respect, at least, it was successful. Lord Liverpool suspended all transfers of men from Sicily to Spain and Portugal, and in anticipation that the invasion would be supported by the Toulon fleet the British blockade of Corfu was lifted to make more ships available to defend Sicily.[49]

In Calabria, however, Murat faced growing difficulties in keeping the expedition force on station. By August, the War Minister, Daure, had still not prepared a financial estimate, pay for the army was in arrears, and the military contractors had not been paid, nor had the owners or the crews of the transports, which fell easy prey to English and Bourbon warships.

The operation ended in fiasco and more recriminations. By the end of the summer Murat finally realized that the emperor had no intention of allowing him to carry out the invasion. He quarrelled with the French commander, General Grenier, and relations between the French and Neapolitan officers were deteriorating. The Toulon fleet never sailed, and by September the expedition was in danger of falling to pieces while disease, as usual, was taking a heavy toll.

On the night of 17 September General Cavaignac crossed the Straits with 3,500 men, by night, landing at dawn near Messina. When the beach-head came under heavy fire Cavaignac's force re-embarked and made its way back to the Calabrian shore with the loss of 600 men and officers captured. It was widely suspected that the sortie had merely been a feint to provide Murat with an excuse for disbanding the expedition, which he did on 1 October. The news provoked another outburst of imperial fury, and Napoleon accused Murat of disbanding the expedition without orders and as a result of causing Masséna to be defeated by the British in Portugal.[50]

[47] Tulard (1983), 164–6. [48] Rambaud (1911b), 435–47; Valente (1968), 164–9.

[49] PRO, WO 1, 308. Abstract of Royal Navy Intelligence Reports (Messina, 8 June 1810).

[50] Espitalier (1912), 59–80.

IMPERIAL DISCORDS 1809–1811

The crisis between Naples and Paris was coming to a head at a moment when the imperial project was running into problems on all sides. There were many causes: the uncertainties raised by Napoleon's Austrian marriage, the growing difficulties in Spain, and above all the strains felt throughout the empire as a result of renewed efforts to impose the Continental blockade.

In Italy, the empire's position had looked solid when Murat arrived in Naples in 1808. But in the following spring the situation changed dramatically when Austria took advantage of France's military commitments in Spain and Portugal to invade northern Italy. After defeating Prince Eugène at Salice, the Austrians briefly occupied Venetia. The invasion did not last long, but it caused widespread unrest and revealed the underlying fragility of French rule in Italy. At its height the whole of Emilia was in revolt and Bologna under siege, and the situation became even more chaotic in central Italy when Rome was annexed to France in May and Pope Pius VII made a prisoner.[51]

Napoleon's response was the counter-offensive that concluded with the victory at Wagram in July 1809, which quickly restored order in Italy and brought further territorial consolidation. The Kingdom of Italy now attained its fullest territorial reach, placing Prince Eugène in nominal command of territories that stretched from Sessia in the west to the Isonzo river in the east, from the Brenner in the north to Emilia-Romagna in the south.[52]

Stability, however, was never a lasting feature of Napoleon's imperial enterprise, and even in these years when the French empire reached its fullest extent the internal strains and contradictions were very visible. The single most important source of discontent was the emperor's determination to make the Continental blockade effective, which provoked resistance not only in France's imperial possessions but also within France itself, which since 1809 was suffering from economic recession that showed no signs of slackening.[53] Protests from French commercial interests forced the emperor to compromise, and a series of decrees between July and September 1810 introduced a system of special licences for trade with Britain. At the same time, the Fontainbleau Decree imposed severe new penalties in an attempt to control the massive contraband in British goods expanding throughout the empire.[54]

These contradictory measures placed new strains on the fabric of empire and on the system of imperial alliances, and in December 1810 the Tsar withdrew Russia from the Continental blockade. The new measures to enforce the blockade

[51] Zaghi (1986), 620–4.

[52] But still cut in two from west to east by the former Duchy of Parma and Piacenza, which had been annexed to France in 1808 following the Treaty of Schönbrunn (October 1809); Zaghi (1986), 370.

[53] Bergeron (1972), 207–15.

[54] St Cloud decree of July 1810, the Trianon Decrees: Woolf (1991), 141–52.

were also resisted in the satellite and annexed territories, and cost the emperor's brother, Louis, his crown in 1810 when he was forced to abdicate the throne of Holland. In Westphalia and Sweden Jerome and Bernadotte responded more circumspectly, but only the emperor's step-son and Viceroy in northern Italy, Prince Eugène, took the path of abject compliance.[55]

THE CRISIS: JUNE–JULY 1811

Murat's position had already become highly insecure because of the Sicilian expedition and it was rumoured in October 1810 that his French generals in Naples had been ordered to depose him.[56] It was widely expected that he would soon share the fate of the king of Holland, and in Paris the imperial bureaucracy seized on Murat's weakness to press its demands with greater force.

In February 1811 Baron de Durant was sent as imperial Minister Plenipotentiary to Naples with instructions that amounted to a bill of attainder. His orders repeated that the Kingdom's relations to France were fixed by the 'constitution of 30 March 1806', which recognized the Kingdom as part of the empire and made its crown revertible to the emperor's family. They listed the three sets of debts outstanding to the empire.[57] All were in arrears and most had not been paid. Nor had the Kingdom met its obligation to build two warships every year: it had failed to implement the blockade satisfactorily or to agree to a commercial treaty with France. The French minister was instructed to demand the immediate settlement of all debts owed the emperor and the imperial treasury, the immediate delivery of the ships, and energetic measures to enforce the blockade.[58]

A month later Grosbois reported that France was no longer considered a most favoured nation in Naples, that its envoys were treated coldly, the *Code Napoléon* was held openly in contempt, and that Murat did not disassociate himself from such attitudes.[59]

Following the birth of Napoleon's son on 20 March, Murat travelled to Paris but returned to Naples at the end of May before the baptism and despite the emperor's orders that he remain in Paris. The long expected crisis then came to a head on 14 June when Murat decreed that all French citizens in government service must apply for Neapolitan nationality.[60]

The emperor's response was devastating. On 6 July he decreed that all French subjects were citizens of the Kingdom of the Two Sicilies, a measure that

[55] Zaghi (1986), 367–8; Bergeron (1972), 207–15; Schroeder (1994), 402–12.

[56] *Notiziastorica* (1848), 121–3.

[57] These included the annual payment of 500,000 francs to the emperor; the debt to *the Legion d'Honneur;* and the payments owing for the maintenance of French troops in the Kingdom and for the Neapolitan troops serving outside the Kingdom.

[58] On 17 July the emperor was informed that the Neapolitan debt to France had been recalculated at 6,037,500 francs.

[59] AAEP: Naples CP, 136, Grosbois to Cadore, 11 March 1811.

[60] Ibid., 14 June 1811.

'humiliated Murat before the whole of Europe'.[61] When the emperor learned that Murat had ordered his senior officers to take a new oath of loyalty, he gave orders for General Grenier to form an Army of Observation from the French troops already in the Kingdom and take up offensive positions.[62]

This was tantamount to a declaration of war and Naples was again an occupied territory. Faced by the emperor's threat of military action, Murat backed down and agreed to withdraw his decree on French employees. Contemporary accounts suggest he suffered a mental breakdown, threatened to shoot himself with a pistol, and after withdrawing to the palace of Capodimonte refused to speak to any of his ministers. He then dismissed Daure, the War Minister, for plotting against him, and replaced him with Antonio Maghella, a former protégé of Saliceti.[63]

Napoleon now gave the crisis a further twist when he accused Murat of stealing the Spanish crown jewels that Charles IV of Spain had entrusted to him for safekeeping during the uprising at Aranjuez in 1808. Their ownership was now in dispute between the emperor and his brother Joseph Bonaparte, but the jewels had disappeared and Murat was held responsible.[64]

This was the opportunity for Caroline Murat to exert her own power. She was now openly recognized to be the leader of the pro-French faction at Murat's court and in September 1811 she travelled to Paris to intercede with Napoleon on her husband's behalf. But the queen's intervention was not the only reason that Murat escaped the fate of the king of Holland. At the height of the crisis in July 1811 Baron Durand had reported on the strength of anti-French feeling and the growth of a nationalist awareness amongst the Neapolitans in reaction to the Emperor's demands.

> The King in truth deludes himself with the state of his country and seems to believe that he is strong enough to do without the co-operation of the French and rely entirely on the Neapolitans.

But he also warned against pushing the conflict too far since this would benefit only the English and the Court in Palermo.[65]

Durand's warning was heeded in Paris and it was probably the danger that the British and their Sicilian allies would be the main beneficiaries of the rift between Naples and Paris that secured Murat's throne for the time being. In any case, Paris began to make more conciliatory overtures and Marshal Pérignon was sent to inform Murat that the emperor had no intention of changing the status of the Kingdom and that Murat was king because the emperor wished it so. But the Marshal warned Murat to take full note of his duties: 'duties that the king of Holland had for a moment forgotten, with the result that he was immediately removed from the ranks of rulers and his Kingdom ceased to exist'. But Murat was also informed that the emperor had dismissed the Neapolitan ambassador in

[61] Cutolo (1937), 408. [62] Ibid. 411. [63] Ibid. 414. [64] Ibid. 417.
[65] AAEP: CP, Naples 137, Durand to Cadore, 9 July 1811.

Paris, the Duke of Campochiaro, and that Naples would be represented in the future by a mere Minister Plenipotentiary.

Murat continued vigorously to protest his treatment:

> I remain deeply saddened by your suspicions. We are currently working even at night in the shipyards to have the ships built... Sir, you are making impossible demands, and while we shall nevertheless do everything to comply with your orders you have utterly destroyed the equilibrium of my finances.[66]

1812

Paris was still unrelenting. In January 1812 the Imperial Ministry of War and the Navy demanded a further 437,306 ducats for the maintenance of the French Army of Observation. Murat had Agar[67] draw up a report on the contributions made to France that openly challenged the 'untruths' contained in the communications from Paris.

Agar pointed out that although the government's revenues had increased, no less than 80 per cent of the total budget was now being devoted to military expenditures. He argued that the comparisons made in Paris between Naples and France or the Kingdom of Italy were meaningless because they took no account of differences in populations and wealth. Huge areas of the Kingdom were uncultivated, the land tax yielded far less than the 4 per cent of agricultural production estimated for France, and indirect taxes were also lower per capita because consumption was less:

> For the most part the inhabitants of the Kingdom of Naples live off little, the people have few needs and scarcely even need to dress themselves, a luxury that exists only in the Capital, property is less well distributed than elsewhere and at present the majority of the population is made up of men who make a living from casual labour, fishing and public welfare.[68]

The Kingdom of Italy had a far larger annual budget, enjoyed revenues of more than 100,000,000 francs, and supported an army of 60,000 men: it had paid more than 32,000,000 francs in subsidies, but had been at peace since Marengo. The Kingdom of Naples, by contrast, had existed for only three years and had to defend extensive coastlines with fortifications that had to be completely rebuilt. It had raised 40,000 conscripts and amassed 8,000 muskets and 3,000 cannon. It had supplied one 74-gun ship and more than a hundred gunboats. It had repaid 20,000,000 francs in debts to Holland and France, and although it had not yet paid any direct subsidies to the imperial treasury, it had maintained an entire French army.[69]

66 ANP: 31 AP 6, Murat to Napoleon, 21 October 1811.
67 Now Count Mosbourg, thanks to Caroline's intervention in Paris.
68 ANP: 31 AP 43, Mosbourg to Murat, 1 April 1812.
69 ANP: 31 AP 6, Murat to di Gallo, 5 February 1812.

RUSSIA

When in May 1812 Murat left Naples to join the *Grande Armée* for the campaign that would finish in Moscow, Mosbourg warned him that the Kingdom did not have the means to sustain a new war.[70] Writing from Germany, Murat argued that Prussia and Poland had made the sacrifices demanded by the emperor. Mosbourg rejected the comparison: Prussia and Poland were both occupied countries. In any case, the resources of the Neapolitan kingdom were exhausted, he insisted, and no further commitments could be made without recourse to a foreign loan.

For the first time the queen was appointed as head of a regency government during Murat's absence. She had given instructions for personal taxes to be raised in advance and for the land tax to be paid monthly. Mosbourg had also increased revenues by switching certain administrative costs from the Treasury to the provinces, 'which is really an increase in taxation, but will not immediately be seen as such'.[71]

In November, Mosbourg reported to Murat that the budget prevision for 1813 was 73,000,000 lire (new denomination) against expected expenditures of 80,000,000 to 84,000,000 lire. Revenues for 1812 had totalled 72,000,000 lire, less 2,000,000 in rents on state domains that had been used for personal indemnities, road building, and gifts. It would be necessary, therefore, to raise a further 4,000,000 lire. Since there were no more domain lands to sell this could only be achieved through taxes on land sales and greater efficiency in management.

The increase in tax revenues over the previous four years had been considerable: from 57,000,000 lire in 1808 to 61,000,000 in 1809, and 73,000,000 in 1812. This increase had been achieved almost entirely through the additional taxes paid by the provinces, which now contributed 4,000,000 lire a year more than they had in 1808. Any attempt to increase taxes further was, in his opinion 'politically dangerous'. The war budget for 1813 now stood at 57,000,000 lire, roughly equivalent to total state revenues in 1808.[72] Despite the precarious situation, the operation to consolidate the National Debt had been successful, and the government had also paid the fifth instalment owed on the Dutch loan.[73]

Murat did not return to Naples until January 1813. He commanded the cavalry reserve during the advance on Moscow and was appointed Commander-in-Chief when Napoleon left the *Grande Armée* on 5 December, after creating the Principality of Ponte Corvo for 'Prince Lucien, the son of our dearly beloved brother the King of Naples'.[74] Then, without seeking the emperor's permission, Murat handed his command to Prince Eugène and returned to Naples.

70 ANP: 31 AP 43, 18 May 1812. 71 Ibid., 11 July 1811.
72 ANP: 31 AP 34, Mosbourg to Murat, 14 November 1812. 73 Ibid., 28 October 1812.
74 BSPN, Ms XXI B5, Quartier Imperial de Smorgoni, 5 December 1812.

On 27 January *Le Moniteur* in Paris accused Murat of deserting his post in Russia. Murat demanded an apology, arguing that he had agreed to take his troops only as far as the Vistula, and that he had been forced to return to Naples by ill health and the threat of an Anglo-Sicilian invasion of his Kingdom.[75]

All the issues in contention between Paris and Naples came to a head again. On 30 January the Duke of Bassano demanded that Naples should immediately supply 16,000 infantry, 2,500 cavalry, and twenty pieces of artillery for the *Grande Armée*. The Neapolitan Minister Plenipotentiary in Paris, the Duke of Carignano, observed that this was impossible and unlawful since Naples was threatened by the Anglo-Bourbon forces in Sicily and could not put its own existence in peril by allowing further troop withdrawals. He agreed, however, that Murat would impose another round of conscription, but he could not supply cavalry because 'there are no horses left in the Kingdom'. The troops left to defend the Kingdom and keep order were 50 per cent below estimates, and the Kingdom needed to purchase muskets, side arms, and horses from France. The government had also been forced to abandon the arming of its maritime defences for want of funds.

Attached to the memo was a report drawn up by General Tugny, the Neapolitan War Minister, who had calculated that by December 1812 Naples had supplied 11,971 infantry, 2,050 cavalry, and 1,994 mounts to the emperor's forces in Spain and central Europe, and had provided a total of 19,501 men and 2,471 mounts for the emperor's wars since 1808. The Neapolitan government also demanded the immediate return of the Farnese property in the *ci-devant* Papal States that had been ceded to Murat by the secret clauses of the Treaty of Bayonne and which Napoleon had seized after Murat's departure from Russia.[76]

Throughout Murat's absence in 1812 the French consul in Naples, Doriol, had kept up his attacks on the Neapolitan government, reporting regularly to Paris that Naples was breaking the terms of the blockade and trading with Britain. He also argued that the government was trying to prevent French privateers from operating off the coast for fear that their prizes might disclose the scale of the contraband trade.

In May 1813 Doriol escalated the charges, stating that the Neapolitan government had knowingly issued licences to a French commercial house 'notoriously acknowledged to be agents of the house of Scott Burns and Co. of London.... This disregard of the rules of the Continental System, together with the infractions that occur here daily, risks causing the collapse of the entire System.' The trade in British colonial goods was now open and the huge stocks that had been built up in Malta and Sicily were hardly sufficient to meet the rapidly growing demand. Sugar, in particular, was being imported in vast quantities hidden in cargoes of salt from Sardinia. In June, Doriol reported that Naples was trading 'almost openly

[75] ANP: 31 AP 6, Murat to Napoleon, 13 April 1813.
[76] ASN: Min Esteri f.5545, Carignano to Bassano, 30 January 1813.

with Malta'.[77] The Neapolitan government denied the charges and formally requested Doriol's recall.

1813–1814: NEGOTIATING WITH THE ALLIES

Murat was trying to sell his services to the emperor on the best terms he could obtain, but the imperial administration in Paris refused to negotiate.[78] Meanwhile Murat had started negotiating with the Austrians as well and when news reached Naples that the emperor had left Paris on 9 April 1813 to join the *Grande Armée* in Germany, the Neapolitan government refused to send the troops demanded because 'the tranquillity of Italy requires that the King remains in command of a strong force'. There had been a recent uprising in Naples, brigandage was again spreading 'on a scale that threatens to assume the form of a guerrilla war on the frontiers of the Kingdom of Italy and the Empire'. Resistance to conscription was growing throughout Italy, and in Naples the Provincial Legions had flatly refused to join the regiments of the line. As soon as it was known that a regiment was to be sent out of the Kingdom, the desertion rates became massive.[79] Fears of internal unrest led the Neapolitan government to step up its attempts to establish a concordat with the papacy, which it was hoped would 'have important consequences for the internal state of the kingdom at this moment and most especially in the whole southern region where the Catholic Religion and religious sentiments are especially vigorous'.[80]

When in May news reached Naples of Napoleon's victory at Lützen, the tone of the Neapolitan diplomatic correspondence changed. In an ostentatious display of loyalty, the foreign minister, di Gallo, informed the imperial minister of the celebrations being organized for the emperor's victory. But he also rejected Bassano's insinuation that concerns about internal unrest were an excuse for not contributing towards the emperor's campaign. The government was continually discovering new evidence of the subversive plots being organized in Naples and the English garrisons in Sicily and Ponza had been reinforced.[81]

Napoleon's victories persuaded Murat to rejoin the *Grande Armée* in Germany, where apart from a brief return to Naples in August, he remained until October. There was a partial reconciliation, but after a lengthy meeting with Prince Metternich in Dresden Napoleon still refused the peace terms offered by Austria. As a result, when Napoleon was defeated at the Battle of the Nations at Leipzig in October, Murat reopened negotiations with the allies. The emperor attempted to have him arrested, but on 4 November he returned to Naples and on the 11 Neapolitan ports were opened to allied shipping.

77 AAEP: CC Naples, 40, 198, Doriol to Bassano, 21 July 1812; ibid. 360, 10 May 1813; ibid. 375, 5 June 1813.

78 ANP: 31 AP 6, Bassano to Di Gallo, 30 January 1813.

79 ASN: Min. Esteri f.5545, Carignano to Bassano, 1 June 1813.

80 ASN: Min. Esteri f.5545, Di Gallo to Carignano, 26 September 1813.

81 Ibid., Di Gallo to Carignano, 17 May 1813.

CONCLUSION

Murat's defection was not consummated until January 1814, when it was already clear that the end of the empire was imminent. Murat's main concern was to sell his services to the allies in the hope of keeping his Kingdom, but his actions also reflected the deeper contradictions on which the imperial enterprise was founded. In this Naples was not unusual and the frictions between the emperor and his brother-in-law illustrate Paul Schroeder's claim that the empire had little function or purpose beyond Napoleon's military needs, some of which were constant (such as the need for men, mounts, materiel, and money) but most of which were passing.[82]

Murat came close to being a casualty of the imperial system, and on at least three occasions he received some form of ultimatum. If he did not suffer the fate of Louis Bonaparte it was because southern Italy was too far away to be treated like Holland and as Baron Durand had noted, any political change was likely to benefit the British and their Sicilian allies. As the fortunes of the empire declined after 1811, however, the balance of power shifted and as Murat's support grew more important to the emperor so did his bargaining power. But by then the imperial enterprise was rapidly heading for the rocks.

The relations between Naples and Paris reveal an unambiguous audit of Napoleon's empire, although things were not quite as bad as Murat's government made out. The massive increase in military expenditure was a devastating drain on resources, but most of the imperial demands were never met. Nonetheless, the prolonged state of war in the Mediterranean had also devastated trade and virtually every branch of economic activity, which was only partially compensated by the contraband trade that Doriol rightly suspected had become the Kingdom's principal business.[83]

Mosbourg's budget figures clearly reveal the costs of empire. Between 1806 and 1812 the Kingdom's direct fiscal revenues had grown by more than 50 per cent. By 1812 80 per cent of those revenues were devoted to military expenditure, mainly outside the Kingdom, and by 1813 the military budget alone was greater than the total state budget in 1806. Even though Naples avoided paying much of what the emperor demanded, it had still paid a great deal—and not in financial terms alone.

[82] 'The very notion of Napoleon's empire as a conceivable, potentially durable form of European international politics, or as a leading one, is a contradiction in terms.' Schroeder (1994), 394.

[83] See p. 221 below.

9

The Promise of Change

NAPLES: A MODEL OF THE EMPIRE'S MODERNIZING MISSION?

The circumstances of the French occupation of southern Italy could hardly have been less promising. The brief decade of French rule in the South took place against a background of invasive colonial subordination, prolonged commercial economic recession, intermittent warfare, constant political uncertainty, and almost permanent internal unrest. Yet the changes that took place within southern Italy in this brief span of time were remarkable. Pietro Colletta, who had served Murat as an officer and administrator, opened his later account of these years with the simple statement: 'Never has a society witnessed greater upheaval or greater transformation in so short a space of time than the Kingdom of Naples at the beginning of the nineteenth century.'[1]

The reorganization of the monarchy began within months of the establishment of the new regime. Feudalism was abolished, public administration was restructured along French lines, and a new fiscal system based on a standard land tax was introduced. The debts of the former monarchy were liquidated and a new public debt was established, funded by the sale of the lands expropriated from the religious orders and from the crown.

As well as a new system of central and local government, the Napoleonic rulers introduced the Napoleonic *Code Civil*, the French commercial and criminal law codes. They reformed the magistracy and the administration of justice; they passed laws to promote the establishment of schools and colleges in the provinces. They reorganized the Kingdom's vast patrimony of charitable foundations and for the first time introduced military conscription. They established a Feudal Commission that between 1809 and 1811 settled all litigation arising from the abolition of feudalism and oversaw the division of the feudal estates between the former owners and the local communities as well as the division of the former common lands among the inhabitants of the rural villages.

Colletta's claim was an exaggeration, but not a wild one, and in the broader context of Napoleonic Italy and Napoleonic Europe the reforms that took place in

[1] Colletta (Cortese, 1957), ii. 214.

southern Italy in these years had few comparisons. Napoleon's rulers and administrators everywhere loudly proclaimed the modernizing mission of the *Grande Nation*. But the forms of government adopted in the different imperial satellites, principalities, annexed territories, and *départements réunis* varied greatly and were shaped as much by pragmatism as ideology.

To explain why southern Italy was the theatre for an exceptionally broad range of reforms historians have looked to Napoleon's rulers and their administrators. But although the key figures in the government of the emperor's Mediterranean colony were men of wide political and administrative experience, none had the career profile of committed reformers.[2] More recent studies have emphasized the importance of the contribution made by Neapolitans, who were indeed the architects of the most important changes that took place in these years and provided strong lines of continuity with earlier Bourbon initiatives. Of this there was no better demonstration than Giuseppe Zurlo, the key figure in the final season of Bourbon reformism after 1799 and who as Joachim Murat's Interior Minister after 1809 implemented the same reform programme through the Feudal Commission. Zurlo was neither a single nor an isolated example and at every level the generation that had reached political maturity in the decade of Bourbon absolutism and the Republic rallied strongly to the promise of modernity offered by the *Grande Nation*.[3]

Recognition of the importance of the roles played by sections of the Neapolitan elites serves to modify the crudely top-down models of political and institutional change that dominate much of the literature, but does not go far enough. To a much greater degree than has been acknowledged, however, the forces for the institutional changes that took place after 1806 came from within the Kingdom and were not imposed from above.

When Marshal Masséna installed Joseph Bonaparte on the throne of Naples in 1806 the new rulers inherited the crisis of the monarchy that Ferdinand IV had again abandoned in his flight to Sicily. Despite the fine rhetoric of the new regime's modernizing mission, the timing and priority of its interventions were determined by the pressing practical needs posed by the almost complete collapse of public administration and public finances. In a second moment, however, forces from below began to play a much greater part in shaping the outcome of interventions that came to acquire a momentum of their own over which the government and its administrators had little control.

Nor is this surprising. Despite the change in regime, the central issue that the French administrators inherited from the crisis of the *ancien régime* was the enormously sensitive and complex balance between local and central power. The campaign against feudalism in the eighteenth century had attempted to

[2] Rambaud (1911), 555–6; Valente (1965), 231–2.

[3] The most detailed accounts can be found in Villani (1986/1995); De Martino (1984); De Lorenzo (1984 and 1997); Scirocco (1978).

replace the complex devolved power-sharing of the *ancien régime* with more centralized and bureaucratic forms of power. This had been a critical issue in the civil war that followed the founding of the Republic in 1799, where it became clear that the struggles against feudal power in the provinces were also struggles for greater local autonomy, not greater central power; hence the collision between the aspirations of the republican capital and the royalist provinces.

The crisis of the *ancien régime* monarchy had left these issues unresolved, but the uncompromisingly centralist and autocratic administrative templates that the French rulers sought to impose once again put them at the centre of the political agenda. Which is why the short period of French rule cannot be considered either as a clean break with the past or as a simple exercise in 'rational' modern governance, as the French and their supporters like to claim. Indeed, despite appearances the initiatives of the new government were not driven by the neatly interlocking logic of the new regime's promise of modernity, nor by the well-tried administrative templates that it introduced, nor even by the remarkable zeal shown by many of its agents. Ideology provided the models but contingent necessities dictated the priorities. The greatest and most pressing problems facing the new regime were direct consequences of the collapse of the *ancien régime* monarchy, which was the principal reason why political and administrative change in the South took different and distinctive forms. It was also why in 1815 there could be no turning back in the South. But that situation also offered different social groups opportunities to develop their own agendas and negotiate their own roles, making the South the theatre for an experiment in constructing a post-feudal order that was contradictory but in some respects also unique.

ESTABLISHING THE NEW ORDER

Within weeks of their arrival in Naples, Joseph's ministers were busy gathering information from every source to acquire a better understanding of their new Kingdom. They received detailed reports from the former French ambassador in Naples, read the works and descriptions of leading authorities from Gaetano Filangieri to Francesco Maria Galanti, and consulted with those who had rallied to the new regime.[4]

Joseph's rapid tour of the provinces in April 1806 yielded a further crop of reports, and on his instructions 'statistical surveys' were drawn up for selected provinces, giving details of the population of the principal towns and the state of trade and agriculture.[5] In April, Antoine Christophe Saliceti, the Minister of

[4] See especially De Martino (1984), 3–71.

[5] See the papers and reports collected by Roederer and Miot de Melito that form the introductory section of the papers of Joseph Bonaparte (now in the ANP, Fonds Joseph Bonaparte, 381 AP 2 and ibid. 381 AP 5: Aperçu Statistique (Province de Bari, Capitanata, Molise, Terra di Lavoro, Principato Ulteriore)).

Police, instructed the former royal governors (*Presidi*) to make regular reports on the general conditions and statistics for each province.[6]

The new government set to work to refashion the *ancien régime* monarchy using templates honed and tried in France. In March, the Council of State was established and the central government was organized around five ministries. The major juridical reforms that paved the way for the reorganization of the state were introduced during the summer, starting with the law of 2 August 1806 that abolished feudalism. As in France, this was the juridical premise for everything that followed. By ending all forms of independent and private jurisdiction the abolition of feudalism established the absolute sovereignty of the state and opened the way for reconstructing the Neapolitan monarchy from the foundations up.

The natural sequel was the law of 8 August that introduced the French system of central and local administration. The Ministry of Justice was stripped of its previous administrative functions and the Kingdom was divided into fourteen provinces and the former royal *Presidi* took the title of *Intendents* (equivalent to the French 'Prefect'). Each Intendent presided over a Provincial Council. Below these a new administrative substructure of *Sotto-Intendenti* assisted by District Councils was established.[7]

The new system was centralized. Every town, village, and hamlet was assigned its place in an administrative hierarchy based on population and importance. The municipal *parlamenti* that had formerly elected local officials were abolished, and new municipal councils were established in every town, recruited from the propertied classes and headed by a mayor (*sindaco*) appointed by the *Intendent*.[8] On 16 September the *Monitore Napoletano* explained the 'former *Presidi* have become *Intendents*' but these officers were now solely responsible for overseeing local administration, answered only to the Minister of the Interior, and no longer had any role in the courts, which were now run exclusively by magistrates.[9]

The law also provided for the establishment of provincial and local assemblies whose functions, like those of their counterparts in France, were purely administrative. Their task was to gather information on local conditions and to organize the distribution of the new land tax (*fondiaria*). Since time was needed to draw up the lists of qualified persons and then to nominate the members of the provincial and district assemblies, they were to meet for the first time in the summer of 1808.[10]

THE KING'S MEN

The men who were principally responsible for reorganizing the Kingdom after the conquest were all seasoned political survivors with a range of different administrative

[6] See below pp. 167–8, 171. [7] The law of 28 Pluviôse Year VIII (16 February 1800).

[8] Those appointed to serve on the District Councils needed to have an annual income of at least 24 ducats: the qualification doubled for communities with more than 3,000 and quadrupled for those over 6,000. The membership of these bodies changed every four years. See Villani (1986); Scirocco (1978). [9] *Monitore Napoletano*, 16 September 1806.

[10] Scirocco (1978); De Lorenzo (1996); De Martino (1984).

experience. Joseph Bonaparte had been trained in the hard school of Corsican factional politics and had become a skilled diplomat and political broker, but he had little experience as an administrator. When he first reached Naples, he showed a certain amount of energy and was the first ruler to tour his provinces. But he was happy to delegate administrative responsibility to the men he chose—or who had been selected by the emperor—to serve him.

This was not a bad decision and the three senior administrators sent by Napoleon to assist his brother were certainly not lightweights. Although they loathed one another, they were all very well equipped to act as what Stuart Woolf terms the vectors of the administrative *mentalités* of the new order.[11] Two of them, André Francois Miot, and Antoine Christophe Saliceti, were chosen by the emperor, the third, Pierre Louis Roederer, by Joseph.

Born at Versailles in 1762, André Francois Miot was the son of a *grand commis* of the *ancien régime* who won preferment at an early age in the Ministry of War as had his father and uncle. Like many high-ranking but non-noble officials, Miot initially supported the Revolution but was soon horrified by its violence.[12] He survived the coup of Thermidor, and in February 1795 the Directory appointed him Minister Plenipotentiary in Tuscany. Miot was already a friend of Joseph Bonaparte and came to know both Napoleon Bonaparte and his civil commissar, Antoine Christophe Saliceti, in Italy in 1796. In December 1796 Napoleon sent Miot to help Joseph impose order in Corsica, but also to replace Saliceti, which was the origin of their subsequent enmity. Miot then served as ambassador to Turin before joining the French diplomatic mission in Holland.

A firm supporter of the Coup of 18–19 Brumaire, Miot was well rewarded.[13] His relations with Joseph Bonaparte grew closer and in October 1800 he was sent again to Corsica with instructions 'to bring the Corsicans into civilization'. In his second mission to Corsica from March 1801 to September 1802 Miot's task was more simply to destroy the enemies of the Bonaparte clan, which he did with brutal efficiency. The administration and courts were purged of Bonaparte's opponents who were imprisoned, exiled, or executed as enemies of France.[14]

A proven Bonaparte loyalist, after returning to France in 1802 Miot worked on the new Code Civil and was appointed Prefect of the left bank of the Rhine. He was put in charge of security (*haute police*) during Joseph Bonaparte's preparations for the invasion of Britain in 1805, and Napoleon chose him to be his brother's principal minister in Naples. Joseph made him Count of Melito, and first named him Minister of War then Minister of the Interior with responsibility for reorganizing the central administration. Miot's political and administrative experience suited him to the task, and as a particularly fervent anti-clerical

[11] See Woolf (1991), 72–4.

[12] To avoid denunciation by the Jacobins, he took part in the brutal repression of the counter-revolution in the Vendée in 1792 and then moved to the Foreign Ministry.

[13] He was appointed Secretary General at the War Ministry in November 1799, then to the *Tribunat*, and in September 1800 to the Council of State.

[14] Renucci, Francesco Ottaviano *Memorie e Storie di Corsica*, cited in Poli (2003), 7–11.

he pressed for the immediate suppression of religious houses to solve the government's dire financial difficulties.[15]

Of Joseph's three senior administrators, Pierre Louis Roederer had the broadest administrative experience.[16] A close ally of Sièyes, Roederer was a firm supporter of the Coup of 18–19 Brumaire in 1799 and of the Constitution of Year VIII (December 1799) that established the position of First Consul. From December 1799 to September 1802 he served in the Council of State and oversaw the re-organization of public administration into Prefectures, Sub-prefectures, and Municipalities. With Joseph Bonaparte in March 1800 he negotiated with the delegation from the United States, and in 1801 drafted the constitution for Napoleon's Italian Republic.[17] It was at Joseph's request that Roederer travelled to Naples in February 1806, although it was not until November that Napoleon finally agreed to a permanent transfer.

Roederer was the principal architect of the major reforms introduced in the summer of 1806: the reorganization of central and local administration along French lines, the introduction of a standard progressive land tax (*fondiaria*), abolition of the tax-farms and *arrendamenti*, and the redemption of the debts of the former monarchy through sales of public land and the suppression of the remaining possessioner houses and convents in the Kingdom. In 1808 he followed Joseph Bonaparte to Spain, by which time progress had been made with the sales of crown and Church lands, but most of the rest of Roederer's legislation had still to be implemented and was already attracting strong criticism. Later in his memoirs he expressed nothing but contempt for Naples, probably in an attempt to distance himself from criticism raised by his successors.

Miot also left with Joseph, so that the only senior French official left when Joachim Murat reached Naples was the Corsican Antoine Christophe Saliceti. The only one not to write his memoirs, Saliceti was also the most powerful but least visible of the senior French officials in Naples and deserves some closer attention since his career is not well known but offers important insights into the means used to establish the French regime in Naples.

In Corsica Saliceti had been a leading opponent of Paolo Paoli and the separatists, and hence an early patron of the Bonaparte family.[18] Despite his Jacobin

[15] Miot de Melito, *Mémoires* (1880), i. Introduction; ii. 286.

[16] Born in Metz in 1754, Roederer's career began with managing the family's glass works, but he became actively involved in the political and public debates of the 1780s and won acclaim for a pamphlet calling for a unified system of taxes. In 1789 he was elected to the Constituent Assembly and to the Tax Committee in 1790. In August 1792 he was denounced by Marat, but survived thanks to Thermidor. See Roederer (ed. Forsyth, 1989), and Roederer (ed. Margerison, 1983).

[17] Napoleon had not liked Roederer's proposals for an electoral system based on lists of notables for each province, and when he clashed with Chaptal over education policy he was dismissed in March 1802 and sent to the Senate. But he continued to be entrusted with important tasks, and in 1803 drafted the constitution for the Swiss Confederation.

[18] Elected as a delegate to the Estates General in 1789, he became procurator general in Corsica two years later and in September 1791 was elected to the Convention where he voted for the death of the king.

past he survived Thermidor and by December 1795 had established close ties with Paul Barras, the most powerful figure in the Directory, who sent him to Genoa to establish contacts with the Italian republicans and prepare for the French invasion of northern Italy. When the invasion began in January 1796, Saliceti acquired the powerful and lucrative post of Civil Commissar to the *Armée d'Italie* and many believed that his ability in raising money and providing supplies and equipment was the key to Napoleon's military successes. In Genoa he developed an extensive network of contacts with Italian republicans and patriots that made him very powerful.

Contemporaries described him as an imposing figure:

> five foot six inches tall, thin, with abundant black hair that he often wore powdered, a long, pallid, jaundiced and pock-marked face, somewhat anaemic, constantly plagued by piles but with fine features, a high forehead, a straight and rounded nose, pale lips but a vigorously shaped mouth and flamboyant black eyes.

He was considered incorruptible—'inaccessible to pleasure and money'—but highly ambitious, a committed patriot and a 'jacobin à outrance'.[19]

Unlike Bonaparte, Saliceti believed that war was an instrument of revolution, whose purpose was to liberate peoples still oppressed by tyrants. He saw the founding of 'sister-republics' as a step toward the creation of a universal Republic and believed the support of the Italian revolutionaries to be crucial for France's military success. In January 1796 he worked with Filippo Michele Buonarroti[20] and others to organize republican risings in Piedmont and with the Milanese patriots to prepare the French entry into the city.[21]

In July 1796 Saliceti directed the French occupation of Livorno and with Joseph Bonaparte led the expedition that recaptured Corsica from the English. He then assumed dictatorial power, and reorganized the entire Corsican administration so that it was controlled by his own followers and the Bonaparte clan. He recommended a French army be maintained permanently on the island and organized a gendarmerie composed of local men 'accustomed to scaling the mountains'.[22]

Saliceti was still close to Joseph, but his brother Napoleon sensed that he was becoming too powerful. When he was replaced by André Miot, Saliceti's relations with Napoleon deteriorated rapidly and in January 1797 he and Commissar Garrau were recalled to Paris. In November 1799 Saliceti openly opposed the Coup of 18–19 Brumaire and was dismissed.[23] Saliceti was only partially rehabilitated and

[19] Godechot (1937), i. 245. [20] See above p. 81.

[21] By now Saliceti and his fellow commissar Garrau were responsible for the 'systematic exploitation of the conquered territories to the benefit both of the *armée d'Italie* and of the Directorial Republic that was on the verge of bankruptcy'. He conducted delicate diplomatic negotiations with the Republic of Genoa, the Papacy, and the Grand Duke of Tuscany and organized the pro-French revolt in Reggio at the end of 1796; Godechot (1937), i. 402–4. [22] Ibid. 480.

[23] He was appointed ambassador to Lucca and then to Genoa in 1801, and again sent to assist Miot to repress the supposed counter-revolution in Corsica.

Napoleon was still very suspicious of him when Joseph left for Naples. But Joseph trusted him and believed that their experience of Corsican politics made Saliceti and Miot exceptionally well qualified for the task of organizing his new Kingdom, while the fact that they detested one another would ensure that neither became too powerful.

As Minister of Police, Saliceti quickly acquired a sinister reputation in Naples. He took little or no part in the major legislative debates and remains a shadowy figure in the central administrative archives. But the local archives tell a different story and reveal that Saliceti was omnipresent in the political reconstruction of southern Italy after the invasion. As he had done in Liguria, he built up a powerful personal network. Thanks to his long-standing contacts with the Italian revolutionaries, he already knew many of the Neapolitan exiles who now returned in search of jobs. He placed these men in key positions, knowing that they were dependent on him alone and had no alternative patrons. He took no notice of jurisdictional boundaries, infuriated the magistrates by intervening in judicial appointments, and interfered in every branch of the administration. Rightly the Bourbons saw him as their most dangerous enemy and repeatedly tried to assassinate him: in 1808 he narrowly escaped a bomb that destroyed much of his house.

Of the men who had accompanied Joseph Bonaparte to Naples, Saliceti was the only one who seemed ready to settle there. He married the daughter of a Neapolitan nobleman, the Duke of Lavello, and easily accommodated to the new regime since he had been a confidant of Caroline Bonaparte since childhood. But that also aroused the emperor's suspicions, which was why he was recalled to Paris in 1809. Shortly after returning to Naples in December 1809 he died, probably of a seizure, although poisoning was suspected and Paris demanded an autopsy.[24]

Joachim Murat's arrival in Naples a year earlier coincided with a new burst of legislative and military activity. This has often been attributed to the new rulers, but this seems unlikely.[25] In imperial circles he was widely referred to simply as 'the pillaging cavalier' and 'an administrator of exceptional ineptitude'.[26] Murat's skills were those of a soldier, and although he had performed some important diplomatic missions, his record as an administrator in Berg was dismal.[27]

Saliceti's death left Murat with few senior French administrators he could trust, and the choice was further complicated by his determination to keep Caroline Bonaparte's political role to a minimum. In this he was not very successful. His most loyal adviser, the rather shadowy fellow Cahorsin, Jean-Antoine Agar, who had been his former administrator in Berg, was the queen's protégé, while he was unaware that

[24] Colletta (Cortese, 1957), ii. 331–2.

[25] Valente's (1941) 'heroic' portrait of Murat is reproduced uncritically in Tulard (1983).

[26] 'Le cavalier pillard'; 'administrateur incapable par excellence'. See Espitalier (1910), 2, 16, 19—cited in Ermice (2005), 61.

[27] Schmidt (1905), 63.

his most trusted adviser, the Minster of War Hectore Daure, was also one of the queen's quite numerous lovers.[28] Among the other French officials and officers who remained after Joseph's departure, few had administrative skill or experience.

THE NEAPOLITANS

As Murat's relations with Paris deteriorated he was widely accused of preferring Neapolitans to Frenchmen, but of the many accusations levelled against Joachim Murat this was among the least well founded. He did appoint Neapolitans to a number of key positions, but because there were no Frenchmen with the necessary skills or experience needed to implement the many reforms left unstarted by Joseph.

Neapolitans had also held many senior positions under Joseph Bonaparte, especially those requiring skills and local knowledge the French officials lacked. After the conquest Joseph's Minister of Justice was Michelangelo Cianciulli, a leading Neapolitan jurist whose brilliant career had brought him into the closed circle of the *togati* at an early age. Cianciulli had held a series of senior government positions under the Bourbons and played no part in the Republic, but in 1801 was appointed Crown Attorney. In February 1806 he negotiated the peaceful entry of the French troops into the Kingdom. Joseph refused to accept his resignation and appointed him Minister of Justice, enabling Cianciulli to play an active role in the Council of State. He drafted the law abolishing feudalism and was responsible for reorganizing the courts and the magistracy. In 1807 Joseph made him a privy councillor, and in May 1808 Cianciulli was nominated to preside over the Council of State until the arrival of the new king. He resigned in 1809 and was replaced by another former *togato* who had also held high office under the Bourbon monarchy, Giuseppe Zurlo.[29]

Joseph entrusted the equally delicate post of Minister of Ecclesiastical Affairs to the Archbishop of Taranto, Giuseppe Capecelatro. Like Cianciulli, Monsignore Capecelatro had had a distinguished career under the previous government. A man of learning and wide interests, he became Archbishop of Taranto in 1778. A leading opponent of papal jurisdictions in the Kingdom, Capecelatro had studied with Genovesi at the University in Naples and was a strong believer in the importance of practical knowledge.[30]

[28] Born in 1771 Agar had been captured by the English in Santo Domingo but made his way back to France in 1795 and joined Murat's staff in 1805. In Berg he presided over the Council of State and oversaw the sales of *beni nazionali*, the suppression of the religious houses, the abolition of Church tithes, the creation of savings banks, the reorganization of the magistracy, and the introduction of the *Code Napoléon*.

[29] Tallarico, in *DBI*, xxv. 167–9.

[30] Giuseppe Capacelatro (1744–1836). He deplored the fact that the newly published treatises on agriculture were destined to 'remain on the desks of men of letters and win applause that does not go beyond a room full of university professors, while the peasants are the same as before'. He believed that priests had a critical role in bringing new ideas and practical training to the rural poor. See Stella, *DBI*, xviii. 445–51.

By chance the absentee Archbishop happened to be in his episcopal seat in 1799. He urged compliance with the republican government in Naples on the grounds that 'all governments are in the hand of our Lord', and then used the same argument to appeal for obedience to the monarchy as Cardinal Ruffo and the Russo-Turkish fleet approached the city in March. In October Capecelatro was arrested as a suspected Jacobin and held until February 1801.

In 1806 Joseph Bonaparte appointed him to the Council of State and made him Minister of Church Affairs. Murat persuaded him to become Minister of the Interior in August 1808, but he resigned and was replaced a year later by another former Bourbon minister, Giuseppe Zurlo.

Zurlo had left Naples with the court in 1806 but he and his brother returned, apparently to prevent the sequestration of his property. The circumstances are unclear, but he was fully committed to the principles on which the new system of administration was based and willing to extol them as the realization of the reforms he had attempted to introduce unsuccessfully after 1802. As Interior Minister he played the key role in reactivating Joseph Bonaparte's Feudal Commission, but became a major target of the opposition. As a result of pressure from the queen he was dismissed in 1812, but returned to office when Murat joined the allies in 1814.

When Zurlo became Minister of the Interior he was succeeded as Minister of Justice by Giuseppe Ricciardi, another young lawyer from the provinces who had made his career in Naples. Ricciardi did not participate in the Republic in 1799, but later courageously defended some of those charged with treason. He remained in Naples after the flight of the monarchy and was appointed to the Council of State in 1807. As Minister of Justice after 1809 he played a critical role in the reorganization of the magistracy and the courts and in the introduction of the French legal codes.[31]

FORMING A PARTY

There were many ways in which Neapolitans were incorporated into the new regime, starting from the Council of State. Taken from the French Constitution of Year VIII, a Council of State had been established in the Kingdom of Italy in 1805 and took the same form in Naples. A consultative body whose advice was almost always ignored, it frequently complained that despite lengthy debates the laws adopted were simply translations of their French originals with no concessions to local custom or practice.[32] But the Council of State was an important means both

[31] Shortly before leaving, Roederer told him that he was 'the only truly enlightened person I have had the pleasure to meet in Naples', but urged him to broaden his reading of Montesquieu and other writers of the French Enlightenment: Roederer to Ricciardi (20 July 1808).

[32] See especially De Martino (1984) and Feola (1977). The proceedings of the Consiglio di Stato have been destroyed.

for associating leading figures from the previous regime with the new order and for bringing in new men.[33]

Much more important, in practical terms, was the presence of Neapolitans in key intermediary roles, especially in local administration. This was Saliceti's domain and nearly all the key posts in local administration were held by his men. The government's senior representative in the newly created provinces was the Intendent and of those appointed to this new position only three were Frenchmen: Joseph-Pierre Briot, Joseph Charron, and Simone Collonna de Leca. Charron was a protégé of the emperor, but Briot and Colonna were not only Saliceti's men but part of the Corsican connection as well.[34]

Their careers indicate what it took to succeed in the risky world of imperial administration. Joseph-Pierre Briot would become a major figure in the administration in Naples, but was no admirer of Napoleon. A prominent former Jacobin, he had escaped deportation to Guyana after opposing the Coup of 18–19 Brumaire only because his patrons included Lucien and Joseph Bonaparte as well as the imperial minister Chaptal.[35] He got the chance to show his submission to the new regime when he was sent to reorganize public administration on Elba in 1801. Good results on Elba found him a year later assisting André Miot in the task of 'civilizing' Corsica. But he came to Naples with a recommendation not from Miot, but from his patron Chaptal to Saliceti.[36]

The importance of the Corsican connection was emphasized by the presence of the only other French Intendent, Simone Colonna, who was another of Saliceti's Corsican associates. Without exception the French administrators were also freemasons, a bond that underwrote even the Corsican connection since Joseph Bonaparte and Saliceti had been initiated in the same Corsican lodge in 1793.[37]

The masonic connection played a central role in the imperial networks of patronage, preferment, and recruitment, but was also a means for the French administrators to identify their likely local supporters in newly conquered territories. This was certainly the case in Naples and when in August 1806 Joseph-Pierre Briot, for example, was appointed Intendent of Abruzzo Citeriore the leading families in Chieti who indicated their support for the new regime were all freemasons. All had been prominent in the reform movement and had supported the Republic, and many would serve the new regime in high positions. They included the leading landowners in the province, Pietro and Romualdo de Sterlich, and Baron Antonio Nolli, who in 1788 had founded the local *Patriotic Society*. Pietro de Sterlich had been a friend of Gaetano Filangieri, and would in

33 Castellano (2004), 96. 34 De Martino (1984), 123–8.

35 Mastroberti (1998), 105–27. Pierre Joseph Briot, a former deputy from the Doubs who had opposed Bonaparte's Coup of 18 Brumaire; he was appointed Chief Commissar on Elba in 1803 and then Intendent first of Abruzzo Cit (1 August 1806) and of Calabria Cit (7 July 1807) by Joseph Bonaparte. Murat made him a Councillor of State. 36 Ibid. 137.

37 Ibid. 352.

turn serve as Intendent of the nearby province of L'Aquila and later in the Terra d'Otranto.[38]

As well as bringing the new regime into closer contact with its supporters, freemasonry also brought many former Neapolitan Jacobins into the new administration. This again was primarily Saliceti's doing, as he had done before in Genoa and Corsica. By choosing men whose careers were jeopardized by their Jacobin past, he created a network of officials over whose careers he had complete control. Hence Saliceti's preference for Neapolitans and former Jacobins and his principal Neapolitan protégés—Pietro Colletta, Vincenzo Cuoco, Matteo Galdi, and Giuseppe Poerio—all fitted this description: he recruited them all and they all served at one time or another as Intendents.[39]

Not only were these men deeply loyal to their patron, but they were also deeply committed to the political ideals of the new regime. In addition to performing often extraordinarily demanding administrative duties, for which they had scant resources, they saw themselves as missionaries of the new order. In often remote provincial postings they and their wives took initiatives that went far beyond the immediate calls of duty, setting up elementary schools, homes for foundlings and orphans, public charities, and colleges.[40]

The sense of missionary zeal clearly resonates in the language used by Briot in a circular announcing the visitations that he was about to make to the Abruzzi towns in April 1807. He was coming to them, he stated, in the name of His Majesty and his ministers 'to bring closer to you the means to improve your lot, to explain the new administrative order and the new laws'. His purpose was to see at first hand if the new laws had been understood and properly executed, but also to ask for advice: 'Let the poor, the wretched and the oppressed come to me, I am their friend and protector; but let the rich and powerful come to me also, because I owe everyone the same justice and I am the friend of all those who truly love their sovereign.' He ordered that there be no extravagant welcoming ceremonies, because he did not come to burden the communities with unnecessary expenses: 'Welcome me like a friend as I myself would welcome you in the Intendent's offices.'[41]

Loyal as they were, however, even the most committed of these officials found the workloads overwhelming. Before he left the Abruzzi, Briot himself had complained bitterly of the impossibility of meeting the tasks assigned to his office without more officers and funds. Pietro Colletta and Giuseppe Poerio repeated the same complaints, but they were also alarmed by the lack of physical means to

[38] Romualdo de Sterlich had a library of more than 12,000 titles and had corresponded with all the luminaries of the reform era. Antonio Nolli was in turn closely connected with the group of reformers in nearby Teramo headed by Melchiorre Delfico (who was appointed to the Council of State in 1806), Giuseppe de Thomasis, and the lawyer Nicola Niccolini. Mastroberti (1998), 148.

[39] De Martino (1984), 58–79.

[40] On Poerio see Nardella, in De Lorenzo (ed.) (2003), 663–75.

[41] BNN: Ms Bancone 8B, 26; Intendenza di Abruzzo Citeriore, 8 April 1807.

reinforce the rhetorical appeals of the new order. Both reported that all attempts to raise volunteer militias or to form units of regular mounted gendarmes had failed repeatedly. The volunteers deserted, sold their horses or guns, or simply went hunting. Others brought prostitutes into the barracks and turned the place into a bordello.[42]

THE PROMISE OF CHANGE

These problems were signs that the new regime's modernizing mission could not easily be accomplished, but the promise of change nonetheless took pride of place in its rhetoric. The first issue of the government-financed *Monitore Napoletano* set out the new government's case as liberators and modernizers, and made the promise of emancipation from the *ancien régime* the principal justification for the overthrow of the Bourbon monarchy:

> The Nation will in a very short time witness the emergence of a new order of things that will implant in its midst the virtues of righteousness, watchfulness, justice, generosity, honesty, disinterestedness, and the love of the common good, conjoined with the sincere and effective desire to make the Nation great and happy in deeds, not just in words.[43]

That message was reiterated even more forcibly by Count André Miot de Melito in his first report on the state of the realm delivered to the Council of State on 4 July 1806. The Kingdom's deplorable condition was the inevitable consequence of misgovernment. Nothing demonstrated this more eloquently than the Byzantine chaos of the *ancien régime* monarchy and the poverty of the Kingdom's inhabitants.

Despite the huge endowments of the charitable foundations, 'the spectacle of indigence offered by the Kingdom of Naples might lead one to think that Religion and Philosophy have been parsimonious towards humanity'. There was no rational system of poor relief, nor any means for identifying paupers:

> The Picture of Poverty that greets one on the streets of Naples is truly terrifying. The cries of lamentation, the Nakedness, the Wounds and Deformities from which the eye cannot escape render this Great City utterly disgusting.

The plight of abandoned children was especially distressing. The former government made no provision for them,

> so that these unfortunate creatures are left to die of cold and hunger or are eaten by animals. They are entrusted to wet-nurses for a period of five years, but there is no supervision. They are destined to become a real danger to the state if their wretched condition does not cause them to perish at an early age.

[42] Ibid. [43] *Monitore Napoletano*, 1 April 1806.

The situation was a little more encouraging when it came to public works and the Minister acknowledged that the previous monarchy had undertaken an extensive programme of road-building, primarily for military purposes. The roads were well built and provided a good base for further development. The Bourbons had also made a start at draining the extensive swampland in the area around Nola, but the contractors of the enterprise had gone bankrupt and would need a subsidy of 50,000 ducats to complete the work.

Agriculture, industry, and commerce had all been damaged by the war, but they suffered from more permanent forms of neglect. The ownership of the vast tracts of land was contested between the crown, the barons, and the *università*, 'rendering this most beautiful country inanimate and barren.... While every form of industry and manufacture can be found in this realm, nothing has ever been developed to any point of perfection because nothing is ever done with any degree of continuity.' Attempts had been made to improve the quality of woollen, cotton, and silk products, but little had been accomplished.

The longest part of Miot's report was dedicated to education. 'Despite the brilliance of the Neapolitans, the Bourbons had used every means to prevent the expansion of education.' The University in Naples had been founded in the twelfth century and offered a vast range of courses but 'today it inspires respect only by virtue of its ancient origin': its chairs had once been conferred on the basis of open competition but for some time this had been replaced by a system of interim appointments or by substitutes appointed by the Prefect. There was no system of secular education, so that seminaries and convents continued to be the main providers of education. The education of girls—'that half of the human race that is the principal influence on the other half'—was neglected in Naples more than anywhere else in Europe.[44]

In the style of imperial envoys past and present, Miot's report was above all an ideological manifesto. Poverty, ignorance, an excessive number of monks and convents were all the result of bad government, misguided policies, and defective institutions. The regime's first task, therefore, was to establish the principles of rational administration and bring Neapolitan institutions in line with French models. Rational administration would be the premise for a new partnership between citizens and the state, between public interests and private enterprise that would bring about the Kingdom's regeneration and end the culture of 'idleness and sloth'. Once done, the natural richness of the land and the natural energies of the people would be released and the way to prosperity and progress would be open.

In this textbook statement of liberal principles, the role of government was limited but clearly defined. Its task was to remove the obstacles to free enterprise and private property by abolishing feudalism and by getting rid of the hordes of monks and nuns and those who lived parasitically off public charities. To combat

[44] ANP: Fonds Joseph Bonaparte, 381AP5: Miot's report on public administration, 4 July 1806.

the culture of sloth the government acknowledged, however, special responsibility for promoting education, which alone could provide the people with the knowledge and skills to live independently. Once these conditions were met, the forces of free enterprise and market incentives would be sufficient to create a virtuous new cycle of production and prosperity.

The healing and unifying quality of the new order was also carefully emphasized. Roederer explained to the Council of State how a single land tax would unite the nation and 'transform a Populace into a People':

The tax on land will bind the monarchy most closely to the landowners, and the landowners most closely to the monarchy... it lays the foundations of Government in the prosperity of Agriculture.

The new land tax would be the most tangible sign that all those who owned property are equal. By making all subject to a single tax it would finally

bring to an end the state of unspoken warfare that for so long has set the Monarchy in conflict with the Nobility and the People. By stripping the Nobility of an immunity that has damaged the interests of the Prince, Your Majesty may at a stroke bring peace to the People, the Nobility and the entire Kingdom... so that the populace may finally become a people.

The proportional tax on land, Sire, will make it possible for Your Majesty to make one strong nation out of the two nations that have hitherto confronted and weakened one another. These two nations consist of the mighty and the lowly, who in every other European state are linked by intermediary classes that are so finely graduated that no-one can tell precisely the point where the mighty begin, or the middling sort end. This system of society is the dominant feature of modern civilization: it has brought with it enlightenment and a new sense of decency and honour to even the humblest social orders, and ideas of decency and honour that have given all men a new sense of dignity and to all States a new sense of power: in short, a new system of society that has created new nations and amongst them one single Great Nation'.[45]

The greatest benefit bestowed by the new order was, course, the abolition of feudalism and on 16 August 1806 the *Corriere di Napoli* carried an article by Vincenzo Cuoco, who had recently returned from Milan, celebrating the law of 2 August:

For fifty years the kingdom of Naples has been lacerated by a civil war which was waged as fiercely in the tribunals of the *Sacro Consiglio* and of the *Regia Camera* [*della Sommaria*] as in the fields of Apulia and the mountains of the Abruzzi. In our tribunals there were no fewer than thirty thousand suits of litigation between rural communities and their barons waiting to be heard. There were no fewer than thirty thousand persons in the kingdom engaged either directly or indirectly in sustaining, fomenting and managing these suits. The whole nation was divided into two rival parts, and even if the force exercised by the government prevented them killing one another, it could not stop them from hating

[45] Ibid., Report by Roederer, 26 July 1806.

one another, denouncing one another, and when the occasion arose seizing their goods. This long war can rightly be described as something more than a civil war because it gave rise to permanent evils that made even times of peace cruel. All that anarchy has now finally ended, thanks to the law of August 2nd 1806, which has been welcomed not only by the rural communities but also by the feudatories themselves.[46]

The press played an important role in promoting the modernizing projects of the new regime, but this was no longer the free press of 1799, and the *Monitore Napoletano* and the *Corriere di Napoli* in which Cuoco's article appeared were closely controlled by the government and specifically by Saliceti.[47] The government as a result spoke with a single voice, and the *grand commis* of the empire constantly insisted that reform was simply a technical matter, a matter of reason for which the revolution had provided the models.

Presenting his proposal for reorganizing direct taxation around a single land tax, Roederer insisted that this would be painless and there would be no losers. The new tax would simply distribute the fiscal burden more fairly, while the abolition of feudalism would turn uncertain titles into absolute private property rights and bring vast tracts of uncultivated land into cultivation. But the greatest benefit of all would be the new spirit of enterprise that would be the principal fruit of these changes and would transform the economy, bringing new wealth and prosperity. Meanwhile the government would work to promote that new spirit primarily through measures to improve education and encourage the dissemination of practical knowledge.

The material means needed to achieve this great transformation were already at hand. All that was needed, Roederer argued, was to suppress the monasteries: 'In all these countries that have grown idle under the influence of a mild climate, the natural fertility of the land and the modesty of their needs, to suppress the convents is to use the patrimony of idleness to reconstruct the patrimony of the crown.'[48]

These panaceas would prove neither easy nor adequate, but when the *Grande Nation* spoke the language of the Enlightenment it knew it could count on the support of the Neapolitan supporters of reform.

FINANCIAL CHAOS

When it came to it, however, the government's actions were determined by the financial chaos that was both cause and consequence of the collapse of the former monarchy. The new government had no money and no revenues, and the whole

[46] In Cuoco (1806–15), 255.

[47] Both were edited by Tito Manzi, a Tuscan and trusted confidant of both Joseph Bonaparte and Saliceti. In 1811 they were amalgamated as the *Monitore delle Sicilie*. See De Francesco (1997), 94–5, and Themelly, *DBI*. On Manzi, see Cortese (1965), 197–222.

[48] Roederer (1854), iv. 19: Roederer to Joseph Bonaparte, 28 June 1808.

edifice of public finance threatened to collapse. Coin of all sorts had virtually disappeared, the banks were effectively bankrupt, and the suspension of interest payments on the *arrendamenti* threatened the creditors of the old monarchy with ruin.

To meet its immediate cash needs the government raised a forced loan in Naples and on punitive terms (that Roederer hid from the emperor) negotiated an international loan in Holland.[49] But restoring financial order and rescuing the creditors of the *ancien régime* monarchy was as much a political as a financial necessity, and one for which France offered uncertain guidelines. The National Convention's attempt to 'republicanise the national debt' in August 1793 had resulted in the disaster of the *assignats*, and the decision to cancel two-thirds of the debt in 1797 had seriously undermined the credibility of the Directory.[50]

Reorganization of the public debt had featured high among the measures delivered for the Italian Republic in the constitution that Napoleon set out at Lyons in 1801, but because the new satellite included a large number of separate states each with their own separate debts, this was not a model for the Kingdom of Naples either.[51] On leaving for Naples Joseph Bonaparte had requested Roederer's presence in Naples specifically to tackle the financial crisis. Roederer's experience was theoretic rather than practical, although he was familiar with the procedures adopted in France. But in Naples the task was complicated by the lack of clear figures and by the multitude of different forms that the *ancien régime* debts had taken, of which the *arrendamenti* and venal offices were only the largest part. In his history of the Kingdom's finances Ludovico Bianchini later commented that the 'disorder and confusion' of the royal accounts meant that the total size of the debt could only be approximately calculated, but at the time of the French invasion it was estimated to be around 105,000,000 ducats.[52]

The operation to redeem the old debt and establish a new consolidated debt began on 24 August 1806 when the government recognized all existing state creditors and decreed that all those with valid titles would receive certificates (*cedole*) corresponding to the full value of their credit. These certificates could be transcribed directly on the new *Gran Libro del Debito Pubblico*, which from 1 January 1807 would pay an annual interest of 5 per cent to the holder. Alternatively, the *cedole* could be traded or used in part payment to purchase *beni nazionali*.[53]

This was the largest single operation undertaken by the French administration and resulted in a complete overhaul of the finances of the *ancien régime*. By 1815 the Kingdom's debt had been converted, consolidated, and reduced to less than 1,000,000 ducats, which had been achieved in part through massive sales of Church lands and the wholesale suppression of religious houses. But the creditors of the *ancien régime* had also paid a heavy price, and the most recent study of this

[49] Rambaud (1911), 336. [50] Ermice (2005), 48. [51] Ibid. 161, 147.

[52] Which must be set against total annual revenues that by the end of the 1790s were around 18 million ducats—of which some 6 million went directly to the feudatories, leaving 12 million for the government, of which 3.2 million were devoted to servicing the debt. Bianchini (1839), 404, cited in Ermice (2005), 31.

[53] Ermice (2005), 46.

operation concludes that in the process of conversion about 33% of the original debt was written off.[54] The Neapolitans could comfort themselves only in the knowledge that the French had come off even worse, while the burden of the losses was of course not distributed equally.

The conversion of the debt was very closely connected with the second of the major operations carried out by the French rulers, the dissolution of the religious houses and the sales of their lands, together with former crown property, as *beni nazionali*. Even before the operation of converting the debt began, the government had begun selling crown lands to raise cash to meet its day-to-day needs. In May the *Dogana delle Pecore*, long the target of eighteenth-century reformers, was abolished and the crown sheep-runs on the Apulian Tavoliere were put up for sale.[55] Those who had previously leased the crown grazing lands for farming were entitled to purchase them as quit-rents (emphyteuts) on payment of an annual rent, together with an entry fee equivalent to one year's rent. The *Monitore Napoletano* announced on 27 May that land on the *Tavoliere* would be sold in small plots 'to ensure that the land should not be accumulated in large estates owned by the few'.[56] The proceeds would be transferred 'to the fund that had been established to amortize the public debt'.[57] But there were few buyers and the measure failed.

On 1 July 1806 the *Monitore Napoletano* announced that the government had decided to abolish the former '*arrendamenti*' and accepted full responsibility for these debts. The creditors of the *arrendamenti*, as well as those of the banks that had failed and the numerous venal offices that had been abolished, were to be incorporated into a new National Debt. All those able to show proper title would have their credits transferred to the new *Gran Libro del Debito Pubblico*, on which they were to receive interest at 5 per cent. The *Monitore* announced on 4 July that the capital of the state creditors would be repaid through the sale of *beni nazionali*. Recognized state creditors received certificates (*cedole*) to the full value of their credit, which could be in part payment for the purchase of *beni nazionali*, which were to be sold free of all feudal or other encumbrances.[58]

The following day the sale of lands belonging to the Royal Domain for a value of 10,000,000 ducats was authorized, and then the assets and property of the religious houses.[59] Between 1806 and 1811, 1,300 monasteries, convents, and religious houses were closed and their lands sold by auction.[60]

[54] Ermice (2005), 147: 'the loss suffered by the creditors of the state can be calculated at approximately 75 million ducats in capital'. The devaluation resulted from the reduction in interest rates (from 5 to 3% in 1808) but above all from the fall in the face-value of the *cedole*, which traded at around 18–20% of nominal values.

[55] Marino (1988), 257.

[56] *Monitore Napoletano*, 27 May 1806.

[57] BNN: Ms SQ IV L.31: Legge sul Tavoliere di Puglia (23 May 1806).

[58] *Monitore Napoletano*, 4 July 1806.

[59] In a single day, on 19 September, the government suppressed seven houses of the Dominicans, four Bernabites, two Carmelites, three Conventuals, two Theatines, two Servites, one convent of Somaschi, and two houses of the Cassino Order: the Carthusians were also expelled from the monastery of S. Martino. De Nicola (19 September 1806), 286.

[60] De Rosa (1979), 531–51.

There were few buyers, however, even though Roederer took measures specifically designed to encourage small buyers to participate. In September General Cavaignac, the Director of the Administration of the Royal Domains, was instructed to ensure that the estates put up for sale were divided into their component parts, each separately valued 'so that even the poorest classes may become purchasers and hence increase the number of new proprietors'.[61]

There were still few buyers. The main cause was shortage of cash, the depressed state of the economy, and the doubts over the government's future since the Calabrian provinces were still in open revolt, while the Bourbon government in Sicily threatened reprisals against purchasers of *beni nazionali*. Most of the land sold in 1806 and 1807 was bought by a small group of wealthy purchasers closely connected to the new government. But the revenues from the sales proved inadequate to meet the interest payments on the debt, which in 1806 was estimated at about 6,000,000 ducats a year.[62]

For political reasons it was decided to give priority to private holders of shares in the former *arrendamenti*. These were not the only creditors 'but since the class of small proprietors is the one that has the most numerous holding of *arrendamenti* and is a very large social group consisting of a great number of families that would have no other means of subsistence were they to be deprived of this income and would be reduced to begging'.[63]

Payment of interest to corporate share-holders was suspended, however, with disastrous consequences for the banks and many charitable foundations. But revenues were still insufficient to meet even the reduced cash payments promised to 'pensioners, *giubiliati* and other creditors of the Public Treasury', and in January 1807 Roederer ordered that payments should be made on a discretionary basis. A month later the creditors were instructed to present their claims to the offices of the Commission for the Liquidation of the Public Debt.[64]

When Joachim Murat reached Naples in 1808 only a small part of the state's creditors had been registered on the new Debt, for which they received dividends at 5% while the rest received nothing. Murat's finance minister, Pignatelli della Cerchiara, insisted that Roederer's project was unworkable and that the land sales could never yield enough to liquidate the remaining 50,000,000 of capital debt. He recommended, therefore, that payments be made to all those with recognized credits, but that the rate of interest be reduced from 5 to 3%. When Murat did this without consulting Paris he provoked the wrath of both the emperor and Joseph Bonaparte, but the French minister in Naples agreed that Murat's action meant that at least some creditors were now finally

61 BNN: Bancone 8 B29; *Direzione Generale dei Demani, Circolare* 22 September 1806.

62 See Villani (1964), 12; Ermice (2005), 30–4.

63 ANP: Fonds Joseph Bonaparte 381AP 5 (doc II), Council of State, 1807.

64 BNN: Bancone 8B 29; Roederer to *Direzione Generale Liquidazione del Debito Pubblico*.

receiving some payments even though the nominal value of shares in the new debt had fallen heavily.[65]

All the creditors of the old monarchy lost something, but the biggest losers were the charitable foundations and the banks. It was estimated in Naples alone that the charitable foundations lost a total of a quarter of a million ducats of annual revenue.[66] The losses sustained by the capital's seven private banks were similar. In January 1807 a petition to the government claimed that the bank's 2,000 investors, employees and their families faced utter ruin, and a commission was appointed to investigate. It did not report until November when the government agreed to a subsidy of only 12,000 ducats a year.[67] But the government could find no solution and shortly before he left Naples in May 1808 Roederer ordered the suppression of the private banks, whose assets were assigned to the liquidation of the public debt. The creditors of the banks lost everything, as did their employees. Many smaller credit institutions like the rural 'corn banks' (*monti frumentari*), established in earlier centuries to make non-usurious advances to enable peasants to acquire seed corn, were also ruined.[68]

Private investors at least retained a part of what they were owed, although many like the Serracapriola family had already suffered heavy losses as a result of the impact of the financial crisis of the Bourbon monarchy on the value of the *arrendamenti* in the 1790s. However, it was a sign of the regime's political success that investors preferred to keep their money in the public debt than use it to purchase *beni nazionali*. There were many reasons for this, but the most important was that the low market value of the *cedole* made it unattractive for small investors to use them for part-payment for *beni nazionali*, since they had to pay the balance in cash. The devalued *cedole* were nonetheless bought up in large quantities by those who made the major purchases of *beni nazionali*, which also explains why the lion's share of the sales went to a relatively small minority of purchasers.[69]

In both cases, the regime's main gains were political. The restoration of a financial order and the increased investment in the state debt and in purchases of *beni nazionali* strengthened its fragile political base. But the main beneficiaries were the groups of senior administrators, wealthy nobles, and foreign financiers whose fortunes were being launched throughout Europe by the needs of Napoleon's satellite rulers. The biggest losers where those who had been most dependent on what Roederer called the 'patrimony of the idle', the religious houses and corporations whose assets had gone to pay off the debts of the *ancien régime*.

65 See above p. 145. 66 Petroni (1874), ii. 170–5; Filangieri (1947), 179–80.

67 Filangieri (1947), 179. 68 Ibid.

69 On investment in the debt, see Ermice (2005), 126–7, 150–60. Five per cent of the total number of buyers acquired over 60% of the *beni nazionali* sold in 1807 and 1808. In the later provincial auctions, however, more land was acquired by an emerging class of middling provincial landowners; see Villani (1964), pp. 156–7.

THE LAND TAX

The problem of the state's ordinary revenues was addressed by means of the introduction of the new land tax that Roederer promised would 'turn a Populace into a People'. On 24 July 1806 Roederer informed the Council of State that under the *ancien régime*, of the 4,578,894 ducats paid each year in taxes on property, only 589,934 ducats were paid on feudal property. The taxes paid by the people took the form of 102 different levies that varied from province to province, the most general being the hearth tax (*focatico*). But no property surveys had ever been drawn up, so the tax was raised in different ways in different towns and feudal properties were exempt.

The new tax, Roederer insisted, would not add to the overall tax burden, but would be easier and cheaper to raise and would distribute the tax burden more fairly. He set the yield of the new *fondiara* at 6,000,000 ducats, admitting that on the basis of a direct comparison with France (in terms of land and population) a yield of 8,000,000 ducats might have been expected 'especially since it is generally recognized that the land here is much more fertile than in France'. But prudence suggested that an initial yield of 6,000,000 ducats would be more reasonable, with the expectation that this would rise to 8,000,000 within three years.[70]

Because many parts of the kingdom were still subject to 'disturbances', the new tax was to be introduced on the basis of the estimates used for assessing the Bourbon *decima* of 1792, which 'although not accurate, has at least the merit of covering the entire territory without distinction of ownership and without respecting feudal or ecclesiastical privilege'.[71]

Those who would gain most would be 'the smaller proprietors and poor'.[72] But in March 1808, Melchiorre Delfico submitted a long memorandum to the Council of State pointing out the grave defects of the new tax, which in the absence of a reliable land survey could not be fairly distributed. Roederer flatly rejected Delfico's alternative, however, because it deviated from the French model. Major anomalies could be rectified later, but '*raison d'etat*' dictated that there should be no interference in the meantime.[73]

Every *comune* was instructed to establish a commission to which all local landowners must submit detailed descriptions of their property that would then

[70] ANP: Fonds Joseph Bonaparte, 381 AP 3: Report by Roederer, 24 July 1808. See also Rambaud (1911), 313–16.

[71] BNN: Ms Bancone 8B 29: Ministero delle Finanze: Circolare ai Signori Intendenti, 20 June 1807. See also De Lorenzo (1984).

[72] ANP: Fonds Joseph Bonaparte, 381 AP 2, Legge sui Consigli Comunali, Distrettuali e Provinciali, 8 August 1806 (Doc 1) Council of State, June 1807, 'Relation de M.Roederer sur la contribution foncière'.

[73] ANP: Fonds Joseph Bonaparte, 381 AP 5 (Doc 1), 'Pensieri che si propongono per rimediare agl'inconvenienti prodotti dalla Fondiaria' per Melchiorre Delfico (Council of State, 15 March 1808): 'Memorandum sur les observations de M. Delfico' (by Roerderer).

be registered as the basis for the individual assessment of the *fondiaria*.[74] When the provincial councils finally met in August 1808, they were unanimous in protesting the arbitrary and unfair ways in which the new tax had been assessed and distributed. Alarmed, the government revised the procedure to prevent the councils from protesting in the future, but re-issued the original assessments.

ADMINISTERING JUSTICE

As well as calling for a reorganization of central and local government, the abolition of feudalism in August 1806 required a complete reorganization of the magistracy and the administration of justice. The closure of the *ancien régime* tribunals had caused utter confusion, but in this case the French templates were of little use and the magistrates were in no mood to cooperate. They had been one of the most powerful corporations of the *ancien régime*, and with the abolition of the tribunals they had lost all their former power and privileges. They staunchly opposed all attempts at reform and like the clergy their unbending hostility to civil divorce made the introduction of the French *Code Civil* impossible. Napoleon would not make concessions, so there was little room for manoeuvre. Joseph Bonaparte played successfully for time, pleading the danger of a new *Santafede* if civil divorce was imposed by force. In the meantime the administration of justice remained suspended.

In June 1806 Miot de Melito had warned the Council of State of the urgent need to reorganize the administration of justice immediately.[75] The Minister of Justice, Michelangelo Cianciulli, made a start by sacking the senior judges, all of whom were committed royalists appointed after the fall of the Republic.[76] But replacing the *ancien régime* tribunals was a much more complex affair and since nothing could be done without the assistance of the magistrates, nothing was done.

The situation was also complicated by the fact that the closure of the *ancien régime* tribunals meant that their former employees, almost all of them in Naples, were now without work and a potentially dangerous source of discontent.[77] To remedy this the former employees were retained on full or part pay and in December 1807 the Minister of Justice ordered that they should be given first priority for positions in the new courts and those unable to work because of age should be given pensions. But shortly after becoming Minister of Justice, Giuseppe Zurlo still felt it necessary to issue another circular in May 1809 to 'all the subaltern officers of the former Tribunals and Jurisdictions in Naples that have been abolished' to assure them that the king was deeply aware of their difficult conditions and while seeking a solution had set up a Commission of

74 BNN: Ms Bancone 8B 25: Decree 12 August 1808.
75 ANP: Fonds Joseph Bonaparte, 381 AP 5 (Doc 2).
76 BNN: Bancone 8B 28, Decreto 6 March 1806: nomina dei magistrati.
77 As De Nicola constantly warned in his diaries.

Beneficence to relieve the distress of 'a group of persons whose indigence is before our eyes every day'.[78]

Saliceti tried to resolve the problems posed by the suspension of the tribunals by setting up ad hoc tribunals modelled on the special military tribunals established in 1806 to administer civil and criminal law, but the magistrates refused to serve on them.[79] In May 1807 the first general reform of the *ancien régime* tribunals was attempted. The former *Sacro Reale Collegio* was renamed the *High Court of Cassation* (*Gran Corte di Cassazione*) and divided into two sections, the first of which was responsible for revising laws and making proposals to the government. The same decree established the lesser tribunals of appeal and the new provincial tribunals, nominated royal procurators to all the courts, and appointed the justices of the peace, the first rung of the judiciary, in the provinces. Again the magistrates refused to cooperate.

The complaint raised by the provincial council in Capitanata when it met in the late summer of 1808 gives an idea of the state of confusion that had spread to the entire Kingdom:

> Justice is in total chaos and confusion. A new Code that has not yet been issued and new procedures that are unknown to those who must follow them have thrown the administration of Justice into chaos, and swings without direction between old and new in ways that prevent any judgment being reached and gives rise to arbitrary decisions that offend the liberty of the citizen. A solemn instruction to all judges to follow the new Codes of Criminal, Civil and Procedural law is sorely needed.[80]

On 20 May 1808 a new 'organic law' intended to establish the definitive administration of justice in the Kingdom based on the system of tribunals set out in the French constitution of Year VIII had been introduced. The Council of State was designated the supreme court of justice, below which the Cassation Court was the highest court of appeal. The High Court of Accounts (*Gran Corte dei Conti*) was responsible for overseeing all public expenditure, and new high criminal courts (*Gran Corti Criminali)* were established in Naples and the provinces to replace the former feudal courts. In January 1809 a new Tribunal of Commerce replaced the courts of the trade guilds that had been abolished in 1808.[81]

The magistrates would have none of Cianciulli's proposals, however, and their outraged protests forced his resignation a year later. He was briefly replaced in May 1809 by Giuseppe Zurlo, but he had no support either. In the same year, after a final unsuccessful attempt to exclude civil divorce, Murat bowed to the emperor's insistence and adopted the French legal codes. This was only the start, however, since the new legal codes had first to be translated and

[78] BNN: Bancone 8B 28, Circolare 10 March 1809. [79] Nicolini (1901), pp. xl–xliii.

[80] ASF: B.1 Consigli provinciali e distrettuali. Processi verbali, Consiglio provinciale di Capitanata 1809.

[81] See Feola, in Massafra (ed.) (1988), 487–506; Abbamonte, in ibid. 506–18, and Greco in ibid. 533–48.

the courts that would put them into practice had also to be created. That happened only after Francesco Ricciardi replaced Zurlo as Minister of Justice and for reasons that had little to do with Murat but a great deal to do with Saliceti and with Ricciardi.

Ricciardi, who did have wide support amongst the magistrates, had previously refused to accept the office of Minister of Justice on the grounds of Saliceti's systematic interference in judicial affairs.[82] Once Saliceti was gone, however, Ricciardi and his fellow jurists saw the opportunity to turn the introduction of the new Codes and courts to their own advantage and to write a script that would give the magistracy powerful new roles in the new post-feudal order.

EDUCATION

Amid these pressing administrative and financial emergencies, the time and energy devoted to education are at first sight surprising. But that would be to mistake both the ideological and practical importance of education in the new regime's modernizing project. Not only was education a subject on which the French and their Neapolitan supporters spoke the same language, but it also posed pressing administrative issues since the wholesale suppression of the religious houses had removed the existing source of popular education. Since the government had neither the means nor the intention of taking responsibility for the provision of education, it needed to make a strong moral case for delegating these responsibilities to local administration.

In 1806 Miot de Melito seized on the deficiencies of every form of education to denigrate the former monarchy and made popular education one of the priorities of the new regime. Three years later Zurlo boasted of the progress that had been made in the first years of the new order. Primary schools for boys and girls had been established in every *comune* in the Kingdom under the supervision of the new Intendents, and six new colleges had been opened in Naples and attended by 160 pupils. Two new schools for girls had also been founded, one in Naples and the other in Aversa under the patronage of the queen, where useful arts were taught in addition to religion. Nine new chairs had been established at the University of Naples.[83]

In the same year, 1809, a commission consisting of the Archbishop of Taranto, Melchiorre Delfico, the Bishop of Lettere and Gragnano, Tito Manzi, and Vincenzo Cuoco presented a first proposal for reorganizing public education to the Council of State. The report was written by Cuoco and in it he set out why public education was the premise for the regeneration of the Neapolitan nation.

[82] Nicolini (1901), p. xliv.

[83] Zurlo (1809), in Lalli (n.d.), 63–4.

Once a great kingdom, Cuoco argued, the decline of Naples was the consequence of centuries of corruption, barbarism, and the neglect of education, so that:

> the natural fertility of its soils has become a source of indolence, and the natural energies of its people have become the cause of ferocious and destructive passion. . . . Only education will enable us to retain our ancient greatness and ancient glory. Nature has bestowed on us all the capital we need. We do not lack for industries, but we do lack the knowledge to develop them; yet this, too, education can provide for us.

Concluding with a now familiar theme, he insisted too that education was the only means to overcome the abyss that divided the nation into two different peoples: 'The purpose of educating the masses is to make possible communication between the many and the few.'[84]

In a separate report, Cuoco had shown that the primary schools to which Zurlo had referred existed only in Minister of the Interior's fantasy. However, he recommended that such schools should be established in every *comune* and that they should teach writing, elementary mathematics, and morality: 'Morality is society's first need.' Schools should be free, and teachers should be trained in the methods of Pestalozzi, of whom Cuoco was a great admirer. He also held that schooling should be provided for both sexes, although addressing their different needs: 'Women are and always will be our most powerful educators. But to educate women in the same way as men would be to upset the order of nature, just as to educate all women in the same way would upset the order of society.'[85]

Cuoco's project and his recommendation for the creation of a Directorate of Public Education was rejected by the Council of State, ostensibly because it differed too much from the French model but in reality because his patron, the Archbishop of Taranto, had been replaced as Minister of the Interior by Giuseppe Zurlo. Zurlo was no friend of Cuoco and he promptly commissioned a new report drafted by another former Jacobin, Matteo Galdi, and finally adopted in December 1811.[86]

Its implementation was the responsibility of the local authorities, however, which immediately gave rise to loud protest from the local communities that were to pay the costs of the schools and their teachers.[87] Of the new schools that were opened most were simply classes run by the parish priest. As late as 1828 there were still only twenty-nine schools for boys in Naples, with 1,636 pupils, and twenty-three schools for girls with 3,000 pupils.[88] The royalist observers who at the time of the Restoration in 1815 claimed that the French regime's great school reform existed only on paper were probably not far wrong.[89]

84 'Rapporto al Re Murat e progetto di decreto per l'organizzazione della Pubblica Istruzione', in *Scritti Vari* (Cortese and Nicolini, 1924), ii. 3–95.

85 Cuoco (1809), ii. 3–95. See also Gentile (1909/1964).

86 On Galdi's report, see Lupo (1999), 249–99.

87 Cuoco (1809), 410–15.

88 See Fusco and Nicodemo in Massafra (ed.) (1988), 429–41.

89 See p. 283 below.

CONCLUSION

When Joseph Bonaparte left Naples in 1808, two years of energetic legislating and debate had mapped out a broad set of reform projects only some of which had been started. Feudalism had been abolished as a juridical principle, but the law of 2 August 1806 had, if anything, added to the uncertainties surrounding property rights. The law on the division of the common lands had been declared, but the government lacked the means to implement it. The institutions of the *ancien régime* monarchy had collapsed, but were not yet replaced. When the provincial assemblies met for the first time in the summer of 1808 to distribute the new land tax it became clear that it was one thing to legislate changes, another to implement them. But by then other forces were beginning to shape and redirect these initiatives in ways over which the government and its agents had little control.

10

A Kingdom Remodelled? The Provinces and the Capital

CONFLICTING AGENDAS

The promise of change was premised on the idea that enlightened government and rational administration would bring about the Kingdom's long-awaited regeneration. The logic was clear and even compelling. The abolition of feudalism would free property of the constraints that had prevented the exploitation of what were still considered to be the Kingdom's rich natural resources. Rational government would give rise to a new sense of unity and bring into being for the first time a true partnership between public and private interests:

'What is administration properly understood', asked Vincenzo Cuoco, 'if not the art of ensuring that the wealth, the talents, the moral sensibilities of private citizens can work together for the public good?'[1]

Redressing the historic imbalances between the capital and the provinces that had been a central theme of the reform writers of the previous decades was a primary mission of this project. But the difficulties facing such an enterprise were huge, and certainly not made any easier by the severe economic hardships resulting from the prolonged interruption of Mediterranean trade. But even in more favourable circumstances the obstacles would have been great, while the means at the disposal of the new government were slender. It could barely fund even the skeletal provincial administration carefully put in place by Saliceti, and local administration continued to depend on a handful of desperately overworked Intendents and Sub-intendents. Save only for a few prominent exceptions, the local notables showed little enthusiasm for being co-opted to perform administrative tasks they considered to be onerous and which carried no corresponding rights of consultation.[2]

There were deeper contradictions too. Behind the rhetoric, the government had clear but undisclosed fiscal objectives. The provinces were not only to bear the full of cost of their regeneration, but were in addition to carry a larger share of the expenses of the state. In 1812 Mosbourg acknowledged that this had indeed

[1] Cuoco (1806–15), 227. [2] Scirocco (1987), 102–25.

happened and that the entire increase in state revenue since 1808 had come from the provinces, much of it in forms of deliberately disguised taxation.[3] Similar fiscal motives lay behind the creation of Zurlo's Feudal Commission, since the division of the former feudal estates and the common lands was designed both to provide the local communities with a secure tax base and at the same time to increase the numbers contributing to the new land tax.

To complicate matters further, the capital also posed problems that could not safely be ignored. To bring greater equality and wealth to the provinces, the government was committed to removing the city's economic and fiscal privileges. But most of these had been abolished after 1799, and those that remained proved difficult to remove. Political imperatives also were at war with economic rationale. No less than their predecessors, the new regime needed a capital that reflected both their own glory and that of the empire, while the sheer size of the city meant that any moves that seriously prejudiced the livelihood of its citizens would be very dangerous. As it was, the impact of the war and prolonged commercial recession on the capital had been exacerbated by the unemployment caused by the abolition of the tribunals of the *ancien régime*, by the crisis of the banks and the charitable foundations, and by the competition from French placemen for white-collar jobs. Faced by these dangerous realities, the government was soon forced to look for ways to restore rather than further reduce the capital's former privileges.

THE PROVINCIAL ASSEMBLIES

The law of 8 August 1806 provided for the establishment of local and provincial assemblies for each of the fourteen mainland provinces.[4] The provincial assemblies consisted of up to twenty members nominated by the Intendents from lists of landowners in each province, and were to meet once a year for up to twenty days.[5] These assemblies had no consultative function, but they were charged with the task of distributing the land tax quotas set for each province and reporting on local conditions and needs.

When they first met in August 1808, the government was taken aback by the freedom with which the assemblies expressed their views. The most frequent subject of complaint was, not surprisingly, the new tax quotas, and even the Duke of Canzano, Intendent of one of the most prosperous provinces in the Kingdom, the Terra di Bari, remarked with exasperation that the allocation for his province

[3] See Chapter 8.

[4] Subdivided into 50 districts, 494 *circondarj*, and 1,732 *comuni*. ASN: Min. di Polizia, 1a F 152(2), Parlamento Nazionale 1820; Rapporto al Parlamento Nazionale sulla situazione del Ministero degli Interni, 23 October 1820, p. 7.

[5] Each town was administered by a *Decurionato*, whose members were elected by the principal property owners and then approved by the Intendent: the model was the French *conseils des départments, arrondissements, cantons et communes* of the Constitution of Year VIII. De Martino (1984), 307.

bore no relation to either the distribution or the productivity of the land in individual comunes.[6]

After the new taxes, the most frequent cause of lament was the devastating economic and commercial impact of over a decade of warfare that had brought overseas trade to a standstill. Everywhere the war had exacerbated existing problems and brought ruin to the wealthiest and the poorest provinces alike. The mountainous frontier province of L'Aquila had 'no Sea, no Agriculture, no Manufactures, no Crafts, and only some small Commerce with the neighbouring Papal State from which it receives little in return for sweat and labour except devastating afflictions and epidemics'. But as a result of the political upheavals in the Papal State, the annual value of trade across the border had fallen from a million to less than 80,000 ducats a year.[7]

The Provincial Council of Basilicata, which included Potenza, Matera, and Lagonegro, also stressed 'the unhappy state in which this Province presently finds itself because of the collapse of trade' and the impossibility of meeting the quotas set for the new land tax.[8] This was another mountainous province 'that generally has the appearance of a vast expanse of naked scree, with no settlements and no woodland and little farm land'. It produced some grain, but not enough to meet local needs, and a little wine. The population was healthy but scarce. There were some primary schools, but no teachers and a provincial college was needed to train teachers so that they could instruct the young in 'morality, Logic, History, Geography, Latin, Mathematics and some notions of experimental Physics'. There were numerous small *Luoghi Pii* (charitable foundations) but they lacked adequate funds.[9]

Conditions in the Province of Capitanata, which included Foggia and much of the *Tavoliere* together with the lands formerly subject to the *Dogana delle Pecore*, were more varied. In the poorest district of Larino 'Agriculture is in its infancy, and since there is no School of Agriculture its most rudimentary principles are unknown'. The government was called on to reduce taxes, provide credit, and set up schools of agriculture and animal husbandry, or at least ensure that in each *comune* there was someone 'able to teach a farmer's catechism and on certain days in the year teach the inhabitants how to sow corn, plant vines, make wine and oil and all other matters touching on the science of Agriculture'.[10] But the inhabitants of Serracapriola and Chieuti were 'ricchi' and as well as good land there was plentiful livestock.[11]

Even in the formerly prosperous commercial province of Apulia, the news was terrible. 'There is a shortage of farm labourers and no one to work the land . . . prices

[6] ASN: Min. delle Finanze: f. 2864 (Fondiaria 1808/9); Intendente Terra di Bari to Min. Finanze, 6 December 1808.

[7] Ibid.; Processi Verbali dei Consigli Generali di Provincia: 2nd Abruzzo Ulteriore (L'Aquila).

[8] Ibid.; Consiglio Provinciale di Basilicata (Matera, Potenza, Lagnegro), 25 October 1808.

[9] Ibid.; Consiglio Distrettuale di Lagonegro (Basilicata), 7 October 1808.

[10] ASF: Consigli Provinciali e Distrettuali (Busta 1), Processi Verbali, October 1808.

[11] ASN: Min. delle Finanze: f. 2864 (Fondiaria 1808/9); Consiglio Provinciale di Capitanata: Busta 1, 27 September 1808.

have collapsed and all internal and external trade is at a standstill.' The situation had been exacerbated by brigandage 'a Hydra that is constantly reborn in this kingdom'. The brigand's victims 'are the poor and the rich alike, the master and the servant, but the latter, to avoid the brigand's fury, deserts the plough and flees, leaving the fields unattended'. Another formerly prosperous province, the Terra di Bari, had also been ruined by the collapse of maritime trade. Prices had dropped to less than half their pre-1806 average, rents had fallen, land was uncultivated, and because of the fall in prices crops were left to rot in the fields.[12]

Many provinces took the opportunity to appeal for assistance. In Capitanata, the problem was a plague of insects (*bruchi*) that destroyed wheat, fruit, and vegetables and brought ruin to the prosperous city of Cerignola and to the region around Foggia and Lucera. The Provincial Council appealed for help to encourage the peasants to plant trees to protect the soil from heavy rains, to introduce horse breeding, and also for the land tax to be reduced. But the report concluded with resignation that none of these things would have an effect 'given the complete absence of trade'.[13]

The Provincial Council for Calabria Ultra lamented 'The unhappy state of the Province which has been a Theatre of War and has had to be host to an army come to fight the Enemy and maintain public order'. The council also underlined 'the sad consequences of Brigandage which has seriously damaged the incomes of the landowners, resulted in destruction that has impoverished the Province, brought internal and external trade to a halt, and caused a heavy increase in the cost of local administration'.[14]

Only in the provinces nearer the capital were conditions somewhat better. In the Upper Principato, the condition of agriculture was good but there were serious concerns about the unregulated clearing of woodland and hillsides for farming because this caused frequent landslides that made the lower lying land unfit even for pasture. There were large numbers of sheep in the province, but the wool woven locally was coarse. The province also lacked a decent road, and there were no bridges to cross the rivers Sebeto and Calore at Altavilla and Montemiletto.[15]

Although varied, the economy of the Campania, the province neighbouring the capital, was far from flourishing. It produced much silk, but it was of poor quality because of the 'rough traditional methods' of throwing and reeling the yarn. The peasants lacked training and needed to be encouraged to use Piedmontese organzine spinning machines that would double the value of the yarn, the best of which was spun by women from Sorrento, Piano di Sorrento, and Massa Lubrense. The fishing industry was in deep crisis because of the war, and because the fish markets in Naples were controlled by 'usurious merchants'.

[12] ASN: Min. delle Finanze: f. 2864 (Fondiaria 1808/9); Consiglio Provinciale di Terra di Bari, Presidente Duca d'Andria, 6 December 1808.

[13] Ibid.

[14] Ibid.; Consiglio Provinciale Calabria Ulteriore, 17 October 1808.

[15] Ibid.; Consiglio Provinciale di Principato Ultra (Montefusco), 8 October 1808.

Cotton was grown near Castellamare and Torre Annunziata, but its cultivation had expanded only because there was little demand for other products. Throughout the province demand for timber for building and for firewood had led to extensive clearance of woodland.[16]

As well as providing information on economic matters, the provincial assemblies in 1808 were required to report on social conditions, on the state of public health, roads, and public works, and on public welfare, orphanages, hospitals, prisons, schools, and colleges. In some cases these questions simply aroused some surprise. The district council of Larino in Capitanata, for example, commented that 'The legislation that we have had until now was a Gothic monument composed of elements that generally contradicted one another.' There were no secure prisons in the district and criminals generally went unpunished, nor was there neither a home for the aged nor a shelter for abandoned children. There were no schools, of any sort, 'theatres are unknown' and government needed to combat 'the ignorance of their responsibilities and duties that is evident among all classes of Inhabitants, and especially the bad conduct of the civic administration'. The local population had no contact with the outside world and 'are little better than savages'. Their houses were

> badly kept. From outside they bear only the marks of squalor and poverty, while inside they reveal a lack of cleanliness which is born from ignorance and carelessness. Were this the case only amongst the humblest Citizens it would be expected, but it is horrifying to find it also in the houses of property owners, of people who should know better. Rubbish and filth were the principal cause of disease and epidemics, and bodies were still being buried inside churches within the town walls. Can there be any worse state of barbarity?[17]

The provincial council of Capitanata complained about the neglect of foundlings: they were sent to wet-nurse but few survived and those that did became beggars. It underlined the need for institutions to take care of them until they were old enough to be placed with a craftsman or farmer to learn a trade. It also pointed out that there was no primary schooling in the province, but there were two important colleges. In Foggia, a convent of Theatine Fathers that was suppressed in 1797 had been taken over by the Scolopians and was attended by 400 young men, but the other college at Lucera was much smaller and very poor.

The assemblies called for measures to limit environmental damage and build and repair roads. They complained about poor and non-existent communications, and above all about population shortage in rural areas. This, it was claimed, was why vast tracts of land remained uncultivated, which in turn condemned the rural populations to lives of the most inhuman poverty. But even when natural causes were admitted, the members of the provincial councils placed the blame squarely on the poor. The Provincial Council of Terra d'Otranto, for example,

16 ASN: Min. dell'Interno (I) f. 183 (Consigli Provinciali): Consiglio Provinciale di Napoli, 1808.
17 ASF: Consigli Provinciali e Distrettuali (Busta 1), Processi Verbali, October 1808.

noted that the vast areas of swampland in the province caused pestilences that decimated the population and discouraged the poor from marrying. But they also argued that this encouraged 'immoral libertinism', especially amongst young girls who everywhere were ready to 'yield to seduction and are easily and quickly taken by men who will not release them until they agree to forced marriages'.[18]

TRADE AND MANUFACTURES

Earlier reports on the state of the Kingdom's manufacturing industries had revealed a similar situation, but also showed that the most advanced sectors of the economy had suffered most heavily. The most widespread form of manufacture was textile production, most of which was done on a domestic basis for local consumption. But there were a number of centres where more specialized forms of woollen cloth were produced, including Naples, Arpino, the Isola di Sora, Piedimonte d'Alife, Ceretto, and Avellino. All had been especially badly damaged by the decline in foreign trade, which had removed the only incentive for improvement since 'throughout the Kingdom the wealthier classes used exclusively imported cloth, while the poorer classes made their own so that markets for manufactured cloth were limited'.[19] The district of Arpino, once 'an Emporium for its surrounding areas and all the main cities in the kingdom', was a genuine example of structural decay and after ten years of war it had been reduced 'to a state of total penury: the woollen industry has collapsed because its products remain unsold, there is no capital, and the workers are unemployed'.[20]

Despite the French expectations that the South was a land of untapped resources, the Kingdom had few other industries. There were tanneries in the capital and at S. Maria di Capua, as well as at Solofra in the Cilento and in the Abruzzi, but the quality was described as poor and the methods of production primitive. Soap was manufactured in Naples and in the Abruzzi, but depended on imports of soda from abroad and was now at a standstill. There was fairly extensive production of tobacco, which was dried and pulverized for sale as '*erba santa*', but it was not produced for smoking or chewing. Some coloured glass panes were produced in Naples, but only on a small scale, and to expand, the industry needed new factories located closer to adequate supplies of timber and charcoal.

Iron ores were mined in Calabria at Stilo and at Piano d'Ardena near Montefusco, but the output was small and the quality poor. The main constraint was the shortage of timber, and to avoid exhausting the meagre supplies of timber the Stilo foundries moved peripatetically from site to site. Iron was not much used in agriculture and what was needed for making barrels for muskets and guns for

18 ASF: Consiglio Provinciale d'Otranto, 1808.
19 De Majo, in Lepre (ed.) (1985), 16.
20 ASN: Min. dell'Interno (II) f. 5068 (18 September 1816).

hunting was imported. The Silo foundry did produce ammunition for muskets, but attempts to cast cannon had been unsuccessful, as had the attempts at making steel, while the small quantity of metal blades produced was of extremely poor quality. Gunpowder was made in the arsenal at Torre Annunziata, however, using nitre mined in the Kingdom.[21]

In 1806, M. Riche of Parma was appointed *Inspecteur des manufactures* and commissioned to survey every branch of manufacture to enable the government to decide 'what was needed to revive and reform each branch'.[22] His report stated that the quality of the products of the royal porcelain factory at Capodimonte was poor, the methods of production were unsatisfactory and uneconomical, and the prices too high. A great deal of lace was also made, especially in Naples, but this was done almost entirely at home by women without any form of organization. The demand for these products from both the court and the Church was considerable, but in this case, too, local production was not competitive with foreign patterns and styles.[23]

The silk industry had been the subject of numerous government interventions to improve the quality of silk yarn in the final years of Bourbon rule,[24] and the director of the Royal Silk Factory explained that the Bourbons had wanted the S. Leucio factory to be a model to encourage the adoption of the Piedmontese method for spinning silk throughout the Kingdom. The traditional methods of throwing and twisting silk fibre relied on 'reeling done by the hands of peasants grown rough and calloused by ploughing and digging, which damaged the fibres and halved their value'. But the new spinning techniques threatened to put domestic spinners out of work and had provoked much popular opposition.[25]

The reports showed that the decline of the silk industry had much older origins. A century earlier about two-thirds of the population of Catanzaro had been engaged in the silk industry, but now less than 4,000 ducats were invested in the industry in the entire province and 'a large number of men and women remain without work and rot in idleness and poverty'. The causes were lack of capital and the failure to improve techniques (especially in dyeing), which had caused quality to decline. The industry had also proved unable to respond to changing fashions as cotton replaced silk for summer wear and damask silk cloth was less in demand for winter clothing and furnishings.[26]

Not only raw materials but also skilled and semi-skilled labour were in short supply. Referring to the warships to be built under the terms of the Treaty of Bayonne, the Foreign Minister di Gallo pointed out that there were less than 700 or 800 workers familiar with shipbuilding in the whole Kingdom and that all the

21 Ibid., f. 5067, 'Prospetto delle manifatture da stabilirsi nel Regno di Napoli' (no date but 1807). On the Calabrian iron works, see also Rubino (1978).

22 Ibid., f. 5066, Min. dell'Interno to M. Riche, 29 August 1806.

23 Ibid., Rapport de l'Inspecteur des manufactures, 29 October 1806, 2 December 1806.

24 Ibid., 29 May 1805.

25 Ibid., Tortora al Re, 23 May 1806.

26 Ibid., 'Memoria del abate Gregorio Araccri sull'industria della seta in Catanzaro'.

materials—the oak, iron, nails, lead, leather, canvas, and rope—needed to build a 74-gun ship had to be imported: 'What use are shipyards without materials, and what use are shipyards and materials without workers?'[27]

The new government continued the earlier Bourbon practice of granting subsidies and monopolies to encourage industries considered to be of strategic importance.[28] Murat went further and to the outrage of the imperial administration in Paris in 1809 imitated the emperor's protectionist policies by imposing duties on imported foreign manufactured goods. But these measures were not enough and the Royal Silk Factory at S. Leucio, which employed more than a thousand workers, had by 1813 accumulated huge stockpiles of unsold silk cloth: the government tried to dispose of these by lottery, but there were too few buyers.[29]

In open violation of imperial regulations, Murat's government began to adopt a coherent strategy of import-substitution to protect and develop key industries. The most important of these was textiles, and a number of Swiss cotton manufacturers whose native industries had been ruined by the Continental blockade and the emperor's Berlin Decrees were persuaded to open factories in the Kingdom. Jacques Egg of Elikon der Thur near Zurich set up the first cotton factory in the ex-convent of the Carmine in Piedimonte d'Alife in the Terra di Lavoro. Other Swiss cotton manufacturers did the same in the Salerno region, and similar facilities were offered to the French clothmakers Charles Lambert and Jules D'Escrivan, who opened a woollen cloth factory on the Isola di Sora in the northern Terra di Lavoro.[30]

The foreign textile manufacturers were provided with buildings and investment subsidies, and were guaranteed markets through government contracts for military or naval uniforms. But the results were not encouraging. When the government held a 'Solemn Exhibition of the Most Important National Manufactures in the Kingdom' in Naples in August 1810, Mosbourg commented to Murat, 'a very pompous article has been published on the products of our national industries presented in the Exhibition. Sadly, one has to say that none of these is in any way remarkable. To hold such an Exhibition every year would be too much.'[31]

The situation improved in the years that followed, but the principal victim of the prolonged recession, as the reports of the provincial assemblies in 1808 had revealed, was agriculture.

NEW ADMINISTRATIVE BURDENS

After decrying the economic paralysis caused by the prolonged interruption of trade, the protests of the provincial assemblies were aimed most loudly at the

[27] ANP: 31 AP 27; di Gallo to Duca di Bassano, n.d.
[28] ASN: Min. dell'Interno (II), f. 5068, Winspeare to Luigi de' Medici, 17 April 1805.
[29] ASN: Min. dell'Interno (II), f. 5066, 31 December 1813 (S. Leucio).
[30] See Davis (1981), 106–29; De Matteo (1984), 3–63; Wenner (1953).
[31] ANP: 31 AP 43: Mosbourg to Murat, 23 August 1813.

heavy new administrative costs with which the provinces were being burdened. There was particularly deep resentment at the costs for maintaining public order that had previously been the responsibility of the baronial and royal courts, the new Provincial Guards, and local gendarmerie set up in each town to replace the previous baronial *sbirri*.[32]

Both had been organized by General Rader, who had previously established similar gendarmeries in Corsica and in the Kingdom of Italy.[33] The Provincial Legions replaced the temporary Military Commissions set up immediately after the conquest, and were responsible 'for maintaining public order and security, for keeping exact lists of all vagabonds, unemployed persons, disturbers of the peace, those guilty of riotous behaviour or carrying prohibited weapons, while watching out for Enemies of the State, those guilty of spreading false rumours and causing Alarm, and all those suspected of Brigandage who must be arrested'.[34]

There was no rush to recruit, however, and in June 1806 General de Gambs ordered every *comune* in Abruzzo Citra to draw up a list of 'volunteers', adding that 'His Majesty wishes it known that being enrolled in the Legion will be considered a necessary condition for all those seeking any civil or military employment.'[35] Still no response, and a month later De Gambs threatened to impose conscription on all towns that failed to supply the required number of volunteers.[36]

The carrying of firearms was prohibited, and each town was required to maintain a prison 'with windows, iron doors and a gate with three heavy locks'. The prison guards should be able to read and write, and if there were no former feudal *sbirri* to perform this duty, army veterans could be employed. But few towns could afford this and the instructions were soon countermanded.

There were frequent complaints, however, that the Provincial Guards and the gendarmes were the main cause of public disorder, which was tacitly acknowledged in 1812 when the commander of the *Gendarmerie Reale delle Due Sicilie* reminded his officers that the *Gendarmerie* existed to protect property and persons, that authorization from a magistrate was required before searching houses or private property, and that the civil authorities should be present when deserters or other delinquents were arrested. Full written reports had to be made regularly of all arrests and other activities, and it was strictly forbidden for gendarmes to lend their weapons 'to friends who want to use them for hunting'. The general concluded by pointing out that it had been discovered that many members of the Guard were draft-dodgers, while others 'were accompanied by women who are certainly not their legitimate spouses'.[37]

32 Law of 8 October 1806.

33 Regulations stipulated that recruits should have four years service in a Regiment of the Line, be at least 5 ft. 5 in. in height, be able to read and write, be of 'good moral standing and have a decent public reputation'. Pay was 136 ducats a year for an infantryman and 245 ducats for the cavalry, with higher rates for sergeants and corporals. *BNN*: Ms. Bancone 8: 'Gendarmerie Napoletana', 24 March 1806.

34 Ibid., Commissione Temporanea di Alta Polizia, Cerignola, September 1806.

35 Ibid., Proclama del Gen di Divisione Daniel de Gambs, 23 June 1806 (Chieti).

36 Ibid., 23 July 1806.

37 Ibid., Gendarmeria Reale del Regno delle Due Sicilie, 15 May 1812.

Given the failure of voluntary service, in 1812 the government adopted a form of conscription by ballot for the Civic Guards, an innovation that was denounced by an outraged Vincenzo Cuoco, who considered it to be inefficient, costly, and contrary to the true principles of patriotism.[38]

As well as local gendarmerie and the voluntary *Guardia Civica*, the *comuni* were also expected to pay for a justice of the peace, to establish primary schools and health clinics, and to retain the services of physicians for the poor (*medici condotti*).[39] They also had to implement the new regulations requiring that cemeteries be sited outside the town walls, that drains be provided for household waste, and that animals should not be allowed to graze or be kept in public streets, enforce the use of new weights and measures, and ensure that no meat from animals dying of disease was sold for human consumption.[40]

These were very heavy financial burdens especially for poor communities, and despite the annual visitations by the Intendent or Sub-intendent they were rarely observed. The suppression of many local charitable foundations (*luoghi pii*) also left the local communities responsible for funding for poor relief. It was not until 1813 that the government began the difficult task of auditing the revenues of the provincial charitable foundations, an operation not completed until 1819. Excluding Naples and Sicily, there were 7,224 charitable foundations in the Kingdom with estimated annual revenues of just over 1,000,000 ducats. But there were marked geographical disparities. Roughly half the revenues belonged to institutions in the Terra di Lavoro, Principato Citra, and the Terra di Bari. By contrast, there were only 213 *luoghi pii* in Basilicata, 283 in Primo Abruzzo Ultra, 56 in Calabria Ultra Prima, and only 21 in Calabria Ultra Seconda. Not surprisingly, the poor were much better provided for in the wealthier provinces.[41]

PUBLIC WORKS

Better roads and more effective land reclamation projects topped the list of what the provincial assemblies wanted from the government. These also figured high in the government's pronouncements and in 1810 the Interior Minister, Giuseppe Zurlo, proudly announced that the government was planning to build a new bridge over the Volturno River and another over the river Calore, and

38 Cuoco (1806–15), ii. 184.

39 Ibid. 410–15. See also Lupo (1999).

40 BNN: Bancone 8, Piano di Polizia Municipale che si presenta per Cerignola all'Ilustrissimo Intendente di Capitanata, Sig. Cav. Poerio (October 1806).

41 ASN: Min. di Polizia (1a) 152/2: Rapporto al Parlamento Nazionale (October 1820), 56–7: Terra di Lavoro, 1,418 *luoghi pii* with a total annual revenue of 289, 402 ducats; Principato Citra, 703 institutions with revenues of around 100,000 ducats per year; Terra di Bari, 729 institutions with 123,972 in annual revenue. By contrast, there were only 213 *luoghi pii* in Basilicata (total revenue 52,402 ducats per year), 283 in Primo Abruzzo Ultra (21,451 ducats), 56 in Calabria Ultra Prima (18,325 ducats), and only 21 in Calabria Ultra Seconda (14,743 ducats).

was engaged in a major project to drain the extensive marshlands along the Volturno River and in the region around Fondi:

Amongst the many misadventures that the negligence and ignorance of man has brought to this most beautiful and fertile part of Italy, the most pitiful are the vast swamps that have rendered huge areas uninhabitable and prevent any form of farming.[42]

Responsibility for directing these projects was delegated to two new agencies, the General Directorates of *Bridges and Roads* and *Woodlands and Waterways*.[43] Both imitated French models and were examples of the interventionist administrative mentality of the new regime. But both suffered from severely inadequate funding.

Much was promised but little was done, while the provinces protested that the funds they paid for public works were frequently put to other uses. The Provincial Council of Capitanata, for example, complained in 1809 that the province had raised 180,000 ducats in taxes to repair the road that linked Apulia to Naples and the bridge at Bovino, but the work had never been started.[44] Two years later the same road was still blocked by a landslide, and the bridge at Bovino had still not been repaired either. In other cases the funds never materialized. In Molise, Joseph Bonaparte allocated *beni nazionali* worth 40,000 ducats to fund the building of a new road to link Campobasso with Naples, which the Provincial Council had agreed was the province's greatest need. But the project was never started because there were no buyers for the *beni nazionali* in question and the Provincial Council could not accept the offer of a loan because it had no means to repay it.[45]

A report drawn up in 1813 by Vincenzo Cuoco showed that little progress had been made on the land reclamation projects started under the previous monarchy, and that in many cases the situation had deteriorated. Major reclamation operations had been started, for example, in the flooded territory known as the Vico di Pantanto situated on the southern bank of the Volturno River between Cunia and Castelvolturno that had been under crown administration since before 1806, and where the Bourbon administrator Martucci had begun a number of drainage operations. The main problem was that there was no general plan for the area as a whole, without which, Cuoco argued, time and money were being wasted. In other cases the rulings of the Feudal Commission had disastrous effects on projects that had already been started. As an example Cuoco cited the Eboli plain, which in technical terms was relatively easy to drain, but the whole operation had been jeopardized when the Feudal Commission divided up the properties on which drainage operations had already begun, so that the swamps were taking over again.[46]

The relative neglect of the provinces was evident from the fact that the entire budget for provincial public works in 1815 was a mere 55,000 ducats[47]—a reflection of

[42] Zurlo, in Lalli (n.d.), 69.
[43] *Direzionale Generale de Ponti e Strade* and the *Direzione Generale delle Acque e Boschi.*
[44] ASF: Processi Verbali, Consiglio Distrettuale di Foggia 1809 (B 1).
[45] Cuoco (1806–15), ii. 202–3. [46] Ibid.
[47] ASN: Min. di Polizia (1a) f.152/2: Rapporto al Parlamento Nazionale 1820, 10.

the overwhelming demands of war expenditures in the final phase of Murat's reign. The situation was much better in the province of Bari, but with only a few exceptions the French rulers invested little in the provinces and significantly less than in the capital, while the investments made were paid for by the provinces.

PAYING FOR PROGRESS

The impact of the administrative burdens that were transferred to the provinces was clearly evident from the changing style of the annual reports of the provincial and local councils. After 1810 the government no longer solicited general comments, but delegated that responsibility to more narrowly selected *Economic Societies*.[48] The reports of the provincial and local councils instead became mere lists of expenses that reveal the high costs of emancipation.

The list of expenses recorded by the Provincial Council for Capitanata in 1811 began with a salary increase for the Intendent, the costs of the Intendent's annual visitation of the province, the cost of the households of the Intendent and of the Sub-intendent, and the cost of the vaccination campaign against smallpox ordered by the government. The province also contributed over 9,000 ducats to the cost of maintaining foundlings, whose number had increased 'either because of the critical circumstances of the times which compromise honest girls or because of the seductions that they do not know how to resist'. It had to pay for barracks for the *Gendarmerie Reale* (6,858 ducats), for the cost of collecting the statistics required for the general census ordered by the government, and for the operations to destroy the eggs of the insects that had devastated the region. The report concluded that the province did not have the means to meet these expenses.[49]

Starting in 1810, each *comune* was required to prepare a provisional budget (*stati discussi*), which had to be submitted for approval to the Intendent's office. The preparation and approval of these budgets were the subject of endless disputes, but the resulting budgets clearly showed how new and additional taxes were constantly being added.[50] The sources of income for the *comuni* were, by contrast, relatively fixed, consisting of rents for land and buildings belonging to the *comune* and consumption taxes. In 1815 these were calculated to amount to a total of 1,500,000 ducats for the entire Kingdom (excluding Naples and Sicily). It was difficult to contract out the collection of these taxes, and most *comuni* raised them through capitation taxes, which were 'most burdensome for the least prosperous class of people'.[51]

48 See pp. 244–6.

49 ASF: Consigli Provinciali e Distrettuali, Processi Verbali (Busta 1); Consiglio Provinciale di Capitanata, 1811.

50 These included an annual contribution of 500,000 ducats to the cost of provincial public works. Then in 1812 the provinces were required to contribute an additional tax of 5% of their total revenues to pay for the *Legioni Provinciali* as well as other charges. Ibid. 22, 80.

51 Ibid. 21.

The division of common lands by the Feudal Commission was designed to address at least some of the financial problems facing the rural communities, but that complex and problematic operation provided few immediate and even fewer long-term solutions. In the meantime, the financial costs of the new administrative system introduced by the law of 8 August 1806 were passed onto the provinces, which by 1812 were also contributing over 4,000,000 lire a year more to the land tax than in 1808, a situation that even the finance minister Count Mosbourg considered to be unsustainable and politically dangerous.[52]

THE CAPITAL

At the time of the Restoration in 1815, the Bourbon minister Donato Tommasi judged the reorganization of the administration of Naples to be one of the best innovations made by the French rulers. The changes meant that the government was finally fully in control of the city, making it possible for the first time to regulate building, communications, public health, and commercial activities. The French had introduced new controls over public food markets, as well as street lighting and the streets were being named and numbered. There were even plans for a new cemetery to be built in a 'magnificent enclosed ground that is sufficiently spacious to accommodate all the city's corpses', although by 1815 work had still not started because the project proved to be very costly.[53]

The unfinished cemetery was in many ways a fitting epitaph to the decade of French rule in the capital. Although the French rulers set out to reorganize the city and remove its economic privileges, almost from the start the project ran up against political and administrative difficulties that proved insurmountable. In part these derived from the disastrous state of the city's economy, but the problems were compounded by the contradictions embedded in the policies of the new regime.

When the French entered Naples in February 1806, they found a city that had suffered the impact not only of invasion and civil war but of a prolonged commercial recession that dated from Ferdinand IV's entry into the First Coalition in 1793. In 1793–4 and again in 1801 the city was the victim of severe subsistence crises. After 1799 it had been stripped of its former jurisdictional privileges, its independent government had been abolished, it had lost its exemption from conscription, and more severe measures had been imposed to reduce the flow of migrants and vagrants from the surrounding rural areas.

In the decades following the famine of 1763/4, the city's population had risen dramatically,[54] but after 1800 began to decline again and reached a trough

[52] ANP: 31 AP 34, Mosbourg to Murat, 14 November 1812.

[53] Donato Tommasi, formerly a close friend of Filangieri, was a senior Bourbon administrator who followed the court to Palermo. In 1814 he drafted an extensive commentary on the administrative and juridical reforms introduced by the French rulers: ASN: Archivi Privati, Carte Tommasi.

[54] From 300,000 to about 400,000 by the close of the century.

in 1811.[55] Since there is no evidence of significant out-migration, disease and mortality were the most likely causes, and in 1809–10 and again in 1816–17 the city was the victim of further serious subsistence crises and epidemics.[56] The paralysis of trade caused severe unemployment among all occupational groups, and the Provincial Council in 1811 reported that domestic servants and fishermen had suffered most.[57] Between 20 and 50% of the population were estimated to be either destitute or on the verge of destitution.[58]

The relative distribution of population between the capital and the provinces changed little, however. In 1800, Naples contained just under 10% of the entire mainland population: in 1815 the proportions were much the same, suggesting that the relationship between the capital and the provinces had not changed significantly during the decade of French rule.[59]

SECURING THE CITY

Although there was no repetition of the events of January 1799, when the French entered Naples in February 1806 they were very mindful of the immediate past. A special Police Commissariat was established under the Minister of the Interior and the city was divided into twelve *quartieri*, each with its own Commissar of Police and a force of gendarmes. The *Commissari* were given wide powers to arrest and detain suspected enemies of the state, as well as 'vagabonds, beggars and unknown persons'. The police were charged with surveillance of the mails and censorship of all publications, with granting licences to carry firearms, for street vendors, porters, stevedores, fishermen, and cab drivers; public gatherings were temporarily banned and required permission from the police, as did fairs and markets, and anyone seeking access to the port and docks. Commissars were appointed as police magistrates in each district with the power to impose fines to a maximum of 12 carlini and up to eight days imprisonment for 'crimes that warrant corporal punishment and public disgrace'[60]

The Duke of Laurenzana, who had been arrested as a traitor in 1799, was appointed Commissioner of Police in March. The former Bourbon magistrates were arrested and removed and replaced by 'prominent patriots from 1799'.[61] On 19 July the voluntary *Guardia Urbana* became a permanent *Guardia Civica* in which all 'former military officers and gentlemen, shopkeepers, craftsmen and their sons as well as people in His Majesty's service' were obliged to serve. The cost was to be met by the city, and exemption fees for those not wishing to serve in person were set at 300 ducats: 'From what I hear no-one has paid this', remarked Carlo De Nicola.[62]

[55] The figures were 1806, 378,402; 1809, 305,000/350,000; 1811, 307,173; 1814, 324,986; 1817, 326,557 (Pilati, 1978, 2).

[56] Martuscelli (1979), p. xlv.

[57] Ibid., tables I and F.

[58] Ibid., p. xlviii; Villani (1978), 163.

[59] Martuscelli (1979), p. cxi.

[60] De Nicola, 3 March 1806, 226.

[61] Ibid., 28 March, 237.

[62] Ibid., 27 March 1806, 200; 19 July, 272.

The *Guardia Civica* was reorganized again in 1813, and all males between the ages of 25 and 60 'without exception, from public employees to shop-owners inclusive' were obliged to serve. Citizens were divided into six categories (former volunteers, public employees, professionals, persons of means, merchants, and shopkeepers) and each had to supply a fixed contingent of recruits. Renamed the Public Security Guard, the new force consisted of 48 companies, each with 155 men: 'which is to say 600 for each district in the city'. No exemptions or substitutions were permitted.[63]

In 1808 the policing of the capital was reorganized again on Napoleon's instructions, and a Prefecture of Naples was created on the model of the *Préfecture de la Seine* in Paris. This proved to be extremely costly and to finance it new taxes had to be raised on licences for wine cellars, inns and taverns, playing cards, passports, fishing boats, and draft animals. These were insufficient, and in 1810 'wet-nurses, obstetricians, pharmacists, suppliers of drugs, dyers and weavers' were all required to obtain licences, and new taxes were imposed on houses with doors opening onto the street and on playing cards. Nonetheless, the Prefecture's budget was repeatedly overspent.[64]

MUNICIPAL GOVERNMENT

A new municipal government, known as the *Corpo della Città*, came into being with the law of 8 August 1806. Presided over by a member of the Council of State it consisted of thirty *decurioni*, a mayor, and twelve *Eletti*, one for each *quartiere* of the city, and all nominated by the government. Its functions were limited to matters of 'urban policing', which included the licensing of urban trades and markets, the maintenance of roads, regulation of weights and measures, distribution of the land tax, the appointment of justices of the peace for each district, and after 1809 the organization of conscription quotas.[65]

In 1806 the city's debts were amalgamated with those of the state, and the government established a fixed annual budget.[66] But although taxes continued to increase, they were never sufficient to cover the costs of the new administration. Even so, the capital's contribution to direct taxation remained relatively low in relation to the size of its population: Naples and its province accounted for 12% of the Kingdom's population but contributed only 15% of the land tax, despite the fact that wealth was concentrated disproportionately in and around the capital. Rather surprisingly, the contributions to the capitation tax introduced in September 1809 specifically on incomes from trade and other activities indicate that less than 3% of the total of those registered resided in the capital.[67]

[63] Ibid., 14–20 March 1813, 618–19.

[64] Valente (1940), 263; De Martino (1984), 180–5.

[65] Cutolo (1932), 5–17.

[66] De Rosa (1959), 18.

[67] 29 September 1809; see Villani (1978), 163; the figures for the tax on trade and professions introduced in 1811 are not available.

CHARITY AND WELFARE

The desperate situation of the city's charitable foundations was a consequence of increased demand caused by the prolonged economic recession and then by the suppression of monasteries and convents in the capital. But it was above all the devastating consequences of the suspension of the *arrendamenti* and the abolition of feudal revenues that forced the government to intervene.[68]

The poverty of the capital was one of the most intractable problems facing the new rulers, but it was also one from which they sought to make political capital. The horror that Miot de Melito expressed at the capital's poverty in his report on the state of the realm in 1806 was a constant refrain. In his memoirs Pierre Louis Roederer, for example, commented, 'In Naples, the streets are full of the most infamous *canaille* and people piss everywhere even in the palaces.'[69]

Similar language recurred in the report of the Provincial Council in 1808:

> Every one knows the appearance of the inhabitants of this Metropolis, a mass of evil looking characters and prostitutes who render the streets ugly while bands of naked and disease-ridden children without parents or homes importune the citizens with their laments, live off offal, dead animals and garbage and sleep piled on top of one another in the streets.[70]

The purpose of this language was to make vagrancy, filth, and poverty bludgeons with which to assail the indiscriminate provision of charity. Miot de Melito had been quick to point to the proliferation of charitable institutions as the main cause of poverty and unemployment because they encouraged a culture of sloth and idleness.

Conditions were indeed horrendous. The *Albergo dei Poveri*, the city's principal poorhouse that doubled as a prison for vagrants, was in a state of 'veritable desolation' and had been partly converted into a military barracks. The principal hospital for the poor, the *Ospedale degli Incurabili*, was in a 'terrible state': it had been sacked in 1799 and had then lost most of its revenues as a result of the conversion of the *arrendamenti*. The principal hospice for abandoned infants, the *Ospedale dell'Annunziata*, was in similar decay and the majority of foundlings lodged there 'perish from the cold and hunger or get eaten by wild animals'. Those poor wretches that survived 'are destined, if their poverty does not cause them to perish at an early age, to become the most dangerous subjects in the State'.[71]

The French ambassador, D'Aubusson, was especially scandalized by the death rate amongst the foundlings, which he blamed illogically on the widespread

[68] The Neapolitan religious houses suppressed in 1807 included the monastery of San Martino and the Calmaldoli houses; in January 1808 the government closed the richest nunneries (Santa Maria dei Miracoli and San Marcellino) and in May a further 26 convents, including the largest, the Franciscan convent of the Holy Trinity in via Toledo. Rambaud (1908), 302–4.

[69] Roederer (1854), vi. 73, 103.

[70] ASN: Min. dell'Interno (I), f. 183, Consiglio della Provincia di Napoli, 1808.

[71] ANP: Fonds Joseph Bonaparte, 381 AP 3, Miot de Melito to Joseph Bonaparte, 4 July 1806.

practice among the poor of using herbs to induce miscarriages. In this manner, he claimed, the Neapolitan *lazzaroni* were cheating the emperor's armies of some 2,000 potential conscripts a year, an outrage he called on the clergy to campaign against and on the police to act more severely in cases of suspected infanticide.[72]

A decade later conditions were no better. Of the foundlings and orphans that entered the *Ospedale della Annunziata* 'it is painful to record that nine tenths perish'. Attempts were made to establish schools for the foundlings who survived, but these failed because of 'the habits of idleness and abuse that they have inherited'.[73]

Conditions in the *Albergo dei Poveri* were as bad. It had been built on what was formerly a marsh, and the buildings were damp and unhealthy. The inmates slept 'in the least healthy part of the building, and there was no fresh water'. The building had never been completed and had suffered serious damage in 1799, so that 'on entering the Capital the visitor is greeted by the sight of a vast monument that is unfinished and apparently abandoned'.[74]

The situation became even worse when the French government designated it as the city's '*dépôt de mendicité*'. The object was to cleanse the capital 'of those crooked, deformed and mutilated creatures that plague it, and of the vagabonds and beggars who make it unsafe', and over 5,000 inmates of both sexes ended up being housed there:

> this great family is composed of beggars, vagabonds, men notorious for obscene actions, prostitutes and all the other wretches who give themselves up or are arrested on the public highways of the capital.[75]

Instruction in a range of crafts and skills was provided for the young male paupers, who could train to be 'tailors, shoemakers, barbers, carpenters, woodturners, metal-casters, printers, makers of weapons, weavers and spinners', but there was only lace-making for the girls. New Bell and Lancaster school were later introduced for the younger children, and fifty of the female inmates were sent to work in Signor Egg's cotton-spinning factory in Piedmonte d'Alife. Many of the young boys were sent to the army as drummers and pipers. But the attempts to provide training for the young and find useful work for the paupers failed either because the funds to buy machines and materials were lacking or, more generally, because of the 'force of inertia'.[76]

To round off the catalogue of human suffering, conditions in the city's prisons were described in one government report as 'a shame to Humanity'.To remedy these problems that had been seriously aggravated by assault on the revenues of the charitable foundations, the government looked primarily for administrative

[72] AAEP: CP (Naples) 132, 'Notes sur le Royaume de Naples' (1808).

[73] Ibid., 42; see also *ASN*: Min. dell'Interno Int (I) f. 183, Consiglio della Provincia di Napoli 1808. Of the 1,676 foundlings that entered the Annunziata between January and December 1808, 1,311 died.

[74] ASN: Min. di Polizia (1a) f. 152(2), Rapporto al Parlamento Nazionale sulla situazione del Ministero degli Affari Interni (23 October 1820), 86.

[75] Ibid.

[76] Ibid.

economies. The smaller foundations were suppressed or amalgamated with larger surviving institutions, an operation overseen by a Central Welfare Committee whose members included the Grand Almoner, the Cardinal Archbishop of Naples, the President of the *Corpo della Città*, and four wealthy proprietors 'renowned for their concern for the poor'.[77] Charitable commissions were set up in each *quartiere* of the city, on which leading citizens and wealthy merchants were required to serve. The Commissions received the miserable sum of 16,000 ducats a year from the government, and their task was to raise private donations to support the families of the deserving poor and to organize soup kitchens and other forms of relief for the poor in times of special hardship.[78]

Unemployment continued to rise, however, and new taxes had to be introduced to support the charitable institutions. When the city was faced with a major subsistence crisis in 1810 the government created a further Council of Hospices and introduced another consumption tax that was expected to raise 100,000 ducats a year. But it did not, and by then the crisis had reached deep into the capillary networks of pawn shops, soup kitchens, hospices, conservatories, hospitals, madhouses, and poorhouses on which the majority of urban poor depended for survival. Some were shut down or put to other use. Many of the conservatories that offered shelter for poor women who were permanently or temporarily single were amalgamated or suppressed, 'which caused their numbers to decrease, and while this has benefited two or three institutions it has ruined the rest, whose inmates are forced to beg on the streets to survive'.[79]

The institutions that provided 'home help' for the deserving poor were particularly hard hit. The *Monte della Misericordia*, which had formerly provided alms and food for poor families in their own homes, was, for example, converted into a barracks for French troops. These losses were compounded by the plunder of the assets of the lay confraternities, another traditional source of support for the independent urban poor.[80]

The larger institutions weathered the storm, in part because of mergers with smaller foundations but also because of their important role in the urban economy. These institutions were major providers of work and a major source of demand for victuals, clothing, linen, bedding, beds, furniture, clerical materials, firewood, and so forth. Although their ability to provide for the poor was reduced, they continued to offer employment for the armies of administrators, lawyers, accountants, estate managers, architects, builders, decorators, plasteres, gatekeepers, gardeners, porters, cooks, cleaners, laundry-women, and workmen.

Not only did the charitable foundations play a crucial role in the urban economy, but without the support of those who administered the city's charitable foundations Naples would almost certainly have been impossible to govern.

77 Landi (1977), ii. 806–7. 78 Ibid. 51.

79 ASN: Min. di Polizia (1a) f. 152(2), Rapporto al Parlamento Nazionale sulla situazione del Ministero degli Affari Interni (23 October 1820). 80 Ibid. 52–4.

As a result, while the government seized whatever revenues it could lay its hands on, there was no serious attempt to undermine the corporate structures around which the charities and the life of the city more generally were organized.

1809–10: FEARS OF FAMINE

The French rulers had other reasons for dropping their original projects for reorganizing the city, which were especially evident when in 1810 the city was again threatened by famine. The crisis, which came while Murat was preparing the invasion of Sicily that never took place, came with advanced warning when poor harvests in the summer of 1809 raised fears about the capital's food supplies, just at a moment when Napoleon's campaign against Austria had brought the Kingdom's trade to a complete standstill.

The threatened subsistence crisis in the capital offered the government the pretext for permanently abandoning the liberal economic measures that had been adopted by Joseph Bonaparte. New protectionist measures directed even against French imports followed, while Joseph's attempts to liberalize trade between the capital and the provinces were replaced by new regulations designed to protect consumers in the metropolis.

In Naples, the situation became more threatening when an outbreak of typhoid fever began in the autumn of 1809. As the winter progressed, predictions for the coming harvest became more dire, and in February 1810 the government suspended the free movement of grain and began negotiating with the leading merchants to purchase grain from abroad. The merchants claimed that the risks were too high and refused. Murat begged the emperor for permission to purchase grain from American ships, but this was refused. He then offered the merchants more attractive terms, which they accepted.[81]

The crisis led to the adoption of new regulations for provisioning the capital that became permanent and were designed to ensure once again that the urban consumer would be guaranteed the lowest food prices available. Free trade in cereals was permitted only when the provincial Intendents gave assurance that prospects for the forthcoming harvest were good; otherwise, grain exports were prohibited while imports were freely permitted.[82]

Once again, the capital and the urban consumer were protected at the expense of the provincial grain producers, who were denied access to more lucrative export markets. Free trade was briefly restored after the Restoration, but then abandoned again in favour of the regulations introduced in 1811, which became a major source of conflict between the Restoration government and the southern

[81] AAEP: CC (Naples) 39, 391; ANP: AFiv 1714a, 31 October 1810.

[82] See the detailed description by the French Consul General, Doriol: AAEP: CC (Naples) 39, 390–4, 1811.

landowners. But these problems again revealed why more balanced relations between the capital and the provinces were not easily achieved.

PUBLIC WORKS

For reasons of political expediency and dynastic representation, the capital also continued to absorb the greater part of the government's expenditure on public works. The most ambitious urban development project attempted in these years was the creation of a new public space in the centre of the city and in front of the royal palace, for which the convents of S. Spirito and S. Francesco da Paola had been demolished.[83] New roads were built to connect the capital with the neighbouring settlements of Posillipo and Ottajano. A fund of 240,000 ducats was set up for another road that would link Naples with Calabria, and another 70,000 ducats in 1812 for a road from Naples to Civitella del Tronto on the frontier with the Papal States in the Abruzzi. New administrative bodies were created to prepare and oversee these projects, but lack of funds or regular budgets meant that few were started and none completed.[84]

Nonetheless Carlo de Nicola was outraged:

> The Kingdom is exhausted, the government has turned thirty thousand families into beggars, and yet it still thinks it a good idea to construct a new road that will link the Royal Palace directly with the park of Capodimonte.[85]

Even though few of the projects initiated by the French rulers had been completed by the time of the Restoration, Naples remained the principal beneficiary of the new regime's interest in urban development. In the provinces Bari also underwent extensive rebuilding, but the capital was the main focus of the government's attention and the French rulers were no less determined than their predecessors that their capital should reflect both the glory of the empire and their own dynastic ambitions.[86]

SEEKING ACCOMMODATION

Just as the government's attempts to reduce the city's economic privileges were quickly abandoned, so too were its efforts to replace earlier corporate bodies and regulations with new forms of bureaucratic administration. The nobility's corporate monopoly over municipal government had been abolished by the Bourbons, and this was never restored. When they first took control of the city the French quickly abolished the guilds and confraternities as part of a more general attempt to deregulate the urban economy.

[83] Now Piazza Plebiscito: building of the monumental church of S. Francesco da Paola was started after 1815 to celebrate the Restoration of the Bourbon dynasty.

[84] The *Consiglio di Pubblici Lavori* and the *Consiglio di Edilizio*.

[85] De Nicola, 20 September 1808, 374.

[86] De Seta (1981), 211–25.

In Naples, as in every other major Italian city, the independent municipal tribunals, together with the craft guilds, the lay confraternities, the major convents, the parishes, and the religious orders, continued to dominate and effectively govern most aspects of the public and private lives of the city and its inhabitants.[87] This was normal and of all the Italian cities, only in Habsburg Milan had serious measures been taken by the end of the eighteenth century to dismantle corporate controls and institutions.[88] But that was the model that the French rulers followed and in August 1806 the government decreed that 'all exemptions from taxes and duties' previously enjoyed by the guilds and corporations of the capital were abolished, as were the guilds and lay confraternities.

Forty-five trade guilds and lay confraternities, each with its own patron church or chapel, were abolished and their assets transferred to the state. Writing later in the century, the Marchese Ceva Grimaldi claimed that the abolition of the corporations had resulted in the massive expropriation of the craftsmen of the capital, who were left with a single dowry bank (*monte di maritaggi*) to provide for the needs of daughters of working people.[89]

Although stripped of their resources, the guilds and the confraternities continued to function with the government's tacit approval.[90] When the Consuls of the Wool Guild protested vigorously about the loss of their commercial privileges, M. Riche, the Inspector General of Manufactures, supported them and claimed under the new laws they would have to pay 4,000 ducats a year in taxes to bring raw wool into the city, which would make them uncompetitive with provincial manufacturers. Given the importance of the woollen industry as a source of employment in the city, M. Riche urged that the tax exemptions be restored. The Consuls of the Guilds continued to represent the interests of their members, and in 1808 M. Riche complained that their refusal to cooperate made it impossible to obtain information about the state of manufactures in the city.[91]

The fate of the guilds and the lay confraternities illustrates the more general impact of French rule on the city. Their assets were seized by the government, but the corporations survived albeit without the means to perform their previous functions. To have done away with them altogether would have been extremely difficult, however, since the government did not have the means to create bureaucratic alternatives. The guilds and confraternities also proved to be indispensable allies when it came to governing the city, since they formed an integral part of the networks of patronage around which municipal politics hinged.

This was unintentionally acknowledged by the French ambassador, D'Aubusson, who in July 1808 reported that policing the city depended on mobilizing powerful factions. He believed that Joseph's decision to make the Duke of Laurenzana Police Commissioner had enabled a powerful faction of the old Neapolitan nobility

[87] Astarita (2005). [88] Ibid.; Fallon (1997). [89] Ceva Grimaldi (1845), 57–8.

[90] However, all the documents relating to the guilds and confraternities were destroyed; see Abbamonte, in Massafra (ed.) (1988), 505–16. [91] ASN: Min. dell'Interno (II), f. 5066.

headed by the powerful Duke of Cassano to retain effective control of the city. Saliceti had tried to challenge this by building his own rival networks that included representatives of the guilds, the confraternities, and influential community leaders, the *capo-rioni popolari*.[92] But the French ambassador also complained that Saliceti's agents were notoriously corrupt: 'In every known part of the world it is the general rule that the lower ranks of Police agents are always recruited from the most vile, the most immoral and the most venal sections of humanity.'[93]

Carlo De Nicola confirmed that Saliceti's police had strong popular roots in the city, and played on popular hostility to the middle classes. Anyone who refused to adopt the popular 'Brutus' hair-style 'without powder and cut short' was at risk of random arrest and questioning:

> The lower sorts who are always the enemies of the patriots wear their hair short for comfort and certainly can't afford to get it curled. The gentry and artists prefer to powder their hair and wear it in a short pigtail as in the olden days, but now they are in danger of being stopped by the police and having their hair forcibly cut off.[94]

CONCLUSION

Saliceti had understood the importance of tapping into the networks of power that were the principal forces of cohesion in this teeming metropolis. For political as well as economic reasons, therefore, although the city's older corporate bodies lost many of their assets and resources they not only survived but retained at least a part of their former power. This was a clear sign of the limits of the modernizing mission of the new rulers, and the consequences were evident when the *Corpo della Città* reported in 1809 that it was unable to set the conscription quotas for the capital because it had no reliable information on the inhabitants of the capital, where they lived, their ages, or their occupations. That plea may have been self-serving, but in 1811 a similar lack of information and administrative machinery made it impossible to include the capital in the census that had been planned for the whole Kingdom.[95]

The capital's complex corporate structures resisted the bureaucratic ambitions of the French innovations, while the initial determination to change the capital gave way to measures designed to ensure that the city remained tranquil under conditions that were becoming increasingly threatening with each passing year. That in turn undermined the efforts to redress imbalances between the capital and the provinces, while the attempts to reorganize provincial administration were also running into increasing difficulty. But in both the capital and the provinces, the government's difficulties were creating opportunities for powerful interest groups to carve out their own positions in the post-feudal order.

[92] De Nicola, May 1806, 249.
[93] AAEP: CP (Naples), 132, 20 July 1808.
[94] De Nicola, 4 July 1807, 351.
[95] Cutolo (1932), 15.

11

Disorder

INTRODUCTION

The most central promise of the imperial enterprise was order, but disorder was its most constant companion in southern Italy. In part this was a direct consequence of the Kingdom's role as a frontier of empire, but disorder was also rooted in conflicts that the collapse of the *ancien régime* monarchy had left unresolved. Although the most visible agents of disorder were drawn most frequently from the poorest sections of Neapolitan society, behind them were frequently found more powerful opponents of the new order.

RESISTANCE: 1806

The most widespread form of disorder was brigandage, a term used by the authorities repeatedly and deliberately to confuse a range of very different phenomena. Most of what was initially described as brigandage were forms of semi-institutionalized armed resistance to the occupation, and even though there was no replay of the *levée en masse* of 1799, by early April 1806 the *Monitore Napoletano* carried reports of the activities of royalist *capi-masse* and anti-government insurrections in the northern provinces and even close to the capital. On 11 March martial law was declared in the affected areas, military commissions were set up, and *colonne mobili* were dispatched to put down the revolts.[1]

The reports of the French military commanders underlined the highly decentralized nature of *ancien régime* law enforcement. In early April, the French commander in the Terra di Lavoro—'the largest province in the Kingdom and the most important for us to control, because our principal lines of communication run through it'—reported that responsibility for policing this entire province was shared between no less than 22 royal and 140 feudal governors. The latter relied on small baronial militias that were disorganized and ineffective, although he also noted that the inhabitants of the mountain regions 'had a great propensity to

[1] *Monitore Napoletano*, no. 4, 11 March 1806.

Brigandage' and that the people strongly supported the Bourbon monarchy because they feared that the convents would be suppressed.[2]

All forms of resistance were simply labelled as brigandage. The royal governor of Matera, the marchese Rodio, had orders to raise an insurrection to block the French advance, but for Saliceti's agents he was 'the celebrated Calabrian named Rodio, who in 1799 had won notoriety as a Brigand and for which he was given the title of *marchese* and the rank of General by the Court'. His attempts to organize resistance explained why the 'seeds of brigandage' had been sown throughout the Province of L'Aquila (Abruzzo) before the French entered the Kingdom. His followers were '*Capo-Briganti* and conspirators' who had been involved in the events of 1799 and came 'for the greater part from the class of malefactors and from the lowliest Plebs. Like Rodio, they had been rewarded for their misdeeds by the former monarchy.'

Rodio's attempts to raise a royalist militia met with little success, however, and after various adventures he was captured in April and taken to Naples to be tried by a military commission. The commission hesitated to pass judgment because he had been captured wearing the uniform of a royal officer, but Saliceti had Masséna replace those who opposed conviction on the pretext that Rodio had bribed members of the tribunal: on 27 April Rodio was duly shot as a brigand.[3]

Another famous Sanfedist leader, Colonel Michele Pezza, alias Fra Diavolo, had better claims to be treated as a brigand, although he too had a royal commission when he was landed with men and supplies at Gaeta. He then stole a horse and two dozen mules from the village of Lauro where neither the 'feudal militia' nor the local 'Proprietors and *Galantuomini*' tried to oppose him. His *chevauchée* proved short-lived, but nonetheless it alarmed Saliceti, who feared it was the sign for a major rising in the capital, where he suspected that the Duke of Cassano and the brother of the Cardinal Archbishop were agents of the Court in Sicily.[4]

The conspiracy never materialized, but the situation became more dangerous in May when the British captured the islands of Capri and Ponza, where the Prince of Canosa set up headquarters to direct royalist plots on the nearby mainland. Numerous armed bands were now operating in the Terra di Lavoro and neighbouring provinces, but they were small and their followers quickly deserted. When Gaeta surrendered to Masséna on 18 July, the royalist leaders in the north lost their principal source of supplies, but their operations soon revived following the news that Reynier's army had been defeated by the English in Calabria.

In September Canosa arranged for Michele Pezza to land again at Gaeta with some 300 criminals released from the jail on Ponza. Pezza raised a large following in the San Germano valley, and when he entered the town of Sora

[2] A de G: C(5*) 32 Lettres de Gen. Girardon, *Armée de Naples*: 6 April 1806, Girardon to Min. Guerre, Capua.

[3] ANP: Fonds Joseph Bonaparte 381 AP 4 (doc 4), Correspondance de C Saliceti: Saliceti to Joseph Bonaparte, 27 April 1806.

[4] Ibid., 29 April 1806.

he ordered that the goods of all those unwilling to support him be seized. He had over 400 men with him, among them spies placed by Saliceti who reported that Pezza's supplies were coming from the Papal States and that his men 'were organised like Regular Troops and like the former *masse* take the name of *Corpo Volante*'.

Without Gaeta it was difficult for the royalist bands to survive, however, and as winter approached Pezza was forced to take to the mountains. In October the Intendent of Lucera reported that he had moved into Molise and was trying to raise fresh support but 'The People up to now have not rallied to him. No town or village is currently under his control.' Every town had been ordered to prepare its defences and Campobasso supplied 300 men for the Civil Guard and 150 more came from Bojano.[5] Pezza then tried to join the insurrections in Calabria, but he was captured at Baronessa near Salerno in November and immediately shot. By the end of the winter the government had regained control of the northern provinces.[6]

THE CALABRIAN REVOLT

In the meantime the Calabrian provinces had risen in revolt following Sir John Stuart's victory at Maida on 2 July 1806. When General Reynier's troops pursued the defeated Bourbon army into Calabria in March 1806, the situation had initially been quiet. Reynier reported on 5 March that the royalists' appeal for a *levée en masse* had fallen on deaf ears: 'The inhabitants remained peacefully in their villages as we advanced from Eboli towards Lagonegro. They even seem content to see my troops.' Reynier proceeded by way of Cosenza to Monteleone, where his army met a warm welcome: 'The inhabitants of the villages all along our route have come in crowds to watch us pass, which is an excellent sign of the confidence they have in us.' The general felt sufficiently relaxed to report on the conditions of the country:

> This is a magnificent land, but it has been depopulated by the recent earthquakes and above all by a detestable system of government. We see many fields which have been left uncultivated and allowed to fill with water and become unhealthy.... The towns and villages have been only partially rebuilt and we are surrounded by the most impoverished and wretched-looking peasants in the midst of one of the most beautiful and fertile landscapes imaginable.

On the 20 March his troops entered Reggio, where they were again warmly greeted by the people and the clergy. Reynier was eager to press across the Straits because his troops 'would have preferred a winter campaign in Germany to this little campaign in Calabria, and they cannot bear the idea of returning home by

[5] Ibid., Intendente of Lucera to Saliceti, 21 October 1806.
[6] Ibid., Saliceti to Joseph Bonaparte, 1 November 1806.

the same route that they have taken to arrive here'. But he did not have the means to attempt a crossing and his provisioning problems had become acute.[7] He reported again, however, that the Bourbon monarchy's attempts to 'enlist the leaders of the popular *masse* that had taken part in that sort of Crusade led by Cardinal Ruffo' had completely failed.

The first cases of resistance were isolated and were provoked by military foraging. But when a more concerted revolt began after the battle of Maida, Reynier's assessment quickly changed. Now he was surrounded on all sides by 'brigands led by English officers and by former leaders of the Royalist *masse.* A true war of the poor against the rich has been waged from the moment that the events of war caused the reins of government to slacken. These Peasants live and breathe only Brigandage and assassination. . . . There are no atrocities or crimes that they have not committed.'[8]

On 31 July the Calabrian provinces were declared to be in state of war. Masséna was sent with 15,000 men to reopen the road from Naples to Calabria.[9] But while Reynier waited for Masséna's army to arrive the insurrections gained force and, to make matters worse, the coastal fort of Amantea fell into royalist hands.

THE SILA

As in 1799, the epicentre of the royalist insurrections in Calabria was the villages and townships of the Sila Mountains. Geographically these communities lay on the principal transit routes through the Sila Mountains that linked the Tyrrhenian and Ionian coasts, giving them great strategic importance for the royalists. There was also clear evidence of advanced preparation, and in many villages the retreating Bourbon army had planted royalists agents with precise instructions on 'how to raise and lead the *masses* and organize them into small rapid commando units (*corpicciuoli volanti*), how to disrupt the progress of an enemy army by attacking its supply trains and drawing its forces into ambushes in deep gorges and dangerous passes in the mountains'. Certain individuals had been assigned ranks and uniforms, and each had been instructed to identify individuals who would be 'prepared to take up arms'.[10]

The first revolts took place in Longobucco, which was recognized as the centre for the extensive networks of shepherds who worked in the region and whose tight kinship bonds made them particularly powerful and widely feared:

> All the shepherds in this province come from this town. Their babes are raised with the sheep, weaned exposed to the cold and the open air, and grow up accustomed to live off

[7] ANP: Fonds Joseph Bonaparte 381 AP 4 (doc 4), Reynier to Joseph Bonaparte, 26 March 1806.

[8] Ibid., Reynier to Joseph Bonaparte, 3 August 1806.

[9] Ibid., C(5) 1, Correspondence de Joseph Bonaparte, Joseph Bonaparte to Napoleon, 31 July 1806, 9 August 1806.

[10] BNP: Fonds Italiens, 1127, Brigantage dans la Calabre Citeriore.

a bare diet of the dry bread they carry with them. The cold climate in which they live makes them more robust and renders them capable of confronting any endeavour without fatigue. Longobucco is the sole producer of a type of woollen cloth that is worn by these people and that in all seasons protects them from the wet and the cold. Accustomed to such ways of living, they are prepared to accept any undertaking, no matter how dangerous.

Along with these 'humble Plebs', Longobucco had produced many distinguished men of letters:

But it is nonetheless true that the cultured and wealthy are few in contrast to the uncouth multitude. What has to be noted is that these people are almost all related to one another and share the same ideas, so that a single bold spirit can move them as a single body. They are also skilled in the use of firearms because they hunt game in the surrounding woodlands.

The first revolt came on 9 June when 'twelve uncouth young field hands who owned no land raised the Bourbon standard in the public square'. Their leader was a young shepherd Antonio Sansoro, better known as Coreme. But the move failed and the insurgents fled to the mountains until they received news of Reynier's defeat at Maida on 2 July, which 'reawakened the sedition that had been crushed by the end of June'. Two days after Reynier's defeat a revolt broke out in Pentone, one of the *casali* of Catanzaro, 'a miserable hamlet of the vilest people who earn their living making charcoal, which they sell in Catanzaro, also the residence of many notorious brigand leaders because the town is close to the Sila and in a place that is not easy for the troops to reach'.[11]

As had happened in 1799, the rebellion immediately spread to the other *casali* of Cosenza, at which point Coreme and the twelve original rebels from Longobucco returned from the hills carrying British standards and insisting that every household do the same. Coreme was the undisputed leader and declared that he had been given the rank of Captain by the royalist *Capo-masse* Panedigrano and was a defender 'of the Christian Faith and Religion'. He recruited a band of fifty followers who all adopted the red cockade of the Bourbons: 'Behold once more the Santafede!'[12]

As the insurrections spread those who had organized them became more visible. They included Serafino Visciglia, the identikit of a feudal official who was more royalist than his master, who worked on the estates of the Duke of Corigliano where he was overseer of a factory that processed the valuable crop of liquorice roots:

For this reason he used to receive from the Duke's administration advances of large sums of money to enable him to recruit workers from the *casali* of Cosenza to work in that Factory, in all some three hundred individuals. This gave Visciglia great influence over the *masse* of which he was the acknowledged leader; but he was supported by his numerous sons and relatives, all brazen and lawless people who were all employed in the same factory and

[11] Ibid. 1125. [12] Ibid.

provided him with a band of loyal junior officers. All the others were employed in the numerous industries that existed on the feudal estates of the Duke of Corigliano, numbering no less than five or six hundred men and women who all shared Visceglia's views. They caused it to be rumoured (because this had no truth) that the Duke was greatly attached to the former Dynasty and was one of the principal promoters of the return of the Bourbon family.[13]

Visciglia did not make his move until the insurrections spread from Longobucco to the neighbouring towns of S. Giovanni in Fiore and Bocchigliero where the leader was 'Filippo Barberio, who belonged to one of the wealthiest families in that place'. When other wealthy families tried to stop the revolt, one of Visciglia's associates Tommaso Rizzuti—a leader of the royalist revolt in Bochigliero in 1799 'who had tried then to destroy the leading families of that town'—appealed for help to Coreme, who brought his men from Longobucco. When they reached Bochigliero, Coreme's shepherds burned down the houses of the 'patriots', whom they first shot and decapitated before looting their property, although 'their women were allowed to enter the convent of Santa Chiara, but with only one dress and the rest of their property was confiscated'.[14]

The disturbances next spread to Acri, where there had been no violence in 1799 'because of the true harmony that existed amongst the persons of intelligence and their followers'. But after Maida, the priest Antonino Rosa Cozza had set himself up as a royalist leader with the support of his brother and contacted royalist sympathizers in other towns. In this case, their target was the neighbouring Greek orthodox communities, whose animals they immediately seized. Paying other bands to stay away from the district, Cozza's followers took control over the outlying villages, which they accused of being Jacobin sympathizers and demanded ransoms.

By now the bands were looting and ransoming villages at will. The activities of Cozza's men attracted the attention of other more powerful bands, and on 10 August the brigand known as Francatrippa entered the town with seventy-five armed men. He demanded a gift of 8,000 ducats and ordered that the houses belonging to the Capalbo family, 'with whom he had a long-standing vendetta', be burned down. Francatrippa's supporters were said to come mainly from the outlying villages and hamlets and 'with this encouragement the most infamous section of the people came to worship Francatrippa and called for a general sack of the town'.[15]

Similar events took place in other towns. On 13 August, the bandit Panedigrano occupied Bisignano and demanded cash ransoms from all the surrounding towns. Two days later Francatrippa returned to Acri, where his men murdered the members of the Fusari, Capalbo, and Padula families before moving on to S. Sofia where the Greek Orthodox bishop D. Francesco Bugliari was brutally murdered, together with his brother and four other leading citizens.[16]

[13] BNP: Fonds Italiens, 1127. [14] Ibid.

[15] Ibid.: Memoria sopra le fatali evvenimenti del comune di Acri. [16] Ibid.

Five citizens from Acri managed to reach Cosenza and beg Reynier and Masséna for help. They dispatched a small column that liberated Acri early in September and drove the brigands into the Sila Mountains, but the French commander was unable to control his own men who in their turn sacked Acri again and on their return sold large quantities of the silk they had seized from the brigands in Bisignano.

Meanwhile, Coreme made his summer headquarters at Longobucco:

> There he appointed Captains and showed preference in giving promotions to those he most trusted, which is to say his less fortunate brothers and cousins and his most faithful friends.

He took the rank of General and 'exercised a vast jurisdiction: indeed what might be called an *imperium mero e misto* which extended throughout the neighbouring villages. These were ruled by his Captains.' Coreme was the source of all authority: 'He governed all things, gave dispensations for marriages and divorces, conferred ecclesiastical benefices and filled vacant parishes. Behold a shepherd raised to be king!'

When in August Coreme's men joined the assault on Acri they were surprised by Reynier's troops, but Coreme and his principal followers managed to escape to Sicily: 'so that only the innocent were left to be punished'.[17]

The allies still held Amantea, on the coast, but by September the operations of the brigand bands were more limited and the landowners were complying with Reynier's instructions to establish Civic Guards. Many of the smaller bands were still at large and there were 'frequent kidnappings, damage to property and ambushes. The brigands had prevented the harvest from being brought in, and now interrupted traffic, burned down barns and sometimes grain and dried goods, cut down fruit-bearing trees, destroyed vines, slaughtered cattle and other livestock not only to have something to eat but to damage and destroy. They also carried off many women to use at their pleasure, and then murdered them so that they could not reveal their hiding places.'

In the meantime the authorities had deployed a range of measures to destroy the bands. General Pignatelli and Colonel Manhès 'gave orders that no-one should take with them into the fields or pastures where the flocks were grazed more food than was needed for a single day' in an attempt to starve the brigands out. Reprisals were taken against the relatives of wanted brigands, while amnesties were offered to brigands who gave themselves up voluntarily. Those who surrendered were in theory not to be punished but 'since it could not be tolerated that they should be permitted to live within the felicity of a peaceful society, they were quickly got rid of in different ways'.[18]

Senior officials were also speculating on the underlying causes of the disorders. For the Intendent of Upper Calabria the answer was that 'the Hearts of the

[17] Ibid. [18] Ibid.

Calabrians are governed by two things: vendetta and theft', but he also claimed that the principal vendettas went back to 1799, and were directed against those whom the Bourbons had placed in office. These conflicts were especially violent in the *casali* of Cosenza, where the Bourbons had never dared call for a *levée en masse* because 'It is of no interest to these people whether the present or the former king rules: who rules is a matter of no importance for them, although the ruler that allows them freedom to murder and rob will always be their choice.'

There was great discontent above all because of the heavy taxes paid by the poor, especially the poll-tax (*testatico*), which the people had hoped the French would abolish. But English and Sicilian agents were the principal instigators of the insurrection. They provided supplies for the former leaders of the popular *masse*, and in this were aided and abetted by the priests and friars 'of whom there are very large numbers in this Province and who were frequently the principal organisers of the revolts'.

The Intendent recommended that taxes should be waived for three years, but he also argued that the measures taken so far had benefited only the poorest: 'the very people who in the recent fatal events in this Province far from suffering losses have greatly bettered their situation, since they are the ones who have given themselves over to brigandage and hence to theft and Robberies'. The true victims were not the poor but 'the class of landowners who bear the principal burden of both the old and new taxes'. Amnesties, he argued, did not work. 'These People cannot be controlled or ruled with tenderness.'[19]

Reynier also understood that in most cases his men arrived only after the brigands had already departed a village, 'leaving only peaceful folks and those who support us, who are generally the rich: if we rob and burn, we ruin the people who are our own supporters'.[20] In his view the best way to end the disturbances was to force the landowners to establish permanent Civic Guard units. 'Wherever they have felt themselves to be sufficiently supported by French troops, they have served us very well.' But the landowners feared the people:

> This hatred, which was deliberately stirred up by the former government . . . is the principal source of the spirit of insurrection and Brigandage which can only be destroyed by bringing the people under a severe yoke that will force them to submit, so that they may discover how much they have to gain from the new order of things.

But Reynier also insisted that to destroy brigandage it was necessary first to destroy 'the vices of the former system of government' and he urged the government to abolish feudalism and set up a new administration as soon as possible.[21]

Winter approached and control over Lower Calabria was still tenuous. Coreme had returned to the Sila Mountains, and on the western coast the *capo-massa* De Michele had put up posters calling for an 'independent democratic Republic'.

19 ASN: Min. dell'Interno (II), 2243 (Calabria Citra), Intendent Palumbo to Min. dell'Interno, 22 September 1806.

20 A de G: C(5*) 31*, Reynier to Joseph Bonaparte, Cassano, 9 August 1806.

21 Ibid., Reynier to Joseph Bonaparte, 19 October 1806.

Smaller bands were led by 'the murderer Necco', who was operating in the area between Scalea and Diamante.

These enemies of the Social Order, although deeply divided amongst themselves, are absolutely united in their desire to destroy all the families of the leading Proprietors and to enrich themselves on the spoils. They show no regard for sex or age. Young children are slaughtered at their mothers' breasts, husbands in the arms of their wives, octogenarians are hacked to pieces, virgins raped and massacred... and every time we shoot or hang a pair of the villains by way of reprisal, the brigands massacre another ten or twenty innocents.... The truth is we hold Cosenza, but only a few other towns.... The rest of the province is completely infested with brigands and prey to massacres and arson.

No taxes had been collected in the province, and half of the 2,000 French troops in Cosenza were sick with fever in the military hospital, where conditions were indescribable. Disease was rapidly spreading through the rest of the French army as well. But the Intendent concluded that the brigands had no interest in supporting either the old or the new government: 'their sole ambition is to massacre the wealthy and enrich themselves with their possessions'.[22]

A report to the Interior Minister, Miot de Melito, written in mid-November, revealed a different side of the situation, however, and placed the blame squarely on the fact that the 'public authorities are totally corrupt'. Since Calabria had been declared in a state of war, the military could do as it wished and the civil authorities did the same. There was no control over military requisitioning, the burden of which fell on the 'few towns that support the Government'. Everything the military needed they took 'in such a way that the Right of Property is completely ignored.... The Military Commanders behave like so many Sultans who demand, or more accurately exact, huge sums of money...' Because of the requisitions there was a desperate shortage of animals, and work in the fields had almost ceased. The inhabitants of the *casali* never approached the town for fear of being robbed.

The report went on to argue that so-called patriots had at first been treated with contempt because they were demoralized, but now they needed to be watched carefully. Many were genuine in their support for the government:

but since Private interest is everything in these venal towns, many of them are loyal only for their own purposes and so that they can use the arm of the military Government to revenge.... Many Individuals who have laid down their arms and taken advantage of the Amnesty have then been robbed and imprisoned by the Officers of the Provincial Guards either for personal reasons or through thirst for gain, all of which produces serious unrest and foments the brigandage that everyone seems determined to perpetuate.... The confusion that reigns everywhere is almost impossible to describe, and the only spirit that prevails is that of extortion and robbery on one hand, discontent and diffidence on the other.[23]

[22] *ASN*: Min. dell'Interno (II), 2243, Intendent of Calabria Citeriore to Miot de Melito, 11 October 1806. [23] Ibid., Ilarbelli (Segretario della Provincia) to Miot, 16 November 1806.

By now the winter snows were forcing the brigands out of the mountains towards the coastal forts at Amantea, Belmonte, Fiumefreddo, and Belvedere held by the royalists. Here, in the words of General MacDonald, 'a handful of miserable wretches are withstanding the most battle-hardened troops in Europe and have repulsed their attacks with vigour'. But after a lengthy siege, Amantea fell in February 1807 and the garrison of 'brigands' was taken prisoner.[24] The remaining royalist strongholds fell in quick succession and by the end of April Reynier could report to Joseph that the insurrection in Lower Calabria was over.[25]

His conclusion proved premature, however, and unrest in the Calabrian provinces continued throughout 1807, although the support from Sicily was less effective than in the previous year. The British had refused to participate in any further landings after Sir John Stuart's expedition, while the French occupations of the Ionian islands after the peace with Russia in July 1807 helped secure the Adriatic coast. Combined with Napoleon's alliance with Turkey the British started to fear for the safety of Sicily, whose defences they began to repair.[26]

In January 1808, Saliceti again reported that order had been restored in every province. But with the spring came fresh disturbances in other provinces, the main cause being news of the war in Spain and the French occupation of Rome. Saliceti's greatest concern was for the frontier districts of the Abruzzi, Apulia, Basilicata, and the Cilento, but there were also now reports of small bands of brigands in Molise and in Upper Calabria.[27] Larger bands of brigands were reported to be moving undisturbed through Apulia and Capitanata, threatening to destroy crops and carry off livestock if they were not paid large ransoms. A band of sixty to seventy men led by Vincenzo Pisani, 'known as the Monk of Torremaggiore', entered the province from northern Apulia and Pisani had the audacity to demand that the mayor of Uruni provide his men with food and fodder. 'From the narrative of these events Your Excellency will understand that these are deeds that cannot be ignored: The Bands are acting with such boldness that the Government must intervene at once.'[28]

Saliceti was equally concerned to find ways of making the pacification of the Calabrian provinces permanent, and he acknowledged that more needed to be done to restore confidence amongst those who had been caught up in the brigand wars:

the towns of Lower Calabria have been divided into Parties of winners and losers, and this has caused a great number of Families to go to Messina. In some towns the Emigration has been so great that there is almost no-one left. Bagnara, for example, is like Pompeii: a ghost

24 ANP: 211AP 1, Journal historique des opérations du Siège de l'Amantea, 10 February 1807, General MacDonald. 25 A de G: C(5*) 31*: Reynier to Joseph Bonaparte, 21 April 1807.

26 Bunbury (1854), 274–313.

27 ANP: Fonds Joseph Bonaparte 381 AP 4: Correspondance de C. Saliceti: Saliceti to Joseph Bonaparte, 13 July 1808.

28 ASN: Min. dell'Interno (IIa), f. 5079: Antonio Nelli, Intendente di Capitanata a Miot de Melito, 18 April–22 May 1807.

town (*una solitudine fabbricata*). The number of Families that have emigrated amount to no fewer than six hundred. Since they own much land, I was asked . . . whether they should be sequestered. But my answer was NO! I am convinced that the greater part of these Emigrants harbour no hostile intent, and whole families rarely emigrate unless driven to do so through fear.[29]

CONSCRIPTION

Murat's decision to double the conscription quotas in 1809 was not a principal cause of brigandage, but it certainly created many new recruits for the brigand bands. Except in the frontier provinces, there had previously been no conscription in the Kingdom until 1802 when the Bourbons attempted a more general draft, but without success. Despite intense pressure from the emperor, Joseph Bonaparte had deferred introducing the more extensive French model of conscription because he knew that he did not have the means to enforce it.

Experience showed that conscription could be successfully enforced only with the support of local elites, and once that was achieved conscription became a relatively routine, albeit deeply resented, operation.[30] This was the case in Lombardy and in Tuscany, but where the French could not count on the active cooperation of local elites conscription proved almost impossible to enforce. The most extreme case was the Papal State, where attempts to impose conscription in Rome in April 1810 caused rioting in the streets. About a third of those liable to be drafted fled, and the Castel S. Angelo was mobbed by the mothers and sweethearts of the conscripts demanding their release. General de Tournon brushed aside their protests with the comment that 'it was often a soldier's duty to make pretty girls and loving mammas weep', but as soon as they were escorted out of the city almost all of the conscripts escaped and joined the bands of brigands proliferating in central Italy.

Despite the military commissions and the regular executions of 'refractories' by firing squad in the Piazza del Popolo, resistance to conscription in Rome was a principal cause of the brigandage that spread throughout the former papal provinces in 1810 and 1811.[31] 'We keep arresting them and shooting them, but the real brigands always get away.'[32] But as law and order in central Italy collapsed, brigand bands moved with increasing freedom across the northern frontiers of the Kingdom of Naples and raided deep into Apulia, Capitanata, and Basilicata.

In Naples, Joseph Bonaparte first introduced a form of voluntary conscription in 1807. The conscripts were to be chosen by lottery, and exemptions were available to those willing to pay. But this did not work and in 1808 the quotas were extended for the first time to the capital and the Calabrian provinces.[33]

[29] ANP: Fonds Joseph Bonaparte 381 AP 4: Correspondance de C. Saliceti: 13 July 1808.
[30] See especially Antonielli (1983) and Filippini (1980a, b). On France see Forrest (1987).
[31] Madelin (1906), 303–14, 455. [32] Ibid. 466.
[33] BNP: Fonds italiens, 1126 (January 1808).

The system still proved workable only in the frontier provinces where the older *levée en masse* was familiar. But it was not applied in the Terra di Lavoro or in Basilicata and virtually no attempt was made to enforce it in Calabria or in Naples. Even so, Sir John Stuart informed Lord Castelreagh that conscription was the main cause of 'the frequent risings in the Calabrian provinces that are causing growing alarm amongst the French authorities'.[34]

The Kingdom's conscription quotas were met by sending convicts or captured brigands to the military depots.[35] Then against the background of the campaign against Austria and eager to ingratiate himself with the emperor, Murat doubled the conscription quota in March 1809. In every province internment camps for draft-evaders (*Depots de Refractaires*) were set up, but the civil and the military authorities reported that the rates of desertion were enormous.[36] In the Calabrian provinces conscription simply provoked a mass exodus of men of military age, many of whom fled to Sicily:

> in Sicigliano, Aprigliano, S.Giovanni in Fiore the population has demonstrated its refusal to submit to the law so that not one young man of military age is to be seen in any of these towns.[37]

To meet the emperor's unrelenting demands more criminals and captured brigands were drafted and marched north. Most escaped in transit and went to the hills to join other bands of brigands, while many that made the journey were sent back as unfit to serve in the *Grande Armée*.

ILLICIT PROFITS

One reason for the persistence of brigandage was of course that it was very profitable. The brigands' principal business was demanding cash ransoms, pillaging, and looting, of which they were not necessarily the principal beneficiaries. But brigandage also gave rise to many ancillary industries, not least the system of amnesties that sustained simple protection rackets of which the brigands—but not only the brigands—were the principal targets. Copied or forged certificates of amnesty were freely bought and sold, and large profits were made. Anyone accused of being a brigand or associating with brigands stood to lose not only his or her life, but the property and possessions of their families as well. Genuine brigands could easily obtain fake amnesty certificates, while completely innocent people could be the target of a fake denunciation. The best guarantee was a powerful patron, which put patronage at a premium.

34 PRO: WO 1, 306 (Sicily 1808) General Sir John Stuart to Castlereagh, Messina, 25 May 1808.
35 Cortese (1926), 320.
36 Le Brethon vii. 48; Murat to Reynier, 1 March 1809; Caldora (1960), 407.
37 A de G: C(5*) 42; Rapports au Roi, Naples, 17 April 1810.

While brigandage could take the form of challenging existing networks of power, brigands were more likely to be part of those networks. The mountains and the upland pastures were where the brigands ruled, but these were also where powerful landowners grazed their flocks and maintained their own armed guards to protect their livestock and the pasture. The bands that survived the longest were likely to be those with the most powerful patrons, who could also protect them in other ways. The trade in fake amnesties was only one example, and while many of those involved were corrupt officials powerful patrons were also prominent players. In 1809 Pierre Joseph Briot, the Intendent of Lower Calabria, accused one of the wealthiest landowners in the province, Alfonso Baracco, of making large profits from supplying amnesties to wanted criminals and notorious bandits.

The brigands' need for protection enabled the powerful to take their cut from the lucrative traffic in stolen goods and livestock, and in particular to share in the rich profits offered by the trade in smuggled British colonial goods and manufactures. The proximity of Sicily and Malta made southern Italy the closest and easiest point of entry for banned British goods in southern Europe, and thanks to the emperor's efforts to enforce the Continental blockade the value of this illicit trade continued to rise. Not only many Calabrian landowners, but also senior French civil and military officials were deeply and profitably involved. In 1810 the Intendent Briot accused the senior French commander in Calabria, General Cavaignac, of being the principal protector of the contraband trade in the province.[38] Cavaignac responded by levelling the same accusation against Briot, but there is clear evidence of the involvement of other French officers at the most senior level down to the end of Murat's Kingdom.[39]

These were not small enterprises. The inventory of British manufactured and colonial goods entering Sicily and Malta after 1806 was roughly equivalent to the legitimate British trade that had formerly entered Italy through the ports of Naples, Livorno, and Genoa. Much of that inventory now found its way across the Straits of Messina. From there, the goods were moved throughout the Kingdom, then across the frontier into the Papal States and from there to the Kingdom of Italy.[40] When the British recaptured the Ionian islands in 1810, the Adriatic provinces became a second front for the contraband trade and British goods from Malta to Corfu quickly found their way onto the unguarded beaches of the Gargano peninsula.[41]

Since southern Italy had been invaded in 1806 mainly in order to extend the blockade on British trade, it was more than ironical that many of those French officers who been had sent to rot in a far-flung outpost of empire should instead grow rich by subverting a central pillar of the imperial project.

[38] Heuron (1960), 125–37.

[39] BNP: Fonds italiens, 1125 (add.), Rapports au Roi, 18 October 1809.

[40] Heuron (1960), 125–37; D'Angelo (1988), 47–115; idem (1990), 125–37; Melita (1999), 113–72.

[41] A de G: C(5*) 33; Rapports au Roi, Capitanata, 17 May 1811.

BRIGAND PROFILES

The brigands had faces; however, the ways in which these were carefully recorded by authorities raise many questions about those doing the recording. Most often the descriptions simply retailed set stereotypes, depicting the bandits as inhuman enemies of the modernizing mission of the new order, a subhuman race of atavistic barbarians and monsters that threatened the essence of civilization. This was clearly the intention of the official who in 1812 concluded a report on the bandits captured and executed in Calabria by the gendarmerie since 1810 by stating that their crimes were too heinous to record, but then did so in graphic detail:

> Men flayed alive, mutilated, killed by beating with sticks or stones, torn apart by mastiffs, burned alive and their members eaten, made to die slowly while being turned by knives, as their flesh is stripped from their bodies and the blood from their wounds drunk in bowls: hung upside down from the branches of trees while slivers of cane are forced under their nails and made to suffocate with smoke from fires lit under the trees... these were their daily amusements.[42]

The thumbnail sketches found in these military reports nonetheless reveal many who resembled Eric Hobsbawm's 'social bandits':[43] poor men—but also women—who became involved in a quarrel with a neighbour over property, animals, or women, committed a crime and took to the hills where they joined or formed their own band of followers and then lived off raiding and ransoming landowners and towns in territories that could stretch from Calabria to Apulia, the Abruzzi, and over the frontiers onto the plains of Lazio.

Pietro Perugino of Pantelandotto, known as Auriello, for example, 'lived in utter poverty until 1807' when he killed a neighbour and took to the hills. He formed a small but violent band, which did not stray far from his native village but continued to operate until he was captured and killed by the *Legionari* in 1811. At the age of 14, the future brigand Giacomo Randelli was already 'guilty of many crimes'. He joined the army in 1798, was jailed for crimes of violence in 1799, then escaped in 1806, and became a brigand but was captured and killed.

Giovan-Battista Mancino from Castelpoto was a miller who became leader of a band in 1806, but then surrendered and was amnestied. Carmine Carrattelli from Solotia, know as the 'Carter', was a carpenter 'but was always a trouble-maker'. He escaped while serving a fifteen-year jail sentence in 1799, was recaptured, and escaped again in 1806 when he became a brigand until he too was captured and executed in 1811. Achille Santoro, from the village of Liuni, was a blacksmith who formed a band with two fellow villagers. He surrendered during an amnesty in 1807 and killed his former associates, but was shot while trying to escape. Francesco Quartucci was another blacksmith whose band included his son

[42] BNP: Fonds italiens, 1124. Report on brigands killed and captured in Calabria Ultra between November 1806 and 31 March 1811 (8 June 1812).

[43] See Hobsbawm (1959).

Tommaso 'and other miscreants'. When his son was captured, Quartucci surrendered and was shot. The same fate befell Andrea Cucchiarella of Fregene L'Abate, who 'until 1807 lived by honest labour' but then raised an armed band. In October 1810 he and his followers gave themselves up but they too were shot, because 'they had not surrendered in the proper manner'.

Some of the brigands came from a little further up the social order. Francesco Curcio, known as Orlandino, owned a herd of cattle (*massaro di bovi*). Vincenzo Luca, known as Zampogna, was a well-to-do farmer who took to the hills of the Marchesato after killing his father in a brawl. He became infamous for his robberies and violence; his trademark was to rape the daughters of the landowners he held to ransom.[44]

Other descriptions seem to have been more fanciful, as in the case of Giuseppe Rotella, who was ambushed and killed in October 1809. Known simply as 'The Hangman' (*Il Boja*), Rotella's 'custom was to cut off the nose and ears of his victims and give them to his dogs to eat'. His base was the town of Firotello: 'and even today nearly all of his fellow villagers have an ear or nose missing'.

WEBS OF COMPLICITY

These descriptions make it clear that the war against the brigands was also an exercise in propaganda. Like the contemporary term 'terrorist', 'brigandage' and 'banditry' were interchangeable labels whose purpose was to place those deemed responsible for criminal actions beyond the protection of the law. This had been the case since medieval times, and a 'bandit' was a person deemed guilty by public acclaim, who was then 'banned' and hence placed 'outside' the protection of the law. Brigandage and banditry were terms that linguistically obscured the boundaries of the legitimate and the illegitimate, and it was no accident that they should have acquired a new notoriety at a time when the state was seeking to acquire new powers. If in many different parts of Europe in the eighteenth century brigandage became a problem, it was not because it was new or even more visible but because the demarcations between public and private power were changing.

In its origins, brigandage was archetypally a frontier phenomenon, something that occurred primarily on the boundaries of rival jurisdictions. But as rulers looked to extend the power of the state, all forms of public disorder became pretexts for the state to intervene in places that had formerly been subject to private jurisdiction. It is in that context that brigandage in southern Italy takes its wider significance as both a social and a political phenomenon.[45]

[44] BNP: Fonds italiens, 1124. Note essenziali sulle vite dei più famosi capi briganti delle Calabrie: travail fait par l'Adjutant Générale Fanelli.

[45] See also Davis (1989), 71–90.

In this respect, too, the French military occupation in 1806 can be seen as a continuation by other and more forcible means of earlier Bourbon initiatives. Both looked to widen the boundaries of the power of the state by reducing the formal and informal private jurisdictions that had previously existed. This was a very delicate process, not least because those localized systems of power had already been undermined by the forces beginning to reshape the agrarian fabric of the South.

Calabria was not unique in any of these respects, and brigandage was never solely a Calabrian phenomenon. But in the Calabrian provinces all these elements were also present in extreme form. The region was distant from the centres of administrative power, and also on the frontier of empire and hence directly exposed to the disruptions caused by the war, the presence of a foreign force of occupation, and a massive trade in contraband goods.

As in many other parts of the Kingdom, the attempts by the French to assert the authority of the state in Calabria came at a moment when local demarcations of power were also shifting. The complex webs of interests that were inseparable from the transhumant economies of this mountainous region made change especially complex and contentious but did not preclude challenges to the established order. For those who wanted to assert their place in the new order, the administrative innovations of the new regime, and particularly the abolition of feudalism and the division of the common lands, offered opportunities that could not easily be overlooked. Response and reactions were, as a result, contradictory and at least outwardly confused.

As in the previous century, the conflicts focused around competition for scarce resources—pasture, woodland, and water—with consequences that had already been clearly set out in Giuseppe Zurlo's earlier investigation into the causes of lawlessness in the Sila forests in the 1790s. But as that report pointed out, the poor were foot soldiers in wars being waged by powerful landowners intent on asserting and protecting their rights over common pasture and public woodland. Brigandage was both a means for pursuing local conflicts and a cover for those responsible.[46]

Gradually the French officials became aware of the pervasive webs of complicity that enveloped the violence. General Cavaignac repeatedly complained that the deep factional conflicts in the Calabrian towns 'paralyse any attempt to move against the Brigands'.[47] He also reported that in the district around Monteleone all the most dangerous bandits were protected by powerful landowners:

> in general the same individuals support all the brigand leaders and their followers, which is why military force is only a secondary means for destroying the bandits who are protected by the leading citizens who also have the means to help them evade with ease our attempts to catch them.

[46] See Bianchini (1838), viii. 418–19.

[47] BNP: Fonds italiens, 1125 (add.), Rapports au Roi, 13 August 1809.

In 1812 the commander of the Calabrian gendarmerie reached a similar conclusion: 'The supporters of the brigands form two principal categories, one being motivated by their evil disposition and self-esteem but the other includes many amongst the class of the leading landowners, yet their names are always veiled in mystery because there is never sufficient proof for them to be named.'[48]

PURSUING THE POWERFUL

This was true in other provinces too and in Principato Citra the authorities were also convinced that powerful landowners were unwilling to act against the bandits because they were actively protecting them.[49] What gave General Manhès,[50] who in 1810 was given the task of destroying brigandage once and for all, a notoriety that rivalled that of the brigands was that he made their powerful protectors his principal target. The measures Manhès employed were neither new nor exceptional, although he applied them more systematically and was prepared to confront the brigands' powerful patrons, which made him a political target as well.

Manhès had acquired experience in counter-insurgency before he came to Naples, and while serving as Murat's aide-de-camp in 1802 had become a close friend of Saliceti in Liguria. He accompanied Murat to Naples where Saliceti recommended that he be put in command of operations against the brigands in Abruzzo in 1808, where with the aid of powerful local landowner Baron Nolli he persuaded the most powerful brigand leaders to accept commissions in the provincial Guard.[51] Manhès also briefly served in Calabria in 1809, but like Briot he fell out with Cavaignac, who tried to get him recalled, probably because he also knew of Cavaignac's involvement in the contraband trade.

The Sicilian expedition in 1810 and the presence of a large military force had provoked numerous new revolts in Calabria, which was why Murat ordered Manhès to use whatever measures were needed to restore order. A fellow officer claimed that Manhès understood that the brigands could not be beaten by '*colonnes mobiles*' alone and that to defeat them it was necessary to recruit 'the citizens themselves'.[52] The methods were not new, but Manhès took them to their

[48] Ibid., 1125 (vol. ii), Rapporto sul Brigantaggio in Calabria 1809–1812 (Gendarmeria Reale, 24 February 1812).

[49] A de G: C(5*) 42: Rapports journaliers au Roi (1810), Cavaignac to Min. War, 2 May 1810, 3 May 1810.

[50] Charles Antoine Manhès (1777–1852). Born in Aurillac (Cantal), Manhès served as an artillery officer in the Army of the Rhine, then in the Army of Italy, and was wounded at the battle of Novi in 1799. He fought at Austerlitz and in April 1807 he was appointed aide-de-camp to Murat in Berg, and followed him to Spain, then to Naples. He was promoted to colonel in November 1808, *maréchal du camp* in September 1809, then to Lieutenant General in March 1811, and he later received the title of Count. He married the daughter of Principe Pignatelli di Cerchiara and settled in Naples after the Restoration. See De Gxx (1817); Cutolo (1937), 410.

[51] *Notizia storica sul Conte Carlo Antonio Manhès* (1846), 33.

[52] De Rivarol (1817), 52.

logical extreme and anticipating more modern counter-insurgency tactics made the rural communities hostages for the actions of the brigands.

The campaign against the brigands that followed was accompanied by levels of brutality that made contemporaries recoil in horror. As winter approached, Manhès starved the brigands into abandoning their mountain hideouts. Writing much later, Pietro Colletta described how Manhès

> waited for the harvest to end and for the leaves to drop, then in each *comune* he published a list of bandits and made the villages responsible for catching them.

The Calabrian provinces were placed under curfew,[53] the churches were closed, and the priests were removed so that no one could take communion, be baptized, married, or buried until the brigands were caught.[54] On threat of summary execution, no peasant or labourer was to take food into the fields or leave animals unattended. Secret communications even between husband and wife were prohibited on pain of death, shepherds were forbidden to move with their flocks without permission, agricultural work in the fields outside the villages was suspended, and soldiers were billeted in every town, village, and hamlet until the bandits surrendered.[55]

The aim was to starve the brigands into submission, and it succeeded. As winter approached:

> the brigands were forced to live off acorns and wild berries, and had to retreat to remote caves to survive one more day. But the skies, as if weary to witness all this mischief, played their part in bringing about their destruction and hurled down so much snow that even the most hardened of these assassins gave up all hope. Every day brought news of new arrests, killings and surrenders.[56]

Manhès also mounted a carefully prepared propaganda war, deliberately building up the notoriety of the brigand leaders he most wanted to capture. He constantly reminded his assistant, Colonel Ianelli, of the need to concentrate his resources on capturing and killing the *capo-brigante* Benincasa: 'Benincasa must fall under your guns, show me what you can do!' In February 1811 Benincasa was still eluding Ianelli, and Manhès sent reinforcements. Barely a fortnight later the General congratulated Ianelli for killing another wanted brigand, Parafante, and capturing twenty-five of his followers, and from Cosenza he ordered Ianelli to send him the heads of the slaughtered brigands, as well as Parafante's 'women' who had been captured and were subsequently hanged in Cosenza. But he repeated, 'Benincasa in our hands, that will be the crowning glory!' Then on 17 March he

[53] BNP: Fonds italiens, 1124, Note essenziali sulle vite dei più famosi capi briganti delle Calabrie: travail fait par l'Adjutant Générale Ianelli.

[54] *Notizia storica sul Conte Carlo Antonio Manhès* (1846), 66.

[55] Colletta (Cortese, 1957), ii. 342. In 1810 Colletta was serving as Intendent in Monteleone under Manhès's direct command.

[56] BNP: Fonds italiens, 1127, Memoria sopra li fatali avvenimenti del comune di Acri, p. 32.

finally received the 'the happy news of the death of the notorious Beinincasa' at the hands of Ianelli's men.[57]

Manhès claimed to have killed or executed 900 brigands in Calabria during the winter of 1810–11.[58] The report drawn up by the *Reale Gendarmeria* a year later stated that between November 1806 and March 1811, 'the day on which this province was finally freed of these monsters', 5,421 bandits had surrendered or been captured, killed, or executed in the province of Lower Calabria alone. The largest numbers of brigands and their supporters were from the districts of Monteleone, Catanzaro, Reggio, and Gerace.[59]

In January 1811, Manhès's special powers were extended to the sprawling province of Basilicata.[60] As they had done in Calabria, Manhès and his officers identified individual brigand leaders and then used bribes and brought pressure on their protectors to bring about their betrayal and capture. Amnesties and pardons were offered freely to ordinary deserters and draft evaders who surrendered voluntarily.

As summer approached Manhès also recruited the assistance of the bands of reapers who travelled in large convoys as they moved from province to province to work on the harvest. The emergency regulations that banned all movement in the countryside threatened the livelihood of these migrant labourers, but in return for being allowed to go about their normal business they provided the authorities with valuable information on the movements of the brigands. On many occasions the caravans of migrant reapers attacked and captured or killed bandits to collect the ransom money. Their victims included 'the ferocious Big Glass Eye', who was hacked to pieces by the scythes of a band of reapers near Ascoli, and Cesare Rosello of Pescopagano, who was killed in June by reapers near the village of Calitri.[61]

As in Calabria, Manhès was merciless with anyone who provided help for the brigands. In May, he hanged four peasants suspected of taking food to the bandit Taccone: 'This example of severity was necessary to cause fear among those who might be tempted to copy them.' He was no less effective in targeting the wealthier protectors of the brigands and the strategy worked as it had in Calabria.

By early summer, the principal brigand leaders in Basilicata were in his hands. Those captured rather than killed were sent to the Military Commission in Matera, where their trials became the occasion for public display. To celebrate the capture of the bandit Quagliarello, in June Manhès ordered that the other captured bandits were to be taken to Matera where they were to be hanged one a day

[57] BNN: Bancone 8 B 17 Copia delle lettere originali del Sig. Tenente Generale Manhès; 19 December 1810; 24 December 1810; 4 February 1811; 17 February 1811; 21 February 1811; 17 March 1811.

[58] A de G: C(5*) 43, Rapports journaliers au Roi, 7 January 1811.

[59] BNP: Fonds italiens, 1125. Brigands killed and captured in Calabria Ultra (June 1812).

[60] Basilicata stretched from Capitanata and Apulia in the east and north to the Lower Principato and Upper Calabria in the west and south.

[61] A de G: C(5*) 33, Basilicata, 14 May 1811.

throughout the period of the fair. He also organized a great *festa* in Potenza during which dowry portions were distributed to 'four girls from poor families'.[62]

For the single district of Lagonegro, the official figures recorded 366 brigands killed, captured, or condemned to death between June and October 1811 alone, including one woman, Olivia Laurenzana: 'This woman dressed like a man and fully armed followed her lover the Brigand leader known as Francesco Vacca di Guardarella', who had committed endless crimes and was killed by the Civic Guard.[63] In June 1811 Manhès reported that the provinces were now tranquil. But this proved to be only a temporary lull, and the following year the disorders revived and continued until after Murat's reign.

Manhès liked to present himself as the 'champion of the poor, your true protector and defender',[64] but his tactics were effective mainly because he was prepared to expose the powerful figures behind the brigands. In the spring of 1811, for example, he threatened to arrest the leading landowners in the Silan town of Acri unless the brigand leader Francesco Fridizza was found. It was then revealed that the wives of Fridizza and his lieutenant were living openly in nearby Longobucco. They were arrested and when questioned the women revealed the hiding places of their men. Fridizza surrendered and was killed, then his body and those of the other slain brigands were 'exposed in irons in the public square until the flesh was consumed'.[65]

One of Manhès's principal targets in Basilicata in the spring of 1811 was the *capo-brigante* known as Taccone. Taccone's base was the town of Laurenzana where he had many supporters, including the *guardiano* of the Palazzo Baronale and the agent of the Duke of Belgioioso. Another accomplice was 'Signor Don Domenico Asselda, a wealthy *galantuomo* and the commander of the Legion in that town. Asselda was a friend of Taccone, who had done him many services, for which reason he had never persecuted him and indeed they were often seen together.' Two of Taccone's fellow brigands, Sacrola and Pecori, were friends of the commander of the *Legionari* in the town of Sicigliano, who supplied them with lists of landowners who willingly agreed to pay to avoid damage to their property.

Although he was one of the most wanted brigands in Basilicata, Taccone's wife lived openly in Laurenzana, where Taccone also attended the baptism of their infant son. His accomplice Domenico Asselda was responsible for murdering the mayor of the neighbouring town of Abriola, who had imprisoned a brother of one of the bandits. Taccone and his men moved to Calabria, where they raised money from many towns and burned down those that refused to pay, but they received supplies from many landowners. As well as sending ammunition, Domenico Asselda recruited men to join Taccone's band and paid them 5 *carlini* a day. Asselda also agreed to have the arch-priest of Abriola murdered because he had

62 A de G: C(5*) 33, Basilicata, 5 June 1811.
63 BNP: Fonds italiens, 1125, Répression, vol. ii.
64 *Notizia storica sul Conte Carlo Antonio Manhès* (1846), 72.
65 BNP: Fonds italiens, 1127, Memoria sopra li fatali avvenimenti nel comune di Acri.

forced Taccone's lover, Rosa di Stefano, to enter a convent on the grounds that Taccone was already married.[66]

Taccone was captured alive in June 1811, and there was great alarm when Manhès travelled to Potenza to interrogate him before he went to the gallows because it was widely feared that he would reveal his network of protectors.[67] Reporting the killing of the brigand Giuseppe Russo of Montepane, 'a tyrant with no soul'; who was held responsible for more than a hundred murders in the area around Catanzaro, in February 1811, Manhès noted that Russo had been found while hiding in the house of a wealthy landowner: 'this infamous protector of so cruel a man escaped but we are pursuing him and have demolished his house'.[68]

In December 1810 he told Ianelli that he was unable to join in the pursuit of the bandit Benincasa because he had to pay an important visit to a certain 'Signor Barracco'.[69] This was Don Alfonso Barracco, a wealthy landowner who was one of the largest purchasers of *beni nazionali* in Lower Calabria and would emerge from the French period as the epitome of the new *latifundist* with suitable noble titles to match.[70]

Barracco had purchased huge tracts of land in the Sila forest where he had extensive interests in sheep grazing. His property had been attacked in 1806, but he later received substantial compensation for supporting the French. In 1809 the Intendent Briot had accused Barracco of trading pardons and amnesties with known brigands, and he informed Manhès that Barracco was almost certainly the leading protector of the brigands operating in the region.[71]

Hence the General decided to visit Signor Barracco on his estates in December 1810. During the meeting, the General informed Don Alfonso that he was suspected of being an enemy of the state and that without immediate proof of his loyalty his previous good services would count for nothing. Two events followed that may, or may not, have been connected. The remaining bandits in the Sila region were captured and killed by Manhès's men within the next two months, while Barracco (in return?) received a military safe-conduct from Manhès in 1811 and a further cash compensation of 200,000 ducats—a very large sum—from the government. As a token of his esteem, Don Alfonso presented General Manhès with two white stallions bred on his estates.[72]

Manhès's willingness to identify and challenge the brigands' supporters made him widely feared, but also made him powerful enemies and it is hardly surprising that he became a target of defamation. The tactics he used were part of the armoury of counter-insurgency methods employed by the military that had been refined during the campaigns against the Breton *chouans* and were not essentially different from those used by other commanders in Italy.

[66] Ibid. 1124.
[67] A de G: C(5*) 33 Manhès: Rapports généraux au Roi, Calabria Citra, 25 May 1811.
[68] Ibid., C(5*) 43: Rapports journaliers au Roi (1811): Manhès to Murat, 15 February 1811.
[69] BNN: Bancone 8 B: Copia lettere del Signor Tenente General Manhès, 19 December 1810.
[70] On the Baracco family, see Petrusewicz (1978), 339–44.
[71] Ibid. See also Caldora (1960), 424.
[72] Caldora (1960), 424; Petrusewicz (1978), 344.

Nonetheless, Manhès was repeatedly singled out for his barbarity. De Nicola noted in April 1811 that he had heard it said in Naples that in the region around Potenza alone, Manhès had executed 600 brigands in the space of barely two months.[73] In July, the envoy of the Kingdom of Italy in Naples, Tassoni d'Estense, also referred to Manhès with revulsion:

I must confess that my heart and pen flee from describing the excesses of cruelty that he has used and which outdo the worst crimes committed by the Brigands.... He has violated young girls, has allowed his soldiers to enter the jails to have their vile way with women unjustly condemned to death, has caused fathers to kill their own sons, in short he has shed rivers of blood in which that of the guilty has been mixed with the innocent.[74]

The episode that most fully epitomized the brutality of Manhès's repression was later recounted by Colletta, who claimed that Manhès's men had executed eleven young girls from the village of Stilo after it was discovered that they were carrying loaves of bread in a basket as they went to the fields to glean corn.[75]

Whether or not these stories are true, they indicate that Manhès had made powerful enemies in his pursuit of the brigands' protectors. There were many reasons why he was politically exposed. His patron, Saliceti, had died in 1809, while his closeness to Murat and his rapid promotion made the other senior French generals jealous, especially Cavaignac whose own murky operations were in danger of being exposed by Murat's unduly energetic aide-de-camp. It was no coincidence, however, that the campaign against Manhès reached its height in the summer of 1811 at the moment when the crisis between Naples and Paris came to a head and the pro-French and mainly French party at Court led by the queen took power. As one of the very few French officers who remained loyal to the king, Manhès was an obvious target.

CONCLUSION

Behind these cruel and seemingly pointless chronicles of random violence and barbarity can be glimpsed the impact of Napoleon's enterprise on the civilian populations of Europe. The horrors of war that Goya captured in Spain were repeated on a Continental canvas, and it was the misfortune of the rural communities of southern Italy that the war came to them in at least two different forms. They were caught between the contending forces: the emperor's enemies in Sicily were constantly engaged in provoking and inciting disorder, while the ever-growing flows of contraband placed further strains on the fragile sinews of authority. In Calabria these external disasters were imposed on a region where social tensions were

[73] De Nicola, 28 April 1811, 559.
[74] Cited in Cutolo (1937), Tassoni Estensi, 15 July 1811, 410.
[75] Colletta (Cortese, 1957), ii. 342.

already inflamed, and where powerful landowners were able to turn the prevailing lawlessness to their own advantage.

Brigandage was not, as some contemporaries claimed, the last gasp of feudalism—an attempt by the former feudal landowners to preserve the independence that had formerly been enforced by their retainers and their feudal *mastrodatti*. Many of the brigands had formerly served the feudatories as armed retainers, but their masters were as likely to be private landowners, new families like the Barracco and the Quintieri who were amassing vast estates in these troubled times and who saw the opportunities to impose their own order irrespective of the rules of either the feudal past or the bureaucratic present.[76] The disorders were inseparable from the emergence of new elites, who were staking out their property claims and at the same time renegotiating their place in the new order. When Manhès tried to call their game, the reactions revealed the reach of the interests he had threatened but not destroyed.

All these things made the scale of disorder in Calabria particularly intense, but not unique. The northern frontier provinces were similarly exposed to incursions from brigand bands from the Papal States that penetrated deep into Capitanata and Apulia with impunity. Once the British regained control of the Ionian islands, the Adriatic provinces were similarly at risk. But the scale of banditry in provinces like Basilicata and the Principato Ultra, which were not close to the frontiers, also shows that conflicts rooted in the transformation of the agrarian order were being felt in most parts of the South, just as the campaigns against the brigands revealed that the face of authority was everywhere insecure.

The webs of complicity that gradually became visible behind the faces of the common brigands showed how more powerful figures were taking the opportunities presented by the prevailing disorders to stake out their own interests and secure their own claims. As a result the vast new estates were acquired by means that were facilitated rather than impeded by the prevailing conditions of disorder.

[76] Montroni (1996), 31–3.

12

A Kingdom Divided

THE POLITICS OF DIVISION

The emperor's wars posed major obstacles to administrative reorganization in southern Italy, while the prolonged interruption of trade severely damaged the Kingdom's fragile economies. But these difficulties were also aggravated by Murat's insecurity within the imperial enterprise. The confrontation with Napoleon in the summer of 1811 proved to be especially damaging, and although unlike Louis Bonaparte Murat survived, the encounter left his position in both the politics of empire and the emperor's own dynastic plans uncertain.[1]

The constant tensions with Paris undermined Murat's attempts to give his regime a more secure political base, and his very public humiliation by the emperor in the summer of 1811 enabled the pro-French faction led by the queen to take control of the government. All those close to Murat—Giuseppe Zurlo and Antonio Maghella—lost their jobs while others like Manhès came under fierce attack. As Murat's position weakened, the incentives for turning to his Neapolitan supporters to create an independent political base increased, but this in turn provided the Neapolitan elites with important opportunities to reshape the political agenda to fit their own interests.[2]

Murat's confrontation with the emperor revealed deeper divisions within his own government that dated from his arrival in Naples. Saliceti had played a critical role in containing those divisions, but after his death in 1809 things quickly fell apart. Murat's main concern was to prevent Caroline Bonaparte from exercising independent power, which with the exception of Agar made him wary of the Frenchmen who had her confidence.[3] But this proved far from easy and his choice of Antonio Maghella to succeed Saliceti as Minister of Police in 1809 was particularly maladroit. A protégé of the former minister with whom he had then publicly quarrelled, Maghella was widely suspected of poisoning his former master and Murat was soon forced to transfer most of his powers to his trusted follower

[1] On the chronic political uncertainty of the imperial enterprise see, e.g., Schroeder (1994), 394.

[2] On the concept and realities of Napoleonic 'state-building' see especially Breuilly in Rowe (ed.) (2003), 121–52.

[3] Saliceti's recall to Paris in 1809 was allegedly the result of his attempts to strengthen the power of Caroline Murat at the king's expense. See Colletta (Cortese, 1957), ii. 331–2.

Hector Daure, the Minister of War. The result was that Daure and Maghella became mortal enemies, and at the height of the crisis with Paris in June 1811 it was Maghella who informed Murat that both Daure and General Vanguyon were the queen's lovers.[4]

Maghella's attempt to discredit the queen led to his downfall, but Murat's efforts to exclude Caroline Bonaparte from power also failed. The emperor's favourite sister had strongly resented the purely ceremonial role assigned to her, and had made it known that she wanted to be a ruler in her own right like her sister Elise Bacciocchi, the Grand Duchess of Tuscany.[5] In this she had her brother's support and the crisis with Paris in 1811 enabled Caroline Bonaparte not only to emerge as the undisputed leader of the pro-French faction at Court but also to mediate between Murat and the emperor and hence establish her own independent role in the government in Naples. She was now Murat's equal and henceforth in his absence would rule as regent.

Murat survived, but the French party led by the queen was now in control. This increased the power of General Cavaignac, the Director General of Domains, whom Tassoni Estense described as the embodiment of the corruption and profiteering that now became the most distinctive feature of the French administration. But all the leading ministers, officers, and officials, Neapolitans included, had received rich bounties, mainly in *beni nazionali* either as gifts or sold at prices far below market values.[6]

Only three senior Neapolitans administrators survived the crisis, among them the Prince of Serra Gerace, the director of the *Cassa di Ammortizzazione del Debito Pubblico*, and an able financier who, as well as his wife, had made great personal fortunes.[7] Francesco Antonio Ricciardi, the Minister of Justice and a forthright critic of Giuseppe Zurlo, also survived,[8] as did the Neapolitan Talleyrand, the marchese di Gallo, who retained his role as Foreign Minister. Di Gallo had also amassed a large fortune, and although he was not a major force in domestic affairs, Tassoni claimed that he was the government's indispensable

[4] The main source for the political divisions in Murat's court was Giulio Tassoni Estense, who served as the diplomatic representative of the Kingdom of Italy at the Neapolitan Court from 1809 to December 1811, when Napoleon ordered his expulsion for participating in a duel fought between the Russian *chargé d'affaires* and a French diplomat following a dispute at a New Year's Eve party. Ibid. 407; also Weil (1912).

[5] *Notizia storica sul Conte Carlo Antonio Manhès* (1846), 121.

[6] Cavaignac never presented proper accounts and 'had enriched himself exorbitantly and his rapacity is proverbial'. Cutolo (1937), 401.

[7] Tassoni claimed that Serra Gerace had made huge personal profits and was one of the largest purchasers of *beni nazionali*. He also claimed that Serra Gerace's wife had received licences to export goods from her vast estates in Calabria in direct violation of the Continental blockade, a charge repeated in the Tommasi papers (see Chapter 14). For the lists of investors in the public debt see Ermice (2005), 150–60 and 173–260, where the Serra Gerace family appears with the Tocco, Muscettola, Spinelli, and Zunica as the largest private shareholders in the public debt, along with many foreign investors and speculators.

[8] Tassoni described Francesco Antonio Ricciardi, Conte dei Calmaldoli (1758–1842), as arrogant and concerned only 'to leave his family with a big patrimony' but claimed that no one could accuse him of venality; Cutolo (1937), 401.

intermediary with both the imperial administration in Paris and the Bourbon court in Palermo.[9]

Of Murat's inner group of advisers only Agar, who had always enjoyed the queen's confidence, remained.[10] The most prominent victim of the crisis, however, was the former Bourbon minister, Giuseppe Zurlo, Murat's Neapolitan Minister of the Interior. Arrogant and aloof, Zurlo was hated by both the French and the Neapolitans, but the immediate reason for his fall was the Feudal Commission, which both Agar and the queen believed Zurlo had turned into an instrument of personal vendetta to ruin the old nobility that had seriously jeopardized the regime's security and reputation.

THE FEUDAL COMMISSION

Caroline Bonaparte's intervention had Agar's support and reflected a broader concern that Murat had allowed Zurlo to alienate the great landowners who were considered the new regime's most powerful allies. Between February and August 1806 Joseph Bonaparte had assured his brother that 'The seigneurs and the wealthy landowners [who] were the enemies of the former Court and are friends of the new order . . . for that reason I should avoid causing them offence by making too many changes with respect to either property or the persons in my employ.'[11]

As in the other Napoleonic states, the new regime's initiatives were gauged specifically to win the support of the landowners, who were among the principal beneficiaries of the partial rescue of the creditors of the *ancien régime* and of the sales of the *beni nazionali.* For the same reason, Joseph Bonaparte had been unwilling to seize the lands of those who had followed the Bourbons to Palermo, while the law of 2 August abolishing feudalism bent over backwards not to harm the interests of the landed classes.[12]

As in the rest of the empire, the law deprived the ex-feudatories of their political powers, fiscal privileges, and some feudal revenues but left them with almost everything else. All rights or monopolies not feudal in origin were converted to private property or rents. Rivers and waterways became public property, but not the 'mills, mill wheels, olive presses, tanning works, paper-making shops, mineral and dye-works, workshops for beating copper and similar constructions' that simply became the private property of the former barons. Similarly 'all rents or taxes and other payments for the use of land whether in cash or in kind remain as they

[9] See Croce, 'Il marchese Caraccciolo' (di Gallo's uncle), in *Uomini e cose della vecchia Italia* (1956), 82–111.

[10] Jean Antoine Agar, Conte de Mosbourg (1771–1844); Tassoni thought he was out of his depth, relied uncritically on French models, and had little knowledge or experience of matters financial or commercial; Cutolo (1937), 401.

[11] ANP: AFiv 1714c; 22 February, 31 July, 8 August 1806.

[12] Villani (1964), 44–7; Ermice (2005), 126–9.

are, and are to be paid as due and to be considered private property'. One of the most controversial sections of the new law stipulated that:

> [T]he *demani* that formed part of the abolished feudal estates will remain the property of their former owners. The local population will retain their common use rights on these same estates and all other rights that they are entitled to until such time as the *demani* shall be the subject of a new law that will lay down the terms for their division.... In the meantime, it is expressly forbidden that any changes or innovations be made.[13]

However, the law of August 1806 demonstrated that it was one thing to abolish feudalism where it no longer existed, but something quite different in Naples where it was a pervasive and deeply contentious reality. The most critical weakness of the new law was that it failed to take account of the questionable legality of most of what was claimed by feudal title. This made the legitimacy of all property rights—feudal or otherwise—uncertain and contentious, and was the issue that had bedevilled every earlier attempt at reform. Had the law of August 1806 been implemented it would have converted feudal property and rights into private property and rents without recognizing the claims of the local communities. Effectively, the disputes between the local communities and neighbouring lay and ecclesiastical feudatories that for half a century had brought conflict and tension to the rural South would have been settled exclusively in favour of the latter.

It soon became clear that the new law was likely to provoke serious unrest, because of both the expectations raised and what was actually promised. The government was faced with the questions that had confronted all previous attempts at reform and had overwhelmed the courts of the *ancien régime*: they had to find the means to distinguish feudal from non-feudal rents, rights, and property, and to determine the legitimacy of all these highly contentious titles and claims.

Unsure how to proceed but alarmed by the growing unrest, in January 1807 the government suspended those sections of the law relating to the compensation of feudal exactions and the division of the *demani*. But the way forward was unclear. The *ancien régime* tribunals had been abolished, but the new legal codes had not yet been introduced. In November 1807 the government therefore created a Feudal Commission to review the contentious sections of the law of August 1806, but when Joseph left for Spain in 1808 no progress had been made.[14]

By the time of Murat's arrival the issue could not safely be deferred much longer, while the meetings of the provincial assemblies in the summer of 1808 revealed additional fiscal imperatives for settling outstanding disputes over rights on both former feudal estates and the common lands. The disastrous state of local finances that became evident when the provincial assemblies met demonstrated that the reorganization of local administration could not progress without a more general reorganization of local finances, which in turn could not be done without

[13] Law on feudalism, 2 August 1806.

[14] Its members were Davide Winspeare, Luigi Dragonetti, Giuseppe Raffaeli, Domenico Franchini, and Vincenzo Cuoco.

resolving the controversies over ownership of the common lands of the local communities and their use-rights on former feudal estates.

Giuseppe Zurlo now proposed that Joseph Bonaparte's Feudal Commission be given a new brief to enable it to carry out both the definitive division of the former feudal estates and also the division of the former common lands. For Murat the political advantages of the project were clear. At very little cost it would enable the government to claim that it had realized its most ambitious modernizing promise, while the reform could also be expected to bring significant but less strongly advertised increases in tax yields for both local government and the state.

In many respects Zurlo also seemed ideally well qualified to carry the operation through. He had been the architect of the Bourbon decree of 1792 ordering the division of the common lands, while his former absolutist training well equipped him as a Napoleonic administrator.[15] He had complete confidence both in absolutist measures and in a reform project that many critics believed to be too abstract to accommodate the widely varying circumstances of the South and in any case probably impossible to implement.[16]

These were not criticisms to which Zurlo paid much attention, although to the irritation of the French party at court he did openly acknowledge the defects of Joseph Bonaparte's law on feudalism:

> although a centuries-old experience had exposed the true nature of the evils of feudalism, [the law of 2 August] not only failed to define what it was abolishing and what it was preserving, but . . . left all these rights subject to exactly the same state of litigation and dispute that had existed before the law was introduced.[17]

In the past the state had been weak and unable to prevent powerful landowners from usurping lands that rightfully belonged to the local communities: 'the village commons were in the hands of the barons. . . . Most of the land held in feudal title was leased on the most onerous terms . . . all forms of industry were reserved exclusively to the barons and it was this that brought devastation to our agriculture.'[18]

Zurlo claimed that although Joseph had recognized the problem, he feared that any attempt to rewrite this fundamental law would be dangerous. The new government was prepared to act more decisively, however, and in this sense the Feudal Commission also played a part in the attempt to present Murat as a more effective and active ruler.

The premise for the new operation was the decrees of 6 December 1808 that made it legal to enclose all private property, which was freed from former rights of open pasture and other collective and customary use-rights. That decree struck at the use-rights on which the economies of the rural communities throughout the South depended, and was followed by a second decree ordering the division of all former feudal and public common lands between the former feudatories and

[15] On the edict of 1792 see Corona (1995), 105–19; see also ANP: Fonds Joseph Bonaparte 381AP2; Council of State, Report of the Demani, June 1806. [16] See Aliberti (1987), 35–6.
[17] Zurlo, in Lalli (ed.) (n.d.), 38. [18] Ibid. 59.

the local communities in proportion to the rights formerly exercised. Then on 24 February 1809 Murat reactivated the Feudal Commission to implement these decrees, empowering it to settle all disputes relating to former feudal rights, and to apportion former feudal estates between the owners and those claiming use-rights. Those decisions would be made and carried out by a Commission for Reallocation (*Commissione dei Repartitori*), which would divide the lands allocated to the local communities amongst the inhabitants in the form of quit-rent smallholdings.[19]

In October 1809 the membership of the Commission was again revised and its five commissioners then set off to travel the length and breadth of the Kingdom to hear and settle outstanding litigation and oversee the division of both the former feudal estates and the common lands.[20] There were to be no appeals against their judgments and the entire operation was to be completed within a year. This was actually achieved and the Feudal Commission was indeed disbanded in August 1810, although the division of the common lands was extended to December 1811, after which its functions were taken over by the ordinary courts and the regional Intendents' councils.[21]

Murat's government moved energetically to gain maximum publicity for an operation hailed as the ultimate demonstration of the benefits that imperial rule had brought to southern Italy. Davide Winspeare was commissioned to write a *History of the Abuses of Feudalism*, the first and only volume of which was published by the government in 1811. This was a self-seeking work that larded a defence of the Feudal Commission with an anecdotal history of feudalism selected at random from the litanies of feudal abuses made familiar by the reform writers of the previous century, including such Gothic horrors as the *jus prima noctis*.[22] But Winspeare's main concern was to point out that this operation was not directed against the landowners, and indeed had their full support. The lay feudatories had long since converted feudal rents and personal services to money rents. Feudalism had survived, Winspeare argued, only because of the Church which was the principal owner of feudal property in the Kingdom and was deaf to modern principles. This rather clumsy piece of propaganda closed by praising the altruism shown by the Neapolitan feudatories who had fully supported the law of August 1806 because they, like the government, considered feudalism an anachronism:

> The present day owners of feudal estates are quite different from their predecessors in their culture and behaviour. Inspired by a new sense of public duty, they can no longer tolerate these hateful feudal rights, although they remain determined to preserve and protect all their revenues. As a result, they often condemn those very rights which in practice they continue to exact.[23]

19 Trifone (1909), 181–98; La Volpe (1930), ii. 125.

20 Davide Winspeare was President with five commissioners: Paolo Nicola Giampaolo, Giuseppe de Thomasis, Giuseppe Poerio, Girolamo Dumas, and Biase Zurlo.

21 Trifone (1909), 318.

22 A feudatory's claim to sleep with his vassals' brides on their wedding night.

23 Winspeare (1811), 86–9.

The same message was repeated in Zurlo's Report on the State of the Realm in 1811. The Feudal Commission and the division of the *demani* had finally brought to an end:

centuries-long litigation which almost from the time of the foundation of the monarchy has fuelled the spirit of rivalry between the rural populations and the barons. As a result of the two operations carried out by the Feudal Commission the property of the former feudatories has been guaranteed; the rights they exercised on the common *demani* have been separated from those of the local communities and the different forms of *servitù* and other abusive rights exercised on public and private land have been suppressed.[24]

Both Winspeare and Zurlo had got it wrong, however. The Feudal Commission began operating just as Manhès had been sent to repress the massive resurgence of brigandage in Calabria that then spread to other provinces. Far from strengthening support for the regime, the actions of the commissioners outraged the nobles who claimed that they had been despoiled of property owned for centuries. Those complaints led to Zurlo's dismissal, which necessarily also undermined the successful implementation of the reforms.

Even those closest to Zurlo acknowledged that the government did not have the practical means to enforce the Commission's rulings. Early in 1811 Angelo Masci,[25] the Intendent of Lower Calabria, reported that powerful landowners had easily subverted the rulings of the Feudal Commission when these threatened their interests:

The torpor and inaction that Your Excellency has had cause to remark on in this province . . . does not derive from ignorance but from the most horrible intrigues. The Barons, the landowners and the owners of the biggest herds of sheep have all joined forces to subvert the excellent measures taken to bring about the division of the common lands, and the means that they have used to this end are all the more damaging because they have also succeeded in deceiving the people so that they too agree in opposing them.[26]

Four months later Masci returned to the same subject:

The people in this province are so deeply accustomed to subservience that if the public authorities are not constantly vigilant in checking the overbearing behaviour of the powerful there is no-one who has the courage to raise his head to assert the rights which the Law confers on him. It is therefore extremely probable that notwithstanding the rulings [of the Feudal Commission] previously referred to, if the authorities in each locality do not constantly remain alert to ensure that they are observed, the former abuses will immediately return.[27]

[24] The Neapolitan Commission, he argued, had faithfully followed the French laws of 25 August 1792, which had also been applied by imperial decree to Piedmont, Genoa, Tuscany, Parma, and Rome; Zurlo, in Lalli (ed.) (n.d.), 78.

[25] Masci had been one of the Economic Visitors in 1801–3, and was one of Zurlo's confidants.

[26] ASN: Carte Winspeare, Affari Demaniali f. 74: Masci to Zurlo, 2 February 1811.

[27] Ibid., Masci to Zurlo, 13 June 1811.

From the Terra d'Otranto, the Intendent Domenico Acclavio wrote in almost identical terms about the failure of the ordinary courts to enforce the decrees of the Commission:

I have lacked neither energy nor zeal in preventing similar abuses, but if the ordinary Courts continue to allow these laws to be neglected I seriously doubt that all my vigilance will be sufficient to prevent the accumulation of precedents in the Province that will enable feudalism to be reborn from its ashes. The vast number of small landowners are totally without the means to enter into litigation and hence may easily fall again under the former yoke.[28]

Acclavio's predictions proved accurate and in most parts of southern Italy the rural poor lost either immediately or within a short space of time the access to the common lands on which the livelihood of the rural communities depended. Instead of ending the expropriation of the lands and assets of the local communities as was intended, the reform if anything accelerated the speed at which they were coming under private control, a process that would be the major cause of social unrest in the rural South in the decades that followed.

The reason, Vincenzo Cuoco argued, was that the criteria on which the rulings of the Feudal Commission were based were deeply flawed. Cuoco was no friend of Zurlo, and in his report as Intendent of the province of Molise in 1812 he denounced the devastating impact of the Commission's rulings:

The common lands belonging to the local communities that were already cultivated made up a about a third of the agricultural land in the Kingdom. Those who worked them were not Barons, nor were they over-mighty: they were drawn from that rank of citizens who have the most to offer the State because they are the most industrious. As the emperors Valentiniano, Teodoso and Arcadio well understood, these are the citizens who are best able to bring together private interest and the public good. But to these same people, who number a full quarter of the population of this Kingdom, we now say: Leave the lands that you have hitherto legitimately owned and cultivated and that are still steeped in the sweat of your fathers.

The expectation that the common lands would be 'converted into private property and emancipated from feudal exactions or collective use-rights in return for a simple quit-rent, thereby protecting both agriculture and industry' had proved to be 'vain dreams':

The land has passed from the hands of those who cultivated it to those who lack the means to cultivate it. The land has changed hands, but the capital needed to cultivate the land has not. So what will happen? The result will be disaster, because it is a disaster to own land that cannot be cultivated when the owner must at the same time pay both rents to the local community and taxes to the State.... The obligation to pay is inescapable; the ability to plough and sow the land is uncertain; hence the land becomes a source of anguish.[29]

[28] Ibid., f. 81, Acclavio to Zurlo, 4 February 1811.

[29] Cuoco (1806–15), 199–200.

The division of the commons would, he warned, inevitably give rise to innumerable new lawsuits and even where small farms had been established they were unlikely to survive. The new tenant farmers were burdened by the entry taxes, by the cost of equipment and seed, and also by the land tax to which they were obliged to contribute in addition to local taxes. As their debts accumulated, they were rarely able to survive the first bad harvest or fall in prices, at which time their land was easily absorbed by the wealthier landowners.[30]

Cuoco's predictions proved right on both counts. Without a very broad and general plan the work of the Feudal Commission could never have been completed. But the very short time in which it was required to issue its rulings resulted in judgments that were arbitrary and inconsistent that gave rise to protest and litigation that in some cases remained unresolved until over a century later.[31] In the meantime, without access to credit, tax concessions, or loans to buy equipment and crops few of the small farms that came into being as a result of the division of the commons and the former feudal estates lasted for long, and most were quickly incorporated into the properties of the wealthier landowners. As Cuoco and others also warned, the division of the common lands and the ending of older regulations also dramatically accelerated woodland clearances and exacerbated the damage to the fragile infrastructures of the southern economies in ways that had already caused alarm amongst the economists of the previous century.[32]

MAGISTRATES AND THE RULE OF LAW

Vincenzo Cuoco was not the only supporter of the regime who denounced the operations of the Feudal Commission. The Minister of Justice, Francesco Ricciardi, also detested Zurlo and denounced the Feudal Commission as an institution which he described as a throwback to the absolutist tribunals of the *ancien régime* and a flagrant violation of the rule of law on which the new regime claimed to be premised. But Ricciardi's denunciation of the juridical premises of the Feudal Commission—and also of the special powers conferred on Manhès—also revealed the ways in which the magistrates were beginning to establish new public roles.

As we have seen, when Joseph Bonaparte left for Spain in 1808 the reorganization of the administration of justice was completely stalled.[33] But the situation changed rapidly in the years that followed and by 1811 the magistrates had emerged as one of the most powerful professional groups in the new state. This was the result of initiatives taken by the magistrates themselves, however, who

[30] Giuseppe Palmieri had given the same warning in the 1790s; Tocci (1971), 68–9.
[31] Trifone (1909), 490.
[32] See D'Elia (ed.) (1993), 3–80, 150–66, and Palmieri (ed.) (1993), pp. xviii–xxiv, 5–33, 71–7.
[33] See Chapter 9, p. 182–4.

after Murat's arrival dropped their earlier resistance and began not only to cooperate but also to acquire new public roles and power.

The shift in attitude coincided with Ricciardi's appointment as Minister of Justice in 1809 and Murat's decision, under further and now inflexible pressure from Paris, to introduce the *Code Napoléon*. But Murat's decision to give way to the emperor's demands in itself meant little, since as in the other imperial territories the French legal codes had first to be translated while the new tribunals that were to apply the new laws had yet to be created. Murat probably expected that the whole awkward process would be swamped in legalistic technicalities and the pettyfogging that followed, as was the case in much of the rest of Europe.[34]

In Naples something quite different happened. When Murat appointed Ricciardi to head the commission set up to oversee the introduction of the French law codes in 1809, the Neapolitan men of law quickly came to understand that the new codes and the reorganization of the administration of justice provided an important opportunity to reclaim powerful positions in public life.[35] The *Code Civil* and the new administration of justice did not enable the *togati* of the *ancien régime* to reinvent themselves. It was a feature of the new legal codes and especially the French laws of legal procedure that magistrates now became representatives of the state with often no more than token guarantees of tenure. But under Ricciardi's leadership the magistrates and judges carved out important new public roles in the post-feudal state.[36]

Ricciardi was strongly committed to establishing the autonomy of the magistracy, and he also clearly understood that the new legal codes and tribunals offered the magistrates a powerful role in the new state. He began by vigorously asserting the autonomy of the new courts and he acted decisively to ensure that the magistrates were under the exclusive control of his Ministry. The new controls that the state exercised over judges under Napoleonic law gave the minister the means to impose tight corporate discipline on the magistrates, and to insist that they were answerable only to his Ministry. At the same time, Ricciardi vigorously promoted the Justice Ministry's unique function as the principal guardian of the law, which in practice meant the right to monitor all other branches of government to ensure that they did not exceed their jurisdictions.

Ricciardi had refused to accept office while Saliceti was alive, specifically on the grounds that the former Minister of Police had systematically violated jurisdictional boundaries. As Minister of Justice he set about dismantling the police state created by Saliceti, starting with the dismissal of the magistrates appointed by the former Minister of Police. A commission was set up to investigate those who had been appointed simply because they had been anti-royalist in 1799 and

[34] On Germany see, e.g., Farhmeir in Rowe (ed.) (2003), 107–20.

[35] Nicolini (1901), p. xl; in addition to the civil code, the French criminal law code and the codes of civil and criminal procedures had also to be translated and adopted.

[36] See especially Castellano (2004), 7–17.

those who were improperly qualified were dismissed. Every magistrate was subject to close and routine surveillance, and all were required to submit regular reports detailing conditions in the provinces and localities where they were in service and to report on the behaviour of all civil officials.

Once the autonomy of his ministry was secure, Ricciardi began reorganizing the courts. He was strongly opposed to every form of special court outside his jurisdiction, including the military tribunals established in 1809. For that reason he vehemently opposed the special powers conferred on Manhès in 1810 and he challenged military intervention in judicial affairs wherever this occurred. But above all he denounced Zurlo's Feudal Commission as an atavistic return to the absolutist *juntas* of the previous century, which violated both the integrity of the administration of justice and the rule of law.[37]

These initiatives met with enthusiastic support from many of those like Giuseppe Poerio and Vincenzo Cuoco who had formerly been close to Saliceti and who supported the aims of the new regime but not its methods.[38] But in the process of reorganization the magistrates also acquired a distinctive sense of their own corporate identity, accompanied by a very explicit sense of national identity as well.

The French legal codes were not simply translated, for example, but adopted and appropriated. This was not difficult since they were written in the language and principles of the Enlightenment with which the Neapolitan lawyers who had come of age in the years of Bourbon reformism, the debates on feudalism, and the revolution and the Republic of 1799 were deeply familiar.[39] But they also now received a strong nationalist imprint, as was illustrated in the inaugural address delivered by Nicola Nicolini when he was appointed Royal Procurator General at the Criminal Court at S. Maria Capua Vetere in 1809.

Nicolini claimed that the new codes of criminal law and criminal procedure that had been imported from France were entirely Neapolitan in inspiration. All their essential principles had been anticipated in the reforms championed in Naples in the eighteenth century by Gaetano Filangieri, Charles III, Tanucci, and Ferdinand IV. The new norms of procedure in criminal cases were identical to the royal decrees of 1735 and 1738 regarding the interrogation of accused persons. Tanucci had established new rules of conduct for all lawyers and magistrates, and the use of torture had been abolished in 1789. For Nicolini, the law of 1774 that required judges to give written justification of their sentences was the basis for the reform of criminal and civil law procedures that culminated in the law of 1808.

The ground has, therefore, been well prepared and the road has been made ready by the studies of our most distinguished native jurists, so that our minds have for many years been

[37] Nicolini (1901), p. xlii; see also Zurlo (1809), 53.

[38] Castellano (2004), 87–99. On Poerio, see *ASN*: Archivi Privati, Carte Tommasi, B5, where Poerio was described as Saliceti's protégé, 'the most eloquent speaker in the Council of State and a dangerous man to have as an opponent'.

[39] See Rao (1984), Ajello (1976), and Cammissa in Massafra (ed.) (1988), 519–24.

educated in ways to prepare them to receive the new legislation. These do not come to us as the beginning of a new civilization, but enable us to move forward with the civilization we already enjoy, finally rid of the difficulties posed by the presence of too many contradictory laws that were confused by the unclear guidance of obscure authorities.

The real innovation was that the new procedures and laws were now 'set forth in the light of day by simple, coherent and fecund principles, made certain by reliable forms of interpretation, and in addition made intelligible and popular thanks to the adoption of the universal language of Italian'.[40]

This was an exceptionally clear statement of the new sense of identity and indeed autonomy that the magistrates had acquired as a result of the crisis of the *ancien régime* monarchy. As Murat's relations with Paris deteriorated, the lawyers' autonomy grew as did their control over the administration of justice. New measures were introduced to formalize entry into the profession, to regulate university courses, and to establish a general register of attorneys.[41] At the same time Ricciardi and a close group of supporters set out new guidelines for magistrates and made numerous revisions of the French codes to bring them into line with Neapolitan custom and procedure.[42]

In some cases new laws were circumvented, the most obvious being partible inheritance, and as in most of the rest of Europe Neapolitans simply drew up their wills in ways that indirectly retained the system of primogeniture.[43] In others this was not possible and the consequences were far-reaching, especially the abolition of feudal entails that after the Restoration was considered throughout Italy to be the single greatest blow to the wealth of the old nobility.[44]

In Naples, as in the rest of Italy, civil divorce remained a major sticking point. It was opposed not only by the clergy and the magistrates, but also more generally by the propertied classes who were concerned by the implications for inheritance and marriage strategies.[45] Although divorce finally did become law, it was ignored. By 1815 only three petitions had been filed in Naples: the first divorce was granted on 17 June 1810, and the second and last were granted in 1814. In the provinces there were more petitions but no divorces were granted. In June 1815 the abolition of civil divorces was the first legislative act of the restored monarchy.[46]

The reorganization of the state offered the Neapolitan jurists the opportunity to acquire powerful new public positions. Their power was no longer that of the former *togati*, but the jurists and judges of the new administrative monarchy were much more numerous than their eighteenth-century forebears. They filled

[40] Nicolini (1850), 13. [41] Castellano (2004), 201–3.

[42] Nicolini (1901), p. xlvii. The commission for revising the French codes included Giuseppe Poerio, Davide Winspeare, Nicola Nicolini, Michele Agresti, Tito Manzi, Giustino Fortunato, and Nicola Libetta.

[43] For example, by allowing women a lifetime interest in an inherited estate but excluding them from a share in the assets. [44] Davis (1988), 114–15.

[45] On marriage strategies see esp. Macry (1988), 153–8.

[46] Croce (1942); see also Volpe, in Di Leo (1995), 153–8, and Parente (1990).

the high offices of state and claimed to be both the guardians of the law and the overseers of all those who stood in authority. The creation of new provincial tribunals and the new office of Justice of the Peace increased career opportunities, while there were openings for commercial lawyers both in Naples and in the provinces.

By no means were all the magistrates new men, however. Of the 137 new magistrates appointed between 1808 and 1815, nearly 50 per cent had begun their careers in the service of the former monarchy.[47] But the men of law had been transformed into a professional corps with a strong sense of its own identity and interests, while the numbers of students who studied law at the University in Naples was an indication of the growing importance of the profession in the post-feudal state. It was also an illustration, however, of the chronic imbalance between supply and demand for professional employment that would play a major part in undermining the Restoration autocracies in Italy as in the rest of Europe.

CO-OPTING THE NOTABLES

The magistrates navigated the transition from the *ancien régime* with considerable skill to carve out powerful new positions in the post-feudal order, but the government's efforts to integrate the elites more actively into the new regime met with more mixed results. In every province there were prominent families that rallied openly to the new regime, but broader responses amongst the landowners were disappointing. Above all they showed little desire to shoulder the heavy administrative burdens delegated to the provincial and local assemblies, and even less to serve in the provincial militias.[48]

The government had been taken aback by the freedom of the criticisms voiced in the provincial assemblies in 1808, and in order to narrow participation established what were called *Economic Societies*. Unlike the provincial assemblies that reported to the Ministry of the Interior though the Intendents, the Economic Societies reported instead to a committee of experts and agronomists nominated by the king from the members of the *Reale Istituto d'Incoragiamento* in Naples, a body that had no executive or advisory powers.[49]

The new associations were dominated by technical experts and senior government administrators. When the *Reale Società Economica di Capitanata* first met in Foggia in July 1810, for example, its president, Giuseppe Rosati, was described as 'A Naturalist of outstanding merit, as his many publications will attest'. The other twelve members included 'a former monk who taught in the religious

[47] See Castellano (2004), 244.

[48] Scirocco (1978), 102–25; De Lorenzo (2201), 289–314.

[49] ASN: Min. dell'Interno (II), f. 5068, 6 February 1810, 6 October 1810; see also De Lorenzo (1998).

schools, and is a professor of physics and mathematics in the college at Foggia, a very able man'. There was also 'a wealthy and zealous landowner who knows a great deal about farming' and another 'enlightened landowner'. Senior government administrators served as corresponding members, including the Duke della Torre, the former Administrator of the *Tavoliere*, and 'a man learned in physics who is a member of the *Accademia di Arcadi* and of the *Accademia dei Georgofili* in Florence';[50] the Administrator of the local depot of gunpowder and saltpetre ('well trained in chemistry') and also M. Briot, 'who currently resides at Cosenza where he is the Intendent of Lower Calabria, but owns property in France and combines great theoretical knowledge with proven administrative skills'.[51]

Capitanata's Economic Society revealed the narrow cross section of government officials and notables that constituted the political foundation of the new regime. The tasks delegated to the Economic Societies carefully focused on highly technical debate of long-term and general issues. The Economic Association for Apulia, for example, in 1810 wrote a detailed survey of the three principal branches of agriculture in the province, and on other occasions reports were frequently delegated to a single expert.[52] While all these reports contained a wealth of important information and recommendations, their only audience was the committee set up by the *Reale Istituto d'Incorraggiamento* in Naples, which had no powers other than to listen.

The census conducted at considerable expense in 1811 met a similar fate, and served mainly to reveal that the regime lacked the means to complete such a survey. The language and repetition evident in the returns indicate that in most cases they were compiled by a single official working in the Intendent's office and on the basis of what information is unclear since few of the local councils completed their inquiries. As in France, these returns are of interest mainly for what they reveal of the values and preconceptions of the administrators. Like the reports of the provincial assemblies in 1808, a dominant concern was rural underpopulation, which was invariably cited as the principal cause of the backwardness of agriculture; as in 1808 this was a pretext for moralizing and often highly prurient denunciations of the immorality of the rural poor. Low fertility rates were blamed on promiscuity, intemperance, and masturbation. Infant mortality was a result of primitive birthing practices, ignorance, and neglect. Even disease was an affliction that the poor brought on themselves through lack of education, lack of concern for simple hygiene and cleanliness, slovenly habits, poorly built and badly maintained housing, ignorance, and indifference.[53] These reports illustrate values shared more widely among the propertied and educated classes, but they were written by lonely officials in understaffed and ill-equipped

[50] The first agricultural association in Italy founded in 1753 by Ubaldino Montelatici.

[51] ASF: *Reale Società Economiche*, F.1, Foggia, July 1810.

[52] Ibid. See also Cuoco (1806–15), 188–90.

[53] For the French provincial census returns, which were very similar in their ideological and anthropological assumptions, see esp. Bourguet (1976), 802–23.

offices that reveal the bureaucratic fantasies but not the administrative realities of the new order.

PUBLIC EMPLOYEES

Public employees were, nonetheless, an occupation group amongst which the new regime looked to develop strong political ties. However, the most immediate impact of the legislation introduced after 1806 was to put the employees of the *ancien régime* tribunals and the feudal administrations out of work. It was expected that this unemployment would be temporary and would soon be offset by the new careers and opportunities for preferment that would result from the reorganization of public administration.

Once the former royal and feudal employees had been reabsorbed, however, the net gains were quite small. Those employed in the new courts were primarily the former employees of the *ancien régime* tribunals. The same occurred in the new provincial and local administrations, which were staffed primarily by former feudal officers, just as the militias and gendarmeries were recruited from the former feudal *sbirri*.[54]

When in 1811 Tassoni Estense referred to Giuseppe Zurlo as the spokesman of the *ceto medio*, he meant specifically the public administrators whom he described as 'a very strong party that is deeply attached to the present government and its ministers'. But he went on to admit that the number of public employees and administrators was too small to constitute a viable political base for the new monarchy. There were major political complications, too, above all the competing claims and preference enjoyed by French nationals. Tassoni Estense claimed that 'some sixteen thousand French employees' were reported to have been given jobs, but added that he had no idea whether the figure was accurate 'since the truth in these matters is shrouded in partiality and polemic'. The figure is certainly wildly exaggerated, as was the smaller number quoted by Murat in February 1811 when he warned Napoleon of the political dangers posed by the horde of French placemen in the Kingdom:

> I cannot hide from Your Majesty that although I have nearly ten thousand men in my service, they are all Frenchmen, Romans, Tuscans or from other parts of Italy, while the Neapolitans are without jobs, they are dying of hunger and need the bread that is being eaten by the foreigners. Sire, Charles III had to contend with a major revolt in Naples for the same reason and I must fear the same outcome.[55]

Despite the inflated numbers, Murat saw sufficient political capital in winning the support of the Neapolitans to take the decision in June 1811 to require all Frenchmen to obtain Neapolitan nationality or leave the Kingdom. That move

[54] See, for example, BNP: Fonds Italiens 1126, Rapports au Roi (September 1808).
[55] ANP: 31 AP6: 18 January 1811.

precipitated the crisis with the emperor, and Napoleon's humiliating response severely undermined attempts further to establish a significant political base among the public employees. But this was never completely abandoned and when Murat defected to the allies in 1814 he immediately reintroduced the law requiring all public officials to have or to acquire Neapolitan nationality.[56]

THE POWER OF REPRESENTATION

Despite the weakness of the new regime's political base, like its absolutist predecessors it placed great store on the powers of representation. It looked to impress the masses with displays of regalian splendour and paternalist munificence, while adopting more cultured profiles to woo the propertied and educated classes. Both Joseph Bonaparte and Joachim Murat patronized the arts and the sciences, with special emphasis on useful scientific knowledge. In Naples a botanical garden was opened, somewhat incongruously in the grounds of the *Albergo dei Poveri*, as well as the astronomical observatory at Capodimonte, and in 1813 the city's first zoo. The excavations at Pompeii and Herculaneum, the archaeological museum, and the city's music conservatories were also meticulously reorganized along French lines.[57]

Caroline Bonaparte played the role of art patron with enthusiasm. She founded a new musical academy and brought Davide's brilliant young pupil, Jean-Auguste-Dominique Ingres, to Naples.[58] The emperor's most popular Italian artist, Antonio Canova, also received numerous commissions that included an equestrian statue of Joachim Murat.[59] The San Carlo opera house once again became an important setting for the royal display, which acquired a new and more daring dimension when Murat persuaded the famous Milanese impresario Domenico Barbaja to take over the contract for the theatre. As he had done in Milan, Barbaja opened gaming rooms and ballrooms in the theatre to help subsidize rapidly escalating production costs.[60] Reactions were divided and many were scandalized, but the new San Carlo served to underline the modernity of the new regime and its willingness to enter the marketplace. The theatre also continued to offer the most visible and frequent venue in which the royal family appeared surrounded by the Court, the high officers of state, the nobility, the prelates and clergy, uniformed army officers, and public officials and their families: the new post-feudal order in microcosm.[61]

[56] Colletta (Cortese, 1957), ii. 432–5.

[57] Torinni (1994), 44–9.

[58] Jean-August-Dominique Ingres (1780–1867). See Tinterow and Conisbee (1999) and Vigne (1997), 39–82.

[59] This did not arrive until after the fall of Murat's government and the face had to be changed to fit the likeness of Ferdinand IV; on Canova and the empire, see Valente (1965), 329–30 and also Johns (1998), 93–120.

[60] Rosselli (1984), 95–8; Davis (2005), 579.

[61] Sorba (2001).

The new rulers also maintained the populist traditions of the past, staging public galas and banquets for the Neapolitan poor, which were paid for not by the government, but by its wealthy supporters. In December 1810, for example, a lavish gala and banquet was organized as a benefit for the families of sailors and fishermen who had been killed during the Sicilian expedition. The feast was paid for by the leading merchants of the city, and the families of the fishermen were offered 'a bowl of macaroni with *ragù* and a quarter piece of kid', followed by a ball in the piazza and free entry for all to the San Carlo theatre. The high spot of the evening was the lottery, from which fifty dowries of twenty-five ducats each were distributed to the orphans of the drowned sailors.

The increasingly morose diarist Carlo De Nicola recorded that the response was sullen: as soon as the food was displayed the people seized it and took it away, along with the table linen and anything else they could carry off. No one returned for the dancing or the theatre.[62] The government organized many similar events to distract attention from high food prices, and De Nicola gloomily recorded in February 1811 that two major balls were held each week organized at huge personal expense by government ministers. Prince Pignatelli was believed to have paid 14,000 ducats for a single public reception at his palace.

'This is an insult to a Nation that is overwhelmed with taxes and impoverished, and it is a terrible sight to see one man drunk and another dying of hunger on the same street.' On 24 February the government held 'a popular *festa* at the expense of the city, but at the king's request', for which the entire square facing the royal palace was turned into a model village with fountains running with wine and bags of flour piled into great towers and then distributed to the poor.[63]

Tassoni Estense believed that the new political order had little popular support, however. Murat, he claimed, was personally popular because of his swashbuckling style and also because there were fewer executions than under Joseph Bonaparte. His government had also resumed the payment of pensions to veterans, widows, and orphans that Joseph had suspended. But beneath it all he was convinced that the people as a whole were still attached to the former monarchy, and it was only the memory of the terrible events of 1799 and the terror they inspired among the propertied classes that discouraged open opposition to the French government.[64]

THE MASONIC CONNECTION

Following the example set by the absolutist rulers in the late eighteenth century, Murat's regime in Naples—like its counterparts throughout the empire—looked on freemasonry as a means for strengthening bonds with the propertied and educated classes. When the French reached Naples in 1806 they quickly reopened

[62] De Nicola, 10 December 1810. [63] Ibid., 9 February 1811, 547.
[64] Ibid. Also Tassoni to Testi, 25 July 1809, in Cutolo (1937), 391.

the lodges that had been shut down more than a decade before, and closed the popular royalist associations that had flourished in the meantime.

As we have seen, the masonic networks in Naples and the provinces enabled the new regime to quickly identify potential allies and supporters and freemasonry played an important but scarcely acknowledged role in the establishment of the new regime. As Murat's relations with Paris deteriorated, however, his government showed even greater interest in strengthening and expanding both the numbers and the membership of the lodges.

These efforts reached a high point right at the height of the confrontation between Paris and Naples in June 1811 when the royal family presided over a major public gathering in Naples of masons from all over the Kingdom. More than 200 masons attended the ceremony, after which food was distributed to the poor and Daure, the War Minister, claimed that the rally had been 'remarkable for the unequivocal signs of good relations and perfect harmony between Neapolitans and Frenchmen which it exhibits'.[65]

A report prepared later for the Bourbon government claimed that by then masonic associations were 'very numerous in every part of the kingdom'. Their members came from 'every social class, except for the humblest members of the Nation, but the nobility and public employees took part in large numbers, and all their proceedings were closely followed by the Police. The king was the Grand Master, his Ministers the Grand Officers while all the Leaders of the provincial lodges were landowners and public officials. Rather than something to be feared as a state within the State, the lodges were closely amalgamated to and controlled by the Government.'[66]

That observation proved unduly optimistic, however, and as political opposition to Murat's government grew the masonic lodges provided the constitutional movement with a means to organize and disseminate its programme. When Murat's government in 1812 moved to outlaw its political opponents, the masonic lodges became the model for the secret societies that took up the demand for political reform and constitutional government.

THE CHURCH

The Church was the institution that from the very beginning the new regime had feared most, yet despite repeated attempts to establish a dialogue the alliance with sections of the clergy that had been realized in 1799 was never renewed. At the time of the French conquest, the clergy constituted the largest occupation and corporate group in the Kingdom, where it was estimated that they numbered around 100,000, of which about half were regulars.[67]

[65] A de G: C(5*) 33: Correspondance et Police, 22 June 1811.

[66] ASN: Archivi Privati; Archivio Tommasi B V: Memorandum 6, 'La Polizia Generale del Regno'.

[67] There were 21 archbishops, 110 bishops, and 53 abbots in the Kingdom (not including Sicily); Rambaud (1908), 296.

From the start, the French rulers were obsessed by the notoriety of the *Santafede*, and Miot de Melito later argued that fear of another counter-revolution had been the main reason that his proposals for suppressing the monasteries and convents had been the most contentious issue at the first meetings of the Council of Ministers in 1806. In fact the feared Santafedist reaction never materialized, but in both the capital and the provinces the closures of the religious houses were deeply unpopular, especially when they affected the mendicant orders, and even Napoleon had been shocked by what he considered to be the unnecessary scale of the closures.[68] They also caused the Kingdom to be flooded with dispossessed monks, nuns, and friars who, according to Tassoni Estense, in 1811 were still 'numerous, discontented, utterly without resources and for some time also without means, since for some months their pensions have not been paid'.[69]

Although the secular clergy were not greatly moved by the fate of their regular brothers and sisters, they also were a source of major problems for the new regime. Not least of these was the Pope's decision in 1806 to invoke the papacy's claims to feudal sovereignty over the Kingdom and the refusal to acknowledge Joseph Bonaparte as the legitimate ruler. Pius VII's action infuriated the emperor and contributed to the decision to occupy Rome two years later. In the Kingdom it caused a very awkward political crisis, since many bishops refused to swear the oath of loyalty to the new king, including the Cardinal Archbishop of Naples.[70] Far from resolving the problem, the French annexation of Rome in 1809 and the imprisonment of Pope Pius VII gave rise to new anxieties in Naples, and in March 1810 the Council of State discussed the urgent need for a new concordat with the papacy.

The case for a new concordat was put exclusively in terms of public order and the fear of a recurrence of 1799:

> The brutal and atrocious events of that year had a fatal effect because those most guilty were not punished, and instead the most evil deeds were rewarded, applauded and honoured as virtues.... Many ministers of the altar were converted into armed brigands, while their most worthy brothers were exposed to the gravest dangers when, animated by the spirit of peace, they tried to calm the people by whom they were hunted down, imprisoned, vilified and mistreated.

The spirit of ferocity had survived and was still bringing new disorders to the Kingdom: 'If we delay further in repairing this damage their insubordination will get worse and become a true Pandora's box so that the People will once more return to a state of barbarity.'

[68] Rambaud (1908), 302. [69] Tassoni, in Cutolo (1937), 392.

[70] See Rambaud (1908), 294–307: The Archbishop of Naples, Cardinal Ruffo of Scilla, was the brother of Fabrizio Ruffo of Bagnara—the former supported the French in 1799 but refused the oath to Joseph Bonaparte in 1806; his brother led the counter-revolution in 1799, but took the oath to Joseph in 1806.

The government had, therefore, to take energetic measures to establish proper education for every class of citizen, but for that to happen the Church needed serious reforms:

> morality is the foundation of all education . . . But what morality can there be without sanctions? And what sanctions can substitute for the force of Religion? If morality is reduced simply to be taught as a scientific discipline, what will happen to the most numerous Class of the People? No matter how many schools, grammar schools and colleges Your Majesty may build, these will never bring instruction to the most numerous classes of the Nation.

The remedy was to repair the damage done to the Church. This must start from the many cathedrals in the Kingdom that were without bishops. 'Abandoned for years to temporary vicars, they have been taken over by vagabonds and useless Priests: there is no discipline and without this the Body of the Church is like a man whose nerves have been cut.' Even where there was an incumbent, many of the bishops were aged. The need for clergy was greater than ever. 'It is true that amongst the secular clergy there are still today many learned and virtuous priests who are worthy of their positions, but the majority of them are of more than mature age and if steps are not taken soon they will have lost the energy to do good.'

The Kingdom's legislation, courts, and military had been reorganized along the lines of 'the first Empire in the World', and it was time to follow the example of Napoleon's Concordat with Pius VII 'that had brought peace once again to France'.[71]

Acting on that advice, the government proposed reducing the number of bishoprics, the reorganization of seminaries and the suppression of small dioceses which attract only 'unsuitable teachers'. Bishops and archbishops would be nominated by the king, and the Supreme Pontiff's canonical authority would be delegated to the Archbishop of Naples. The bishops would undertake a complete reform of all the parishes in their diocese to make them 'fit to meet the needs of the People', which would be done under the supervision and control of the Government.[72]

The papal authorities in Paris never replied and the reforms were never implemented. Nonetheless, the concerns expressed gave an unusually candid assessment of the weakness of the regime's popular support and the disastrous condition of the clergy.

THE ARMY

The army was the single largest source of public employment in the Kingdom, and was the institution to which Murat in particular looked to create an independent base for his dynastic Kingdom. But in practice this proved both difficult and dangerous.

[71] ASN: Min. degli Affari Esteri, f. 5691—memorandum attached to letter re Concordat from Di Gallo to Duca di Campochiaro, 30 March 1810.

[72] Rambaud (1908), 296.

Like all the imperial regimes, the style of Murat's government was overwhelmingly militaristic and this at least in theory offered important opportunities for bonding with the younger male sections of the local elites.[73] In some respects this was successful, and it was amongst the military that Murat found some of his most enthusiastic Neapolitan admirers. But the relationship was deeply contradictory, since Murat's attempts to create a dynastic army were viewed with the deepest suspicion by the emperor.

This again illustrates how the Kingdom's uncertain and contradictory status in the imperial enterprise undermined Murat's efforts to give his regime more permanent political roots. In this case, the contradictions were increased by the fact that there were two armies in Naples: a French army of conquest, which the Kingdom maintained when the emperor did not need its services, and the remnants of the defeated Bourbon army. Neither Joseph nor Murat ever held command over the French forces in their Kingdom, while for the Neapolitan army Napoleon had only contempt: 'The Neapolitan army is nothing, has never been anything and could never become anything.'[74]

Despite the disasters of 1798–9, however, the Bourbon army in 1801 could still muster 28,000 infantry and 5,000 horse.[75] That left it heavily outnumbered by the 40,000 men who crossed the Neapolitan frontier with Masséna in February 1806, and after the second defeat in 1806 very little was left while the Bourbon navy was in Sicily with the Bourbons.[76] Thereafter the task of rebuilding the Neapolitan army was made even more difficult by the Kingdom's obligations to both the French army of occupation and to France. The first Neapolitan contingent sent to join the *Grande Armée* in July 1807 was made up of convicts and pardoned brigands. They served in the capture of Barcelona and in the siege of Girona, and when Joseph Bonaparte moved to Madrid in 1808 he took with him two more Neapolitan infantry regiments and the elite *Guardia Reale*.

After Murat's arrival the situation was even more onerous. Under the terms of the Treaty of Bayonne, Naples was obliged to supply the *Grande Armée* with 16,000 infantry, 2,500 light cavalry, and twenty pieces of field artillery.[77] As a first instalment, 2,000 infantry and 400 cavalry were sent to Spain in 1808, but almost all were convicts and a thousand were rejected by Napoleon as unfit for service.[78] By 1810, one and a half divisions of Neapolitans were serving in Spain, and in 1812 and 1813 a similar force was sent to Germany, Russia, and Poland. In all some 9,000 Neapolitans served in Spain, and a further 13,000 in Germany and Russia, much less than the emperor had demanded but few returned.[79]

[73] On the pervasive militarism of the court of Eugène Beauharnais in Milan, see Zaghi (1986), 539–58.

[74] Cortese (1926), 320.

[75] 59 infantry battalions, 36 cavalry squadrons, and 2 regiments of artillery; Blanch, in Croce (ed.) (1945), 22–3.

[76] Rambaud (1911), 247.

[77] Cortese (1926), 220–1; Valente (1965), 308–11; Rao (1996), 255–98.

[78] Cortese (1926), 220–1.

[79] Ibid. 318.

On top of this the Kingdom had to pay for the French army of occupation which when Murat reached Naples in 1808 had received no pay for nine months: Joseph had not held any reviews and his generals had freely plundered the military coffers.[80] However, the departure of the regular French troops for the campaign against Austria in the spring of 1809 gave Murat an excuse for establishing a National Guard to maintain order. He also planned to recruit 20,000 men into what were now called the Select Volunteers (*Corpi di Volontari Scelti*), but this met with stubborn resistance from the landowners who considered it to be 'a form of conscription'.[81]

When Murat decided to create a new elite corps of *Veliti* to replace the Royal Guards that Joseph had taken to Spain, the emperor again became suspicious. The new corps was to consist of 4,000 cadets and officers, who were to form an elite body-guard recruited exclusively from the nobility and the wealthiest landowners. In 1809 a major rally was held in Naples to celebrate the founding of this praetorian guard, but Napoleon's suspicions only grew when he learned that Murat had also created a new military *Order of the Two Sicilies*.[82]

Those suspicions were fed by Murat's French generals and contributed to Napoleon's decision to humiliate his brother-in-law whom he stripped of command of the Sicilian expedition in 1810.[83] Orders were then given that the French and Neapolitan armies should be completely separated: in no circumstances were Neapolitan officers to command French troops, no French subject was to serve in the Neapolitan army without the emperor's authorization, and French military commissars were to be sent to Naples to ensure that convicts were not sent as conscripts for the *Grande Armée*.[84]

The command structure of the force assembled for the invasion of Sicily clearly demonstrated the subordinate positions assigned to the Neapolitan officers: all the divisional commanders were French,[85] and only two battalion commanders were Neapolitans.[86] The emperor's intervention also greatly increased the hostility that already existed between the small number of Neapolitan career officers and their French counterparts. Murat's attempts to reconstruct the Neapolitan army were warmly welcomed, therefore, not only by serving officers but also by the landed classes more generally. Like Joseph he supported the military academy at the *Nunziatella*, and founded a new corps of military engineers (*Genio Militare*) and a School of Military Engineering that offered important opportunities for training civil as well as military engineers.[87] This greatly consolidated the army's function as the principal provider of training for a wide range of professions, from

80 AAEP (Paris) CP: D'Aubusson to De Champagny, 22 January 1809.

81 Le Brethon, viii. Murat to Napoleon, 13 February 1809 (no. 3793).

82 Cortese (1926), 312.

83 Rambaud (1911b), 695–709.

84 Colletta (Cortese, 1957), ii. 337–40; Le Brethon, vi. Napoleon to Murat, 2 October 1808, 360; see also Cutolo (1937), 395–6.

85 Partouneaux, Lammarque, Dery, and Cavaignac.

86 Amato and Tenandi: Colletta (1848), 134; and Espitalier (1912), 78–80.

87 See Russo (1967) and Cortese (1965), 197–273.

physicians and chemists to veterinary surgeons and engineers, and it was hardly surprisingly that the military became the preferred career for the sons of the post-feudal landowners. But, as in the rest of Europe, the gap between expectations and openings was enormous.

By 1815 Murat's army had grown once more, on paper at least, to 17,000 men and officers. But it soon became clear that the emperor's wrath was not the only danger that Murat ran into in attempting to create a dynastic army. As relations with Paris deteriorated, Murat looked to create closer ties with his generals, all of whom held commissions in the *Grande Armée*, but these were valid only while on active service in the imperial campaigns outside the Kingdom.[88] Murat offered these men an alternative and better career, and they provided Murat with the means to rebuild his army after 1811. The generals supported Murat's own dynastic ambitions, but not without conditions and both freemasonry and support for the constitutional movement gained strength in Murat's army. By 1814 Joachim Murat had joined the long list of soldier-kings at risk of becoming prisoners of their generals, a danger that derived in part from Murat's own dynastic ambitions but which also reflected the deeper political inadequacies of the narrowly autocratic formula established in the wake of the collapse of the *ancien régime* monarchy.

CONCLUSION

This did not make the South different, however, and in its essential contours the Kingdom of Naples was in most respects similar to the other imperial satellite Kingdoms. The new regime was premised on a bureaucratic model of the state, in which the military and public employees were to be additional elements of political cohesion in a system that depended on the support of the great landowners and remained uncompromisingly autocratic.

The obstacles that undermined Murat's attempts to build political alliances derived most obviously from the Kingdom's colonial subordination and the uncertainty of his own place in imperial politics. But these were not the only ones. The new bureaucratic institutions were too weak to function effectively as an alternative source of political patronage. By 1815 the total judicial hierarchy, including the humble justices of the peace, consisted of no more than 800 to 900 judges and magistrates. The entire body of central administrators was made up of fifteen provincial Intendents, thirty-eight Sub-intendents, and eight ministers of state with twenty-four employees apiece. On paper the army employed 17,000 men, but only a small number were officers or had permanent commissions.[89]

[88] Andrea Pignatelli di Cerchiara, Vincenzo Pignatelli di Strongoli, Francesco Pignatelli, Florestano and Guglielmo Pepe, Luigi Blanch, Pietro Colletta, Michele Carrascosa; see Cortese (1926), 312.

[89] Castellano (2004), 244.

Underlying the weakness of the new bureaucratic structures was, of course, also the material difficulty of maintaining these structures at a moment of dire economic crisis and in contexts of overwhelming poverty. Not surprisingly when the revolutions came to the South in 1820 the most widespread complaints focused on the fiscal burdens that were the most tangible legacies of administrative change. But this was a vicious circle since despite increased tax burdens the revenues were not sufficient to make the new bureaucracies either efficient or effective.

For similar reasons the regime raised expectations of professional employment that could not be realized, and when it came to the army this was especially dangerous. It was no small irony of the Napoleonic episode in the South that Murat's strongest political supporters were also the foremost in demanding constitutional government and an end to subordination to the *Grande Nation* and its emperor. But if Murat's generals who supported the demand for a constitution in 1814 were the regime's most powerful opponents, behind them could be heard the voices of the propertied classes and the local notables more generally who saw in constitutional government the best way to protect the needs and interests of the provinces against the pretensions of a rigidly autocratic and bureaucratic government.

Naples was by no means the only case where these developments proved highly contradictory. Everywhere in Italy French autocracy and bureaucratic centralization met with resistance from the elites, but only in the South did that take the form of demands for constitutional government. In part that was a consequence of the weakness and isolation of Murat's regime within the empire, which gave the opposition in his own Kingdom greater freedom to organize and articulate its demands. But the constitutional project also gave expression to forms of political mobilization that as yet had no parallels elsewhere in Italy.

PART III

RESTORATION AND REVOLUTION

13

Losing Naples

'ON TOP OF THE VOLCANOES': NAPOLEON AND MURAT, 1814–15

The final chapter in the saga of Napoleonic Naples began in January 1814 when Joachim Murat defected to the allies. A year later he again rallied to Napoleon after the flight from Elba, but in May that venture ended definitively in military defeat on the battlefield at Tolentino. The finale came five months later when on the morning of 13 October 1815 Murat was executed by a firing squad against the perimeter wall of a small hill-top fortress at Pizzo on the Calabrian coast.

After Napoleon's victories at Lützen and Bautzen in May 1813, Murat rejoined the emperor's armies in Germany where, apart from a brief return to Naples in August, he remained until October. There was a partial reconciliation, but Napoleon still refused the peace terms offered by Austria and after the emperor was defeated at Leipzig in October Murat reopened negotiations with the allies. Napoleon tried to have him arrested, but on 4 November Murat returned to Naples and on 11 November opened the Neapolitan ports to allied shipping. Two days later he informed the emperor that the situation in his Kingdom had changed completely during his absence. Revolutionary placards were circulating in Calabria and a revolt was imminent: 'Sire, we are not only close to the volcanoes, but right on top of them.'[1]

Napoleon then sent his former Minister of Police, Joseph Fouché, to persuade Murat to honour his obligations to the empire.[2] Fouché reached Naples in December 1813 and reported that Murat was likely to join the offensive that the Austrian General Nugent was about to launch against Prince Eugène in northern Italy. But he clearly stated his belief that the emperor's actions had forced Murat into the allied camp. The emperor had repeatedly and publicly humiliated his brother-in-law, deprived him of his military command in his own Kingdom, and forced him to send troops to Germany even when his own Kingdom was under

[1] ANP: 31 AP 6: Murat to Napoleon, 13 November 1813.

[2] Joseph Fouché (1759–1820), a protégé of Barras who became Napoleon's chief of police and in 1808 was made Duke of Otranto. Disgraced and dismissed in 1810, he was appointed Governor of the Illyrian Provinces three years later, and then acted as mediator with Prince Metternich. See Colletta (Cortese, 1957), ii. 406–7.

threat of attack by the English. While the emperor threatened and bullied, the allies offered rewards and guarantees. The most fundamental problem, Fouché insisted, was that the Kingdom of Naples was exhausted and needed peace. If he took up the cause of the empire, Murat risked facing a revolt: 'Peace is what is needed here and it is what everyone wants.'

Fouché also commented on the growth of Italian nationalism and the hostility he had found towards France everywhere in Italy:

Here, as everywhere in Italy now, the word independence has acquired a magic force. It is a banner around which many different interests converge, of course, but all people want some form of local government. Everyone here complains that they have to go to Paris for every petty request. The government in Paris is distant and represents heavy costs for which there are no visible compensations. Conscription, taxes, vexations, privations, and sacrifices, that—say the Romans—is what being governed by France means for us.[3]

It was Murat's turn on 16 December to explain why he had refused to obey the emperor's order to take his army north to the Po.

Italy is seething with agitation, the events in Spain and Germany have filled every head with ideas of independence, an Italian League, the Reunification of Italy and freedom from the foreign yoke—these are the words that have mobilised nearly everyone . . . the most numerous classes have everything to gain from disorder and want revolution, while the propertied classes hope by all means to avoid this. The latter want to preserve the monarchy, but the others are using secret societies like the *Carbonari* to propagate republican ideas, and the English urge them on with promises of money and support.

Murat pointed out that his was the only army left in Italy and everyone looked to him for a lead. In these circumstances, to rally to the empire would be to sacrifice 'not only my troops, but the very existence of my Kingdom'. Public opinion was flatly opposed, and so he must try to find ways of overcoming that opposition: 'I must flatter them . . . I will make vague references to independence and territorial expansion.' But all Italy wanted was peace.

Then Murat made his bargaining pitch. He could not hide his dismay that the emperor had spoken in favour of allowing the English to retain Sicily and of the Austrians' intention to 're-establish the Pope and the little princes in Italy. What will be the outcome of such an organisation, or rather disorganization? That Austria will be free to intervene when it chooses, in which case France will have to oppose it and Italy will continue to be a battlefield between the two empires?'

Murat closed with the reminder that while they were campaigning together in Germany he had personally confided in the emperor that the best political solution would be to divide Italy into two kingdoms, one in the North and the other in the South whose frontiers would be the Po River. The English, he claimed, were prepared to support this, and he could not fight in the emperor's cause for less.[4]

[3] Fouché to Napoleon, 27 December 1813; cited in Weil (1902), iii. 296.
[4] ANP: 31 AP 6: Murat to Napoleon, 16 December 1813.

Although biographers have tried to recruit him as an Italian nationalist, Murat's correspondence reveals a self-seeking opportunist who was bargaining with both the allies and the emperor for the best deal. His somewhat unrealistic hope was that the collapse of French rule in northern Italy would enable him to realize the Bourbon dream of a southern kingdom stretching northwards through central Italy and to the Po River.[5]

The emperor never replied and when the Austrian offensive against Prince Eugène began in December 1813, the political and military situation in Italy was transformed. The strength of Prince Eugène's army and of the Austrians' was relatively equal, leaving a clear opportunity for Murat.[6] On 3 January 1814 the king of Naples wrote to tell Napoleon that 'the most painful day of my life' had arrived. He had received no reply from Paris, but had been offered terms by Austria and an armistice by the English. Naples was crying out for peace. He could not take the side of the empire and found himself with no alternative but 'to enter into relations that are in appearance contrary to your interests'.[7]

Murat was being economical with the truth and this was part of a more fully formed project. In December 1813 he had warned the Grand Duchess of Tuscany, Elise Bacciochi, that a Neapolitan force would occupy the Tuscan fortresses, asking for her cooperation and warning her not to acknowledge further orders from Prince Eugène.[8] Elise Bacciochi wrote to Napoleon for advice:

> The Tuscans do not like the Neapolitans, but I cannot permit that they take up arms against them. The ideas of independence had spread so widely in Italy in the last two months and hopes of change are so high . . . that much as the Tuscans may hate to be subject to the Neapolitans they will submit so long as they finish up being ruled by a prince of their own.[9]

On 11 January 1814 Murat signed a treaty with the Austrians, and three weeks later entered Bologna at the head of a Neapolitan army.[10] Popular revolts had been staged in the papal territories to justify the Neapolitan occupation, and the Neapolitan commanders now openly adopted the rhetoric of Italian nationalism. In February, Giuseppe (now Baron) Poerio proclaimed in Bologna that the King of the Two Sicilies was the provisional ruler of the Roman States, Tuscany, and the 'Southern Italic Departments' under the terms of the treaty with the allies. The provisional government guaranteed the protection of all 'Ministers of Religion, all public buildings, all persons and private property'. It also proclaimed freedom of trade, promised that there would be no new taxes, and concluded with a call to action: 'Political Independence, the first right of all Nations, is yours to seize.'[11]

5 See Valente (1965), 331–79, and Tulard (1983), 185–202.
6 Bianchini (1839), 531–2.
7 ANP: 31 AP 6: Murat to Napoleon, 3 January 1814.
8 Weil (1902), iii. 250: Murat to Elise Bacciochi, 15 December 1813.
9 Ibid., Elise Bacciocchi to Napoleon, 5 January 1814.
10 Ibid. 442.
11 BSPN: XXI B5 'Proclama del Barone Poerio ai popoli de'Dipartimenti Italici Meridionali', 9 February 1914.

The political situation in Italy changed again following Napoleon's abdication on 6 April 1814. Louis XVIII returned to France, Victor Emmanuel I to Piedmont, Grand Duke Ferdinand III to Tuscany, and Pope Pius VII was reinstated in Rome. On 16 April Prince Eugène sued for an armistice and the Austrians occupied Lombardy.[12]

Murat still held the papal Marche, but the allies now had little use for him, and he was not even mentioned in the Peace signed in Paris on 30 May 1814.[13] The Treaty between Naples and Vienna guaranteed the Kingdom of Naples to Murat and his heirs, but the British governor of Sicily, Lord William Bentinck, had specifically refused to guarantee that Murat would retain Naples and for that reason had agreed only to an armistice.[14] In March Bentinck led an expedition to Tuscany and tensions were heightened when he refused to allow the Neapolitans to enter Livorno but then appealed to the Italians to follow the example of the Spanish and rise up against the French oppressor.[15]

For Bentinck Murat was 'the most treacherous of all the Gauls' and his suspicions were not misplaced. Murat had been careful to keep his own lines of communication with Napoleon open, despite the latter's fury on hearing of his brother-in-law's treachery:

> You are a brave soldier on the battlefield, but off it you have no courage and no integrity. I hope that you are not one of those who think that the lion is dead and that you can piss on him. That would be a serious mistake. The king's title has completely turned your head—but if you want to keep it, behave yourself and stay loyal.[16]

Murat reassured Napoleon by claiming that he was playing a double game, that his alliance with the Austrians and British was a feint to gain time, and that his army 'will never fight against France'.[17]

Murat did well to keep his options open, because when the allies finally met in Vienna in November 1814 to discuss the Peace his position looked hopeless. The decision to restore the Bourbon rulers in France and Spain had destroyed his hopes of retaining Naples, while his continuing refusal to evacuate papal territory despite the Pope's return to Rome outraged the allies who held him responsible for the collapse of law and order in Central Italy.

The British government had been irritated in equal measure by both Murat and Bentinck, and their appeals to Italian nationalism in particular had infuriated Lord Castlereagh:

> how intolerably prone he [Bentinck] is to Whig Revolutions everywhere. I am confident his mismanagement at least doubled all the natural dangers of Murat's rascality; and my

[12] Grab (2003), 202. [13] Johnson (1904), i. 256–327.

[14] BSPN: Ms. XXI B5: Min. Plenipotente du Roi de Naples (Duca di Campochiaro) à Castelreagh, 29 December 1814; Comte Metternich à Comte Mier, 28 October 1813. The armistice was signed on 3 February 1814.

[15] Rosselli (1956), 133–41; See also ANP: 31 AP 43, Mosbourg to Murat, 20 March, 8 and 23 August 1814. [16] BSPN: Ms. XXI B5: Napoleon to Murat, February 1814.

[17] Ibid.

persuasion is, if the war had gone on much longer in France, we should have had the most disastrous complication in Italy.... He seems bent upon throwing all Italy loose. This might be well against France, but against Austria and the King of Sardinia, with all the new Constitutions which now menace the world with fresh convulsions, it is most absurd.[18]

Castlereagh's comments accurately reflect the principles guiding the resettlement of Europe after Napoleon's defeat, and they were repeated in similar terms by the French foreign minister. In December Talleyrand informed Castlereagh that the Bourbon king Ferdinand IV had the only legitimate claim to the Kingdom of Naples, which if denied would fatally compromise the principle of legitimate monarchy.[19]

The great and final objective to which Europe is moving, and the only one that France can support, is to bring the Revolution to an end and establish a lasting peace. The 'principle of Monarchy' must triumph totally over the 'principles of the Revolution'. For that reason the legitimist dynasties must be restored, the king of Saxony in Saxony, the king of Naples in Naples.[20]

There was no space left for the dynastic ambitions of Joachim Murat, and in January 1815 Prince Metternich formally complained that the presence of Neapolitan troops in Central Italy went 'beyond what is needed'. But Murat still refused to withdraw, even though the Neapolitans were by now faced by popular revolts throughout central Italy and Tuscany. Then came the news that in February Napoleon had escaped from Elba and had reached Lyons, which led Murat to gamble on Napoleon's success. On 17 March he left Naples to rejoin the Neapolitan forces in Central Italy, taking with him his foreign minister, the Marquis di Gallo, Giuseppe Zurlo, the Minister of the Interior, and his finance minister Count Mosbourg; however, Mosbourg told the king that the Treasury had no means to support his campaign and asked to resign.[21]

Murat's chief of staff was the French General Millet de Villeneuf, and the three divisions of his army were commanded by Generals Carrascosa, Ambrisio, and Lecchi, with three other recently formed divisions commanded by Generals Livron, Pignatelli, and Prince Pignatelli Cerchiara. From Rimini Murat issued an appeal (dated retrospectively to 30 March) that called for a national Italian rising against the Austrian invaders:

The hour has come when destiny will be accomplished. Even Providence itself calls you to liberty. Let a single cry be heard from the Alps to Sicily, the cry of Italian Independence.[22]

Murat's appeal had little effect. On 11 April he warned Caroline that the English considered his declaration against Austria to be a breach of the armistice and that they were preparing to attack Naples. Shortly afterwards he wrote

[18] Castlereagh to Liverpool, 5 May 1814: quoted in Rosselli (1956), 142.
[19] BSPN: Ms. XXI B5, Talleyrand to Castlereagh, 15 December 1814.
[20] Ibid., 26 December 1814. [21] ANP: 31 AP 43: Mosbourg to Murat, March 1815.
[22] Ibid., Decret de Rimini, 30 March 1815.

complaining that the Italians had failed to support him, that he was short of arms and money, that he was alone and hopelessly outnumbered against the Austrian forces. He had no alternative but to retreat under the pretence of changing positions.[23]

Murat's forces took Modena, but an offensive against Ferrara failed and popular opposition forced the Neapolitans to abandon Bologna and fall back on Ancona. The army was demoralized and for Murat's generals the enterprise was doomed. 'The war was considered to be lost even before it started', Luigi Blanch later recalled. The long series of campaigns in Spain, Germany, Russia, and the Tyrol and then in Italy had decimated the Neapolitan officer corps. The army had been brutalized by the campaigns against the brigands in Calabria, and corruption was widespread.[24] Most serious of all, the army was disintegrating. The *Observateur Autrichien* commented on the extraordinarily high rates of desertion from even its most seasoned units: 'Desertion from these units is unparalleled, even though they include some brigades of Royal Guards. The artillery train is small and mediocre.'[25]

The end came when Murat's forces were routed by the Austrians near Tolentino on 3 May. Revolts against both the French and the Neapolitans spread through central Italy, and were especially violent in Livorno where the mob attacked the Jewish ghetto 'to vent their fury on those unfortunates, accusing them of being pro-French and supporters of the Neapolitans'.[26]

Bentinck declared war on Naples and on 13 May Caroline Bonaparte surrendered the Neapolitan fleet. On 20 May representatives of King Ferdinand IV signed the Treaty of Casalanza with the Austrians, which restored the Bourbons to the throne of Naples. Two days later Caroline Bonaparte, her children, and their possessions were transported under safe conduct to Trieste on a British warship. Murat spent two weeks in hiding before boarding a French ship at Baia that carried him to France.[27]

In Marseilles he immediately became a target of the White Terror for his part in the execution of the Duke of Enghien. He fled to Corsica and from there set sail with a small group of followers in October to raise a revolt against the Bourbons and regain his Kingdom. He and his followers were blown off course and beached near Pizzo in Calabria, where they were immediately captured. Acting on instructions received by the new system of semaphore telegraphy from Naples, on the morning of 13 October the commander of the Pizzo garrison presided over Murat's execution by firing squad, bringing the *episode napoléonniene* in southern Italy to a final end.[28]

[23] ANP: 31 AP 43: Murat to Caroline Bonaparte, 1815.

[24] Blanch, in Croce (ed.) (1945), i. 308.

[25] BSPN: *Observateur Autrichien*, 27 April 1815.

[26] Ibid., 7 May 1815.

[27] The detailed account of Murat's escape is in Weil (1915), v. 178–202. In Austria Caroline Bonaparte adopted the title of Duchess of Lipona (an anagram of Napoli).

[28] Bianchini (1839), vii. 534.

THE SECRET SOCIETIES

Even before Murat's defeat, opposition to his government in Naples had increased. When Murat was in Germany in October 1813, Mosbourg had written to inform him that the situation in the Kingdom was alarming. Armed robbers who had attempted to steal the cash deposits of the city of Naples had tried to give their conspiracy 'the appearance of a revolutionary project linked to the Society of Charcoal-burners that your Majesty has long since banned, but which we have continued to tolerate'. The plot proved to have wide ramifications. One of the leaders, Capobianco, fled to join a band of brigands in Calabria, where he was captured by Manhès and executed in Cosenza. The queen had issued an edict banning the Carbonarist lodges and the military commissions were investigating other suspects.

The history of the secret societies has been deliberately buried in layers of mystery and myth-making, but it seems reasonably certain that they were offshoots from the masonic lodges that Murat's government had promoted until 1813.[29] Their earlier origins are more open to speculation. One interpretation claimed that the Carbonarist[30] lodges started in the Swiss *Tugendbund*, where they had recruited Neapolitan exiles after 1799 and French officers opposed to the Bonapartist regime in France. They observed strict secrecy and were supposedly imported into Naples in 1806 by a Swiss regiment in Masséna's army stationed at Capua.[31]

Others claimed that the Carbonarist societies had been founded by anti-Bonapartist officers after the battle of Jena, and had been brought to southern Italy by the ubiquitous Mr Broadbent, who was described as 'an English Quaker who came to Sicily to trade with the Americans'.[32]

Whatever the origin, the first Carbonarist lodge established in Naples in 1810 was organized on the model of the existing masonic lodges and followed the Scottish rite.[33] The first provincial Carbonarist lodge was founded in Basilicata in 1811 and its aim was 'to bring Light to the ignorant and make men better able to understand and exercise their Rights'. Lodges spread from there to other parts of Basilicata, Abruzzo, and Calabria, and there was also competition from societies of other political persuasions and origins, with names like 'Veri Amici, Filantropi, Amici della Felicità dell'Uomo, but the Carbonari had the widest following'.[34]

[29] Johnson (1904), ii. 29–34; see also Roberts (1974), 289–307.

[30] The name comes from the corporation of charcoal burners (Charboniers) in the Swiss Jura.

[31] Caldora (1960), 620; Godechot (1976), 266–9; Johnson (1904), ii. 29–34.

[32] The same Mr Broadbent (described variously as English and American) negotiated sales of American wheat with Murat's government. See d'Angelo (1990), 112.

[33] ASN: Archivio Tommasi, B XI, Memorandum segreto di Domenico Bocchini sulle origini della setta dei'Carbonari.

[34] BSPN: Ms. Varia XXII a.6: Saggio storico delle società denominate Carboneria, Vera Amicizia e Colonia, istituite nel Regno di Napoli sotto il governo dell'occupazione militare.

The Carbonari are a Sect that has split off from the Freemasons and taken another name. It is more simple, has fewer ranks, is less expensive to join, less exclusive and accepts people from the lowest social orders and tolerates all religions although in Naples it is almost exclusively Catholic... it has many followers in the Kingdom.[35]

By 1815 the Carbonarist lodges were estimated to have no fewer than 30,000 members, but this was pure guesswork. The Bourbon minister Donato Tommasi believed that both the police commissioner Saliceti and his successor Maghella had deliberately fostered these societies in which they planted informers to keep an eye on public opinion. Maghella was certainly a strong supporter of Freemasonry,[36] and Tommasi believed that Daure's successor as Minister of Police, the Duke of Campochiaro, had also seen the lodges as a valuable means for keeping an eye on opponents of the regime. For this reason he had given the Carbonari semi-official recognition and from their members had selected for key positions 'persons who are strongly committed to maintaining public order... and in this way the government believes it can keep an eye on the discontented'.

Tommasi's interpretation would square with the fact that the first Carbonarist lodge in Calabria was almost certainly founded in 1813 by the Intendent Pierre-Joseph Briot, a member of the Council of State, but also an opponent of Bonapartism with longstanding Jacobin and Masonic credentials.[37]

In May 1813 Murat's government changed course and the Carbonarist lodges were outlawed, but repression only increased their number and political fragmentation.[38] Some of their members now rallied to the government and re-entered the official masonic lodges, but others opted for clandestinity and adopted the programme of constitutional reform. While many still looked to Murat to achieve constitutional reform, others turned to the Bourbon monarchy that in 1812 had granted a constitution in Sicily. In anticipation of a Bourbon Restoration older ultra-Catholic royalists secret societies were also being re-established, the most important being the *Trinitarj*, which the Carbonari referred to as the *Calderai*. Support came from the ever-active Principino of Canosa, who was still directing the Bourbon espionage operations on the mainland.[39]

At first the government tried to maintain the distinctions between membership of the masonic lodges and the secret societies by banning the second but not the first. But this proved impossible, and in October 1813 the Intendents were instructed to ban meetings of any form of secret society. Public employees were prohibited from joining secret societies or attending their meetings, and were obliged to inform the authorities if they had knowledge of any such gatherings.[40]

Pietro Colletta commented that measures taken against the secret societies were similar to those employed against the brigands: 'but while the brigands included

[35] ASN: Archivio Tommasi, B. 5, Memorandum sulla Polizia Generale.

[36] A de G: C(5*) 42, Rapports au Roi: Min. Police to M. D'Azzia, Commissaire de Police, Cosenza, 28 May 1810.

[37] On Briot, see Chapter 9, p. 171 n. 35.

[38] A de G: C(5*) 42.

[39] ASN: Archivio Tommasi, B XI, Memorandum segreto.

[40] ASN: Min. dell'Interno, f. 213: Circolare agli Intendenti, 2 October 1813.

the worst elements of society, the *Carbonari* were the best'.[41] The first insurrection associated with the *Carbonari* took place in Calabria in September 1813, a clear sign that the political solutions that Joseph Bonaparte and Joachim Murat had attempted to establish in the Kingdom were beginning to unravel as demand grew for Murat to concede a constitution.

CONSTITUTIONAL MODELS: SPAIN AND SICILY, 1812

The demand for constitutional government derived most directly from the Treaty of Bayonne, which stated that a National Parliament would be established in the Kingdom. Similar parliaments were proposed for France and for the Kingdom of Italy, but for Miot de Melito they were all 'an example of the emperor's growing preference for reviving feudal institutions and of the aversion, about which he made no secret, for anything that might offer the citizen liberty or political independence'.

The clause in the Treaty that promised the establishment of a parliament had supposedly been drafted by Joseph Bonaparte, but the imperial chancellery is its more likely place of origin. The parliament was to consist of a single Chamber divided into five 'orders': the clergy, nobility, landowners, 'savants', and merchants. Members of each section were nominated by the ruler, and while each order was numerically equal, their votes were not. Members of the first three sections had fixed tenure, but not the other two. Miot de Melito considered that this was an accurate 'indication of the political principles the emperor had adopted and was if anything even worse than its Italian and French counterparts'.[42]

Murat never honoured the requirement to establish a parliament, but by 1812 there were two alternative models of constitutional government, one from Spain and one from Sicily. The emperor also had devised a parliament for Spain at Bayonne, but this had been rejected, and in March 1812 an Extraordinary General Cortes convened near Cadiz under the protection of the British navy promulgated a constitution that caught the attention of Napoleon's opponents in Europe as well as liberal revolutionaries in Latin America.

The Constitution of Cadiz was an anti-Napoleonic document that was both liberal and nationalist: it proclaimed the sovereignty of the Spanish Nation and made a clear association between 'Nation' and 'Liberty'.[43] It guaranteed the freedom of the press, the freedom from arbitrary arrest, and the right of property. It established the basis for 'moderate monarchy' through the creation of a unicameral Cortes elected by indirect male suffrage (only servants; the insane and criminals were excluded from voting). For deputies, there were minimum property requirements, but the king could not veto bills passed by the Cortes more than three times,

[41] Colletta (Cortese, 1957), ii. 396.
[42] Miot de Melito (1888), iii. 339.
[43] Herr, in Woloch (1996), 86–7.

and his ministers were responsible to it. Municipal offices were made elective, and annually renewable.[44]

When the Spanish king, Fernando VII, returned to Spain after Wellington's victory at Vittoria (21 June 1813), the Cortes had abolished all forms of seigneurial jurisdiction and fiscal exemptions and recommended the abolition of the Inquisition. The anger this provoked among the reactionary forces within the Church and the military enabled the king to bring the short season of constitutional government in Spain to an end in May 1814 when both the constitution and the Cortes were proclaimed illegal.[45]

Nonetheless, the Spanish constitution attracted wide attention and news of it was relayed to Naples by the many Neapolitan officers who had served in the emperor's campaigns on the peninsula. The text was known only at second-hand and by hearsay, but it quickly won broad support within Murat's army, the masonic lodges, and the secret societies in Naples.

The other constitutional model was even closer at hand. This was the constitution that in 1812 the British authorities in Sicily forced on the exiled Bourbon ruler Ferdinand IV. Since 1806 Sicily had been under the protection of British forces, and by 1812 relations between the British and the Bourbon rulers had deteriorated to breaking point. Demands for a constitution had come mainly from a section of the Sicilian aristocracy, however, and were closely bound up with the struggles between the Bourbon monarchy and the Sicilian nobility that went back to the eighteenth century.[46]

The central issue was still the privileges and independence of the Sicilian aristocracy, whose institutional foundation was the Sicilian Parliament.[47] The defenders of aristocratic privilege had defeated the monarchy in the 1780s, but the conflict had left a residue of political bitterness and division that revived immediately when in 1799 the Bourbon rulers and their court arrived in Palermo under the protection of the British navy. They were accompanied by hordes of Neapolitan refugees, officials, place-seekers, and ministers, all of whom the Sicilian treasury was called on to support as well as to raise taxes to finance the reconquest of the mainland.[48]

When the Bourbon monarchy returned in similar circumstances in 1806, the struggles resumed, but with a new twist. In 1799 Maria Carolina had looked to Sir William Hamilton, Lady Hamilton, and Lord Nelson as her saviours, but in 1806 she blamed the English for abandoning the mainland and for the loss of half her Kingdom. The British government, for its part, was infuriated by the attitude of the Court in Palermo, and refused to commit itself to the restoration of the Bourbon monarchy in Naples. Maria Carolina in turn became convinced that the British planned to occupy Sicily and make it an English colony.[49]

[44] Herr, in Woloch (1996), 88. [45] Ibid. 91–2. [46] See Chapter 3 above.

[47] Giarizzo (1985).

[48] See esp. John Rosselli's (1956) study of Lord William Bentinck in Sicily. For British politics in Sicily after 1806, see Romeo (1950), 140–2. [49] Rosselli (1956), 10.

In fact, William Drummond, the British envoy at Palermo in 1806, did seriously consider 'measures that would have made Sicily a province of Great Britain'.[50] But the Foreign Office would have none of that, and once the Peace of Tilsit consolidated France's control of the Italian peninsula, the British government showed little further interest in Sicily or Italy. Drummond's successor, Lord Amherst, attempted to negotiate with the Neapolitan Court without success, while the two successive British military commanders[51] were convinced that the queen was having treasonable conversations with Murat's government with the aim of trading Sicily for Naples. Their suspicions were increased by Napoleon's marriage to Marie Louise of Austria in 1810 and when the Bourbon Court refused to contribute to the defence of Messina against Murat's threatened invasion that year, Amherst too was convinced that 'jealousy of the designs of Great Britain predominates in the Queen's mind over the hatred she may entertain for Bonaparte'.[52]

The political crisis began in January 1810 when the Sicilian Parliament refused to grant taxes for the defence of the realm and the opposition called for the dismissal of the king's Neapolitan ministers and their replacement by Sicilians. Although these demands were supported by the king's son-in-law, Louis Philippe, Duke of Orléans,[53] the Court refused to consider them. To break the dead-lock, the Sicilian reform party turned to Lord Amherst, but he had had enough and resigned in July, followed in October by Sir John Stuart.[54]

These resignations brought the seriousness of the situation in Sicily home to the Foreign Office, and the Marquis of Wellesley nominated a senior British administrator and former Governor of Madras, Lord William Bentinck, to represent the British government in Naples. The new governor was given clear instructions. He was to inform their Sicilian Majesties that their misgovernment was the principal cause of the unrest on the island that threatened to jeopardize the safety of British soldiers. If their Sicilian Majesties wished to continue this misrule, Britain could not commit itself to working to ensure their restoration to Naples after the fall of the French usurper.

Bentinck was strongly influenced by the writings of G. F. Leckie, a fervent advocate of Britain's imperial mission, and he was convinced of the need to confront Bonapartist tyranny with the virtues of constitutional government. He firmly believed that once a constitutional government was established in Sicily, the island would become an ideological base from which the allies could appeal to the Italians to rise up against their French oppressors.[55]

When Bentinck arrived in Sicily in the summer of 1811 he assumed dictatorial powers, demanded that the queen leave Palermo and that the king delegate his powers to the Hereditary Prince Francis.[56] On 16 January 1812 British troops were transferred from Messina to Palermo, forcing the reluctant king to appoint his son Francis Vicar General.

50 Ibid. 51 Sir John Moore and, from 1808 to 1811, Sir John Stuart. 52 Ibid. 12.
53 The future king Louis Philippe of France. 54 Rosselli (1956), 16–17.
55 Ibid. 20–1. 56 Ibid. 27–9.

In July, the Sicilian Parliament proposed fifteen fundamental articles (known as the 'Bases') modelled on the British constitution. The new constitution separated Sicily from Naples and established the separation of powers between king and Parliament, with the latter retaining the sole power to raise taxes and legislate. The Parliament was to meet annually. All feudal dues, jurisdictions, and privileges were abolished, although abolished feudal monopolies and other dues were subject to compensation.[57]

Like the king of Spain, Ferdinand IV soon found ways to subvert the constitution, which he abolished before returning to Naples in 1815. But in the meantime the new constitutional regime in Sicily heightened expectations that a Bourbon Restoration would bring constitutional monarchy to the mainland. However, the nationalist and liberal tones of the Spanish constitution made it more popular amongst the Neapolitan advocates of reform, and it was the one most widely endorsed by the secret societies on the mainland. In Sicily, by contrast, the British constitution had a wide following, because it guaranteed Sicily's autonomy from Naples.

LOSING NAPLES

When Murat's army marched north in January 1814 to join the allies in Central Italy, few troops were left to maintain order in the Kingdom. Attempts to reorganize the provincial militias in the previous year had failed, and the Minister of Police authorized the Intendents to offer pardons to brigand leaders willing to serve in the anti-brigand militias.[58] But in January as Murat's army marched north, hundreds of deserters swarmed back towards Naples. In February, General Manhès, who had been left in command of the capital, attempted to close the Neapolitan frontiers and set up military commissions to pursue brigands, deserters, and escaped conscripts.

Before leaving, Murat had issued a circular to explain that he had put himself at the head of his troops 'not in the service of foreign interests but to obtain the salvation of the Kingdom'. All public functionaries were instructed to assist the king in his bid to ensure the independence and tranquillity of the Kingdom.[59]

Murat's decision to join the allies in 1814 was widely supported by the Neapolitan elites, especially by his generals who saw the alliance as the only means of escaping subordination to France. But it was also an opportunity to press demands for a constitution. On three occasions during the campaign of 1814 (at Reggio Emilia, at Borgo San Donnino, and at Ancona) Generals Michele Filangieri, Michele Carrascosa, Pietro Colletta, and Florestano Pepe formally requested that the king grant a constitution. Murat's refusal on each occasion cost him the support of his only remaining political allies.[60]

[57] Rosselli (1956), 60. [58] Colletta (Cortese, 1957), ii. 421.
[59] *ASN*: Min. dell'Interno, f. 213—22 January 1814. [60] Weil (1909–10), v. 49–50, 524.

The generals' demands revealed the dangers of making the army an instrument of dynastic politics. But by now the constitutional movement had spread more widely, and when the government was faced by the first serious threat of insurrection in March 1814, the army showed its sympathy with the rebels.

In December 1813, the Sub-intendent of Sulmona claimed to have discovered a conspiracy for a royalist rising in the village of Pacentro, whose leader, a shoemaker named Cercone, was captured and guillotined in L'Aquila on 3 December. The priest who officiated at his execution warned the people 'to live good and upright lives, to observe the law and their lawful rulers and to heed the example of Cercone'. But in January anonymous posters appeared in Sulmona announcing the imminent arrival of Ferdinand IV with an army.[61]

In March, a more serious uprising started near Teramo. The first protesters declared for 'Ferdinand IV, the Constitutional King', but revolts in the neighbouring villages of Penne and Città San Angelo took explicitly republican tones. The government was convinced that the revolts had been organized by the Carbonarist societies and on 4 April Zurlo issued a decree condemning the *Carbonari* as enemies of the state.[62]

General Florestano Pepe was ordered to return from Central Italy to put down the revolt in Abruzzo. But as Pepe approached Teramo he was met by a delegation of the insurgents who had the support of influential notables in the Teramo region. There was also a strong Carbonarist connection. At this point Florestano Pepe declared his own sympathies with the insurgents: in his report to Murat he stated that 'the great landowners generally wish to ensure that things are resolved for the best: they have agreed to lay down their arms and they will do everything in their power to ensure that the Carbonarists and their followers will do the same'.[63]

Two envoys sent by the queen had in the meantime reached Teramo: the councillor of State, Baron Antonio Nolli, and Cavaliere Delfico. Both were major landowners in the Abruzzi and prominent members of the administration. They allowed General Pepe, whose sympathies with the insurgents were now more or less public, to withdraw, came to terms with the local notables, and then had the French general Montigny invoke the emergency measures to find some scapegoats amongst the lesser insurgents.[64]

Florestano Pepe's sympathies for the Carbonarists and the demands for a constitution were widely supported in the army, and in May Murat returned to Naples to investigate the situation. The political climate in the capital was tense. In April, De Nicola recorded, 'Things go badly here: every day there is some new alarm and the people give signs of an excitement that rouses fear.' The following day he noted reports of popular demonstrations in support of the Bourbons, while

[61] BSPN: 30 Corr, XIVB. 2 (Documenti 1799–1815) Testimonianza di R. Battaglino, contadino, al Sig. A. Siciliano, Sotto Intendente di Sulmona, 28 January 1814.

[62] Zurlo was reinstated as Minister of the Interior when Murat joined the allies.

[63] Pepe (1896), i. 149.

[64] Ibid. See also Colletta (Cortese, 1957), ii. 421–3 (especially Cortese's notes).

the arrival of the first consignment of oranges from Sicily in the port had been greeted with cries of 'Long live the Big Nose, our one and only King.'[65] On 23 April there were disturbances in the Mercato district and rumours were sweeping the city that Murat had agreed to grant a constitution.

Murat introduced measures designed to make his government more popular by reducing taxes, making more changes to the legal codes, and temporarily suspending conscription. But the government also sent out demands for the immediate settlement of all tax arrears.[66] De Nicola reported that police activity had greatly increased: 'Everywhere they are throwing the so-called Carbonari into jail, and this includes people of all ranks.'[67] In July, the first execution by guillotine took place in Naples and two days later De Nicola remarked 'I hear the prisons are full of gentlemen who have been arrested by the Police.'[68]

The treasury was exhausted and the army could only be kept on a war footing by looting and plundering in the territories where it was quartered, which was now provoking serious popular resistance. In Naples, Murat now reintroduced the requirement that all French employees obtain Neapolitan nationality that in 1811 had almost led to war with France but in September conscription was reintroduced on terms even more onerous than before.[69]

De Nicola reported that Naples was full of rumours about the intentions of the Congress of Vienna, and was divided into pro-Murat and pro-Bourbon parties. The government was again receiving disturbing reports of the revival of brigandage in many of the provinces and in mid-October issued a circular to the Intendents expressing the king's dismay at the 'general lack of energy in repressing disorder' on the part of local officials who had fallen 'into a sort of torpor'.[70]

THE TRANSITION OF POWER: 1815

Despite the growing unrest and political opposition, the transition of power in southern Italy in 1815 proved remarkably peaceful. Luigi Blanch, who had served as one of Murat's staff officers in the campaign of 1815, later posed the question: 'Why was there not the slightest disorder in the Kingdom? The established authorities were everywhere respected, the French officials went unmolested in their persons and property, indeed the change took place as though this was happening in some cold and gentle country like Holland.'[71]

[65] De Nicola (1899–1905), 20 April, 21 April, 711. ('Nasone' was the popular nickname for Ferdinand IV.)

[66] ASN: Min. dell'Interno Appendice I, f. 213: Circolari agli Intendenti, 16 May, 21 May, 25 May, 28 May 1814.

[67] De Nicola (1899–1905), ii. 3 July 1814, 741.

[68] Ibid., 28 July, 30 July 1814, 743.

[69] Ibid., 3 September 1814.

[70] Ibid., 19 October 1814. ASN: Min. dell'Interno Appendice I, f. 213, Min. Interno agli Signori Intendenti del Regno.

[71] Blanch, in Croce (ed.) (1945) i. 382.

Blanch suggested three reasons for this. First, the propertied classes were determined to prevent any recurrence of popular violence. Second were the secret societies: 'The sect of the *Carbonari* placed the people in close communication with the upper classes and as a result removed that hatred and war to the death that in 1799 had been waged against any who were not of the people.'[72] Finally, both the Austrians and the Bourbons deliberately avoided anything that might foment civil war or civil disorder. Even the Court of Palermo 'had avoided exciting passions and had not employed men associated with the horrors of the past'. Blanch also thought that Napoleon's seemingly miraculous recovery after the escape from Elba served to restrain any desire for vendetta or vengeance for fear that the emperor might again return to Italy to punish any 'momentary excess'.[73]

Blanch's emphasis on the measures taken to maintain order were supported by De Nicola's account of events in the capital. When Murat left Naples on 17 March 1815 to join the army, he had appointed Manhès as military command, with Maghella responsible for maintaining public order: 'The Police are very active', De Nicola noted: the civic guard was mobilized and the soldiers began to mount regular patrols.[74]

On 17 April the civic guard reserves were called up and public employees who failed to appear for duty were threatened with immediate dismissal. Long lists of political suspects were compiled by Manhès and Maghella, and included many 'noblemen and gentlemen'. News was circulated of the enthusiastic reactions to Murat's appeals for 'Italian Independence' in the North, but De Nicola claimed that 'the word that circulated in the city is that Joachim had not found the support he hoped for and that the Italians understood full well that under the banner of Italian Independence they would become provinces of the Kingdom of Naples.'[75]

On 20 April the government raised another forced loan from the wealthier citizens, followed on the 27th by a new wave of arrests. On 1 May the city was full of contradictory rumours and alarms. The following day the Interior Minister Giuseppe Zurlo returned from Murat's headquarters and was believed to have brought with him a constitution. De Nicola recorded on 4 May that 'The Internal Security Guards patrol day and night.... Twenty or thirty thousand men serve in the guard.' The Intendent of the city, Michele Filangieri, announced publicly that when the Austrian advance guard reached Capua he would personally hand over the keys of the city, 'not wishing that the city should be exposed to military violence'.[76]

Rumours circulated the next day that a Council of War had refused to allow the queen to take refuge in the fortress of Gaeta 'because this might have caused a Revolution'.[77] On 9 May General MacDonald marched the remaining French troops from Naples to Gaeta, and on the following day the commanders of the Internal Security Guard established procedures for surrendering the city to the

[72] Ibid. [73] Ibid. [74] De Nicola (1899–1905), ii. 17 March 1815, 784.
[75] Ibid., 12, 15, 16 April, 800. [76] Ibid., 1, 2, 3, 4 May 1815, 809–10.
[77] Ibid., 4 May 1815, 811.

Austrians. Signals would be given by rounds of cannon fire. At the first round 'all the so-called *lazzaroni* must get off the streets. At the second, all citizens required to maintain order must report for duty. At the third no one may circulate in the city and the guards have orders to shoot anyone who does.'[78]

A squadron of English frigates entered the Bay of Naples on 12 May and threatened to shell the city unless it surrendered within forty-eight hours. On the 17th news arrived of Murat's capitulation to Bentinck and groups of unemployed sailors staged a hostile demonstration outside the house of the Interior Minister, Zurlo. The mayor, Michele Fliangieri, arranged for 500 selected Austrian troops to reinforce the Internal Security Guard and when it became known on the 20th that Murat had fled, the political prisoners were released from the jails. The common prisoners, who had been without food for three days, rioted but the police quickly surrounded the jails with artillery, fired on the demonstrators, and seized the ringleaders who were summarily executed.

After destroying their papers, Maghella and Zurlo were permitted to leave the city under safe conduct. Early in the morning of 21 May Austrian troops entered the city: 'It is two o'clock in the morning and the only sound is of patrols of cavalry and the Civic Guards. It must be said that we are very much obliged to the Guard and to the many distinguished gentlemen, heads of families, public servants, and tradesmen who have worked day and night. While we sleep soundly they watch over our security.'[79]

Later that day, Ferdinand IV entered the city escorted by the Internal Security Guard. The Austrians imposed tight discipline on their troops, but De Nicola soon noted that 'the Civic Guard has greatly abused the People and indulged in vendettas'. Most of those in the civic guard were 'committed Patriots who took out their fury on the People whom they kill, wound and beat without any reason causing much discontent'. But the supporters of the monarchy were also angered that the employees of the previous government were to keep their jobs. 'The supporters of the Bourbons are angry because they feel they have been ignored and slighted.'[80]

The transition of power took place less dramatically in the provinces, but again without major upheaval. On 29 April Manhès ordered the propertied classes in each province to form companies of armed and mounted men in every *capoluogo* to reinforce the provincial and civic guards and help maintain order. A month later, on 24 May, the Intendents were ordered to announce the restoration of 'Our August Sovereign, Ferdinand IV'. All public officials were ordered to return to their posts and the local authorities were instructed to take whatever measures were required to maintain public order. 'His Majesty places his absolute trust in the zeal and firmness of the Internal Security Guards, the Provincial Legions and all honest Citizens.'[81]

[78] De Nicola (1899–1905), ii. 9, 10 May 1815, 813.
[79] Ibid., 20 May 1815, 830.
[80] Ibid., iii. 21, 22, 24, 29 May 1815, 2–11.
[81] ASN: Min. dell'Interno Appendice I, f. 213: Circolare, 24 May 1815.

14

Restoration

Italy in 1815, from G. Holmes (ed.), *The Oxford Illustrated History of Italy* (Oxford: Oxford University Press, 1997).

AMBIGUOUS LEGACIES

Nowhere in Italy was the Restoration greeted with higher expectations than in Naples. When Murat's regime collapsed there were high hopes that the Bourbons would extend the Sicilian constitution to the mainland, but as soon as King Ferdinand left Palermo he abolished the Sicilian constitution and in Naples appointed the reactionary Principino of Canosa as Minister of Police. Metternich, Caroline Bonaparte's former lover and now the Austrian Chancellor, had anticipated these moves, however, and Canosa was forced to resign.

There was therefore no repetition of the purges of 1799, and the restoration of the Bourbon monarchy in 1815 made no attempt to reinstate the *ancien régime* in the South. In part this was Austria's doing and the Treaty of Casalanza by which the European powers restored Ferdinand IV to his throne obliged the Neapolitan government to issue a general amnesty for those who had held office during what was now termed 'the recent sad military occupation' and to confirm the commissions of all who had served in Murat's army.[1] On 19 July the government's official bulletin, the *Giornale delle Delle Due Sicilie*, announced that the state was to be reorganized on the basis of 'criteria very different from those of the monstrous system consecrated to the principles of the French Revolution'.[2] However, except for the law on civil divorce, the juridical and administrative changes introduced by the French rulers were preserved. Commissions were set up to investigate the principal innovations of the French period—specifically the rulings of the Feudal Commission, the sales of *beni nazionali*, the new central and provincial administration, and the new legal codes. The *legge organica* of 12 December confirmed the structures of central and provincial administration and in January 1817 the central administration was reorganized around eight ministries of state.[3]

The only major change was the abolition of the French Council of State, which was stripped of its judicial powers and became simply an extension of the council of ministers.[4] The French system of provincial and local administration was retained with minor adjustments, the Intendencies and Sub-intendencies were preserved, as were the Provincial and District Councils. As before, they exercised no consultative rights and all appointments, including membership of the municipal councils, were by nomination by the government. No attempts were made, however, to oust those appointed during the French period.[5]

Ninety possessioner houses and four nunneries were reopened, but the new government did not try to restore the suppressed monasteries. It did move quickly

[1] Romeo (1963), 511–14; Scirocco (1986), 647–50. On Canosa see Postigliola, in *DBI*, xviii. 458–9.

[2] Addeo (1984), 836.

[3] Laws of 4 January and 10 June; Scirocco (1986), 647.

[4] Ibid. See also Feola, in Massafra (ed.) (1988), 487–92, 494–9.

[5] Laws of 6 January, 10 June, 1 May, 12 December 1816; Scirocco (1986), 647–50.

to mend relations with Rome, however, and the concordat reached with the papacy in 1818 was negotiated personally by Luigi de' Medici and Francesco Ricciardi. Although widely seen by liberals as a betrayal of the monarchy's anti-curial policies of the previous century, the Concordat of 1818 followed terms very similar to those unsuccessfully proposed by Murat's government. The central concern was to strengthen the discipline exercised by the bishops. In 1818, 43 of the Kingdom's 131 bishoprics were vacant, and over the next fifteen years fifty of the smaller diocese were abolished. New measures were taken to strengthen the authority of the bishops and to improve the quality and behaviour of the clergy.[6] The Concordat of 1818 enabled the Restoration government to succeed where Murat's government had failed in making the secular clergy into an arm of the bureaucratic state, but liberals were especially angered that the clergy regained a dominant hold over primary and secondary schooling, and effective control over the university and censorship.[7]

Nonetheless, the institutional and political reforms made during the period of French rule were retained more fully in the South in 1815 than in any of the other Italian states, consolidating a form of government described by contemporaries as an 'administrative monarchy'. Not only were the innovations of the French period retained on the mainland, but they were now extended to Sicily as well. On 11 December 1816, the formerly independent crowns of Naples and Sicily were unified and Palermo became simply the residence of a Royal Lieutenant General. In the words of Luigi Blanch, Sicily was now 'a posthumous conquest of Napoleon'.[8]

In all the Restoration states the continuities with the Napoleonic past were considerable, but in almost every other Italian state the French model of a centralized bureaucratic state met with firm opposition. The legitimist apologists of the Restoration were advocates of absolutism, but also of a corporatist vision of society in which religion and paternalist values were seen as the key defences against the ideas and innovations believed to have been the principal cause of the Revolution and disasters that had followed. For the champions of the legitimist rulers the rapid collapse of Napoleon's empire was in itself a clear demonstration of the weakness of a political system based solely on bureaucracy and the army.

The Napoleonic model of centralized bureaucratic autocracy was now denounced not only by legitimist conservatives like Joseph de Maistre, but also liberals like Jean Charles Léonard Simonde de Sismondi, who saw the Napoleonic state as an instrument of tyranny that threatened to deprive civil society of all effective autonomy.[9] These debates reflected the different ways in which the

[6] See Rocchina, in Di Leo (1995), 162.

[7] On Restoration censorship in Naples, see Davis, in Goldstein (ed.) (2000), 81–124.

[8] Blanch, in Croce (ed.) (1945), ii. 14–15; see also Rosselli (1956), 153. It was Blanch who coined the term 'administrative monarchy'.

[9] On Sismondi, see Lyttelton, in Teich and Porter (eds.) (1993), 63–105, and Pazzagli (2003).

Italian elites had responded to and adapted French models. Even in the most reactionary states, there was no attempt to reverse the closure of the monasteries or the land sales, or the new organization of public finances. But except in the Duchy of Parma, which the Congress of Vienna granted to the former empress Marie Louise of Austria, the ideological reaction against French rule was uncompromising, as were the purges of all those who had held office or given support to the Napoleonic administrations.

The Habsburg territories reverted to Habsburg administrative practice and custom, and the other Italian rulers followed suit. In Piedmont, the House of Savoy abolished all legislation that had been introduced since 1770, an attempt to restore the *ancien régime* not imitated even in papal Rome.[10] But it was not only in the states that were most fully committed to the ideological propositions of the Restoration that the reactions against French rule went deep. Indeed, one of the most explicit political debates took place in Tuscany where the restored Grand Duke acknowledged that the sovereign's power was rooted in a hierarchical ordering of society best safeguarded by the principles of religion and paternalism. In practice that meant recognizing the right of the Church and the landowners to govern at a local level, albeit under the surveillance of the Grand Duke. It is hardly surprising, therefore, that Sismondi's celebration of the medieval Tuscan city states as models of local autonomy and a historical alternative to Napoleonic centralism and tyranny should have been avidly read and applauded in the Grand Duchy.[11]

Reactions in the South were different, and here there was much broader support in principle for the new 'administrative monarchy'. The reason was that the leading ideologists of the Restoration acknowledged that in the South the paternalist foundations on which the Tuscan, the Piedmontese, and the Habsburg rulers looked to rebuild the post-feudal state no longer existed. In the South the state had, therefore, a larger role to play in reshaping society, a view also shared by the reformers who continued to look on the state as the critical agent of change in the South. However, the trust that they had formerly placed in the enlightened prince had by now been undermined by the experience of the revolutionary years and of Napoleonic autocracy and imperialism. The advocates of reform still looked to the state as the necessary agent of change, but they also saw in the constitutional project the means to impose checks and balances that would modify the rigidly centralizing assumptions on which the reforms of the late eighteenth century and of the Napoleonic period were premised. By extending greater political autonomy at the provincial and local level, the constitutional project looked to restore the political role of the post-feudal notables. But the danger, as

[10] For Lombardy, see Meriggi (1963) and Rath (1967); for the Papal State, Reinerman (1979/1989) and Hughes (1994); for Rome, Boutry, in Ciucci (ed.) (2000).

[11] See especially Soldani's preface to Kröll (2005), pp. xiii–xxv, and the chapters by Contini, Coppini, Greco, Porciani, in Fasano Guarini, Petralia, and Pezzino (eds.) (2004).

many also recognized, was that those same local autonomies were also opportunities for resurrecting the monopolist power formerly exercised by the feudatories.

In many respects, the South was confronted by problems that would come to face other parts of Italy only much later. The crisis of older forms of paternalism and deference in the rural South was not unique, but when compared with much of central and northern Italy those processes had been precocious and peculiarly disruptive. But while this had created incentives for developing new forms of bureaucratic power earlier than in other Italian states, this was not easily achieved. The poverty of the southern economies made the bureaucratic project difficult to achieve, while moves to tighten bureaucratic centralization provoked powerful local resistance. When in 1816 the Congress of Vienna decided to unify the formerly independent crowns of Naples and Sicily, those tensions were further heightened.

None of these developments were unique to the South, however, and in all the Italian states the Congress of Vienna took the opportunity to amalgamate, annex, and integrate formerly independent states, territories, and towns. The aim was to strengthen the Italian principalities, but the process of incorporation and administrative centralization was everywhere the most serious cause of political unrest in the Italian Restoration regimes. Without constant external support, these internal tensions proved difficult to contain, and the problems were exacerbated when the defence of local autonomies found a broader and more compelling platform in the nationalist projects that gained force in the 1840s.

REFLECTING ON THE REVOLUTION

The terms of the Restoration settlement in Naples in 1815 were dictated by Vienna, but they also closely followed the recommendations of two men who would play a central role in the politics of the Restoration government, Luigi de' Medici and Donato Tommasi. After the Restoration they served respectively as Ministers of Finance and Justice, but from much earlier they had already been following and studying the change taking place on the mainland from Palermo. When Napoleon's Continental project began to fall apart, they had carefully begun to plot the course that the Restoration should take.

De' Medici and Tommasi had both begun their careers in the final decades of enlightened absolutism, both were disciples of Gaetano Filangieri, and both had been directly involved in the final Bourbon reform initiatives after 1801. Their politics and outlook were very similar to those of Giuseppe Zurlo, and like Zurlo they had followed the Court to Palermo in 1806. Unlike Zurlo they had remained in Sicily, where they had been caught in the bitter struggles among the queen, the British, and the Sicilian barons.

De' Medici and Tommasi were both deeply hostile to the constitutional experiment in Sicily and like the eighteenth-century reformers they considered the Sicilian Parliament to be a bastion of the reactionary feudal nobility that was the principal enemy of progress. Like Zurlo and Ricciardi in Naples, both Tommasi and de' Medici believed that enlightened autocracy offered the safest and most rational form of progressive government. Although they considered the French regime on the mainland to be little better than a military dictatorship, they still found it far preferable to what the English had tried to impose on Sicily.

Both men saw the Restoration as an opportunity to create a new alliance between throne and altar, but they were agreed that this must be done without alienating those who had rallied to the French regime. It was no accident that among the documents collected in Palermo by Tommasi was an original copy of the 'King's Orders given from the Road of Naples' to Cardinal Ruffo in July 1799, which had authorized the White Terror. This was precisely the precedent to be avoided, and both men agreed that the political divisions that had lacerated the nation between 1799 and 1806 had fatally weakened the monarchy and were the reason 'why the Government that succeeded that of His Majesty King Ferdinand won the applause of the Neapolitan Nation'.[12]

The two Bourbon ministers accepted the underlying soundness of the changes made by the French rulers, and indeed the central refrain in the memoranda prepared in Palermo, and later repeated in the politics of the Restoration, was that the French innovations had simply realized the reforms that had originally been proposed by the Bourbon rulers in the previous century. This was a formula that enabled the Bourbon ministers to accept the new administrative system in principle, while rejecting the ways and the means by which these changes had been implemented by the French.

For example, while it was acknowledged that the new Interior Ministry was sound in principle, it was also claimed that it typified the failure of the French rulers to carry through their reforms. The Ministry was above all an example of:

> the mania to create everything in a single moment and on a scale that is quite disproportionate to existing resources, with the result that great quantities of money have been consumed, yet everything remains chronically short of funds so that very few objectives have been achieved. Decrees that have never been enforced and things that have been demolished but never rebuilt are rightly the targets of public criticism. . . . The publication of a new decree and the announcement of a new project served primarily to fill the page of some report that would appear in France to boast of the improvements made in this State, in contrast to the views of the Nation that cried out against the money wasted to flatter the self-image of the Court and its vainglorious ruler.

Allowing for the strong ideological stances taken in these reports, they did nonetheless pinpoint key weaknesses in the administrative innovations on the mainland. The reports prepared in Palermo confirmed, for example, that jurisdictional boundaries between the new central ministries of state remained uncertain

[12] ASN: Archivi Privati, Carte Tommasi B IV, 'Istruzioni del Re per il Suo Luogotenente e Capitano Generale al Cardinale Ruffo, date dalla Rada di Napoli', 24 July 1799.

and that they had often been given powers they had no means to enforce. The Interior Ministry, for example, was also responsible for the promotion of trade, but since the Kingdom had no colonies its trade consisted almost entirely in the export of agricultural products. What agriculture needed first and foremost was roads, but 'in nine years not one new road has been built and those that exist are still in a terrible state'. The new Administration of Bridges and Roads was hailed as the institutional solution adopted by the whole of Europe, yet had so far produced little: 'Roads are needed and will be built, but for that we do not need to maintain this extensive General Staff of costly and useless employees.'

Changes in the administration of justice were judged more positively and it was acknowledged that this had created a clearly organized hierarchy that worked from the lowest rung, the local Justice of the Peace, upwards through the provincial courts, the four Appeal Courts, and finally reaching the Cassation Court in Naples. The lower and higher criminal courts that had been created in each province were also cited approvingly, as was the office of the Procurators Royal who acted on the crown's behalf in criminal and civil cases, and were responsible for ensuring that the courts followed proper procedure and interpreted the law correctly.[13] The new provincial tribunals were also praised for making access to the courts easier for citizens, while increasing the opportunities for young lawyers and judges to receive training and experience.[14]

The standardization of the Kingdom's legal codes was also welcomed, although the report insisted that the new laws needed a firmer Neapolitan imprint: 'The Revolution that has brought so many evils, has also brought us this advantage', but 'opportune reforms' were needed so that once 'refashioned by the paternal care of His Majesty the King' the new codes could properly be described not as Napoleonic but as Neapolitan.

CHURCH AND CLERGY

The conditions of the Church and the clergy were a matter of special concern. But although the alliance between throne and altar was to be the foundation of the Restoration order, the approach was essentially pragmatic and there was no suggestion that the changes made by the French should be undone. In part this was because the observers in Palermo shared the hostility of the eighteenth-century reformers toward the regular clergy and papal jurisdiction in the Kingdom. They noted that with the exception of the mendicant orders, virtually all the religious houses had been suppressed, save only the monasteries of Monte Cassino and Cava dei Tirreni, which had been allowed to survive because of the important libraries and documents they possessed. Other monasteries had been stripped of

[13] The reference was to the office of the Public Minister.

[14] ASN: Archivi Privati, Carte Tommasi, Memorandum VII: Sul Ministero di Culto e Giustizia.

their furnishings and books to deck out royal palaces and the new Royal Library in Naples. But they went on to argue that 'even if there were the means to restore everything to what it had once been, after nine years, it is no longer clear whether this would be a good or a bad thing'. Many young monks would resist attempts to make them return to the cloister, and those who now received public stipends considered that they had benefited from the changes. They were also a valuable supply of teachers for schools, colleges, and seminaries, and of administrators for charities and hospitals.

The heaviest losses, it was claimed, were felt less by individuals than by families 'who used to dedicate one of their members to this State and can no longer make use of this resource'. That loss was partially compensated by the increase in the size of the army, but the report also took the opportunity to raise a more general concern on that score: the army was an expense that the government could not sustain and so must somehow seek to reduce without creating discontent.

The wider moral impact of the suppression of the monasteries was a matter of greater concern, however, and especially for Naples 'where the need for the influence of religion is especially necessary, since it is essential to have a means to check the imaginations of a people who become volcanic and dangerous when left to their own devices'. The suppression of the monasteries had seriously reduced the provision of education and instruction for the poor. The new schools created by the French were 'inactive, lacking teachers and without funds'. As a result primary education was completely neglected. The founding of new colleges 'only affects the higher forms of learning' since they would not increase the supply of new teachers for the poor. Nor could the teacher shortage be resolved by the secular clergy since they had other functions. Only the 'idle life of the cloister fitted people for this form of public teaching which brought learning to the poor. There had always been a monk willing to teach the alphabet, some grammar and the Catechism, but the secular clergy have no time for this.... What poor Father who works for a living and what Neapolitan mother has the skills? As a result Your Majesty has many subjects and citizens who are ignorant of why they exist and of what they owe to their Creator, to Society and to their Sovereign.'

The writers of the memorandum also warned that it would be dangerous and inadvisable to attempt to restore the property of the religious orders, arguing that it was preferable that the clergy be paid by the state since this reduced the power and influence of the Court of Rome. But new measures were needed to improve the behaviour of the regular clergy, who too often caused scandal and were a threat to public order.

When it came to the secular clergy, the observers in Palermo shared the concerns that had led Murat's government to seek a new concordat. Many bishoprics, canonries, and abbacies had suffered heavily from the loss of feudal revenues and the division of the feudal *demani*. Although many bishops now received stipends from the government, some as much as 1,400 ducats a year, most of the bishoprics in the Kingdom remained vacant. Parish priests had been assigned good stipends by the state, but these were rarely paid. A thorough reorganization of the secular hierarchies was urgently needed to make the authority of the bishops more effective and—by implication—to make the secular clergy a more effective and disciplined branch of public administration.[15]

WELFARE AND EDUCATION

The reports were especially scathing when it came to the shortcomings of the French government's initiatives to promote welfare and education. Endless decrees, it was claimed, had been issued establishing primary and secondary schools, colleges, grammar schools, universities, libraries, and printing works, but all were in a state of total confusion and abandon. The University was in disorder, and was avoided by both students and professors. There were no great advocates practising in Naples, nor physicians, mathematicians, classical scholars, or literary figures of renown. Manufacturing had received some encouragement, but remained in its infancy and needed help to grow stronger.

They also underlined the irreparable damage done to the charitable institutions that had been one of the Kingdom's greatest resources.

> There is a decree prohibiting begging, yet the streets of the capital are full of the most public displays of suffering and have become a Kingdom of unfortunate creatures whose plight must wrench the heart-strings of any sensitive person.

The inmates of the hospices often went without food, yet despite the French reforms the number of those employed by the charitable foundations was excessive and they were grossly overpaid: 'the principal beneficiaries of the charities are still those who run them'.

The astronomical observatory and the botanical gardens were cited as examples of useful innovations, likewise the standardization of weights and measures using the metric system, although it was to be deplored that this had been accompanied by barbarously Italianized French names. It was agreed too that the French rulers had also introduced sound new regulations on public hygiene and town planning. The siting of food and livestock markets was now subject to public control, and towns were required to build cemeteries outside inhabited urban spaces, to ensure that night-soil and refuse were regularly disposed of, and to issue permissions for all public and private construction. But the means to oversee and enforce these regulations were wanting.

Too often *ancien régime* regulatory bodies had been abolished without being replaced. The *Protomedicato* that had, for example, formerly regulated medical practitioners and apothecaries had been abolished, but since it was not replaced by any new body 'the unlicensed trade in drugs means that a handful of unscrupulous

[15] ASN: Archivi Privati, Carte Tommasi, Memorandum VII: Sul Ministero di Culto e Giustizia.

people who know more about alchemy than chemistry now produce medicines for the sick' and the regulations on who could practice medicine had been relaxed 'to the point that even an out of work notary could set up as a physician'.[16]

THE FEUDAL COMMISSION

The Feudal Commission was the principal target on which the commentators in Palermo focused their scorn. They acknowledged and welcomed without reservation the abolition of feudalism, which was again described as the realization of the most fundamental reform pursued by the previous Bourbon monarchy. But the Feudal Commission itself was held up as an example of the arbitrary and despotic nature of French rule:

> The Minister of the Interior and the Procurator General Winspeare, on the pretext of revolutionary ideas embellished by philanthropic references to the benefits of a general and equal distribution of land, have committed one of the greatest injustices. The abuses of feudal privilege were an offence to the Sovereign and to public law, but the seizure of land in an attempt to carry through an Agrarian Law has been the most unjust, the most anti-monarchical, and the most damaging action to the interests of the State.

The operation was carried out by corrupt judges who in a single day issued 270 judgements without appeal and without due process in response to a simple appeal by the mayor or the representative of a *comune*. In this fashion 270 people were deprived of property they had owned for centuries.

> The nobility has been ruined, and how many of the great landowners have been left without brood-mares or ewes from which to breed? What forests, what pastures have been left to sustain the pastoral economy after the division of the common lands carried out by the Minister of the Interior? To destroy the big estates so that every citizen may have a part in the belief that this will cause industry to increase is a chimera in which only someone who does not know the Neapolitans could indulge.
>
> If there is no-one to pay the farm workers, if there is no-one to make loans, all industry will perish, there will be no-one left to pay the taxes, and if there is no vast Army to absorb the resources of the State and feed at least part of those left without work, the number of criminals will grow as will the scale of public poverty.

It would have been much better to have undertaken major land reclamation projects 'that would help clothe the naked instead of a remedy that simply strips naked those that are already clothed'.[17]

Despite their heavy ideological charge, these criticisms were similar to those levelled against the operations of the Feudal Commission in Naples by Francesco Ricciardi and Vincenzo Cuoco.

[16] *ASN*: Archivi Privati, Carte Tommasi, Memorandum VIII: Ministero dell'Interno.
[17] Ibid., Memorandum V: L'Amminstrazione Civile.

THE QUESTION OF COST

Not surprisingly there were also many significant silences in the reports drawn up in Palermo. There was no mention, for example, of the reorganization of public finances, of the conversion of the debts of the *ancien régime* monarchy, or of the consolidation of a new National Debt that had fundamentally changed the structure of public finances. Nor was there any reference to the reorganization of direct taxation following the introduction of the *fondiaria*. Nor was much said about the small but important initiatives taken by Murat's government to build up native industries and reduce dependence on imports in key sectors like textiles.

These silences were in part due to the fact that there was no disagreement over the utility of these innovations, while it was also agreed that the new system of administration had immeasurably strengthened the government's control over the provinces and local government. There was praise for the new municipal government in Naples and for the new provincial administrations, especially for the Provincial Councils, 'where the Intendent takes executive decisions subject to confirmation by the Council of State' on all local affairs and on all questions relating to the fiscal obligations of individuals, towns, and local administrations.[18]

The reports did draw attention, however, to the heavy costs of these new forms of bureaucratic administration, and questioned how these could be sustained given the Kingdom's slender economic resources. Despite heavy increases in taxation, the Kingdom's fiscal revenues were insufficient to support the new administrative structures, let alone the many other new projects that the French rulers had proposed. No one doubted the need for investments in road-building and land reclamation projects, it was argued, but no one had shown how such endeavours could be funded from existing resources. As a result, the French had left in their train a long series of projects either never started or else soon abandoned.

In this the Bourbon ministers were not wide of the mark, and the project of administrative reorganization begun by the French rulers in many critical respects outran the resources of the southern economy. Nor is this surprising, since even in much wealthier regions like Lombardy the costs of the new forms of central and local administration were the main reason for the heavy tax increases that made French rule very unpopular in the closing years of the empire.[19] In the South, the depressed state of the economy made the additional fiscal burdens imposed to support the new bureaucracies even more difficult to sustain, while the problems were seriously aggravated by the tendency to pass additional tax burdens on to the provinces. These new costs would be one of the principal targets of protest during the revolutions of 1820–1 in Sicily and on the mainland.[20]

[18] Ibid. [19] Zaghi (1991), 519—see also Antonielli (1983) and Grab (1997).
[20] Spagnoletti (1985), 953–1019.

PUBLIC ORDER AND PRIVATE ORDER

The reports prepared for Tommasi and de' Medici in Palermo revealed a sensitive understanding of the material difficulty of sustaining a modern bureaucratic state in an impoverished Kingdom. But they also acknowledged the difficulties that the seemingly irreversible breakdown of informal systems of power in many parts of the South posed for the construction of a post-feudal order. Factionalism, political and party rivalries, and public order in general were, therefore, a major source of concern, but while it was recognized that the French had strengthened the apparatus of policing it was also acknowledged that this could not offer effective solutions.

Before the Revolution, it was argued, the Governor of the Vicaria tribunal and prison in Naples had exercised all the powers needed to keep the peace and punish wrongdoers.[21] But in a modern state, what the French called *Alta Polizia*—essentially the policing of ideas—had become a necessity.

> Because of the infection caused by new principles, because men of letters began to challenge errors and prejudices only to replace them with inappropriate philosophies that gave rise to strange fruits in a Nation that still lacks education, and because the trade with foreigners that is necessary for the nation's prosperity also became a source of highly dangerous contagion, new forms of policing that are vigilant, impartial but truly patriotic have become necessary and indispensable.

The threat to the modern state no longer came from common criminals, but from individuals with political motives, which left the government with no alternative but to police ideas and behaviour. In a modern state, therefore, the police were indispensable 'to protect the State from rebellion, to maintain order and to encourage a spirit of reconciliation in Society'.

But how to do this without exacerbating political divisions? The choice of a Chief of Police was obviously of critical importance, and it was recommended that only persons from a distinguished family with property should be chosen for such a position, since such individuals were less 'likely to be associated with Parties'. The example to be avoided at all costs was that of Antoine Christophe Saliceti, whose time as Minister of Police had been 'a terrible epoch in the history of the kingdom. Despotism, terror, immorality, unlimited ambition and a Chaos of Horrors formed the code by which he lived.'

The pervasiveness of factional and party divisions in the South indicated deeper problems, however, that called for other measures. In political terms, these divisions made it advisable to continue the politics of *ralliement* and *amalgame* adopted by the French rulers. The last of Murat's police chiefs, the Duke of Campochiaro, had included both former Jacobins and former Sanfedists in his

[21] On the Vicaria and policing in Naples at the end of the *ancien régime* see Alessi (1993).

administration, for example, and had relaxed the formerly rigid 'surveillance of political opinions' in an attempt to overcome the factionalism encouraged by his predecessors.[22] That approach had worked best in the provinces, it was argued, where the Intendents were generally honest and loyal and were less affected by political ambitions than their French counterparts in the capital. The Intendents provided regular reports on the state of public opinion, which were carefully cross-referenced with reports from 'honest men from the same Province'. With the change of regime it would be necessary to ensure that there was no 'falling off in either principle or practice'.[23]

A benign and watchful state could give the lead, but the roots of factionalism lay in the fractured structures of local power, of which the most alarming symptom was the ubiquity of the secret societies. For the observers in Palermo this posed a simple but critical question: were the secret societies a means for overcoming the crisis of the paternalist order in the South, or were they simply the instruments of factionalism and division? The writers of the reports were unable to answer that question, but they concluded with a warning that the diffusion of the secret societies was now so great that any attempt to destroy them would be very dangerous.[24]

These reports show that contemporaries had a clear understanding of the broader changes taking place. The monarchy's principal advisers welcomed the end of the feudal order and saw the Restoration as the opportunity to build a new post-feudal order and a new political consensus. But on what terms?

> Monarchies in the Bonaparte style are military dictatorships, made up of the Sovereign and the Plebs with no intermediaries. They lead either to despotism or revolution. The return of his Majesty King Ferdinand IV to the throne of Naples will reflect the ideas of this century. It will not establish a new form of military government, but rather a paternal government that is the fruit not of maxims but of experience and founded in a true understanding of the character of the Nation that He governs. But there is only one true intermediary between the ruler and the Nation: 'There is no Monarchy without Nobility, and there is no Nobility without hereditary Property, which is the indispensable foundation of the whole Edifice.'[25]

That meant repairing the organic and paternalist social bonds that had been shattered by the Revolution and by Napoleonic bureaucracy. But in the political and economic circumstances of the Restoration, it was far from clear how such a project could be realized.

NAPLES, VIENNA, AND LONDON

Not least of the difficulties facing the restored Italian rulers in 1815 was the subordinate and dependent role assigned them by the European peacemakers.

[22] Maghella and Daure.
[23] ASN: Archivi Privati: Carte Tommasi, Memorandum VI, 'Sulla Polizia generale del Regno'.
[24] Ibid. [25] Ibid.

When it came to Italy, the overriding concern of the Vienna settlement was to prevent any revival of French territorial ambitions on the peninsula. For that reason, the European powers entrusted the Italian states to the protection of the Habsburg monarchy, and although Austria ruled directly only in the newly formed Kingdom of Lombardy-Venetia, from the formidable redoubts of the Quadrilateral fortresses in the central Po valley its armies could be dispatched speedily to any part of the peninsula. Military might, moreover, was reinforced by networks of kinship that made every Italian ruler either a cousin or a client of the Austrian imperial family. For the first time in modern history, the Italian states were dominated by a single foreign power, a situation that left the Italian rulers little room for political or diplomatic manoeuvre.[26]

In the South, the terms of the Restoration reflected the Bourbon dynasty's greatly reduced importance in European politics. Despite lip-service to the principles of dynastic legitimacy, Ferdinand IV had been restored to the throne of Naples in 1815 only because it suited the political interests of the allies, who only a year before had been prepared to consider the claims of Joachim Murat. In Naples, the terms of the Treaty of Casalanza were considered to be so humiliating that the Neapolitan envoy, the Duke of Serracapriola, had refused to sign them. The Bourbons finally lost the territorial claims that had inspired Murat's adventures in central Italy in 1814 and 1815 and were confined to the boundaries set by the 'Holy See and the salt sea'.[27] The Tuscan *Presidi* were lost without compensation, the Papacy's claim to suzerainty over the Kingdom was not challenged, and the Neapolitan claims to the territories of Pontecorvo and Benevento were not acknowledged.[28]

Austria's support for the dynasty's restoration came at a high price. Following Napoleon's example, the Austrians stationed an army of occupation in the Kingdom, which remained there until 1818 at the Neapolitan government's expense. In addition, Naples was required to pay the full costs of Austria's military operations in 1814 and 1815.[29] But the English had demanded their quittance too. Finally in possession of a secure base in Malta, Britain was now the undisputed naval power in the Mediterranean, whose strategic importance for communication with its colonial empire in India and the Orient became a permanent concern of successive British governments. Britain's aim was to prevent any political unrest in Italy that other powers, namely France, might try to exploit.

[26] France managed to regain a foothold when it sent an army to defend the Pope against an insurrection in 1831 and occupied Ancona. However, the situation changed completely when in 1849 the French Republic sent another army to destroy the Roman Republic and restore Pope Pius IX: this army remained in Rome until 1870 and enabled the emperor Louis Napoleon to become a major player in the politics of Italian unification.

[27] The Holy See being the Papal State; see Astarita (2005).

[28] Blanch, in Croce (ed.) (1945), ii. 14–15. See also Romeo (1963), 65–96; Cingari (1966); Scirocco (1986).

[29] Between 1815 and 1825 the debt rose to 100 million ducats, five times the Kingdom's annual revenues. See Ostuni (1992), 329–32.

For that reason, Britain was willing for Austria to act as *gendarme* of the Italian states, even though in British eyes Austria's hostility to liberalism and its commitment to legitimist autocracy at home and abroad was a major cause of Italy's political unrests. But despite the growing sympathy on the part of English public opinion for the cause of Italian independence, down to 1859 British governments remained unswerving in their support for the political status quo in Italy.[30]

When it came to Naples and the Bourbon monarchy, British attitudes were particularly mixed. The ten years of joint rule in Sicily had left few happy memories, while at the same time strengthening British convictions that poverty and discontent in Italy in general, and in the South in particular, were the inevitable consequences of despotism and misrule. On that subject successive British governments continued to make their feelings known, although to avoid compromising relations between London and Vienna they made do with lecturing the Neapolitan rulers and the Pope on how to run their states.

British support for the Bourbon restoration in Naples had come at a high price, however. During the Napoleonic wars, Britain's trade with southern Italy had grown mainly thanks to the traffic in British contraband goods stocked in Sicily and Malta. A number of British commercial ventures had flourished in Sicily, including the enterprise of James Woodhouse and Benjamin Ingham, two Englishmen who had begun exporting dessert wines from Marsala before the Revolution. These became very popular first with the British navy and then after the war were in high demand in British drawing rooms. From this profitable business, Woodhouse and Ingham branched out into other fields, including the export trade in citrus fruits and in sulphur, for which industrial demand was increasing.[31]

Britain's compensation came, therefore, in the form of commercial privileges and there was no clearer demonstration of the Bourbon Kingdom's continuing colonial status after the Restoration than the humiliating commercial privileges demanded by its allies. The treaties signed in September 1816 conceded 10 per cent on all customs duties on goods loaded on and off any British, French, or Spanish vessel. Since Neapolitan ships did not enjoy the same privilege, the Kingdom's commercial interests were ruthlessly subordinated to those of its principal commercial partners. By the 1830s most of the Kingdom's foreign trade, exports as well as imports, was carried on foreign and mainly on British merchant vessels.[32] These commercial privileges were the ones that both Joseph Bonaparte and Joachim Murat had refused to grant even to Napoleon. As Vincenzo Cuoco and others had warned two decades earlier, in the rapidly evolving new world of international economic competition, southern Italy's political and diplomatic insecurity made it especially vulnerable to the risk of colonial subordination to its powerful foreign commercial partners, especially Great Britain.[33]

[30] Mack Smith (1954/1985), 31–6.

[31] Trevelyan (1973); D'Angelo (1988, 1990). On British merchants in Naples, see also Dawes (1991).

[32] Pontieri (1965), 318–36.

[33] Cuoco (Villani, ed., 1980), 58–9.

The crisis at the close of the eighteenth century had irreversibly compromised the autonomy to which the eighteenth-century rulers of Naples had aspired. In 1815 the Restoration freed the Kingdom of the Two Sicilies from colonial subordination to Napoleonic France only to make it a political satellite of the Habsburg Empire and part of Britain's new informal commercial empire. But in this respect too the Bourbon Kingdom in the South again differed little from the other Italian states, and down to 1848 even the two Italian princes who enjoyed the greatest degrees of diplomatic autonomy—the House of Savoy and the Pope—both chose to make Austria their protector.

There were also important differences. Unlike the Bourbon Kingdom in the South, the diplomatic and territorial integrity of both the papacy and the House of Savoy was guaranteed by the European Powers. After 1815, as before, it was a premise of European diplomacy that the Piedmontese territories formed a necessary buffer between France and Austria, which meant that in 1848 and 1849, and again in 1859 the Piedmontese monarchy could go to war with Austria in the knowledge that military defeat would not jeopardize the existence of the Piedmontese state. Similarly, for so long as the papacy had powerful international supporters the survival of the Pope's temporal powers in Central Italy was guaranteed, no matter what the strength of local opposition. This was why after 1860 Rome would remain outside the new Italian Kingdom, until the defeat of the emperor Louis Napoleon in September 1870 by the Prussians at the battle of Sedan removed the Pope's last international protector.[34] The rulers of the Bourbon Kingdom of the Two Sicilies enjoyed no comparable diplomatic security, however. Apart from the alliance with Austria the monarchy had few friends but many powerful adversaries, a situation that would cause the Bourbon government in the South to follow strategies that were significantly different from those of their fellow Italian rulers.

THE ECONOMICS OF RESTORATION

The political and diplomatic challenges facing the restored monarchy in 1815 were compounded by the economic and financial problems facing the Kingdom. From the first days of the Restoration the government was faced by a crippling financial crisis, while the commercial recession that had dragged on since the start of the revolutionary wars not only continued, but in some respects deepened.

As well as the massive costs of Murat's final campaigns and the undisclosed but lavish personal bribes the Bourbons paid to Prince Metternich and Talleyrand to secure their throne, the Neapolitan rulers had to repay the costs of Austrian military occupation in 1815, a large cash indemnity to Prince Eugène, and the cost of

[34] According to Bismarck Italy's Unification was the result of three S's: the battles of San Martino, Sadowa, and Sedan.

maintaining the Austrian army, which remained in the Kingdom for two years (at a cost of 4,200,000 ducats). To pay for these 'extraordinary expenditures', between 1815 and 1820 the government had to find some 23,000,000 ducats in excess of its annual revenues.[35]

The high price of the Kingdom's fragile independence came on top of the heavy financial and fiscal strains imposed by the empire and Murat's wars. The Finance Minister, Luigi de' Medici, made deep cuts in government spending that were damaging especially for those whose fortunes had risen under Murat. Public employees were dismissed, others were placed on part or supplementary time, salaries were cut and paid in heavy arrears. Reductions in the army budget and in commissions were another major cause of discontent, as was the government's decision to disband many of the technical agencies created by Murat, including the Directorate of *Ponti e Strade* and the *Scuola di'Ingegneria*. Heavy cuts in the budget for public works were a further blow to the depressed provincial economies and resulted in often irreparable damage once more to numerous land reclamation projects that had been started or restarted.

The government's financial problems were severely aggravated by the commercial recession that followed the war. Throughout Europe prices fell, and just as Vincenzo Cuoco and Luigi Blanch had predicted the cause was the grain from Egypt, the Morea, and the Black Sea that for the first time began to reach European markets. Not for the last time, the Mediterranean economies were the principal victims of these early examples of globalization. In this case the impact was made more severe by Luigi de' Medici's decision to remove restrictions on the import of foreign grain, which caused prices to fall even more heavily. To make matters worse, there was an outbreak of what was believed to be the plague on the mainland in 1816, while a year later the poorest harvests in living memory brought more disease and starvation. The government lacked the means to intervene, but although conditions in the provinces became even more precarious, de' Medici nonetheless followed Mosbourg's strategy and continued to load them with additional fiscal burdens.

THE POLITICS OF RESTORATION

Austria's determination in 1815 to prevent Ferdinand of Naples repeating the political errors of 1799 did not imply sympathy with political change. Quite the opposite. Austria was vehemently opposed to the Sicilian constitution of 1812 and under the terms of a secret Treaty of Friendship between Vienna and Naples signed on 12 June 1815 the king of Naples agreed not to make any changes that were not 'compatible with the political institutions of the Habsburg monarchy'.

[35] Colletta (Cortese, 1957), iii. 18–21 (see Cortese's notes); Scirocco (1986), 647–52. See also Ostuni (1992), 64–9 and Bianchini (1839), 536.

This was the pretext for abolishing the Sicilian constitution, and ensured that the expectations of constitutional government would not be realized. If this provided the supporters of the revolutions of 1820 on the mainland and in Sicily with their principal demands, the Treaty of 1815 also provided Austria with the pretext for military intervention to overthrow the constitution granted by Ferdinand IV—after 1816 Ferdinand I of the new Kingdom of the Two Sicilies—in July 1820 and which his son had taken a solemn vow to uphold.[36]

There was little space for public debate in Restoration Naples, although the restored dynasty followed the models of representation set by their French predecessors. As it had been in the decade of French rule, the San Carlo opera house in Naples played a critical role in defining the national and modern attributes of the monarchy and was the site where the royal family was most frequently seen in a carefully choreographed setting. Domenico Barbaja's services were retained and the San Carlo theatre was the most modern and lavish in Italy, the scene of Rossini's early triumphs and another reflection of both the glory and the modernity of the new monarchy. When the opera house was burned down in 1816, Stendhal recognized that the decision to rebuild it immediately was guided by political not artistic considerations and in his view did more than anything else to consolidate the monarchy's popularity.[37]

The indefatigable diarist Carlo de Nicola repeatedly noted how warmly the restored monarchy was welcomed in the popular districts of the capital, although the cycles of bread and circuses maintained by the French rulers were never restored to their former lavishness. Outside the capital things were different. In Palermo, for example, the decayed state of the San Carlino theatre contrasted with the glories of the San Carlo in Naples and became an important symbol of the city's loss of status following the Act of Union in 1816.[38]

The union of the two crowns had been a direct response to the humiliations suffered by the monarchy during the long exile in Palermo, but had been imposed by Austria and endorsed by the European powers. The resentments over the loss of autonomy gave rise in Sicily to the most serious political challenges to the restored monarchy and marked the latest, although not yet the final chapter in the struggles with the Sicilian grandees. But the Act of Union also revived older divisions within Sicily and at least initially was widely supported by those opposed to the reactionary autonomist pretensions of the nobility and to the dominant role in Sicilian politics that Palermo sought to retain. Messina and Catania in particular looked to gain greater independence from the union with Naples and to challenge their subordination to Palermo.

Although the Act of Union abolished feudalism in Sicily, no Feudal Commission was created to adjudicate contested rights and in most cases the former feudal estates

[36] Scirocco (1990), 9–105; idem (1986), 643–82.

[37] Stendhal, *Rome, Naples et Florence*, cited in Di Lernia (1988), 160; on the social and political role of the theatre in Restoration Italy see Sorba (2001), 93–154.

[38] Davis (2005), 578–80.

and the feudal and village *demani* passed directly to the ex-feudal landowners and the *galantuomini* without compensation to the rural communities. Although by the time of the revolutions in 1820 the process had barely begun, by challenging numerous jealously preserved privileges unification had created a groundswell of powerful discontents that quickly involved Sicily in the political events that began when the monarchy conceded a constitution in Naples on 7 July 1820.[39]

Despite the apparently peaceful transition of power in 1815, serious problems had also developed in the mainland provinces. Brigandage not only revived, but began to assume unprecedented proportions. In part this was a direct consequence of the breakdown of order in central Italy, where the French withdrawal had been followed by Murat's invasion and occupation of papal territories in 1814. The restoration of Pope Pius VII in May 1814 had made little difference, while Murat's military operations in 1815 left a further residue of popular revolts, deserters, and armed bands who moved freely across the frontiers into the northern provinces of Terra di Lavoro, the Abruzzo, and Molise, even raiding deep into Basilicata, Capitanata, and Apulia. Although no longer promoted by the English or the royalists, brigandage was still also endemic in the Calabrian provinces, where smuggling continued to provide abundant work for the brigands.[40]

The situation was aggravated by the government's decision in 1815 to disband Murat's Provincial Legions, which it mistrusted, and to abolish the military commissions on the grounds that those whom the French had called bandits were in reality Bourbon loyalists. That proved to be completely false, and within a year the military commissions and the Provincial Militias were reinstated. But the landowners refused to serve and instead sent substitutes so that the anti-brigand militias consisted mainly of amnestied bandits and other delinquents who proved more energetic in pursuing their own criminal activities than bandits.[41]

Once again the military authorities published lists of wanted outlaws, sold amnesties, and recruited bandits who surrendered voluntarily to hunt those who did not. As in the past, however, these measures fuelled rather than checked the lawlessness, which by 1817 had reached particularly alarming proportions in Capitanata and Apulia. The scale of the disorders can be glimpsed from the correspondence of the Neapolitan ambassador in St Petersburg, the Duke of Serracapriola, who in 1817 appointed a new administrator to run his estate in Capitanata. The new agent made the journey from Naples but when he reached the Duke's property in Chieuti he discovered that the estates had for some time been taken over by the kinsmen of a former administrator. In fear for his life, the Duke's new agent turned on his heel and hurried back to the safety of the capital.[42]

39 Romeo (1950), 148–54, 163–9. See also Romano (1952), Renda (1968), and De Francesco (1992).

40 Colletta (Cortese, 1957), iii. 108–17; Blanch (Croce, ed., 1945), ii. 190–5.

41 Lucarelli (1942), 50–64.

42 ASN: AP Maresca di Serracapriola B 131, 132, 137. There has been a long history of disputes, between the feudatories and the 'naturali' of Chieuti.

In an attempt to restore order in Apulia, in 1817 the government commissioned an Irish general, Richard Church, to do what Manhès had done for Murat. When Church arrived in Bari, he reported that the province was in state of civil war, and he warned the government that the brigands were in close communication with the Carbonarist lodges. In December, he occupied Lecce, rounded up all suspect *Carbonari*, and set up military tribunals to try and execute all suspected brigands.[43] But the measures were not successful, and the government instead tried making deals with brigand leaders. They included a secret pact with one of the most notorious bands operating in Apulia led by Gaetano Meomartino (known as Vardarelli) and Ciro Annichiarico, who secretly agreed to accept government pay for turning in their opponents. But the military used the agreement as a lure to ambush and kill the leaders in Foggia,[44] an event recorded by the English traveller Henry Keppel Craven who arrived just in time to witness the shootout.[45]

When the Austrian army finally withdrew in 1817 the situation became even worse, and in the following year the reintroduction of conscription provided the bands with a fresh supply of recruits. But while these disorders reflected the desperate state of economic conditions, they were also inseparable from the conflicts that surrounded the divisions of the former common lands and feudal estates throughout the Kingdom. In many cases, the issues left unresolved by the Feudal Commission and the French reforms were settled by force. Nor was it a coincidence that brigandage intensified in Sicily as well precisely at the moment when feudalism was abolished on the island.[46]

As had been the case during the years of French rule, brigandage offered powerful landowners with opportunities to rebuild local networks of power and autonomy. Like the French before them, the Bourbon government now looked to the secret societies as means to combat these networks. But although Luigi Blanch had argued that the secret societies had acted as a critical force for order during the Restoration, in the years that followed they became the principal vehicles for promoting and disseminating the constitutional programme in southern Italy and in Sicily.[47] Even their enemies, who deliberately exaggerated their power and influence, paid the compliment of imitating them. During his brief tenure in the Ministry of Police at the start of the Restoration, the Prince of Canosa had busily promoted numerous royalist secret societies and he was a staunch advocate of popular royalist militias.

Fearing that his measures would lead to civil war, the Austrians insisted that Canosa be removed. As brigandage escalated and as the secret societies grew in number both in the mainland provinces and in Sicily, the South became a theatre for disorder on a scale not seen since 1799. But when the revolutions began in June 1820, on the mainland at least they took place under conditions of remarkable tranquillity.

43 Lucarelli (1942), 124: Palumbo (1911), 265.
44 Themelly (1979), 62 n. 42.
45 Keppel Craven (1824), 111–15.
46 Fiume, in Davis and Ginsborg (ed.) (1991/2002), 70–91.
47 Blanch, in Croce (ed.) (1945), ii. 190–5.

15

Revolution

1820: AN UNUSUAL REVOLUTION

The revolutions in Naples and Sicily in 1820–1 were the most direct and explicit response to the changes that had taken place in southern Italy during the years of Napoleonic rule, which after the Restoration had been exported to Sicily as well. They must rank, however, amongst the more unusual political happenings in nineteenth-century Europe. The revolutions took place almost without bloodshed and in less than a week a revolt that started as a protest in an army barracks in Nola in July 1820 led to the concession of a constitution and inspired a separate revolution in Sicily.

On the mainland, the revolution took place with little upheaval or violence. Supporters divided into rival conservative, moderate, and radical camps, but never quite came to blows, and the popular violence and peasant *jacqueries* that had come to be thought of as standard accompaniments of political upheaval in southern Italy were strikingly absent. The situation was different in Sicily, but mainly because the revolution there had different objectives, specifically the Act of Union of 1816. When Palermo refused to acknowledge the constitutional government in Naples, it set a collision course not only with Naples but also with the other major Sicilian towns that refused to follow its lead.

Nonetheless, the nine months of constitutional government from July 1820 to March 1821 were the first moment of freedom of speech in southern Italy since the time of the Republic of 1799. In Sicily, the debates focused primarily on the island's autonomy and the political terms of the Restoration. On the mainland, however, the revolution was an opportunity for a searching review of the political and administrative changes that had been introduced during the years of French domination and preserved after the Restoration. These debates revealed how the political events of the previous decades had given rise to new forms of political awareness in many different parts of the South. In this the secret societies had played an important role. The masses by and large remained silent, but membership of the secret societies nonetheless reached well beyond narrow confines of the patrician elites. Like the masonic lodges before them, the secret societies were responsible not only for spreading awareness of the constitutional programme but also for actively planning the revolutions and maintaining control once they had occurred.

After the event, the royalists would mock the absurdity of the political debates that took place in the South in 1820, and a new generation of democrats would follow Mazzini in dismissing the secret societies as a Gothic anachronism. Yet the debates in 1820 articulated a clear understanding of the political issues posed by the attempts to build a post-feudal order in the South, while also revealing powerful new national and local identities. These debates had no parallel elsewhere in Italy. The debates in the National Parliament and in the provincial Deputations focused on the political and administrative models on which the post-feudal monarchy in the South had been constructed. They exposed how the French bureaucratic models exceeded the Kingdom's narrow economic resources and showed why the project of reorganizing the southern state could not be achieved without the cooperation of the elites. They also demonstrated how the crisis of the old agrarian order had complicated the transition to more bureaucratized forms of power, creating opportunities for new political monopolies to replace or replicate those formerly exercised by powerful feudatories. But the increase in centralized state power had also given rise to forms of 'arbitrary government' that were a frequent target of protest in 1820, as was the domination of local government by powerful factions. Although the remodelling of the southern monarchy had not resolved the political problems posed by the crisis of the old order in the South, it had nonetheless inspired forms of political awareness that in other parts of Italy would develop only later.

TAKEN BY SURPRISE

When the revolution came in July 1820, the senior diplomatic representatives in Naples were taken by surprise. The Austrian minister, Prince Jablonski, claimed that a revolution seemed more likely to occur on the moon than in Naples.[1] Prince Metternich, who had been lavishly entertained in Naples in the previous year during an official visit by the Austrian Emperor, Francis I, expressed surprise and contempt in equal measure:

> A people that is still half barbarous, ignorant, superstitious without limit, ardent and passionate like Africans, that knows neither how to read nor to write and whose final word is the stiletto, offers a fine example for the application of constitutional principles!

The outcome, he predicted, would be 'torrents of blood'.[2] The British ambassador William A'Court was astonished that a kingdom 'in the highest degree flourishing and happy, under the mildest of governments and by no means offended by the weight of taxation, [should] crumble before a handful of insurgents that half a battalion of good soldiers would have crushed in an instant'.[3]

[1] Cited in Acton (1956), 675. [2] Metternich, cited in Addeo (1989), 357–8.
[3] Acton (1956), 675. See Curato (1958), i. 250–1.

THE CARBONARI

Mr A'Court was misinformed in every particular. The government had been warned of the imminent danger of a revolution for some time. For at least two years it was feared that the *Carbonari* were trying to organize a revolution, which they were, and the revolt that began in Nola in July 1820 was one of the few nineteenth-century political revolutions that had been planned in some detail.

In 1816 the government had tried to ban the Carbonarist lodges, but the royalist general Vito Nunziante reported that there were more than 50,000 *Carbonari* in Calabria alone and advised against a frontal assault. The estimate was a wild exaggeration, but two former Muratist generals, Guglielmo Pepe and Pietro Colletta, gave exactly the same advice two years later when they were sent to reorganize the militias in Capitanata and Basilicata. They too warned against any frontal attack, recommending instead the tactics of infiltration employed by Murat's government.[4] De' Medici agreed and even the king reputedly exclaimed that 'Everyone else seems to be in the Carbonari, so I should join too!'[5]

The lead in planning the revolution was taken by two men, Rosario Macchiaroli, a surgeon who also worked in the office of the provincial Intendent in Salerno, and Pietro Serra. Former Jacobins, both were members of the Carbonarist lodge in Salerno. In 1817 they convened a secret meeting of Carbonarist leaders from different provinces in the suitably cloak-and-dagger venue of the ruins of Pompeii, where Macchiaroli and Serra proposed that they adopt a single national programme. According to Luigi Minichini, a Carbonarist priest who would later play a leading part in the early phases of the revolution, a Carbonarist Diet was then held in Salerno in January 1818 where Macchiaroli's programme was endorsed by the representatives of lodges from all over the Kingdom. The representatives agreed to take the Spanish constitution of 1812 as the basis for the Carbonarist constitution and to coordinate revolts that would occur simultaneously in Salerno, Naples, Foggia, and Bari.[6]

Beyond its general principles, familiarity with the Spanish constitution of 1812 was hazy and relied heavily on the ways in which its contents were conveyed by Serra and above all Macchiaroli. The general belief in any case was that it would be both democratic and federalist within the general frame of a constitutional monarchy, would guarantee universal suffrage, place the army and the magistracy under the control of elected assemblies, guarantee freedom of speech and religion, and emancipate women from their exclusion from civil life and education, although without giving them the vote.

[4] See esp. Minichini (Themelly, ed.) (1979), pp. ix–xv; Colletta (Cortese, 1957), iii. 124–40; Blanch, in Croce (ed.) (1945).

[5] Moscati (1971), 36.

[6] See Minichini (Themelly, ed.) (1979), pp. xiv, 60.

The constitution's principal aim, however, was to 'imprint a national identity on the people' and turn then into active citizens. For that reason, great emphasis was placed on creating autonomous and democratic local and provincial government. For his own province, Macchiaroli proposed the creation of a self-governing federal 'Republic of Eastern Lucania' that would include the existing provinces of Principato Citeriore and Basicilata. These self-governing provincial federations, or 'Supreme Magistracies', were to be based on directly elected municipal assemblies that would in turn collectively constitute the nation that would take the form of a constitutional monarchy. Macchiaroli also firmly insisted on the sanctity of private property.[7]

Alarmed by reports of seditious meetings, in 1818 the government sent General Nunziante to Salerno to make a show of force. Arrests were made, followed by some unsuccessful revolts. But none found wider support until 1820, when Minichini persuaded two young subalterns named Michele Morelli and Giuseppe Salvati, whose cavalry regiment was stationed in Nola, to lead what was in effect a mutiny.[8]

The protest in Nola triggered a sympathetic response in other regiments, reflecting deep discontent among the junior officers in particular. The reasons for this were partly de' Medici's economies, which had damaged promotion prospects especially for younger officers. But there was a deeper underswell of these grievances that originated from the ways in which Murat's army had been integrated with the royalist army after 1815.

Under the terms of the Treaty of Casalanza (which had been negotiated on Murat's behalf by Generals Colletta and Carrascosa), the king had sworn to maintain the commissions and ranks of all those serving in Murat's army. In practice, however, the Muratist officers were marginalized. As Luigi Blanch put it, 'Ferdinand's army had gown old on the streets of Palermo', while the officers appointed by Murat were generally young. For those who had not already risen to high rank like the Pepe brothers, Pietro Colletta, Luigi Blanch, and Michele Carrascosa, career prospects after 1815 were dismal. The officer corps was oversized and the royalists received preference, with the result that the junior officers who had looked for promotion and glory under Joachim Murat now found their careers blocked by the geriatric staff that the king had brought back from Palermo.[9]

The Carbonarist lodges found many recruits among these discontented officers who now looked to Murat's former generals for a lead. In 1814 and 1815 Michele Carrascosa, the brothers Guglielmo and Florestano Pepe, and Pietro Colletta had taken the lead in demanding that Murat grant a constitution. Once they had accepted commissions in the royal army in 1815, however, their enthusiasm for constitutions seems to have diminished notably. Nonetheless, they were the leaders to whom the junior officers now turned and they could not easily remain uninvolved.

[7] See Minichini (Themelly, ed.) (1979), pp. xxvi–xxix.

[8] Ibid.

[9] Saverese (1941), 72.

How exactly Murat's former generals planned to respond is not clear, but it seems likely that Generals Pietro Colletta and Guglielmo Pepe had begun preparing for a revolution they believed to be inevitable but not necessarily desirable. In the two areas where the two generals were given the task of reorganizing the provincial militias in 1818, respectively the Salernitano and Basilicata, and Irpinia and Capitanata, there were also high numbers of Carbonarist lodges. From what happened in 1820 it seems that Colletta and Pepe deliberately put men closely connected to the *Carbonari* in command of the militias, making them in effect an embryonic National Guard.[10] The epicentres of revolts that started the revolution in July 1820 were precisely the towns where Colletta and Pepe had been active two years earlier—Salerno, Nola, Avellino, and Foggia.[11]

It seems likely that Pepe and Colletta believed that the *Carbonari* could be recruited to control a revolt that was unavoidable. But not all the Muratist generals reacted in the same way. Michele Carrascosa and Luigi Blanch had both been enthusiastic constitutionalists before 1815, but saw no future in a revolution that had little internal coherence and no external support. That was also the view of the former Muratist ministers Giuseppe Zurlo and Francesco Ricciardi, who had agreed to serve in the Provisional Constitutional Government in July 1820 only with the greatest reluctance.[12]

THE REVOLUTIONS

When Lieutenant Morelli launched his appeal for a constitution at Nola on 2 July his protest was immediately taken up by the Carbonarist lodges in the area around Avellino. The military commander of Avellino, Colonel De Concilii, also joined the protestors, which threw the government in Naples into a state of indecision. After long debate General Carrascosa was ordered to march to Avellino to negotiate with the insurgents and bring the insurrection to an end.

Pietro Colletta later claimed that Morelli's advance 'was not a march but a triumph'. Morelli had been joined by 200 *Carbonari* raised by the priest Luigi Minichini, and when on 3 July he advanced towards Avellino the Royal Samnite Regiment stationed in the city joined the mutiny. By the time he entered Avellino, Morelli had more than a thousand armed men. Nonetheless, he acted throughout with scrupulous legality, placed himself under the orders of Colonel De Concilii, and issued certificates to the mayors of the towns through which his followers passed to guarantee their good behaviour and pay for any damage they caused.[13]

10 Themelly, in Minichini (ed.) (1979), p. xxxi.

11 On Colletta, see Scirocco, *DBI*, xxvii. 27–34; on Pepe see Minichini (Themelly, ed.) (1979), p. xiv.

12 Colletta (Cortese, 1957), iii. 147–51.

13 Colletta (1848), 6.

Amongst its many claims to originality, 'the revolution travelled by post, or rather by telegraph'. Indeed, in his enthusiasm to use the new system of semaphore telegraphy Colonel De Concilii unwittingly spread news of what had occurred in Avellino to the capital and the Apulian provinces.[14] As support for the revolt spread, General Carrascosa began to fear that his own troops were about to join the insurgents and began to play for time, 'sticking as resolutely to his pen as his sword stuck to its scabbard'.[15]

Generals Campane and Nunziante were sent from Naples to reinforce Carrascosa, but when they received news on 3 July that Foggia, the chief town in Capitanata, had declared for the constitution and that the revolution was spreading rapidly in neighbouring provinces they turned round and headed back to Naples. This was the cue for Salerno to declare for the constitution, and its lead was then followed by the principal towns in Terra di Lavoro, Basilicata, and Calabria.[16]

On 5 July noisy demonstrations were held in the capital, led by armed citizens supported by Carbonarist officers and NCOs from the Royal Regiment of Dragoons and the Royal Naples Battalion. The decisive turn came when Guglielmo Pepe, who had risen to the rank of Field Marshal, left Naples at night and joined the rebels in Avellino. The insurrection spread to other regiments and on 6 July the king announced that a constitution would be introduced within eight days. Then on the pretext of ill-health, he delegated full powers to his son, Francis, Duke of Calabria.[17]

In Naples, the decision to defer the constitution aroused fears of treachery. The *Carbonari* suspected the Court's motives, and many believed that General Pepe had joined the rebels to prevent rather than promote a revolution. As rumours spread, the city rang with 'the shouts of the Internal Security Guard that were matched by those of the students who, inflamed by love of their country and by the sacred rights of the citizen, marched through the streets and in loud voices demanded the Constitution of Spain'.[18]

On 6 July a provisional governing junta was set up that included Generals Carrascosa and Colletta, Giuseppe Zurlo, and Francesco Ricciardi. But these appointments only heightened fears that a counter-revolution was being prepared, and the situation risked getting out of control. On 7 July the Duke of Calabria (now the prince regent) proclaimed the concession of a constitution that would be 'the same as the one adopted by His Majesty the King of Spain in 1812 and sanctioned by His Catholic Majesty in March of this year, except for those modifications which the Nation's representatives when constitutionally convened may deem it appropriate to propose to adapt it to the particular circumstances of this Kingdom'.[19]

[14] Colletta (1848), 12. It is also claimed that Murat's execution in October 1815 was the first to be authorized by semaphore telegraphy.

[15] Cited in Johnson (1904), ii. 81–2; see 'Michele Carrascosa', in *DBI* (V. Sperber).

[16] Colletta (1848), 10–12. [17] Ibid. 13. [18] Ibid. 14.

[19] Cited in Corciulo (2000), 39–49.

On 9 July, a Sunday, thousands of armed *Carbonari* from the neighbouring towns and provinces poured into Naples. After marching through the streets, the *Carbonari* were addressed by the prince regent who, like the rest of his family, was dressed in the colours of the constitution to which he now solemnly swore allegiance. The procession was followed by a rally in the *Campo di Marte*, but in the days that followed General Pepe took measures to ensure that the Carbonarists dispersed and returned to their homes.[20]

SICILY

When the news of events on the mainland reached Palermo on 6 July the ruling classes were uncertain how to react. Some radicals and democrats favoured the Spanish constitution adopted in Naples, but the more conservative forces lined up in support of the Sicilian constitution of 1812 since this would have restored the island's autonomy and Palermo's privileged status as capital. On 11 July, however, Messina followed Naples in declaring for the Spanish constitution and was followed by Catania, Siracusa, Modica in eastern Sicily, and by Caltanisetta, Agrigento, and Trapani in the West.

Palermo was isolated, but popular agitation intensified and came to a crescendo during the feast of Santa Rosalia on 15 July. The Bourbon Lieutenant Governor, General Naselli, tried to restore order but two days later was forced to abandon the city. A supposedly popular government dominated by a group of conservative aristocrats headed by the Archbishop of Palermo, Cardinal Gravina, set up a new municipal junta which declared the constitution of 1812 and Sicily's independence from Naples. It also began to prepare military measures against the Sicilian towns that supported the provisional government in Naples and the Spanish constitution.[21]

In August the provisional government in Naples sent General Florestano Pepe with an army to Palermo, but Pepe refused to use force and early in October recommended that Sicily have a separate constitution and a separate parliament. But Palermo's separatist programme met with strong opposition in many other Sicilian towns and in September the government sent the leader of the revolt at Nola, Luigi Minichini, to rally support for the constitution and the National Parliament. He was hailed as 'the Liberator of the Fatherland', and in both Messina and Catania mass public rallies were held in his honour and to celebrate the opening of the National Parliament in Naples.

When news reached Messina on 10 October that Florestano Pepe had 'capitulated' to Palermo, there was a tremendous outcry. The leaders of the city government told Minichini that the terms agreed with Palermo would bring ruin to their city. The civil and religious authorities proclaimed their support for the

[20] Minichini (Themelly, ed.) (1979), 275.
[21] Renda (1968); Romeo (1950); Romano (1952).

constitution and the city's commitment to a single parliament. Five days later Minichini was greeted by a similar public gathering in Catania, where more than 3,000 citizens were estimated to have greeted him. Here too the authorities denounced Palermo and declared their loyalty to the constitution and the National Parliament.[22]

When the National Parliament in Naples finally met in October, it rejected the terms offered by Pepe and sent General Pietro Colletta to renegotiate. Like Pepe, Colletta tried to avoid a confrontation and agreed that Sicily should have a separate parliament. These terms were again rejected by the National Parliament in Naples, and after Colletta's withdrawal in January 1821 an open rift between Naples and Palermo seemed unavoidable.

THE REVOLUTION ON THE MAINLAND

On the mainland, the revolt spread quickly but proved more cohesive and less disorderly. News of the protests in Nola and Avelllino arrived in Foggia not by the new system of semaphore telegraphy but with the mail coach from Naples a day later on 3 July. When it was known that General Pepe had joined the 'military revolution', the commander of the Royal Regiment of Cavalry in Foggia, Colonel Giovanni Russo, declared his own support.[23] He set up a volunteer Public Security Guard to maintain order, which—according to an account drawn up after the Bourbon restoration in September 1821—was the signal for the leading Carbonarists of Foggia to take control.

As well as Colonel Russo, they included Colonel marchese de Rosa and the priest Don Francesco Paolo Iacuzio, described in the later Bourbon police document as 'President of the Tribe of Sectarians of the District of Foggia, together with his cousin Carmelo Jacuzio, the military surgeon Don Vincenzo del Musico, Don Paolo Vitale, Don Luigi Pavone and others'. They had all been 'especially energetic in preparing materials for the Revolution, such as proclamations, tricolour banners and the like'. They ordered the printer Pasquale Russo to prepare their proclamations. He in turn asked the Intendent for advice: 'but in the fog of events this official knew not what advice to give, except to close the print works and hide the type-face, but the Printer thought it better to yield to the Danger and do what he had been asked'.[24]

People were pouring into Foggia from the surrounding towns and settlements. On 4 July, Colonel Russo left to join the insurgents in Avellino, after first establishing an armed militia of *patrioti* under the command of Major Pisa. That evening

22 Minichini (Themelly, ed.) (1979), 318.

23 Pepe's defection was on 5 July, so the report was inaccurate.

24 ASF: Intendenza, Governo, Prefettura: Atti di Polizia (Part 1): f. 2495—Inchiesta sugli evvenimenti successi nella provincia nel luglio 1820.

the soldiers, the *gendarmeria* and the Carbonarists paraded fully armed in the Piazza della Porta Reale and unfurled the tricolour flag to the sound of *tamburri*. The priest Jacuzi made a short speech that was greeted with wild applause 'and everyone repeated his final words: *Viva la Costituzione! Viva il Re!*' This was followed by a Carbonarist rally, during which an appeal was made to all the 'members of the secret societies' in the province to take up arms and make their way to Foggia.

The next day, a delegation was sent to the Intendent who was found in his office 'much perplexed as to his fate'. He explained that as an officer of the crown he could not be associated with any party. Nonetheless, he was persuaded to don a tricolour sash and show himself to the people from the balcony, and he was then forced to go to the house of the priest Jacuzio 'where he was met by a picket of armed *Carbonari* and other leaders of the revolt'.

On 5 July groups of armed *Carbonari* arrived from San Severo and San Nicandro, accompanied by the provincial Sub-intendent, Don Gaetano Rodinò, who had 'plotted the downfall of the Intendent'. The still-confused Intendent had taken refuge in the house of Marchese Don Tommaso Antonio Celentano, but Rodinò sent his 'thugs' who 'abused and threatened' him and he was spared injury only by the determined intervention of his servants.

Rodinò had in the meantime taken over the Intendent's residence, from where the *Supreme Magistracy of the United Provinces of Daunia* was proclaimed, under the presidency of Don Francesco Paolo Casiti of Lucera, of Rodinò himself, and of Colonel Russo. They began printing the decrees and laws and organized the administrative duties formerly performed by the Intendent into four ministries. Once that was accomplished, the military detachments and the provincial militia set out for Naples.

Everything, it seems, had been carefully prepared in advance. The two key figures in the insurrection in Foggia, Russo and Rodinó, had been appointed by Colletta in 1818. The declaration of the Supreme Magistracy of Daunia echoed the Republic of Eastern Lucania proclaimed in Salerno by Machiaroli, and both were models of the autonomous federal self-government advocated by the *Carbonari*.

According to the Bourbon official who later drew up the report, however: 'the absolute legislative and executive powers that the Supreme Magistracy had independently abrogated for itself gave rise to general disgust'. A delegation was sent to Naples to protest the abuse of power by Rodinò's followers and the prince regent ordered Russo to return to Foggia with the power of interim Intendent to suppress the Magistracy and take control of the administration. But the Magistracy remained in existence and continued to have some influence. Russo subsequently returned to Naples where he was elected as Foggia's representative in the National Parliament and was replaced in Foggia by the Duke of Montejasi. The anonymous royalist report concluded: 'No other event of note occurred in the Province during the period of the Constitution . . . except for the expulsion of the Missionary Fathers of Deliceto.'[25]

[25] Ibid.

AN ORDERLY REVOLUTION

Pietro Colletta wrote later in exile that the concession of the constitution on 7 July meant that 'a revolution that began without a conspiracy and without a plan and had no single leader was completed in five days. In those five days not a single crime was committed: the lives, property and the rights of all citizens were religiously respected, and the established authorities all remained at their posts.'[26] Despite a degree of exaggeration, it was true that the political events of July and August were remarkably orderly on the mainland. This was partly because of the king's decision to grant the constitution almost immediately after the protest at Nola, for which there was little alternative once Guglielmo Pepe's decision to join the rebels faced the government with the threat of a general mutiny. But the solemn public oaths to uphold the constitution taken by the prince regent had conferred full legitimacy on the constitutional regime established almost without a revolution. Even an official like the Intendent of Capitanata who was 'perplexed as to his fate' now had no alternative but to support the constitutional municipalities that apparently had the full approval of the monarchy.

The government's decision to adopt the radical Spanish constitution of 1812 is less easy to explain. It was in some respects a remarkably democratic although extremely complex and confused document whose content was not known in detail in Naples.[27] However, the key provisions were for an elected National Parliament and elected local and provincial governments, in both cases giving votes to all males over the age of 21 whether or not they were literate.

From the monarchy's point of view the constitution had the imprimatur of a Bourbon monarch, the king of Spain, and was certainly preferable to the detested constitution that the English had established in Sicily in 1812, although this was the one the Sicilian separatists adopted. Although democratic in its elective processes, the Spanish constitution did not threaten the unity of the monarchy.

The king was in any case playing for time, since the terms of the secret Treaty of Friendship of June 1815 obliged Austria to intervene if the constitutional regime remained in force. Not only was the constitution not recognized by any of the major powers, but England and France even placed a fleet at the disposal of the king should he need it. Having publicly and freely sworn allegiance to the constitution, however, neither the king nor the prince regent could easily overthrow it without clear justification. What they needed, therefore, was a pretext.

This was also well understood by the constitution's supporters, who represented a broad cross section of the propertied and educated classes. The revolt had begun in the army, but had never taken the form of a military *pronunciamento* nor

[26] Colletta (1848), 14. [27] Venturi (1952), 203–22; Spini (1960).

had there ever been any suggestion that the army could or should take power. Nor indeed had the July protestors seen themselves as rebels. Their slogan was 'Viva Dio, Re, Costituzione—Long Live God, the King and the Constitution' and Luigi Minichini, who had organized the revolt and was the link between the soldiers and the *Carbonari*, emphasized the legality of their cause and its respect for the established order by carefully giving pride of place to the effigy of St Theobald, whom the *Carbonari* had adopted as their patron.[28]

Its supporters also knew that the government was working to rally those regiments that had not supported the constitution, and that once the monarchy was confident that the army would obey the least sign of public disorder or violence would be sufficient pretext for intervention. For that reason in both Foggia and Naples the constitution's supporters went to great lengths to avoid any form of public disorder. In Naples, the prince regent's announcement on 9 July that the members of the provisional constitutional government would include Zurlo, Ricciardi, and Tommasi—all of whom were now deeply unpopular—caused great outcry in the capital, and the houses of the new ministers were threatened by hostile crowds. However, the *Carbonari* had already established a General Assembly in opposition to the provisional government, which now intervened to restore order in the city.

The same occurred when the National Parliament was inaugurated on 1 October. The General Assembly of the *Carbonari* declared itself to be the true voice of the constitutional movement, but although it closely monitored the activities of the Parliament—above all through the extremely lively periodical press and broadsheets that proliferated following the abolition of censorship and the declaration of the freedom of the press—the General Assembly continued to assume responsibility for maintaining order in the capital.[29]

Luigi Blanch later claimed that as in 1815, the Carbonarist lodges enabled the local elites to control a broad cross section of provincial society. The claim is difficult to prove or disprove, since the clandestine nature of the lodges means that information about their membership is vague. In many places artisans and tradesmen were certainly well represented, but contemporary estimates also greatly exaggerated the size of membership. In Foggia, the group that initially took control of the town was quite small in number and the report drawn up later by the Bourbon police admitted that initially there had probably been no more than fifty *Carbonari* in the town. Except for the 'Great Masters of the Order' little was known about them, although by the end of the revolution their number was presumed to have risen to 'a thousand or fifteen hundred by common belief'. However, a list compiled by the police two years later, which included not only the *Carbonari* but all those suspected of 'sympathy with liberalism or the secret societies', included only seventy-four names, nearly all of whom were landowners

28 Minichini (Themelly, ed.) (1979), 177.

29 Colletta (Cortese, 1957), iii. 196–201 (especially Cortese's notes).

(only a few were described as 'small' or 'very small' landowners), lawyers, priests, or doctors.[30]

The often outlandish contemporary estimates notwithstanding, membership of the lodges seems to have been relatively small, which probably explains their ability to retain control over events. When peasants in the Val di Lucania in the Cilento tried to occupy contested *demani* in December, for example, the local Carbonarist lodges voluntarily closed and invited the militias to restore order. In other towns, collective and peaceful symbolic occupations were staged in the presence of the local authorities to protest the privatization of former *demani* or refusals to permit the exercise of use-rights generally believed to be illegal.[31]

THE NEW ORDER UNDER SCRUTINY

The elections for the National Parliament were based on male suffrage and were held in August in every town and village on the mainland and in Sicily. Despite the South's notorious reputation for political violence, the elections took place with little disorder.

The number of delegates was small in relation to the population, and the social and professional backgrounds of those elected to the National Parliament were certainly much narrower than those of the Carbonarist lodges. The seventy-two delegates elected for the mainland constituencies were all provincial notables.[32] The absence of the aristocracy reflected a clear reluctance to be associated openly with a constitutional government that few considered likely to last.[33]

The Parliament met on 1 October and first had to deal with the defection of Palermo, then review and revise the Spanish constitution in line with Neapolitan custom and conditions. It then called on the two senior representatives of Murat's government who were now members of the provisional government—Giuseppe Zurlo and Francesco Ricciardi—to assess the changes in public administration that had been introduced during the decade of French rule.

Ricciardi addressed the Parliament on 16 October and staunchly defended the soundness of the new administration of justice and the legal codes. He conceded that there were some minor problems, in particular that there were too many circuits without a judge and many judges were too old to be effective or else did not understand the new codes or procedures. He also admitted that there was a severe shortage of qualified individuals to act as Justices of the Peace, and that since the workload was enormous and the pay miserable all too often people unsuited to

30 ASF: f. 2495; *Elenco delle Vendite de' Carbonari in Foggia* (1821).

31 Lepre (1968), 143–65.

32 Scirocco (1986), 661. According to Fontanarosa (1910), 32, they included 1 cardinal, 9 priests, 24 landowners, 8 'professors of science', 11 magistrates, 2 government employees, 9 doctors, 5 soldiers, and 3 merchants. Only 6 were noblemen, although 5 of the 24 Sicilian delegates were nobles.

33 There was a much higher percentage of nobles among the Sicilian representatives.

the function took it on.[34] In response to complaints from the provinces, Ricciardi also admitted in a later session that the powers of the circuit judges were too wide, that their number needed to be increased, and that more provincial civil appeal courts were needed.[35]

On 23 October it was Zurlo's turn to report on the Ministry of the Interior. This was mainly an exercise in self-congratulation and an unbending defence of the reforms that he had been responsible for introducing during the years of French rule. He again insisted that these reforms were no more than the continuation of the innovations begun earlier by the Bourbon rulers, which would have resulted in a 'complete reform in line with the true interests of the Nation had the French Revolution not interrupted the direction in which we were already headed'.

However, the reforms were introduced by the French on exactly the same terms, with immediate and dramatic effects: 'As a result of this Reform the Kingdom has changed its appearance in every respect. Public opinion has taken shape, a common interest has been reborn, everyone seeks to promote the general good, and all take an interest in the activities and progress of the Government.'

Zurlo admitted that the burden of expenses and taxes faced by the local administrations should be reduced, and calculated that the total taxes raised from the local communities had increased. He admitted that the increase had been paid disproportionately by the poorest and that local government was still plagued by mismanagement and dishonesty. But otherwise he saw no case for changing an administrative system that had transformed a 'kingdom into a Nation'.[36]

He was prepared to concede that the French had made some errors, however. They had been mistaken in stripping the Kingdom's charitable institutions, hospitals, orphanages, and conservatories of their assets, although he firmly rejected the idea that poverty could be solved through alms: 'It is more useful to create means for employing the poor than to encourage inertia and the disinclination to work.' What was needed was better management of the charities' remaining assets, although he acknowledged that the register of the revenues of the *opere pie* that had been started in 1813 was still incomplete.[37]

He also noted approvingly the government's actions to reduce the number of beggars and vagabonds. He had first proposed creating *Depositi di Mendicità* in 1802, although they were not operational in Naples until 1817. In the six months that followed, 1,294 beggars had been arrested, and 4,046 more between May 1818 and August 1819. Over a thousand beggars were being held in the Royal Hospice for the Poor in Naples, and similar provision was being made in the

[34] ASN: Min Polizia Ia Ripartimento, f. 152 (1) Rapporto al Parliamento Nazionale sulla riforma della Magistratura, 16 October 1820.

[35] Ibid., f. 94: Rapporto e progetto di legge sul riordinamento del potere guidiziario November 1820.

[36] Ibid., from 1,472,819 ducats in 1815, to 1,760,789 ducats in 1818.

[37] The accounts of *opere pie* that had been examined by 1819 indicated that there were 7,224 of these institutions in the mainland provinces, whose collective annual revenues amounted to 1,081,435 ducats; see pp. 196, 202–5.

provinces where male foundlings were held until they reached the age of seven, when they were sent to the army, 'which relieves the provinces of the responsibility for providing the same number of conscripts, to the great benefit of agriculture'. Yet despite the intervention of the government, most provinces still had no homes for abandoned children, and the legislation forbidding burials in churches and requiring that cemeteries be built outside the inhabited areas had been ignored.

Zurlo also admitted that expenditure on public works had imposed heavy burdens on local finances, although he claimed that these were offset by the new roads in the Terra di Bari that would increase trade and prosperity. As he had done many times during the French period, Zurlo recited the government's achievements, with the curious conclusion that the theatre was the surest indicator of the capital's flourishing commercial and cultural condition:

> Theatres are both the indication of, and the means to achieve progress (*incivilmento*), and not as once used to be thought merely a source of innocent entertainment for the idle and the curious. In any great city theatres are a moral and a political necessity that distracts the multitude from more dangerous meetings, and in Naples they have for some time made the metropolis celebrated and have played an important role in attracting the valued presence of foreign visitors.[38]

PROVINCIAL PROTESTS

Zurlo's confidence in the system that he had played a major part in creating was not reflected in the petitions submitted to the Parliament from the Provincial Deputations. These set out the discontents of every section of provincial society, and taken together presented a remarkably full and critical commentary on the impact of the changes introduced during the years of French rule.

The most frequent protest, of course, was against the land tax, but hardly less frequent were protests at the disproportionate increases in provincial and local taxes. The petitions depicted the familiar story of the chaos of local administration, the inability of most communities to meet the costs of local administration, the devastating effect of brigandage and public disorder, the damage caused by the military and the militias, and—not least—the continuing rivalries over administrative status and privileges.

These concerns were clearly set out by the Deputation for the Terra d'Otranto. It acknowledged that the old system of municipal government elected by open parliaments needed reform, but bitterly attacked the system that had replaced it: 'civic freedom has been replaced by ministerial supervision which like the iron law of the Roman *patria potestà* will of necessity degenerate into tyranny; our towns

[38] ASN: Min Polizia Io Ripartimento, Busta 152 (2): G. Zurlo, 'Rapporto al Parlamento Nazionale sulla Situazione del Minstero degli Affari Interni', 23 October 1820.

are trapped between the voracious impertinence of their administrators and the oppression of those in power'.[39]

In response, the Parliament moved to reduce the land tax quotas and to transfer many of the costs charged to local administrations back to the Treasury. On 16 February 1821 it voted to establish elected provincial and local government, a measure immediately vetoed by the provisional government.

IDENTITIES

National and regional identity also assumed great importance in the debates in the National Parliament. A committee was set up to recommend a suitable name for the new constitutional Kingdom, on the grounds that:

> The lack of a name that accurately conveys what the different Peoples who inhabit the kingdom have in common is of little matter in a form of Government in which a single figure rules, but when a Nation regains its rights and wants everyone to feel part of it, then it is important to find a name that is both inclusive and distinctive.

The 'Kingdom of the Two Sicilies' and its more recent form, the 'United Kingdom of the Two Sicilies', were rejected out of hand as political and geographical misnomers. If the Kingdom of Sicily made sense, the Kingdom of Naples made none: was France the Kingdom of Paris? Since the Kingdom covered more than two-thirds of 'the entire land area of Italy' a more appropriate title would be 'The Kingdom of Italy'. But since such a name would cause 'diplomatic disputes', the committee instead proposed the 'Kingdom of Southern Italy'.

It also recommended that the names of the provinces be changed since most of them had originally been imposed by the Romans when they had conquered the South, were colonial in origin, and had 'assumed that everything revolved around and was subordinate to Naples'. To reflect their true identities the provinces should wherever possible return to their pre-Roman names: for example, Sannium instead of Molise; Daunia instead of Capitanata; Lucania in place of Basilicata. Where pre-Roman names did not exist, the names should be topographical.[40]

National identity also figured prominently in the report that Luigi Blanch made to the Parliament after he had been sent to investigate the political situation in the other Italian states in the summer of 1820. In his report Blanch repeatedly emphasized the cohesiveness of the South as a nation and the lack of unity in the other Italian states.

He claimed that the Papal States were in a state of turmoil and paralyzed by internal divisions because the restored papal government faced fierce opposition in all the territories that had formerly been part of Napoleon's Kingdom of

[39] Ibid., Min Polizia I Ripartimento, f. 71: Rapporto della Deputazione Provinciale di Terra d'Otranto, 10 November 1820.

[40] *Atti del Parlamento dell Due Sicilie 1820–1*, ii. 62–4.

Italy: the Marche, the Duchy of Urbino and the Legations. The Duchies of Modena and Parma and the Tuscan Grand Duchy he dismissed as mere Austrian satellites, and he claimed that the Kingdom of Lombardy–Venetia held together only because of the presence an Austrian army of 60,000 men. He acknowledged that Piedmont was 'the only Italian State that has an independent government and a well organized army', but it lacked internal unity because it was composed of Genovese, Sardinians, and Savoyards, all of whom wanted to be what they had formerly been: 'the Genoese want their Republic, the people of Savoy want to be French and the Sardinians want to be left with their old laws.'[41]

Luigi Blanch's insistence on the relative cultural homogeneity of the southern Kingdom revealed other important cultural legacies of the political upheavals in the South in the previous decades. A rediscovered sense of southern national identity could be traced back to the writers of the previous century, and in 1820 this was not seen to be incompatible either with the equally strong sense of Sicilian separateness or with the demands of the provinces for greater autonomy. Indeed, the strong federalist tone of the Carbonarist programme explicitly assumed that the two could be reconciled. Whether that was practical is beside the point since the downfall of the revolution was already being plotted from outside and for quite different reasons.

THE REVOLUTION BETRAYED

Even at the time, the nine months of constitutional government in Naples and Sicily between July 1820 and March 1821 had an aura of the unreal that was first broken as the threat of conflict between Naples and Palermo grew. For one group within the provisional government, this offered the opportunity for a pre-emptive strike against the constitution to avert the threat of another Austrian invasion that many considered inevitable.

The principal advocates of this strategy were Giuseppe Zurlo and Michele Carrascosa, who began sounding out the regiments traditionally loyal to the king. But they were opposed by Guglielmo Pepe and Giuseppe Poerio, both of whom feared that an attack on the Parliament would precipitate civil war.[42] That view was shared by Pasquale Borrelli, the Director of the Commission for Public Safety, who feared that a coup against the Parliament would give the ultra-royalists the pretext they were waiting for to incite another Sanfedist counter-revolution.[43] Others argued that the best hope was for a negotiated settlement brokered by Britain and France. This had been the true purpose of Luigi Blanch's diplomatic mission which took him to Rome, Turin, Switzerland, Baden, Württemberg, and

[41] Ibid., iii, *Rapporto a S.E. Il Ministro degli Affari Esteri*, 17–21.
[42] Savarese (1941), 91–2.
[43] On Borrelli see Minichini (Themelly, ed.) (1979), 292.

Paris to test the reactions of other Italian and European governments, but he had found no foreign support for the constitutional government in either Naples or Spain.[44]

In early October Metternich cut short these speculations when he summoned the representatives of the European powers to Troppau to discuss the situation in Naples and Spain. On 19 November the governments of Russia, Prussia, and Austria issued a joint Protocol authorizing Austria to intervene, if necessary by force, to restore order in the Kingdom of the Two Sicilies. Metternich then invited King Ferdinand of Naples to attend a conference to be held in January at Laybach (Lubjana) to seek a negotiated settlement.[45]

This was a trap to which the king of Naples was a willing accomplice. If the king did not attend, Austria had a pretext for invading the Kingdom to 'liberate' him: if he did, Austria could still claim legitimate cause for invading the Kingdom to restore the king to the title and powers conferred on him by the Congress of Vienna.

On 7 December the prince regent published a letter in Naples in which the king announced his decision to attend the conference in Laybach in order to make 'necessary and wise adjustments to the constitution'. This news caused the *Carbonari* to mobilize a massive demonstration in Naples and the *piazze* of the capital rang with cries of 'the Spanish Constitution or Death'. Zurlo and Carrascosa believed that the time had now come for a coup, which Carrascosa enthusiastically described as 'another 9 Thermidor to destroy the anarchists'.[46] On 8 December, Zurlo presented to Parliament the king's request to leave the Kingdom, and two days of heated debates followed. But plans for a coup were abandoned when Carrascosa reported that the army still could not be relied upon. The moderates Poerio and Borelli then proposed that the Parliament permit the king to travel to Laybach 'to defend the Constitution' and after a fierce debate this fictional hope was carried and Ferdinand left for Trieste on a British warship.[47]

The trap was now sprung. On 4 February, Marshal Frimont crossed the Po at the head of an Austrian army corps whose mission was to restore order in the Kingdom of the Two Sicilies. On 13 February the Neapolitan Parliament met and amid great enthusiasm declared war against Austria to free the king who was a 'prisoner of the Sovereigns'.

THE LAST CALL

As the Austrian army drew closer, the Parliament published a last defiant statement on 2 March. It was addressed simply to 'The People of the Two Sicilies' and set out what had been accomplished since October.

44 See the entry on Luigi Blanch in *DBI* (x. 771–6) by Cortese.

45 Minichini (Themelly, ed.) (1979), p. li.

46 Ibid.

47 Savarese (1941), 93–6.

The Parliament had worked 'to make our systems more free, to make local administration less arbitrary and to establish a National Guard capable of guaranteeing our Independence. We have tried to relieve you of the heavy fiscal burdens you are asked to bear, to promote trade, agriculture and industry and to find ways of providing public education that has a practical not an illusory foundation in line with the requirements of true wisdom and true philosophy.'

The Parliament had approved the Spanish constitution, removing only the 'dangerous provision' that in Spain permitted female succession to the throne. The constitution had established trial by jury, religious toleration, and freedom of the press. Every *comune* was to have an elected local magistrate. Provincial administration was reorganized: the Intendents' Councils were abolished and their powers transferred to elected Provincial Deputations, while every *comune* was run by an elected government. Delegates were to receive stipends to avoid the Provincial Deputation being dominated by 'the wealthiest citizens of the province and those who live in the provincial capitals'.

The Parliament had relieved municipal administrations of 'many expenses that were not related to local administration and which were calculated to amount to 800,000 ducats a year'. These expenses were the consequence of 'arbitrary ministerial power' that had caused the local communities to carry the burden of the cost of maintaining local circuit judges, the upkeep of prisons, prisoners, and warders, the upkeep of troops stationed in each province, and of the Austrian army down to 1817, as well as stipends for the parish priest and his assistant. The Treasury would now pay all of these costs, while additional obligations to supply and billet the army were abolished.

The Parliament had also renewed the struggle against feudalism, which it claimed was dead only in theory: 'It would take an army of administrators, as well as a complete moral and political revolution of the people, to destroy the Hydra of the barons.' The Parliament had introduced new laws to abolish entails that had survived despite previous legislation. It had abolished feudalism in Sicily, as well as the tithes collected by the Church, and had also banned 'gambling which threatens to ruin our citizens and the innocent and inexpert manners of our youth'.[48]

The declaration on 2 March was supposed to rally support to the rapidly disintegrating revolution. The appeals that 'the courageous officers of the companies of the National Militias disbanded after the Restoration' reform their battalions to defend the Nation from the advancing foreign invader were hardly realistic, however, and the National Guard to which it referred had not yet been created. Nor did the proposals to reduce the land tax, the financial burdens on local communities, and the tithes paid to the Church take any account of the desperate state of public finances. By September 1820, Luigi de' Medici's carefully balanced budget had been hopelessly compromised and every government department faced huge

[48] ASN: Min. Polizia I° Ripartimento: Il Parlamento Nazionale ai Popoli del Regno delle Due Sicilie, a Napoli, 2 March 1821.

deficits. By March of the following year the situation was even worse, not least because the nine months of the constitutional government had been a prolonged tax holiday.

Many of the measures adopted by the Parliament had made mortal enemies. The Cardinal Archbishop of Naples led the attack on religious toleration and freedom of the press, both of which were guaranteed by the constitution. If these freedoms were to come about, the Cardinal warned, 'There will be nothing to restrain the insolent Libertine. Married women will no longer be respected, honest virgins will no longer blush with shame, the innocent child will lose all sense of modesty and everything will be in disarray and combustion. A pestilent plague of infamous books worthy of the city of Pentapolis will contaminate the public squares and private houses of our beloved Naples and infect every mind and every heart throughout the Kingdom.'[49]

In fact, virtually all of the Parliament's liberal measures had been vetoed by the provisional government. Giuseppe Zurlo made no secret of his contempt for constitutions and parliaments which, like de' Medici and Tommasi, he considered to be a throwback to the corporate bodies of the *ancien régime* that had blocked the reform initiatives of an enlightened prince. Parliaments, he believed, served only to breed 'parties', faction, self-interest, and disunity. The monarchy was the only guarantee of the unity of the nation, and for that reason Zurlo remained opposed to any decentralization of the French administrative reforms and opposed every attempt to introduce elected provincial and municipal assemblies. Francesco Ricciardi was even more contemptuous of the constitution, which he considered to be 'madness'.[50]

THE THIRD RESTORATION

When it came to repulsing the invasion, the Parliament's rallying cries were of little avail and the revolution that had never happened now simply disintegrated. Initially there had been great patriotic enthusiasm for the war, and in Naples the theatres staged patriotic plays, while patriotic hymns and songs were heard throughout the city. Even the son of the prince regent volunteered to enlist to defend the constitution and for days the capital was full of popular patriotic demonstrations and parades.

These demonstrations did not translate into action, however. Some of the *Carbonari* advocated a national uprising against the foreign invader, but even the fearless Luigi Minichini acknowledged that such a rebellion was impractical. The army was paralysed by divisions between supporters of the constitution and the monarchy, between moderates and radicals, and the influence of the *Carbonari* amongst many of the officers and NCOs was causing the chains of command to break down everywhere.

49 Addeo (1989), 174. 50 Savarese (1941), 91–2.

Divisions amongst the military commanders made planned response to the Austrian advance impossible. Guglielmo Pepe, the senior commander, favoured an offensive, but it was widely suspected that his real aim was simply to draw the radical elements of the *Carbonari* away from Naples to reduce the risk of civil war. Meanwhile Carrascosa, supported by Blanch, favoured a defensive strategy, and refused to move his troops, leaving Pepe without reserves or supplies. The *Carbonari* refused to accept orders and many regiments suddenly rediscovered their loyalty to the crown. Pepe, Colletta, and Carrascosa all reported massive desertions, indiscipline, and mutinies and Luigi Blanch described the situation as one of 'mass desertion'.[51]

On 7 March, without the government's authorization or knowledge, Pepe attacked the Austrians near Rieti and his army fell apart. The Austrians crossed the frontier in the Abruzzi Mountains and when the king called on the Neapolitan army to lay down its arms and welcome the Austrian ally the garrison at Capua raised the royal standard and on 23 March yet another Austrian army entered Naples.

This was King Ferdinand's third restoration, all three achieved thanks to foreign military assistance: in 1799, from the British navy with Russian and Turkish ground forces; in 1815 and 1821 from the Austrians, with naval assistance from Great Britain. The Austrian army would again stay on at the Kingdom's expense, this time until 1827.

If the revolution of 1820 had been the epilogue to the decade of French rule and innovation, the restoration of 1821 was the opportunity for the political purges and vendettas that had been avoided in 1815. This time there was no pretence of compromise and the king, who remained in Florence, made his views clear: 'The only expedient is a severe military government for at least a year that will use terror and overwhelming force, and I would happily order this and forgo returning to my Kingdom where my life is constantly in danger.'[52]

The aged Marchese Circelli headed a provisional government and in May Prince Canosa resumed the Police Ministry. Only those of less exalted social standing like Lieutenants Morelli and Salvati paid with their lives. Guglielmo Pepe and Luigi Minichini both wisely sailed for Barcelona before the Austrians reached Naples. Pietro Colletta, Giuseppe Poerio, Luigi Blanch, and Michele Carrascosa were amongst those exiled, and the last was condemned to death *in absentia* in 1823. They continued their feuds in exile. Carrascosa and Pepe fought a duel in London in 1823, but the weapons were more often pens rather than sabres, and it was primarily in their memoirs, histories, and biographies that the survivors of 1820–1 refought the battles of the French decade and revolutions.

For accepting office under the constitution (even though this had had the full endorsement of the crown) de' Medici, Ricciardi, and Tommasi were also exiled, while systematic purges of all those who had supported the constitutional

[51] Minichini (Themelly, ed.) (1979), p. lvii.

[52] Cingari (1966), 22.

government or had been members of the Carbonarist lodges now began. All public employees and teachers came under scrutiny, and most of the students at the University in Naples were rusticated. An extensive purge of the magistracy resulted in the dismissal of judges and law officers of every grade, both in the capital and in the provinces. All those suspected of supporting the revolution were banned from practising their professions and kept under police surveillance, which put many more lawyers out of work. The clergy came under no less close scrutiny, and when the bishops were ordered to investigate the conduct of those in their diocese they seized the invitation with relish. The parish churches throughout the Kingdom were reorganized along lines suggested by the Bishop of Pozzuoli, and in general the power of the bishops was greatly increased. A number of bishops also appealed to the government to recall the Jesuits.[53]

To the applause of the clergy, censorship was reintroduced. Canosa's police seized and destroyed the papers of the National Parliament, and a royal decree of 7 May made the possession of 'emblems, papers, books or other devices belonging to the Secret Societies' an offence punishable by exile for ten years or more. The same decree banned all 'the poisonous texts that had dealt with matters that are contrary to religion, morality and the principles of governance'. A decree of 2 June 1821 obliged printers to submit copies of all printed material to the Junta of Examination, which had been established to compile an index of all books to be destroyed. Every library was to supply the police with a copy of its catalogues. A decree of 4 December 1821 required that all printed matter be submitted to the police for authorization, including theatre tickets and invitations to private gatherings. Any printed document of more than ten pages was to be submitted to the Junta for Public Education, which was empowered to raid private houses, hand over any prohibited books to be burned by the public hangman, and imprison anyone found in possession of such material.[54]

The Minister of Police acknowledged with gratitude that the reforms of the French rulers had made it possible for the government to enforce censorship more effectively than in the previous century, and he warned against the misguided sense of 'indulgence' that had caused Italy's recent disasters:

> It was because of that indulgence that the fanaticism of innovation was spread by books. These were the source of the poison that was present in the guise of reform, regeneration, progress and freedom. It was in this way that the spirit of revolution brought desolation to our people, undid morality and destroyed religion. Everyone knows that there never has been, nor ever will be, any open attempt to subvert a legitimate government by force, unless this has been prepared carefully over time... an aim that has always been, and always will be, the purpose of books and printed writings, as to which there can be no shadow of a doubt since we all have before us the tearful memories of what has befallen us in the recent past.[55]

[53] Rocchina (De Leo, 1995), 161–5. [54] Addeo (1984), 185.

[55] ASN: Ministero di Polizia, Min. Interno I° Ripartimemto, Diversi 1824–5: f. 2912. Revisione dei libri, opuscoli, fogli volanti e periodici di attribuzione alla polizia.

The most severe purges were reserved for the army, however. All those who had supported the constitution or been members of the *Carbonari* were dismissed or imprisoned. Every officer was required to give a full account of his political activities since 1793, and nearly all of those appointed during the French occupation were dismissed. Fourteen infantry and five cavalry regiments were disbanded and replaced by three new infantry regiments composed entirely of foreigners. Conscription was abolished, to general acclaim, and three regiments of Swiss volunteers were recruited to act as the Royal Guard and to garrison the city of Naples.[56]

Despite the orderliness of the revolution, its collapse threw every branch of central and provincial administration into confusion. While the Austrian troops effectively repressed brigandage and disorder on the mainland, Sicily was in open revolt. To defuse one of the most persistent demands of the revolution, Metternich had forced the king at Laybach to introduce a dual consultative body known as the *Consulta*—one for the mainland and one for Sicily. But once Ferdinand was back in control of the Kingdom these commitments were ignored and the *Consulta* existed only on paper.

The restored government could not ignore the disastrous state of the Kingdom's finances, however. De' Medici's careful work of financial stabilization had been shattered, and after the Austrian invasion the financial situation became disastrous. To meet its current account deficits and to repay the costs of the Austrian occupation and of maintaining the Austrian army that remained in the Kingdom, Vienna helped the Neapolitan government raise loans from the Rothschild Bank, which in turn acquired a large share of the Kingdom's public debt. But that was only a stop-gap. No one in the government set up by Ferdinand I in 1821 had the expertise or ability to address the financial situation that deepened as the market value of the government's paper collapsed. In response to appeals from Vienna, in December 1822 Luigi de' Medici was recalled from exile.[57]

Until his death in 1830, de' Medici remained in control of the Kingdom's finances and its commercial policies. Ferdinand I died in 1825 after a reign that with interruptions had lasted fifty-eight years. He was succeeded by his son, the former Duke of Calabria who took the title of Francis I. Despite his flirtation with the constitution in 1820, Francis I continued the repressive and reactionary policies of the last years of his father's reign until his death in 1830. The Austrian army withdrew in 1827, but an attempted uprising in the Cilento resulted in new measures of repression. Only with the accession of Ferdinand II in 1830 did the political climate of the Kingdom begin to change, and for the first time some of the exiles of 1821 were permitted to return. But hopes that the new king would take up the cause of constitutional government and reform were to be disappointed.

[56] Pieri (1962), 58–9. [57] Ostuni (1992), 329–32; Cingari (1966), 144.

Conclusion: States of Insecurity

Italy in 1861, from G. Holmes (ed.), *The Oxford Illustrated History of Italy* (Oxford: Oxford University Press, 1997).

The revolutions of 1820 and 1821 have generally been seen as part of the sequence of southern 'failures' that confirmed the impossibility of achieving change in the South.[1] But that is to wrench these events out of context and to ascribe to them goals they did not have. Indeed, it is not really clear whether 'revolution' is the appropriate term for what happened in 1820–1. The main protagonists went out of their way to insist on the legitimacy of their protests and to maintain order, while the monarchy's speedy concession of the constitution made everything that followed legitimate except for the king's violation of the sacred oath to uphold the constitution. Nor did internal events have anything to do with the outcomes because the fate of the short-lived constitutional experiment was a foregone conclusion and the Austrian invasion in March 1821 simply another reminder of the degree to which Italian politics in the early nineteenth century were shaped by external forces.

The revolutions of 1820–1 were also the epilogue to the years of French rule, and if the political protests heard as much in the provinces as in the capitals were directed against the terms of the Restoration of 1815 their main targets were the innovations dating from the Napoleonic decade. In Sicily, where those changes derived from the more recent Act of Union of 1816, the debates were complicated by the emergence of a powerful separatist movement that brought Palermo into conflict not only with Naples, but also with many of the other Sicilian towns and cities. In Sicily this resulted in a great deal of violence, but on the mainland the debates took place in a surprisingly orderly environment and demonstrated how far removed the historical experience of the South was from the later imagery of the 'passive revolution'.

The nine months of constitutional government were the first moments of freedom of speech in the South since the Republic of 1799, and they offered the opportunity for a searching critique of the legacies of Napoleonic rule that had been preserved and extended after the Restoration. The debates and the different political projects proposed revealed how the upheavals of the previous decades had given rise to forms of political awareness that as yet had no parallels elsewhere in Italy. By contrast, the insurrections that took place a year later in Piedmont found little support outside the army, while the conspiracy discovered by the Austrians in Milan in 1821 was also a narrow patrician affair. In the South, the protests had a much wider reach and they brought more sharply into focus the centralizing logic that had driven the attempts to refashion the southern state from the absolutist reforms of the *ancien régime* monarchy to the Republic of 1799, the French occupation between 1806 and 1815, and finally the legitimist Restoration of 1815.

The debates that took place on the mainland and in Sicily in 1820 exposed the contradictions that surrounded the attempts to create a bureaucratic state in the South. In part, the obstacles were political, and the revolutions revealed how

[1] See Croce (1967), 220.

the attempts to shift the balance of power away from the peripheries toward the centre had given rise to an awareness of local and regional identities that was new and was accompanied by political demands incompatible with autocracy. The prevailing demands in 1820 were not for a return to the *ancien régime*, and feudalism was repeatedly identified with the monopolistic exercise of power at a local level. Indeed, the new political institutions were criticized above all for not going far enough in destroying the vestiges of feudalism, while broader political participation at a local level was repeatedly invoked as the best means to ensure that local government did not fall into the hands of powerful individuals or factions.[2]

The revolutions also underscored the material obstacles to the establishment of an effective bureaucratic state in the South, and by 1820 it was evident that the costs of sustaining even the rudimentary new forms of bureaucratic administration exceeded the Kingdom's slender human and material resources. But this was not unusual; indeed it was a problem that faced much wealthier states too, and even in Italy's most prosperous regions the new administrative bureaucracies imposed fiscal burdens that were not easily sustained. In Lombardy, for example, heavy increases in local taxation were one of the main causes of popular unrest and protest in the closing years of French rule. The high cost of maintaining many of the administrative innovations made during the years of French rule was as important as ideological prejudice in encouraging the Restoration rulers throughout Italy to reduce the levels of bureaucratic administration and the numbers of administrators. But because they seriously reduced opportunities for public employment, those economies would prove a major cause of political disaffection among the career hungry and underemployed Italian professional and middle classes.[3]

The situation in the South was different, but again only by degree. The political debates of 1820 illustrated how the innovations of the previous decades had left southern Italy caught uneasily between an older agrarian order that had been seriously destabilized and newer forms of bureaucratic power that were in large part still to be created. The crisis of the *ancien régime* monarchy and the administrative reforms of the French decade had embarked the South on a path of political development that was both precocious and precarious. In most of the states of northern and central Italy, government bureaucracies were developing slowly and in partnership with relatively resilient forms of agrarian paternalism. In the South, by contrast, the parallel but closely interconnected crisis of the *ancien régime* monarchy and the agrarian order had made the transition to a bureaucratic organization of the state much more problematic and dangerous. The crisis of the old agrarian order had also given rise to social conflicts not easily contained, making the balance between the centralizing efforts of the state and the centrifugal reactions of the provinces even more uncertain.

[2] Cf. Giarrizzo (1983), 21–33.

[3] See Lyttelton (ed. Davis, 1979) 104–34. For Lombardy see Antonelli (1997), 193–219, and Meriggi (1983, 1987). For Tuscany, see Kröll (2005).

As had been clearly revealed in the protests of 1820, the weakness of the new bureaucracies left them vulnerable at a local level to infiltration and domination by powerful individuals or factions. That danger had been foreseen by the eighteenth-century reformers, and was one of the reasons they had seen the enlightened absolutist ruler as the ideal instrument of reform. By 1820 confidence in the ruler had been weakened: hence the insistence that constitutional government was the solution. Now the answer seemed to lie in a federalist reorganization of the state that would guarantee greater regional autonomy. This was an alternative way of addressing the problems posed by the prevalence of factionalism and the monopolistic exercise of power at a local level, which were features of the post-feudal order in the South, but not necessarily an effective alternative.[4]

The transition from the *ancien régime* to the post-feudal order in the South had proved particularly difficult and painful, but it must be emphasized that the most fundamental problems facing southern society were the consequence of change and not its absence. Similar challenges faced all European states and societies in these years, and if the impact of change in the South was especially traumatic the reason was that an agrarian order that in much of the rest of Italy would remain intact until after Italy's Unification had been deeply compromised almost a century earlier. It was not until the 1850s, for example, that the conservative Lombard Catholic Stefano Jacini adopted a distinction first made in France to bemoan the dangers posed for the survival of the face-to-face paternalist rural order—the 'real Italy'—that he believed still survived in much of northern Italy by the expansion of an impersonal and distant bureaucratic state—the 'legal Italy'.[5] In parts of the Veneto the state would remain remote and almost unknown until well into the twentieth century.[6]

In the South, the state had sought to acquire greater power in the localities from much earlier, but with ambiguous and contradictory results. These were evident in 1820–1, and became even more so in the decades that followed. After the revolutions the Bourbon rulers set their faces firmly against any form of political dialogue, and the Kingdom of the Two Sicilies followed the reactionary models set by the other Italian rulers. For reasons of economy as well as ideology, the bureaucratic project was put on hold and the provincial voices that had played an increasingly important political role since the end of the eighteenth century were again silenced. The project of bureaucratic centralization was maintained, but became increasingly dependent on narrow groups of professional administrators and nobles whose loyalty to the dynasty was beyond reproach.

[4] On factionalism, see especially Pezzino (1992) and Fiume (1984) and in Davis and Ginsborg (eds.) (1991), 70–91.

[5] Jacini (1857). In an important recent study of local government in Sicily after Unification Lucy Riall argues that the South had experienced a different process of state formation (Riall (1997), 228). But although problematic the process of state formation in the South was essentially the same as in other parts of Italy, the difference being that the changes came earlier. See also Sabetti (1984), 3–18.

[6] See, e.g., Lanaro (1984) and Fumian (1990).

As in the other Italian states, the reactionary turn in the South after 1821 narrowed the monarchy's political base, and left the Church and the army to take up the slack. Even the rulers' closest advisers were well aware of the dangers this posed, and in the climate of growing apprehension before the revolutions of 1848 the king's principal adviser, the marchese Ceva Grimaldi, warned Ferdinand II that:

> Luigi de' Medici described our government very well when he called it a monarchy 'à la Napoléon'.... Without any effective support from the Aristocracy or the Church, its only real foundation is in the Army and the Public Officials. But public employees are generally happy to watch revolutions take place from the window, so long as someone goes on paying their wages.[7]

That description could have been applied to every other Italian state in the same period, but the reassertion of reactionary absolutism after 1821 had triggered a particularly vicious cycle in the South. When loyalty to the regime became the sole criterion for public service, corruption grew as did new forms of monopolistic controls over public administration. In the absence of alternative forms of economic activity, the resources of local government became the focus for fierce struggles between competing local factions.[8] These tendencies had all been present earlier but they now became more intense, as did social tensions. In part these were the result of the depressed state of the economy, which showed no sign of recovery until the 1830s. But they were also rooted more specifically in popular resentment at the ways in which the abolition of feudalism, the division of the common lands, and the disappearance of customary use-rights had deprived the rural communities of their scarce but only assets.

Similar tensions were evident in other parts of Italy in the same period. Everywhere the steady advance of new forms of farming, together with new measures designed to reduce promiscuous grazing and collective land use, threatened the economies of the rural poor.[9] The situation in the South was therefore only a variant, albeit often a more extreme one, on patterns of development at work on a wider scale on the Italian peninsula and in other parts of Europe. As elsewhere, the Bourbon monarchy's attempts to mediate between the conflicting forces of the market and the threats these posed to the security of rural communities proved ineffective. As in the previous century, the government's interventions were more likely to inflame than resolve local conflicts, in ways that did little for the poor but angered the landowners. There was little space for compromise, and these disputes served mainly to expose the government's inability to impose its will against powerful local interests.[10]

[7] ASN: Archivio Borbone f. 607, Parte II inc 823: C. Ceva Grimaldi a Ferdinando II, 10 August 1843.

[8] Pezzino (1992), 9–23; Davis (1981), 296–329. On corruption and the state in Latin America see also Macfarlane, in Little and Posada-Carbó (eds.) (1996), 40–63.

[9] See Grossi (1981), 121–71.

[10] See especially Cassese, in Cestaro and Laveglia (eds.) (1970), 191–266.

As in the rest of Italy, the divisions of the former feudal estates and the sales of Church and crown lands in the South had resulted in a redistribution of land primarily among those who already owned property. Many of the old feudal families suffered heavy losses, in some cases because of the loss of significant incomes from feudal levies, but above all because of the abolition of feudal entails and primogeniture that resulted in the rapid dispersion of noble patrimonies. This was the main cause of the breakup of many older noble estates, although in some parts of the Kingdom this was offset by the formation of vast new estates known as *latifundia*.[11]

Latifundia had existed in southern Italy—and in other parts of Italy as well—from much earlier. As the name indicates, the institution was Roman in origin although it had been an important instrument of Spanish colonial settlement in the New World and in southern Italy. However, latifundist estates also existed in central Italy—notably in Lazio and the arid plain around Rome—and in different form in the Veneto as well.[12] But the *latifondo* was particularly well suited to the natural conditions that prevailed in many parts of central and southern Italy, where the vast size of these estates made possible economies of scale that helped to offset the limits posed by poor soils, inadequate rainfall, and slight and fragile natural resources.

The land sales of the French period and the difficulties facing many of the old feudal families provided the opportunities for the creation of new latifundist properties in the early nineteenth century, and it was not by chance these developed especially in areas where the purchase of the government's new administrative apparatus was most weak. On the mainland, they were especially prominent in Calabria, where a number of new families—the Barracco, the Campagna, and the Quintieri—pushed their way into the agrarian hierarchy, buying land from the crown, but above all by acquiring the debts of the great feudatories.[13]

The new estates were not simply a continuation of earlier feudalism, and their economic management was often geared to exploiting new commercial opportunities while at the same time offering protection against the unpredictable swings of the market—the single greatest problem facing producers in marginal economies subject to the unpredictable yet potentially devastating swings in external demand. Yet the underlying logic of these enterprises was monopolistic: over huge areas the essential means of production—land, labour, livestock, water, pasture, and credit—came under the monopolist control of the *latifondo* and its masters, giving these estates the character of a state within a state. The power of the landowners was absolute and when challenged was imposed by force. But that was rarely necessary because the system depended less on coercion than on the monopolies exercised by the great landowners and their agents who controlled not only the land but above

[11] Montroni (1996), pp. vii–ix, 31–4.

[12] On the Veneto, see Lanaro (1984) and Fumian (1984).

[13] Montroni (1996), 37–4; Petrusewicz (1996), 33–59. On the Quintieri see Rienzo (2004), 20–5.

all the resources needed to work the land, and especially credit. It was this that made the economic, social, and cultural lives of the communities who lived and worked on the great estates dependent in every respect on the owners of the estates.[14]

Such relations of dependence were not unusual in nineteenth-century Italy and indeed throughout Europe debt was most commonly what tied the post-feudal rural poor to the land and the interests of the landowners.[15] But there were clear signs that in the South the landowners were adopting new measures to reimpose hierarchies of rural dependence that had been threatened by the crisis of the old agrarian order.

Before 1860 new *latifundia* were located primarily in those regions of the mainland where brigandage had previously proved most difficult to eradicate. But as early as the 1830s Bourbon officials noted similar developments in western Sicily. Here, too, the abolition of feudalism had provided powerful Sicilian landowners with opportunities to engross and privatize lands that had previously been subject to collective use. From the reports of Bourbon officials, it is also possible to identify what would only later come to be known as *mafia*, a system of power relations in which estate bailiffs and their armed retainers acted as powerful intermediaries who oversaw the management of the estates and their labour force on behalf of generally absentee landowners. They were responsible for enforcing monopolies over scant resources—water and pasture in particular—but they also engaged in a range of illicit commercial activities, especially the trade in rustled livestock and meat, while maintaining order on the estates and enforcing local codes of discipline and deference.[16]

Neither *mafia* nor the reconstruction of the latifundist estates on the mainland were legacies from the feudal past. Both are better understood as responses to the challenges posed by change and the incursion of unpredictable and uncertain market forces in the fragile agrarian economies of the South. One consequence was to accentuate the differences within the South. In Sicily the slowly expanding commercial economies of Messina and Catania in eastern Sicily and even of the citrus growing Conca d'Oro near Palermo contrasted with the *mafia*-dominated estates of the arid interior. On the mainland, the relatively closed Calabrian *latifundia* contrasted with the more open commercial world of Bari and the Adriatic ports.[17]

[14] The reporter for the 1882 parliamentary inquiry on the state of agriculture who visited the Quintieri estates in Calabria commented, 'The fable of Midas who turned to gold everything he touched, that telling allusion to the torments of avarice and the power of saving, is still a reality here in distant Calabria due to the absence of any awareness of the needs and costs of more refined forms of civilization.' Virtually every landowner in the province, he noted, was indebted to the Quintieri family; see *Atti della Giunta per l'Inchiesta Agrària* (1882) vol. ix, p. xvi, cited in Davis (1979), 75. For similar but also contrasting descriptions of the 19th-century *latifondo*, cf. Lupo (1990), and Petrusewicz (1996).

[15] See, e.g., Malatesta (1988), 111–25.

[16] See the report by the Bourbon Procurator General, Pietro Cala-Ulloa, in 1838, in Pontieri (1965), 239–77, cited in Fiume (1984) and Davis (1988), 84–7.

[17] Benigno (1982, 2001); Cancila (1991); D'Angelo (1988); Salvemini (1995); Massafra (1981, 1995).

In fact, there were many points of contact between these two apparently contrasting worlds. Since the most advanced sectors of southern agriculture were those most heavily engaged in export activities, they were also the most heavily exposed to the unpredictable swings of international markets. As a result wise investors sought safer and more protected opportunities, and the continuing preferences for investment in land, in loans secured by mortgages on land, or in contracts for public works were clear indications of the high risks involved in other commercial activities.[18]

The poverty of internal markets made the most advanced sectors of the southern economies dependent on export markets whose uncertainty was the main obstacle to economic growth. These problems faced all the Italian economies, which were reduced to marginal and subordinate roles in a new world of unprecedentedly competitive markets. But the impact on the fragile economies of the South was especially disruptive and gave rise to conditions of chronic uncertainty and insecurity.

Insecurity would become an increasingly central feature of the lives of many southerners, and it was also reflected in the Kingdom's dynastic and diplomatic vulnerability. The central aim of Bourbon dynastic strategies in the eighteenth century had been to give substance to the Kingdom's theoretic autonomy. Murat shared similar illusions, but in the crisis that followed the revolution in France those dreams of autonomy had been lost for ever. The Kingdom first became a satellite of its British ally and then a colony partitioned between Britain and France.

After 1815, the Bourbon monarchy's claims to autonomy were no more than a mask while the events of 1820 would brutally reveal its internal and external weaknesses. The situation that faced the Bourbon rulers after their third Restoration by a foreign army in the space of twenty-two years was desperate, and the obligation to meet both the military costs of the Restoration and the maintenance of an Austrian army of invasion for an indeterminate period threatened financial collapse. To avert this, the Rothschild Bank in 1821 at the request of the Austrian government agreed to open its first Italian agency in Naples, and with de' Medici's assistance proceeded to take over the Neapolitan debt, which was floated on the European security markets.[19]

Financial disaster was averted, and de' Medici knew that opening the public debt to foreign investors gave the monarchy a degree of security. But this also meant that interest payments on the debt drew capital away from the Kingdom, while the concession of management of the Kingdom's debt to a leading international bank was a dangerous further step toward economic dependency. To break out of the threatened poverty trap, Luigi de' Medici embarked on a high-risk

[18] Davis (1981), 296–340. Lupo (1990) shows how the expansion of the Sicilian *latifondo* was linked to persistent market uncertainties. See also Sabetti (1984), 93–4. Macry (1997), Marmo (1994), Caglioti (1994) also stress the constant precariousness of Neapolitan society.

[19] Cingari (1966), 140–76; Ostuni (1993), 329–32.

economic strategy when in 1823 the Kingdom of the Two Sicilies adopted one of the highest protectionist regimes in Europe.

The tariffs targeted imported manufactured goods, looking to import substitution as a means to promote the development of national industries, especially textiles, shipbuilding, and engineering. The strategy was a continuation by other means of less coherent policies followed by the eighteenth-century Bourbons, and above all of Murat's earlier efforts to reduce colonial subordination to France. Indeed, most of the numerous community of foreign merchants and textile masters that had settled in the Kingdom had first arrived during the years of French rule and at Murat's invitation.[20]

As those earlier initiatives had made clear, the threats of commercial and colonial dependence were the most serious challenges to the Kingdom's autonomy. De' Medici now combined these earlier experiments at import substitution with a more ambitious attempt to reverse the Kingdom's commercial and political subordination. The key aim was to expand the merchant fleet, but this was linked with measures designed to equip the Kingdom with a modern navy and a reorganized army. The naval shipyards in Naples would build the first steamships in Italy, and were also designed to produce modern artillery for the army as well as Italy's first railway. Dynastic loyalty became the test for all those who sought commissions in the army, while regiments of foreign mercenaries were recruited to provide greater internal security and protect the monarchy against a repetition of the mutinies of 1820.

By the early 1830s Naples as a result had the largest industrial base of all the pre-Unification Italian states. The largest shipyards and engineering works in Italy were in Naples, while numerous cotton and wool textile factories had been established in the Apennine foothills where water-power was abundant.[21] Two decades before their counterparts in Piedmont–Savoy the Bourbon rulers in the South had embarked on a programme of economic development and military reorganization. But the strategy proved impossible to sustain. It brought the Kingdom into conflict first with its most powerful commercial partner, Great Britain, and then with the most powerful economic interests in the Kingdom, the landowners.

Both reactions revealed the obstacles facing the survival of small dynastic states in an age of growing international economic competition and political rivalry. The policies adopted by the Bourbon rulers in Naples met with a fate very similar to that visited on the Egyptian ruler Mehemet Ali in the same period, and for similar reasons. The Bourbon government's protectionist measures immediately became the target of punitive reprisals against the Kingdom's prime exports, in particular olive oil, by the British and resulted in a prolonged commercial war that dragged on until June 1840 when the two countries nearly came to war.

20 Cingari (1966), 140–76; Davis (1981); Dawes (1991), 226–37.

21 On the Neapolitan shipbuilding industry, see De Rosa (1968); on the textile industry De Matteo (1984) and Davis (1981), 108–32.

The immediate cause was the decision by the Neapolitan government to grant a monopoly over the export of sulphur from Sicily to a French company in 1839. The 'Affair of the Sicilian Brimstones' caused a furore in England, since the commercial treaty with Naples in 1816 had given British shipping a virtual monopoly over the Kingdom's carrying trade. On the pretext that British commercial interests had been unfairly damaged, in June 1840 Lord Palmerston dispatched a squadron of British gunboats to the Bay of Naples. Under threat of bombardment the Neapolitan government was forced to climb down, agreeing under duress to pay heavy indemnities for losses suffered by British merchants that later turned out to be fictitious, and also to abandon its protectionist tariffs.[22]

This was the fourth time in just over a century that the British navy had threatened to bombard Naples and although the 'Affair of the Sicilian Brimstones' has hardly earned a footnote in the history of the imperialism of free trade and British gunboat diplomacy it starkly revealed the obstacles to the survival of an independent dynastic state in southern Italy. The situation was further complicated by the fact that de' Medici's bid to develop a modern industrial sector and promote a national shipbuilding industry had aroused fierce opposition from the southern landowners as well. The government's protectionist measures had caused the price of imported goods to rise, cut southern agricultural producers off from access to foreign markets, and made the Kingdom's most valuable agricultural exports the principal target of British reprisals. The landowners' discontents also focused on the government's decision to maintain control on grain exports introduced by the French rulers in 1810, which permitted exports only after the needs of the domestic market had been met. These measures were designed to prevent popular unrest by ensuring plentiful supplies of cheap bread, but they were especially damaging for those engaged in the export trades. The landowners' discontents did not take overtly political form, but they did give rise to growing demands for the government to adopt more liberal economic measures and contributed to a more general disaffection with Bourbon rule.[23]

The difficulty of maintaining some degree of dynastic independence in a rapidly changing world faced the Bourbons rulers in the South with challenges that were not unique, and similar problems faced all the other Italian rulers although in most cases these were disguised by Austrian protection. But this was not why the Kingdom collapsed in 1860, and when the Bourbons lost their throne it was because Austria's defeat in 1859 sealed the fate of all the Italian rulers, except for the Pope and the House of Savoy.

This is not to deny that powerful political tensions had developed within the Bourbon Kingdom, but these did not differ significantly from those facing the other Italian rulers. Indeed, after the outbreak of the revolutions in 1848 Ferdinand II of Naples was the first Italian ruler to restore order without outside

[22] Davis (1982), 5–24. [23] Ibid.

help. The monarchy did not repeat the mistakes of 1820, in large part because in 1848 both the army and the Swiss guards remained loyal to the monarchy. As a result, the insurrections in the southern provinces were quickly put down, as were the revolutions in Sicily.

In 1849 the royalist counter-revolution prevailed in southern Italy, as it did in every other Italian state with the single exception of Piedmont. But the most serious outcome of the revolutions of 1848–9 was that the monarchy's success in crushing the revolutions earned Ferdinand II the epithet of 'King Bomba' in the European liberal press. William Gladstone's ringing denunciation of the Bourbon dynasty as the 'negation of God set up as a system of government' on account of the mistreatment of the liberals held as political prisoners after the revolutions made that reputation stick and made the Neapolitan Bourbons the pariahs of liberal Europe.[24]

When in 1854 the war in the Crimea revealed how deeply the revolutions of 1848 had weakened the Habsburg monarchy, the Bourbon monarchy in the South became even more dangerously isolated. The Neapolitan government could hardly have misjudged things more badly, however, when it made overtures for an alliance with St Petersburg, a move that was bound to make Britain even more hostile. It was not by chance that in May 1860 Garibaldi's volunteers chose to land at Marsala, a port dominated by British merchants that was also protected by two British men-o'-war.[25]

After 1849, the political conditions in the southern Kingdom were as bleak and reactionary as in any of the other Italian states, except in Piedmont, the only Italian state in which constitutional government had survived. Had the Neapolitan Bourbons followed the lead of the House of Savoy and played the nationalist card things might have turned out differently. But the question has only to be asked to reveal why this was never an option. The most compelling obstacle was the dynasty's continuing dependence on the protection of Austria and the support of the Pope. But even had foresight made that gamble worth taking, any concessions to liberal demands would have reopened the issues of regional and Sicilian autonomy that had dominated the agenda of the revolutions in the South in 1848.

There was no obvious exit strategy from the endgame facing the Neapolitan Bourbons after 1850. But with the exception of Victor Emmanuel II of Piedmont, the other Italian rulers found themselves in similar situations which is why none of them survived. Not even the centrifugal forces that were the immediate cause of

[24] See Moe (2002), 131–9. However, it is less widely known that Gladstone's intervention was by no means unpartisan. In 1839 he had been the spokesman in the House of Commons for the British merchants interested in the Sicilian sulphur trade, whereas earlier he had written a more positive account of Bourbon rule in Naples!—see Foot (ed.) *Gladstone Diaries*, ii (October–November 1838), 484–502.

[25] Mack Smith (1954/1985), 23–36; Martucci (1999), 165–8. On relations with Russia, see Giura (1967).

the downfall of the Neapolitan Bourbons in 1860 when Sicily made its third and finally successful bid for autonomy were peculiar to the South. During the revolutions of 1848 similar demands for regional or municipal autonomy had been the principal cause of political unrest in all the Italian states. In Piedmont, the Genoese revolt against Turin was put down in 1849 no less bloodily than the Bourbon assaults on Messina and Palermo. Almost identical struggles were played out in the Veneto when the cities of the Venetian *Terraferma* took the opportunity to break free from subordination to Venice, in Tuscany when Livorno made its bid for freedom from Florence, and in the Papal States where virtually every city rebelled against Rome.[26]

The tensions between the capital and the provinces and between Sicily and the mainland that in 1860 overwhelmed the Bourbon Kingdom of the Two Sicilies were only one example, therefore, of internal tensions that faced every Italian ruler and contributed in no small part to the collapse of the pre-Unification Italian states. In each case, moves toward greater centralization and the incorporation of previously independent states, cities, and territories were the principal causes of political unrest. Resentments at lost regional and municipal autonomy had dominated the course of the revolutions in 1848–9, and Italy's political Unification would succeed at least in part because it proved better able to accommodate these deeply felt local and municipal identities.

Nor can it be assumed that social and economic conditions in the South were significantly worse than in the rest of Italy at the time of Unification. Down to the end of the century poverty was the common condition of most Italians and at the time of Unification there was little to choose between the poorest regions in the South and those of the North and Centre.[27] There were also a number of relatively advanced commercial regions in the South, even though these did not benefit to the same degree from the commercial boom of the 1850s that brought important changes to the more developed commercial centres in the North—especially in Piedmont and Lombardy. But in 1860 the economic differences between the North and the South were still much less than they would be forty years later, and before the new Italian state dismantled the protective barriers that had enabled the southern textile, engineering, and shipbuilding industries to develop. The numbers engaged in 'industry'—although the term is very misleading—were actually higher in the South than anywhere else in Italy in 1860.[28]

There were also important structural differences, although these would not become evident until later. Even in those parts of the South where commercial agriculture was most developed—the Terra di Bari, the regions closest to the

[26] On the Veneto in English see Ginsborg (1979) and more recently Laven (2002). For Tuscany see especially Lo Romer (1987) and Kröll (2005). On Rome see Carnavale and Caracciolo (1978).

[27] Bolton King and Thomas Okey in their survey of Italy in 1902 believed that the country's poverty was its most distinctive feature amongst the western European industrialized states.

[28] De Rosa (2004), 3–19.

capital and around Reggio Calabria on the mainland, Messina, Catania, Palermo's Conca d'Ora, Marsala, Trapani, and a number of other western Sicilian ports—the resources and infrastructures that would turn the lower Po valley into the principal motor of Italy's economic growth in the years after Unification were lacking. The South had no cash crop comparable to the silk of Lombardy and Piedmont—Italy's 'white coal'—that would remain its principal export commodity down to the Great War and the main source of the commercial wealth and capital investment in both agriculture and industry in the North.[29] The fact that the southern Kingdom's foreign trade was the lowest of all the Italian states in per capita terms at the time of Unification was another indicator of underlying economic weakness, although the figures are to some extent distorted by the fact that this was most populous of the Italian states.[30] A more telling sign came perhaps from the decision of the Rothschild Bank in the 1850s to close down its offices in Naples, on the grounds that apart from government stock the Kingdom no longer offered attractive commercial or industrial investment opportunities.[31]

The reasons for the Kingdom's collapse in 1860 were military, diplomatic, and political, therefore, although after the event this came to be seen as the consequence of backwardness and of decades, even centuries of misrule, oppression, and corruption. That was an oversimplification that nonetheless fed the parallel myth that economic liberalism was the best remedy for the ills of the South. But this was to disregard the lessons that had been painfully learned at the beginning of the century. Both the laissez-faire principles that had guided the enlightened reformers of the eighteenth century and the confident belief of the French rulers that rational governance was all that was needed to unlock the natural wealth of the South had proved inadequate solutions to the problems posed by rapid change in the Mezzogiorno. These problems had little to do with immobility, but everything to do with the extreme fragility of the Kingdom's economic foundations when exposed to new forces of change.

The Bourbon monarchy had neither the vision nor the means to address these problems and its own desperate attempts to survive added new contradictions and conflicts. But once the Kingdom ceased to exist, the myths of an immobile and unchanging South were invoked to justify panaceas that had already been tried and found wanting. When these failed again, the blame was laid on the backwardness of the South. It would be more accurate to say, however, that the South embodied in extreme form conditions common to most of Italy—poverty, low levels of consumption, a marginal and subordinate position on international markets.

It was by no means only in the South that the new state failed to address those problems, but in the South the consequences of that failure would prove especially damaging. As in many of Europe's peripheral regions, the challenges posed by the new era of industrialization and international commercial markets threw the

[29] Cafagna (1994), 17–49. [30] Graziani (1960), 1–89.
[31] 'Les opérations semblent y avoir étés suspendues pendant longtemps': Gilles (1965), ii. 49.

economic fabric and existing social hierarchies of many parts of the South into confusion, creating conditions not only of conflict but also of uncertainty and insecurity. If these changes created new opportunities, the prevailing conditions of insecurity also encouraged the development of forms of monopolist exploitation that would become the most pathological features of the Southern Problem.

It was no coincidence that these developments should have become increasingly visible in the years that followed the great agricultural crisis of the 1880s, whose devastating impact on the fragile economies of Spain, Greece, the Balkans, and southern Italy has frequently been underestimated.[32] The mass emigrations of the following decade revealed the deep structural impact of the crisis, which struck the most profitable and advanced sectors of the southern economies most heavily, creating new incentives to monopolize the scant resources that remained.[33]

The crisis of the 1880s exposed the underlying fragility of the southern economies and the responses that followed were typical of impoverished economies in times of insecurity and uncertainty. A direct consequence was the extension of monopolist powers from the economy to politics in ways charted by observers from Gaetano Salvemini to Antonio Gramsci. But this was not the story of a death foretold, not was it the consequence of some supposed deficit of social capital.[34] The vulnerabilities of the South had been evident from much earlier, and the short period of Napoleonic rule at the beginning of the century had dramatically revealed why change tended to be both abrupt and disruptive. The Napoleonic decade had also exposed the South's vulnerability to political and economic subordination, even though against every intention of empire the Neapolitans in those years had acquired important autonomies. But in the changed political and economic conditions after Unification the South would become the prisoner of its insecurities, such that when the oldest and largest of the Italy's pre-Unification states ceased to be a kingdom it became a problem: the Southern Problem.

[32] See Morilla Critz, Olmstead, Rhode (1999), 316–25. The devastating impact of international competition in markets where Mediterranean producers were previously well represented merits comparison with the earlier post-Napoleonic recession caused by the arrival of Egyptian and Russian grain on European markets.

[33] For an important analysis of the links between insecurity and the rise of *mafia* in the 20th century, for example see Gambetta (1993), 75–98.

[34] The term is from Putnam (1993).

Bibliography

PRIMARY SOURCES

Archives

Paris

Archives des Affaires Etrangères (AAEP)

Correspondance politique (CP) (Naples), vols. 126–38 (1789–1812)

Correspondance consulaire (CC) (Naples), vols. 38–41 (1793–1811)

Mémoires et Documents (Naples), vols. 1–6

Archives Nationales, Paris (ANP)

AFiv 1714a	Secrétaire d'état imperial
AFiv 1714b	Joseph Bonaparte
AFiv 1714c	Correspondance de Joseph Bonaparte–Napoléon
AFiv 1714d	Papiers André Miot
F(12)	Commerce et industries, ff. 549–50, 625–9, 2192
F(2)	Cottons napolitains, ff. 625–9

ANP: Archives Privées

29 AP	Papiers Roederer
31AP 5–43	Archive Murat
33AP	Papiers Berthier
211AP	Papiers de Jean Louis Ebenezer Reynier
381 AP	Fonds Joseph Bonaparte

Archives de la Guerre (Chateau de Vincennes) (A de G)

C(5) 1–18	Correspondances de Joseph Bonaparte
C(5*) 31–2	Reynier
C(5*) 33–44	Correspondance et Police
B(3*)	Armée d'Italie 1799, ff. 221–331–322 (MacDonald) 325 (Championnet)

Bibliothèque Nationale, Paris (BNP)

Fonds Italiens 1124–7

London

Public Record Office (PRO)

WO 1–280, 304, 306, 308, 315

FO 67 (Sardinia 1783–4)

FO 70 (Naples and Sicily) 4, 12, 13, 33, 38

FO 165

Naples

Archivio di Stato di Napoli (ASN)

Archivio Ministero dell'Interno (I Inventario), f. 183

Archivio Ministero dell'Interno (II Inventario), ff. 2206, 2243, 5066, 5067, 5068, 5079 (brigantaggio)

Archivio Ministero dell'Interno Appendice1, ff. 150, 213

Archivio Ministero dell'Interno Appendice II, f. 585 (Commissar Paolo Giampaolo)

Archivio Ministero dell'Interno Carte Winspeare, Affari Demaniali, ff. 74–89

Archivio Ministero di Polizia (1a Parte), ff. 94, 152, Rei di Stato, 265–349

Archivio Ministero dell'Interno, Catasti Onciari, ff. 4658, 5921–2, 5986, 7122

Archivio Ministero delle Finanze 1627–1649 (Carte Zurlo), ff. 2366, 2529, 2717, 2724, 2735, 2737, 2745, 2790, 2864, 2802, 2812, 4959

Archivio Ministero degli Affari Esteri, ff. 5512–45, 5600 (Marchese di Gallo), 5521, 5534 (consular correspondence), 5691 (correspondence with Paris), 5732, 5602 (di Gallo)

Commissione per la Liquidazione del Debito Pubblico, ff. 3527, 5589, 5595, 4959, 4242, 4512

Bollettino delle Sentenze della Commissione Feudale (1808–59), 71 vols.

Bolletino delle Ordinanze de'Commissari Ripartitori (1858–67), 24 vols.

Rei di Stato, ff. 265, 276, 323–4

Archivi Privati

Archivio Tommasi, B V–XI

Archivio Maresca di Serracapriola, B 16–22, 29–32, 38–9, 40–2, 46–51, 130–3, 167, 176, 217–19

Archivio Serra Gerace, B60–175

Archivio Di Toccò di Montemiletto, B 59, 87–9, 102, 123, 126, 130, 135, 157, 190–4, 198

Biblioteca Nazionale V. Emanuele II, Naples (Sezione Manoscritti) (BNN)

Sezione Ms: Bancone 8B: ff. 17, 18, 19, 20, 21, 22, 23, 25, 26, 27, 28, 29, 30, 33

Mss Cuoco XX

Mss rari: SQ IV L 31

Ms varie: xxii a.6

Biblioteca Storia Patria, Naples (BSPN)

Mss XXVI A.8 Documenti originali: 24, 33, 37, 41, 43, 47, 53, 61, 74, 79, 94, 96, 117, 195

Mss C2 fasc 3: Notamento dei monasteri soppressi 1806–9

Mss XXI B 5 (Codice diplomatico: dominazione francese)

Documenti 1799–1815. Mss: 3 Corrispondenza XIV, Busta 2

SD. X. c.17 (1–64), Min. Interno 1806–15

Ms varia XXXIII 6 Saggio storico delle società denominate Carboneria ecc

Archivio di Stato di Foggia (ASF)

Consigli Provinciali e Distrettuali; Processi Verbali, Buste 1–2

Intendenze di Capitanata: Carte Varie: Busta 5; Fascic.1 (*Reale Società Economiche*); ff. 332, 346

Atti di Polizia: ff. 355, 396

Edited Collections of Original Documents

Atti del Parlamento delle Due Sicilie, 1820–1, ed. Alberti Annibale, 2 vols. (Rome–Bologna: Accademia dei Lincei, 1931).

Bonaparte, Joseph. *Mémoires et correspondance politique et militaire du Roi Joseph*, ed. A. Du Casse, 10 vols. (Paris, 1853–4).

Bonaparte, Napoleon. *Correspondance de Napoléon Ier*, 32 vols. (Paris, 1858).

Di Gallo, Marzillio Mastrilli. 'Memorie del Duca di Gallo': *ASPN* a xiii. Fii (1888), 207–382.

Jullien, Marc-Antoine. *Segretario Generale della Repubblica Napoletana. Lettere e documenti* ed. Mario Battaglini (Naples: Vivarium, 1998).

La Riconquista del Regno di Napoli nel 1799. Lettere del Cardinale Ruffo, del Re, della Regina e del Ministro Acton, ed. B. Croce (Bari: Laterza, 1943).

La Repubblica Napoletana. Diari, memorie, racconti, ed. Mario Battaglini, 2 vols. (Naples: Istituto Italiano per gli Studi Filosofici, 2000).

Leggi, Atti, Proclami ed altri documenti della Repubblica Napoletana 1798–1799, ed. M. Battaglini and A. Placanica (Cava dei Tirreni: Di Mauro Editore, 2000–1).

L'invasione francese negli Abruzzi 1798–1810, ed. Luigi Coppa-Zuccari, 4 vols. (L'Aquila, 1927).

Murat, Joachim. *Lettres et documents pour servire à l'histoire de Joachim Murat 1767–1815*, vols. vi–viii, ed. Paul Le Brethon (Paris: Plon-Nourrit, 1911–14).

Il Parlamento Nazionale Napoletano per gli anni 1820 e 1821, ed. V. Fontanarosa (Rome: Biblioteca di Storia del Risorgimento, 1910).

U. S. Consular Correspondence: Naples, vol. i (December 1796–October 1832).

Published Sources and Memoires

Anon. *Notizia storica del conte Carlo Antonio Manhès* (Naples: Giovanni Ranucci, 1846).

Arrighi, G. M. *Saggio storico per servire di studio alle rivoluzioni politiche e civili del Regno di Napoli* (Naples, 1809).

Beyle, Henri (Stendhal). *Rome, Naples et Florence en 1817* (Paris, 1817).

Bianchini, Ludovico. *Della storia della finanze del Regno di Napoli*, 3 vols. (Naples, 1859) (republished as *Storia delle Finanze del Regno delle Due Sicilie* (Naples, 1971).

Blanch, Luigi. *Scritti Storici*, ed. B. Croce, 3 vols. (Bari: Laterza, 1945).

Bunbury, Sir Henry. *Narratives of some passages in the great war with France 1799 to 1810* (London 1854).

Calà Ulloa, Pietro. *Il Regno di Ferdinando II* (Naples: ESI, 1967).

Capasso, Bartolomeo. *Sulla circoscrizione civile ed ecclesiastica e sulla popolazione della città di Napoli* (Naples, 1882).

Ceva Grimaldi, G. *Del Lavoro degli Artigiani* (Naples, 1845).

——. *Memorie storiche di Napoli dal Tempo della sua Fondazione* (Naples, 1857).

Colletta, Pietro. *Cenno storico intorno alla rivoluzione napoletana del 1820* (Napoli, 1848).

——. *Storia del Reame di Napoli*, ed. Nino Cortese (Naples, 1957), 3 vols. (Original edn.: *Storia del Reame di Napoli dal 1734 al 1825*, ed. G. Capponi (Firenze, 1834), 3 vols.)

Courier, Paul Louis. *Mémoires, correspondances et opuscules inédits*, 2 vols. (Paris, 1828).
Craven, Richard Keppel. *Sketch of the late Revolution at Naples by an eye-witness* (London, 1820).
Cronache segreti dela polizia toscana, ed. G. Marcotti (Florence, 1898).
Cuoco, Vincenzo. *Scritti Vari*, ed. N. Cortese and F. Niccolini, Parte Prima (Periodo milanese, 1801–6); Parte Seconda (Periodo napoletano 1806–15) (Bari: Laterza, 1924).
——. *Saggio storico sulla rivoluzione napoletana del 1799*, ed. Pasquale Villani (Bari: Laterza, 1980).
——. *Saggio Storico sulla Rivoluzione di Napoli*, ed. Fulvio Tessitore (Naples: Itinerario, 1988).
——. *Saggio Storico sulla rivoluzione di Napoli*, ed. Antonino De Francesco, (Manduria–Bari–Rome: Lacaita, 1998).
De Gxx. *Notice historique sur M. le Lieutenant Géneral Charles Antoine, Comte Manhès* (Paris, 1817).
De Nicola, Carlo. *Diario Napoletano 1798–1825* (*ASPN* 1899–1905), 3 vols. (Naples, 1906). Partially rpt. as *Diario Napoletano: Dicembre 1798–Dicembre 1800*, ed. R. Riccis (Milano, 1963); full rpt. and Introduction: *Diario Napoletano 1798–1825*, 3 vols., ed. R. De Lorenzo (Naples: Luigi Regina Editore, 1999).
De Rivarol, Auguste. *Notice historique sur la Calabre pendant les dernières revolutions de Naples* (Paris, 1817).
Drusco, abate Pietrabonda. *Anarchia popolare a Napoli del 21 dicembre 1796 al 23 gennaio 1799*, ed. M. Arcella (Naples, 1884).
Dumas, Alexandre. *I Borboni di Napoli*, 10 vols. (Naples, 1862–4).
Duret de Tavel. *Séjour d'un officier français en Calabre* (Paris, 1820).
Filangieri Raveschieri, Teresa. *Storia della Carità a Napoli* (Naples, 1878).
Galanti, Giuseppe Maria. *Nuova Descrizione Storica e Geografica delle Sicilie*, 4 vols. (Naples, 1786).
——. *Breve Descrizione di Napoli e del Suo Contorno* (Naples, 1792).
——. *Memorie del mio tempo* (1805), ed. A. Placanica (Cava dei Tirreni: Di Mauro Editore, 1996).
——. *Testamento Forense*, 2 vols. (Venice, 1806; rpt. Naples, Istituto per gli Studi Filosofici, 1977).
——. *Descrizione del Molise*, ed. Francesco Barra (Cava dei Tirreni: Di Mauro Editore, 1993).
——. *Scritti sulla Calabria*, ed. A. Placanica (Cava dei Tirreni: Di Mauro Editore, 1993).
Gladstone, W. E. *The Gladstone Diaries*, ed. M. R. D. Foot (Oxford: Clarendon Press, 1968), ii.
Helfert, Freiher von. *Fabrizio Ruffo: Rivoluzione e controrivoluzione di Napoli dal novembre 1798 all'agosto 1799* (Florence, 1885).
Hüffer, Hermann. *La Repubblica napoletana dell'anno 1799*, ed. Renata De Lorenzo (Naples: Liguori Editore, 1999).
Jacini, Stefano. *La proprietà fondiaria e le popolazioni agricole in Lombardia* (Milan, 1857).
Lomonaco, Francesco. *Rapporto al Cittadino Carnot*, ed. Antonino De Francesco (Bari–Rome–Manduria: Lacaita, 1999)
Lumbroso, A. *Gioacchino Murat e le aspirazioni unitarie italiane del 1815* (Rome, 1899).

Manzoni, Alessandro. *Dell'Indipendenza dell'Italia*, ed. Fausto Ghisalberti (Milan, 1947).
Maria Carolina. *Carteggio di Maria Carolina con Lady Emma Hamilton* (Naples: Pironti, 1999).
Masci, Angelo. *Esame politico legale dei dritti e delle prerogative dei Baroni del Regno di Napoli* (Naples, 1792).
Metternich, Clemens Wenzel Lothar, Furst von. *Memoirs of Prince Metternich 1773–1835*, ed. Prince Richard Metternich (New York: Fostig, 1973).
Micheroux, Antonio. 'Il cavaliere Antonio Micheroux nella reazione napoletana del 1799', ed. R. Maresca, *ASPN* 18–19 (1893–4), 494–526; 106–248, 652–90.
Minichini, Luigi. *Luglio 1820. Cronaca di una rivoluzione*, ed. Mario Themelly (Rome: Bulzoni Editore, 1979).
Miot de Melito. *Mémoires*, ed. Fleischmann, 3 vols. (Paris, 1858).
Monnier, Marc. *Histoire du brigandage dans l'Italie méridionale* (Paris, 1862).
Murat, Caroline. *My Memoirs* (London, 1910).
Nicolini, Nicola. *Del passaggio dall'antica alla nuova legislazione nel Regno delle Due Sicilie* (Discorso di Nicola Nicolini, 7 January 1809) (Naples, 1850).
Nisco, N. *Storia del Reame di Napoli* (Naples, 1888).
Pepe, Gabriele. *Memorie* (Paris, 1847).
Pepe, Guglielmo. *Memoirs of General Pepe*, 3 vols. (London, 1896).
Petroni, Giulio. *De' Banchi di Napoli*, 2 vols. (Naples, 1871).
Pignatelli, Francesco. *Memorie di un generale della Repubblica e dell'Impero: Francesco Pignatelli, Principe di Strongoli*, ed. Nino Cortese, 2 vols. (Bari: Laterza, 1927).
Roederer, Pierre-Louis. *Oeuvres du comte P-L Roederer*, ed. A. M. Roederer, 8 vols. (Paris, 1854).
——. *Political Thought and Practice during the French Revolution*, ed. K. Margerison (Philadelphia: Transactions of the American Philosophical Society, 73, Part I, 1983), pp. vii–162.
——. *The Spirit of the Revolution of 1789*, trans. and ed. M. Forsyth (Aldershot: Scolar Press, 1989).
Sacchinelli, Domenico. *Memorie storiche sulla vita del Cardinale Ruffo* (Naples, 1836).
Salfi, Francesco Saverio. *L'Italie au Dix-neuvième siècle* (Paris, 1821).
Savarese, G. *Tra Rivoluzione e Reazione. Ricordi di Giusepe Zurlo 1759–1828*, ed. A. Romano (Turin: Einaudi, 1941).
Southey, Robert. *Life of Nelson*, 2 vols. (John Murray: London 1813).
Swinburne, Henry. *Travels in the Two Sicilies*, 2 vols. (London, 1783–5).
Winspeare, Davide. *Storia degli Abusi Feudali* (Naples, 1811).
Young, Arthur. *Travels in France and Italy*, ed. T. Okey (London, 1915).
Zurlo, Giuseppe. *Rapporto sullo Stato del Reame di Napoli*, ed. Renato Lalli (Isernia, no date).

Newspapers

Monitore Napoletano, 2 February 1799–8 June 1799 (Naples) (available on http:www.repubblicanapoletana.it)
Monitore Napoletano, 1806–15 (Naples)
Monitore delle Due Sicilie (Naples)
Corriere di Napoli (Naples)

Reference Works

BER *Bibliografia dell'età del Risorgimento 1970–2001*, 4 vols. (Florence: Leo Olschki, 2003).

DBGAF *Dictionnaire Biographique des Genéraux et Amiraux français*, ed. G. Six, 2 vols. (Paris, 1934).

DBF *Dictionnaire de Biographie Française* (Paris, 1932).

DBI *Dizionario Biografico degli Italiani (Rome: Istituto dell'Enciclopedia Italiana).*

SECONDARY SOURCES

'Abrial, André-Joseph, 1750–1828'. *Dictionnaire de Biographie Française* (Paris, 1932).

Abbamonte, O. 'I tribunali di commercio', in Angelo Massafra (ed.), *Il Mezzogiorno preunitario. Economia, società e istituzioni* (Bari: Edizioni Dedalo, 1988), 507–18.

Acton, H. *The Bourbons of Naples 1734–1825* (London: Methuen, 1956).

——. *The Last Bourbons of Naples (1825–1861)* (London: Methuen 1962).

Addeo, G. 'La libertà della stampa nel nonimestre costituzionale a Napoli'. Parte I, *ASPN*, 107 (1989), 337–80; Parte II, *ASPN*, 110 (1992), 193–274.

'Agar, Jean-Antoine-Michel, Comte de Mosbourg, 1771–1844'. *Dictionnaire de Biographie Française* (Paris, 1932).

Ajello, Raffaele. *Arcana Juris. Diritto e politica nel Settecento italiano* (Naples: Jovene, 1976).

——. 'I filosofi e la regina. Il governo delle Due Sicilie da Tanucci a Caracciolo (1776–1786)'. *RSI*, 103(2) (1991), 399–452; 103(3) (1991), 657–740.

Alessi, G. *Giustizia e polizia. Il controllo di un capitale, Napoli 1779–1803* (Naples: Jovine, 1993).

Aliberti, Giovanni. 'Economia e società da Carlo III ai Napoleonidi (1734–1806)', in *Storia di Napoli* (Naples, 1969), viii. 77–164.

——. *Lo stato post-feudale. Un secolo di potere pubblico nel Mezzogiorno d'Italia 1806–1910* (Naples: Guida, 1993).

——. *Potere società locale nel Mezzogiorno dell'800* (Bari–Rome: Laterza, 1987).

Allum, P. A. *Politics and Society in Post-war Naples* (Cambridge: Cambridge University Press, 1973).

Antonielli, Livio. *I Prefetti dell'Italia Napoleonica* (Bologna: Il Mulino, 1983).

——. 'Il primo arruolamento nella Gendarmeria italica: le cause di un insuccesso', in Giovanni Luigi Fontana and Antonio Lazarini (eds.), *Veneto e Lombardia tra rivoluzione giacobina ed età napoleonica. Economia, territorio, istituzioni* (Rome: Cairiplo-Laterza, 1992), 504–38.

——. 'L'amministrazione nell'Italia rivoluzionaria e napoleonica. I tre momenti di un grande progetto', in *L'Italia nell'età Napoleonica*, Atti del LXVII Congresso di Storia del Risorgimento Italiano (Milan, 2–5 ottobre 1996) (Rome: Istituto per la storia del Risorgimento Italiano, 1997), 193–219.

Astarita, Tommaso. *Between the Salt Sea and the Holy Water: A History of Southern Italy* (New York: Norton, 2005).

Atteridge, A. Hilliard. *Joachim Murat. Marshal of France and King of Naples* (New York: Brentano, 1911).

Atti del Convegno sul tema: Napoleone e l'Italia, 2 vols. (Rome: Accademia Nazionale dei Lincei, a ccclxx, 1973).

Aymard, Maurice. 'L'abolition del la feodalité en Sicilie: le sens d'une réforme'. *Annuario dell'Istituto Storico per l'Età Moderna e Contemporanea* (Rome, 1971–2), 67–85.

——. 'Une famille de l'aristocratie sicilienne au XVI et XVIIe siècles: les ducs de Terranova. Un bel exemple d'ascension seigneuriale'. *Revue Historique*, 19 (1972), 187–252.

——. 'La transizione dal feudalismo al capitalismo', in Ruggiero Romano and Corrado Vivanti (eds.), *Storia d'Italia, Annali I* (Turin: Einaudi, 1978), 1131–82.

Barberis, Walter. *Le armi del Principe. La tradizione militare sabauda* (Turin: Einaudi, 1988).

Barra, Francesco. *Il brigantaggio del Decennio francese (1806–1815). Studi e ricerche*, 2 vols. (Salerno: Plectica, 2003).

——. *Il Mezzogiorno e le potenze europee nell'età moderna* (Milan: Elio Sellino Editore, no date), i.

Bartoccini, F. 'Maria Annunziata Carolina Bonaparte (1782–1839)'. *DBI*.

Battaglini, Mario (ed.). *I giornali giacobini* (Rome: Borzi, 1988).

——. *La Repubblica napoletana. Origini, nascita, struttura* (Rome: Bonacco Editore 1992).

Beales, D. E. D. *Joseph II* (Cambridge: Cambridge University Press, 1987).

——. *Property and Plunder: European Catholic Monasteries in the Age of Revolution 1680–1815* (Cambridge: Cambridge University Press, 2003a).

——. *Enlightenment and Reform in Eighteenth-Century Europe* (London: I. B. Tauris, 2003b).

Benigno, Francesco. *Il Porto di Trapani nel Settecento. Rotte, traffici, esportazioni 1674–1800* (Trapani: Gervasi–Modica, 1982).

——. *Ultra Phara. Famiglie, commercio e territori nel Meridione moderno* (Rome: Meridiana, 2001).

Bercé, Yves-Marie (ed.). *La fin de l'Europe napoléonienne. 1814—la vacance de pouvoir* (Paris: Henri Veyrier, 1990).

Bergeron, Louis. *L'Episode Napoléonien. Aspects interieurs 1799–1815* (Paris: Editions du Seuil, 1972).

Bevilacqua, Piero. 'Acque e bonifiche nella prima metà dell'Ottocento', in Angelo Massafra (ed.), *Il Mezzogiorno preunitario. Economia, società e istituzioni* (Bari: Edizioni Dedalo, 1988), 337–60.

—— (ed.). *Storia dell'agricoltura italiana in età contemporanea*, iii: *Mercati ed istituzioni* (Venice: Marsilio Editore, 1991).

——. *Breve Storia dell'Italia Meridionale dall'Ottocento a oggi* (Rome: Donzelli, 1993).

——. 'La storia economica e l'economia', in Pierluigi Ciocca and Gianni Toniolo (eds.), *Storia Economica d'Italia* (Rome–Bari: Laterza Editore, 1998), i. 159–96.

——, and Gabriella Corona (eds.). *Ambiente e risorse nel Mezzogiorno contemporaneo* (Rome: Donzelli, 2002).

Biagianti, Ivo. 'Riforme ecclesiastiche e pratica religiosa dall'assolutismo illuminato all'età napoleonica', in *L'Italia giacobina e napoleonica. Storia della società italiana* (Milan: Teti Editore, 1985), xiii.

Bibliografia dell'età del Risorgimento 1970–2001, 3 vols. (Florence: Leo Olschki Editore, 2003).

Black, Jeremy. *Italy and the Grand Tour* (London and New Haven, Conn.: Yale University Press, 2003).

Blinkhorn, Martin. *Carlism and Crisis in Spain 1931–1939* (Cambridge: Cambridge University Press, 1975).

Bonney, Richard (ed.). *The Rise of the Fiscal State in Europe c. 1200–1815* (Oxford: Oxford University Press, 1999).

Botti, Gabriella, Laura Guidi, and Lucia Valenzi. *Povertà e beneficenza tra Rivoluzione e Restaurazione* (Naples: Morano Editore, 1990).

Bourguet, Marie-Noëlle. 'Race et folklore. L'image officielle de la France en 1800'. *Annales ESC* no. 4 (1976), 802–23.

Boutry, Philippe. 'La Restaurazione 1814–1848', in Giorgio Ciucci (ed.), *Roma Moderna* (Rome–Bari: Laterza, 2000).

Boyle, Nicholas. *Goethe. The Poet and the Age*, i: *The Poetry of Desire* (Oxford: Oxford University Press, 1992).

Breuilly, John. 'Napoleonic Germany and State-Formation', in Michael Rowe (ed.), *Collaboration and Resistance in Napoleonic Europe: State Formation in an Age of Upheaval (c. 1800–1815)* (London: Palgrave, 2003), 121–53.

Broers, Michael. *Europe under Napoelon 1799–1815* (London: Arnold, 1995).

——. *Politics and Religion in Napoleonic Italy: The War against God 1801–1814* (London: Routledge, 2002).

——. 'Centre and Periphery in Napoleonic Italy: The Nature of French Rule in the *départments réunis*', in Michael Rowe (ed.), *Collaboration, Resistance in Napoleonic Europe: State Formation in an Age of Upheaval (c. 1800–1815)* (London: Palgrave, 2003), 55–73.

——. *The Napoleonic Empire in Italy 1796–1814* (London: Palgrave, 2005).

Burke, Edmund. 'The terror and religion in Brittany and Algeria', in Gregory Blue, Martin Bunton, and Ralph Croizier (eds.), *Colonialism in the Modern World* (New York: Sharpe, 2002), 41–8.

Cafagna, Luciano. *Il Nord nella Storia d'Italia* (Bari: Laterza, 1962).

——. *Dualismo e sviluppo nella storia d'Italia* (Venice: Marsilio, 1989).

——. *Nord e Sud. Non fare a pezzi l'unità italiana* (Venice: Marsilio, 1994).

——. 'The industrial revolution in Italy 1830–1914', in Carlo Cipolla (ed.), *The Fontana Economic History of Europe* (London, 1973), iv. 279–325.

Caffiero, Marina. *La Repubblica nella città del papa. Roma 1798.* (Rome: Donzelli, 2005).

Caglioti, Daniela Luigia. *Il Guadagno Difficile. Commercianti napoletani nella seconda metà dell'Ottocento* (Bologna: Il Mulino, 1984).

Calabria, Anthony. *The Cost of Empire: The Finances of the Kingdom of Naples in the Time of Spanish Rule* (Cambridge: Cambridge University Press, 1991).

Calaresu, Melissa. 'Images of Ancient Rome in Late Eighteenth-Century Neapolitan Historiography'. *Journal of History of Ideas* (1997), 641–61.

——. 'Looking at Virgil's tomb: the end of the Grand Tour and the Cosmopolitan Ideal in Europe', in J. Elsner and J. P. Rubies (eds.), *Voyages and Visions: Towards a Cultural History of Travel* (London: Reaktion Books, 1999), 138–60.

Caldora, Umberto. *Calabria Napoleonica (1806–1815)* (Napoli, 1960).

——. 'Per la storia della spedizione sanfedista del Ruffo nel 1799'. *Calabria Nobilisssima*, 19 (49/50) (1965), 11–60.

——. 'La statistica murattiana del Regno di Napoli. Le relazioni sulla Calabria', ed. Vincenzo Cappelli (Rende, 1995).

Cammisa, F. 'La giurisdizione delle Grandi Corti Criminali', in Angelo Massafra (ed.), *Il Mezzogiorno preunitario. Economia, società e istituzioni* (Baris: Edizioni Dedalo, 1988), 519–24.

Cancila, Oreste. *L'economia della Sicilia. Aspetti storici* (Palermo: Il Saggiatore, 1991).

Capra, Carlo. 'L'età napoleonica', in G. Levi, U. Levra, and N. Tranfaglia (eds.), *Storia d'Italia* (Florence, 1978), 364–70.

—— (ed.). *L'età rivoluzionaria e napoleonica in Italia 1796–1815* (Turin: Loescher Editore, 1978).

——. 'Nobili, notabili, elites: dal modello francese al caso italiano'. *Quaderni Storici*, 37 (1979), 12–42.

——. 'Habsburg Italy in the Age of Reform'. *JMIS*, 10(2) (2005), 218–33.

Caracciolo, Alberto. 'La storia economica', in Ruggiero Romano and Corrado Vivanti (eds.), *Storia d'Italia*, iii: *Dal primo settecento all'Unità*, (Turin: Einaudi, 1973), 512–687.

Carnavale, M. and A. Caracciolo. *Lo Stato Pontificio da Martino V al Pio IX*, in G.Galasso (ed.), *Storia d'Italia* (Turin: UTET, 1978), xiv.

Cassani, C. 'Eleonora Fonseca di Pimentel (1752–1799)', in *DBI*, xlviii. 595–600.

Cassese, Leopoldo (ed.). *La statistica del Regno di Napoli: La relazione sulla Provincia di Salerno* (Salerno, 1955).

——. *Scritti di Storia meridionale*, ed. A. Cestaro and P. Laveglia (Salerno: Laveglia, 1970).

Castellano, Carolina. *Il Mestiere del giudice. Magistrati e sistema giuridico tra i francesi e i Borboni (1799–1848)* (Bologna: Il Mulino, 2004).

Cestaro, Antonio. *Aspetti della questione demaniale nel Mezzogiorno* (Brescia, 1963).

——. 'La revoluzione nelle provincie di Basilicata e Salernitano', in Anna Maria Rao (ed.), *Napoli 1799. Fra Storia e Storiografia* (Naples: Vivarium, 2002), 757–76.

Chabod, Federico. *Storia della politica estera italiana dal 1870 al 1896* (Bari: Laterza, 1962). Translated as *Italian Foreign Policy: The Statecraft of the Founders*, trans. William McCuaig (Princeton, NJ: Princeton University Press, 1996).

Chadwick, Owen. *The Popes and the European Revolution* (Oxford: Clarendon Press, 1981).

Chaney, Edward. *The Evolution of the Grand Tour: Anglo-Italian Cultural Relations since the Renaissance* (London/Portland, Ore.: Frank Cass, 1998).

—— and Ritchie, N. (eds.). *Oxford, China and Italy: Writings in Honour of Sir Harold Acton on his Eightieth Birthday* (Thames and Hudson, 1984).

Chiosi, Elvira. *Andrea Serrao. Apologia e crisi del regalismo nel settecento napoletano* (Naples: Jovene, 1981).

——. 'Il Regno dal 1734 al 1799', in Giuseppe Galasso and Rosario Romeo (eds.), *Storia del Mezzogiorno*, iv: *Il Regno dagli Angioini ai Borboni* (Rome: Edizioni del Sole, 1986), Part II, 371–467.

——. *Lo Spirito del Secolo. Politica e religione a Napoli nell'età dell'illuminismo* (Naples: Giannini, 1992).

——. 'Intellectuals and Academies', in Girolamo Imbruglia (ed.), *Naples in the Eighteenth Century. The Birth and the Death of a Nation* (Cambridge: Cambridge University Press, 2000), 118–34.

——. 'Massoneria e politica', in Anna Maria Rao (ed.), *Napoli 1799. Fra Storia e Storiografia* (Naples: Vivarium, 2002), 217–37.

——. 'Giuseppe Maria Capece Zurlo (1711–1801)'. *DBI*, xviii. 462–4.

Chorley, Patrick. *Oil, Silk and Enlightenment: Economic Problems in Eighteenth-Century Naples* (Naples: Istituto per gli Studi Storici, 1965).

Ciasca, Raffaele. 'Per la storia delle classi sociali nelle provincie meridionali durante la prima metà del secolo XIX', in *Studi storici in onore di Michelangelo Schipa* (Naples, 1926), 631–51.

Cingari, Gaetano. *Mezzogiorno e Risorgimento. La Restaurazione a Napoli dal 1821 al 1830* (Bari: Laterza, 1966).

——. *Brigantaggio, proprietari e contadini nel Sud (1799–1900)* (Reggio Calabria, 1976).

——. *Giacobini e sanfedisti in Calabria nel 1799* (Messina, 1957/Reggio Calabria, 1978).

——. *Mezzogiorno e Giustino Fortunato* (Florence, no date).

Ciocca, Pierluigi, and Gianni Toniolo (eds.). *Storia Economica d'Italia*, 2 vols. (Rome–Bari: Laterza Editore, 1998).

Ciucci, Giorgio (ed.). *Roma Moderna* (Bari: Laterza Editore, 2000).

Civile, Giuseppe. *Il comune rustico. Storia sociale di un paese del Mezzogiorno nell'800* (Bologna, 1990).

——, S. De Majo, G. Montroni, R. Pilati, M. Storchi, and M.-A. Visceglia. *Studi sulla società meridionale* (Naples: Guida, 1978).

Clark, Peter, and Bernard Lepetit (eds.). *Capital Cities and Their Hinterlands in Early Modern Europe* (Aldershot: Scolar Press, 1997).

Clemente, V. 'Melchiore Delfico (1744–1835)', in *DBI*, xxxvi. 527–39.

——. *Rinascenza teramana e riformismo napoletano (1777–1798)* (Rome: Edizione di Storia e Letteratura, 1981).

Cobb, Richard. *The Police and the People: French Popular Protest 1789–1820* (Oxford: Clarendon Press, 1970).

Cochrane, Eric W. *Florence in the Forgotten Centuries, 1527–1800; a History of Florence and the Florentines in the Age of the Grand Dukes* (Chicago: University of Chicago Press, 1973).

Cohen, Jon, and Giovanni Federico. *The Growth of the Italian Economy 1820–1960* (Cambridge: Cambridge University Press, 2001).

Colapietra, Raffaele. 'Le insorgenze di massa nell'Abruzzo in età moderna'. *Storia e Politica*, 1 (1981), 1–48.

——. *Per una rilettura socio-antropologica dell'Abruzzo giacobino e sanfedista* (Naples: La Città del Sole, 1995).

Colley, Linda. *Britons: Forging the Nation 1701–1837* (New Haven, Conn.: Yale University Press, 1992).

——. *Captives* (London: Pantheon, 2002).

Collins, Jeffrey. *Papacy and Politics in Eighteenth-Century Rome. Pius VI and the Arts* (Cambridge: Cambridge University Press, 2004).

Conolly, Owen. *Napoleon's Satellite Kingdoms* (Ontario: Free Press, 1965).

Constantine, David. *Fields of Fire: A Life of Sir William Hamilton* (London: Wiedenfeld and Nicolson, 2001).

Cooper, J. P. 'Patterns of Inheritance and Settlement by Great Landowners from the Fifteenth to the Eighteenth Centuries', in Jack Goody, Joan Thirsk, and E. P. Thompson (eds.), *Family and Inheritance: Rural society in Western Europe 1200–1800* (Cambridge: Cambridge University Press, 1976), 192–326.

Coppini, Paolo Romano. *Il Granducato di Toscana. Dagli anni francesi all'Unità*, in Giuseppe Galasso (ed.), *Storia d'Italia* (Turin: UTET, 1993), xiii.

Corciulo, M. S. 'Aspetti politici e istituzionali della rivoluzione napoletana del 1820–1', in *Bollettino del diciannovesimo secolo* (Naples: aV, 2000), n.6, 39–49.

Corona, Gabriella. *Demani ed individualismo agrario nel Regno di Napoli (1780–1806)* (Naples: ESI, 1995).

Cortese, Nino 'Luigi Blanch (1784–1872)', *DBI*, x. 771–6.

——. 'L'esercito napoletano nelle guerre napoleoniche'. *ASPN* (1926), 164–339.

——. 'Il governo napoletano e la rivoluzione siciliana del 1820–1'. *Archivio Storico Messinese*, 35 (Messina: Officine grafiche messinese, 1934), 191–214.

——. *La prima rivoluzione separatista siciliana, 1820–1821* (Naples: Libreria Scientifica Editrice, 1957).

——. 'Il Murat e la carboneria napoletana nella prima metà del 1814', in *Studi in onore di Gioacchino Volpe* (Florence, 1958), i. 211–20.

——. *Il Mezzogiorno e il Risorgimento italiano* (Naples: Libreria Scientifica Editrice, 1965).

Criscuolo, Vittorio. 'L'esperienza della Repubblica napoletana nel quadro del triennio 1796–9', in Anna Maria Rao (ed.), *Napoli 1799. Fra Storia e Storiografia* (Naples: Vivarium, 2002), 279–94.

Croce, Benedetto. *Studi Storici sulla Rivoluzione napoletana del 1799*, 2nd edn. (Roma, 1897).

——. *Storia del Regno di Napoli* (Bari: Laterza, 1924/1943/1967).

——. 'Il divorzio nelle provincie napoletane', in *Aneddoti di varia letteratura* (Bari: Laterza, 1942), iii. 67–85.

——. *La Riconquista del Regno di Napoli nel 1799* (Bari: Laterza, 1943).

——. *I teatri di Napoli dal Rinascimento alla fine del secolo decimottavo* (Bari: Laterza, 1947).

——. *Uomini e cose della vecchia Italia* (Scritti di storia lettereraria e politica xx) (Bari: Laterza, 1956), i.

Curato, F. 'La situazione interna delle Due Sicilie nel 1817 secondo i dispacci degli inviati francesi ed inglesi a Napoli', in *Studi in Onore di G. Volpe* (Florence, 1958), i. 227–60.

Cutolo, A. *Il Decurionato di Napoli* (Naples, 1932).

——. 'Il Regno di Napoli ai tempi di Gioacchino Murat. Dalle lettere di un diplomatico contemporaneo' *ASPN*, (2nd series) 22 (1937), xxvi. 380–407.

Dainotto, Roberto. '"Tramonto" and "Risorgimento": Gentile's Dialectics and the Prophesy of Nationhood', in A. Ascoli and K. Henneberg (eds.) *Making and Remaking Italy* (Oxford: Berg, 2001).

D'Alessio, C. 'Matteo Galdi (1764–1821)', in *DBI*, li. 374–7.

D'Angelo, Michela. *Mercanti inglesi in Sicilia. Rapporti commerciali tra la Sicilia e la Gran Bretagna nel periodo del blocco continentale* (Milan: Giuffré, 1988).

——. *Mercanti inglesi a Malta 1800–1825* (Milan: Franco Angeli, 1990).

Dante, Umberto. *Insorgenza ed Anarchia: Il Regno di Napoli e l'Invasione Francese* (Salerno: Cooperativa universitaria editrice, 1980).

D'Antone, Leandra (ed.). *Radici storiche ed esperienze dell'intervento straordinario nel Mezzogiorno* (Naples: Bibliopolis, 1996).

Davis, John A. (ed.) *Gramsci and Italy's Passive Revolution* (London: Croom Helm, 1979).

——. *Merchants, Monopolists and Contractors. A Study of Economic Activity and Society in Bourbon Naples (1815–1860)* (New York: Arno Press, 1979).

——. 'The South, the Risorgimento and the Origins of the "Southern Problem"' in idem (ed.) *Gramsci and Italy's Passive Revolution* (London: Croom Helm, 1979), 67–103.

——. 'Palmerston and the Sicilian Sulphur Crisis of 1848. An episode in the imperialism of free trade', in *Risorgimento* (Brussels) (1982) (1/2), 5–24.

——. 'Naples during the French Decennio: A Problem Unresolved?', in *Villes et Territoire pendant la période napoléonienne (France et Italie)* Collection de *l'Ecole Française de Rome* (96) (Rome, 1987), 327–54.

——. *Conflict and Control. Law and Order in Nineteenth Century Italy* (London: Macmillan, 1988).

Davis, John A. 'England, the Mediterranean and the Italian States', in *L'Italia alla Vigilia dela Rivoluzione Franecese* (Atti del LIV Congresso di Storia del Risorgimento taliano, Milan, 1988) (Rome: Istituto per la Storia del Risorgimento Italiano, 1990), 91–114.

——. 'The political role of the Neapolitan army in the *decennio francese*', in Anna Maria Rao (ed.), *Esercito e società nell'età rivoluzionaria e napoleonica* (Naples: Morano Editore, 1990) 151–72.

——. 'La fin du royaume de Murat à Naples', in Yves-Marie Bercé (ed.), *La fin de l'Europe napoléonienne. 1814—la vacance de pouvoir* (Paris: Henri Veyrier, 1990), 219–34.

——. 'The Napoleonic era in southern Italy: An ambiguous legacy'. *Proceedings of the British Academy* (Lectures and Memoirs), 80 (1991), 133–48.

——. '1799: The Santafede and the crisis of the Ancien Regime in southern Italy', in John A. Davis and Paul Ginsborg (eds.), *Society and Politics in the Age of the Risorgimento: Essays in Honour of Denis Mack Smith* (Cambridge: Cambridge University Press 1991/2002), 1–25.

——. 'Remapping Italy's Path to the Twentieth Century'. *JMH*, 66 (June 1994), 291–320.

——. 'The Mezzogiorno and Modernization: Changing Contours of Public and Private during the French *decennio*', in Paolo Macry and Angelo Massafra (eds.), *Fra Storia e Storiografia. Scritti in Onore di Pasquale Villani* (Bologna: Il Mulino, 1994).

——. 'Changing Perspectives on Italy's Southern Problem', in Carl Levy (ed.), *Italian Regionalism in Context* (London: Berg, 1996), 53–68.

——. 'Great Britain and Italy in the Napoleonic era', in *L'Italia nell'età Napoleonica.* Atti del LXVII Congresso di Storia del Risorgimento Italiano (Milano, 2–5 ottobre 1996) (Rome: Istituto per la storia del Risorgimento Italiano, 1997), 385–400.

——. 'Casting off the "Southern Problem": Or the peculiarities of the South Reconsidered', in Jane Schnieder (ed.), *Italy's Southern Question. Orientalism in One Country* (Oxford/New York: Berg, 1998), 205–24.

——. 'Rivolte popolari e controrivoluzione nel Mezzogiorno continentale', in Anna Maria Rao (ed.), *Folle controrivoluzionarie. Le insorgenze popolari nell'Italia rivoluzionaria e napoleonica* (Rome: Carocci, 1999), 349–68.

——. 'The Neapolitan Revolution of 1799: Between History and Myth'. *JMIS*, 4(3) (Fall 1999), 350–7.

——. 'L'Inghilterra, Nelson e la Repubblica napoletana del 1799', in Anna Maria Rao (ed.), *Napoli 1799. Fra Storia e Storiografia* (Naples:Vivarium, 2002), 393–430.

——. 'Italy', in Robert J. Goldstein (ed.), *The War for the Public Mind. Political Censorship in Nineteenth Century Europe* (Westport, Conn.: Praeger, 2000), 81–124.

—— (ed.). *Italy in the Nineteenth Century* (Oxford: Oxford University Press, 2000).

——. 'The Many Faces of Modernity: French Rule in Southern Italy 1806–1815', in Michael Rowe (ed.), *Collaboration and Resistance in Napoleonic Europe. State Formation in an Age of Upheaval c. 1800–1815* (London: Palgrave, 2003), 74–89.

——. 'Opera and Absolutism in Restoration Italy, 1815–1860'. *Journal of Interdisciplinary History*, 36 (4) (Spring 2006), 569–94.

——, and Paul Ginsborg (eds.). *Society and Politics in the Age of the Risorgimento: Essays in Honour of Denis Mack Smith* (Cambridge: Cambridge University Press, 1991/2002).

Dawes, Barbara. *British Merchants in Naples 1820–80* (Naples: ESI, 1991).

De Divitiis, Gigliola Pagano. *Mercanti inglesi nell'Italia del seicento* (Venice: Marsilio, 1990).

——, and Vincenzo Giura. *L'Italia del secondo settecento nelle relazioni segrete di William Hamilton, Horace Mann e John Murray* (Naples: ESI, 1997).

De Felice, Renzo. *Il triennio giacobino in Italia (1796–1799). Note e ricerche* (Rome: Bonaccci Editore, 1990).

De Francesco, Antonino. *La guerra in Sicilia. Il distretto di Caltagiorne nella rivoluzione del 1820–1* (Catania: Bonnano Editore, 1992).

——. 'Ideologie e movimenti politici', in Giovanni Sabbattucci and Vittorio Vidotto (eds.), *Storia d'Italia 1. Le premesse dell'unità. Dalla fine del Settecento al 1861* (Bari–Rome: Editori Laterza, 1994), 229–335.

——. *Rivoluzione e costituzioni. Saggi sul democratismo politico nell'Italia napoleonica 1796–1821* (Naples: ESI, 1996).

——. *Vincenzo Cuoco, Una vita politica* (Bari: Laterza, 1997).

—— (ed.). *Francesco Lomonaco. Rapporto al cittadino Carnot* (Manduria–Bari–Rome: Pietro Lacaita Editore, 1999).

——. 'How Not to Finish a Revolution', in Girolamo Imbruglia (ed.), *Naples in the Eighteenth Century. The Birth and the Death of a Nation* (Cambridge: Cambridge University Press, 2000), 167–82.

D'Elia, Costanza (ed.). *Il Mezzogiorno agli Inizi dell'Ottocento* (Bari–Rome: Editori Laterza, 1992).

——. *Stato padre, stato demiurgo. I lavori pubblici nel Mezzogiorno (1815–1860)* (Bari: Edipuglia, 1996).

Delille, Gérard. *Famille et proprieté dans le Royaume de Naples, XVe–XIXe siècle* (Rome: Ecole Française de Rome, 1984).

——. 'Migrations internes et mobilité sociale dans le Royaume de Naples (XVe-XIXe)', in Paolo Macry and Angelo Massafra (eds.), *Fra Storia e Storiografia. Scritti in Onore di Pasquale Villani* (Bologna: Il Mulino, 1994).

De Lorenzo, Renata. *Proprietà fondiaria e fisco nel Mezzogiorno: la riforma della tassazione nel decennio francese (1806–1815)* (Salerno: Centro Studi per il Cilento e il Vallo di Diano, 1984).

——. 'L'amministrazione centrale e periferica nel Regno di Napoli' *L'Italia nell'età Napoleonica*. Atti del LXVII Congresso di Storia del Risorgimento Italiano (Milano, 2–5 ottobre 1996) (Rome: Istituto per la storia del Risorgimento Italiano, 1997), 145–92.

——. *Società economiche e istruzione agraria nell'Ottocento meridionale* (Milan: Franco Angeli, 1998).

——. *Un regno in bilico. Uomini, eventi e luoghi nel Mezzogiorno preunitario* (Rome: Carocci, 2001).

——. 'I giacobini abruzzesi da uomini di confine a uomini di frontiera', in Anna Maria Rao (ed.), *Napoli 1799. Fra Storia e Storiografia* (Naples: Vivarium, 2002), 654–711.

—— (ed.). *Risorgimento, democrazia, Mezzogiorno d'Italia. Studi in onore di Alfonso Scirocco* (Milan: Franco Angeli, 2003).

De Majo, S. 'Manifattura, industria e protezionismo statale nel decennio', in Aurelio Lepre (ed.), *Studi sul Regno di Napoli nel Decennio francese* (Liguori Editore, 1985), 13–33.

Demarco, Domenico (ed.). *La Statistica Murattiano del Regno di Napoli nel 1808*, 4 vols. (Rome: Fonti e Ricerche di Storia Economica, Accademia dei Lincei, 1988).

De Martino, A. *La nascita delle intendenze. Problemi dell'amministrazione periferica nel Regno di Napoli (1806–1815)* (Naples: Jovene, 1984).

De Matia, F., and F. De Negri. 'Il Corpo di Ponti e Strade dal decennio francese alla riforma del 1826', in Angelo Massafra (ed.) *Il Mezzogiorno Pre-Unitario. Economia, società e istituzioni* (Bari: Dedalo, 1988), 449–68.

De Matteo, Luigi *Politica doganale e industrializzazione nel Mezzogiorno (1845–1849)* (Naples: Pironti Editore, 1982).

De Matteo, *Governo, credito e industria laniera nel Mezzogiorno. Da Murat alla crisi post-unitaria* (Naples: Istituto italiano per gli Studi Filosofici, 1984).

De Rosa, Luigi. 'Un caso di conversione di rendita pubblica nel secolo XVIII', in *Studi in onore di Riccardo Filangieri* (Naples, 1958).

——. *Studi sugli arrendamenti del Regno di Napoli. Aspetti della distribuzione della ricchezza mobiliare nel Mezzogiorno continentale (1649–1806)* (Napoli, 1958; new edn., Naples: Istituto per gli Studi Filosofici, 2005).

——. 'Il debito pubblico della città di Napoli e le riforme di Giuseppe Bonaparte 1806–7'. *Bollettino dell'Archivio Storico del Banco di Napoli*, f.111 (Naples: Banco di Napoli, 1959), 6–20.

——. *Iniziativa e capitale straniero nell'industria metalmeccanica del Mezzogiorno (1800–1904)* (Naples: Giannini, 1968).

——. *La rivoluzione industriale in Italia e il Mezzogiorno* (Bari: Laterza, 1974).

——. 'Property rights, institutional change and economic growth in southern Italy in the XVIIIth and XIXth centuries'. *Journal of European Economic History*, 8 (3) (Winter 1979), 531–51.

——. *Economisti Meridionali* (Naples: Istituto per gli Studi Filosofici, 1995).

——. *La provincia subordinata. Saggio sulla questione meridionale* (Rome–Bari: Editori Laterza, 2004).

De Seta, Cesare. *Architettura, ambiente e società a Napoli nel '700* (Turin: Einaudi, 1981a).

——. *Napoli* (Rome–Bari: Editore Laterza, 1981b).

—— (ed.). *L'Italia nello specchio del Grand Tour*, in Ruggiero Romano and Corrado Vivanti (eds.), *Storia d'Italia: Annali*, v: *Il Paesaggio* (Turin, 1982), 227–53.

——. *L'Italia del Grand Tour da Montaigne a Goethe* (Milan: Electra, 1996).

——. *Vedutisti e viaggiatori in Italia tra settecento e ottocento* (Turin: Bolati Boringhieri, 1999).

—— and L. Di Mauro. *Palermo*, in C. De Seta (ed.), *Le Città nella storia d'Italia* (Bari: Laterza, 1980).

Di Benedetto, Renato. 'Music and Enlightenment', in Girolamo Imbruglia (ed.), *Naples in the Eighteenth Century. The Birth and the Death of a Nation* (Cambridge: Cambridge University Press, 2000), 135–53.

Di Ciommo, Enrica. *La Nazione Possible. Mezzogiorno e Questione Meridionale nel 1848* (Milan: Franco Angeli, 1993).

Di Leo, A. (ed.). *Riformismo e rivoluzione: il Mezzogiorno tra due Restaurazioni* (Naples: ESI, 1995).

—— *Il Modello napoleonico e l'amministrazione pubblica nel Mezzogiorno: La Basilicata*, in idem (ed.), *Riformismo e rivoluzione: il Mezzogiorno tra due Restaurazioni* (Naples: ESI, 1995).

Di Lernia, Luciana. 'La visita a San Carlo del viaggiatore straniero', in *Il Teatro del Re: Il San Carlo da Napoli a l'Europa* (Naples: ESI, 1988), 159–71.

Di Rienzo, Eugenio. *Marc-Antoine Jullien de Paris (1789–1848): Una biografia politica* (Naples: Guida, 1999).

Dickie, John. *Darkest Italy. The Notion and Stereotype of the Mezzogiorno 1860–1900* (London: Macmillan, 1999).

Dito, Oreste. *La campagna muratiana dell'Indipendenza d'Italia* (Milan–Rome–Naples: Biblioteca storica del Risorgimento italiano, 1911).

Dombroski, Robert S. 'Re-writing Sicily. Post-modern Perspectives', in Jane Schneider (ed.), *Italy's Southern Question. Orientalism in One Country* (Oxford: Berg, 1998), 261–76.

Doyle, W. *The Old European Order 1660–1800* (Oxford: Oxford University Press, 1978).
——. *Venality. The Sale of Office in Eighteenth Century France* (Oxford: Clarendon Press, 1996).
Duggan, Christopher. *Francesco Crispi. From Nation to Nationalism* (Oxford: Oxford University Press, 2002).
Dwyer, Philip (ed.). *Napoleon and Europe* (London: Longman, 2001).
Ebner, P. *Storia di un feudo del Mezzogiorno* (Rome, 1973).
Emsley, Clive. *Napoleonic Europe* (London: Longman, 1993).
Ermice, Maria Cristina. *Le origini del Gran Libro del debito pubblico e l'emergere di nuovi gruppi sociali (1806–1815)* (Naples: Arte Tipografica Editrice, 2005).
Espitalier, Albert. *Napoléon et le roi Murat 1808–1815. D'après de nouveaux documents* (Paris, 1910); English trans., *Napoleon and King Murat* (London, 1912).
Fahrmeir, Andreas. 'Centralisation versus particularism in the Third Germany', in Michael Rowe (ed.), *Collaboration, Resistance in Napoleonic Europe. State Formation in an Age of Upheaval (c. 1800–1815)* (London: Palgrave, 2003), 107–20.
Fallon, Olivier. *La ville des destinés croisés. Recherches sur la societé milanaise du xixième siècle (1811–1860)* (Rome: Ecole Française de Rome, 1997).
Fasano Guarini, E., G. Petralia, and P. Pezzino (eds.). *Storia della Toscana. Parte II: Dal Settecento a Oggi* (Rome–Bari: Laterza, 2004).
Feola, Raffaele. 'Donato Tommasi tra illumunisimo e restaurazione. Aspetti e problemi della riforma della legislazione nelle Due Sicilie'. *ASPN*, 3rd series, 10 (1971), 9–114.
——. *Dall'Illuminismo alla Restaurazione. Donato Tommasi e la legislazione delle Sicilie* (Naples: Jovine, 1977).
——. 'La giurisdizione nel nuovo equilibrio dei poteri', and 'L'amministrazione contenziosa', in Angelo Massafra (ed.), *Il Mezzogiorno preunitario. Economia, società e istituzioni* (Bari: Edizioni Dedalo, 1988), 487–506.
——. 'I riformatori meridionali e il modello giuseppino', in A. Di Leo (ed.), *Riformismo e Rivoluzione: il Mezzogiorno tra due Restaurazioni* (Naples: ESI, 1995), 10–15.
Ferrone, Vincenzo. *I profeti dell'illuminismo* (Rome–Bari: Editori Laterza, 1989/2000).
Filangieri, Riccardo. *I banchi di Napoli dalle origini alla costruzione del Banco delle Due Sicilie (1539–1808)* (Naples, 1947).
Filippini, J. P. 'Difesa dell'impero o difesa della società? Le misure di "Haute Police" nella Toscana napoleonica', in *Rivista Italiana di Studi Napoleonici*, 17 (1980); 20–45.
——. 'Ralliement et opposition des notables toscanes à l'empire francaise'. *Annuario dell'Istituto Italiano per la Storia Moderna e Contemporanea*, 23–4 (1971–2), 332–54.
Fiume, Giovanna. *Le bande armate in Sicilia (1819–1849). Violenza ed organizzazione del potere* (Palermo: Annali della Facoltà di Lettere e Filosofia, Università di Palermo, 1984).
——. 'Bandits, Violence and the Organization of Power in Sicily in the Early Nineteenth Century', in John A. Davis and Paul Ginsborg (eds.), *Society and Politics in the Age of the Risorgimento: Essays in Honour of Denis Mack Smith* (Cambridge: Cambridge University Press, 1991/2002), 70–91.
Fiumian, Carlo. *La città del lavoro. Un'utopia agroindustriale nel Veneto contemporaneo* (Venice: Marsilio Editore, 1990).
Flayhart, William H. *Counter-point to Trafalgar. The Anglo-Russian Invasion of Naples 1805–6* (Columbia, SC: University of South Carolina Press, 1992).
Forges Davanzati, Domenico. *Giovanni Andrea Serra. Vescovo di Potenza e la lotta dello Stato contro la Chiesa in Napoli nella seconda metà del Settecento* (Naples: Lacaita, 1999).

Forrest, Alan I. *Conscripts and Deserters: The Army and French Society during the Revolution and Empire* (Oxford: Oxford University Press, 1989).

Fortunato, Giustino. 'Il 1799 in Basilicata.' *ASPN*, 24 (1899), 223–45.

Fothergill, Brian. *Sir William Hamilton. Envoy Extraordinary* (London: Faber and Faber, 1969).

Frigione, M. 'I banchi di Napoli e la loro fusione in Banco delle Due Sicilie sotto Giacchino Murat'. *ASPN*, 27 (1941), 37–98.

Fugier, A. *Napoléon et l'Italie* (Paris, 1947).

Fusco, F., and R. Nicodemo. 'Scuola primaria in Basilicata e Napoli', in Angelo Massafra (ed.), *Il Mezzogiorno Pre-Unitario. Economia, società e istituzioni* (Bari: Dedalo 1988), 429–41.

Galasso, Giuseppe. 'La legge feudale napoletana del 1799'. *Rivista Storica Italiana* (1964), 507–29.

——. *Mezzogiorno medievale e moderno* (Turin: Einaudi, 1965).

——. *Potere e istituzioni nella storia d'Italia* (Turin: Einaudi, 1974).

——. *Il Mezzogiorno nella storia d'Italia* (Florence: Le Monnier, 1977).

——. *Il Mezzogiorno d'Italia. Lineamenti di storia meridionale e due momenti di storia regionale* (Florence: Le Monnier, 1984).

——. 'I giacobini meridionali'. *RSI*, 46 (1) (Jan. 1984), 69–105.

——. *Intervista su Napoli* (Rome–Bari: Laterza, 1987).

——. *La Filosofia in succorso de'governi. La cultura napoletana del settecento* (Naples: Guida, 1989).

——. *Alla Periferia dell'Impero. Il Regno di Napoli nel periodo spagnuolo (secoli XVI–XVIII)* (Turin: Einaudi, 1994).

——. *L'Altra Europa. Per un'antropologia storica del Mezzogiorno d'Italia* (Lecce: Argo, 1997).

——. *Napoli capitale: identità politica ed identità cittadina. Studi e ricerche 1266–1860* (Naples: Electra, 1998).

——. 'Stato nazionale e democrazia latina: il modello italiano', in Pierluigi Ciocca and Gianni Toniolo (eds.), *Storia Economica d'Italia* (Rome–Bari: Laterza Editore, 1998), i. 328–95.

——. *Il Mezzogiorno. Da 'Questione' a 'Problema Aperto'* (Manduria–Bari–Rome: Lacaita, 2005).

—— and Rosario Romeo (eds.), *Storia del Mezzogiorno*, iv: *Il Regno dagli Angioini ai Borboni* (Rome: Edizioni del Sole, 1986).

Gallo, Francesca Fausta. *Dai gigli alle coccarde. Il conflitto politico in Abruzzo (1770–1815)* (Rome: Carocci, 2002).

Gambetta, Diego. *The Sicilian Mafia. The Business of Private Protection* (Cambridge, Mass.: Harvard University Press, 1993).

Gangemi, Maurizio. 'Uomini e boschi nel Regno durante l'ultima dominazione borbonica'. *Rassegna degli Archivi dello Stato*, 44 (3) (Rome, Istituto Poligrafico e Zecca dello Stato, 1985), 477–95.

——. 'Progetto illuministico e realtà ottocentesca: le società economiche calabresi', in M. Augello and M. Guidi (ed.), *Associazionismo economico e diffusione dell'economia politica nell'Italia dell'Ottocento*, i. (Milan: Franco Angeli, 2000), 369–93.

Genoino, A. *Francesi e realisti nel Salernitano nel 1799* (Cava dei Tirreni, 1931).

——. *Studi e Ricerche sul 1799*, ed. Franceso Barra (Cava dei Tirreni: Avagliano, 1999).

Gentile, Giovanni. *I profeti del Risorgimento italiano*, in *Opere Complete* (Florence: Sansoni, 1944).
——. 'Il Pensiero politico e pedagogico di Vincenzo Cuoco', in Vincenzo Cuoco, *Studi e Appunti* (1909), in *Gentile Opere* (Florence: Sansoni, 1927), xxii. 3–83; rpt. as *Vincenzo Cuoco: studi e appunti* (Florence: Sansoni, 1964).
Giarrizzo, Giuseppe. *Un comune rurale nella Sicilia etnea. Biancavilla 1810–1860* (Catania, 1963).
——. 'Borghesia e provincia nel Mezzogiorno durante la Restaurazione', in *Atti del 3 Convegno di Studi sul Risorgimento in Puglia: L'età della Restaurazione 1815–31* (Bari, 1983), 231–3.
——. 'Sicilia e Napoli nel'700', in *I Borboni di Napoli e I Borboni di Spagna* (Naples: Guida, 1985), 193–214.
——. *Mezzogiorno senza meridionalismo. La Sicilia, lo sviluppo, il potere* (Venice: Marsilio, 1992).
——. *Massoneria e Illuminismo nell'Europa del Settecento* (Venice: Marsilio, 1995).
Giglioli, Constance H. D. *Naples in 1799. An Account of the Revolution of 1799 and of the Rise and Fall of the Parthenopean Republic* (New York: Dutton; London: John Murray, 1903).
Gilles, B. *Histoire de la Maison Rothschild*, 2 vols. (Geneva: Droz, 1965).
Ginsborg, Paul. *Daniel Manin and the Venetian revolution of 1848–49* (Cambridge: Cambridge University Press, 1979).
——. *Italy and its Discontents: Family, Civil Society, State 1980–2001* (London: Palgrave Macmillan, 2003).
Gioachino Murat, protagonista nella storia di Napoli (Naples: Elio de Rosa editore, 1994).
Giura, Vincenzo. *Russia. Stati Uniti e Regno di Napoli* (Naples, 1967).
Godechot Jacques. *Les Commissaires aux Armées sous le Directoire*, 2 vols. (Paris: Editions Fustoer, 1937).
——. *The Counter-Revolution. Doctrine and Action 1789–1804*, trans. S. Attanasio (New York: Fertig, 1971).
——. 'Saliceti, ministre du Royaume de Naples sous Joseph Bonaparte et Murat', in *Studi in Memoria di Nino Cortese* (Rome, 1976), 255–73.
Goody, Jack, Joan Thirsk, and E. P. Thompson. *Family and Inheritance. Rural Society in Western Europe 1200–1800* (Cambridge: Cambridge University Press, 1976).
Grab, A. 'La politica finanziaria nella Repubblica e nel Regno d'Italia sotto Napoleone (1802–1814)', in *L'Italia nell'età Napoleonica*. Atti del LXVII Congresso di Storia del Risorgimento Italiano (Milano, 2–5 ottobre 1996) (Rome: Istituto per la storia del Risorgimento Italiano, 1997), 37–114.
——. 'From the French Revolution to Napoleon', in John A. Davis (ed.), *Italy in the Nineteenth Century* (Oxford University Press, 2000), 25–50.
——. *Napoleon and the Transformation of Europe* (London: Palgrave, 2003).
Gramsci, Antonio. *Sul Risorgimento*, ed. Elsa Fubini (Rome: Editore Riuniti, 1959).
——. 'Alcuni temi della quistione meridionale', in Franco de Felice and Valentino Parlato (eds.), *La Questione Meridionale* (Rome: Editori Riuniti, 1966), 131–60.
Graziani, Augusto. 'Il commercio estero del Regno del Due Sicilie'. *Archivio economico del'Unificazione italiana*, ser. 1, 10 (1960), 1–89.
Greco, G. 'Istituzioni e procedure delle Grandi Corti Criminali', in Angelo Massafra (ed.), *Il Mezzogiorno preunitario. Economia, società e istituzioni* (Bari: Edizioni Dedalo, 1988), 533–48.

Gross, Hans. *Roma nel Settecento* (Rome–Bari: Laterza, 1990).

Grossi, Paolo. *An Alternative to Private Property. Collective property in the juridical consciousness of the nineteenth century* (Chicago/London: University of Chicago Press, 1977).

Guerci, Luciano. *Le monarchie assolute.* Parte II, *Permanenze e mutamenti nell'Europa del Settecento* (1986: UTET, Turin).

——. 'Catechismi repubblicani a Napoli nel 1799', in Anna Maria Rao (ed.), *Napoli 1799. Fra Storia e Storiografia* (Naples: Vivarium, 2002), 431–68.

Guerra, A., E. Molteni, and P. Nicolasi. *Il trionfo della miseria. Gli alberghi dei poveri di Genova, Palermo, Napoli* (Naples: Electra, 1996).

Gutteridge, H. C. *Nelson and the Neapolitan Jacobins. Documents Relating to the Suppression of the Jacobin Revolution in Naples June 1799*, Navy Record Society 25 (London, 1903).

Hanlon, Gregory. *The Twilight of the Military Tradition: Italian aristocrats and European conflicts 1560–1800* (New York: Holmes and Meier, 1998).

Hardmann, W. *A History of Malta during the Period of the French and British Occupations 1798–1815* (London: Holland Rose, 1908).

Haskell, Francis. *Patrons and Painters: A Study in the Relations between Italian Art and Society in the Age of the Baroque* (London: Chatto and Windus, 1963).

——. 'Art Patronage and Collecting in Naples during the Eighteenth Century', in *The Golden Age of Naples: Art and Civilization under the Bourbons 1734–1805* (Detroit Institute of Arts with the Art Institute of Chicago, 1981), 15–22.

Herr, R. 'The Constitution of 1812 and the Spanish Road to Parliamentary Monarchy', in Isser Woloch (ed.), *Revolution and Meaning of Freedom in the Nineteenth Century* (Stanford, Calif.: Stanford University Press, 1996), 65–99.

Heuron, Marc. 'Le contrebande en Calabre durant la période napoléonienne', in *Atti del 2 Congresso Storica Calabrese* (1960) (Naples, 1961), 125–37.

Hoare, Q., and G. Nowell Smith (eds.). *Selections from the Prison Notebooks* (London: Lawrence and Wishart, 1971).

Hobsbawm, E. J. *Primitive Rebels. Studies in Archaic Forms of Social Movements in the Nineteenth and Twentieth Centuries* (Manchester: Manchester University Press, 1959).

——. *Bandits* (New York: Norton, 1969/2000).

Hughes, S. C. *Crime, Disorder and the Risorgimento. The Politics of Policing in Bologna* (Cambridge: Cambridge University Press, 1994).

Imbruglia, Girolamo (ed.). *Naples in the Eighteenth Century. The Birth and the Death of a Nation* (Cambridge: Cambridge University Press, 2000).

——. 'Vita religiosa e lotta politica a Napoli nei mesi della rivoluzione', in Anna Maria Rao (ed.), *Napoli 1799. Fra Storia e Storiografia* (Naples: Vivarium, 2002), 295–324.

Incarnato, Gennaro. *Le illusioni del progresso nella società napoletana di fine Settecento.* Parte Prima, *La crisi aristocratica.* Parte Seconda, *Tra rigori modernizzatori e aspettative di assistenza* (Naples: Loffredo editore, 1991–3).

——. ' "Brava gente" alla prova. La borghesia di Pisciotta ed i suoi tormenti nei primi anni del decennio francese (1806–1809)', in Renata de Lorenzo (ed.), *Risorgimento, democrazia, Mezzogiorno d'Italia. Studi in onore di Alfonso Scirocco* (Milan: Franco Angeli, 2003), 663–75.

——. *Borghesia "Brava Gente". Pisciotta e i suoi tormenti nel primi anni del decennio francese (1806–1809)* (Naples: Controcorrente, 2004).

Jenkins, Ian. '"Contemporary Minds": William Hamilton's affair with antiquity', in Ian Jenkins and Kim Sloan (eds.), *Vases and Volcanoes: Sir William Hamilton and His Collection* (London: British Museum Press, 1996), 40–64.

——, and Kim Sloan. *Vases and Volcanoes: Sir William Hamilton and His Collection* (London: British Museum Press, 1996).

Johns, Christopher M. S. *Antonio Canova and the politics of patronage in revolutionary and Napoleonic Europe* (Berkeley, Calif.: University of California Press, 1998).

Johnson, R. M. *The Napoleonic Empire in Southern Italy and the Rise of the Secret Societies*, 2 vols. (London: Macmillan, 1904).

King, Bolton, and Thomas Okey. *Italy Today* (London: J. Nisbet, 1901).

Kröll, Thomas. *La Rivolta del Patriziato. Il liberalismo della nobilità nella Toscana del Risorgimento* (Florence: Leo S. Olschki, 2005).

Landi, G. *Istituzioni di diritto pubblico del Regno delle Due Sicilie 1815–61*, 2 vols. (Milan: Giuffré, 1977).

La Sorsa, M. *La Carboneria in Terra di Bari* (Rome: Bollettino di Statistica Amministrativa, 1919).

Lauria, F. *Demani e feudi nell'Italia meridionale* (Napoli, 1924).

Laven, David. 'The age of the Restoration', in John A. Davis (ed.), *Italy in the Nineteenth Century* (Oxford: Oxford University Press, 2000), 51–65.

——. *Venice and the Venetia under the Habsburgs 1815–1848* (Oxford: Oxford University Press, 2002).

La Volpe, G. 'Gioacchino Murat, re di Napoli. Amministrazione e riforme economiche (1808–1815)'. *NRS* (1930), 539–57; Part 2, 124–41.

Leoni, Francesco. *Storia della controrivoluzione in Italia 1789–1854* (Naples, 1975).

Lepre, Aurelio. *La Rivoluzione Napoletana del 1820–1821* (Rome, 1967).

—— (ed.). *Studi sul Regno di Napoli nel Decennio francese* (Naples: Liguori Editore, 1985).

Levy, Carl (ed.). *Italian Regionalism in Context* (London: Berg, 1996).

Librandi, Rita. 'La communicazione con le Plebe', in Anna Maria Rao (ed.), *Napoli 1799. Fra Storia e Storiografia* (Naples: Vivarium, 2002), 493–513.

Lisanti, Nicola, Tommaso, Russo, and Rosa Maria Salvia. *Il feudo, la coccarda e l'intendenza. La Basilicata dal 1789 al 1821* (Milan: Franco Angeli, 2000).

Lisio, Pasquale Alberto (ed.). *Francesco Saverio Salfi. Un calabrese per l'Europa* (Naples: Società Editrice Napoletana, 1981).

L'Italia giacobina e napoleonica. Storia della societa italiana, xiii (Milan: Teti Editore, 1985).

L'Italia nell'età Napoleonica. Atti del LXVII Congresso di Storia del Risorgimento Italiano (Milano, 2–5 ottobre 1996) (Rome: Istituto per la storia del Risorgimento Italiano, 1997).

Litchfield, R. B. *Emergence of a Bureaucracy. The Florentine Patricians 1530–1780* (Princeton, NJ: Princeton University Press, 1986).

Lomonaco, Fabrizio. 'L'anti-curialismo di Gianfranco Conforti dalle riforme alla rivoluzione', in Anna Maria Rao (ed.) *Napoli 1799. Fra Storia e Storiografia* (Naples: Vivarium, 2002), 167–200.

Lo Romer, David G. *Merchants and reform in Livorno 1814–1868* (Berkeley, Calif.: University of California Press, 1987).

Lo Sardo, Eugenio. *Napoli e Londra nel XVIII secolo. Le relazioni economiche* (Naples: Jovene, 1991).

——. *Il mondo nuovo e le virtù civili. L'espistolario di Gaetano Filangieri 1772–1788* (Naples: Federiciana Editore, 1999).

Lucarelli, Antonio. *La Puglia nel Risorgimento*, 4 vols. (Bari, 1931–53), *La rivoluzione del 1799* (Bari, 1934) ii.; rpt. Pietro Laciata Editore (Manduria–Bari: Rome, 1998).
Luise, Flavia. *Librai ed editori a Napoli nel XVIII secolo* (Naples: Liguori Editore, 2001).
Lumbroso, G. *I moti popolari contro i francesi alla fine del secolo XVIII (1796–1800)* (Florence: Le Monnier, 1932).
Lumley, Robert, and Jonathan Morris (eds.) *The New History of the Italian South: The Mezzogiorno Revisited* (Devon: Exeter University Press, 1997).
Lupo, Maurizio. 'Reorganization of public education in the Kingdom of Naples during the French period'. *JMIS* 4/3 (Fall 1999), 229–49.
Lupo, Salvatore. *Il giardino degli aranci. Il mondo degli agrumi nella storia d'Italia* (Venice: Marsilio, 1990).
——. *Storia della Mafia dalle origini ai nostril giorni* (Rome: Donzelli, 1993).
Lynch, John. *Bourbon Spain 1700–1808* (Oxford: Blackwell, 1989).
Lyttelton, Adrian. 'Landlords, peasants and the limits of liberalism', in Davis (ed.) (1979) 104–34.
——. 'The National Question in Italy', in Mikulas Teich and Roy Porter (eds.), *The National Question in Europe in Historical Context* (Cambridge: Cambridge University Press, 1993), 63–105.
McFarlane, Anthony. 'Political Corruption and Reform in Bourbon Spanish America', in W. Little and E. Posada-Carbó (eds.), *Political Corruption in Europe and Latin America* (London: Macmillan, 1996), 40–63.
Mack Smith, Denis. *Cavour and Garibaldi: A Study in Political Conflict* (Cambridge: Cambridge University Press, 1954/1985).
——. *Victor Emanuel, Cavour and the Risorgimento* (Oxford: Oxford University Press, 1971).
Mackesy, Piers. *The war in the Mediterranean 1803–1810* (Cambridge, Mass.: Harvard University Press, 1957).
Macry, Paolo. *Mercato e società nel Regno di Napoli: commercio del grano e politica economica del Settcento* (Naples: Guida, 1974).
——. *Ottocento. Famiglia, elites e patrimoni a Napoli* (Turin: Einaudi, 1988).
——. 'Studi recenti sul Mezzogiorno ottocentesco', in Paolo Macry and Angelo Massafra (eds.), *Fra Storia e Storiografia. Scritti in Onore di Pasquale Villani* (Bologna: Il Mulino, 1994), 151–62.
——. *Giocare la Vita: storia del lotto a Napoli tra Sette ed Ottocento* (Rome: Donzelli, 1997).
——. (ed.). *Quando Crolla lo Stato. Studi sull'Italia Preunitaria* (Naples: Liguori Editori, 2003).
——. and Angelo Massafra (eds.). *Fra Storia e Storiografia. Scritti in Onore di Pasquale Villani* (Bologna: Il Mulino, 1994).
Madelin, Louis. *La Rome de Napoléon. La domination française à Rome de 1809 à 1814* (Paris, 1906).
Maiorini, Maria Grazia. 'The capital and the provinces', in Girolamo Imbruglia (ed.), *Naples in the Eighteenth Century: The Birth and the Death of a Nation* (Cambridge: Cambridge University Press, 2000), 4–21.
Malatesta, Maria. *I signori della terra. L'organizzazione degli interessi agrari padani 1860–1914* (Milan, 1988).
Marandel, J. P. 'Foreign figure painters in Naples', in *The Golden Age of Naples: Art and Civilization under the Bourbons 1734–1805* (Detroit Institute of Arts with the Art Institute of Chicago, 1981), 156–82.

Marin Brigitte. 'Naples: Capital of the Enlightenment', in Peter Clark and Bernard Lepetit (eds.), *Capital cities and their hinterlands in early modern Europe* (Aldershot: Scolar Press, 1997), 143–216.
——. 'Town and country in the Kingdom of Naples 1500–1800', in S. K. Epstein (ed.), *Town and Country in Europe 1300–1800* (Cambridge: Cambridge University Press, 2001), 316–30.
Marino, John. *Pastoral Economics in the Kingdom of Naples* (Baltimore: Johns Hopkins University Press, 1988).
Marmo, Marcella. 'Tra carceri e i mercati. Spazi e modelli storici del fenomeno camorrista', in Paolo Macry and Pasquale Villani (eds.), *La Campania* (Storia d'Italia. Le Regioni dall'Unità a Oggi) (Turin: Einaudi, 1990), 691–726.
Martelli, S. 'Riformatori e giacobini molisani tra provincia e capitale', in Anna Maria Rao (ed.), *Napoli 1799. Fra Storia e Storiografia* (Naples: Vivarium, 2002), 717–43.
Martucci, Roberto. *L'invenzione dell'Italia unita 1855–1864* (Milan: Sansoni, 1999).
Martuscelli, S. *La Popolazione del Regno di Napoli nella Statistica del Re Murat* (Naples, 1979).
Masi, G. *Strutture e società nella Puglia barese del secondo settecento* (Matera, 1966).
Massafra, Angelo. 'Fisco e baroni nel Regno di Napoli alla fine del secolo XVIII', in *Studi in Onore di G. Pepe* (Bari, 1969), 624–75.
——. 'Giurisdizione feudale e rendita fondiaria nel settecento napoletano'. *Quaderni Storici* (1972), n.19, 187–252.
—— (ed.). *Problemi di storia delle campagne meridionali nell'età moderna e contemporanea* (Bari: Dedalo Libri, 1981).
—— (ed.). *Produzione, mercato e classi sociali nella Capitanata moderna e contemporanea* (Foggia, 1985).
—— (ed.). *Il Mezzogiorno preunitario. Economia, società e istituzioni* (Bari: Edizioni Dedalo, 1988).
——. 'Una stagione degli studi sulla feudalità nel Regno di Napoli', in Paolo Macry and Angelo Massafra (eds.), *Fra Storia e Storiografia. Scritti in Onore di Pasquale Villani* (Bologna: Il Mulino, 1994), 103–30.
Mastroberti, Francesco. *Pierre Joseph Briot. Un giacobino tra amministrazione e politica (1771–1827)* (Naples: Jovene, 1998).
Matarazzo, Pasquale. *Catechismi repubblicani. Napoli 1799* (Naples: Vivarium, 1999).
Mayer, Arno J. *The Persistence of the Old Regime. Europe to the Great War* (New York: Pantheon, 1981).
Melita, Maria Carla. 'Il Regno di Napoli e le violazioni del Blocco Continentale', in *Storia Economica*, anno II (1) (1999), 113–72.
Menozzi, Daniele. 'La chiesa e la rivoluzione francese', in *L'Italia giacobina e napoleonica. Storia della società italiana* (Milan: Teti Editore, 1985) xiii.
Meriggi Marco. *Amministrazione e classi sociali nel Lombardo-Veneto 1814–1848* (Bologna: Il Mulino, 1983).
——. *Il Regno Lombardo-Veneto* (Turin: Einaudi, 1987).
——. 'Società, istituzioni e ceti dirigenti', in Giovanni Sabbattucci and Vittorio Vidotto (eds.), *Storia d'Italia 1. Le premesse dell'unità. Dalla fine del Settecento al 1861* (Rome–Bari: Editori Laterza, 1994), 119–28.
——. *Breve Storia dell'Italia Settentrionale dal'Ottocento a oggi* (Rome: Donzelli, 1996).
Merlin, P., C. Rosso, G. Symcox, and G. Ricuperati. *Il Piemonte Sabaudo. Stato e territori in'età moderna*, in Giuseppe Galasso (ed.), *Storia d'Italia* (Turin: UTET, 1994) viii.

Miele, M. 'La scelta del episcopato meridionale', in P. Scaramella (ed.) *Il Cittadino Ecclesiastico. Il Clero nella Repubblica Napoletana del 1799* (Naples: Vivarium, 2000), 3–41.

Miglione, Marino Rodinò di. *Storia finanziaria del Comune di Napoli nel secolo XIX* (Naples: Luigi Pierro Editore, 1908).

Migliorini, Luigi Mascilli. *Il sistema delle Arti. Corporazioni annonarie e di mestiere a Napoli nel Settecento* (Naples: Guida, 1992).

——. 'Brotherhoods and Guilds in Naples in the Eighteenth Century: Religious Devotion and the Protection of Crafts', in Alberto Guenzi, Paola Massa, and Fausto Piola Caselli (eds.), *Guilds, Markets and Work Regulations in Italy (16th–19th Centuries)* (Aldershot: Ashgate, 1998), 395–408.

——. *Napoleone* (Rome: Salerno Editrice, 2002).

Mineccia, Francesco. 'L'agricoltura italiana nella seconda metà del settecento', in *L'Italia giacobina e napoleonica. Storia della società italiana* (Milan: Trti Editore, 1985) xiii.

Miot, André Francois (1762–1841). See http://www.acccademiacorsa.org.

Moe, Nelson. *The View from Vesuvius. Italian Culture and the Southern Question* (Berkeley, Calif.: University of California Press, 2002).

Montroni, Giovanni. *Gli uomini del re. La nobiltà napoletana nell'Ottcento* (Rome: Donzelli, 1996).

—— (ed.). *Agricoltura e commercio nel Mezzogiorno tra '700 e '800* (Naples: Liquori Editore, 1996).

——. 'The Court: Power Relations and Forms of Social Life', in Girolamo Imbruglia (ed.), *Naples in the Eighteenth Century. The Birth and the Death of a Nation* (Cambridge: Cambridge University Press, 2000), 22–43.

Moricola, Giuseppe. *L'industria della carità. L'albergo dei poveri nell'economia e nella società napoletana tra '700 e '800* (Naples: Liguori Editore, 1994).

Morilla Critz, José, Alan L. Olmstead, and Paul W. Rhode. '"Horn of Plenty": The Globalization of Mediterranean Horticulture and the Economic Development of Southern Europe 1880–1930'. *Journal of Economic History*, 59 (2) (June 1999), 316–52.

Moscati, Ruggiero. 'Su la rivoluzione napoletana del 1820–1', in *Scritti in onore di Leopoldo Cassese* (Naples, 1971), ii. 29–37.

Mozzillo, Atanasio. *Viaggiatori stranieri nel Sud* (Milano: Edizioni di Comunità, 1964).

——. *Passaggio a Mezzogiorno:Napoli e il Sud nell'immaginario barocco e illuminista europeo* (Milan: Leonardo, 1993).

——. *Cronache della Calabria in Guerra 1806–1811*, 3 vols. (Naples: ESI, 1972).

——. *Frontiera del Grand Tour. Viaggi e viaggiatori nel Mezzogiorno borbonico* (Naples: Liguori Editore, 1992).

Murdock, Richard K. 'Un rapporto sull' economia napoletana presentato a Napoleone da un mercante francese nel 1801'. *ASPN*, 12 (1973), 281–90.

Nada, N. 'Il Regno di Napoli nell'età della Restaurazione secondo un giudizio di Tito Manzi'. *RSI*, 57(4) (1961), 626–45.

Naddeo, Barbara Ann. 'Cultural capitals and cosmopolitanism in eighteenth century Italy: the historiography and Italy on the Grand Tour'. *JMIS*, 10(2) (June 2005), 183–99.

Nardella, Tommaso. 'Giuseppe Poerio primo intendente di Capitanata e del Contrado di Molise', in Renata de Lorenzo (ed.), *Risorgimento, democrazia, Mezzogiorno d'Italia. Studi in onore di Alfonso Scirocco* (Milan: Franco Angeli, 2003), 663–75.

Nardi, Carla. *Napoleone a Rome. La politica della consulta romana* (Ecole Française de Rome, 1989).

Nicolini, Fausto. *Nicola Nicolini e gli studi giuridici nella prima metà del secolo XIX* (Naples, 1901).
Nicolini, Nicola. 'La spedizione punitiva del Latouche-Tréville (16 dicembre 1792) ed altri saggi', in G. Gentile and M. Menghini (eds.), *Studi e documenti di storia del Risorgimento* (Florence: Le Monnier, 1939).
Notario, Paolo, and Narcisco Nada. *Il Piedmonte Sabaudo. Dal Periodo Napoleonico al Risorgimento*, vol. viii, part II, of Giuseppe Galasso (ed.), *Storia d'Italia* (Turin: UTET, 1993).
Nuzzo, Giuseppe. 'John Acton (1736–1811), ' in *DBI*, i. 206–10.
——. 'Il mancato trattato di commercio tra l'Inghilterra e Napoli nella seconda metà del Settecento', in *Scritti in Memoria di Leopoldo Cassese* (Naples, 1971), i. 280–318.
——. *La monarchia delle Due Sicilie tra Ancien Regime e Rivoluzione* (Naples: Bevison, 1972).
——. 'L'ascesa di Giovanni Acton al governo dello stato'. *ASPN*, 19 (1990), 437–535.
Occupants et Occupés 1792–1815 (Brussels: Centre d'Histoire Economique et Sociale, 1969).
Ostuni, Nicola. *Finanze ed economia nel Regno delle Due Sicilie* (Naples: Liquori Editore, 1992).
Ouvrand, R. 'Briot, Pierre-Joseph (1771–1827)' http://www.carboneria.it.
Pagden, Anthony. 'Francesco Maria Pagano's Republic of Virtues. Naples 1799', in B. Fontana (ed.), *The Invention of the Modern Republic* (Cambridge: Cambridge University Press, 1994), 140–52.
Palmieri, Walter (ed.). *Il Mezzogiorno agli inizi della Restaurazione* (Rome–Bari: Editori Laterza, 1993).
——. 'La tutela del territorio; il bosco e il parlamento napoletano del 1820–1'. *Storia Urbana*, 80 (1997), 35–61.
Parente, G. 'Il Cardinale Giuseppe Maria Capece Zurlo, Arcivescovo di Napoli (1781–1801)', in P. Scaramella (ed.), *Il Cittadino Ecclesiastico. Il Clero nella Repubblica Napoletana del 1799* (Naples: Vivarium, 2000), 45–106.
Parente, L. 'Dibattito sul divorzio. Una battaglia politica nel Mezzogiorno napoleonico'. *Studi Beneventani* (Benevento, 1990).
Pazzagli, Carlo. *L'agricoltura toscana nella prima metà dell'800* (Florence: Leo Olschki, 1973).
——. *Sismondi e la Toscana del suo tempo (1795–1838)* (Siena: Protagon Editori Toscani, 2003).
Pedio, Tommaso. *Giacobini e sanfedisti in Italia meridionale: Terra di Bari e Terra d'Otranto nelle Cronache del 1799*, 2 vols. (Bari: Adriatica Editrice, 1974).
Pepe, L. 'Ignazio Ciaia (1766–1799)'. *DBI*, xxv. 100.
Pescosolido, Guido. 'L'economia e la vita materiale', in Giovanni Sabbattucci and Vittorio Vidotto (eds.), *Storia d'Italia 1. Le premesse dell'unità. Dalla fine del Settecento al 1861* (Rome–Bari: Editori Laterza, 1994), 5–118.
Petraccone, Claudia. *Napoli nel 1799. Rivoluzione e Proprietà* (Naples: Morano Editore, 1989).
Petrusewicz, Marta. 'Signori e briganti. Repressione del brigantaggio nel periodo francese in Calabria: Caso Baracco', in *Studi in onore di Umberto Caldora* (Cosenza, 1978), 333–46.
——. 'Agronomia, innovatori agrari nelle periferie europee nell'Ottocento', in Piero Bevilacqua (ed.), *Storia dell'agricoltura italiana in età contemporanea* (Venice: Marsilio Editore, 1991), iii. 255–344.

Petrusewicz, Marta. *Latifundium. Moral economy and material life in a European periphery* (Ann Arbor, Mich.: University of Michigan Press, 1996).

——. 'Before the Southern Question: "Native" Ideas on Backwardness and Remedies in the Kingdom of the Two Sicilies 1815–1849', in Jane Schneider (ed.), *Italy's Southern Question. Orientalism in One Country* (Oxford: Berg, 1998), 27–49.

Pezzino, Paolo. *Il paradiso abitato dai diavoli. Società, elites, istituzioni nel Mezzogiorno contemporaneo* (Milan: Franco Angeli, 1992).

Piero, Pieri. 'Il Regno di Napoli dal luglio 1799 al marzo 1806' *ASPN*, 51 (1926), 7–309.

——. *Storia militare del Risorgimento: Guerra e insurrezioni* (Turin: Einaudi, 1962).

Pii, Eluggero. *Antonio Genovesi. Dalla Politica Economica alla 'Politica Civile'* (Florence: Leo Olschki, 1984).

Pilati, Renata. 'La popolazione di Napoli dal 1770 al 1820', in G. Civile, S. de Majo, G. Montroni, R. Pilati, M. Storchi, and M.-A. Visceglia (eds.), *Studi sulla società meridionale* (Naples: Guida, 1978), 1–46.

——. 'Delitti e ordine pubblico durante il decennio francese: gli atti della gran corte criminale di Napoli'. *ASPN*, 11 (1984), 389–419.

Piscitelli, Enzo. 'Fabrizio Ruffo e la riforma dello stato pontificio'. *Società Romana di Storia Patria*, 74 (Rome, 1951), 71–148.

Placanica, A. *Cassa Sacra e beni della Chiesa nella Calabria del Settecento* (Naples: Biblioteca degli Annali di storia economica e sociale, 1970).

——. *Uomini e strutture economiche in Calabria nei secoli xvi–xviii*, 2 vols. (Catanzaro: Editore Meridionali Riuniti, 1974).

——. *Alle origini dell'egemonia borghese in Calabria. La privatizzazione delle terre ecclesiastiche 1784–1815* (Salerno–Catanzaro: Società Editoriale Meridionale, 1979).

——. *Il filosofo e la catastrophe: un terremoto del Settecento* (Turin: Einaudi, 1985).

Platania, M. 'Instabilità sociale e delinquenza', in Angelo Massafra (ed.), *Il Mezzogiorno Pre-Unitario. Economia, società e istituzioni* (Bari: Dedalo, 1988), 1069–86.

Pocock, Tom. *A Thirst for glory. The Life of Admiral Sir Sidney Smith* (London: Pimlico, 1998).

Poletta, Luciana. 'Il neoclassicismo', in *L'Italia giacobina e napoleonica. Storia della societa italiana* (Milan: Teti Editore, 1985), xiii.

Poli, Jean Pierre. 'Portrait d'André François Miot', in *Accademia Corsica* (January 2003), 1–18. Available at: http://www.accademiacorsica.org.

Pontieri, Ernesto. *Il riformismo borbonico nella Sicilia del Sette e del'Ottocento*, 2nd edn. (Naples, 1965).

Postigliola, A. 'Antonio Capece Minutolo, Prince of Canosa (1768–1838)' in *DBI*, xviii. 451–8.

Puca, A. 'La Calabria nel decennio francese', in Augusto Placanica (ed.), *Storia della Calabria* (Roma–Reggio, 1992), 411–44.

Putnam, Robert D. *Making Democracy Work: Civic Traditions in Modern Italy* (Princeton, NJ: Princeton University Press, 1993).

Rambaud, Jacques. 'L'église de Naples sous la domination napoléonienne'. *Revue d'histoire ecclésiastique*, 9 (1908), 294–312.

——. *Naples sous Joseph Bonaparte (1806–1808)* (Paris: Plon, 1911).

——. 'Il tentativo di Murat contro la Sicilia nel 1810'. *ASPN*, 36 (1911b), f. iii, 454–50; f. iv, 695–709.

Rao, Anna Maria. *L'Amaro della Feudalità. La devoluzione di Arnone e la questione feudale a Napoli alla fine del '700'* (Naples: Guida Editore, 1984a).

——. 'Galanti, Simonetti e la riforma della giustizia nel Regno di Napoli (1795)' *ASPN*, 102 (1984b), 281–341.

——. 'La Repubblica napoletana del 1799'; 'La Prima Restaurazione borbonica', in Giuseppe Galasso and Rosario Romeo (eds.), *Storia del Mezzogiorno. Il Regno dagli Angioini ai Borboni.* (Rome: Edizioni del Sole, 1986), iv. Now rpt. in Anna Maria Rao and Pasquale Villani (eds.), *Napoli 1799–1815. Dalla Repubblica alla Monarchia amministrativa* (Naples: Edizioni del Sole, 1995).

——. 'Esercito e società a Napoli nelle riforme della seconda metà del settecento'. *Studi Storici*, 28 (1987), 623–77.

——. 'Il problema della violenza popolare in Italia nell'età rivoluzionaria', in *Rivoluzione francese. La forza delle idee e la forza delle cose* (Milan, 1990), 247–66.

—— (ed.). *Esercito e società nell'età rivoluzionaria e napoleonica* (Naples, Morano Editore, 1990).

——. 'Antiche storie e autentiche scritture. Prova di nobilità a Napoli nel Settecento', in M. A. Visceglia (ed.), *Signori, Patrizi, Cavalieri nell'età moderna* (Rome–Bari: Laterza, 1992), 279–88.

——. *Esuli. L'emigrazione politica italiana in Francia (1792–1802)* (Naples: Guida, 1992).

——. 'Mezzogiorno e rivoluzione: trent'anni di storiografia'. *Studi Storici*, 37 (1996), 981–1041.

——. 'Le strutture militari nel Regno di Napoli durante il decennio francese', in *L'Italia dell'età napoleonica.* Atti del LVIII Congresso di storia del Risorgimento italiano (Milan, 1996) (Rome: Istituto per la Storia del Risorgimento, 1997), 255–98.

—— (ed.). *Editoria e Cultura a Napoli nel XVIII secolo* (Naples: Liguori Editore, 1998).

—— (ed.). *Folle controrivoluzionarie. Le insorgenze popolari nell'Italia rivoluzionaria e napoleonica* (Rome: Carocci, 1999).

——. 'Popular Societies and the Neapolitan Republic of 1799'. *JMIS*, 4/3 (1999), 350–69.

——. 'The Feudal Question, Judicial Systems and the Enlightenment', in Girolamo Imbruglia (ed.), *Naples in the Eighteenth Century: The Birth and the Death of a Nation* (Cambridge: Cambridge University Press, 2000), 95–117.

——. 'Enlightenment and Reform', in John Marino (ed.), *Early Modern Italy* (Oxford: Oxford University Press, 2002), 229–52.

—— (ed.). *Napoli 1799. Fra Storia e Storiografia* (Naples: Vivarium, 2002).

——. 'Tra civiltà e barbarie: storie inglesi della Repubblica napoletana del 1799', in Renata de Lorenzo (ed.), *Risorgimento, democrazia, Mezzogiorno d'Italia. Studi in onore di Alfonso Scirocco* (Milan: Franco Angeli, 2003), 708–39.

——. 'Enlightenment and Reform; An Overview of Culture and Politics in Enlightenment Italy'. *JMIS* 10(2) (June 2005), 142–67.

Rath, R. J. *The Provisional Austrian Government in Lombardy-Venetia 1814–21* (Austin: University of Texas Press, 1967).

Reinerman, Alan. *Austria and the Papacy in the Age of Metternich*, 2 vols. (Washington, DC: Catholic University Press, 1979/1989).

Renda, F. *Il movimento contadino nella società siciliana* (Palermo, 1956).

——. *Risorgimento e classi popolari in Sicilia 1820–1* (Milan: Feltrinelli, 1968).

Riall, Lucy. *Sicily and the Unification of Italy. Liberal Policy and Local Power 1859–66* (Oxford: Clarendon Press, 1997).

——. 'Garibaldi and the South', in John A. Davis (ed.), *Italy in the Nineteenth Century* (Oxford: Oxford University Press, 2000), 132–53.

Ricchioni, Vincenzo (ed.). *La statistica del reame di Napoli del 1811: le relazioni sulla Puglia* (Trani, 1942).

Rienzo, Maria, Gabriella. *Banchieri ed imprenditori nel Mezzogiorno. La Banca di Calabria (1910–39)* (Rome: Donzelli, 2004).

Ringrose, David. 'Capital cities and their hinterland: Europe and the Colonial Dimension', in Peter Clark and Bernard Lepetit (eds.), *Capital Cities and Their Hinterlands in Early Modern Europe* (Aldershot: Scolar Press 1996), 217–40.

Roberts, J. M. *The Mythology of the Secret Societies* (London: Paladin, 1974).

Robertson, John. 'The Case for the Enlightenment'. Scotland and Naples (1680–1760). (Cambridge University Press 2005).

Rocchina, Maria Abbondanza. 'Il clero', in A. Di Leo (ed.), *Riformismo e rivoluzione: il Mezzogiorno tra due Restaurazioni* (Naples: ESI, 1995), 161–5.

Rodolico N. *Il Popolo agli inzi del Risorgimento nell'Italia Meridionale 1799–1801* (Florence: Le Monnier, 1926).

Romani, George T. *The Neapolitan Revolution of 1820–21* (Evanston, Ill.: Northwestern University Press, 1950).

Romano, Ruggiero. *Le commerce du royaume de Naples avec la France et les pays de l'Adriatique au XVIIIe siècle* (Paris: A. Colin, 1951).

——. *Prezzi, salari e servizi a Napoli nel secolo XVIII (1734–1806)* (Milan: Banca Commerciale, 1965).

Romano, S. *Momenti del Risorgimento in Sicilia* (Messina: G di Anna, 1952).

Romeo, Rosario. *Il Risorgimento in Sicilia* (Bari: Laterza, 1950).

——. *Mezzogiorno e Sicilia nel Risorgimento* (Naples: ESI, 1963).

——. *Momenti e problemi della Restaurazione nel Regno delle Due Sicilie* (now in Romeo, 1963).

Ross, Michael. *The Reluctant King. Joseph Bonaparte King of the Two Sicilies and Spain* (London: Sidgwick and Jackson, 1976).

Rosselli, John. *Lord William Bentinck and the British Occupation of Sicily 1811–1814* (Cambridge: Cambridge University Press, 1956).

——. *The Opera Industry in Italy from Cimarosa to Verdi: The Role of the Impresario* (Cambridge: Cambridge University Press, 1984).

——. 'Artisti e impresari', in *Il Teatro di San Carlo* (Naples: Giuda, 1987).

——. 'Opera production 1780–1880', in Lorenzo Bianconi and Giorgio Pestelli (eds.), *Opera Production and its Resources* (Chicago: University of Chicago Press, 1998), 81–164.

Rossi, Lauro. *Mazzini e la rivoluzione napoletana del 1799. Ricerche sull'Italia giacobina* (Manduria–Bari–Rome: Pietro Laciata Editore, 1995).

Rotondo, A. 'La censura ecclesiastica e la cultura', in Ruggiero Romano and Corrado Vivanti (eds.) *Storia d'Italia* (Turin: Einaudi, 1984), v., part 2, 1479–503.

Rousseau, G. 'The sources of Priapus: Anti-clericalism, Homosocial Desire and Richard Payne Knight', in G. Rousseau and R. Porter (eds.), *Sexual Underworld of the Enlightenment* (Manchester: Manchester University Press, 1987), 101–42.

Rovito, Pier Luigi. *Respubblica dei togati. Giuristi e società nella Napoli del seicento*, i: *Le garanzie giruridiche* (Naples, 1982).

Rowe, Michael. *From Reich to State. The Rhineland in the Revolutionary Age 1780–1830* (Cambridge: Cambridge University Press, 2003).

—— (ed.). *Collaboration and Resistance in Napoleonic Europe State Formation in an Age of Upheaval (c. 1800–1815)* (London: Palgrave, 2003).

Rubino, Gregorio. *Archaeologia industriale e Mezzogiorno* (Naples, 1978).
Ruggiero, M. *Briganti del Piemonte napoleonico* (Turin, 1979), 69–70.
Russo, G. *La Scuola d'Ingegneria in Napoli 1811–1857* (Naples: ESI, 1967).
Russo, Saverio (ed.). *La Capitanata nel 1799* (Foggia: Claudio Genezii Editore, 2000).
——. *Tra Abruzzo e Puglia. La transumanza dopo la Dogana* (Milan: Franco Angeli, 2002).
Sabbattucci, Giovanni, and Vittorio Vidotto (eds.). *Storia d'Italia 1. Le premesse dell'unità. Dalla fine del Settecento al 1861* (Rome–Bari: Editori Laterza, 1994).
Sabetti, Filippo. *Political Authority in a Sicilian Village* (Brunswick, NJ: Rutgers University Press, 1984).
Saine T. P., J. L. Sammons. *Johan Wolfgang von Goethe's Italian Journey* (New York: Suhrkamp Publishers, 1989).
Salvemini, Biagio. 'Note sul concetto dell'Ottocento meridionale'. *Società e Storia*, 26 (1984), 917–45.
——. *L'innovazione precaria. Spazi, mercati e società nel Mezzogiorno tra Sette e Ottocento* (Rome, 1995).
——. 'The Arrogance of the Market: The Economy of the Kingdom between the Mediterranean and Europe', in Girolamo Imbruglia (ed.), *Naples in the Eighteenth Century. The Birth and the Death of a Nation* (Cambridge: Cambridge University Press, 2000), 44–69.
——, and Maria Antonietta Visceglie. 'Fiere e mercati. Circuiti commerciali nel Mezzogiorno', in P. Bevilacqua (ed.) *Storia dell'agricoltura italiana in età contemporanea*, iii: *Mercati ed istituzioni* (Venice: Marsilio Editore, 1991), 55–122.
Savarese, G. *Tra Rivoluzioni e Reazione. Ricordi di Giuseppe Zurlo 1759–1828*, ed. A. Romano (Turin: Einaudi, 1941).
Scaramella, Pierroberto (ed.) *Il Cittadino Ecclesiastico. Il Clero nella Repubblica Napoletana del 1799* (Naples: Vivarium, 2000).
Schipa, Michelangelo. 'Cause ed importanza della rivoluzione napoletana del 1820'. *ASPN*, ns anno vi, xlv (1920), 110–27.
——. *Il Regno di Napoli al tempo di Carlo di Borbone*, 2 vols. (Milan, 1926); rpt. (Cosenza: Editori Brenner, 1994).
Schmidt, C. *Le Grand Duché de Berg (1806–1813). Etude sur la domination française en Allemagne sous Napoléon Ier* (Paris, 1905).
Schneider, Jane (ed.). *Italy's Southern Question. Orientalism in One Country* (Oxford: Berg, 1998).
——, and Peter Schneider. *Culture and Political Economy in Western Sicily* (New York: Academic Press, 1976).
Schroeder, Paul W. *The Transformation of European Politics 1763–1848* (Oxford: Clarendon Press, 1994).
Scirocco, Alfonso. 'Il problema dell'autonomia locale nel Mezzogiorno durante la rivoluzione del 1820–1', in AAVV *Studi in Memoria di Nino Cortese* (Rome: Istituto per la Storia del Risorgimento Italiano, 1976), 485–528.
——. 'I corpi rappresentativi nel Mezzogiorno dal *decennio* alla Restaurazione: il personale dei consigli provinciali'. *Quaderni Storici*, 37 (1978), 102–25.
——. *Dalla Seconda Restaurazione alla Fine del Regno*, in Giuseppe Galasso and Rosario Romeo (eds.), *Storia del Mezzogiorno*, iv: *Il Regno dagli Angioini ai Borboni* (Rome: Edizioni del Sole, 1986), 643–789.
——. 'Il brigantaggio meridionale nel Decennio e la repressione di Manhès', in A. Motta (ed.), *Della Capitana e del Mezzogiorno* (Manduria, 1987), 153–64.

Scirocco, Alfonso. *L'Italia del Risorgimento 1800–1860* (Bologna: Il Mulino, 1990).
——. 'Collegi e licei nel Mezzogiorno 1806–1860', in *Il Risorgimento*, 8 (Milano: Tipografia Editrice CENS, 1996), 7–21.
——. 'Pietro Collettta (1775–1831)', in *DBI*, xxvii. 27–34.
Scott, H. M. (ed.). *Enlightenment Absolutism: Reform and Reformers in Late Eighteenth Century Europe* (Ann Arbor, Mich.: University of Michigan Press, 1990).
Sereni, Emilio. *Storia del Paesaggio Italiano* (Bari: Laterza, 1961/1989; published in English as *History of the Italian Agricultural Landscape*, trans. R. Burr Litchfield (Princeton NJ: Princeton University Press, 1997).
Simioni, A. 'L'esercito napoletano dalla minorità di Ferdinando IV alla Repubblica del 1799'. *ASPN* (1920), 88–125; 295–321; (1921), 171–205; 295–321.
——. *Le Origini del Risorgimento Politico dell'Italia Meridionale* (Palermo, 1925; new edn., Naples: Società Storia Patria, 1995).
Sloan, Kim. ' "Observations on the Kingdom of Naples": Sir William Hamilton's Diplomatic Career', in Ian Jenkins and Kim Sloan (eds.), *Vases and Volcanoes: Sir William Hamilton and His Collection* (London: British Museum Press, 1996).
Sofia, Francesca. 'Una scienza per l'Amministrazione. Statistica e pubblici apparati tra età rivoluzionaria e Restaurazione', in *Quaderni di Clio* (Rome: Carucci, 1988), i.
Sorba, Carlotta. *I Teatri. L'Italia del melodrama nell'età del Risorgimento* (Bologna: Il Mulino, 2001).
Spagnoletti, Angelantonio. 'Il controllo degli Intendenti nelle amministrazioni locali nel Regno di Napoli', in *L'Amministrazione nella Storia Moderna* (Istituto per la Scienza dell'Amministrazione Pubblica, Archivio n.s 3) (Milano: Giuffrè, 1985), i. 953–99.
——. 'Centri e periferie nell stato napoletano del primo Ottocento', in Angelo Massafra (ed.), *Il Mezzogiorno Pre-Unitario. Economia, società e istituzioni* (Bari; Dedalo 1988), 379–410.
——. *Storia del Regno delle Due Sicilie* (Bologna: Il Mulino, 1997).
——. 'Monarchia e republicanismo in Puglia', in Anna Maria Rao (ed.), *Napoli 1799. Fra Storia e Storiografia* (Naples: Vivarium, 2002), 638–52.
Sperber, V. 'Michele Carrascosa (1770–1852)', in *DBI*, xx. 714–16.
Spini, Giorgio. *Miti e realtà della Spagna nelle rivoluzioni italiane 1820/1* (Rome, 1960).
Spinosa, N. 'Neapolitan painting under Charles and Ferdinand Bourbon: continuity and crisis within tradition' in *The Golden Age of Naples: Art and Civilization under the Bourbons 1734–1805* (Detroit Institute of Arts with the Art Institute of Chicago, 198I), 55–155.
Steegmuller, Francis. *A Woman, a Man and Two Kingdoms. The Story of Madame D'Epinay and the Abbé Galiani* (Princeton, NJ: Princeton University Press, 1991).
Stella, P. 'Giuseppe Capecelatro (1744–1836)', in *DBI*, xviii. 448–51.
Storchi, M. R. 'Grani, prezzi e mercati nel Regno di Napoli (1806–1852)', in Angelo Massafra (ed.), *Il Mezzogiorno Pre-Unitario. Economia, società e istituzioni* (Bari: Dedalo, 1988), 133–48.
Talamo, Giuseppe. *Napoli agli inizi dell'800. Il Regno di Giuseppe Bonaparte 1806–1808.* (Rome, 1971).
——. 'Napoli da Giuseppe Bonaparte a Ferdinand II', in *Storia di Napoli* (Cava dei Tirreni: ESI, 1972), viii.
Tallarico, M. A. 'Michelangelo Cianciulli, 1743–1819'. *DBI*, xxv. 167–9.
Tarrow, Sydney. *Peasant Communism in Southern Italy* (New Haven, Conn.: Yale University Press, 1967).

Tescione, G. *San Leucio e l'Arte della Seta nel Mezzogiorno d'Italia* (Naples, 1961).
Tessitore, Fulvio. 'Vincenzo Cuoco e le origini del liberalismo "moderato"', in *L'Italia giacobina e napoleonica. Storia della società italiana* (Milano: Teti Editore, 1985), xiii. 329–69.
The Golden Age of Naples: Art and Civilization under the Bourbons 1734–1805 (Detroit Institute of Arts with the Art Institute of Chicago, 1981).
Themelly, Mario. 'Vincenzo Cuoco (1770–1825)', in *DBI*, xxxi. 388–402.
Thompson, E. P. *Whigs and Hunters: The Origins of the Black Act* (New York: Pantheon, 1975).
——. 'The moral economy of the English crowd in the 18th century', in *Customs in Common. Studies in Traditional Culture* (New York: The New Press, 1993).
Tinterow, G., and P. Conisbee (eds.). *Portraits by Ingres: Image of an Epoch* (New York: Metropolitan Museum, 1999).
Tocci, U. *Terra e riforma nel Mezzogiorno moderno* (Bologna, 1971).
Tognarini, I. 'La rivoluzione francese e la crisi del riformismo italiano', in *L'Italia giacobina e napoleonica. Storia della società italiana* (Milan: Teti Editore, 1985), xiii.
—— (ed.). *La Toscana nell'età rivoluzionaria e napoleonica* (Naples, 1985).
Torrini, M. 'Le arti e le scienze. L'orto botanico, l'osservatorio, i musei', in *Gioacchino Murat* (Naples: Elio De Rosa, 1994), 44–9.
Trevelyan, R. *Princes under the Volcano* (New York: William Morrow, 1973).
Trifone, R. *Feudi e demani; eversione della feudalità nelle provincie napoletane* (Milan, 1909).
Tsoukas, C. M. *I 'torbimenti' del Trasimeno del 1799* (Milan: Franco Angeli, 1988).
Tulard, Jean. *Murat ou l'éveil des nations* (Paris: Hachette, 1983).
Turi, Gabriele. *Viva Maria. Riforme, rivoluzione e insorgenze in Toscana (1790–1799)* (Florence: Leo Olschki, 1969; Bologna: Il Mulino, 1999).
Ungari, Paolo. *L'età del Codice Civile: lotte per la codificazione e scuole di giurisprudenza nel Risorgimento* (Naples: ESI, 1967).
——. *Storia del diritto della famiglia in Italia* (Bologna: Il Mulino, 1974).
Valente, Angela. *Gioacchino Murat e l'Italia Meridionale* (Turin: Einaudi, 1941/1965).
Valenzi, Lucia. *Poveri, ospizi e potere a Napoli (XVII–XIX secoli)* (Milan: Franco, 1995).
Venturi, Franco. 'La circolazione delle idee'. *Rassegna Storica del Risorgimento*, 41 (1954), 203–22.
—— (ed.). *Illuministi Italiani*, v: *Riformatori napoletani* (Milan–Naples: Ricciardi, 1962).
—— *Italy and the Enlightenment: Studies in a Cosmopolitan Century*, ed. S. J. Woolf (Longman: London, 1972).
——. '1764: Napoli nell'anno della fame'. *RSI*, 81 (1973a), 394–472.
——. 'L'Italia fuori d'Italia', in R. Romano and C. Vivanti (eds.), *Storia d'Italia* (Turin: Einaudi, 1973b), iii. 985–1481.
Vigne, Georges. 'Ingres e la Corte di Napoli', in *Civiltà dell'Ottocento. Cultura e società* (Naples: Electra, 1997), 39–82.
Villani, Pasquale. *La vendita dei beni dello stato nel Regno di Napoli 1806–1815* (Bologna: Il Mulino, 1964).
——. 'Giuseppe Zurlo e la crisi dell'antico regime nel Regno di Napoli', in *Annuario dell'Istitito italiano per l'età contemporanea e moderna* (Rome, 1965), vii. 17–78; rpt. in Villani (ed.) (1974).

Villani, Pasquale. *Feudalità, riforme, capitalismo agrario* (Bari: Laterza, 1967).

——. 'Il Regno di Napoli nel decennio francese', in *Studi in onore di G. Pepe* (Bari, 1969), 689–702.

——. 'Qualche aspetto dell'economia italiana nell'età napoleonica'. *Annuario dell Istituto per l'età moderna e contemporanea*, 23–4 (1971–2), 19–61.

—— (ed.). *Economia e classi sociali nella Puglia moderna* (Naples, 1974).

——. *Mezzogiorno tra riforme e rivoluzione* (Bari: Laterza, 1974).

——. Introduzione a V. Cuoco, *Saggio Storico sulla rivoluzione napoletana del 1799* (Bari: Laterza, 1980).

——. *Italia Napoleonica* (Naples: Guida Editore, 1978).

——. 'Le imposte dirette e la distribuzione del reddito nel Regno di Napoli e nella Calabria Napoleonica', in idem, *Italia Napoleonica* (Naples: Guida Editore, 1978).

——. *Il decennio francese*', in Giuseppe Galasso & Rosario Romeo (eds.), *Storia del Mezzogiorno*, iv: *Il Regno dagli Angioini ai Borboni.* (Rome: Edizioni del Sole, 1986): rpt. in Anna Maria Rao and Pasquale Villani (eds.), *Napoli 1799–1815. Dalla Repubblica alla Monarchia amministrativa* (Naples: Edizioni del Sole, 1995), 179–282.

——. *Società rurale e ceti dirigenti (XVII–XX secolo)* (Naples: Morano Edirore, 1989).

——. 'Bilancio storiografico' *L'Italia nell'età Napoleonica.* Atti del LXVII Congresso di Storia del Risorgimento Italiano, Milano, 1996 (Rome: Istituto per la storia del Risorgimento Italiano, 1997), 19–36.

——. 'Il 1799 nella storia d'Italia', in Anna Maria Rao (ed.), *Napoli 1799. Fra Storia e Storiografia* (Naples: Vivarium, 2002), 841–53.

——. *Rivoluzione e diplomazia. Agenti francesi in Italia (1792–1798)* (Naples: Vivarium, 2002).

——. 'Ludovico Bianchini' (1770–1823)', in *DBI*, x. 208–12.

——. 'Gianfrancesco Conforti (1743–1799)' in *DBI*, xxvii. 793–803.

Villari, Lucio. *Il pensiero economico di Antonio Genovesi* (Florence: Le Monnier, 1959)

Villari, Rosario. 'Per la storia rurale del Mezzogiorno nel secolo XVII'. *Movimento Operaio* 6 (4) (1954), 513–38.

—— (ed.). *Il Sud nella storia d'Italia: antologia della questione meridionale*, 2 vols. (Bari: Laterza, 1961).

——. *Mezzogiorno e contadini nell'età moderna* (Bari: Laterza, 1961).

Volpe, F. 'Aspetti di vita socio-religiosa', in A. Di Leo (ed.), *Riformismo e rivoluzione: il Mezzogiorno tra due Restaurazioni* (Naples: ESI, 1995), 147–58.

Vovelle, Michel. *Il Triennio rivoluzionario italiano visto dalla Francia* (Naples: Guida, 1999).

——. 'La rivoluzione francese e la rivoluzione napoletana', in Anna Maria Rao (ed.), *Napoli 1799. Fra Storia e Storiografia* (Naples: Vivarium, 2002), 855–84.

——. *Les républiques-soeurs sous le regard de la Grande Nation 1795–1803* (Paris: L'Hamattan, 2000).

Wahnbaeck, Till. *Luxury and Happiness. Political Economy in the Italian Enlightenment* (Oxford: Oxford University Press, 2004).

Weil M. H. *Le prince Eugène et Murat*, 5 vols. (Paris: A. Fontemoign, 1902).

——. *Joachim Murat, roi de Naples: la dernière année de règne (mai 1814-mai 1815)*, 2 vols. (Paris: A. Fontemoign 1909–10).

——. *Antoine Maghella* (Paris: A. Fontemoign, 1912).

Woloch, I. *The New Regime. Transformations of the French Civil Order 1789–1820s* (New York: Norton, 1994).
—— (ed.). *Revolution and Meaning of Freedom in the Nineteenth Century* (Stanford, Calif.: Stanford University Press, 1996).
Woolf, Stuart J. *A History of Italy 1700–1860: The Social Constraints of Political Change* (London: Methuen, 1979).
——. *The Poor in Western Europe in the 18th and 19th centuries* (London: Methuen, 1986).
——. *Napoleon's Integration of Europe* (London: Routledge, 1991).
Zaghi, Carlo. *L'Italia napoleonica dalla Cisalpina al Regno,* in Giuseppe Galasso (ed.), *Storia d'Italia* (Turin: UTET, 1986/1991), xviii. 1.
Zazo, A. 'Giuseppe Poerio e il brigantaggio in Molise'. *Samnium,* 24(4) (1951), 152–77.
Zilli, Illaria (ed.). *Risorse umane e Mezzogiorno. Istruzione, recupero e formazione tra '700 e '800* (Naples: ESI, 1999).

Index